E–Government Website Development:
Future Trends and Strategic Models

Ed Downey
SUNY College at Brockport, USA

Carl D. Ekstrom
University of Nebraska at Omaha, USA

Matthew A. Jones
Portland State University, USA

INFORMATION SCIENCE REFERENCE

Hershey · New York

Director of Editorial Content:	Kristin Klinger
Director of Book Publications:	Julia Mosemann
Acquisitions Editor:	Lindsay Johnston
Development Editor:	Christine Bufton
Publishing Assistant:	Deanna Zombro / Jamie Snavely
Typesetter:	Michael Brehm
Production Editor:	Jamie Snavely
Cover Design:	Lisa Tosheff

Published in the United States of America by
Information Science Reference (an imprint of IGI Global)
701 E. Chocolate Avenue
Hershey PA 17033
Tel: 717-533-8845
Fax: 717-533-8661
E-mail: cust@igi-global.com
Web site: http://www.igi-global.com

Library of Congress Cataloging-in-Publication Data

E-government website development : future trends and strategic models / Ed Downey, Carl D. Ekstrom and Matthew A. Jones, editors.   p. cm.
  Includes bibliographical references and index.
  Summary: "This book provides fundamental clues about the direction forward in electronic government needed to achieve even greater value from websites and assist the continuing transformation of governmental interaction with citizens"--Provided by publisher. ISBN 978-1-61692-018-0 (hardcover) -- ISBN 978-1-61692-019-7 (e-book) 1. Internet in public administration. 2. Government Web sites. 3. Electronic government information. 4. Political participation--Technological innovations. I. Downey, Ed, 1945- II. Ekstrom, Carl D. III. Jones, Matthew A., 1975-
  JF1525.A8E239 2010
  352.3'8028567--dc22
                              2010000635

British Cataloguing in Publication Data
A Cataloguing in Publication record for this book is available from the British Library.

All work contributed to this book is new, previously-unpublished material. The views expressed in this book are those of the authors, but not necessarily of the publisher.

This book is dedicated to Walter Balk (1924-2008)

For two of the editors, Walter was a teacher, mentor, and friend. Walter came to teaching after a rich professional career with International Business Machines (IBM). As an early pioneer in the computing and technology field, Walter brought both enthusiasm and skepticism about technology to the classroom. It is the balancing of these two views that dominates this volume.

Table of Contents

Section 1
Concepts that Influence E-Government Development

Section 2
Evidence from Current Practice

Section 3
Future Directions

Detailed Table of Contents

Section 1
Concepts that Influence E-Government Development

Chapter 1

A Framework for Considering the Market and Political Value of E-Government Websites:

Ed Downey, The College at Brockport State University of New York, USA

A framework for understanding the value of government websites is presented that considers both market and political value. Market value is the extent to which a site saves citizens on transaction costs and promotes the economic growth within a government jurisdiction. Political value is measured in terms of cost savings that websites make to government operations and the strengthening of democratic value through civic engagement. This chapter concentrates on the civic engagement aspect of political value by examining three government website studies at the state, county, and city levels.

Chapter 2

F. Dianne Lux Wigand, University of Arkansas at Little Rock, USA

Noting the absence of concerted movement toward transactional systems in E-Government, this chapter develops a framework to design, manage, and evaluate the development of future websites relying on interaction between end-user, task, and channel. The framework draws on three overarching theories: Use and Gratification Theory; Technical Acceptance Model; and Diffusion of Innovation Theory. The resulting recommendations provide important considerations for the development of citizen-centric government websites.

Chapter 3

J. Scott McDonald, University of Texas at El Paso, USA
Gerald A. Merwin Jr., Valdosta State University, USA
Keith A. Merwin, Merwin Associates, USA
Regina K. Morris, University of Texas at El Paso, USA
Edris L. Brannen, Valdosta State University, USA

In this chapter the authors evaluate the implementation of Executive Order 13166 on local government websites. The goal of this order is to improve access to services for persons with limited English proficiency. Using a sample of cities and counties across the United States, they assess government web pages for 10 key services that are available in Spanish.

Chapter 4

Rodney Erakovich, Texas Wesleyan University, USA

The chapter incorporates the issue of administrative ethical decision making and an organization's use of technology. Erakovich offers that the relationship between technology use and administrative governance can shift the values of an organization and impact its ethical climate. He provides the reader with a theoretical query that considers how web based and Internet technology could result in value shifts in power distribution, social equity and persuasiveness of citizens as government websites are forged.

Chapter 5

Ourania I. Markaki, National Technical University of Athens, Greece
Dimitris E. Charilas, National Technical University of Athens, Greece
Dimitris Askounis, National Technical University of Athens, Greece

The chapter proposes a decision-making framework to evaluate the quality of e-government websites. Employing Multi-Attribute Decision Making (MADM) methods and Fuzzy Sets Theory they maintain the proposed model has the ability to overcome the subjectivity and inaccuracy of previous website evaluation methods. They also offer the framework has the ability to provide comparisons of different website implementation across and between national and international levels.

Chapter 6

Meena Chary, University of South Florida, USA

Early in the development of e-government websites the issue of the digital divide was recognized as a limiting factor. As value is provided on government websites it becomes more available to those citizens who have the capacity to take advantage of the expanded opportunities offered. Those who lack the capacity may fall behind. This chapter focuses on those who may fall behind and the concerns for them that are affecting the impact of e-government in India, the largest democracy in the world.

Section 2
Evidence from Current Practice

Chapter 7

Abebe Rorissa, University at Albany, State University of New York, USA
Dawit Demissie, University at Albany, State University of New York, USA
Mohammed Gharawi, University at Albany, State University of New York, USA

More than 56% of the world's population resides in Asia. This means that any consideration of global e-government is incomplete without adequate consideration of the state of affairs in the countries of Asia. This chapter involves a descriptive analysis of website content from a cross-section of 939 e-government websites drawn from a sample of 3,551 websites from 52 Asian countries. The findings indicate that Asian nation-states have wide-ranging efforts to incorporate website development into an e-government strategy for their respective areas.

Chapter 8

Akhlaque Haque, University of Alabama at Birmingham, USA

The chapter explores the factors that might shape the next generation of e-government in developing countries using Bangladesh as a focus. The study examines e-readiness by comparing the results of two studies by the Government of Bangladesh in 2004 and 2008, and identifies progress but demonstrates that substantially more must be done to achieve greater penetration of e-government. The chapter indicates that in order to reach the grass roots level more effectively government must partner with civil society organizations. In addition, resources are seen as inhibiting progress but the study anticipates that the use of widely used devices like the mobile telephone will help overcome deficits.

Chapter 9

Debjani Bhattacharya, Northern Institute for Integrated Learning in Management, India
Umesh Gulla, Teri University, India
M. P. Gupta, Indian Institute of Technology Delhi, India

The chapter provides an overview of recent developments in information and communication technologies in India, develops a conceptual model for evaluating e-government websites and then applies this model to Indian States (28) and Union Territories (7). The authors describe some of the problems of introducing e-government websites in India, such as the sheer size and diversity of the country. Despite these difficulties e-government websites are growing in numbers and functionality. The findings suggest a wide variation in these websites.

Chapter 10

Asım Balcı, Selçuk University, Turkey
Tunç Durmuş Medeni, METU, Turkey

E-Government initiatives could be said to have started in Turkey in 1998 with the Kamunet project to establish a national information system. Following this a series of nationwide initiatives were taken and in 2006 the State Planning Organization, Devlet Planlanma Teşkilatı or DTP set ambitious goals for the use of e-government websites called the E-Government Gateway (EGG). This chapter follows the ongoing development of EGG and provides insights into factors that affect its progress and future.

Chapter 11

Franz Foltz, Rochester Institute of Technology, USA
Rudy Pugliese, Rochester Institute of Technology, USA
Paul Ferber, Rochester Institute of Technology, USA

In assessing the website Recovery.gov, a website created to provide information on the implementation of the American Recovery and Reinvestment Act of 2009, the authors identify the difficulties of creating a website that satisfies the objectives of facilitating transparency and interaction. The chapter provides a useful framework for evaluating interactive features of optimal websites.

Chapter 12

J. Ramon Gil-Garcia, Centro de Investigación y Docencia Económicas, Mexico
Francisco R. Hernandez-Tella, Universidad Autónoma del Estado de México, Mexico

The creation of a number 1 ranked state website is in itself an interesting story. However, the fact that the Indiana State website was developed and continues to be maintained by a public-private partnership is compelling. This case study can provide a template for any level of government that does not wish to completely outsource its website and must use limited financial resources in a way that leverages the technical expertise available in the private sector. This chapter shows how a public-private partnership can deliver value to citizens and government.

Chapter 13

Matthew A. Jones, Portland State University, USA
Melchor C. de Guzman, State University of New York, USA

This chapter discusses the relationship of comprehensive websites with community co-production of public safety. A content analysis of the websites of police departments employing 250 or more sworn officers serving a municipal population in the U.S.is undertaken. Using previously employed measures of website evaluations as well as some developed for this research, the authors find that overall, police organizations are lacking in their web presence. They subsequently discuss the need for a stronger police presence on the web and provide policy recommendations for administrators.

Chapter 14

The author utilizes a survey sent to a sample of chief administrative officers in five Mid-Western states and performs content analysis of their websites to research whether deliberative features of local government websites reflect city officials' beliefs and funding for Internet-based citizen participation. Aikins findings suggest that overall, the deliberative contents of a municipality's website do reflect the beliefs and funding on the part of city officials to use the Internet in an effort to support citizen participation. He offers the proposition that deliberative features of websites are low because officials are more willing to engage citizens through traditional means.

Section 3
Future Directions

Chapter 15

This chapter discusses the need for standardized frameworks of e-government portals. It proposes a comparison framework that adopts and extends current approaches to the national standardization framework's needs. In this effort, the authors provide a comprehensive review of some of the most significant standardization efforts for e-government portals undertaken worldwide. They propose that National Standardization Frameworks for Electronic Government Service Portals can be broken into five clusters: (a) content; (b) structure; (c) technology; (d) security; (e) organizational. Sarantis and Askounis further posit that these frameworks can provide strategic directions, standards and specifications for the design, development and support of the operation of government portals that offer electronic services to citizens and businesses.

Chapter 16

The development of more effective means of communication between citizens and government is one of the primary purposes of any government website. Determining how government sites can employ the technologies that have enabled the dramatic increase of interpersonal communication over the Web, a phenomenon often referred to as Web 2.0, is the focus of this chapter. Readers will find a carefully developed framework for improving the value of government websites by implementing Web 2.0 technologies in a thoughtful, constructive way.

Chapter 17

Even the most simple government website can develop into a complex and seemingly uncontrollable entity that can take on a life of its own. In some ways this is to be expected since the Internet, itself seems to behave in this way. The use of Extensible Markup Language (XML) can assist in website content management in government settings. This chapter provides explanations and examples of the role XML can play in dealing with the increasingly complex content on government websites.

Chapter 18

The presentation of budgetary information on government websites is a clear way to increase the value of the sites. The major studies of government website content include measures of the extent to which budgetary information is available. The chapter presents a survey of current practices and provides a template for achieving budgetary transparency on government websites. This is achieved by examining process based information including the means for citizen participation and the presentation of budgetary outcomes.

Chapter 19

The chapter develops a model that assesses the level of transparency in websites. The authors apply this model to assess transparency of five state lottery websites. The results illustrate that website development in the latter years of a lottery website was more transparent. The authors suggest the likelihood that not only do programs become similar as administrators learn from the experiences of others but also administrative expectations of transparency are integrated into the adopted programmatic design.

Kenneth A. Klase, University of North Carolina at Greensboro, USA
Michael John Dougherty, West Virginia University Extension Service, USA

Using the lens of legislative websites in U. S. state governments, this chapter assesses these websites
on their ability to provide useful information to citizens about state budget deliberations. The assumption is that such information is vital to enhance citizen involvement in the budgetary decisions made at
the state level. The analysis is two-staged incorporating a content analysis of state legislative websites
followed by a web survey of members of state legislative research offices. The analysis also incorporates a longitudinal perspective looking at 2005 and 2009. The authors conclude that the evidence from
individual states is mixed although most states have made progress in improving the information provided. Despite this progress in the availability of information, there is little evidence that efforts have
enhanced citizen participation and civic engagement. In a concluding section the authors provide some
guidance on how this flaw may be corrected in the future.

Foreword

The seventh annual update (see State and Federal Government Report, 2007, Taubman Center for Public Policy, Brown University) on the features that are available online through American state and federal government websites indicates that considerable progress has been made in placing services and information online but many websites are still poorly organized while some outlying sites, like the Ethics Commission, Elections, or Consumer Protection, do not receive the same attention and suffer structurally and from a dearth of information. Other areas of concern include lack of effective search engines, lack of explicit privacy policies, poor navigation protocols etc. Also only about 50% of the web sites comply with the World Wide Web Consortium's (W3C) disability guidelines.

This book which is a collection of refereed papers authored by researchers from around the world is aimed at highlighting and explaining many of the factors and situations that lead to some of the above limitations in E-Government Website development. The papers are forward looking and a timely addition to the literature as they provide a framework for policy makers, at the state and federal level, who are involved in developing information dissemination policies. They also afford valuable insights to web site developers who can utilize them in designing sites that avoid clutter and do not overwhelm the citizens as they navigate the web sites. More importantly since government web sites cater to a variety of stakeholders, the papers provide, in an easy to read format, different perspectives one should keep in mind as the web sites are developed. Of special interest are papers by authors from South Asian countries that provide an emerging country perspective of E-Government web sites.

The papers are especially useful to researchers in E-Government as they identify future trends that could influence the growth and development of government web sites. Specifically the areas that could see more attention include judicious use of multimedia tools, mainly audio and video clips, along with intellectual games for several age levels and Web 2.0 technologies. It is reasonable to assume that these sites would offer Personalization and Customization tools which would allow citizens and other users to customize and tailor their web accounts specifically to their needs and interests. Clearly these developments would engender many opportunities for researchers to assess and evaluate the efficacy of these features and technologies.

In the final analysis it is my opinion and hope that this book would be a great read for the practitioner and the policy maker alike while being a good reference to the E-Government researcher.

Giri Kumar Tayi
SUNY Albany, USA

*Giri **Kumar** Tayi is a Professor of Management Science and Information Systems in the School of Business at the State University of New York at Albany. He obtained his PhD from Carnegie Mellon University and his research and teaching interests are interdisciplinary and span the fields of Information Systems, Operations Management and Operations Research. His current research streams include Economics of Information Systems (Information Security, Software Sample Design, Pricing of Information Goods), Modeling of Online Communities (Creative Commons, Digital Copyright Policies), Geographically Distributed Software Development (Process Choice, Software Quality), IS Project Outsourcing (Risk Management, Engagement Models), Data Quality and Data Mining, Models and Algorithms for Mobile Computing Environments, Online Auctions, Grid Computing, Modeling of Supply Chains (Reverse Logistics, Product Recovery and Return Architectures). He has published about 45 refereed journal articles and several book chapters covering the above three fields. Many of the articles appear in top-tier academic journals such as Operations Research, Management Science, klIS Quarterly, IEEE Transactions, Networks, Naval Research Logistics, EJO R, Journal of Combinatorial Optimization, INFO Rit1S Journal of Computing, Journal of Computer Security, Government Information Quarterly, Communications of the AClvl. He serves on the Editorial Board of several academic journals such as Information Systems Research, Decision Sciences Journal, AClvl Journal of Data and Information Quality, Information Technology Management, Information Systems Frontiers, Information and Management, International Journal of Shipping and Transport Logistics. He has co-guest edited several special issues for EJOR, Communications of the ACA1, Information Technology Management, Information Systems Frontiers and Government Information Quarterly covering topics such as Multistage Production-Inventory Systems, Data Quality, Communication Networks, Mobile Computing, Information Integration and Digital Government. He regularly serves on the Program Committee of several academic conferences and workshops including WITS, CIST, C-SWIM, AMCIS, ICIQ, IEEE Services Computing, dg.o, ICE-Gov, ECIS, HICSS, ISIS. He is regularly invited to present his research at major research universities around the world. He also serves as esi External Reviewer of Research Grant Proposals to the National Science Foundation (NSF), University Research Grants Council of Hong Kong, Natural Sciences and Engineering Research Council of Canada, National Research Grants Council of Singapore.*

Preface

OVERVIEW

The digital world has altered the way all of us gain access to information, education, and entertainment; conduct business and personal interactions and transactions; and either engage in or withdraw from the world around us. The central focus of this collection of individually written chapters is on governmental websites as they facilitate or fail to facilitate these communications and interactions objectives. In addition to providing selected information about the state of affairs, the chapters provide special insights about strategic models and ideas that might guide future efforts and refinements.

This book has been put together at a time of great potential transition. The actual printed version is an artifact of old technology that will probably be replaced by electronic based media or some mode yet to be developed. Despite this one foot in the past element, the book was put together using the digital advantages of the world. The interaction among the editors was largely conducted in a variety of electronic ways, the individual authors were initially solicited electronically, and all chapters were written and reviewed using electronic means of communications and transmission. The final product is a traditional printed volume that will be handled and read in a manner that has changed little over almost six centuries. Despite this anomaly, the content of the book is focused on what is an emerging field of study and certainly a focus of a reasonable amount of time and resources in many governmental entities—websites.

Websites provide the electronic entry to governmental information and transactions worldwide. The degree of sophistication and the utility of individual websites vary but the way forward is clearly premised on continuing substantial investment. Evidence suggests that individual participants in the business world have been quick to adapt to using the digital world effectively or risk being left behind to falter. Governments at all levels have experienced similar pressures to adopt more aggressively the potential presented by the digital world. The website provides a view of the "face" of many of these efforts associated with taking advantage of the possibilities created by a digital era. Much of the energy associated with developing E-Government has been in what might be defined as "product development." Issues such as appropriate content and protocols have dominated much of the thinking. The considerations also include the assumption of a linear sequential development progression from posting of static information to more interactive features. To a large extent, the movement seems to have reached a level of development where further interaction and transactions seems possible but has not been achieved. Some of the difficulty associated with further development is the lack of a full understanding about the current state of affairs. In addition, there is a lack of vision concerning appropriate future models. This book is intended to deal with both of these problems, providing additional insights about the nature of things in various parts of the current E-Government world plus provide some glimpses about what is possible in the future E-Government world. The chapters that make up the book incorporate a combination of thinking about basic concepts that will guide future development of governmental websites, descriptive research about the state of E-Government in various parts of the world, and specific prescription about future direction.

Even a casual glace at most of the literature concerned about E-Government gives the reader ample evidence that most scholars and practitioners are struggling to define a field that is constantly undergoing development and, in many instances, unpredicted change. While many may overrate the potential for E-Government to change the way that governments function, especially with direct interaction with the public served, few deny that computers and information technology have substantially facilitated transactions and enhanced operational efficiency in government. Websites provide the public face of government to the Internet world and have been the focus of much research and investigation. While many of the investigations have been designed to provide basic information about product development, the intent of this book is to look beyond these product development approaches to E-Government and examine emerging trends and strategies in website development.

WHERE THE BOOK FITS INTO THE WORLD

The implicit assumption behind most E-Government websites seems to be "build it and they will come." This is a quote from the 1989 movie Field of Dreams where a mid-western farmer, transformed a corn field into a baseball park that magically attracted players from the past and fans from around the country. Despite the rapid increase in the number of E-Government websites, there is some disappointment that fundamental transformations have not occurred in public-government interactions. While it is true that market values have been enhanced shifting some transactions from "face-to-face" to Internet based, evidence does support the notion that political value is underdeveloped. The chapters in this book provide some additional clues about the direction forward to achieve even greater value from websites and assist the continuing transformation of governmental interaction with citizens.

Much of the development of the Internet and E-Government has been focused on the developed world, especially the United States. This text extends the analysis to the developing world with a number of contributions from authors in South Asia and Turkey. These chapters examine international developments which provide a helpful and unique comparative perspective.

Putting together a book like this always involves a measure of risk—the risk that chapters produced will not be of sufficient quality and a risk that there is little coherence among the various chapters written independently. The editors of this volume were fortunate to have avoided both of these risks. The quality of individual submissions has been high and patterns emerged early in the review process indicating that the chapters could be organized into three foundational issues, each focusing on a different aspect of E-Government websites.

The first focus is on concepts or theories that seem to or should influence and guide E-Government and website development. The chapters that fit into this focus provide insights on several key values and concepts that need to be uppermost in the minds of website developers. These include market and political value, citizen-centric values, language and cultural accessibility, ethical considerations, and social equity.

The second focus is on describing and analyzing E-Government website experience from different national perspectives. This provides a refreshing comparative perspective with indications that the less developed countries of the world have invested in E-Government as a hope for enhancing governmental development.

The third focus is on some possible models that might provide additional direction for future E-Government development. Insights are provided about the future use of E-Government websites in Web 2.0 applications, incorporation of XML features, and enhancing transparency in a variety of applications.

TARGET AUDIENCE

This book is designed for an academic audience of scholars who are engaged in the study of E-Government, both students and professors. At the same time the book treats issues, concepts, and examples that practitioners in government will find helpful. The chapters are written from a variety of cultural backgrounds, involving several nation-states across the globe, and thus provide some comparative perspective which will appeal to a global audience.

PROGRESSION OF THE BOOK

The first section of the book assembles those chapters which provide a special concept or theory to guide E-Government website development. It is appropriate that this section begins with a chapter written by Ed Downey. In this introductory chapter Downey provides an overview framework for considering E-Government websites as they contribute to market and political value. This introductory chapter is followed by F. Dianne Lux Wigand who provides a framework for citizen-centric websites. In this chapter Wigand argues that a framework that incorporates interaction between end-user, task and channel is important. J. Scott McDonald, Gerald A. Merwin, Jr., and Keith A. Merwin examine the important ingredient of language in websites. The central concern is that E-Government websites need to be sensitive to the possibilities of multiple language competence among intended users and the need to be accommodating of different perspectives in order to minimize accessibility problems. Rodney Erakovich adds the consideration of ethical influences in E-Government website development. Erakovich is especially sensitive to the possibilities that technology can result in value shifts in power distributions, social equity and persuasiveness. Meena Chary provides a final consideration that has frequently been cited as the "digital divide." While Chary is writing with India in mind, the considerations she poses resonate in all democratic systems in the world.

The second section of the book contains chapters which use primarily descriptive analysis to provide some understanding of the current state of E-Government websites. Abebe Rorissa, Dawit Demissie, and Mohammed Gharawi provide a good summary examination of government websites in Asia. Their findings suggest that many nation-states in this part of the world have begun investment in E-Government with varying results. Aklaque Haque picks up this theme providing a glimpse at E-Government websites in Bangladesh. He documents the need for greater partnership with civil society organizations and the need to adapt to accessible technology, especially mobile telephones. Debjani Bhattacharya, Umesh Gulla, and M. P. Gupta extend the analysis of South Asia with a consideration of websites in sub-national governments in India. They conclude that E-Government development is progressing in most jurisdictions although functionality varies. Asim Balci and Tunc Durmus Medeni provide a look at E-Government websites in Turkey. Franz Foltz, Rudy Puglise and Paul Ferber turn the attention to the

United States with an examination of the recently developed Recovery.gov website at the national level and related state government websites suggesting that these efforts have met significant challenges and overpromised results that have yet to be realized. J. Ramon Gil-Garcia and Francisco R. Hernandez-Tella examine the case of the public-private partnership that was used to develop the State of Indiana website. Matthew A. Jones and Melchor C. de Guzman explore the case of E-Policing among police officers serving municipalities in the United States. Stephen K. Aikins examines the connection between municipal websites and city officials' beliefs and funding for Internet-based citizen participation in five Midwestern states.

The final section of the book contains chapters that begin to provide some templates or ideas concerning the way forward. Dementros Sarantas and Dimitris Askounis discuss the need for standardized frameworks for E-Government portals and propose a National Standardization Framework for Electronic Government Service Portals. Heasun Chun and Daejoong Kim provide a carefully developed framework for improving the value of government websites by implementing Web 2.0 technologies. J. Ramon Gil-Garcia, Jim Costello, Donna Canestraro, and Derek Werthmuller discuss the use of Extensible Markup Language (XML) to assist website content management in governmental settings. M. Emita Joaquin and Thomas J. Greitens turn to the use of budgetary information in governmental websites to enhance citizen participation and presentation of budgetary outcomes. Charles E. Menifeld and Joy Clay develop a model for transparency in websites and then use this model to assess the transparency of five state lottery websites. Kenneth A. Klase and Michael John Dougherty examine state legislative websites and their usefulness in providing information to citizens about state budget deliberations in state legislatures, concluding that the evidence about success is mixed.

These chapters provide a wide ranging examination of issues and concepts, descriptions of developments in E-Government websites in various parts of the world, and some limited prescriptions about how to move the developments forward.

Some observations:

- Progress is occurring although there seems to be an expectation that since E-Government involves computers, the pace of change should be much faster. There is an abiding impatience and expectation that results should be greater than is obvious.

- While everyone talks about interactive web developments, there is little evidence that this is taking place on E-Government websites. This necessitates even more effort directed at developing a clear vision. The expectation is that citizens want a greater connection to governmental activity. Such an assumption belies the actual data on citizen participation available on E-Government websites.

- It is possible that interaction is not really desired. Some decry the absence of effective channels and suggest that government is resistant to citizen involvement. Closer examination indicates that at least some of these critics are confusing access with control. Vincent Homburg even suggests that the focus on electronic service delivery may paradoxically widen the gap between citizens and public administrators. (Homburg, 2008)

- The research agenda seems to be overly focused on the issue of why policy makers have not invested more resources in website development. This is the argument that, "build it and they will come." There are plenty of opportunities for access to information--if anything an overload. Consider the number of local governmental jurisdictions a citizen lives in (county, local, school district, and special districts), and assume that each had a well structured website. How many times would even a conscientious citizen be likely to access each? Most of the readers of this volume are actively involved in public policy (informed observers) but do all have time to fully access all relevant information? Most of us simply do not have the time to spend keeping up with original sources and instead, rely on intermediary sources like the press and perhaps social media like Twitter and Facebook to keep us informed. Maybe the focus should be how to reduce the number of websites and promote cooperative efforts (one option might be a county portal which links to cities, towns, and villages as well as school districts). Perhaps there is the need to have some research focused on how citizens gain information and how we effectively promote education of citizens on governmental issues.

- On the issue of information overload there is a reciprocal concern from the point of view of government actors. If citizens are provided with more and more sophisticated opportunities for dialogue through E-Government websites there may be serious burdens placed on the response capabilities of government actors. If government responses are inadequate the effect on citizen participation levels could be to diminish them.

The Internet is still relatively new and there is little to suggest that either the technology or those who use it have achieved an optimal fit. Technological and social change will continue as, for example, evidenced by the rise of social media and considerations of how it impacts governance. Staying ahead of this kind of change is problematic, however, learning from it is clearly possible and desirable and that is the underlying goal of this book.

Ed Downey
SUNY College at Brockport, USA

Carl D. Ekstrom
University of Nebraska at Omaha, USA

Matthew A. Jones
Portland State University, USA

REFERENCE

Homburg, V. (2008). *Understanding e-government: Information systems in public administration.* London: Routledge.

Acknowledgment

The editors would like to acknowledge the authors, reviewers, and members of the Editorial Review Board for making this book possible. In addition we wish to thank Christine Bufton, Editorial Communications Coordinator, and Beth Ardner, Assistant Director of Marketing, at IGI Global for their guidance.

Ed Downey
SUNY College at Brockport, USA

Carl D. Ekstrom
University of Nebraska at Omaha, USA

Matthew A. Jones
Portland State University, USA

Section 1
Concepts that Influence
E–Government Development

Chapter 1

A Framework for Considering the Market and Political Value of E-Government Websites:
A Focus on the Current Political Value on State, County, and City Sites in the U.S.

Ed Downey
The College at Brockport State University of New York, USA

ABSTRACT

This chapter starts with the assumption that E-Government implementation requires public administrators to respond to stakeholder value considerations. A theoretical value framework is described that is based on market and political value concepts. After describing the value framework the chapter narrows its focus to active political value, defined in terms of civic engagement, in E-Government web sites. Three recent studies are discussed that show that the active political value on E-Government web sites is underdeveloped in the U.S. at the State, County, and City levels of government. The chapter concludes with some suggestions as to why the active political value is underdeveloped and suggests how public administrators might go about determining how and whether or not it should be enhanced on E-Government web sites.

INTRODUCTION

The purpose of the chapter is to provide E-Government web site decision makers and developers strategies they can use to increase the value of site content. This is not a chapter on web site design in the sense of making the site more attractive or easier to navigate. Though those issues are important, and much is written about them, they

cannot be the starting point for considering E-Government web site content. The starting point must be a consideration of the kind of value that the site will provide stakeholders, the many individuals, organizations and institutions that use E-Government web sites.

The discussion is based on a conceptual framework for considering the value of E-Government web sites which suggests two kinds of value: market and political (Downey, 2008). Market value is conceived both in terms of the ease with which

DOI: 10.4018/978-1-61692-018-0.ch001

markets work and as proprietary value production. This suggests two market value sub-categories. The first ease with which markets work is defined as economizing on the cost of legally mandated exchanges between individuals, organizations, or institutions and government by making these transactions on a web site. The second, proprietary value production, is growing the proprietary business economies within government jurisdictions (i.e. increasing the value of products and services produced). Political value is also conceived in two sub-categories: improving government efficiencies and promoting civic engagement. The first sub-category, improving government efficiencies, is making better use of fiscal resources by governments through savings from the use of web sites. The second is promoting civic engagement to tap the capabilities of citizens, institutions and other stakeholders to pursue the core values of liberal societies-individual freedom, a more genuinely participatory political system, a critical culture, and social justice (Benkler, 2006). This second sub-category of political value, civic engagement to tap the capabilities of citizens, institutions and other stakeholders to pursue the core values of liberal societies, is called active political value and is the focus of this chapter.

Why focus on the second sub-category of political value and not on the other three sub-categories? The reason for this focus is that the second sub-category of political value, promoting civic engagement, appears to be much less developed than the other three categories. For the first market value sub-category, economizing on the cost of legally mandated transactions, the development of E-Government web sites that allow citizens to do things like pay for automobile registrations and other fees and taxes on-line are examples in common use. Also, the second sub-category of market value, encouraging the growth of proprietary business economies in the jurisdiction, is frequently found in site content designed to attract tourism, business, and prospective residents to the jurisdiction. The first

category of political value, improving government efficiencies, is the reciprocal of the first market value sub-category, economizing on the cost of legally mandated transactions. For example, when a citizen makes a mandated transaction on line such as paying the required user fee for the use of a camp site in a public park, not only does the citizen benefit from lower transaction costs but the jurisdiction also benefits from the increased efficiencies of processing the transaction. The second sub-category of political value, promoting civic engagement, appears to be less in evidence on E-Government web sites.

Some E-Government sites provide some information necessary to the promotion of civic engagement but very few provide interactive forums despite the availability of the technology (i.e. Wikis, Blogs, and RSS feeds). This chapter explores the existence of civic engagement on E-Government web sites and hopes to provide some understanding as to why it might be underdeveloped. Three recent studies are discussed to show that the active political value on E-Government web sites is underdeveloped in the U.S. at the state, county, and city levels of government. The chapter provides some suggestions as to why the political value is constrained and thus underdeveloped. Finally ideas on how and whether or not political value might be enhanced are considered.

BACKGROUND

The Conceptual Framework for Considering the Value of E-Government

Since the idea of looking at E-Government web site content in terms of market and political value is new it is restated and further discussed here. As previously mentioned, market value is defined in two sub-categories, they are: (1) economizing on the cost of legally mandated exchanges and (2) proprietary value production. Economizing on the cost of legally mandated exchanges is viewed as decreasing transaction costs in the market (Coase, 1988, Williamson, 1995) and the cost of accessing government information to individuals, organizations and institutions. Proprietary value production is changing economic arrangements in ways that grow a jurisdictions economy by attracting people, businesses, other governments, and institutions to spend money in the jurisdiction[1].

The first of the market value sub-categories is called passive market value. For passive market value, financial transactions and data access queries are both called exchanges. The exchanges considered here are those that are legally imposed on individuals, organizations, or institutions. These legally imposed exchanges are fundamentally the same whether or not they are done on E-Government web sites. However, web exchanges provide more efficient ways of doing things than non-web exchanges (e.g. pay taxes, fees, fines, obtain required forms). The term passive is chosen to describe this since no fundamental change in the nature of the exchange due to the introduction of web site technologies takes place and in most instances there are non-web exchange alternatives. Passive market value is found in on-line exchanges that reduce the cost (e.g. travel, waiting in line, and mail) to the individuals, organizations, or institutions who must engage in a mandated exchange with a government jurisdiction.

The term active is used where the exchange is not legally imposed and the nature of the relationship is fundamentally changed by the introduction of web site technology. The active market sub-category implies proprietary value production due to new business and change that is unlikely without the presence of a web site. Market enhancement and development efforts (Grant, 2005) within a jurisdiction are sub-categorized as active market value since they envision an increase in business through new customers and new relationships. Two examples of active market value found on New York State county[2] web sites are information to

increase tourism and to encourage business creation or relocation to the county. In these instances while brochures exist with similar information, the use of hypertext on county sites allows for browsing capabilities with the potential for new understandings and relationships that go beyond those that may be formed with the use of printed material alone.

Two Kinds of Political Value

As with market value, political value is conceptualized in two sub-categories. First, improving government efficiencies by making better use of county resources and secondly, tapping the resources of citizens, institutions and other stakeholders through civic engagement to pursue the core values of liberal societies (Benkler, 2006). As with market value, political value can be sub-categorized as either passive or active. Passive political value includes government fiscal value (Schware, 2003) and refers to legally imposed exchanges with individuals, organizations, or institutions which have not fundamentally changed but become less costly to government with the introduction of web site technologies. The exchanges considered here are those that are legally imposed on the jurisdiction. An example of this for New York State counties is the reduced costs to the counties of making property records available to citizens on-line rather than devoting the administrative time, space, and material costs associated with the provision of this service without on-line capability.

The active political value sub-category suggests civic engagement and includes social value (Schware, 2003) and citizen empowerment (Grant, 2005) in so far as they search out and test value definitions among citizens. Savoie (2004) indicates that the organizational boundaries within government as they affect policy making fundamentally change with the arrival of E-Government initiatives related to social value (Schware, 2003) and the value testing and search aspects of citizen empowerment (Grant, 2005). These ideas are based on the paradigm shift in civic agency and democracy described by Boyte (2005, p. 537) where: "The shift can be conceived as a move from seeing citizens as voters, volunteers, clients, or consumers to viewing citizens as problem solvers and co-creators of public goods."

As with market value the determination as to whether political value is sub-categorized as passive or active is related to the extent to which there is a fundamental change in the nature of the exchange due to the introduction of web site content. An example of active political value for New York State counties is the provision of county budget data along with, in some instances, considerable explanation which provides the information for civic engagement and the potential for change that might otherwise not have taken place.

A Value Framework for E-Government Web Sites

In the previous sections four value sub-categories of market and political value were developed: passive market and political value, and active market and political value. In this section the four sub-categories are integrated into a comprehensive model called the Value Framework for E-Government Web sites. In the framework, passive market and political value are shown to be reciprocal. The framework also includes three assumptions of how the sub-categories manifest themselves in E-Government web sites which will be discussed.

The value framework considers the value of exchanges made on E-Government web sites between individuals, organizations, or institutions and government jurisdictions. The concept of exchange used here is based in Social Exchange Theory (SET) which views any interaction between individuals as an exchange of resources (Homans, 1958). Of course the difference is that the

exchanges considered can go beyond individuals and be among organizations, or institutions and government jurisdictions. There is precedence for this in the SET literature. For example, Lambe (2001) reviews SET as it is used to examine business-to-business exchanges and points out that the theory has been central to the study of marketing since the early 1970's. The underlying assumption of SET is that parties enter into an exchange relationship with the expectation that it will be rewarding (Blau, 1968; Homans 1958). The value framework looks at the rewards or value to the individuals, organizations, or institutions and government jurisdictions who are parties to exchanges on E-Government web sites is summarized in Figure 1.

Another important aspect of SET in so far as it is related to the value framework is that resources exchanged may not be only tangible (EG. goods or money), but also intangible (EG. social amenities or friendship). This suggests that an exchange, as viewed from the perspective of the value framework, may provide value in more than a single value category (see Figure 1). For example, downloading a form on-line results in both passive market value (savings in travel and waiting time to the citizen) and passive political value (savings in office expenses to the government). Furthermore as a consequence of downloading a form a citizen may very well see and use an on-line blog thus enhancing active political value (value due to civic engagement).

Passive market value web site features are those that reduce the cost of legally imposed exchanges on individuals, organizations, or institutions. These are financial or non-financial exchanges where the costs to individuals, organizations, or institutions making the exchanges with a particular governmental jurisdiction are reduced by using an E-Government web site. In many instances the cost reduction of the exchanges can be considered as increasing the convenience of making the exchanges and thus reducing costs (i.e., costs

Figure 1. The Value Framework

Market or Political → ——————— Passive or Active ↓	Market Value-improved ease of transactions; proprietary value production	Political Value-better use of resources; pursue core values of liberal society
Passive-legally imposed; no fundamental change in the nature of the exchange	Passive Market Value-decrease exchange costs to individuals, organizations, or institutions	Passive Political Value-increase the efficiency of government operations
Active-not legally imposed; the relationship is fundamentally changed by web site technology	Active Market Value-improve the economy of a jurisdiction	Active Political Value-enhance civic engagement

such as travel to a government office, waiting in a line, and using the mail).

Passive political value E-Government web site features are those that reduce the cost of legally imposed exchanges on governments. For example, on-line access to property databases by citizens saves government administrative time, space, and material costs.

As already suggested passive market and political value enhancement are reciprocal and will occur together. Thus, a value increase in one will likely find a reciprocal increase in the other. A savings to citizens in travel time, waiting in line, or using mail will correspond to a savings to governments in administrative time, space, and material costs.[3] Legally imposed citizen-government exchanges cost less for both parties with the use of E-Government websites. The dotted line between passive market and political value illustrates this concept in Figure 1.

Active market value web site content attempts to affect aggregate demand in the market of a jurisdiction to grow the economy by taking new initiatives and/or forming new relationships. For state, county, and city web sites this includes encouraging tourism, individual, and business relocation and new business creation. These aspects of E-Government web sites are designed to increase aggregate demand and thus grow the economies of jurisdictions. Examples of active

market value content on county web sites include tourism, and business creation and relocation information.

Active political value is found on web sites that provide the information needed and/or the forum for civic engagement. Terry L. Cooper of the USC Civic Engagement Initiative provides the following definition of civic engagement: "… people participating together for deliberation and collective action with an array of interests, institutions and networks, developing civic identity, and involving people in governance processes." (2005, p. 534) Examples of civic engagement opportunities on county web sites include such things as opportunities to interact with government officials, availability of relevant policy and program implementation information, dispute resolution, and opportunities to volunteer.

The active political and active market value sub-categories are distinguished from the passive market and political category in two distinct ways. First, for the active value sub-category exchanges are not legally imposed. Secondly, the active sub-categories create value through new exchanges and relationships made possible by web sites, while the passive sub-category creates value by reducing web exchange costs below those for non-web exchanges.

The value framework uncovers how E-Government web sites provide different kinds of value and what value site developers believe is important. While the value framework is not a predictive model, its application (Downey, in press) suggests that E-Government sites conform to the three following assumptions:

1. E-Government web sites provide value in more than one sub-category and, in most instances, in all the sub-categories.
2. Within jurisdictions there will be some variability in the way E-Government web sites provide value in each of the value sub-categories.
3. E-Government web sites are likely to provide more aggregate value in one or perhaps two sub-categories than in the others.

The four sub-categories of value (active political, passive political, active market, and passive market value) and the three assumptions described above constitute a value framework for understanding the kind of value offered by E-Government web sites. The framework is not intended to be normative and is descriptive rather than prescriptive. However, recent studies on E-Government web site content at state, county, and city levels of government indicate the presence of relatively low levels of active political value (Downey, in press; Holzer, 2009, 2009a).

MAIN FOCUS OF THE CHAPTER

Three E-Government web site studies done in 2008 and their findings regarding active political value in state, county, and city jurisdictions are discussed here. The county study was done by the author and employed the value framework. The city and state studies were done by the E-Governance Institute, National Center for Public Performance at Rutgers University, Campus at Newark. The state and city studies did not employ the value framework; however the findings are translated in terms of the framework.

The Study of Active Political Value in New York State County Web Sites

Study Sample and Methodology

During the summer and fall of 2008, New York State county web sites were reviewed by the author. Data for 46 items was collected to describe the kind of value offered by each site in accordance with the value framework sub-categories (active political, passive political, active market, and passive market value).

New York State has 62 counties, 5 of which are contiguous with the boroughs of the City of New York. The web sites for the 5 boroughs are not distinguishable from the New York City site and were excluded from the analysis. The primary reasons for selecting New York state counties were researcher familiarity and county diversity. Evidence of county economic and demographic diversity is readily available.

The 57 counties in the sample have a median population of 81,916 (2004 estimated, http://www.epodunk.com/), a median county budget of $138.8 million, and a median income of $37,272 (2000 census, U.S. Census Bureau). There is considerable variability in these numbers and in the physical realities in the counties. The smallest county is Hamilton, population 5,227; county budget, $15.5 million, and median income of $32,287. The largest counties are Suffolk and Nassau which are on Long Island, near New York City. These counties have populations of 1.5 and 1.3 million; county budgets of $1.6 and $2.7 billion; and median incomes of $65,288 and $70,020, respectively. The counties have diverse economies which are largely driven by their proximity to the City of New York. Cayuga and Clinton counties are at the sample median in terms of population with 81,916 and 81,875 respectively. They have county budgets of $138 and $147 million and median incomes of $37,487 and $37,028. Cayuga is located in the western part of the state and Clinton is located in the northeast corner of the state on Lake Champlain and the Canadian and Vermont borders.

While there is considerable economic and demographic diversity, that diversity is not normally distributed. Measures of skewness for population, county budget and median income are positive at 2.95, 3.21, and 1.94, respectively. These numbers are caused by the fact that frequency distributions tend to tail off to the right (higher side) because of the influence of the counties around New York City.

This chapter will look at the data collected for some of the more interesting items in the active political value sub-category, which is defined as web site content that promotes civic engagement:

1. Available contact with county officials
2. Really Simple Syndication (RSS) and listserv capability
3. Types of communication channels used
4. Availability of budget information
5. Program evaluations and/or audit reports available
6. Sustainability Issues Content

The next section presents an analysis of these items for New York State county web sites.

Analysis of the Active Political Value of New York State County Web Sites

A frequency distribution for the available contact with county officials is shown in Table 1.

For the scale in Table 1 the ranking was done so that all the capabilities below it are present except for 1. For example a 3 indicates that a Mailto comment or information request form is available as well as addresses, phone numbers, and/or email addresses.

Facilitating contact with county officials is fundamental to civic engagement, and 56 counties provided directory information or more. Twenty of the 56 county sites (35.09% of all 57 counties) had on-line contact, and five of these sites offered blogs. In all instances the blogs were relatively

Table 1. Available contact with county officials

Ranking	Web sites	%
1. There are no opportunities to interact	1	1.8%
2. Addresses, phone numbers, and/or email addresses are available	36	63.2%
3. Mailto comment/ information request form	15	26.3%
4. Blog or threaded conversation	5	8.8%
5. On-line synchronous communication (chat room)	0	0.0%
N=	57	

inactive and primarily used as a vehicle for county press releases and announcements. None of the county sites had a chat room and only 1 site did not provide contact information for county officials.

A gamma of .556 (Approx. sig. =.001) was obtained for the relation between the first 4 ranks of contact with county officials and county population in quartiles, suggesting that the larger a county's population is the more likely it is to have more contact options in site content. A similar relationship was found between contact options in site content and the size of the county budget in quartiles with a gamma of .500 (Approx. sig. =.001). Since the size of the budget is related to the size of population, this is expected and tends to confirm the conclusion that larger counties have more budget explanation site content.

More populated counties in New York also tend to have higher median incomes and we would expect a positive gamma between median income and the contact options in site content. This expectation is not realized with a gamma of .201 (Approx. sig. =.293). Larger county population, budget, but not median income is associated with more contact options in site content on county web sites.

Notification, which may result in a response and thus dialogue, is another important aspect of civic engagement. In this regard the existence of RSS and listserv features was surveyed. A cross

Table 2. RSS and listserv capability

	No Listserv Capability	Listserv Capability	Total
No RSS Capability	41/ 71.9%	6/ 10.5%	47/ 82.5%
RSS Capability	4/ 7.0%	6/ 10.5%	10/ 17.5%
Total	45/ 78.9%	12/ 21.1%	57/ 100%
N=	57		

Table 3. Opportunities to retrieve information for civic engagement

Information Opportunities[1] Count	Web sites	%
1. 0-1 out of 4	16	28.1%
2. 2 out of 4	23	40.4%
3. 3 out of 4	16	28.1%
4. 4 out of 4	2	3.5%
N=	57	

[1] Information Opportunities: FAQ (text), Video and/or Audio of deliberations, Meeting agendas (text), Meeting minutes or transcripts (text)

tabulation of RSS and listserv capability is done in Table 2.

The cross tabulation of RSS and listserv capabilities in Table 2 shows that 10 sites (17.5%) had RSS and 12 sites (21.1%) offered listservs. Only 6 sites (10.5%) offered both features. On the other hand 47 sites (82.5%) offered no RSS; 45 sites (78.9%) offered no listservs; and a total of 41 sites (71.9%) offered neither option. Lambdas were done to determine if one item could be used to classify another and they were not significant. This suggests that RSS and listserv capability are independent in terms of whether or not they are found in site content.

Opportunities to retrieve information for civic engagement from the content on county sites are summarized in Table 3.

The greater number of information opportunities used the more amenable the site is to the interactions that promote civic engagement. The table shows that 39 sites (68.5%) use between 2 and 3 of the information opportunities, however 16 sites (28.1%) used 1 or fewer.

A gamma of .413 (Approx. sig. =.004) was obtained for the relation between the opportunities to retrieve information for civic engagement and county population in quartiles, suggesting that the larger a county's population is the more likely it is to have more opportunities to retrieve information for civic engagement. A similar relationship was found between opportunities to retrieve information in site content and the size of the county budget in quartiles with a gamma of .335 (Approx. sig. =.037). Since the size of the budget is related to the size of population, this is expected and tends to confirm the conclusion that larger counties have more budget explanation site content.

More populated counties in New York also tend to have higher median incomes and we would expect a positive gamma between median income and opportunities to retrieve information in site content. This expectation is not realized with a gamma of .200 (Approx. sig. =.222). Larger county population, budget, but not median income is associated with more opportunities to retrieve information in site content on county web sites.

Perhaps one of the most important kinds of information for civic engagement is the county budget and an explanation of the process and priorities that went into creating it. Thirteen county sites (22.8%) provided no budget information, 44 sites (77.2%) made budget information available. The availability of budget information and the level of explanation provided are in Table 4.

Budgets, alone, are not as useful as budgets with explanation in helping citizens understand county priorities. With explanation budgets become a potentially valuable tool for those who wish to be involved in civic engagement, and 24 sites (42% of all county sites) did provide some degree of budget explanation. The variability in Table 4 is, in part, explained by county differences in population, budget, and median income.

Table 4. Availability of budget information

Explanation of Budget	Web sites	%
No budget information	13	22.81%
Budget w/ no explanation	20	35.09%
Budget w/ some explanation	16	28.07%
Budget w/ considerable explanation	8	14.04%
N=	57	

Table 5. Program evaluations and/or audit reports available

Number of Reports Available On-Line	Web sites	%
1. 0-1	41	71.9%
2. 2-5	6	10.5%
3. 6-10	6	10.5%
4. 11 or more	4	7.0%
N=	57	

A gamma of .478 (Approx. sig. =.000) was obtained for the relation between the level of budget explanation in site content and county population in quartiles, suggesting that the larger a county's population is the more likely it is to have more budget explanation site content. A similar and stronger relationship was found between budget explanation content and the size of the county budget in quartiles with a gamma of .510 (Approx. sig. =.001). Since the size of the budget is related to the size of population, this is expected and tends to confirm the conclusion that larger counties have more budget explanation site content.

More populated counties in New York also tend to have higher median incomes and we would expect a positive gamma between median income and the level of budget explanation. This expectation is realized with a gamma of .405 (Approx. sig. =.004). Larger county population, budget, and median income are associated with higher levels of budget explanation content (i.e., higher functionality) on county web sites.

As with information about the budget, information about the evaluation of county programs and audit reports are important to civic engagement. The number of program evaluations and audit reports available on county sites is reported in Table 5.

As can be seen from the table the vast majority of counties (71.9%) provided few if any program evaluations and/or audit reports.

Sustainability issues and programs (e.g. commodity and/or natural resource conservation, housing rehabilitation, climate change, environ-

mental maintenance or improvement) for local governance go hand in hand with civic engagement (Cooper, 2005; Portney, 2005). The study reviewed county web site content to determine how many sustainability issues were included in site content. Table 6 shows variability in the distribution of the number of sustainability issues covered by county web sites.

This variability in Table 6 may be related to county demographic and economic differences. A gamma of .473 (Approx. sig. =.001) was obtained for the relation between the number of sustainability issues in site content and county population in quartiles, suggesting that the larger a county's population is the more likely it is to have more sustainability issues in its site content. A similar, though not as strong relationship was found between sustainability content and the size of the county budget in quartiles, with a gamma of .413 (Approx. sig. =.008). Since the size of the budget is related to the size of the populations, this is expected and tends to confirm the conclusion that larger counties have more sustainability issues in site content.

Again, as previously mentioned more populated counties in New York also tend to have higher median incomes and we would expect a positive gamma between median income and sustainability content. This expectation is realized with a gamma of .344 (Approx. sig. =.029). Larger county population, budget, and median income are associated with higher levels of sustainability content on county web sites.

Table 6. Number of sustainability issues on site

Number of Sustainability Issues Treated	Web sites	%
1. 0-1	25	43.9%
2. 2	18	31.6%
3. 3	7	12.3%
4. 4	7	12.3%
N=	57	

Conclusions Regarding Active Political Value on New York State County Web Sites

In terms of the information required for civic engagement, there is modest value available from contact options or capability with county officials, opportunities to retrieve information for civic engagement, budget information, and sustainability issues content. For these four items, demographic and economic variables were positively associated with two exceptions. A significant relationship between median income and the contact options in site content was not found. A significant relationship between median income and opportunities to retrieve information for civic engagement was also not found in the data. These findings are in part supported by the literature suggesting a positive relationship between population and E-governance capacity at local levels of government (Moon, 2002; Moon and deLeon, 2001; Musso, 2000).

There is less value from the availability of on-line audit or program evaluation information and RSS and listserv capability. Almost 72% of the county sites surveyed provided few if any program evaluations and/or audit reports and 72% of the sites offered no RSS and listserv capabilities. As noted only 5 sites offered blogs which were inactive, and none of the sites had chat rooms.

Civic engagement requires relevant information and a forum where engagement can take place. In general, active political value is enhanced by county sites to the extent that they provide modest levels of information with the clear exception of program evaluations and/or audit reports. However, the sites offer lower levels of value in that the use of communication channels such as RSS, listservs, and chat rooms are underutilized.

The Study of Active Political Value in U. S. State and City Web Sites

In the early summer of 2009 a study of U.S. city web sites (Holzer, 2009) was released by the E-Governance Institute, School of Public Affairs and Administration at Rutgers University, Newark, and the Department of Public Administration at San Francisco State University. Soon after, a similar study of U.S. state web sites was released (Holzer, 2009a). The data for both studies was gathered in 2008 and the author was an evaluator for the city study. Following is a description of the studies and their findings with particular focus on the active political value found on state and city sites.

Study Sample and Methodology

The studies replicate global surveys done by the E-Governance Institute in 2003, 2005, and 2007, and are designed to evaluate the practice of digital government. Both the U.S. city and state web sites reports rank cities and states based on scores from a 98 item evaluation format.

The 98 items are in 5 equally weighted categories: Privacy/Security; Usability; Content; Services; and Citizen Participation. Each category has 18 to 20 items. Items are coded on a scale of four-points (0, 1, 2, and 3) or a dichotomy of two-points (0, 3 or 0, 1). Higher total point scores indicate higher levels of digital government capacity on a site.

Two evaluators were used to score each site and a third evaluator was used where a significant variation between evaluator scores was found. In order to overcome the differential weighting effect of the different number of items in each of the 5 categories, scores are indexed so that the maximum score for a category is 20, and thus the maximum overall score for any city or state is 100 (i.e. 20 points X 5 categories).

The five categories (Privacy/Security, Usability, Content, Services, and Citizen Participation) used in these studies to measure digital government capacity are described as follows:

The discussion of Privacy/Security examines privacy policies and issues related to authentication. Discussion of the Usability category involves traditional web pages, forms and search tools. The Content category is addressed in terms of access to contact information, public documents and disability access, as well as access to multimedia and time sensitive information. The section on Services examines interactions that allow users to purchase or pay for services, and the ability of users to apply or register for municipal events or services online. Finally, the measures for Citizen Participation involve examining how local governments are engaging citizens and providing mechanisms for citizens to participate in government online (Holzer, 2009, p. 21).

The sample for the cities study included 101 U.S. cities. These are the two largest cities, in terms of population, in each of the 50 states and the city of Washington in the District of Columbia. The state study surveyed all 50 states in the U.S.

Analysis of the Active Political Value on City and State Web Sites

The 20 items in the Citizen Participation category of the E-Governance Institute evaluation instrument are considered by the author to be measures of active political value. They are as follows:

1. Online feedback forms to individual departments or agencies (Score: 0-3)
2. Site allows for feedback to elected officials (Score: 0-3)
3. A newsletter is available (Score: 0-3)
4. A listserv is available (Score: 0-1)
5. An unsubscribe option for the newsletter or listserv (Score: 0-1)
6. An online bulletin board (Score: 0-2)
7. An online discussion forum on policy issues (Score: 0-3)
8. Discussants on online forums include public officials, issue experts, a moderator (Score: 0-3)
9. Features of online forums such as email notice, discussion summaries, and citizen option to suggest topic (Score: 0-3)
10. E-meetings in real time (Score: 0-3)
11. Number of online forums or discussions for the previous year (Score: 0-3)
12. Online surveys or polls (Score: 0-3)
13. Number of online surveys or polls in the last year (Score: 0-3)
14. Synchronous video of public events (Score: 0-3)
15. Online satisfaction survey (Score: 0-3)
16. Survey results published on site (Score: 0-3)
17. Tools for online decision making such as e-petition, electronic citizen juries, and e-referenda (Score: 0-3)
18. Availability of performance measures, standards, or benchmarks (Score: 0-3)
19. A jurisdiction wide performance measurement system on the site (Score: 0-3)
20. Results of performance measurement are published (Score: 0-3)

These items are similar to those used to measure site content to promote civic engagement in the author's New York county study but are not identical. There are 4 major differences. First, the county study attempts to measure "civic engagement" while the E-Governance Institute evaluation instrument refers to "citizen participation." While these terms are similar they are not synonymous. Secondly, the county study uses 6 items while the Institute uses 20. On the surface it appears that the Institute's instrument is drilling deeper by using more items, however it may be that some of the

Table 7. Top, middle and lower city scores

Overall Ranking	City	State	Total Score (overall mean= 42.04)	Participation Ranking	Participation Scores (overall mean=3.57)
1	Washington	District of Columbia	67.64	1	11.64
2	Portland	Oregon	62.23	4	8.73
3	New York	New York	61.66	9	6.18
49	Tucson	Arizona	43.25	67	2.73
50	Henderson	Nevada	42.97	33	4.18
51	Fargo	North Dakota	42.76	42	3.64
99	Gulfport	Mississippi	18.36	101	0.00
100	Rutland	Vermont	18.30	100	0.55
101	Hilo	Hawaii	13.23	85	1.64

items overlap others or attempt to measure features that only rarely occur. Thirdly, the county study includes items on contact information, meeting minutes, availability of budget information, and sustainability. In the Institute study there is contact information, meeting minutes, and several budget items in the content category (thus not counted as part of citizen participation) but no items directly related to sustainability. Fourthly, the county study is descriptive, not prescriptive while the Institute studies suggest criteria that result in a "good" E-Government web site. The appropriateness of site content is an open question and considerations of what should and should not be included in E-Government web sites will be discussed in the chapter conclusions.

While the county study and the E-Governance Institute studies measure somewhat different attributes it is argued that they both measure some aspect of active political value defined as web site content that provides the information needed and/or the forum for civic engagement. While civic engagement and citizen participation are not identical certainly participation is a prerequisite to engagement.

The maximum score for the 20 citizen participation items above for the Institute's cities study is 55 points. The overall mean score for city web sites for privacy (maximum score=25), us-

ability (maximum score=32), content (maximum score=48), service (maximum score=59), and citizen participation (maximum score=55) combined is 42.04 and the mean for citizen participation alone is 3.57. Top, middle and lower total scores and scores for citizen participation along with rankings are shown in Table 7 to give the reader an understanding for the variability in the data.

For the E-Governance Institute's state study the overall mean score for state web sites is 50.1 and the mean for citizen participation is 4.33. As before top, middle, and lower total scores and scores for citizen participation along with rankings are shown in Table 8 to give the reader an understanding for the variability in the data.

The mean scores by category from the city and state studies along with the percentage of the total possible score they represent are reported in Table 9. Participation is at a relatively low level compared to the other categories for both the city (3.57 representing 17.9% of total possible score) and state (4.33 representing 21.7%) studies.

In terms of facilitating contact and interaction, 94% of the state sites used feedback forms. However, as Table 10 shows only 11% of the cities used this feature and both city and state sites are at relatively low percentages for the use of bulletin boards and policy forums.

Table 8. Top, middle, and lower state scores

Overall Ranking	State	Total Score (overall mean=50.1)	Participation Ranking	Participation Scores (overall mean=4.33)
1	Maine	69.17	1	12.73
2	Oregon	66.46	2	10.73
3	Utah	63.17	28	3.10
24	Texas	50.91	23	4.37
25	Louisiana	49.22	16	4.91
26	Idaho	48.73	26	3.64
48	Montana	38.52	41	2.18
49	S. Dakota	35.26	36	2.37
50	Wyoming	35.18	45	2.00

Table 9. Scores by category from city and state studies

Categories of Digital Government Practice	Cities Mean Score	% of Possible Score (20 for each category)	States Mean Score	% of Possible Score (20 for each category)
Privacy	7.97	39.9%	11.02	55.1%
Usability	12.1	60.5%	14.24	71.2%
Content	10.18	50.9%	11.62	58.1%
Services	8.18	40.9%	8.90	44.5%
Participation	3.57	17.9%	4.33	21.7%

Table 10. Selected participation items

Item	Cities Average	States Average
Feedback Form	11%	94%
Bulletin Board	5%	11%
Policy Forum	10%	10%
Performance Measurement	16%	25%

These data support the concerns regarding citizen participation which appear in the overall conclusions to the city and state reports. The city report makes the following observations:

Similar to our finding in the global surveys, citizen participation has recorded the lowest score among the five categories (Holzer & Kim, 2007). Cities have yet to recognize the importance of involving and supporting citizen participation online. A promising finding in terms of citizen participation however is the growing tendency among municipalities to publish performance measurement data on their websites (Holzer, 2009, p. 79).

The state report makes similar observations:

States have yet to recognize the importance of involving and supporting citizen participation online. We therefore recommend developing a comprehensive policy that should include capacity building for states, including information infrastructure, content, applications and access for individuals, and educating the residents with appropriate computer education (Holzer, 2009a, p. 61).

In the next section a summary of the findings of the state, county, and city findings is presented along with some of the possible constraints and responses to the low level of active political value on E-Government web sites.

SOLUTIONS AND RECOMMENDATIONS

A Summary of the Active Political Value Findings for the State, County, and City Studies

The three studies found that county, city, and state web sites generally provide low or modest active political value in site content. Some active political value does exist. The county study uncovered modest value available from contact options or capability with county officials, opportunities to retrieve information for civic engagement, budget information, and sustainability issues content. The city study found that the increased use of performance measurement data in site content was promising (see Table 10 above). However, the conclusions of the state study indicate that there is much to be done to increase citizen participation with the use of web site content. For the city and state studies average participation scores of 3.57 and 4.33 out of 20 certainly indicate some form of deficiency in this category both in absolute and relative terms (i.e. relative to the other 4 categories). In the county study the very low instances of blogs and complete lack of chat rooms (see Table 1); the lack of RSS and listserv capabilities (see Table 2); the modest opportunities to retrieve information for civic engagement (see Table 3);

the modest availability of budget information (see Table 4); the very modest availability of program evaluations and/or audits (see Table 5); and the rather low level of content concerning sustainability issues suggest that active political value on New York state county web sites is at best only moderately available in site content.

Certainly the study methodologies differ. The county study is based on the value framework with its 4 sub-categories of value: passive and active market value; and passive and active political value. The state and city studies are based on a site content taxonomy of 5 categories: privacy/security; usability; content; services; and citizen participation. The last category, citizen participation, is conceptually very similar to active political value which is defined in terms of civic engagement in the county study. There are however some differences. In the State and City studies contact information, meeting minutes, and budget information are in the content category while in the county study these are aspects of active political value since they are information required for civic engagement. In addition the state and city studies do not have items directly related to sustainability.

While to some degree the methodologies differ with respect to active political value there is enough similarity to allow for cross study comparisons and all three studies point to the existence of active political value constraints on E-Government web sites. The next section looks at these constraints.

Constraints on Active Political Value

The three studies were not designed to uncover the cause for modest levels of active political value on E-Government web sites and so to a great degree the analysis here must be speculative. Despite this, speculation is useful as it may lead to some future insights into what might constrain active political value in E-Government web site content.

In *e-governance: styles of political judgment in the information age polity*, perri 6 considers five common factors that may explain the constraint of the progress of E-Government (2004) as follows:

1. Information network flow explanations: Policy makers are not aware of the potential uses
2. Perceived cost/benefit ratio explanations: systems cost too much, returns are negligible
3. User skill and willingness deficiency explanations: decision makers are not or do not see themselves as sufficiently skilled
4. Design weakness explanations: systems are not or are not perceived as being designed sufficiently to support decision making in government
5. Institutional explanations: formal rules, informal norms, custom and prior commitment preclude progress

The use of these explanations to discuss the causes for active political value constraint seems reasonable and the author suggests that a sixth common factor be added to the list for this discussion:

6. Broader system explanations: the existence of extra-governmental capabilities preclude to some degree the need for the development of those capabilities by government (EG. for active political value MoveOn.org and TaxDayTeaParty.com)

Generally the first 4 of perri 6's five common factors should become less constraining to the development of E-Government web sites and active political value over time. Presumably as time goes on it is likely that the first factor (information network flow explanations) will mitigate as policy makers become more aware of the potential for active political value content on E-Government web sites. Likewise the second common factor (perceived cost/benefit ratio explanations) should be reduced in effect as costs come down and the perceived value is increased, though admittedly

the value of citizen input may not be universally appreciated.

That cost may be a factor for what is in county E-Government web site content is demonstrated by the fact that a considerable amount of active market content was offered by links from county government sites to county tourism and chamber of commerce sites where the cost of maintaining content is not born by county government. In like manner a considerable number of county sites had GIS and property database search capabilities and the cost of these was, in part, subsidized by the state. It is not possible to conclude with any certitude that these content were there solely or partly due to low cost but this suggests hypotheses worthy of future consideration.

The third and fourth common factors, user skill and design weakness explanations, can also be overcome with the passage of time. As time goes on one would expect E-Government decision makers to gain more skill and understanding regarding E-Government web sites. Likewise we would expect design weakness explanations to diminish especially for information and communications technologies that can enhance active political value many of which currently exist but are underutilized (Kumar, 2009). This might happen in two ways. First vendors may develop new products and capabilities or modify existing ones to meet perceived needs for E-Government web site features. Secondly, E-Government decision makers may find more applications for existing technologies and innovations as they become more familiar with the technologies.

There are efforts to overcome the common factors of user skill and design weakness explanations for slow E-Government innovation to enhance active political value and the other categories of value as well. For example, the state study makes the following recommendations:

We therefore recommend developing a comprehensive policy that should include capacity building for states, including information infrastructure, content, applications and access for individuals, and educating the residents with appropriate computer education (Holzer, 209a: p. 61).

Of course recommendations do not always result in action or change and this brings us to the fifth common factor suggested by perri 7, which is institutional explanations: formal rules, informal norms, custom and prior commitment preclude progress. Perhaps there is no single issue that has been as discussed and debated in the field of Public Administration as the appropriate nature of the relationship between the public and public administrators in American governance. In attempting to determine what kind and how much active political value or citizen participation might be in E-Government web site content we also come to some understanding of the appropriate nature of this relationship. The technical capability to facilitate the dialogue between the public and public administrators exists but is underutilized (Kumar, 2009). Perhaps this is in part the result of the assumptions currently being made by E-Government web site decision makers and developers regarding the appropriate nature of the relationship between the public and public administrators.

The sixth common factor, added by the author, for the lack of more active political value on E-Government web sites are broader system explanations: the existence of extra-governmental capabilities preclude to some degree the need for the development of those capabilities by government (EG. for active political value MoveOn.org and TaxDayTeaParty.com). The lack of active political value on E-Government web sites may mean that other extra-governmental organizations or institutions are already filling this need. MoveOn.org and TaxDayTeaParty.com are but two examples of these phenomena and of course the 2 major political parties and their surrogates in the U.S. maintain web sites at the national and sub-national levels that are largely devoted to providing active political value.

Taken together the institutional and broader system explanations may explain the low level of active political value or citizen participation content on E-Government web sites. These suggest that for E-Government web site decision makers and developers the appropriate nature of the relationship between the public and public administrators in American governance is not unrestrained. Rather than direct dialogue utilizing E-Government website technologies, a dialogue largely filtered through extra-governmental organizations or institutions is the more likely reality at this point.

How can we increase active political value? The strategy of increasing the levels of interactivity and the amount of information available on E-Government web sites is a questionable one. Considering the number of government jurisdictions in which a citizen lives (e.g. federal, state, county, town, city, school district, special districts) it is unrealistic to think that increased information and interactivity on all related web sites is likely to bring substantially more people into any useful dialogue that would increase active political value. The assumption that E-Government web site developers can "build it and they will come" is probably wrong and cannot be used as a justification for allocating resources for content designed to increase active political value. Indeed the findings that active political value is relatively underdeveloped in the three studies discussed in this chapter may be the result of this calculation made by the thousands of people involved in the development of the web sites studied. This suggests a research agenda focused on how citizens gain information and how we can effectively promote education on governmental issues.

FUTURE RESEARCH DIRECTIONS

As indicated, the previous discussion is largely speculative. We do not have a great deal of information regarding the preferences of E-Government web site decision makers and developers. First, the decision makers and developers of E-Government web sites must be identified. For a particular jurisdiction or agency this may be a group whose membership is fairly fluid, and whose members have differing perspectives on what should constitute site content. In this regard future research might answers questions such as:

1. Who is involved in deciding what goes into site content?
2. Has this group changed over time?
3. What is the role each person plays in the agency or jurisdiction?
4. What is the role each person plays in determining site content?
5. What assumptions to web site developers make about civic engagement?

Once it is determined who is in the group of decision makers and developers for the E-Government web site content for a particular jurisdiction or agency, determining what kinds of value they want to provide are important research questions. It is suggested that the value framework discussed earlier in this chapter is the conceptual model that would be most useful here as it allows for the understanding of value priorities in the four categories of passive market and political value, and active market and political value. Once the value priorities of the decision makers and developers are measured they can be compared to the actual value offered on the site using methodologies similar to those described in this chapter. Such research would uncover some of the relationships between theory and practice resulting in a contribution to the field of Public Administration in its understanding of the development of E-Government web sites.

CONCLUSION

The state, county, and city studies discussed in this chapter found modest to low levels of active politi-

cal value or citizen participation on E-Government web sites. There has been some speculation on why this is the case however there has not been any consideration of whether or not the lack of active political value is problematic and should be remedied in some fashion. The state and city studies were done for the express purpose of creating a ranking in 5 equally weighted categories: Privacy/Security; Usability; Content; Services; and Citizen Participation. The E-Governance Institute, which conducted the state and city studies, believes that more citizen participation on E-Government web sites is better since this will contribute to a higher overall ranking for a given site. The author's study on New York State counties did not rank sites and was more descriptive than prescriptive in nature.

In considering the three studies it may well be that more is not necessarily better when it comes to the active political value available on E-Government sites. As has been already discussed there are two broad reasons for this. The first is that a less restrained and largely untested relationship resulting from the application of web technologies between the public and public administrators, though technically possible may not be desirable. This is because this relationship is not understood to the extent that it should be and may have unintended negative consequences such as cost, time, and the potential of creating hostility toward government (Irvin, 2004). Secondly, the seeming vacuum created by the lack of active political value on E-Government web sites may well be taken up by extra-governmental organizations or institutions, so any increase on E-Government web sites may in part be duplicative and thus wasteful of the resources required to build and maintain this capacity.

Perhaps more active political value on E-Government web sites is desirable for some sites and not for others. More research and a thoughtful discussion are required to better understand the kinds of value offered.

REFERENCES

Benkler, Y. (2006). *The wealth of networks: How social production transforms markets and freedom*. New Haven, CT: Yale University Press.

Blau, P. M. (1960). *Exchange and power in social life*. New York: John Wiley & Sons, Inc.

Boyte, H. C. (2005). Reframing democracy: Governance civic agency, and politics. *Public Administration Review*, *65*(5), 536–546. doi:10.1111/j.1540-6210.2005.00481.x

Coase, R. H. (1988). *The firm the market and the law*. Chicago: University of Chicago Press.

Cooper, T. L. (Ed.). (2005). Articles from the civic engagement initiative conference. *Public Administration Review*, *65*(5), 534–623. doi:10.1111/j.1540-6210.2005.00480.x

Downey, E. (2008). A conceptual framework for considering the value of e-government. In Anttiroiko, A. V. (Ed.), *Electronic government concepts methodologies tools and applications* (pp. 843–852). Hershey, PA: IGI Global.

Downey, E. (in press). An assessment of the value of county web sites in new york state. In Garson, C. G., & Shea, C. M. (Eds.), *Handbook of public information systems* (3rd ed.). New York: CRC Press.

Grant, G., & Chau, D. (2005). Developing a generic framework for e-government. *Journal of Global Information Management*, *13*, 1–30.

Holzer, M., & Kim, S. T. (2007). *Digital governance in municipalities worldwide: A longitudinal assessment of municipal web sites throughout the world*. Newark, N.J.: E-Governance Institute, Rutgers University.

Holzer, M., Manoharan, A., Shick, R., & Stowers, G. N. L. (2009). *U.S. municipalities e-governance survey 2008: An assessment of municipal websites*. Newark, N.J.: E-Governance Institute National Center for Public Performance School of Public Affairs and Administration. Rutgers University.

Holzer, M., Manoharan, A., Shick, R., & Stowers, G. N. L. (2009a). *U.S. states e-governance survey 2008: An assessment of state websites*. Newark, N.J.: E-Governance Institute National Center for Public Performance School of Public Affairs and Administration Rutgers University.

Homans, G. C. (1958). Social behavior as exchange. *American Journal of Sociology*, *63*(May), 597–606. doi:10.1086/222355

Irvin, R., & Stansbury, J. (2004, January). Citizen Participation in Decision Making: Is It Worth the Effort? *Public Administration Review*, *64*(1), 55–65. doi:10.1111/j.1540-6210.2004.00346.x

Kumar, N., & Vragov, R. (2009, January). Active Citizen Participation Using ICT Tools. *Communications of the ACM*, *52*(1), 118–121. doi:10.1145/1435417.1435444

Lambe, C., Wittmann, C., & Spekman, R. (2001, July). Social Exchange Theory and Research on Business-to-Business Relational Exchange. *Journal of Business-To-Business Marketing*, *8*(3), 1. doi:10.1300/J033v08n03_01

Moon, M. J. (2002). The evolution of e-government among municipalities: Rhetoric or reality. *Public Administration Review*, *62*(4), 424–433. doi:10.1111/0033-3352.00196

Moon, M. J., & deLeon, P. (2001). Municipal reinvention: Municipal values and diffusion among municipalities. *Journal of Public Administration: Research and Theory*, *11*(3), 327–352.

Musso, J., Weare, C., & Hale, M. (2000, January). Designing Web Technologies for Local Governance Reform: Good Management or Good Democracy? *Political Communication, 17*(1), 1–19. doi:10.1080/105846000198486

Perri 6 (2004). *E-governance styles of political judgment in the information age polity.* New York: Palgrave McMillan.

Portnry, K. (2005). Civic engagement and sustainable cities in the United States. *Public Administration Review, 65*(5), 534–623.

Savoie, D. (2004, Spring). 2004. Searching for accountability in a government without boundaries. *Canadian Public Administration, 47*(1), 1–26. doi:10.1111/j.1754-7121.2004.tb01968.x

Schware, R., & Deane, A. (2003). Deploying e-government programs: the strategic importance of "i" before "e". *Info-The Journal of Policy. Regulation and Strategy for Telecommunications, 5*(4), 10–19. doi:10.1108/14636690310495193

Williamson, O. (1995). Transaction cost economics and organization theory. In Williamson, O. (Ed.), *Organization theory from chester barnard to the present and beyond* (pp. 207–256). New York: Oxford University Press.

ENDNOTES

[1] The term jurisdiction will refer to State, City, or County governments in the US, since these are the categories of government in the studies reviewed in this chapter.

[2] County examples are used here because the author's research has been done on county web sites in New York State.

[3] Where 2 or more government jurisdictions make exchanges on and E-Government web site with each other political value is enhanced for the government jurisdictions involved. This can be the case for both active and passive political value.

Chapter 2
A Framework for Citizen–Centric Government Websites

F. Dianne Lux Wigand
University of Arkansas at Little Rock, USA

ABSTRACT

This author argues for a stronger end-user and citizen-centric approach to the development and evaluation of e-government services provided via the Internet. Over the past decade government agencies at all levels have created web sites that provide primarily information and only offer few two-way transactions. The predicted and hoped for resulting transformation of government at all levels due to the advent of Internet services seems yet to occur. The overall development of e-government services has been slow and uneven. To add value to existing and future government web sites, public administrators need to come to grips with a framework presented here and to understand the nature of and relationships among three variables: End-user, task, and channel characteristics and then consider their respective role and impact on channel selection. This framework along with an end-user perspective enables public administrators to assess not only the value of current information and service channels, but newer information and communication technologies such as those found in Web 2.0 or social media developments. Recommendations are offered.

INTRODUCTION

The purpose of this chapter is to provide public administrators with a framework to design, manage and evaluate web sites from an end-user and citizen-centric perspective. Accordingly, the underlying fundamental question addressing this perspective is: Why and how do citizens (and other stakeholders) contact government? In answering this critical question, public administrators need to understand and grapple with the nature of and relationships among three variables: End-user characteristics, task characteristics, and channel characteristics (Wigand, 2007). The importance of this framework for public administrators is that web sites as well as other communication chan-

DOI: 10.4018/978-1-61692-018-0.ch002

nels must be designed to provide all stakeholders with the information and services they want, when they want it, and to be delivered through their preferred channel. By evaluating web sites from the perspective of the end-user, public administrators will be able to access and manage citizens' information needs, existing channels as well as emerging information and communication technologies (ICT) and channels such as social network sites, blogs, Wikis and Twitter. Public administrators at all levels of government can use this approach not only to evaluate channels, but to allocate resources to channels that will deliver outcomes (information and/or services) to citizens in an efficient and effective way for government. This emphasis on citizen-centric orientation is reflective of a fundamental communication principle, i.e. all communication efforts must start with the end-user. The end-user is the person for whom the technology or application was intended. In this chapter the term end-user is used interchangeably with citizen.

The importance of the end-user has been recognized in several fields (communication, information management, sociology, organization behavior, computer and information science and government). End-user orientation (sometimes referred to as 'audience orientation') is the alpha and omega of fields dealing with ICT use. Only the end-user can evaluate the value of the channel(s) used for communication (Zeithaml, Parasuraman and Malhorta, 2000). Accordingly, the end-user has a message, selects the appropriate channel to reach a receiver who responds, i.e. provides feedback, within a specified time frame and closes the communication loop. Moreover, this shift to an end-user orientation for government web sites will provide added value for all stakeholders.

The focus of this chapter is to place the end-user at the very center of the development, provision and evaluation of electronic public services. To accomplish this, the nature of and interrelationships among three variables: end-user characteristics, task characteristics and channel

characteristics are examined to determine their respective impact on channel selection and the use of e-government services. First, though, a theoretical overview describes three overarching theories: *Uses and Gratifications Theory, Technology Acceptance Model (TAM)*, and *Diffusion of Innovations Theory*. These theories provide an appropriate theoretical background to explain the characteristics of end-users, channel and task characteristics as well as variables that affect the adoption of a technology. A brief review of the relevant research on government web sites over the past decade is presented to examine why the adoption and use of e-government services are slow to take off in most countries. Next, relevant research on end-user and citizen characteristics such as age, education, sex, habits, and access, is examined to determine how these characteristics impact channel selection and the use of e-government services. Then task characteristics (complexity, ambiguity, routineness, and urgency) are explored to demonstrate end-user channel preferences for specific tasks. In addition channel characteristics (richness, social presence, and synchronicity) are reviewed to determine their relationship to channel selection and adoption of e-government services. Lastly, the relationship among these variables and their respective impact on channel selection is discussed. These interrelationships among the three variables provide guidance for building a framework of government web sites and to harness their value and investment for the future. The chapter concludes with a framework in which these efforts can be viewed conceptually.

Theoretical Overview

Three theoretical approaches, Uses and Gratification Theory, Technology Acceptance Model (TAM), and Diffusion of Innovations Theory offer insights into the role of the end-user and channel selection. *Uses and Gratification Theory* (Blumler & Katz, 1974) posits that media users actively take part in the communication process, are goal oriented in choosing a media source that maximally fulfills their needs. Moreover, the assumption is made that the user has alternative choices to satisfy his or her needs. Although *Uses and Gratification Theory* was applied originally to radio and television, the basic features of this theory can be applied to a certain degree for citizens' efforts to contact and communicate with government as well.

This theory lends itself partially for the present setting in that channel choices made by citizens are also likely to be made in the sense that gratification is achieved. For Blumler and Katz such gratification is derived from the particular program watched on television or listened to on the radio. Moreover, media consumers are assumed to have a free will to decide and choose how they will use the media and how it will impact them. In the present context, however, gratification is derived when a solution or partial solution is found to a citizen's problem while using a particular communication channel. The nature of such overall gratification achieved by Blumler and Katz's media user differs considerably from the nature of gratification derived by the citizen's channel choice. The citizen deliberately chooses and uses a channel as a means to an end, i.e. to solve a problem. *Uses and Gratification Theory*, however, then makes inferences subsequently how the medium (e.g., television) may have an impact on our lives, how we view reality and the world and may influence our behavior. This latter notion then also differs and cannot be applied to the present setting when citizens choose a communication channel to contact government. Thus it can be seen that *Uses and Gratification Theory* offers some inherent limited utility for the present setting such as channel choice, but we cannot apply this theory as originally conceived by Blumler and Katz (1974) to provide similar gratifications, and certainly not the assumed inferences and impacts on an individual's life, world view and behavior.

The *Technology Acceptance Model (TAM)* developed by Davis (1989) models how users come to accept and use technology. This theory has been applied to broader information technology (IT) environments and numerous studies supported this model. There is, however, still ongoing criticism and controversy about the use of this model. TAM posits that there are a number of factors that will influence the user as to whether or not to adopt the technology. Davis (1989) found two most common factors: *Perceived usefulness* (the degree to which a person believes that using a particular system would enhance his or her job performance), and *ease of use* (the degree to which a person believes that using a particular system would be free from effort) would account for the adoption of a technology. Later studies, Venkatesh and Davis (2000) expanded the model to TAM2 and explained usage intentions in terms of social influence. Then Venkatesh et al. (2003) developed the Unified Theory of Acceptance and Use of Technology (UTAUT) to explain user intentions to use an information system and usage behavior. The four key components of this model are: Performance expectancy, effort expectancy, social influence, and facilitating condition. Social demographic variables such as gender, age, experience, and voluntariness of use were found to mediate the four key constructs. This model has been used to account for variation in usage intention. TAM, TAM2, and UTAUT are useful models to explain the end-user's intentions and channel characteristics and channel selection discussed later in this chapter, there is no evidence, however, that these models have been used to explain the government to citizen relationship (Pieterson & van Dijk, 2007).

The third theory applicable to understanding the role of the end-user and the adoption of a technology is *Diffusion of Innovations Theory*. This theory explains how, why, and the rate of adoption for new ideas and technologies to spread through networks. The model of the innovation-decision process has four stages: *Knowledge* – awareness of an innovation and some understanding of its use; *persuasion* - the user has a favorable or unfavorable attitude toward the innovation; *decision* – a choice is made to adopt or reject the innovation; and *confirmation* – seeks reinforcement for the decision to adopt or not to adopt (Rogers with Shoemaker 1971, p. 103). According to these authors, the five most important characteristics of innovations explaining the rate of adoption (the speed by which members of a social system adopt an innovation) are: Relative advantage (amount of improvement over existing technology), compatibility (ability to incorporate the technology into an individual's life), complexity (how difficult will it be to adopt), trialability (how easy is it to experiment with the technology), and observability (how visible is the technology to other users). These four stages and five characteristics certainly provide a foundation to understand and explain the end-user, task, and channel characteristics framework proposed for this chapter.

These three theoretical approaches, *User Gratification Theory, Technology Acceptance Model, and Diffusion of Innovations Theory,* provide conceptual guidance in developing the overall framework for citizen-centric government web sites.

The Challenging Landscape of E-Government

E-government covers a broad array of dimensions and can refer to government's use of all forms of ICT to facilitate the daily administration of government. The Organisation for Economic Co-Operation and Development (OECD) defines e-government as: "The use of information and communication technologies, particularly the Internet, as a tool to achieve better government (OECD, 2003, p. 23). E-government, analogous to e-commerce, is the application of ICT from the point of origin to the endpoint along the value chain of government processes conducted electronically to achieve a goal (based on Wigand, 1997). The processes may encompass the reciprocal (at least potentially) relationships of government to

citizen, government to business, or government to government. For the purposes of this chapter, e-government as a term will be limited to the use of the Internet to deliver information and services by all levels of government to its citizens.

The National Performance Review (1997) encouraged government agencies to employ the Internet to improve service, cut red tape and increase access to government. At the time, many researchers and visionaries speculated that the utilization of government web sites would evolve from an information stage, to a transaction stage, and finally to a transformation stage (Moon, 2002; Norris & Moon, 2005). The implication was that the Internet would revolutionize the delivery of government services. This, however, was a *field of dreams* perspective: If we build it, they will come and use it. Over the past decade research findings demonstrate that even though access and usage of government web sites have increased steadily, in-person and phone use are still the preferred channels for citizens to contact government (Smith, 2010; Ebbers, Pieterson & Noordman, 2007; Accenture, 2006; U.S. General Services Administration Report, 2005; Horrigan, 2004). According to Lucas (2008) most government web sites are still in the provision of information stage of development. Moreover, Norris and Moon (2005) as well as Coursey and Norris (2008) demonstrated that while web sites are common place for local and state governments, their primary function is to provide information and very few transactional services are provided. A longitudinal study of the 70 largest city governments in the U.S. West (2004) found that only 40 percent of these web sites offer services that are fully executable online. West (2007) concluded in his analysis of global adoption of e-government that reality falls far short of the somewhat utopian aspirations for transforming government. Furthermore West (2007) demonstrated that less effort has been expended on interactive features that would improve the delivery of services. West's findings are also supported by the United Nations'

2008 e-government survey finding that governments around the world are moving forward in e-government development, but that only a few governments have made the necessary investment to move from e-government applications *per se* to the more integrated connected governance stage (United Nations, 2008). Even though in some developed countries significant resources have been invested in increasing the number of online government services, citizens have been slow to adopt e-government services (Osimo, 2008). In a longitudinal survey of large American cities, the 2008 U.S. Municipalities E-Governance Report found increased attention to usability and content, but services, privacy and citizen participation still received lower scores and require further attention (Holzer et al., 2009). The US findings also reflect the results of the global survey of cities. All of these studies demonstrate that the move to more interactive services at all levels of government is slow and the predicted transformation stage of e-government has yet to be attained.

Models of E-Government Services

Coursey and Norris (2008) found in their review of models of e-government over the past decade that most models predicted a linear progression from information to transaction and ultimately to the transformation. Moreover, there was the belief that fully transactional systems are better and will yield more citizen interaction, translating into improved services and user satisfaction. Thus the predicted movement from information to transformation is either moving at a slow pace or not at all. Furthermore, their data revealed that local governments were not reporting the expected impact of reduced costs, increased online transactions and citizen participation. The models appeared to be speculations based on a technological determinism perspective and were not grounded in the research of information technology or government (Coursey & Norris, 2008). While Coursey and Norris (2008) do not offer a new model, they

do provide some general statements based on their findings that illuminate the current e-government environment. First and most importantly for this chapter, they conclude, "E-government is mainly an add-on to traditional ways of delivering government information and services, not a substitute for them" (Coursey & Norris, 2008, p. 533). The addition of new channels, while they may redirect some traffic from other channels, cannot supplant the traditional channels. Instead, new channels add to the costs, both for technology and management personnel, to maintain them. This may explain why these researchers did not find local governments reporting reduced costs or positive changes as a result of introducing new and additional e-government services as well as the slow and incremental adoption of these services. Secondly, these authors claim that e-government does not follow a linear progression (as predicted by earlier models) as later adopters can learn from early adopters and leap-frog to new technologies and uses. Finally, Coursey's and Norris's (2008) argument supports Kraemer's and King's (2006) assertion that e-government will probably not lead to governmental reform and/or transformation but instead support the dominant and existing political and administrative structures within governmental organizations. While Coursey and Norris only analyzed responses from government officials, these researchers propose that future research should focus on "citizen uptake and use of e-government" (Coursey & Norris, 2008, p. 535).

Critics of electronic public services emphasize that too much attention has been focused on the supply side factors and technological possibilities rather than on the needs of the end user (Verdegem & Verleye, 2009; Bertot & Jaeger, 2006; Reddick, 2005a). As a response to this technological, supply-side perspective of e-government services, some research suggests that the focus of e-government should shift towards user-centered services that cross governmental boundaries, and provided through multi-channels (Accenture, 2006, 2007; U.S. General Services Administration, 2005;

Horrigan, 2004). This leads to the examination of two recent empirical studies focusing on the acceptance and use of e-government services (van Dijk et al., 2008), and the development of a model to measure user satisfaction (Verdegem & Verleye, 2009).

An analysis of a 2006 survey on the use of government Internet services found the following primary predictors of e-government services: (1) The availability of Internet services, (2) the knowledge of this availability, (3) the preference for a digital channel, and (4) the ability and experience to use this channel (van Dijk et al., 2008). Moreover, this study found that, "People will stick to their habits of using traditional channels unless they happen to learn a better alternative" (van Dijk et al., 2008, p. 397). In addition to having access to a digital channel in the first place, citizens must have a preference for a digital channel. The preference to migrate to a digital channel comes from a satisfactory experience with the channel such as achieving the outcome of the task. Interestingly, van Dijk et al. (2008) report that social demographic factors were less significant in their model than other studies had reported (Horrigan, 2004; Pieterson & van Dijk, 2007; U.S. General Services Report, 2005). Van Dijk et al. (2008) argue that governments should move from the supply-side to a demand-side orientation to achieve not only a better measurement of the continuing usage of e-government services by citizens, but also to determine which services should be offered via the Internet. While government websites need to be attractive and easy to use, awareness of their availability is part of the learning process to entice citizens to use a digital channel.

In the development of their user-centered e-government model, Verdegem and Verleye (2009) found similar results. A 2006 survey of 1,651 citizens was conducted to determine the needs and expectations of citizens towards e-government and to discover the important determinants for measuring e-government satisfaction from an end-user perspective. Respondents reported that they were generally satisfied with the electronic services and accessed them more frequently at the local level rather than the regional or federal level. The researchers found eight key indicators for user satisfaction: (1) Technical aspects such as speed and reliability of the system (2) customer friendliness, (3) integration of services (4) use of multiple channels (5) possibility for personal contact (6) security (7) recent content and (8) usability. In addition to the on-line and off-line survey, these researchers conducted three focus groups with 28 respondents. The results of these focus groups revealed that while the eight determinants of user satisfaction were still important, the respondents indicated a lack of trust in e-government services and that the citizens received too little in return. Respondents wanted government to be more forthcoming with services and information. They also wanted a one-stop centralized portal from which they could easily get to the information and services they needed. More importantly, these respondents wanted to be able to contact a person via phone which argues for a multi-channel approach. From the focus group perspective, respondents felt that access to the service, usage of the service, and impact of the service were the most important factors. Verdegem and Verleye (2009, p. 14) concluded that there is a gap between interest of potential users and the actual use of e-government services, and that attention should be directed toward the non-users of electronic services. While potential users report a lack of awareness as a key factor for non use, these researchers argue that further investigation of citizens' needs and channel preference need to be conducted. A channel preference approach would be useful for government decision makers to find the most effective and efficient channel for the delivery of services particularly in light of newly emerging channels.

Verdegem and Verleye (2009) demonstrated that the move to fully executable online services is slow and uneven. This slow and patchy growth of e-government services at all levels of government not only in the U.S., but worldwide is supported by recent surveys (Lucas, 2008; Accenture, 2006; United Nations, 2008). The findings from these surveys reveal that e-government is far from transforming public administration and has not yet made the wants and needs of citizens or the use of multi-channel services a major focus of these e-government initiatives. Government agencies are now at a crossroads to determine which services should be delivered through which channels and to develop a multi-channel communication and service delivery strategy. If government web sites are to provide value to stakeholders, then government agencies need to analyze the entire process, starting from the citizen's perspective. To further this move towards e-government, the next step is to examine the relevant research on end-user characteristics.

End-User/Citizen Characteristics

Specific demographic characteristics of citizens may determine which channel is preferred (Thomas & Streib, 2003; Horrigan, 2004; U.S. General Services Report, 2005; Pieterson & van Dijk, 2007). The 2003 PEW Internet and American Life Project survey of 2,925 government patrons, i.e. people who contacted government for reasons other than mailing in a tax return, found that demographic characteristics can be related to how and why people contact government:

Demographically, those who contact the government are better educated, wealthier, younger and more likely to be male than the general population. … Among the factors that do not come significantly into play in people's tendencies to contact government are race, political affiliation, and marital status or being a parent. (Horrigan, 2004, p. 7)

Horrigan (2004) also reported that government patrons with broadband access to the Internet were more likely to contact government and use the Internet indicating that access as well as the speed of access was important for these patrons. Similar findings, i.e., demographic characteristics of high-income and well-educated Internet users as well as access and speed of access, also were found by the 2009 Pew Internet and American Life Project survey (Smith, 2010). The ease of use and familiarity with a channel also predicted channel choice. Pieterson and van Dijk (2007) found that personal characteristics, specifically age and education as well as habit (patterns of behavior based on previous experience or familiarity with a channel), and perceived ease of use were important predictors of channel choice. Only van Dijk et al. (2008) reported that end-user demographic characteristics were less important than other predictors, yet they still played an important role in understanding the adoption of e-government services.

The U.S. General Services Report (2005) also reported similar demographic characteristics related to channel selection. For example, 54 percent of Americans contact government in a typical year; most contacts are made by citizens between the ages of 30 and 49 followed by the 50 to 64 age group; telephone was the most preferred communication channel across all age groups; the younger citizens (less than 30) demonstrate a preference for the Internet as well as the telephone, while the older demographic (65 plus) preferred the phone and face-to-face contacts. While telephone was a preferred channel for all age groups, the preference for the Internet was increasing. This shift in channel preference appeared to be related to age and experience with electronic media. Moreover, citizens expect to use all current channels in the future as well as use new channels as they are developed. Significantly, citizens expect to use a combination of channels to contact government. Consequently, this report recommended that governments start planning for newer technologies that will result in new channels to manage. Furthermore, the report suggested that more research is needed into the service-level expectations of those citizens less likely to contact government and to address the digital divide.

For government agencies it is a difficult choice to move a process to on-line exclusively, but consideration and understanding of the target population characteristics as well as knowing how to access this population can help in that decision and bridge the digital divide. For example, a local government housing authority decided to move the application process for low income housing vouchers solely to an on-line application to avoid long lines which in turn previously resulted in fights, and to create an efficient and effective application process. By not considering the demographic characteristics as well as the limited access to the Internet by the target population, the housing authority created barriers for the target audience it served (Hillen, 2008). Non-profit organizations and local libraries were recruited to assist patrons. Although it may be obvious, a primary lesson from this example is to learn for whom the on-line process is efficient and effective. Thus demographic information and an understanding of communication and information seeking behavior of a target audience are useful for the design and ultimately the usage of a web site or any other channel to deliver information and services. Some local, state, and federal agencies are beginning to hire administrators who can manage social network sites, blogs, Twitter, and other social media to accommodate the expectations of their stakeholders with different demographic profiles. More importantly, these end-user characteristics are related to the nature of the task which is discussed next.

Task Characteristics

The literature on task characteristics indicates that the nature of the task is an important factor for channel selection (Reddick, 2005a; Pieterson & van Dijk, 2006, Wigand, 2007). In a comparison of the use of communication by phones versus communication by web sites Reddick (2005b)

discovered that when people have a problem they typically contact government by phone and use the web for information and transactions. Pieterson and van Dijk (2006) found that task complexity (multiple issues) and ambiguity (lack of clarity) are determinants for channel selection. These findings reflect earlier research (Daft, Lengel & Trevino, 1984, 1986, 1987; Bystrom & Jarverlin, 1995; Horrigan, 2004; Estabrook, Witt & Rainie 2007) on the interaction between task characteristics and channel selection. The 2003 Pew and American Life Survey reports that 49 percent of people who contacted government for very complex or urgent problems prefer to use the phone followed by in-person visits. Moreover, these government patrons also reported that the telephone was preferred for contacting government to solve a problem, to conduct transactions, and to search for information. The Web was the second most preferred channel for contacting government (Horrigan, 2004, p. 6). While more recent studies ((Smith, 2010; Ebbers et al., 2007; Accenture, 2006; U.S. General Services Administration Report, 2005) demonstrated that citizens still preferred the phone and in-person channels to contact government, the Pew Internet 2003 survey was the only study examining these tasks characteristics. This Pew Internet Study demonstrates that for complex (multiple issues), non-routine (infrequent occurrence), ambiguous (vague) and urgent (immediacy) tasks citizens prefer richer channels such as in-person or phone, and for simple (single issue), routine (frequent occurrence), and clearly defined tasks can be resolved via other channels, but overall citizens still prefer the phone. Hence, there appears to be a relationship between the nature of the task and channel selection.

When the U.S. General Services Report (2005) study conducted focus groups with 225 participants, similar results were discovered:

... Channel preferences, both for today and for the future varied by reason for and nature of contact. ... Cell phones/telephone is the preferred current

channel of contact for a simple, urgent expression of opinion (highway), while in-person is the preferred channel of contact for a complex, urgent problem (passport). ... Citizens expect to use the most convenient, competent, and timely channels as determined by specific reason and the nature of the interaction. (U.S. General Services Report, 2005, p. 57)

Verdegem and Verleye (2009) also echo the same relationship between type of task and channel preference and argue that governments should consider these channel-related impacts as they rethink electronic service delivery. The importance of task characteristics for public administrators is to understand the nature of the task that can range from simple (seeking information), non urgent (time not a factor) to complex (multiple issues), ambiguous (unclear or multiple solutions) and urgent (short time frame) so that the right channel can be used to resolve an issue, and in many cases offer a multi-channel strategy, since citizens are likely to use multiple channels to seek information and to achieve a response. Smith (2010) also found that a combination of online and offline channels are used to gather information and access government services.

Next, the channel characteristics are examined that can be matched with the task characteristics so as to build an understanding which channel might deliver convenient, competent and timely results.

Channel Characteristics

Research emphasizing the attributes of channels examines the degree of social presence, media richness, and synchronicity. Social presence theory ranks media channels on the degree to which each medium conveys physical presence, such as non-verbal and social cues of the participants required for a task (Short, Williams & Christie, 1976). The social presence scale ranges from face-to-face communication, i.e. the most social presence, to text-based communication exhibiting

the least social presence. Consequently, media with higher social presence are preferred for complex and ambiguous tasks such as conflict resolution. This line of research led to the concept of *media richness*.

Media Richness Theory builds on social presence theory and proposes that a medium is considered *rich* if it can reduce ambiguity in the following ways: (1) facilitating feedback, (2) communicating multiple cues, (3) using natural language to convey nuances and subtleties, and (4) creating individually tailored messages. The rank order of the media (i.e. from highest to lowest) on the media richness scale is face-to-face, telephone, written text (letters and memos), documents and bulletins, and computer printouts (Daft, Lengel & Trevino, 1987). Media richness theory posits that task characteristics should be matched with a medium's *richness* or "its capacity to facilitate shared meaning" (Daft, Lengel & Trevino, 1987). Although the social presence and media richness theories were developed prior to the Internet, their applicability is still relevant to this relatively new medium. Later studies focusing solely on the Internet also demonstrate that more personal and social cues enhance communication particularly for complex and ambiguous tasks (Pieterson & van Dijk, 2006; Ebbers, Pieterson & Noordman, 2007).

Channel characteristics vary according to their social presence and richness. The phone and front desk channels can offer interpretation of the contextual situation for the citizen as well as enable civil servants to ask probing questions to gain a better understanding. The Internet can provide more complex information that might be difficult to convey over the phone or in person. After a review of media richness and social presence research Robert and Dennis (2005, p.16) argue that there is an inverse relationship between user's attention and motivation with the ability to process information. These authors conclude:

The use of rich media high in social presence induces increased motivation but decreased abil-

ity to process, while the use of lean media low in social presence induces decreased motivation but increased ability to process. This runs counter to past research ... that as task complexity increases, so should social presence of the media used. ... By understanding the paradoxical effects of rich media high in social presence, we may be better able to select and use the most appropriate sets of media to accomplish our goals. (Robert and Dennis, 2005, p.16)

If a receiver of a message needs time to reflect and to process complex information, then the sender should select a channel with less social presence for the receiver to process the information. Furthermore, Robert and Dennis (2005) propose that switching between high and low social presence media will enhance the probability that the task will be achieved successfully. Again, this argues for using mixed media for channel choice for different types of tasks. In addition to media richness and social presence, Pieterson and van Dijk (2007) found that speed was frequently mentioned as a channel characteristic important to respondents. Speed was divided into two categories: (1) Speed of contact and (2) feedback speed.

Synchronicity, the timing and speed of a response, is a factor that determines a channel's likely use. Media synchronicity theory (Dennis & Valacich, 1999) focuses on the differences in preferred media for complex tasks. Media may vary in the ability to convey information and for information processing (convergence of shared meaning) to accomplish a task. A channel with high synchronicity, i.e. providing immediate feedback such as face-to-face and telephone, will result in more effective communication in which convergence of shared meaning is required. Similarly, asynchronous (or low synchronicity) channels, i.e. e-mail, listservs, voice mail, written mail and bulletin boards, are more effective for conveying information. DeLuca and Valacich (2008) suggest: "No one channel is always the richest, a channel may vary by the way it is used, the context in

which it is used, and the convenience of its use" (p. 795). Consequently, to develop a web site from an end-user perspective appropriately requires an understanding of the synchronicity of a channel that is linked to task and channel characteristics. The following section presents solutions and recommendations.

SOLUTIONS AND RECOMMENDATIONS

The framework presented in this chapter proposes the concept that public administrators need to consider the development and value of a web site from the end-user perspective and to understand the nature of and relationships among the end-users, tasks, and channel characteristics as well as the impact on channel selection. This first and foremost requires answering the questions: Why do citizens contact government? Which channels do citizens prefer? How can we match the channel with the reason for contact and channel preference? The value of this approach is that public administrators can evaluate and manage existing channels as well as make decisions regarding new ICT's and channels, e.g., blogs, emerging social networking technology, web chats and Twitter. Since traditional channels will continue to be used, this approach can enable public administrators to allocate resources to the channels that will deliver services to citizens in an efficient and effective way for government and for citizens.

The first recommendation is that government agencies need to consider ways to persuade citizens to adopt electronic government services, if the channel is a correct match for the task and end-user characteristics. While some critics feel that the adoption of e-government services has been slow and uneven, it may be that the adoption process may take longer than a decade. This may not be all that surprising when comparing this innovation to others (Rogers with Shoemaker, 1971). Rogers and Shoemaker present numerous examples of innovations taking various lengths of time. They also suggest potential efforts and interventions correspondingly may steepen the S-shaped diffusion curve. Relative advantage (perceived value of the innovation) is a key element in the diffusion process (Rogers with Shoemaker, 1971). Gourville (2004) asserts that an innovation must be perceived to be nine times better than a current channel in order for it to be adopted. The end-user must perceive that a new channel will yield a more reliable, faster and consistent response than a previously preferred channel. The new channel or web site must be compatible with existing values, past experiences, and needs of the citizen. Complexity, i.e. how difficult or easy a channel is to use, also will impact the rate of adoption. Ease of use is a consistent determinant in channel choice research. Moreover, if end-users can experiment on a limited basis with a new channel they are more likely to develop further their expertise and use. Likewise, if citizens observe others using a website successfully, they are more likely to adopt this channel. Observing others using a new channel indicates an awareness of its existence, and awareness is a key predictor to adoption (van Dijk et al., 2008; Verdegem & Verleye, 2009). Consequently, the perceived characteristics of a new channel (the innovation) may determine the rate of adoption. This is consistent with the five basic characteristics for the rate of adoption proposed in the *Diffusion of Innovations Theory*. Also the provider of an innovation (in this case the government agency) needs to decide which channel will be best for either providing information or persuading the end-user to adopt it. Using Rogers' with Shoemaker's (1971) innovation decision process model in conjunction with the framework of end-user, task and channel characteristics may enable public administrators to discern why or why not a new channel is being used and create motivation for adoption.

The second recommendation is that if e-government services are to add value and transform government, then specific organizational change will need to occur. This means that government organizations will need to restructure their processes to meet the citizens' needs and expectations. This may require new personnel with new e-government skills or retraining existing personnel to meet the demands of the proposed change. An example of government organizations changing to meet the needs of new channels is reflected in their efforts to hire administrators skilled to work with social networking media. Organizations, like citizens, are slow to adopt new processes and channels and need to appreciate the value, especially the added value, of such a change. To date most e-government services are a mirror image of existing paper-based processes. Very little attention has been given to citizen-initiated contacts with government and how to respond with the required information and services via an appropriate channel. As new channels appear on the horizon, the evaluation of the channel, task, and end-user characteristics will become even more important to the use and adoption of a new channel. For diffusion and adoption to occur there must be changes on both the supply-side and demand-side of the equation.

FUTURE RESEARCH DIRECTIONS

This research review demonstrates that channel choice and adoption of new channels is a complex issue requiring further research. First, more empirical research needs to focus not only on the end-users of e-government services, i.e. their satisfaction and expectations, but on the motivation, or lack thereof, of the non-users as well. There is a need to examine the slow rate of adoption of government web sites and e-government services. Attention should also be placed on how to increase awareness of the availability of e-government services as well as demonstrating the added value that this channel may provide over traditional channels. Citizens need not only to be aware of channels that will meet their needs; they need to be motivated to use them. Research has demonstrated that experience with a channel and channel choice impacts the adoption of a channel (van Dijk et al., 2008; Ebbers et al., 2008). Hence citizens need to have a positive experience with a channel that will motivate them to use it in the future. Second, more research on the interrelationships among end-user, task and channel characteristics and channel choices should be conducted to develop a strategy for the delivery of information and services through a preferred channel that matches these characteristics. Moreover, multi-channel approaches, i.e. different channels are used for different steps for information-seeking behavior, should be examined. When evaluating whether to adopt new channels, government agencies need to examine whether the channel is appropriate for intra-organizational, inter-organizational or external communication. The channel needs to be evaluated from a user-centric perspective and for its ability to convey the information and service for which it is intended. Finally, research using the proposed framework should be conducted to measure a channel's effectiveness and efficiency. Emphasis also should be placed on the resulting organizational changes required to implement a new channel.

CONCLUSION

Citizen-initiated contact with government and channel selection are complex topics that involve multiple concerns including end-user, task, and channel characteristics. Citizens still prefer to use traditional communication channels such as the phone to contact government as well as to use different channels for different purposes (Reddick, 2005). Ebbers, Pieterson and Noordman (2007) demonstrate that there is a gap between the communication channels governments prefer and those preferred by citizens. To close this gap, public administrators can apply this proposed framework to evaluate the target audience's de-

mographic information, the preferred patterns of channel choice, and link this knowledge with the nature of a task and the attributes of a channel to deliver quality information and services. Consequently, once government agencies understand that the starting point is the end-user, i.e. the citizen, public administrators can make decisions about the value of web sites and other channels based on this perspective in a regression-like fashion such as utilizing the best predictors of channel choice.

REFERENCES

Accenture (2006). *Leadership in customer service: Building the trust*. Retrieved April 30, 2009, from http://www.accenture.com

Accenture (2007). *Leadership in customer service: Delivering on the promise*. Retrieved March 12, 2008, from http://www.accenture.com

Baum, C., & Di Maio, A. (2000). *Gartner's four phases of e-government model*. Retrieved April 30, 2009, from http://www.gartner.com

Bertot, J. C., & Jaeger, P. T. (2006). User-centered e-government: Challenges and benefits for government web sites. *Government Information Quarterly*, *23*(2), 163–168. doi:10.1016/j.giq.2006.02.001

Bertot, J. C., & Jaeger, P. T. (2008). The e-government paradox: Better customer service doesn't necessarily cost less. *Government Information Quarterly*, *25*(2), 149–154. doi:10.1016/j.giq.2007.10.002

Blumler, J. G., & Katz, E. (1974). *The uses of mass communications: Current perspectives on gratifications research*. Beverly Hills, CA: Sage.

Bystrom, K., & Jarverlin, K. (1995). Task complexity affects information seeking and use. *Information Processing & Management*, *31*(2), 191–213. doi:10.1016/0306-4573(94)00041-Z

Coursey, D., & Norris, D. (2008). Models of e-Government: Are they correct? An empirical assessment. *Public Administration Review, 68*(3), 523–536. doi:10.1111/j.1540-6210.2008.00888.x

Daft, R. L., & Lengel, R. H. (1986). Organizational information requirements, media richness and structural design. *Management Science, 32*(5), 554–571. doi:10.1287/mnsc.32.5.554

Daft, R. L., Lengel, R. H., & Trevino, L. K. (1987). Message equivocality, media selection, and manager performance: Implications for information support systems. *Management Information Systems Quarterly, 11*, 355–366. doi:10.2307/248682

Davis, F. D. (1989). Perceived usefulness, perceived ease of use and user acceptance of information technology. *Management Information Systems Quarterly, 13*(3), 319–340. doi:10.2307/249008

DeLuca, D. C., & Valacich, J. S. (2008). Situational synchronicity for decision support. In Adam, F., & Humphreys, P. (Eds.), *Encyclopedia of decision making and decision support technologies* (*Vol. II*, pp. 790–797). Hershey, PA: Information Science Reference.

Dennis, A. R., & Valacich, J. S. (1999). Rethinking Media Richness: Towards a theory of media synchronicity. In HICSS-32, *32nd Annual Hawaii International Conference on System Sciences*. Los Alamitos CA: IEEE Computer Society.

Ebbers, W. E., Pieterson, W. J., & Noordman, H. N. (2008). Electronic government: Rethinking channel management strategies. *Government Information Quarterly, 25*(2), 181–201. doi:10.1016/j.giq.2006.11.003

Estabrook, L., Witt, E., & Rainie, L. (2007). *Information searches that solve problems: How people use the Internet, libraries, and government agencies when they need help*. Pew Internet and American Life Project. Retrieved May 1, 2009 from http://www.pewinternet.org

Gourville, J. (2004). Why consumers don't buy: The psychology of new product adoption. *Harvard Business School Note #504-056.*

Hillen, M. (2008, February 18). Housing voucher forms go on Web. *Arkansas Democrat-Gazette, 9*(11).

Holzer, M., Manoharan, A., Shick, R., & Stowers, G. (2009). *U.S. municipalities e-governance report (2008): An assessment of municipal websites*. Newark, N.J.: National Center for Public Performance, Rutgers University.

Horrigan, J. (2004). *How Americans get in touch with government. The Pew Internet and American Life Project.* Retrieved May 1, 2009, from http://www.pewinternet.org

Layne, K., & Lee, J. (2001). Developing fully functional e-government: A four stage model. *Government Information Quarterly, 18*(2), 122–136. doi:10.1016/S0740-624X(01)00066-1

Lucas, E. (2008, February 16). The electronic bureaucrat: A special report on technology and government. *The Economist*, 3-18.

Moon, M. J. (2002). The evolution of e-government among municipalities: Rhetoric or reality? *Public Administration Review, 62*(4), 424–433. doi:10.1111/0033-3352.00196

Norris, D. F., & Moon, M. J. (2005). Advancing e-government at the grassroots: Tortoise or hare? *Public Administration Review, 65*(1), 64–75. doi:10.1111/j.1540-6210.2005.00431.x

OECD. (2003). *OECD, the e-government imperative*. Paris: OECD e-government studies.

OECD. (2005). *OECD, e-government for better government*. Paris: OECD e-government studies.

Osimo, D. (2008). *Web 2.0 in government: Why and how?* European Commission Joint Research Center. Retrieved August 28, 2009 from http://ftp.jrc.es/EURdoc/JRC45269.pdf

Pieterson, W., & van Dijk, J. (2006). Governmental service channel positioning. In A. Gronlund, H. Scholl, K.V. Andersen, and M.A. Wimmer (Eds.), *Communication Proceedings of the Fifth International EGOV Conference 2006*. Krakow, Poland: Trauner Druck.

Pieterson, W., & van Dijk, J. (2007). Channel choice determinants: An exploration of the factors that determine the choice of a service channel in citizen initiated contacts. In *Proceedings of the 8th annual international conference on digital government research: bridging disciplines & domains*. Digital Government Society of North America, Vol. 228, 173-182.

Reddick, C. G. (2005a). Citizen-initiated contacts with government: Comparing phones and websites. *Journal of E-Government, 2*(1), 27–49. doi:10.1300/J399v02n01_03

Reddick, C. G. (2005b). Citizen interaction with e-government: From the streets to servers? *Government Information Quarterly, 22*(1), 38–57. doi:10.1016/j.giq.2004.10.003

Robert, L., & Dennis, A. (2005). Paradox of richness: A cognitive model of media choice. *IEEE Transactions on Professional Communication, 48*(1), 10–21. doi:10.1109/TPC.2004.843292

Rogers, E. M., & Shoemaker, F. (1971). *Communication of Innovation: A Cross-Cultural Approach* (2nd ed.). New York: Free Press.

Short, J., Williams, E., & Christie, B. (1976). *The social psychology of telecommunications*. London: John Wiley.

Smith, A. (2010). Government online. *The Pew Internet and American Life Project*. Retrieved May 1, 2010, from http://www.pewinternet.org.

Thomas, J., & Streib, G. (2003). The new face of government: Citizen-initiated contacts in the era of e-government. *Journal of Public Administration: Research and Theory, 13*(1), 83–102. doi:10.1093/jpart/mug010

United Nations. (2008). *United Nations e-government survey 2008: From e-government to connected governance*. Retrieved June 23, 2009 from http://unpan1.un.org/intradoc/groups/public/documents/UN/UNPAN028607.pdf

U.S. General Services Administration. (2005). *Citizens' service-level expectations: Final report. (USGSA Publication No. 99-D-00005)*. McLean, VA: MITRE Corporation.

van Dijk, J. A. G. M., Peters, O., & Ebbers, W. (2008). Explaining the acceptance and use of government Internet services: A multivariate analysis of 2006 survey data in the Netherlands. *Government Information Quarterly, 25*(3), 379–399. doi:10.1016/j.giq.2007.09.006

Venkatesh, V., & Davis, F. D. (2000). A theoretical extension of the technology acceptance model: Four longitudinal field studies. *Management Science, 46*(2), 186–204. doi:10.1287/mnsc.46.2.186.11926

Venkatesh, V., Morris, M. G., Davis, G. B., & Davis, F. D. (2003). User acceptance of information technology: Toward a unified view. *Management Information Systems Quarterly, 27*(3), 425–478.

Verdegem, P., & Verleye, G. (2009). User-centered e-government in practice: A comprehensive model for measuring user satisfaction. *Government Information Quarterly, 26*(3), 487–497. doi:10.1016/j.giq.2009.03.005

West, D. M. (2004). E-Government and the transformation of service delivery and citizen attitudes. *Public Administration Review, 64*(1), 15–27. doi:10.1111/j.1540-6210.2004.00343.x

West, D. M. (2007). Global perspectives on e-government. In Mayer-Schonberger, V., & Lazer, D. (Eds.), *Governance and information technology: From electronic government to information government*. Cambridge, MA: MIT Press.

Wigand, D. (2007). Building on Leavitt's diamond model of organizations: The organizational interaction diamond model and the impact of information technology on structure people and tasks. *AMCIS 2007 Proceedings.* Paper 287. Retrieved from http://aisel.aisnet.org/amcis2007/287

Wigand, R. T. (1997). Electronic commerce: Definition, theory and context. *The Information Society, 13*(3), 1–16. doi:10.1080/019722497129241

Zeithaml, V., Parasuraman, A., & Malhorta, A. (2000). A conceptual framework for understanding e-service quality: Implications for future research and managerial practice. *Marketing Science Institute*, 00-115.

KEY TERMS AND DEFINITIONS

Citizen-Centric E-Government: The focus of the provision of e-government services shifts from the supply-side to the demand-side, i.e. the end-user.

End-User Characteristics: The individual social demographic characteristics such as education, age, sex, income level, channel habits as well as experience with and access to the Internet.

Task Characteristics: Tasks can be described as complex, non-routine, ambiguous and urgent or as simple, routine, clearly defined, and non-urgent. The nature of the task will require different channels to derive the desired response.

Channel Characteristics: The channel attributes examined are social presence (degree to which a channel conveys physical presence, i.e. non-verbal and social cues); media richness refers to the ability of a channel to reduce ambiguity by its capacity to facilitate shared meaning via feedback, multiple communication cues, use of natural language to convey nuances and subtleties, and creating individual tailored messages; and synchronicity, i.e. the timing and speed of a response.

Multi-Channel Strategies: The use of more than one channel of communication, e.g., web sites, phone, and in-person to provide information and services.

Chapter 3
Serving Constituents with Limited English Proficiency (LEP) in the U.S.:
Challenges and Implications for Local Government Websites

J. Scott McDonald
University of Texas at El Paso, USA

Gerald A. Merwin Jr.
Valdosta State University, USA

Keith A. Merwin
Merwin Associates, USA

Regina K. Morris
University of Texas at El Paso, USA

Edris L. Brannen
Valdosta State University, USA

ABSTRACT

This chapter evaluates the implementation by local government websites of President William Jefferson Clinton's Executive Order 13166, Improving Access to Services for Persons with Limited English Proficiency (LEP) (Clinton, 2000). The purpose of Executive Order 13166 is to facilitate access to federally funded services. In the U.S., local governments are the most important basic service providers. This assessment is fundamentally important in light of the growing number of non-English speakers who reside in the country. The chapter looks at a diverse set of local governments and focuses on availability of information in Spanish, by far the predominant non-English language, spoken in about 12 percent of households in the U.S. in 2006. Government Web pages are assessed in terms of the degree to which 10 key government service areas are accessible in Spanish. The chapter identifies best practices for governments to make sites accessible to individuals with limited English proficiency.

DOI: 10.4018/978-1-61692-018-0.ch003

INTRODUCTION

If we humans are in fact what we read, a substantial share of U.S. citizens and residents fall short of their potential because important information located on local government websites is unintelligible: these websites lack accessibility to persons with limited English proficiency. The largest effected group in the U.S. are immigrants new to English, and little research has been directed at this group. In many other countries, such as the E.U. member states, research has focused on the issues mostly concerning languages spoken by indigenous peoples (Oeter, 2007).

President William Jefferson Clinton responded to this condition when he issued Executive Order 13166, Improving Access to Services for Persons with Limited English Proficiency (LEP), in August 2000 (Clinton, 2000). The goals of the Executive Order include facilitating access to services funded by the federal government and assisting individuals with LEP in their development of English language skills. The order requires all entities accepting federal funds to be accessible to persons with LEP, and notes general criteria, that is, numbers of persons with LEP and the critical nature of access among others. Yet, there are only limited guidelines and, to our knowledge, no federal actions to force compliance. However, as the U.S. continues to grow more diverse, the importance of language accessibility will increase. This chapter investigates local government actions in this arena and seeks to identify best practices that local governments, seeking to provide cost effective services to persons with LEP, might employ. Spanish language speakers and websites are the primary focus of the chapter because these individuals represent the predominant non-English language group in the U.S.

BACKGROUND

The relationship between language and the roles and rights of the governed is the focus of a relatively limited body of literature. This section briefly reviews the most relevant of this literature with regard to the present study. Brugger (1996) and Arzoz (2007) both credit German jurist Georg Jellinek with a system of categorizing human rights. Brugger, who traces the development of human rights to the American and French revolutions, summarizes three types or categories of rights: *status negativus,* most simply, liberty; *status activus,* the right to participate in the democratic process; and *status positivus,* relating to social and economic freedoms (1996, p. 597).

The specific issue of language rights is addressed by Xabier Arzoz (2007):

The theory of fundamental rights distinguishes three basic functions (which correspond to three basic normative structures) in the relation between the individual and the state: status negativus, status positivus and status activus (Pieroth and Schlink, 2003). The status negativus concerns freedom from interference from the state. The status positivus refers to the circumstances in which the individual cannot enjoy freedom without the active intervention of the state: one of the most important rights belonging to the status positivus is judicial protection, but it also extends nowadays to many forms of social protection and social services (schooling, housing, health care and so on). The status activus refers to the exercise of the individual's freedom within and for the state. These concepts, which have been construed to structure the relation of the individual and the state, also provide a useful analytical tool to approach the special needs of protection of minorities' characteristics (status positivus) and of institutional representation and participation of minorities (status activus) (Enke, 1931). The underlying idea is that the general ban on discrimination and other classical individual rights are not sufficient for the protection of minorities, and that their unique position within society justifies providing them additional constitutional safeguards (Sadurski, 2003). Thus, tolerance versus promotion proves a useful conceptual distinction in sociolinguistic and legal assessments of minority language policies, since it takes into account the special needs of minorities. (pp. 6-7)

Within the context of the Arzoz framework (2007), the intent of Executive Order 13166 is "status positivus." Arzoz's interpretation of protections covering social services such as education, housing, and health care (p. 6), correspond to services generally provided by local governments in the U.S. that are all or partially funded by the federal government. The intent of the Executive Order is clear: it establishes within the context of federal funding that individuals with LEP presently have limited access to government services. Therefore, it is essential that information be available in a language they can read and understand.

The nature of target populations is a fundamental difference between U.S. efforts to provide language rights via Executive Order 13166 and provisions for language rights in the European Union. Arzoz (2007) writes regarding the European Charter for Regional or Minority Languages (ECRML), created in 1992: "… the aim of the ECRML is not to guarantee human rights per se, but the protection of regional and minority languages as an integral part of the European cultural heritage (p. 16)."

Oeter (2007, p. 2) is more specific regarding the ECRML, noting, "…diversity of situations is not only striking if one looks into the language policy of different European states, but occurs also within individual states - one might think of the discrepancies between the situations of Danish and Frisian in Germany, between Welsh and Scottish Gaelic in the United Kingdom, between Catalan and Asturian in Spain, between German and Al-

banian in Italy." The principle focus of language rights protections within the European setting is indigenous peoples rather than immigrants.

In the United States a broad diversity of languages is spoken. Over a million people representing more than 70 countries obtained legal permanent-resident status in the U.S. in 2008 alone. People with LEP who speak Spanish, Russian, French or other languages, are overwhelmingly first generation immigrants and are therefore the primary beneficiaries of Executive Order 13166. For these individuals, if the information essential to accessing services is not available in their native language, they are precluded from realizing the benefits of government programming.

The federal government recognizes local governments as most persons' primary point for government access. Furthermore, the federal government acknowledges that with growth in LEP population, language is becoming an increasingly important barrier to access to government information and services.

The primary mission of local government websites is to take the government to the people, but if a website and a share of the population operate in different languages, the site fails in at least a portion of its mission. Language availability is more complex with websites than many other forms of government communication. For example, in the more traditional office setting, government units assisting persons with LEP might employ the services of a staff person to serve as translator. When LEP persons are seeking information or assistance via a local government's website, this one-on-one translation service is clearly not an option.

Local government websites have become an instrument to enhance accessibility and participation, and therefore democratization, and are the focus of increasing attention (Weare, Musso, & Hale 1999; Welch & Wong 2001; La Porte, Demchak, & de Jong 2002; Ho & Ni 2004; Streib & Navarro 2006; Bolivar, Perez & Hernandez 2007; Carrizales 2008). In the U.S., Internet accessibility is most often defined in terms of differently abled individuals' ability to access and understand Web content as defined by the Web Accessibility Initiative (W3C, 2009). Another aspect of accessibility is readability of presented information. Principal 3 of Web Content Accessibility Guidelines (WCAG) 2.0 (W3C, n.d.) specifies that Web content should fit the reading skills of users. Typically a 5th grade to 8th grade reading level is recommended for most general use websites, although today, these decisions are algorithm driven. A third aspect of accessibility, underappreciated and not well understood, yet greatly impacting participation, is the language(s) available on the site. Is the site exclusively in English or is equivalent content available in one or more alternative languages? Ordinarily, the use of a translation program such as Google translator or Babelfish yields less than stellar results (Accessibility NZ, 2008) although recent improvements are a major leap forward (Fallows, 2007).

Data from the 2006 American Community Survey suggest a language other than English is spoken in 19.7 percent of U.S. households (U.S. Census Bureau, 2008). This chapter samples city and county government websites from some of the most language diverse communities in the U.S. We focus on the availability of Spanish language content because Spanish is the predominant second language in U.S., spoken in 12.2 percent (2006) of households.

According to the U.S. Census Bureau, 54.8 million people (19.5 percent) speak a language other than English at home (2006 American Community Survey). Of this population approximately 14.9 percent speak English well or very well, leaving approximately 40 million who potentially require a language other than English to function well.

Executive Order 13166

President William Jefferson Clinton issued Executive Order 13166, Improving Access to Services for Persons with Limited English Proficiency, on August 11, 2000 (Clinton, 2000). Goals of the Executive Order include facilitating access to services funded entirely or partially by the federal government and assisting individuals with LEP in their development of English language skills. The Executive Order follows in the footsteps and mindset of the Civil Rights Act of 1964, and specifically Title VI which prohibits discrimination on the basis of national origin.

The Executive Order states "The federal government provides and funds an array of services that can be made accessible to otherwise eligible persons who are not proficient in the English language. The federal government is committed to improving the accessibility of these services to eligible LEP persons" (Clinton, 2000, Section 1. Goals). While the federal government provides these services and funds, it is clear that without accessible, multi-lingual sites, opportunity for all users is unlikely. Agencies and organizations accepting federal funding are responsible to make the information about services and funds accessible to targeted populations.

Online information on meeting the requirements of the Executive Order is collected and disseminated at www.lep.gov (U.S. Department of Justice, 2009a). The Civil Rights Division of the Department of Justice (DOJ) maintains the site providing LEP implementation standards to federal agencies based on the Executive order requirements. One page, "Federal Agency LEP Guidance & Language Access Plans" (U.S. Department of Justice, 2009b), provides links to LEP guidance prepared by federal departments. At present, many departments of the federal government itself, including Agriculture, Defense, and Homeland Security, list only "pending" and provide no links (U.S. Department of Justice, Civil Rights Division 2009). Others, for example, DOJ Civil Rights Division has an extensive LEP implementation plan in place (U.S. Department of Justice, Civil Rights Division 2001).

The U.S. Department of Justice's (2002) guidelines are suitable for most local governments providing a four-factor analysis to determine the level of LEP services needed/required:

1. The number or proportion of LEP persons eligible to be served or likely to be encountered by the program or grantee;
2. the frequency with which LEP individuals come into contact with the program;
3. the nature and importance of the program, activity, or service provided by the program to peoples' lives; and
4. the resources available to the grantee/recipient and costs. (p. 41459)

The DOJ Guidance is intended for law enforcement agencies (police and sheriffs' departments), jails, courts, and similar public safety or emergency organizations. In applying the analysis above, recipients of federal funding are advised to work at delivering language services to those most in need. "The greater the number or proportion of these LEP persons, the more likely language services are needed" (U.S. Department of Justice, 2002, p. 41459). However, the DOJ Guidance acknowledges that smaller agencies with limited budgets will be unlikely to provide the same levels of service as entities with larger budgets and resources (U.S. Department of Justice, 2000):

A recipient's level of resources and the costs that would be imposed on it may have an impact on the nature of the steps it should take. Smaller recipients with more limited budgets are not expected to provide the same level of language services as larger recipients with larger budgets. In addition, 'reasonable steps' may cease to be reasonable where the costs imposed substantially exceed the benefits. (p. 41460)

Employing DOJ guidance, in essence, standards, and other information, the following hypotheses were tested on the information above.

Figure 1. Language spoken at home; 2000 and 2005-2007 (Source: U.S. Census, 2000 Census and 2005-2007 American Community Survey 3-Year Estimates)

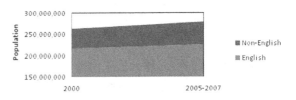

Figure 2. Language spoken at home, percent change 2000 and 2005-2007 (Source: U.S. Census, 2000 Census and 2005-2007 American Community Survey 3-Year Estimates)

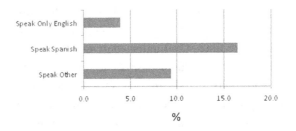

- As the proportion of LEP persons increases within a local government's service area, the likelihood of that local government website being LEP accessible increases.
- As the size (population) of the local government increases, the likelihood of that local government website being LEP accessible increases.

MAIN FOCUS OF THE CHAPTER

Population

The United States is increasingly multicultural as evidenced in Figures 1 and 2. As displayed in Figure 3, over 19 percent of the U.S. population speaks a language other than English at home, almost two-thirds of these being Spanish speakers. The group of individuals who speak a language

Figure 3. Language spoken at home 2005-2007 (Source: U.S. Census, 2000 Census and 2005-2007 American Community Survey 3-Year Estimates)

other than English at home is increasing more than twice as fast as those who speak only English, and Spanish speakers at home are increasing at more than three times the English-only rate. Speaking a language other than English at home does not in and of itself indicate that an individual does not speak English fluently. In fact, 56 percent of those who speak a language other than English at home self-report as speaking English *well*. However, this means more than 24 million persons have some disadvantage in speaking English. Moreover, Spanish speakers are the less likely to speak English well, with almost half (47.5 percent) reporting they speak English less than well. We should not overlook that ordinarily one will speak a language with high proficiency, in this case English, prior to reading with a similar level of proficiency.

Sample

To identify if and how local governments employ websites that provide information to non-English language speakers and to identify best practices, three conditions were sampled: proportions of the population who were non-English speakers, rate of growth in population most associated with being non-English speakers i.e., Hispanics), and large population governments with notable non-

English speaking populations. We opted for this diverse mode of developing a sample to afford some opportunity for generalization and to ensure a diverse sample of governments. We operational-ized these conditions via three samples, two based on a single measure from the U.S. Census and one based on media and other reports of diversity. Two samples are based on county level data and focus on county governments.

The first sample consisted of the 30 (of 3,086) counties with the highest percentage of popula-tion (five years or older) who spoke a language other than English at home. The sample counties are presented in Appendix 1. The counties ranged from 93.1 percent to 41.8 percent of population speaking a language other than English at home. As one might expect, the sample was dominated by counties in the four Mexico/U.S. border states: California (11 counties), Texas (6 counties), New Mexico (3), and Arizona (2). However, the sample was regionally diverse with three counties from New York, two each from New Jersey and Florida, and one county from Washington State.

A second sample consists of the five counties meeting two conditions: the fastest rate of growth of Hispanic population (2000-2007), and Hispanic populations in excess of 1,000 persons (2007). These counties, displayed in Figure 4 and Ap-pendix 2, had Hispanic population growth rates averaging 295 percent.

The third sample consisted of the principal unit of government within metro areas noted for diversity by various media. These include Bro-ward County, FL, and the cities of Miami, FL, Phoenix, AR, Los Angeles, CA, Chicago, IL and Seattle, WA. These six units, each with significant non-English speaking populations, were sampled based on size of non-English speaking population (rather than the percentage of population speak-ing languages other than English) to achieve a regional distribution.

Finally, while not a formal portion of any sample, we added the city of Tampa, FL for two reasons: the presence of a significant LEP

Figure 4. Percent change Hispanic pop % change Hispanic population 2000-2007 (Source: U.S. Census, 2000 Census and 2005-2007 American Community Survey 3-Year Estimates)

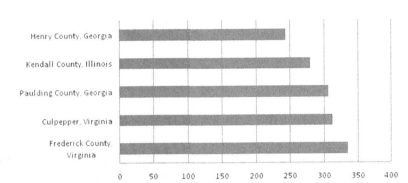

population, reported at 28 percent of the population speaking Spanish at home report they speak English not well or not at all; and more interestingly, because the city's website has a history of excellence, receiving numerous rewards over an eight-year period. For example, in 2007 alone, the city site took third in the 250,000 or more population category of the Digital Cities Survey, *Best of the Web* from the Center for Digital Government, and A+ in National Policy Research Council Excellence in E-government Project (City of Tampa, 2009). Based on the extraordinary performance of this site, the authors anticipated that the site might serve as a "best practices" model to meet Executive Order 13166 requirements.

Protocol

The protocol employed to evaluate sites, displayed in Appendix 3, uses a seven- point rating scale from zero to six. A zero rating indicates the lowest rating a website can receive, representing a placeholder. Many small governments have only basic local government contact information, such as telephone and address, and perhaps e-mail. This is the beginning level of setting up a site for constituents to contact the local government, but has very little information. A rating of one indicates a site with English only information. The two rating is given to a site that has Spanish on the

home page but only English on subsequent pages. Generally, the Spanish on these pages is machine translated. Someone who is fluent in Spanish would likely notice many translations errors, for instance incorrect grammar and awkward syntax which may yield errors in meaning as well.

A rating of three indicates a site that is likely to be useful to LEP persons. This type of page has Spanish that is machine translated and subsequent pages with more specific machine translated information in Spanish. These pages might require the user to click to get to the Spanish page from the page in English. A four rating represents pages with original Spanish created by someone fluent in the language and on some linked pages.

Websites with ratings of five and six both meet the criteria of the four rating and also have methods for someone to request information or submit forms in Spanish. Forms on the pages with a five rating must be downloaded, then manually completed and submitted, while a six indicates Spanish language forms linked with a database.

Evaluation of Local Government Sites

Reviewing Websites: An Example

We used a number of methods to evaluate local governments' websites in use of languages other

*Figure 5. Summary of Web page scores [n=36]
(Source: 2005-2007 American Community Survey
3-Year Estimates)*

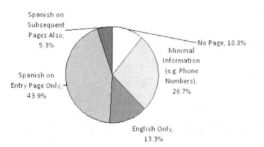

Figure 6. Website scores by state

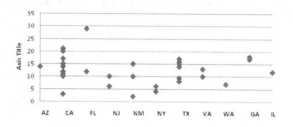

than English. First, we reviewed a government's home page for any indication of alternate language options. For example, on the City of Miami homepage (2009a), at the top left side of the page, the first menu item is "En Español" which links to the same homepage in Spanish (City of Miami, 2009b). Headings and menu items on this second page are in Spanish, however many subheadings, for example under "Noticias," are in English. Following the links under "Noticias" yields information in a strange combination of English and Spanish. The first item under "Noticias" yields the page with a news story in both Spanish and English, while headline and photo caption are in English only (City of Miami, 2009c).

Another page from the same list of "Noticias" yields a page totally in Spanish. The Spanish language side of the Miami website is clearly a work in progress.

Data and Interpretation

Samples 1 and 2

Assessments of the first two samples of counties (n = 36) are summarized in Figure 5. Assessments were conducted for as many as ten Web pages for each county website: home page, jail/corrections, juvenile justice, public defender, district attorney, sheriff, tax appraiser/assessor, tax collector, water department, county clerk employing the rating scale described above.

Almost 95 percent of Web pages reviewed scored two or less, indicating low accessibility for persons with LEP. Only 5.3 percent of pages scored in the three to six range (some Spanish on subsequent pages) representing pages that would be accessible to persons with LEP. Homepages were most likely to offer some access to Spanish language information, with 16.7 percent scoring three or above.

In Figure 6, each of the 11 states with sampled counties is represented by a column, with a diamond-shaped symbol (♦) for each county within that state, for example, Florida, the third state from the left, has two counties within the sample. The figure obviates that no state jumps out as either a high or low performer.

We hypothesized that counties with larger populations would provide more language accessibility. As Figure 7 displays, this was clearly not the case. The distribution is almost random and, in fact, larger populations tended to yield lower scores.

Finally, we tested whether proportion of households speaking Spanish or Spanish Creole within a county impacted the accessibility of a county's websites. Figure 8 displays data indicating that this is not the case; increased use of Spanish at home does not impact the availability of Spanish on a county's websites.

Sample 3

Ratings results for local government Websites in the third sample are summarized in Figure 9.

Figure 7. Website scores by county population (Note: Los Angeles County [population = 9,165,930] omitted for scaling purposes)

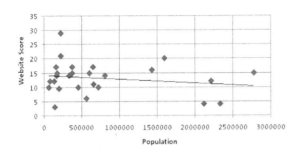

Figure 8. Total Web site scores by percentage Spanish or Spanish Creole language spoken at home

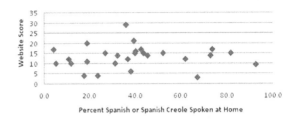

Figure 9. Selected city site scores

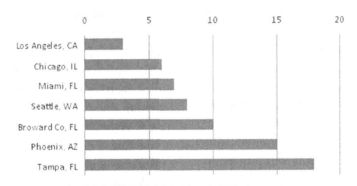

While the rating scale is the same used for the prior two samples (0 to 6), the specific pages used for the ratings are different for this sample. Local governments in Sample 3 are comprised of both city and metropolitan county governments in various states, therefore these entities have different responsibilities. In other words, not all city governments are responsible for assessing and collecting real estate taxes. Furthermore, many municipal governments do not have the same offices and/or services, such as courts, district attorneys and public defenders, jails, and water, because those are provided by other entities.

Figures 10 and 11 place total website score within the context of population size and percentage of LEP population for the seven metropolitan areas studied. As with the counties (Samples 1 and 2), site score did not increase with population size.

In fact, as Figure 10 displays, site scores tend to decrease with population increases, although this observation must be qualified in light of the small sample size. Likewise, site scores are inversely related to percentage LEP population. Both these findings go counter to our expectations.

True to their reputation, the City of Tampa site had the highest site rating and the highest home page rating—the only page to achieve a score of six, in any of the 43 websites we reviewed. Tampa achieved this notable feat, despite it having the smallest population and second lowest proportion of LEP of the seven metro areas studied. This seems to demonstrate that local governments can provide useful information to LEP residents even if they are not the largest by population or have the highest proportion of LEP population.

Figure 10. Website score by population

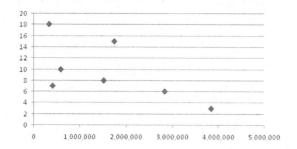

Figure 11. Website score by percentage LEP

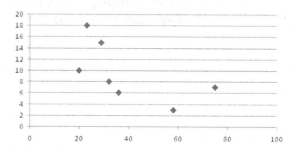

SOLUTIONS AND RECOMMENDATIONS

A guide to "best practices" is urgently needed to assist local government and other entities in addressing the needs of their LEP populations. Additionally, many governments, particularly those with smaller populations and/or rapidly expanding LEP populations, will need to target their limited resources carefully. The following discussion of methods for better serving constituents with limited English skills will provide an initial road map to local governments wishing to enhance their sites.

BEST PRACTICES

A first recommendation for local governments and entities seeking to better serve LEP constituents is to have clearly marked links on the home page leading to translations of the most important information. A first step is for each government to prioritize Web pages and focus resources on the most important information from the perspectives of LEP populations. Ideally these links will be at or near the top of the page highlighting the non-English languages in a user friendly manner, such as "En Español" rather than "In Spanish." At a minimum, these pages may be machine translated, even though this method tends to yield a lower

quality product. Nevertheless, it is at least a start in the right direction.

A second step, taken in conjunction with the first, is to prioritize Web pages and focus translation and page development resources on the most important information from the perspectives of LEP populations. The pages outlined in our ratings of city and county sites are suggested as potential starting points for prioritization; however each local government and the population it serves is unique. For city governments the important pages are likely to include those for services such as Police, Fire, Water, and Housing. The pages that might be most useful to residents of county governments would include Sheriff, Jail, Juvenile Justice, Public Defender, District Attorney, Water, Tax Appraisers and Collector, and Clerk. Governments are advised to consult with citizen groups, especially those serving LEP populations, or to conduct focus groups of LEP populations to determine which services to prioritize and address first.

A third step that may improve Web accessibility for all residents is to provide a clear site map with the departments or services listed and cross-referenced in ways that might make sense to residents. For instance, it is likely better to list Water (e.g., "How do I get my water turned on?") by itself, even if water service falls under a Public Utilities Department. Otherwise, residents who do not understand the structure of their local government might remain in the dark. A parallel site map should be considered for each language used by a significant proportion of local residents. The parallel maps might show what is available in say, Spanish (en Español), and what is English-only.

A fourth step to improve accessibility is to hold focus groups and ask local residents for feedback regarding the site, especially its usability. By compiling the information gathered from these groups it is likely that the website can be improved in many ways that the government employees might not consider. This is a marketing practice commonly employed by the private sector.

There are numerous other activities that may be undertaken to improve local government sites. It is not within the scope of this chapter to cover all of them. Some of these may be found in the "Suggested Readings" at the end of the chapter.

Meeting the Needs of Small or Rapidly Growing Communities

Each state, in cooperation with local municipal and/or county advocacy organizations, can establish templates to assist local governments in providing information to the residents with LEP. These templates can be translated by fluent individuals (in those primary languages spoken by residents of the area) from samples based on the "Best Practices" and any other local guidelines. Through this effort local governments can begin to "fill in the blanks" with contact information or other details specific to the departments or services covered.

States may choose to assist small and/or poorer local governments by providing Web hosting for the local government sites at no cost or low cost, perhaps through grants funded by federal funds. This will likely be the fastest route to meeting the intent of the Executive Order 13166. Efforts to meet the Executive Order requirements are important not only to avoid any Federal penalties,

but in a larger context these efforts are to better meet the needs of residents.

FUTURE RESEARCH DIRECTIONS

LEP accessibility of government websites is a subject matter ripe for both action and study. We expect as governments become more attentive to LEP access to web based information, they will need the support of researchers to effectively and efficiently address this matter. There is ample opportunity for researchers with diverse backgrounds, such as computer science, linguistics, public policy, and anthropology to name a few, to contribute to these efforts.

The study reported herein barely scratched the surface of the LEP issue both in terms of number of cases and scope. The study employed relatively small sample sizes, analyzing and discussing barely forty governments of the 3,034 county and 19,429 municipal governments, not to mention the 65,000 other units of local government. Studies employing larger samples and samples of other units, such as school systems, are warranted. Studies focused on specific governmental services/issues may also be warranted, such as criminal justice and housing.

With the U.S. becoming increasingly diverse, researchers and practitioners may want to review the experiences of other multicultural communities, such as Canada (especially Quebec), England, Belgium, Malaysia, portions of the E.U., as well as other locales. Additionally, government may learn a good deal from the private sector in addressing LEP populations.

As a civil rights issue, LEP access to the Web will not be going away. Good faith or even more stringent standards will likely be required as the issue matriculates through state and federal agencies and possibly the courts. Efficiency and effectiveness will depend on applying best practices that other governments developed.

CONCLUSION

Whether a local government is proactive in providing language accessibility to LEP populations is not a function of the overall size of population service or the size of LEP population. Motivation, often driven by a single individual, seems to be the key determinant of a serious effort at LEP accessibility.

REFERENCES

W3C (2008). *Web content accessibility guidelines 2.0*. Retrieved March 20, 2009, from http://www.w3.org/TR/WCAG20/

W3C (2009). *Web Accessibility Initiative (WAI) Highlights*. Retrieved March 20, 2009 from http://www.w3.org/WAI/

Accessibility, N. Z. (2008). *Consider the ease of reading, and language level*. Retrieved March 18, 2009, from http://accessibility.net.nz/blog/ease-of-reading-language-level/

Arzoz, X. (2007). The Nature of Language Rights. *Journal on Ethnopolitics and Minority Issues in Europe*, 2. Retrieved August 21, 2009, from http://www.ecmi.de/jemie/download/2-2007-Arzoz.pdf

Bolivar, M., Perez, C., & Hernandez, A. (2007). E-government and public financial reporting: The case of Spanish regional governments. *The American Review of Public Administration, 37*(2), 142-177. Retrieved March 23, 2009, from http://arp.sagepub.com/cgi/reprint/37/2/142

Brugger, W. (1996). The Image of the Person in the Human Rights Concept [Electronic version]. *Human Rights Quarterly, 18*(3), 594–611. doi:10.1353/hrq.1996.0034

Carrizales, T. (2008). Critical factors in an electronic democracy: A study of municipal managers. *The Electronic Journal of e-Government, 6*(1), 23-30. Retrieved March 25, 2009, from http://www.ejeg.com/volume-6/vol6-iss1/Carrizales.pdf

City of Miami. (2009a). *City of Miami* (Home Page – English Language Version). Retrieved June 24, 2009, from http://www.miamigov.com/cms/

City of Miami. (2009b). *Ciudad de Miami* (Home Page – Spanish Language Version). Retrieved June 24, 2009, from http://trans5.convertlanguage.com/miami/enes/?24;http://www.miamigov.com/cms/

City of Miami. (2009c). *Noticias*. Retrieved June 24, 2009 from: http://trans5.convertlanguage.com/miami/enes/?24;http://www.miamigov.com/cms/comm/1724_6034.asp

City of Tampa. (2009). *Tampa Announcements*. Retrieved 9 June 2009 from: http://www.tampagov.net/appl_tampa_announcements/default.asp?page=1&hide=yes&VF=0&numResults=10&typeID=WEB&searchDate=6%2F9%2F2009+1%3A41%3A25+PM

Clinton, W. J. (2000). *Executive Order 13166*. Retrieved May 10, 2009 from http://www.usdoj.gov/crt/cor/Pubs/eolep.php

Fallows, J. (2007, April). One-button translation. *The Atlantic*. Retrieved March 24, 2009 from: http://www.theatlantic.com/doc/200704/fallows-translators

Florida Center for Community Design + Research, School of Architecture and Community Design, University of South Florida (2005). *Hillsborough Community Atlas: City of Tampa*. Retrieved 9 June 2009, from http://www.hillsborough.communityatlas.usf.edu/demographics/default.asp?ID=1205771000&level=mncplty#elp

Gummesson, E. (2000). *Qualitative Methods in Management Research (2nd)*. Thousand Oaks, CA: Sage.

Ho, A., & Ni, A. (2004). Explaining the adoption of e-government features: A case study of Iowa county treasurers' offices. *The American Review of Public Administration, 34*(2), 164-180. Retrieved March 27, 2009, from http://arp.sagepub.com/cgi/reprint/34/2/164

La Porte, T., Demchak, C., & de Jong, M. (2002). Democracy and bureaucracy in the age of the web: Empirical findings and theoretical speculations. *Administration & Society, 34*(4), 411-446. Retrieved March 25, 2009, from http://aas.sagepub.com/cgi/reprint/34/4/411

Migration Policy Institute. (2007). *MPI Data Hub: Migration Facts, Stats, and Maps.* Retrieved January 28, 2009, from http://www.migrationinformation.org/DataHub/charts/6.1.shtml

Oeter, S. (2007). Minority Language Policy: Theory and Practice. *Journal on Ethnopolitics and Minority Issues in Europe*, 2. Retrieved August 21, 2009, from http://www.ecmi.de/jemie/download/2-2007-Oeter-Introduction.pdf

Office of Immigration Statistics. (2008). *2008 Yearbook of Immigration Statistics*. Washington DC: Department of Homeland Security. Retrieved August 25, 2009, from http://www.dhs.gov/xlibrary/assets/statistics/yearbook/2008/ois_yb_2008.pdf

Streib, G., & Navarro, I. (2007). Citizen demand for interactive e-government: The case of Georgia consumer services. *The American Review of Public Administration, 36*(3), 288-300. Retrieved March 29, 2009, from http://arp.sagepub.com/cgi/reprint/36/3/288

U. S. Department of Justice. (2002, June 18). Guidance to Federal Financial Assistance Recipients Regarding Title VI Prohibition Against National Origin Discrimination Affecting Limited English Proficient Persons. *Federal Register, 67*(117).

U.S. Census Bureau. (2008). *2005-2007 American community survey 3-year estimates* Washington, DC: US Department of Commerce. Retrieved January 30, 2009, from http://factfinder.census.gov/servlet/DatasetMainPageServlet?_program=ACS&_submenuId=&_lang=en&_ts=

U.S. Department of Justice. (2002). Guidance to federal financial assistance recipients regarding Title VI prohibition against national origin discrimination affecting limited English proficient persons. *Federal* Register 67:117, 41455-41472. Retrieved 25 January 2009 from http://www.usdoj.gov/crt/cor/lep/DOJFinLEPFRJun182002.pdf

U.S. Department of Justice, Civil Rights Division. (2001). *Departmental plan implementing Executive Order 13166*. Retrieved January 25, 2009, from http://www.usdoj.gov/crt/cor/lep/dojimp.php

U.S. Department of Justice, Civil Rights Division. (2009 a). *Federal Agency LEP Guidance & Language Access Plans.* Retrieved September 19, 2009, from http://www.lep.gov/guidance/guidance_index.html

U.S. Department of Justice, Civil Rights Division. (2009 b). *Limited English Proficiency A Federal Interagency Website.* Retrieved September 19, 2009, from http://www.lep.gov

Weare, C., Musso, J., & Hale, M. (1999). Electronic democracy and the diffusion of municipal web pages in California. *Administration & Society*, 31(1), 3–27. Retrieved from http://aas.sagepub.com/cgi/reprint/31/1/3. doi:10.1177/009539999400935475

Welch, E., & Wong, W. (2001). Global information technology pressure and government accountability: The mediating effect of domestic content on website openness. *Journal of Public Administration Research and Theory, 11*(4), 509-538. Retrieved March 14, 2009, from http://jpart.oxfordjournals.org/cgi/reprint/11/4/509

Yin, R. (2003). *Case Study Research: Design and Methods (3ʳᵈ)*. Thousand Oaks, CA: Sage.

ADDITIONAL READING

W3C (2008). Web content accessibility guidelines 2.0. Retrieved March 20, 2009, from http://www.w3.org/TR/WCAG20/

W3C (2009). *Web Accessibility Initiative (WAI) Highlights*. Retrieved March 20, 2009, from http://www.w3.org/WAI/

Accessibility, N. Z. (2008). *Consider the ease of reading, and language level*. Retrieved March 18, 2009, from http://accessibility.net.nz/blog/ease-of-reading-language-level/

Bolivar, M., Perez, C., & Hernandez, A. (2007). E-government and public financial reporting: The case of Spanish regional governments. *The American Review of Public Administration, 37*(2), 142-177. Retrieved March 23, 2009, from http://arp.sagepub.com/cgi/reprint/37/2/142

Cardi, V. (2007). Regional or Minority Language Use before Judicial Authorities: Provisions and Facts. *Journal on Ethnopolitics and Minority Issues in Europe*, 2. Retrieved August 21, 2009, from: http://www.ecmi.de/jemie/download/2-2007-Cardi.pdf

Carrizales, T. (2008). Critical factors in an electronic democracy: A study of municipal managers. *The Electronic Journal of e-Government, 6*(1), 23-30. Retrieved March 25, 2009, from http://www.ejeg.com/volume-6/vol6-iss1/Carrizales.pdf

City of Tampa. (2009). *Tampa Announcements*. Retrieved June 9, 2009, from http://www.tampa-gov.net/appl_tampa_announcements/default.asp?page=1&hide=yes&VF=0&numResults=10&typeID=WEB&searchDate=6%2F9%2F2009+1%3A41%3A25+PM

Civil Rights Division, U.S. Department of Justice. (2000). *Federal Agency LEP Guidance & Language Access Plans*. Retrieved May 10, 2009, from http://www.usdoj.gov/crt/lep/guidance/guidance_index.html

Clinton, W. J. (2000). *Executive Order 13166*. Retrieved May 10, 2009, from http://www.usdoj.gov/crt/cor/Pubs/eolep.php

Clinton, W. J. (2000). Statement on the Executive order to improve access to services for persons with limited English proficiency. *Weekly Compilation of Presidential Documents, 36*(33), 1857.

Cornell, D. (1999). The imaginary of english only. [from http://www.csa.com]. *University of Miami Law Review, 53*(4), 977–982. Retrieved August 21, 2009.

Curtin, G. G., Sommer, M. H., & Sommer, V. V. (Eds.). (2003). *The world of e-government*. New York: Haworth Press.

deLeon, P., & deLeon, L. (2002). What Ever Happened to Policy Implementation? An Alternative Approach [Electronic version]. *Journal of Public Administration: Research and Theory, 12*, 467–492.

Department of Justice. (2002, June 18). Guidance to Federal Financial Assistance Recipients Regarding Title VI Prohibition Against National Origin Discrimination Affecting Limited English Proficient Persons. *Federal Register, 67*(117).

Fallows, J. (2007). One-button translation *The Atlantic*. Retrieved March 24, 2009, from http://www.theatlantic.com/doc/200704/fallows-translators

Florida Center for Community Design + Research, School of Architecture and Community Design, University of South Florida (2005). *Hillsborough Community Atlas: City of Tampa*. Retrieved June 9, 2009, from http://www.hillsborough.communityatlas.usf.edu/demographics/default.asp?ID=1205771000&level=mncplty#elp

Garson, G. D. (2006). *Public information technology and e-governance: Managing the virtual state*. Boston: Jones & Bartlett.

Graham, H. (1990). Race, language, and social policy: Comparing the Black and Hispanic experience in the U.S. *Population and Environment, 12*(1), 43–58. doi:10.1007/BF01378551

Ho, A., & Ni, A. (2004). Explaining the adoption of e-government features: A case study of Iowa county treasurers' offices. *The American Review of Public Administration 34*(2), 164-180. Retrieved March 27, 2009, from http://arp.sagepub.com/cgi/reprint/34/2/164

Info Tech Research Group. (2006). *Government: 2006 IT Budget and Staffing Report*. London, Ontario.

Ingram, D. (2003). Between Political Liberalism and Postnational Cosmopolitanism: Toward an Alternative Theory of Human Rights [Electronic version]. *Political Theory, 31*(3), 359–391. doi:10.1177/0090591703031003002

La Porte, T., Demchak, C., & de Jong, M. (2002). Democracy and bureaucracy in the age of the web: Empirical findings and theoretical speculations. *Administration & Society, 34*(4), 411-446. Retrieved March 25, 2009, from http://aas.sagepub.com/cgi/reprint/34/4/411

Liu, R., & Schachter, H. (2007). Mobility Information Needs of Immigrants with Limited English Proficiency (LEP) in New Jersey. *Journal of Immigrant & Refugee Studies, 5*(2), 89–108. doi:10.1300/J500v05n02_05

National Academy of Sciences. (1999). *Funding a Revolution: Government Support for Computing Research*. Washington: National Academy Press. Retrieved October 15, 2006, from http://newton.nap.edu/books/0309062780/html

National Association of Community Health Centers. (2008). *Serving patients with limited English proficiency: Results of a community health center survey*. Retrieved August 7, 2009 from http://www.calendow.org/uploadedFiles/Publications/By_Topic/Culturally_Competent_Health_Systems/Language_Access/NACHC-NHeLP.pdf

Paulston, C. B. (1997). Language Policies and Language Rights. *Annual Review of Anthropology, 26*, 73–85. doi:10.1146/annurev.anthro.26.1.73

Rosenbaum, S. (2004). Reducing discrimination affecting persons with limited English proficiency: Federal civil rights guidelines under Title VI of the 1964 Civil Rights Act. *Public Health Reports, 119*, 93-96. Retrieved August 8, 2009 from http://www.pubmedcentral.nih.gov/picrender.fcgi?artid=1502263&blobtype=pdf

Seifert, J. (2003). *A Primer on E-Government: Sectors, Stages, Opportunities, and Challenges of Online Governance*. Washington, DC: Library of Congress, Congressional Research Service.

Shiu-Thorton, S., Balabis, J., Senturia, K., Tamayo, A., & Oberle, M. (2007). Disaster preparedness for limited English proficient communities: Medical interpreters as cultural brokers and gatekeepers. *Public Health Reports, 122*(4), 466–471.

Streib, G., & Navarro, I. (2007). Citizen demand for interactive e-government: The case of Georgia consumer services. *The American Review of Public Administration, 36*(3), 288-300. Retrieved March 29, 2009 from http://arp.sagepub.com/cgi/reprint/36/3/288

U.S. Census Bureau. (2008). 2005-2007 American community survey 3-year estimates Washington, DC: U.S. Department of Commerce. Retrieved January 30, 2009, from http://factfinder.census.gov/servlet/DatasetMainPageServlet?_program=ACS&_submenuId=&_lang=en&_ts=

U.S. Department of Justice. (2002). Guidance to federal financial assistance recipients regarding Title VI prohibition against national origin discrimination affecting limited English proficient persons. *Federal Register, 67*(117), 41455-41472. Retrieved January 25, 2009, from http://www.usdoj.gov/crt/cor/lep/DOJFinLEPFRJun182002.pdf

U.S. Department of Justice, Civil Rights Division. (2001*). Departmental plan implementing Executive Order 13166*. Retrieved 25 January 2009 from http://www.usdoj.gov/crt/cor/lep/dojimp.php

Vieytez, E. J. R. (2007). New minorities and linguistic diversity: Some reflections from the Spanish and Basque perspectives. *Journal on Ethnopolitics and Minority Issues in Europe*, 2. Retrieved August 21, 2009, from http://www.ecmi.de/jemie/download/2-2007-Vieytez.pdf

Wainright, M. E., Brown, C. V., DeHayes, D. W., Hoffer, J. A., & Perkins, W. C. (2005). *Managing Information Technology* (5th ed.). Upper Saddle River, NJ: Prentice Hall.

Weare, C., Musso, J., & Hale, M. (1999). Electronic democracy and the diffusion of municipal web pages in California. *Administration & Society, 31*(1), 3–27. Retrieved from http://aas.sagepub.com/cgi/reprint/31/1/3. doi:10.1177/009539999400935475

Welch, E., & Wong, W. (2001). Global information technology pressure and government accountability: The mediating effect of domestic content on website openness. *Journal of Public Administration Research and Theory, 11*(4), 509-538. Retrieved March 14, 2009, from http://jpart.oxfordjournals.org/cgi/reprint/11/4/509

Zavodny, M. (2000). The Effects of Official English Laws on Limited-English-Proficient Workers [Electronic version]. *Journal of Labor Economics, 18*(3), 427–452. doi:10.1086/209965

KEY TERMS AND DEFINITIONS

Executive Order: In the United States there are three branches of government: executive, legislative, and judicial. The president is the head of the executive branch and can issue orders that are generally carried out by the departments in the executive branch, such as Justice, State, Agriculture, Labor, Defense, and others. The executive orders are not law, but are generally intended to clarify the ways a specific law will be enforced. Executive orders have been issued by U.S. presidents since 1789.

Limited English Proficiency (LEP): Limited English proficiency (LEP) is used here in relation to Executive Order 13166, intended to promote communication of information about government services to everyone, despite the level of English comprehension. LEP is used to describe someone who primarily speaks and understands a language other than English and might in some cases have problems understanding information presented only in English.

Indigenous Peoples: Indigenous peoples are members of ethnic groups who are the earliest known inhabitants of an area, region, or country that is now shared by others with different ethnic backgrounds. In many cases the predominant culture and language of the country is not representative of the indigenous peoples.

W3C: The World Wide Web Consortium, generally abbreviated as W3C, is an international organization that oversees operation of the web. The W3C creates and updates standards for implementation of web pages and sites and provides information for those who use and create these pages and sites.

Best of the Web: The "Best of the Web" (also abbreviated as "BOTW") is a directory found at: http://botw.org/ that provides information on sites that are chosen as the best within their category. Some of the categories are arts, business, computers, and many others, with all having sub-categories.

Center for Digital Government: The Center for Digital Government, located at: http://www.centerdigitalgov.com/, is an organization that provides information on the ways that government agencies use information technology. Information is disseminated through reports, surveys, and events.

Local Government: As used here, local government refers to either city or county governments in the United States of America. While there might be other units of government below the state level, the focus of this chapter is on city and county governments.

Template: The concept of a template, as used here, is that a web page would be created in such a way that it could be used by a variety of different organizations by filling in the blanks with appropriate and specific information. For instance, a template for a local government home page would list those officials, departments and services that are generally part of a local government unit. Ideally templates for other pages (such as those specific to the departments and services) would also be provided to simplify the production of a site by a local government.

APPENDIX 1. COUNTIES WITH HIGHEST LEVELS OF LANGUAGE OTHER THAN ENGLISH SPOKEN AT HOME

			Population 5 Years and Older			
				Language Spoken at Home		
	Percent Who Speak a Language Other Than English at Home	Rank	Total	Speak only English	Spanish or Spanish Creole	% Spanish or Spanish Creole
Maverick County, Texas	93.1	1				
Webb County, Texas	93.1	2	197,943	13,714	182,977	92.4
Hidalgo County, Texas	82.5	3	606,893	106,264	494,812	81.5
El Paso County, Texas	75.7	4	653,549	159,059	481,155	73.6
Cameron County, Texas	73.7	5	336,704	88,657	245,577	72.9
Miami-Dade County, Florida	70.8	6	2,216,286	646,365	1,377,231	62.1
Imperial County, California	68.9	7	143,347	44,575	96,292	67.2
Rio Arriba County, New Mexico	62.8	8				
Apache County, Arizona	62.4	9				
McKinley County, New Mexico	59.0	10				
Los Angeles County, California	56.3	11	9,165,930	4,006,477	3,652,510	39.8
Hudson County, New Jersey	56.0	12	560,314	246,272	213,399	38.1
Bronx County, New York	55.6	13	1,261,778	560,127	575,689	45.6
Queens County, New York	54.5	14	2,122,988	965,290	498,948	23.5
Dona Ana County, New Mexico	53.8	15	178,033	82,280	92,964	52.2
Monterey County, California	51.5	16	372,931	180,973	162,006	43.4
Santa Clara County, California	49.8	17	1,597,306	802,452	300,801	18.8
Merced County, California	48.7	18	220,645	113,223	86,775	39.3
Yuma County, Arizona	46.9	19	169,259	89,856	76,351	45.1
Tulare County, California	46.6	20	374,510	200,015	158,276	42.3
Kings County, New York	46.1	21	2,332,439	1,257,290	408,171	17.5
Franklin County, Washington	46.1	22				
San Francisco County, California	45.5	23	718,962	391,887	85,871	11.9
Passaic County, New Jersey	44.4	24	455,562	253,300	142,091	31.2
San Mateo County, California	44.3	25	654,938	364,669	123,080	18.8
Orange County, California	43.6	26	2,775,583	1,565,158	743,879	26.8
Bexar County, Texas	43.1	27	1,425,203	810,885	570,147	40.0
Kings County, California	42.4	28	134,238	77,356	49,354	36.8
Osceola County, Florida	42.4	29	225,442	129,929	80,750	35.8
Fresno County, California	41.8	30	809,469	470,768	261,604	32.3
United States	**19.5**		**278,276,723**	**223,949,581**	**33,701,181**	**12.1**

Source: 2005-2007 American Community Survey 3-Year Estimates.

Blank cells indicate missing data. ACS sample n too small for reporting.

NOTE. Although the American Community Survey (ACS) produces population, demographic and housing unit estimates, it is the Census Bureau's Population Estimates Program that produces and disseminates the official estimates of the population for the nation, states, counties, cities and towns and estimates of housing units for states and counties.

(1) Pew @ http://pewhispanic.org/docs/?DocID=17

APPENDIX 2. COUNTIES WITH HIGHEST RATES OF GROWTH IN HISPANIC POPULATION 2000-2007

	Language Spoken at Home 5 Years of Age and Above					
	Total	Speak only English	Spanish or Spanish Creole	% Spanish or Spanish Creole	Rank % Change in Hispanic Population 2000-2007	% Change Hispanic Pop 2000 - 2007
Kendall County, Illinois	80,173	68,023	8,658	10.8	1	335
Henry County, Georgia	162,150	148,492	6,734	4.2	2	312
Frederick County, Virginia	66,080	61,457	3,441	5.2	3	306
Culpeper County, Virginia					4	279
Paulding County, Georgia					5	243

* Source: 2005-2007 American Community Survey 3-Year Estimates.

Blank cells indicate missing data. ACS sample n too small for reporting.

NOTE. Although the American Community Survey (ACS) produces population, demographic and housing unit estimates, it is the Census Bureau's Population Estimates Program that produces and disseminates the official estimates of the population for the nation, states, counties, cities and towns and estimates of housing units for states and counties.

(1) Pew @ http://pewhispanic.org/docs/?DocID=17

APPENDIX 3. WEBSITE EVALUATION PROTOCOL

	Description	Operationalized*		
		Page	Links	Linked Pages
0	Placeholder	Listings of address, phone, email only		
1	English only	Page in English	English Only	
2	English with translation by program, no Spanish on linked pages	Page in English with translation (Spanish) (machine) by clicking	In Spanish	In English only (no translation)
3	Spanish by translation throughout	*Same as 2*	*Same as 2*	In English, translation (Spanish) by clicking
4	Spanish originals (not translated) on linked pages	*Same as 3*	*Same as 3*	In Spanish
5	Full Spanish (online requests for assistance, forms to do licenses, etc., forms must be printed for submission)	*Same as 4*	*Same as 4*	PDF forms in Spanish
6	Full Spanish with fillable forms (database forms accept data entered online)	*Same as 5*	*Same as 5*	Data submitted in forms

*Spanish is most frequent "other language."

Chapter 4
Ethical Influences of E–Government Website Development:
Sustaining an Ethical Climate in Public Organizations

Rodney Erakovich
Texas Wesleyan University, USA

ABSTRACT

Complementary and competing values of political, legal and public interest issues define administrative ethical decision-making in public organizations. Organizational values create an ethical climate that prescribes acceptable ethical norms of behavior. The relationship between technology and administrative governance can influence and shift organizational values that affect the ethical climate in public organizations. This theoretical inquiry considers how web based and Internet technology can result in value shifts in power distribution, social equity and persuasiveness of citizens as government web sites are forged. Discussions of these value shifts suggest ethical considerations in decisions by public managers that focus on building an ethical climate to support democratic governance goals.

INTRODUCTION

The strength in the recognition of the use of information technology to influence organizational ethical public organizations encourages us to evaluate organizational functions with this in mind. Dr. Paula Gordon (1977) suggests an approach to value-based ethics brought on by technical rationality. Rather than the "reactive perspectives and approaches that are current today" (p.1) we need to evaluate public administration technology roles in terms of value-based ethics.

Science should be a tool that frees man, not a tool that leads to his subjugation, or as Thoreau warned, that 'makes man a tool of his tools.' Science should be used in human ways to meet human needs, not in ways that deny, show disdain for, and effectively destroy man's freedom, man's spirit, man's intrinsic humanness, and the very meaning of his life. Science should not be used

DOI: 10.4018/978-1-61692-018-0.ch004

in ways that needlessly destroy or threaten life and with it, man's peace and peace of mind (p.3).

Complementary and competing values of political, legal and public interest issues define the administrative ethical decision-making in public organizations (Van Wart, 1998). Political authority infers public ownership, which in turn provides a distinctively different approach to organizational control from that of private organizations. For example, the economic resources for public organizations come from legislative bodies that reach collaborative agreement based on their policy decisions.

Law creates public organizations to carry out policy and administer the law. These legal principles create values of subordination to elected and appointed officials, the law, legislative intent, and the courts (Van Wart, 1998). While managers in private organizations can act, unless a law or rule prescribes otherwise, compliance with laws in public organizations is compulsory (Erakovich, Kavran & Wyman, 2006).

Public interest requires systematic democratic governance, division of political and administration power through federalism and protection of individual rights from governmental abuses. Public interest suggests an implicit agreement on decision-making that resolves questions of what is the common good and in the public interest partially through the free market and partially through representative government. Public interest suggests an implicit agreement concerning the rules of conduct and decision-making in society. (Schumpeter, 1942; Downs, 1962; Gardner, 1990)

The work of government is to facilitate the continual readjustment of competing and conflicting values and influences (Schumpeter, 1942). The environment in which a public organization works develops values that guide decision making to implement technology and the values brought about by web based technology applications. Past shifts in public organizational values have occurred with increased technological complexity

and growth of society. For example, in the 1990s, technology produced a flow of information that brought new public management into the public reform efforts (Fountain, 2001) and value shifts toward a market approach to management and businesslike principles. The main contention here is that these value perspectives, while meeting the political, legal and economic influences, are based on econometric assumptions that neglect a public administration focus of democratic building and issues of plurality, equality and a public interest focus that considers all citizens (Gregory, 1999).

This paper proposes we can gain a fuller understanding of value shifts and ethics in public service by drawing from concepts built in organizational forms of inquiry. This inquiry considers how the use of e-government web based and Internet technology can result in value shifts in power distribution, social equity and persuasiveness of government web sites as they are forged. Ideas about the relationship between technology and ethical climates in public organizations are described in the organizational processes and a normative view of public administration ethics.

Approaches to Ethical Decision Making in Public Organizations

Public managers focus on two main objectives in managing ethics in public organizations:

1. Develop organizational systems that encourage and support ethical behavior, and
2. Provide training and orientation to support these organizational systems (Gortner, 1991).

To keep public organizations focused on public service, rather than its own special interest, the values and principles of a democratic political process in the administration of government must provide reference points. Decisions must include the legally mandated mission of the organization. However, the manager is also concerned with the ethical conduct of the public employees and development of an organizational ethical climate. The fear is that a large public organization can begin to run with self-serving tendencies and not in the public interest. This fear suggests that whatever is good for individuals must come from a large organization and therefore all behaviors must benefit the organization (Cooper, 1990).

Ethical controls in public organizations focus on two general approaches. In a structural or micro approach, the focus is on codifying codes, laws and rules based on the structure of the workplace. By creating a systematic process, a structural framework attempts to ensure continuity and consistency. Structural arrangements are significant to elaborating key values from legislative frameworks of accountability and organizational control based on codes of ethics (Erakovich, Kavran & Wyman, 2006). The focus of this approach is to react to unethical actions and seek to punish breaches of core public service values.

Less precise than the structural perspective, a normative or macro view of public administration ethics is proactive and relies on three Meta values: citizenship, public interest and social equity (Van Wart, 1998). Citizenship involves membership in a community that involves rights and obligations prescribed by the values of society (Cooper, 1990). The notion of public interest, a term discussed without much precision, (Lippman, 1955) suggests that public interest is what people would choose if they saw clearly and thought rationally as a collaborative effort by society on a course of action that benefits its members. It is a viable representation of a democratic framework and a key value in a normative approach to ethics. Social equity notes a spirit of "fairness, justness and right dealing which regulate the intercourse of men" (Hart, 1984, p. 112).

The process in a normative approach to ethical decision-making involves principle and outcome. A public manager searches for a principle to guide the decision-making process to rationalize the action as long as the outcomes meet those selected

principles. This approach provides a framework to guide and give reason for a decision. Most importantly, this approach employs principles drawn from values inherent in the society and governance system in which the individual lives (Erakovich, Kavran & Wyman, 2006). For example, a police officer can, by law, stop and issue a citation for an individual driving above the posted speed limit. If that individual is on the way to a hospital with an expectant wife, the decision to issue a traffic citation can be moderated by the situation and outcome.

Ethical problems occur where there is a conflict between competing values. It is not so much making a decision of right versus wrong, but making a decision of right versus right. Efficiency of individual decision-making versus a group process, social equity versus public interest and security versus transparency are principle conflicts based on values intrinsic in most policy decisions. Further, conflicts between a focus to strictly follow the law or rule without regard to outcomes conflicts with outcome considerations (the greatest good for the greatest number) where consideration of the outcome is primary. While ethical analysis involving these competing values will not provide a right or wrong answer, it does create a moral focus that is central in public service beyond matters of technical expertise to function on behalf of the citizenry.

The role of the Internet and websites to facilitate the relationship between government and citizens, between governments and as a link to business creates new avenues of social and governmental interactions. It also creates consideration of key value shifts and how these shifts influence public service ethics.

Organizational Ethical Climate as a Measure of Public Organization's Ethics

Victor and Cullen (1987) developed a typology of organizational ethical climate using dimensions or levels of criteria similar to Kohlberg's moral theory. Kohlberg (1981) found individual development follows a multistage sequence from an individualistic view to a wider concern for universal rights and even humanity as a whole. In Victor and Cullen's typology, ethical determinants (moral reasoning) and ethical analysis (boundary framework) are the criteria used to create an organizational ethical climate.

First, the moral focus can be termed ethical if the decision strictly follows a law or rule. Second, the boundary framework can range from the individual to the broadest of social systems. Employees and managers make a judgment about which course of action is correct based on the ethical climate dimension that includes belief the action is socially and personally preferable in the organization and community (Erakovich & Wyman, 2009). Ethical conflict occurs when a decision is based on one level of ethical focus and results in an unacceptable outcome. For example, citizens may want inclusion into a policy decision process and at the same time want efficiency of process.

While formal codes of ethics offer some standards of conduct and guidelines for ethical decision-making, a normative approach suitable with a structural framework establishes an ethical climate that supports the organizational processes and goals. Such strategies might include:

1. Develop employee accountability and establish trust within the organization and with citizen groups.
2. Promote decision-making participation of citizens and employees establishing cooperation and trust.
3. Develop an internal and external supportive environment that builds partnerships.
4. Support cohesion within the organization to build integrity.
5. Within the legal and regulatory constraints of the public bureaucracy, support innovation through risk taking (Erakovich & Wyman, 2009).

Technology is influential in the ethical climate in a public organization and may create a shift in values toward power distribution within the public organization and between the government and its citizens.

POWER DISTRIBUTION

The exercise of power is when an individual has the capacity to influence the actions of another. An employee, for example, might have acted different ethically if he or she were not influenced by norms found in the organizational ethical climate. A greater reliance on electronic information and technology and its implementation can create conditions for information control and a movement away from value based organizational leadership and management. The use of web-based information sources through websites to improve citizen communication has the possibility of providing significant support for undertaking and continuing moral discussions on key issues of concern to citizens and at the same time, it provides new and serious impediments. The significant assessment by public managers of Web based information services in public organizations is to contribute efficiently as a means to interact with external stakeholders (Drake, Yuthas & Dillard, 2000). To assess choices of what information is available, who is able to access and manipulate the information affects the balance of the ethical influence both inside and outside the public organization. Decisions about the development, implementation and updating of information presented confer power on those in control of the system. To some extent, it may alter the culture of the public organization by creating an unintended outcome of conferring power on a technological elite group of professionals that have educational and skill expertise (Garson, 2003).

Results of a study done by Stone and Henry (2003) examining information technology ethical work climates found a high focus on individual and workgroup egoistic climates regardless of the outcomes. These climates stress individual and workgroup self-interests in making ethical decisions. Organizational principles did not empirically emerge. Although these findings are not inherently positive or negative, the key findings as it relates to this discussion is the role of expert power certainly present in development of web based products is not an empirical reason for discussion. The analysis of outcomes, such as the power to deliver intellectual capital (Brynjolfsson, 1994) through the display of information on websites, was not identified as a significant issue.

Both internal and external exercise of power does influence the ethical standards that govern the behavior of individuals in the public organization and sets the ethical norms in the ethical climate. Information technology and specifically the use of web sites alter the manner in which influence occurs between organizational members and the citizens the organization serves. While this may enhance a pluralistic distribution of power, it can also have a negative impact by strengthening those with technological expertise.

The bureaucratic administrative processes found in public organizations deliver power according to a known hierarchical and task oriented process. Those responsible for the organization's ethical and moral decisions may be taking an unintended shift toward where technical expertise gains power and control of web-based information that is equal to public managerial authority (La Porte, 2001). The right to control the information published access to this information and the timeliness of its display in web-based services may be establishing a norm of technical power based on one level of ethical focus to the exclusion of outcome analysis. Considering ethical outcomes are needed to create a balanced ethical climate.

Technological pace of change in the development and use of websites for government use takes us beyond the current assumptions of simply examining the efficiency and effectiveness of information technology to present information. It

requires that public managers consider the patterns of authority between technical application and how the power of information technology affects the power balance. The key issue is to include in decisions of ethical considerations that which represents values of democratic governance, such as transparency, and bring the exercise of power out into the open.

Social Equity

Bovaird (2007) discusses what he terms as the emerging pattern of coproduction and argues a key issue that relates to social equity, a key public administration value, and web based technology: "…the ability of community members to engage in coproduction is not simply a given (p. 855). In coproduction, public service often takes on an "enabling role, so that the client actually performs the service task" (p. 847). The service recipient becomes a co producer of the service. Typical private sector examples include automatic teller machines (ATMs) and the self-service checkout at stores.

In a world of increasingly competent Internet users, Bovaird (2007) predicts that such relationships will become more prominent. He argues "much evidence" exists that the idea of coproduction may not be equitably distributed and proportionally it is "in the hands of better-off members" of communities (p. 856). Economically we can see where coproduction through a web-based environment would be efficient. Thus, there is some mediating of power in the "role between public organizations and individual co producers" (p. 855). This would have a greater social influence in a local community where the public administrator is closer to the citizen than in a state or federal government agency.

Though there has been impressive growth in the number of people accessing the Internet over the past decade, this growth has not been uniform. Access to the Worldwide Web offered to customers by telecommunications firms have traditionally underserved poorer urban and rural communities (Abhijit, Mandviwalla & Banker, 2007), creating technological "have" and "have not's."

There is a continuing digital divide in the United States. Socioeconomic status continues to be a primary factor that determines Internet access (Garson, 2003). While two-thirds of US households have broadband access as of May 2009, an increase from one-fifth five years ago (LRG, 2009), only 37 percent of households with income under $30,000 have broadband access compared with 89 percent of households with over $75,000 annual income according to the same study. Higher-income households remain most likely to subscribe to a broadband service.

The digital divide remains a factor in government providing equitable service and closing the gap will increasingly become a factor in addressing the need for equality, economic development and educational access. It is important to remind ourselves that technology does not create the gap, but the general underdevelopment of policy keeping up to date with technological developments to address technology social equity seems to be influential.

Legitimacy for ethical considerations in social equity development is found in public interest values. Important in government is how much it improves the welfare of society as a whole. A key process value of public interest is direct democracy and the ability of web based means to create forums for citizen discussion and decisions. More importantly, websites can strengthen representative democracy by providing the forum where citizens can provide input for elected officials in making policy decisions.

Two specific value sources that influence ethical climate in public organizations are important in considering social equity, organizational and public interest values. Internally, the relationship between an organization's value system and information technology is bureaucratic in nature (Fountain, 2001) with an end focus on efficiency, stability and control through information manage-

ment (Van Wart, 1998). Technology ethical climates in the public bureaucratic structure overlook the organizational values that guide processes toward public service. Whether the structure or process of website implementation change the ethical climate, the responsibility to ensure web site use is congruent with public service values rests with the public manager. This neglect creates an ethical climate focused on application of information technology to further individual and work group interests regardless of the larger or cosmopolitan ethical outcomes. The only pressure for change may come from efforts to privatize the technology systems to create efficiency.

Historically, municipalities have often provided utility service for citizens (e.g., electricity, water, health clinics, and education). This provides a high-tech extension of existing services provided by the municipality's local government. In 2004, the City of Albuquerque started offering wireless access around the city, allowing residents and visitors open access to the Internet. Recently Edmonton, Canada created "wifi" hotspots downtown to support its citizens. The program has since expanded to other locations.

From an efficiency standpoint, providing Internet access benefits to citizens is in the public interest and legitimized by following the rule by two British Economists, Nicholas Kaldor and John Hicks (Gramlich, 1990). What is simply stated as the Kaldor-Hicks rule is that a public manager's decision in implementation *"has positive net benefits if the gainers could compensate the losers and still be better off"* (p. 38). Creating a web-based means of government-to-citizen communication can provide means of information flow through access to computer systems in libraries, city hall and other public places for example. While it would not provide a direct benefit to those with Internet access, it would provide a means for those without Internet to access government websites. The indirect compensation for those with access is to further the maturity of demand that can create added emphasis on government accountability.

With municipal provided access, these public interest efforts can lessen the digital divide.

The potential of Web access to build trust and public interest into the relationship between the public organization and its citizens is significant. While bureaucratic norms dictate implementation designs that promote the existing notion of efficiency and responsiveness based on pre-existing notions of government-to-citizen relationships, inclusion of values of social equity and public interest provide the best possible use of web technology. Not only can technology change existing information systems, it can also change the ethical values considered. Consideration of civic integrity that reflects a belief in a democratic social contract, can be a value conflict and mutually exclusive to the strategic needs of web based development. Eventually, the public manager must instill a strong civic integrity in the organizational value system with the basis for legitimacy founded in law. A democratic social contract that ethically supports the society it serves goes beyond principle and is an ethical outcome norm that should be part of the ethical climate norms.

PERSUASIVENESS OF CITIZENS BY GOVERNMENT WEBSITES

Most considerations in the use of government web sites does not start with the intent to persuade citizens, businesses and other governments that are primary users of the information. Often, governmental websites serve as an online phone directory of individuals, forms for use by citizens and businesses and occasionally, data on past performance. Yet the persuasiveness of web sites can be an unintended outcome and should not be ignored.

Campeau, Higgins and Huff (1999) found significant relationships between use of technology and outcome expectations. Their findings explain that social cognition, the social influence of outcomes based on information, is influenced by web-based information. From a public administration perspective, evidence suggests web sites could be effective in influencing policy development and implementation (Morgeson and Mithas, 2009). Current research by Matsuo and Yamamoto (2009) consider the interaction of trust among consumers and developing social networks through the Worldwide Web. Their theoretical development of *community gravity* supports how strongly a user is attracted to an online community.

Fountain (2001) describes how the quickened delivery of government services and information by means of the Internet create, organize and filter information in collaborative fashion to shape economic, political and social policies. In a democratic process of collaboratively deciding policy, influencing the users of information provided through web sites can leverage "the big efforts of the few" (Fountain, 2001, p. 23). Both the content and selectivity of information increases political and organizational inertia to continue in the direction charted regardless of the ethical outcomes and democratic process. In essence, it creates value of information in promoting an ethical climate of organizational interests while the role of web-based technology should strengthen principles of democracy without undue social persuasiveness.

From an organizational examination, the ethical climate of a public organization may focus on rational compliance with existing regulations and laws, fact-based decision-making and centralized management of web-site development. This would be consistent with the technical requirement that builds an internal ethical focus and stability in the management process. Further, the changing nature of public-sector organizational values toward market-oriented principles represents movement toward efficiency and effectiveness and less resolve to ensure democratic processes. What is weakened is the relationship between values and maneuvering the social environment to create and control information.

The ethical reflection is that information provided by web sites can persuade citizens and groups by reducing human variability and preserving expected behavior patterns. Expressing beliefs through web-based presentation can alter information processing, opinion and action in the social environment by citizens (Sharma, 2009). While there is a gap in the research in the public sector, literature examining this influence in markets in the private sector is readily available. This persuasiveness of public opinion represents a fundamental shift in not only organizational control, but also in social transformations.

THE RESEARCH NEED

In the public organization, research must consider whether websites and Internet technology are creating value shifts that drive governance toward or away from democratic principles. While following a law or rule is needed as part of the principled ethical approach, outcome analysis is also needed to ensure an ethical climate established balanced norms of ethical reference. To what extent is power inside and external to the public organization affected? Does it promote a technocratic culture with a focus only on organizational outcomes and preserving self-interest? Alternatively, is the distribution of power more equitable because of increased information content and speed of access? Does technical power have an effect on representative bureaucracy?

As noted, the digital divide remains and does not seem to be closing. What ethical role do public organizations have in considering this gap in information technology development? Is the surge of websites and Internet traffic creating greater divergence of socioeconomic groups in society? To what extent do websites affect users of the information presented?

In the private sector, market analysis of online buyers reflects a trend to create influence among virtual communities. Social websites, blog and other virtual developments are providing a forum for dissemination of opinion and seemingly valid data that affects policy direction. Little research is available on persuasiveness of citizens by government websites. To what extent do government websites influence their environment? What pluralistic benefit is created by the content and display of government websites as it relates to information provided to citizens? Alternatively, do websites create elitist groups with increases in relative power to influence policy decisions? How much do websites and their content persuade citizens to accept or reject political and policy considerations?

CONCLUSION

Contained within Dwight Waldo's (1974) list of responsibilities of public managers are two themes present in all ethical problems faced by public servants: the individual and the organization. Public service ethics reflects one's duty by "balancing attention to virtue, principle and good consequences" (Svara, 2007, p. 16). Moore (1981) reflects this best:

The duties of public officials are not simply to be passive instruments in policymaking but to work actively in establishing goals for public policy in their area, and in advocating those goals among the people who share their responsibility (p.5).

The development of the ethical climate by web-based technological dimension remains at the point of this analysis. Websites can be an essential tool to inform citizens. However, moral judgment requires ethical decision-making beyond simply putting information on the website that may have transformative and persuasive potential.

The research in the private sector on market behaviors explains an increasing influence on social behavior. It may be we are witnessing a social phenomenon in developing technological social capital. The potential benefits of government websites must be balanced against outcome risks to democracy and social equity externalities.

Web-based information raises issues of fairness, justice, and equity that have always been a part of public administration. The government's development and use of the Internet influences the digital divide. Equal access and process equity that guarantees consistency in the level of service delivery regardless of the process are important ethical considerations.

The exercise of analysis in the development, implementation and maintenance of government web based information requires an ethical examination by public managers to prevent unintended consequences; it should not be left to information technology experts. By recognizing technology's affect on power, we can manage from an ethical strength and build transparency in the process that will create a more efficient and effective workplace. A strong sense of civic integrity coupled with a sense stewardship of government processes for the benefit of the citizenry sets up the public interest focus that is the essential value ingredient in the public organization's ethical climate.

REFERENCES

Abhijit, J., Mandviwalla, M., & Banker, R. D. (2007). Government as catalyst: Can it work again with wireless internet access? *Public Administration Review, 67*(6), 993–1005. doi:10.1111/j.1540-6210.2007.00790.x

Bovaird, T. (2007). Beyond engagement and participation: User and community coproduction of public services. *Public Administration Review, 67*(5), 846–860. doi:10.1111/j.1540-6210.2007.00773.x

Brynjolfsson, E. (1994). Information assets, technology and organization. *Management Science, 40*(12), 1645–1662. doi:10.1287/mnsc.40.12.1645

Compeau, D., Higgins, C., & Huff, S. (1999). Social cognitive theory and individual reactions to computing technology: A longitudinal study. *Management Information Systems Quarterly, 23*(2), 145–158. doi:10.2307/249749

Cooper, T. L. (1990). *The responsible administrator: An approach to ethics for the administrative role* (3rd ed.). San Francisco: Jossey-Bass.

Downs, A. (1962). The public interest: It's meaning in a democracy. *Social Research: An International Quarterly of Political and Social Science,* 1-36.

Drake, B., Yuthas, K., & Dillard, J. (2000). Its only words: Impacts of information technology on moral dialogue. *Journal of Business Ethics, 23*(1), 41–59. doi:10.1023/A:1006270911041

Erakovich, R., Kavran, D., & Wyman, S. (2006). A normative approach to ethics training in Central and Eastern Europe. *International Journal of Public Administration, 29*(13), 1229–1257. doi:10.1080/01900690600928060

Erakovich, R., & Wyman, S. (2009). Implications of organizational influence on ethical behavior: An analysis of the perceptions of public managers. In Cox, R. W. III, (Ed.), *Ethics and integrity in public administration: Concepts and cases* (pp. 77–91). Armonk, NY: M. E. Sharpe, Inc.

Fountain, J. E. (2001). *Building the virtual state: Information technology and Institutional change.* Washington, DC: The Brookings Institution.

Gardner, J. W. (1990). *On leadership.* NY: The Free Press.

Garson, G. D. (2003). Toward an information technology research agenda for public administration. In Garson, G. D. (Ed.), *Public information technology: Policy and management issues* (pp. 331–357). Hershey, PA: Idea Group Publishing.

Gordon, P. (1977). *Public administration in the public interest.* Paper presented at the National Conference of the American Society for Public Administration, Atlanta, GA.

Gortner, H. F. (1991). *Ethics for public managers*. New York: Praeger.

Gramlich, E. M. (1990). *A Guide to benefit-cost analysis* (2nd ed.). Englewood Cliffs, NJ: Prentice Hall.

Gregory, R. J. (1999). Social capital theory and administrative reform: Maintaining ethical probity. *Public Administration Review*, *59*(1), 63–75. doi:10.2307/977480

Hart, D. K. (1984). The virtuous citizen, the honorable bureaucrat and public administration. *Public Administration Review*, 111–120. doi:10.2307/975550

Kohlberg, L. (1981). *Philosophy of moral development*. New York: Harper and Row Publishers.

La Porte, T. (2001). Politics and inventing the future: Perspectives in Science and government. In W. Bruce (Ed.), *Classics of administrative ethics* (393-409). Boulder, CO: Westview.

Lippman, W. (1955). *Essays in the public philosophy*. Boston: Little, Brown and Co.

LRG Research Studies. (2009). *Leichtman Research Group*. Retrieved June 1, 2009, from www.leichtmanresearch.com/research.html#studies

Matsuo, Y., & Yamamoto, H. (2009). Community gravity: Measuring bidirectional effects by trust and rating on online social networks. *International World Wide Web Conference*. Retrieved June 1, 2009, from http://www2009.eprints.org/76/1/p751.pdf

Moore, M. H. (1981). Realms of obligation and virtues. In Fleishman, J. L., Liebman, L., & Moore, M. H. (Eds.), *Public duties: The moral obligation of government officials* (pp. 1–15). Cambridge, MA: Harvard Press.

Morgeson, F., & Mithas, 2. (2009). Does e-government measure up to e-business? Comparing end user perceptions of U.S. federal government and e-business web sites. *Public Administration Review*, *69*(4), 740–752. doi:10.1111/j.1540-6210.2009.02021.x

Schumpeter, J. (1942). *Capitalism, socialism and democracy*. New York: Free Press.

Sharma, S. (2009). *The ethics driven spatial management in multiculturalism through ICTs*. Unpublished paper.

Stone, R., & Henry, J. (2003). Identifying and developing measures of information technology ethical work climates. *Journal of Business Ethics*, *46*(4), 337–350. doi:10.1023/A:1025632614084

Svara, J. (2007). *The ethics primer for public administrators in government and nonprofit organizations*. Sudbury, MA: Jones and Bartlett.

Van Wart, M. (1998). *Changing public sector values*. New York: Garland Publishing, Inc.

Victor, B., & Cullen, J. B. (1987). A theory and measure of ethical climate in organizations. *Research in Corporate Social Performance and Policy*, *9*, 51–71.

Waldo, D. (1974). Reflections On Public Morality. *Administration & Society*, *6*, 267–283. doi:10.1177/009539977400600301

KEY TERMS AND DEFINITIONS

Moral Reasoning: The process of discerning thought with the objective of determining what is right or wrong.

Boundary Framework: Determining the boundary of the ethical analysis. In ethical climates, the boundary can limit consideration to individual morals, group norms, or organizational needs and further to include a global focus.

Stewardship: The careful and responsible management of citizen's resources entrusted to the care of public officials.

Coproduction: The idea that citizens working together develop a strong community and starts when those that are users of government services and products are involved in their production.

Direct Democracy: Refers to citizens making policy decisions and law in person, without going through representatives and legislatures.

Representative Democracy: The exercise of the democratic rights of citizens by a subset of the people, usually political officials based on elections.

Digital Divide: A term used to define a gap between those individuals and communities that have access to information technologies and those that do not.

Community Gravity: Illustrates how strongly a user might be attracted to a virtual community.

Democratic Social Contract: A theoretical basis that describes agreed-upon social arrangements that provides basic security and access to information for individuals in modern societies. One such agreed on need is transparency.

Chapter 5
Evaluating the Quality Attributes of E–Government Websites

Ourania I. Markaki
National Technical University of Athens, Greece

Dimitris E. Charilas
National Technical University of Athens, Greece

Dimitris Askounis
National Technical University of Athens, Greece

ABSTRACT

The purpose of this chapter is to address the issue of e-government website evaluation in terms of providing a decision making framework. Built around the concepts of website evaluation and e-government, the proposed framework deploys Multi-Attribute Decision Making (MADM) methods and Fuzzy Sets Theory to overcome the subjectivity and inaccuracy that characterizes the conventional models for e-government website quality assessment. The framework offers also the possibility of performing comparisons with regard to the overall quality of different implementations either at national or international level. The chapter presents a holistic and scalable approach to e-government website evaluation and it is anticipated to be of great interest to both researchers and practitioners requiring an understanding of the factors influencing the quality of e-government websites or allocating resources to the relevant implementations respectively.

INTRODUCTION

The Internet and particularly the World Wide Web has evolved for both private and public organizations all over the world from a basic tool of displaying information into a means of providing added value services to customers. However, while an effective presence on the web appears as a competitive advantage for private organizations, for public organizations it constitutes rather an obligation toward citizens. As public authorities at all government levels around the world attempt to embrace the digital revolution and place a wide range of materials on the web, from mere informa-

DOI: 10.4018/978-1-61692-018-0.ch005

tion to actual online services for the convenience of citizens, expectations of the performance levels that e-government websites should provide have been considerably raised, bringing up the issue of their quality evaluation.

To address this issue, this chapter provides a decision making framework for evaluating and comparing e-government websites that is based on Fuzzy Sets Theory and MADM methods. The proposed framework constitutes a holistic approach and is characterized by scalability.

The discussion in this chapter proceeds as follows. Section 1 is an introduction to the issues addressed in this chapter. Section 2 provides an overview of current evaluation approaches as well as an insight to fuzzy numbers and MADM methods, which are the tools adopted to establish the evaluation framework. Section 3 sets the grounds of the framework by identifying the individual factors that compose the overall quality of an e-government website and may thus serve as evaluation criteria. Section 4 presents the evaluation framework, which is based on the afore-mentioned tools, while Section 5 exposes the basic guidelines for performing comparisons with regard to the overall quality of different implementations through the use of MADM methods. Section 6 presents an alternative approach for establishing a highly dynamic comparison framework, using Fuzzy Inference Systems. Lastly, the chapter concludes with a summary of ideas presented.

BACKGROUND

This chapter presents a decision making framework for evaluating and comparing e-government websites. For this purpose, in this section we first discuss the current website evaluation approaches and specify the reasons for adopting tools such as MADM methods and Fuzzy Sets Theory in order to establish the evaluation framework. We then provide fundamental information on the aforementioned tools, so that the reader acquires a basic understanding of the relevant concepts before proceeding with the evaluation methodology.

Literature Review

Although there is already an extensive literature on website evaluation (Alexander & Tate, 1999; Bauer & Scharl, 2000; Nielsen, 2000), only lately have there been attempts to address the issue under the prism of specific business sectors and website categories. Within this frame, a few attempts have also been made recently to propose and use specific metrics for assessing the websites of public authorities. Despite that several different criteria and metrics are utilized, it is obvious that the authors generally agree on a specific set of concepts such as usability, content, technical characteristics, online services and citizens' participation (Bauer & Scharl, 2000; Fei, Yao & Yu, 2008; Peters, Janssen & Van Engers, 2004; Soufi & Maguire, 2007; Wang, Bretschneider & Gant 2005).

Moreover, recent research points out that evaluating the quality of an e-government website is a process of organizing in a hierarchical structure (Alshawi, Alahmary & Alalwany, 2008; Fei et al., 2008; Peters et al., 2004) multiple criteria that serve as surrogates to deduce the overall quality and weighting them appropriately; that what differs is the method of assessment adopted. Nevertheless the methods used to define the weights of the selected criteria are usually not clarified or the weights are simply determined based on the researchers' own personal opinion (Panopoulou, Tambouris & Tarabanis, 2008). In other cases, the proposed schemes rely on citizens to define such weights through questionnaires (Barnes & Vidgen, 2004).

Panopoulou et al. (2008) propose a holistic approach for evaluating the websites of public authorities that applies three different levels of detail (axes, factors and metrics) and to define the overall score of each website they employ for all three levels a weighting scheme that is based on the authors' personal experience. Barnes and Vidgen (2004) present eQual, an instrument designed to analyze user perceptions of the quality of a national website. In the context of eQual website users are asked to rate target sites against each of a range of qualities and to rate each one of these qualities in terms of their importance. On the other hand, Bauer and Scharl (2000) argue on the importance of using software tools for website evaluation; such tools that automatically classify and evaluate websites are more objective than human evaluators and more efficient in that they allow the fast evaluation of hundreds of samples.

Evaluating the quality of an e-government website is unquestionably a process of weighting multiple criteria. This process involves human subjectivity and constitutes a multiple attribute decision making (MADM) problem in the presence of many quantitative and qualitative attributes. MADM involves the selection of a series of criteria that impact the decision process and the specification of the relative significance of these criteria by assigning weights that reflect their importance in the final decision. The MADM nature of the evaluation problem may be indeed reflected in conventional evaluation models for e-government website quality assessment; however these models are still too subjective and inaccurate, and thus uncertainty is an inevitable component of the evaluation process. As a result, in this chapter the authors establish a framework for the evaluation of e-government websites by combining MADM methods with Fuzzy Sets Theory to address the former insufficiency.

The main characteristic of fuzziness is the grouping of individuals' judgments into classes that do not have sharply defined boundaries (Zadeh, 1965). In this frame, the relative importance of selected evaluation criteria is modeled as a fuzzy number since objective judgment cannot be guaranteed and vagueness should not be overlooked. Crisp weights are finally applied through the process of defuzzification.

Fuzzy Numbers

The Fuzzy Sets Theory, introduced by Zadeh (1965) to deal with vagueness, imprecision and uncertainty in problems, has been used as a modeling tool for complex systems that can be controlled by humans but are hard to define precisely. The main characteristic of fuzziness is the grouping of individuals' judgments into classes that do not have sharply defined boundaries. An uncertain comparison can be represented by a fuzzy number. A fuzzy set is one that assigns grades of membership between 0 and 1 to objects using a particular membership function $\mu_A(x)$. A triangular fuzzy number is a special type of fuzzy number whose membership is defined by three real numbers, expressed as (l, m, u), where l is the lower limit value, m is the most promising value and u is the upper limit value. Particularly, when $l = m = u$, fuzzy numbers become crisp numbers. The triangular fuzzy numbers are represented as shown in Figure 1.

Multi-Attribute Decision Making Methods

Multi Attribute Decision Making (MADM) involves the selection of a series of criteria that influence the decision process and the specification of their relative significance by assigning weights that reflect their importance in the final decision, so that the best option among a set of alternatives can be pointed out based on its weighted score on the selected criteria.

Numerous types of MADM algorithms exist and several of them may be suitable for solving a decision problem so that the decision maker may encounter the task of selecting amongst a number of feasible methods the most appropriate one. The choice of the most suitable model depends on the problem at hand and may be as well to some extent dependent on which model the decision maker is most comfortable with.

Figure 1. Triangular fuzzy number

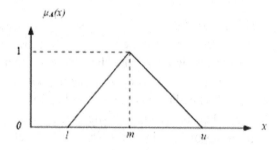

$$\mu_A(x) = \begin{cases} (x-l)/(m-l), & l \le x \le m \\ (u-x)/(u-m), & m \le x \le u \\ 0 & otherwise \end{cases}$$

In general, one could distinguish two different types of MADM methods, based on their scope. On the one hand, methods, such as the Analytic Hierarchy Process (AHP), aim at determining the importance that each criterion yields in the final decision. This is accomplished by comparing elements and determining their corresponding weights. No final selection or ranking of the alternatives is performed here, but it is possible that the extracted weights are used later on so that a decision is reached. AHP is the most indicative method of this category and will be briefly presented in the following paragraph so that the reader may acquire an understanding of how the comparison process is implemented.

On the other hand, most MADM methods, such as ELECTRE, SAW, TOPSIS etc, rely on a series of metric performances and a set of weights to compare all alternatives with one another and finally point out which one is the best. Therefore, combinations of MADM methods are often encountered in the literature, since the first one of them is employed to provide weights as input to the second one that actually performs the ranking of alternatives under examination (Charilas, Markaki, Psarras & Constantinou, 2009; Mahmooodzadeh, Shahrabi, Pariazar & Zaeri, 2007).

Analytic Hierarchy Process (AHP)

The Analytic Hierarchy Process (AHP) is one of the extensively used multi-attribute decision-making methods. Since Saaty (2008) proposed AHP as a decision aid to help solve unstructured problems in economics, social and management sciences, the method has been applied in a variety of contexts. One of the main advantages of this method is the relative ease with which it handles multiple criteria. In addition to this, AHP is easy to understand and it can effectively handle both qualitative and quantitative data. Finally, its use does not involve complex mathematics.

The AHP decision problem is structured hierarchically at different levels, each level consisting of a finite number of decision elements. The top level of the hierarchy represents the overall goal, while the lowest level is composed of all possible alternatives. One or more intermediate levels embody the decision criteria and sub-criteria. The relative importance of the decision elements is assessed indirectly through a series of comparative judgments. The decision-maker is required to provide his/her preferences by comparing all criteria, sub-criteria and alternatives with respect to upper level decision elements. The standard preference scale used for AHP ranges from 1 that indicates "equal importance" to 9 representing "extreme importance"; however sometimes different evaluation scales can be used, such as the Direct Weighting scale that allows the completion of tables with any values, without the use of strictly predefined values. The values of the weights and scores are elicited from these comparisons and represented in a decision table, as in Table 1.

Table 1. AHP Matrix with three selection criteria

	D.E.1	D.E.2	D.E.3	Weights
D.E.1	a_{11}	a_{12}	a_{13}	w_1
D.E.2	a_{21}	a_{22}	a_{23}	w_2
D.E.3	a_{31}	a_{32}	a_{33}	w_3

Practically, each value of the decision matrix implies the extent at which an element is more important to another. More specifically, depending on the elements that are being compared the following cases exist:

- $a_{ij}=1$, since an element is compared with itself
- $a_{ij}>1$ when element i is considered to be more important than element j
- $a_{ij}<1$ when element j is considered to be more important than element i
- $a_{ij}=1/a_{ji}$ for the rest of the values of the table

The way in which the weights of the decision criteria and sub-criteria are calculated via AHP is explained in Appendix A of this chapter.

EVALUATION CRITERIA

There are numerous factors that may be considered in order to evaluate the overall quality of e-government websites. Some of them refer to general characteristics and apply to all types of websites, while others address specific functionalities that particularly an e-government website should support.

A thorough evaluation analysis should take into account as many evaluation criteria and sub-criteria as possible; however such a level of detail would very much degrade the efficiency of the evaluation scheme. As a result, in the frame of this chapter the authors have distinguished the factors that they consider to be more representative

with regard to e-government website evaluation, suggesting that the decision maker can make the necessary amendments or additions according to his focus or according to the particular website implementation.

This section aims at the composition of the problem hierarchy that will be adopted for the application of the evaluation scheme. For this purpose, the first step is to define the key concepts that will constitute the first level of the evaluation hierarchy and then further analyze them in a number of lesser components referring to minor relevant aspects. In this frame, from now on we will be referring to the elements of the first level of the hierarchy as criteria and to the elements of the second level as sub-criteria.

The list of the selected criteria presented here includes the concepts of usability, content, site quality, e-services and e-democracy features. All five criteria along with the relevant sub-criteria are further described in the following paragraphs.

Usability

The Usability of the website of a public authority is evaluated in terms of the visual appearance, (i.e. the website design), which has to follow specific directions and standards, and the search capability, which refers to the existence of internal search engines and external links to the websites of relevant public and private organizations. The provision of navigation aids (i.e. site maps, navigation menus etc.) is also directly connected to the website's functionality and ease of use. The existence of features that ensure accessibility for the disabled, encompassing all different disability types (associated with aging, visual, auditory, speech, motor and cognitive deficiencies) is as well taken into account.

Visual Appearance

The appearance of a website determines the first impression a visitor acquires and is particularly important in e-government implementations, since a respectable number of individuals are not adequately familiarized with computers and the principles of web services. The visual appearance of a website owes to follow specific directions and standards that mainly refer to colors, fonts, thumbnails, coloring of links, web page size and content format. The basic format has to be as simple as possible and must be consistently used throughout the site.

Search Capability

The search capability of a website is usually evaluated in terms of the availability of internal search engines. The latter constitute an important feature since they provide visitors with an easy and quick way for locating the content of their interest (Alexander & Tate, 1999; Gehrke & Turban, 1999) especially in websites that contain large amounts of information.

Navigation

The literature suggests that without an efficient and user-friendly navigation scheme, the user is likely to get confused, lost or frustrated and finally leave the site (Gehrke & Turban, 1999). Moreover, it is generally acknowledged that users should be able to find what they are looking for in three clicks or less (Basu, 2003). As a result, tools such as site maps, navigation menus and alphabetical indices are extremely useful as they provide a quick overview of the pages contained within the entire website (Alexander & Tate, 1999). Of course, full functionality of the former tools is achieved when their contents are simultaneously active links to the web pagers they refer to (Alexander & Tate, 1999).

Access to the Disabled

In the race for more content, colors, graphics, motion pictures, audio, video and other dynamic

elements, it is becoming increasingly difficult for disabled individuals to access websites (Huang, 2003). Thus, the adoption of standards such as the WCAG (Web Content Accessibility Guidelines) standard of the world wide web consortium (W3C, 1999) that ensure an acceptable level of accessibility for the disabled, should be a major concern in e-government website design, in order to avoid digital exclusion.

Content

Almost all literature references on website evaluation refer to some degree to content and width of offered information (Gehrke & Turban, 1999; Henriksson, Yi, Frost & Middleton, 2007; Smith, 2001). In general, the information that appears on a website has to be current, (i.e. regularly reviewed and updated) error-free, explicit and clear, precise and relevant and limited to the absolutely necessary, so as not to weary the user. It is therefore self-evident that content has to be included as a first level criterion in the hierarchy composed in this chapter. The sub-criteria involved are respectively up-to-datedness, validity, comprehensiveness, relevance-accuracy and provision of information at the right level of detail.

Updated Content

The content of a website has to be frequently reviewed and updated (Alexander & Tate, 1999; Smith, 2001). A citizen that finds once information that is out of date and thus no longer valid is bound to lose his trust on the particular e-government website permanently. Moreover, it has to be ensured that links to other web pages are current and working properly. The date when the content was first placed on the web or last revised should also be available.

Validity

Content validity is interpreted as content reliability and does not only refer to error-free, factual and consistent information but it presupposes too that information on the public authority that owns the website as well as the credentials and contact information of the webmaster or another person in the public organization are also provided so that the visitor can ask questions or verify the relevant information (Panopoulou et al., 2008).

Comprehensiveness

The comprehensiveness of information provided, as well as a clear statement of the purpose of the website, are the key points for successful evaluation with regard to this sub-criterion. The efficient organization of information, so that the visitor can easily locate the content of his interest without wandering around and wasting time, is also of great concern.

Accuracy & Relevance

The value of an e-government website is significantly increased when it incorporates precise and relevant information on the mission and priorities of the corresponding authority, details on the authority's internal organization as well as on the services it provides.

Correct Level of Detail

A website should present the relevant content at the right level of detail, thus without forcing the visitor to seek other resources for additional information. Similarly, the visitor should not be overwhelmed with tons of information even for the most simple tasks or services (Gehrke & Turban, 1999; Smith, 2001); in such a case, inexperienced citizens would not be able to easily use the available services. Basic information should be available to all visitors, while more detailed features should be accessible by only those actually seeking for them.

Site Quality

The criterion of Site Quality addresses aspects such as the technical features of a website (i.e. the availability of the website and its response time), which includes both the page loading time and the response speed of the website in case of service requests.

Response Time

Response time is of great importance when dealing with the Internet and particularly with web services. Even the most explicitly designed and intriguing website will surely frustrate the visitor if he/she has to wait several minutes until his/her requests have finally been processed by the system. This metric actually monitors the amount of time needed from the point the user clicks a button or link until the selected content has been loaded and the visitor is able to see it. This suggests that in fact response time covers two different parameters related to the system's delay:

- The web server's response time to the visitor's request, which involves the time needed for the interpretation of the visitor's query, its execution in the database and the retrieval of the selected content.
- The website's loading time that is the time required by the web server to send the selected content to the visitor's browser.

It should be obvious that even if one of the former aspects fails to reach the required performance, the visitor may experience tremendous dissatisfaction.

Availability

It is self-evident that an e-government website has to be always fully accessible and available in order to accomplish its mission. That means that frequent failures of the web server by which it is hosted or prolonged "under construction" periods for the entire website or specific parts of it are not really an option. In the same frame, restrictions such as options for text only, or frames, or suggestions of a particular browser for better viewing are to be avoided. The specific sub-criterion may as well include the availability of links for downloading free software that is necessary for viewing the content offered on a website as this is an important feature with regard to accessibility to information for non internet savvy users (Alexander & Tate, 1999).

E-Services

The e-services axis of the proposed hierarchy refers to the provision of online public services, which in the case of the public sector is an essential prerequisite for e-government to realize its full potential (Jansen, 2005; Sakowicz, 2007). The parameters that are of interest in this case are the percentage of services that are available online, the e-services' sophistication stage, as this is defined in (Cap Gemini, 2007), the degree of personalization offered to the citizens as well as privacy and security issues, which are of particular importance in case of personalized services and full online transactions.

Security and Privacy

The use of mechanisms, such as encrypted connections for the transmission of personal information and transaction data as well as the onsite availability of a privacy and security statement that explicitly explains the way in which citizen data is protected and how it is going to be used are strongly recommended by the relevant literature (Gehrke & Turban, 1999; Smith, 2001) in order to enable the provision of personalized services and full online transactions. In fact, according to recent research findings, it is the citizens themselves that place security and a desire for higher

accountability above convenience or the expansion of services and information and expect government agencies to clearly demonstrate attention to these issues (Moon & Welch, 2005).

Personalization

Web personalization refers in general to the process of customizing the content and structure of a website to the specific and individual needs of each user (Eirinaki & Vazirgiannis, 2003). In the context of e-services, profile-based personalization may be applied. Users may have the possibility of registering and entering personal information (user profiles) such as gender, age, interests etc. in order to receive advanced services.

Percentage of E-Services

There is no doubt that the total number of public services available online is significant for the evaluation of an e-government website. However, although it is quite simple to determine the number of online public services, it is rather difficult to define the number of public services that should be available online, as this may substantially differ depending on the specific government level (local, regional, national or federal) and may be as well restricted due to political or policy reasons. As a result, there is the possibility of evaluating the online availability percentage of e-services either based on a basket of pre-selected public services, such as the one composed by Cap Gemini (2007) for the European Commission, or using the maximum number of services that are currently offered online per authority level (local, regional etc.) (Panopoulou et al., 2008).

Sophistication Stage

Another important aspect of the e-services criterion is the evaluation of the sophistication level at which the services are offered, as there is obviously a huge difference between offering just online information on a service and offering the whole transaction service online. A well established model for the measurement of the sophistication of online public services is the e-service sophistication model adopted in a series of studies performed on behalf of the European Commission (Cap Gemini, 2006; 2007). This model illustrates the different degrees of sophistication of online public services going from "basic" information provision over one-way and two way interaction to "full" electronic case handling and consists of five stages, each one being more advanced compared to the others before it. More specifically,

- Stage 1 corresponds solely to the online availability of the information required to start the procedure to obtain a specific public service.
- Stage 2 indicates that the publicly available website offers the possibility to obtain in a non-electronic way, thus by downloading forms, the paper form necessary to commence the procedures related to the specific public service.
- Stage 3 represents as well the possibility of an electronic intake of an official electronic form in order to obtain the service, implying the existence of an authentication mechanism for verifying the identity of the person requesting the service.
- Stage 4 is indicative of full electronic delivery of services, where no other formal procedure is necessary for the applicant via "paperwork".
- Finally, the 5th level of sophistication, built around the concepts of pro-activity and personalization, gives an indication of fully integrated electronic procedures that help reduce "red tape" and improve data consistency. Of course both stages 4 and 5 represent full electronic case handling.

E-Democracy Features

E-democracy and e-participation emerge henceforth as an important component of e-government (Janssen, 2003; Sakowicz, 2007). In fact, apart from the provision of information and online services, an e-government website should also target the promotion of public participation in decision-making. As a result, e-democracy features are also incorporated as a criterion in the hierarchical structure proposed. The democratic and participatory aspects of a public website are evaluated on the basis of the existence of communication tools that enable and promote citizens' involvement in public issues as well as of democratic decision making tools.

Citizens' Involvement

Citizen participation and involvement in public affairs through the web involves active communication tools such as chats, blogs and e-forums, where citizens are able not only to be informed about current developments but also to express their opinion.

DDM Tools

This sub-criterion is imposed by the i2010 e-Government Action Plan deployed by the EU, that has adopted as one of its five priorities the strengthening of participation and democratic decision-making, demonstrating by 2010 tools for effective public debate and participation in democratic decision-making (European Communication, 2006). Democratic decision making involves tools such as e-polls, e-voting, public surveys etc, as well as the ability for citizens to propose a topic at e-forums and e-polls or for inclusion in the agenda of the local representatives' meeting.

Figure 2. Hierarchy of evaluation factors

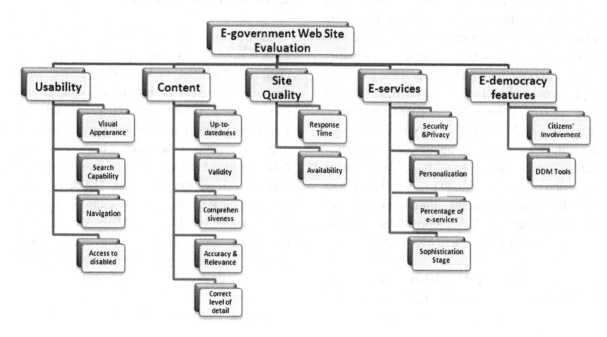

Problem Hierarchy

Figure 2 illustrates the hierarchy of the evaluation problem as it has been discussed in this section. As already stated, the hierarchy consists of two levels, corresponding to criteria and sub-criteria respectively. Of course, the former analysis indicates that several of the sub-criteria described above can be themselves further analyzed into a number of more specific parameters, e.g. the sub-criterion of Navigation may be further analyzed into the specific navigational aids (site maps, navigation menus and alphabetical indices etc) that could potentially be incorporated in an e-government website to enhance its usability. However, such a level of detail escapes the interests of this chapter. The advantage of the evaluation approach proposed is that it offers significant scalability, as additional sub-criteria may be easily added without causing major changes to the evaluation process.

EVALUATION FRAMEWORK

Scope

As stated in the introduction of this chapter, e-government website evaluation is a process of weighting multiple criteria and may be thus confronted adopting MADM methods, such as AHP, that integrate subjective and personal preferences. However, due to the uncertainty and vagueness in subjective judgments of the decision maker, in the role of which we may also place the citizens themselves, the crisp pair wise comparison of AHP seems too insufficient and imprecise to handle the inherent uncertainty associated with the mapping of the decision maker's perception to exact numbers, and thus to reflect human thinking.

A natural way to cope with uncertainty in judgments is to express the comparison ratios as fuzzy sets or fuzzy numbers, which reflect the vagueness of human thinking. In this frame, a vague evaluative judgment resulting from the comparison of any two elements at the same level of the decision hierarchy can be represented by a fuzzy number.

That is why Fuzzy Sets Theory is introduced in the pair wise comparison of AHP to make up for the afore-mentioned deficiency in the original crisp method. The outcome of the combination of AHP and Fuzzy Sets Theory is Fuzzy AHP. The FAHP-based evaluation framework can eventually provide government administrators with a valuable reference for assessing the quality of e-government website implementations.

Acquiring the Citizens' Opinion

As e-government websites address citizens as their main beneficiaries, it is considered rational enough that effort is put in the frame of the relevant evaluation schemes on acquiring the citizens' opinions. Indeed, common evaluation approaches in the field of e-government rely on questionnaires, in which citizens are requested to express their overall experience of a service or their opinion on a specific feature on a predefined evaluation scale (Abhichandani & Horan, 2006) that in several cases consists of numeric values.

The use of numeric values however does not always apply as in some situations the information required may be hard or even impossible to quantify due to its nature, and thus an approximate value can be tolerated. In such cases, information can only be expressed in linguistic terms (e.g., when evaluating the comfort or design of a car, terms like "good", "fair", "poor" can be used) and can be mathematically modeled through the use of Fuzzy Sets Theory. Fuzzy Sets Theory can handle fuzziness by representing qualitative aspects as linguistic variables. That is, variables whose values are not numbers but words or sentences according to a natural or artificial language (e.g. "low", "medium", "high"), that can be afterwards converted to fuzzy numbers using a suitable conversion scale. Processing of the relevant information takes place using these fuzzy numbers, which are finally converted to crisp numbers through the process of defuzzification.

Obviously, the same linguistic terms in different conversion scales can have different crisp values.

Such an approach may be adopted for the purposes of this evaluation framework as well, meaning that the problem analyst may rely on citizens' opinions, obtained through questionnaires, to estimate the importance of the criteria that are involved in the problem hierarchy. More specifically, citizens may be asked to evaluate the importance of a specific criterion over another based on a qualitative preference scale of linguistic variables that ranges from "Unimportant" to "Very Important". Using a suitable conversion scale these variables can be then converted to fuzzy numbers which can be used to form the comparison matrix, as it will be explained in the next paragraph of this section. As already stated, the use of fuzzy instead of crisp numbers is adopted as a means of ensuring that the uncertainty factor that is innate in subjective evaluations is incorporated into the analysis and more reliable results are produced.

Fuzzy AHP (FAHP)

Fuzzy AHP (FAHP), the fuzzy extension of AHP, has been developed to solve hierarchical fuzzy problems (Mikhailov & Tsvetinov, 2004). The fuzzy numbers required to form the judgment matrix in the fuzzy AHP procedure may be determined directly according to the designer's focus or may derive from questionnaires, in which users are prompted to evaluate the selected criteria with regard to their relative importance. In this case subjective evaluations may be expressed in linguistic terms, such as "unimportant", "slightly important", or "very important", which are then to be converted to fuzzy numbers using a suitable conversion scale. In the classic FAHP method the intensity of importance that each criterion or sub-criterion yields in pair-wise comparisons, is assigned to a fuzzy number according to the conversion scale of Table 2. Mean values can be afterwards calculated from the fuzzified form of the weighted arithmetic mean, which for triangu-

Table 2. Fuzzy relative criteria importance

Intensity of importance	Fuzzy number	Definition
1	$\tilde{1}$	Equal importance
3	$\tilde{3}$	Weak importance of one over another
5	$\tilde{5}$	Essential or strong importance
7	$\tilde{7}$	Very strong and demonstrated
9	$\tilde{9}$	Absolute importance

lar fuzzy numbers $\widetilde{A}_1, \widetilde{A}_2, ..., \widetilde{A}_n$ $(\widetilde{A}_i = (l, m, u))$ is defined as

$$\widetilde{A} = \frac{\sum_{i=0}^{n} f_i \cdot \widetilde{A}_n}{\sum_{i=0}^{n} f_i} \tag{1}$$

where f_i are the corresponding frequencies of appearance. An alternative approach would be to collect, instead of linguistic terms, multiple crisp data sets reflecting different opinions and then form the fuzzy numbers as the triplet (*min, mean, max*) deriving from the specific data sets.

Based on a set of standardized answers (linguistic variables) provided through appropriate question forms, the corresponding triangular fuzzy values are defined and the pair wise comparison matrix is constructed as

$$\widetilde{A} = \left(\widetilde{a}_{ij}\right)_{n \times n} = \begin{bmatrix} (1,1,1) & (l_{12}, m_{12}, u_{12}) & \cdots & (l_{1n}, m_{1n}, u_{1n}) \\ (l_{21}, m_{21}, u_{21}) & (1,1,1) & \cdots & (l_{2n}, m_{2n}, u_{2n}) \\ \vdots & \vdots & \vdots & \vdots \\ (l_{n1}, m_{n1}, u_{n1}) & (l_{n2}, m_{n2}, u_{n2}) & \cdots & (1,1,1) \end{bmatrix}$$

where $\tilde{a}_{ij}$ denotes a triangular fuzzy number depicting the relative strength of two elements. Note that the comparison matrix is symmetric, which means that

$$\tilde{a}_{ji} = \left[\tilde{a}_{ij}\right]^{-1} = (l_{ij}, m_{ij}, u_{ij})^{-1} = \left(\frac{1}{u_{ij}}, \frac{1}{m_{ij}}, \frac{1}{l_{ij}}\right)$$

Final weights of alternatives can be acquired from different methods that have been proposed in the literature. One of the most popular is the *Fuzzy Extent Analysis,* proposed by Chang in 1996 (Mahmoodzadeh, Shahrabi, Pariazar & Zaeri, 2007), which is presented in Appendix B.

Application Example

In this section we provide an application example of the proposed evaluation framework based on the problem hierarchy described earlier. As already implied, the top level of the problem hierarchy represents the overall goal, i.e. the overall e-government website quality, while the two lower levels embody the afore-mentioned selected criteria and sub-criteria. The relative importance of the evaluation criteria is determined by performing pair-wise comparisons among them with respect to the overall goal. The same applies for the estimation of the relative importance of the evaluation sub-criteria, which are however pair-wisely compared with regard to the relevant first level criterion. The ratios in pair wise comparisons for each criterion or sub-criterion are expressed using triangular fuzzy numbers and aggregated in a fuzzy comparison matrix.

Obviously, fuzzy comparison matrices need to be constructed for all criteria and sub-criteria involved in the hierarchy. However, since the calculation process is the same for all criteria and sub-criteria, the fuzzy comparison matrix (Table 3), as well as the intermediate and final results of the application of the evaluation framework, are only presented for the criterion of Usability.

Using equations (B.1)-(B.3) and the values of the fuzzy comparison matrix (Table 3), the fuzzy synthetic extents are calculated as $S_1 = (0.179, 0.247, 0.333)$, $S_2 = (0.119, 0.156, 0.223)$, $S_3 = (0.192, 0.28, 0.429)$ and $S_4 = (0.21, 0.317, 0.442)$. The weight vector d for these values is $(0.639, 0.075, 0.854, 1)$, which is then normalized to provide the final weights (see equation (B.6)).

Table 3.Fuzzy comparison matrix for the sub-criteria of Usability

	Visual appearance	**Search capability**	**Navigation**	**Access to disabled**
Visual appearance	(1,1,1)	(1.1,1.3,1.4)	(0.556,0.625,0.909)	(1.1,1.5,1.6)
Search capability	(0.714,0.769,0.909)	(1,1,1)	(0.357,0.526,0.667)	(0.435,0.5,0.714)
Navigation	(1.1,1.6,1.8)	(1.5,1.9,2.8)	(1,1,1)	(0.435,0.5,0.714)
Access to disabled	(0.625,0.667,0.909)	(1.4,2,2.3)	(1.4,2,2.3)	(1,1,1)

Table 4. Local and global priority weights for sub-criteria of Usability

	Visual appearance	*Search capability*	*Navigation*	*Access to disabled*	
Local	0.249	0.029	0.333	0.389	1
Global	0.108	0.013	0.146	0.169	0.436

At this point attention should be drawn to the fact that two different kinds of weights – local and global - are distinguished:

- The *local weights* represent the relative weights of criteria within a group with respect to their "parent" in the hierarchy. The local weights of each group of criteria add up to 1.
- The *global weights* are obtained by multiplying the local weights of the siblings by their parent's global weight. The global weights for all the sub-criteria add up once again to 1.

In this frame, assuming that the application of the evaluation framework for all first level parameters has assigned to the criterion of Usability a weight equal to 0.436, the local weights initially obtained for all sub-criteria involved can be multiplied by 0.436 to provide the corresponding global weights. Both the local and global weights of the Usability sub-criteria are aggregated in Table 4. As seen in Table 4, the local weights of the Usability sub-criteria add up to 1, while their global weights add up to 0.436, which is the weight assigned to the criterion of Usability with respect to the overall goal.

It is obvious that the parameters of Navigation and Access to the disabled are quite important when considering the overall quality of a website, as they possess higher weights. On the other hand, the Search capability is assigned a lower weight, and thus plays a less important role. This observation allows the website designer to focus his efforts on the most promising aspects of a website and thus achieve the maximum benefit when improving certain features.

Using the proposed scheme, weights for all evaluation factors can be extracted. Given that there are measured values for all metrics in question, public authorities may rely on the proposed evaluation scheme to obtain a spherical view on which aspects of e-government websites should be further optimized, as well as on how any refinements would impact on the public opinion.

E-GOVERNMENT WEBSITE COMPARISONS

Scope

So far the chapter has illustrated how two different tools, Fuzzy Sets Theory and MADM, can be combined to provide weights that indicate the importance of each criterion impacting the evaluation of e-government websites. This however is not the only goal of the chapter; as stated in the introduction, apart from providing the reader with the necessary tools to efficiently evaluate the quality attributes of a website and therefore determine the aspects that need further enhancement, the authors aim as well at setting the basic guidelines for performing comparisons between different implementations using MADM methods. As already explained in another section of this chapter, apart from weight extraction, another class of MADM methods relies on a series of pair-wise comparisons that leads eventually to the ranking of alternatives.

The aim is, more specifically, to provide a series of methods for comparing the presence of different public authorities on the web in terms of a common overall quality assessment, so that useful conclusions can be reached, or even for ranking the relevant implementations with regard to their overall performance on the selected criteria, so that the most successful ones can be distinguished and adopted as reference or best practice examples. At this point, attention has to be drawn to the fact that comparisons among different websites either at national or international level are only meaningful for public authorities of the same governmental level (local, regional, national or federal) as well of the same scope and competencies and thus the following analysis has been based on this assumption.

MADM shall be once again deployed in this frame, since multiple factors have to be taken into account and therefore it is not possible to compare or rank the alternatives (a.k.a. e-government implementations) according to preference on a single criterion. In fact, the selected criteria have to be combined and scaled in a meaningful way. That means that in the frame of MADM methods, once the problem hierarchy has been formed and the individual evaluation parameters have been weighted, the overall performance of the alterna-

tives under examination is estimated through the calculation of complex indices.

For the purposes of this study the authors have selected the SAW, ELECTRE and TOPSIS methods, each one of which relies on different indices. Since the calculation of the relevant indices presupposes that there is quantifiable information on the performance of each alternative on each of the evaluation criteria, and the majority of these criteria are qualitative parameters, the next paragraph addresses the issue of the selection of the appropriate measurement scale. A generic mathematical model that applies to all MADM methods is also provided as a starting point and then each method is briefly described, so that the reader may decide which one best fits his/her interests. The analysis that follows is anticipated to be of interest to researchers that are engaged in e-government website evaluation as well as to analysts conducting statistical surveys on e-government performance at national or international level.

Measurement Scale

A significant challenge that the analyst has to tackle before proceeding with the application of a MADM method is the mapping of the performance of the alternatives under examination for each one of the evaluation criteria to a suitable measurement scale. In the case of the problem hierarchy presented earlier, it is obvious that the evaluation parameters of the second level are heterogeneous enough; few of them are fully quantifiable (e.g. response time) and the vast majority are qualitative attributes that may be assessed either on a strictly binary scale (e.g. by assigning 0 or 1 in case a specific sub-criterion is respectively covered or not) or on a suitable nominal qualitative scale that awards proportionally points of score (e.g. in a range from 0 to 1 or 1 to 10) depending on the multitude of the individual sub-features that have been incorporated in the website implementation examined to enhance the specific sub-criterion in question.

The use of MADM methods however presupposes that the values assigned to all sub-criteria are measured on a common scale. As a result, and moreover due to the particular nature of the decision problem, it is suggested that a common scale is employed from the very beginning of the problem design for all individual parameters, being either quantitative or qualitative. The particular rules according to which the performance of both quantitative and qualitative criteria will be mapped to specific values of the common measurement scale as well as the range of the scale are left to be determined by the decision maker, who is free to make the choices that best serve his interests and only committed to apply these choices for all parameters and alternatives under examination, so that evaluation is conducted on the same base. The scores of the relevant criteria and of course the overall performance of each alternative are to be calculated using either one of the MADM methods proposed.

Forming the Decision Matrix

This section addresses the mathematical formalization of the decision problem, which is generally modeled as $P=(A,C,w)$, where

- $A=\{1,...,N\}$ denotes the set of alternatives, in this case e-government websites
- $C=\{1,...,N\}$ denotes the set of criteria impacting the decision process,
- $w=\{1,...,M\}$ denotes the set of weights assigned to the selected criteria, so that $\sum_{i=1}^{M} w_i = 1$.

Based on the scores achieved for each one of the selected criteria (attributes), the i_{th} alternative can be represented by a vector of M decision criteria as follows:

$$DM_i = \begin{bmatrix} C1_i & C2_i & \cdots & CM_i \end{bmatrix}$$

For N alternatives to be considered in the selection process, the decision matrix DM can be formulated as follows:

$$DM = \begin{bmatrix} C1_1 & C2_1 & \cdots & CM_1 \\ C1_2 & C2_2 & \cdots & CM_2 \\ \vdots & \vdots & \vdots & \vdots \\ C1_N & C2_N & \cdots & CM_N \end{bmatrix}$$

The SAW Method

SAW stands for Simple Additive Weighting and is the most well-known and simplest method of MADM. In SAW, the overall score of an alternative is determined by the weighted sum of all attribute values and is calculated by equation (7) where C_{ij} represent the attribute scores and w_j the corresponding assigned weights.

$$A_{SAW} = \max_i \sum_{j=1}^{n} (C_{ij} \cdot w_j) \qquad (2)$$

The ELECTRE Method

ELECTRE was first developed by Bernard Roy and its acronym stands for ELimination Et Choix Traduisant la REalité (ELimination and Choice Expressing REality). A detailed analysis of this method can be found in (Charilas et al., 2009). In ELECTRE, the impact of the relative weights is integrated in the decision process through the calculation of a new matrix DM_w as follows:

$$DM_w = \begin{bmatrix} w_1 C1_1 & w_2 C2_1 & \cdots & w_M CM_1 \\ w_1 C1_2 & w_2 C2_2 & \cdots & w_M CM_2 \\ \vdots & \vdots & \vdots & \vdots \\ w_1 C1_N & w_2 C2_N & \cdots & w_M CM_N \end{bmatrix}$$

The main part of ELECTRE lies in the construction of the concordance and discordance matrices, which provide measurements of satisfaction and dissatisfaction of the decision maker when one alternative is compared to another. The values of the aforementioned matrices are calculated using concordance and discordance sets, where a concordance set constitutes a list of the attributes, for which alternative X is superior to alternative Y and a discordance set is its complementary set, comprising of the list of attributes for which alternative X is worse than the compared alternative Y.

The application of the method proceeds with the calculation of the concordance and discordance indices, where the concordance index constitutes a measure of relative dominance of an alternative *i* over other alternatives when compared to a measure of dominance of other alternatives over the alternative *i* and a discordance index provides a measure of relative weakness of alternative *i* over other alternatives when compared to a measure of weakness of other alternatives over alternative *i*. Alternatives are finally ranked based on the concordance and discordance indices as well by taking the average of these two rankings. The alternative with the highest average ranking is considered to be best solution.

The TOPSIS Method

TOPSIS is based upon the concept that the chosen alternative should have the relative shortest distance to the ideal solution. According to this method, firstly a Euclidean normalized decision matrix *R* is formed, its values are weighted being multiplied by the corresponding weights and finally ideal and negative-ideal solutions are determined. The comparison among the given alternatives is accomplished through calculation of the relative closeness of the alternatives to the ideal solution. The relative closeness is determined as an index lying between 0 and 1. The larger the index value, the better the performance of the alternative. For additional information on this method the reader is prompted at (Mahmoodzadeh et al., 2007).

AN ALTERNATIVE APPROACH: FUZZY INFERENCE SYSTEMS

This final section of the chapter brings into the reader's attention an alternative approach for establishing a highly dynamic comparison framework. This time, instead of using MADM methods, the authors clarify how a decision system can be established with the help of Fuzzy Logic and a set of rules, the essence of which will be explained in the following paragraphs. This approach builds also on the concept of linguistic variables, with the use of which the parameters of the decision system are determined.

As shown in Figure 3, a fuzzy decision system is made up of:

a. A *fuzzifier* that converts input values into linguistic variables matched to membership degrees based on membership functions,
b. An *inference system* that applies the fuzzy rules and
c. A *defuzzifier* that deduces the final decision from the intermediate ones.

Fuzzification makes possible the comparison of the decision parameters. Each input is characterized by a membership function, which measures the degree of membership of a given value to the fuzzy subsets defined. If a variable value changes slightly, the degrees of membership to the fuzzy subsets vary slightly. In fuzzy logic, membership degrees variations are continuous contrary to conventional logic in which membership degrees can be either 0 or 1.

The fuzzy controller uses a list of "IF" – "THEN" rules, that may be based on prior field experience, questionnaires, measurements etc. to control the system. The following example on such rules may be considered: according to

Figure 3. Fuzzy system components

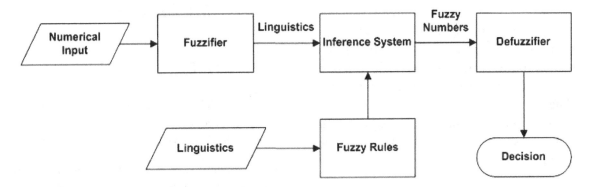

a survey, citizens have provided feedback that may be translated into the following set of rules:

- If the Content of the website is "Good" and the Site Quality is "Very Good" then the website is considered as "Very Good".
- If the Content of the website is "Bad" and the Site Quality is "Good" then the website is considered as "Good".
- If the Content of the website is "Bad" and the Site Quality is "Very Good" then the website is considered as "Very Good".
- If the Content of the website is "Very Good" and the Site Quality is "Very Bad" then the website is considered as "Bad".

This set of rules gives an initial clue that from the citizens' point of view, the overall experience is mainly determined by the Site Quality criterion and Content does not play such an important role. This simple example constitutes of 2 criteria and 4 linguistic variables, providing a total of 4^2 possible combinations. Of course, having all 16 different rules is not obligatory, since for a more complex example the overall complexity would reach unacceptable levels. In general, the maximum number of rules required is N^M, where N is the number of linguistic variables and M the number of criteria. Using a suitable tool, different combinations can be explored. More specifically, changing the value of one criterion while maintaining the others, may

invoke a certain change in the final decision which is quantified by the system. An efficient tool for performing such an analysis is the Matlab Fuzzy Logic Toolbox, as it provides computational and visual aid.

The advantage of such an approach is that it solely requires feedback from the public opinion. Afterwards, rules can be easily formulated or modified. Also, one may easily preview the anticipated impact of the modification in the value of one or more criteria. The behavior of a fuzzy system can be changed by modifying the appropriate rules. Learning techniques can be also applied to improve the decision rules by optimizing the membership functions.

FUTURE RESEARCH DIRECTIONS

This chapter has presented a methodological decision making framework on e-government web-site evaluation, based on the use of questionnaires, MADM methods and Fuzzy Sets Theory. Future studies on the problem at hand should adapt the generic guidelines provided, to cover the particular requirements and characteristics that arise with regard to the evaluation of web-site implementations of public authorities of different levels and competencies as well as apply them in real contexts and use cases. As already implied in the "Fuzzy Inference Systems" section, another potential next step would be to exploit the afore-mentioned solution to set up a highly dynamic evaluation framework, capable of previewing the impact of modifications of individual evaluation parameters on the overall web-site quality. Finally, a future challenge would also be to compare the findings of such an analysis on the evaluation of e-government web-site implementations with their actual success and utilization by the citizens in pure quantitative terms.

CONCLUSION

This chapter addressed the issue of e-government website evaluation. In this context, the authors defined the main factors involved in the evaluation process and presented an evaluation framework for specifying the impact of each one on the overall quality. In fact, since the relative importance of each criterion over another cannot be precisely defined, the adoption of fuzzy numbers in order to integrate the uncertainty of subjective judgment into the problem analysis and the use of Fuzzy Analytic Hierarchy Process, a MADM method, to extract the priority weights of all criteria and sub-criteria, were suggested. Moreover, the chapter exposed the basic guidelines for performing comparisons among different e-government web-sites, suggesting once again the use of MADM methods for calculating the overall performance of the candidate implementations.

As a concluding remark the authors wish to draw attention to the fact that a nicely designed, user-oriented and sophisticated website is only one aspect of increasing the value produced by Public Administration and that e-government web-sites have to be assessed in terms of public outreach and civic engagement as well. In this context, it is self-evident that policy makers and public administration executives should take into account the information and technology literacy of citizens as well as implement training and dissemination activities to assist e-government web-sites in realizing their full potential.

REFERENCES

W3C. (1999). *Web content accessibility guidelines 1.0.* Retrieved June 8, 2009, from http://www.w3.org/TR/WCAG10/

Abhichandani, T., & Horan, T. A. (2006). Toward a new evaluation model of e-government satisfaction: Results of structural equation modeling. *Paper presented at the 12th America's Conference on Information Systems (AMCIS 2006).* Acapulco, Mexico.

Alexander, J. E., & Tate, M. A. (1999). *Web wisdom: how to evaluate and create information quality on the web.* Mahwah, NJ: Lawrence Erlbaum Associates.

Alshawi, S., Alahmary, A., & Alalwany, H. (2008). E-government evaluation factors: Citizen's perspective. *Paper presented at the European and Mediterranean Conference on Information Systems 2007 (EMCIS 2007).* Spain.

Barnes, S. J., & Vidgen, R. T. (2004). Interactive e-government services: modelling user perceptions with eQual. *Electronic Government, an International Journal, 1*(2), 213-228.

Basu, A. (2003). Context-driven assessment of commercial websites. *Paper presented at the 36th Hawaii International Conference on System Sciences (HICSS'03).* Big Island, Hawaii.

Bauer, C., & Scharl, A. (2000). Quantitative evaluation of website content and structure. *Internet Research: Electronic Networking Applications and Policy, 10*(1), 31–43. doi:10.1108/10662240010312138

Cap Gemini. (2006). *Online Availability of Public Services: How Is Europe Progressing? Web Based Survey on Electronic Public Services – Report of the 6th Measurement*. London: Cap Gemini.

Cap Gemini. (2007). *The User Challenge: Benchmarking the Supply of Online Public Services – 7th Measurement*. London: Cap Gemini.

Charilas, E. D., Markaki, I. O., Psarras, J., & Constantinou, P. (2009). Application of fuzzy ahp and ELECTRE to network selection. *Paper presented at the 1st International Conference on Mobile Lightweight Wireless Systems (MOBILIGHT 2009)*. Athens, Greece.

Eirinaki, M., & Vazirgiannis, M. (2003). Web mining for web personalization. *ACM Transactions on Internet Technology, 3*(1), 1–27. doi:10.1145/643477.643478

European Communication. (2006). *i2010 e-government action plan: Accelerating egovernment in europe for the benefit of all. COM(2006) 173 final*. Brussels, Belgium: Commission of the European Communities.

Fei, J., Yao, R., & Yu, L. (2008). Fuzzy analytic hierarchy process application to e-government performance evaluation. *Paper presented at the 5th International Conference on Fuzzy Systems and Knowledge Discovery (FSKD '08)*. Jinan, China.

Gehrke, D., & Turban, E. (1999). Determinants of successful website design: Relative importance and recommendations for effectiveness. *Paper presented at the 32nd Hawaii International Conference on System Sciences (HICSS'99)*. Maui Island, Hawaii.

Henriksson, A., Yi, Y., Frost B., & Middleton, M. (2007). *Evaluation instrument for e-government websites. Electronic Government, an International Journal, 4*(2), 204-226.

Huang, C. J. (2003). *Usability of e-government websites for people with disabilities. Paper presented at the 36th Hawaii International Conference on System Sciences (HICSS'03)*. Big Island, Hawaii.

Jansen, A. (2005). Assessing e-government progress – why and what. In B.J. Tessem and G. Iden og, (Eds), *Proceedings of Christensen (red) NOKOBIT 2005*.

Janssen, D. (2003). Mine's bigger than yours: assessing international e-government benchmarking. In F. Bannister and D. Remenyi (Eds.), *3rd European Conference on e-Government* (pp. 209-218). London: MCIL.

Mahmoodzadeh, S., Shahrabi, J., Pariazar, M., & Zaeri, M. S. (2007). Project selection by using fuzzy ahp and topsis technique. *International Journal of Human and Social Sciences, 1*(3), 25.

Mikhailov, L., & Tsvetinov, P. (2004). Evaluation of services using a fuzzy analytic hierarchy process. *Applied Soft Computing, 5*(1), 23–33. doi:10.1016/j.asoc.2004.04.001

Moon, M. J., & Welch, E. W. (2005). *Same bed, different dreams: A comparative analysis of citizen and bureaucrat perspectives on e-government. Paper presented at the 37th Hawaii International Conference on System Sciences (HICSS'04)*. Big Island, Hawaii.

Nielsen, J. (2000). *Designing web usability: The practice of simplicity*. Indianapolis, IN: New Riders Publishing.

Panopoulou, E., Tambouris, E., & Tarabanis, K. (2008). A framework for evaluating websites of public authorities. *Aslib Proceedings: New Information Perspectives, 60*(5), 517–546.

Peters, M. R., Janssen, M., & Van Engers, M. T. (2004). Measuring e-government impact: existing practices and shortcomings. *Paper presented at the 6th International Conference on Electronic Commerce (ICEC'04)*. Delft, The Netherlands.

Saaty, L. T. (2008). Relative measurement and its generalization in decision making: Why pairwise comparisons are central in mathematics for the measurement of intangible factors. The Analytic Hierarchy/Network Process. *Review of the Royal Spanish Academy of Sciences, Series A. Mathematics, 102*(2), 251–318.

Sakowicz, M. (2007). *How to evaluate e-government: Different methodologies and methods. Paper presented at the 11th Annual NISPA Conference.* Bucharest, Romania.

Smith, A. G. (2001). Applying evaluation criteria to New Zealand government websites. *International Journal of Information Management, 21*(2), 137–149. doi:10.1016/S0268-4012(01)00006-8

Soufi, B., & Maguire, M. (2007). Achieving usability within e-government websites illustrated by a case study evaluation. In Smith, M. J., & Salvendy, G. (Eds.), *Human interface and the management of information. Interacting in information environments* (pp. 777–784). Berlin, Germany: Springer. doi:10.1007/978-3-540-73354-6_85

Wang, L., Bretschneider, S., & Gant, J. (2005). *Evaluating web-based e-government services with a citizen-centric approach. Paper presented at the 38th Hawaii International Conference on System Sciences (HICSS'05)*, Big Island, Hawaii.

Zadeh, L. A. (1965). Fuzzy sets. *Information and Control, 8*, 338–353. doi:10.1016/S0019-9958(65)90241-X

APPENDIX A

Using the decision matrix, the weights, with which the decision elements participate in the configuration of the final objective, are calculated. The vector $\hat{w}$, which constitutes the required estimation of the vector of the final weights, is calculated through the following repetitive process:

1. The elements of each line of the matrix are added up for each i, $s_i = \sum_j a_{ij}$.

2. For each line of matrix the weight of each element is estimated by calculating the quotient of the value s_i via the sum of all elements of the matrix $w_i = \dfrac{s_i}{\sum_i \sum_j a_{ij}}$.

3. The elements of the received vector $\hat{w}$, are normalized, so that their sum is equal to 1.

4. The square of the matrix is calculated and all the procedure steps are repeated until two successive approaches do not differ considerably in the frame of the desirable precision.

APPENDIX B

Final weights of alternatives can be acquired from different methods that have been proposed in the literature. One of the most popular is the *Fuzzy Extent Analysis*, proposed by Chang in 1996 (Mahmoodzadeh et al., 2007). The value of the fuzzy synthetic extent with respect to the i_{th} object is defined with the help of fuzzy arithmetic operations as:

$$\tilde{S}_i = \sum_{j=1}^{n} \tilde{a}_{ij} \otimes \left[\sum_{i=1}^{n} \sum_{j=1}^{n} \tilde{a}_{kj} \right]^{-1} \tag{B.1}$$

The fuzzy addition operation of n extent analysis values as well as the inverse of the vector are given by equations (2) and (3) respectively.

$$\sum_{j=1}^{n} \tilde{a}_{ij} = \left(\sum_{j=1}^{n} l_{ij}, \sum_{j=1}^{n} m_{ij}, \sum_{j=1}^{n} u_{ij} \right) \tag{B.2}$$

$$\left[\sum_{i=1}^{n} \sum_{j=1}^{n} \tilde{a}_{ij} \right]^{-1} = \left(\frac{1}{\sum_{i=1}^{n} \sum_{j=1}^{n} u_{ij}}, \frac{1}{\sum_{i=1}^{n} \sum_{j=1}^{n} m_{ij}}, \frac{1}{\sum_{i=1}^{n} \sum_{j=1}^{n} l_{ij}} \right) \tag{B.3}$$

The possibility of $\tilde{S}_1 \geq \tilde{S}_2$ is defined as $V(\tilde{S}_1 \geq \tilde{S}_2) = SUP_{x \geq y}[\min(\tilde{S}_1(x), \tilde{S}_2(y))]$, x and y being the values on the axis of the membership function of each criterion. This expression can be equivalently written as:

$$V(\tilde{S}_1 \geq \tilde{S}_2) = \begin{cases} 1, & m_1 \geq m_2 \\ 0, & l_2 \geq u_1 \\ \dfrac{l_2 - u_1}{(m_1 - u_1) - (m_2 - l_2)}, & otherwise \end{cases} \quad (B.4)$$

To compare $\tilde{S}_1$ and $\tilde{S}_2$, both the values of $V\left(\tilde{S}_1 \geq \tilde{S}_2\right)$ and $V\left(\tilde{S}_2 \geq \tilde{S}_1\right)$ are needed. The possibility

for a convex fuzzy number to be greater than k convex fuzzy numbers $\tilde{S}_i, \left(i = 1, 2, ..., k\right)$ is defined by:

$$V(\tilde{S} \geq \tilde{S}_1, \tilde{S}_2, ..., \tilde{S}_k) = V\left[(\tilde{S} \geq \tilde{S}_1) and (\tilde{S} \geq \tilde{S}_2) and ... and (\tilde{S} \geq \tilde{S}_k)\right] = \min V(\tilde{S} \geq \tilde{S}_i), i = 1, 2, 3, ..., k$$

$$(B.5)$$

Assuming that $d'_i = \min V(\tilde{S}_i \geq \tilde{S}_k)$, the weight vector is given by $W' = \left(d'_1, d'_2, ..., d'_n\right)^T$.

Via normalization, the normalized (non-fuzzy) weight vector is

$$W = \left(d_1, d_2, ..., d_n\right)^T \quad (B.6)$$

Chapter 6
Social Equity, the Digital Divide and E-Governance:
An Analysis of E-Governance Initiatives in India

Meena Chary
University of South Florida, USA

ABSTRACT

This chapter critically assesses how e-government initiatives in India are attempting to contend with social equity issues posed by the deepening digital divide and draws conclusions regarding the value and reach of e-government initiatives. The chapter summarizes current understandings of the digital divide, and uses those understandings to develop a characterization of those constituents who are not reached by e-government initiatives and services. The chapter asserts that those who do not have the ability to access and use ICT are excluded from using e-government initiatives and services, and discusses examples of actions that begin to mitigate the social equity effects of the digital divide.

INTRODUCTION

This chapter critically assesses how e-government initiatives in India are attempting to contend with social equity issues posed by the deepening digital divide and draws conclusions regarding the value and reach of e-government initiatives.

In order to fulfill these objectives, the chapter first summarizes current understandings of the digital divide, and uses those understandings to develop a characterization of those constituents who are not reached by e-government websites

and services. The global digital divide is defined here to mean the gap between those who have the ability to access and use information and communication technology (ICT) and those who do not. These individuals who fall on either side of the digital divide are characterized by differences in personal wealth, demographics such as race and gender, levels of education and literacy, and access to ICT (Chary & Aikins, 2009). The chapter asserts that those who do not have the ability to access and use ICT are excluded from using e-government websites and services. In this, the chapter aims to contribute to the overall understanding of the digital divide as a critical

DOI: 10.4018/978-1-61692-018-0.ch006

global phenomenon that affects the value and applicability of e-governance.

Second, the chapter critically analyzes Indian e-governance initiatives against those dimensions to draw conclusions regarding the value, reach and applicability of those initiatives, especially in a social equity context. The chapter attempts to contribute to our overall understanding of how to use social equity concerns in a world characterized by a deep and wide digital divide and to evaluate and perhaps enhance the reach of e-government websites. Finally, the chapter draws conclusions regarding how well existing e-governance has addressed digital divide issues and makes recommendations on how those attempts may be further enhanced.

Based on currently held definitions in the literature (Bagchi, 2005; Chinn & Fairlie, 2007; James, 2004; others), the global digital divide is defined here to mean the gap between those who have the ability to access and use information and communication technology (ICT) and those who do not. This chapter limits its discussion to computer-based Internet technologies. Although other communication technologies—such as mobile telephony—have a significant influence on how people can get information and remain connected, this chapter focuses on the Internet aspect of ICT as being most relevant to e-governance.

The digital divide, and how it affects access to ICT, is a fundamental social equity issue. In fact, it might well be the greatest social equity challenge in today's flattened and globalized world where world events are shared online before they are spread through traditional communication channels. In the aftermath of the Iranian election of 2009, the state effectively shut down all traditional journalistic coverage of the bloody protests. In the past, such actions would have effectively blocked the flow of all information to the outside world. In 2009, however, details, images and videos of protests and police actions were still shared with the world through YouTube™, Twitter™ and (we) blogs. People in Iran with the ability to access and

use ICT – those on the "have" side of the digital divide – had the ability to receive life-saving information, while those outside Iran were able to monitor and disseminate current information. Those without access to ICT were left in the dark, literally when the television media were blacked out and metaphorically as they had no access to information.

In a less dramatic though no less important context, individuals who have access to and can use ICT have more avenues to easily educate themselves on the range of government resources and services available to them and to determine their eligibility for government programs. Unfortunately, the very people who generally suffer from lack of access to ICT (those with low personal wealth, low levels of education and literacy) are usually the same constituents who are eligible for many government assistance programs, especially means-tested ones. As such, unless governments actively mitigate the effects of the digital divide, e-governance initiatives will exclude the very constituents that programs are mandated to reach.

BACKGROUND

The methodology used is a case study. The cases in question are the e-government websites and initiatives from both state and central/federal governments in India, with case vignettes from the United States used for some comparisons. At first glance, the digital divide seems to manifest in radically different ways in each country. In the United States, 47% of households boast high speed internet access. In India, less than 2% of the population own personal computers. However, these statistics do not capture the fact that over the last decade, India's economic transformation has significantly changed the way in which the digital divide manifests in that country. The appearance of a 300 million strong tech-savvy middle class and the rapid spread of independently-owned internet kiosks which provide affordable internet access without computer ownership has shifted a massive portion of the population from one side of the divide to the other, while at the same deepening the divide almost insurmountably for those left behind.

This chapter argues that in both countries, significant citizen groups – women and African Americans in the U.S. and those with low personal wealth in India – are left on the wrong side of the digital divide. Consequently, both countries face very similar issues in developing e-governance solutions that reach across the digital divide and offer similar levels of government services to historically under-serviced population groups. The additional element of continual technology intelligence, development and service outsourcing from the United States to India (which serves to deepen the digital divide in both countries, especially how technology education is accessible to under-serviced groups) makes the selection of India an interesting, relevant and important case to serve as a comparison to the United States.

The comparative case study is performed as follows. First, contemporary academic literature is used to develop a working understanding of the various characteristics of the digital divide. Second, governmental and nongovernmental organizations have documented the development and implementation of e-governance in both countries. Such documents will form the basis for case vignettes of the practice of e-governance in India and the United States. Third, the study will assess Indian e-government initiatives within the context of the developed understanding of the global digital divide to assess to what extent these initiatives have addressed the social equity issues, using American initiatives for comparison in some instances. Finally, the study will make recommendations of aspects of e-governance that may be used to mitigate the social equity effects of the digital divide phenomenon.

The digital divide, and those who fall on either side of it, can be characterized using a model which defines those who fall into the "have not"

side of the divide as potential users of ICT, while those who fall into the "have" side are defined as users of ICT (Chary & Aikins, 2009). The model acknowledges that what we have at any given moment is a snapshot definition or characterization of the digital divide. The divide itself is in actuality a rapidly changing phenomenon (Bagchi, 2005) and characterizations of those users and potential users must reflect the phenomenon itself. Understanding characteristics of the potential users of ICT are of particular interest here, since these are the constituents who are excluded (by definition) from access to and use of ICT – and therefore, potentially access to and use of e-governance initiatives.

The characteristics of the global digital divide can be generally grouped into two basic categories, as shown in Figure 1. The first category describes the characteristics of the individuals who are affected by the digital divide – that is, those who fall on either side of that gap in the ability to access and use: users and potential users. The second category of characteristics describes those institutions (private or public) offering the required services to users. These service providers (and potential service providers) may be offering backbone services (such as network capacity) or last-mile services (such as end-user access) (Chandrasekhar, 2003). The combination of these two categories helps us better understand and define the global phenomenon known as the digital divide.

Individual Socioeconomic Characteristics

Those individuals who fall on either side of the digital divide are characterized by four different factors: personal wealth, demographics such as race and gender, levels of education and literacy, and access to ICT (Chary & Aikins, 2009).

Further, having access to and use of the Internet separate these individuals who fall on either side of the digital divide. Certainly, access and use are not mutually exclusive. In fact, having access to

Figure 1. Characteristics of the Global Digital Divide

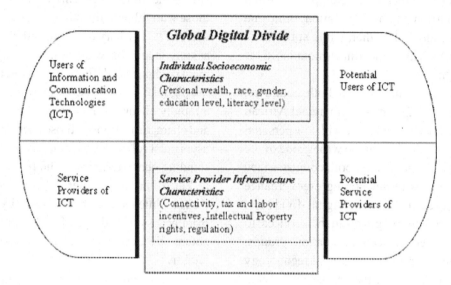

technology tends to facilitate the use of it (Hoffman & Novak, 1998). How we measure access and use, however, is complicated. Two common measures of access to and use of the Internet are penetration rates of computer ownership and Internet subscription (Chinn & Fairlie, 2006; Grondeau, 2007; Hawkins & Hawkins, 2003).

In 2001, the United States ranked among the highest in the world with 62.50 computers per 100 people and 50.15 Internet subscribers per 100 people while India ranked considerably lower at.58 computers per 100 people and.68 Internet subscribers per 100 people (Chinn & Fairlie, 2006; Indiastat, 2003). In India, the divide also manifests along urban and rural lines. Of those who subscribe to the Internet, more than three quarters live in major urban areas (Chandrasekhar, 2003). Only 54% of adults whose annual incomes are less than $30,000 have access to and use ICT, as opposed to over 80% of adults with annual incomes greater than $30,000 (Pew, 2006). Similarly, 40% of adults with lower education levels (less than high school) have access to and use ICT, as compared to 64% of adults with a high school degree and 91% with a college degree (Pew, 2006). In addition, higher education levels are also statistically associated

with higher levels of computer ownership (Chinn & Fairlie, 2007). Even in discussing access to ICT that does not depend on owning a computer, whites generally have greater access to and use of ICT than minorities (Hoffman & Novak, 1998).

Globally, one of the clearest characteristics separating users from potential users is the level of personal wealth (Bagchi, 2005). Personal wealth as a contributing factor to the digital divide is fairly intuitive, since it is reasonable that those with greater personal wealth can better afford for either ownership of or access to Internet technologies.

Simply stated, those with greater personal wealth tend to have more disposable income to pay for access to Internet technologies. They also tend to have greater leisure time (that is, time not committed to activities necessary for survival) to learn to use and then to actually use Internet technologies. In addition, personal wealth is also positively correlated with education and literacy, all of which compound the ease with which users can access ICT (Chinn & Fairlie, 2007). This characteristic is particularly important in the context of e-governance, since many government programs in the realms of social welfare, social insurance, health care and education target constituents with lower personal wealth. Therefore, it becomes particularly crucial to ensure that this demographic is provided with adequate access to information and services. At the very least, if providing additional information access is impractical, governments have a moral responsibility to ensure that information access for constituents with lower personal wealth is not more restricted than that of their wealthier counterparts. That is, governments ought to ensure that constituents with lower personal wealth are not in a worse-off position as a result of the digital divide.

Demographics such as race (or, equivalently caste, in India) and gender have particular significance in the context of the digital divide. In fact, women in general have less access to and use of ICT worldwide (James, 2004; Smith, 2005). Whites tend to fall on the "have" side of the digital divide, while minorities, especially African Americans fall on the "have not" side (Pew, 2006; Fairlie, 2003). Race and gender are also correlated with education and income levels, with white (higher caste) males generally attaining greater levels of education and income than their counterparts (Chinn & Fairlie, 2007).

Intuitively, it is clear that those who have access to technology tend to be able to use it better. Therefore, the final dimension characterizing the digital divide lies in the ability to access ICT, which is often measured by computer ownership and Internet subscription rates (Chinn & Fairlie, 2006; Grondeau, 2007; Hawkins & Hawkins, 2003). In the United States, such measures can appropriately reflect use of ICT – in fact, with over 62% computer ownership and 50% Internet subscription rates in the US, more recent scholarship is considering whether the true digital divide in the US lies between broadband and low-speed access (Chinn & Fairlie, 2006). However, in India, ownership of computers (and Internet subscriptions) is simply not accurate measures of access to ICT. Lack of electricity (Kenny, 2003), space constraints, lack of access to low-cost machines

and lack of privacy (Malhotra & Singh, 2007) in living situations may well account for the huge popularity of independently-owned and operated Internet cafes. Recent estimates suggest that there are four times as many Internet users as Internet subscriptions (Raven, Huang & Kim, 2007) and that 40% of those who used the Internet accessed it not from their own computers but rather from places Internet cafes (Chandrasekhar, 2003).

It is important to note that while income is an important contributor, it is not the only one. Increased schooling, which is associated with increased income, is also associated with increased computer ownership (Chinn & Fairlie, 2007). Further, educational and literacy differences between races in the U.S. also help explain differences in access to computers even when no ownership is implied, such as in work environments (Hoffman & Novak, 1998).

The digital divide also manifests along racial and gender lines. Some scholars suggest the digital divide has already begun to affect the social fabric in undesirable ways (Hoffman & Novak, 1998). Smith (2005) points out that women and African Americans in the United States are socialized to have higher levels of anxiety and lower levels of confidence with computer and software-related management skills while Fairlie (2003) reports only a portion of the differences in American computer ownership (between races) is explained by income. The effects of race (as defined by caste membership) on the digital divide in India are less documented and understood. However, it is well documented that men tend to be able to use and access the Internet more than women in India (James, 2004). In addition, the design of Internet services and software is not free from gender bias. Those who design systems make de facto decisions on priorities for system development. Designer communities dominated by men may well prioritize the needs of male users, and consequently design to those needs (Oudshoorn, Rommes & Stienstra, 2004).

In a developed country such as the United States, computer ownership and Internet subscription rates may be a fairly accurate measure of Internet usage. However, in developing countries such as India, using computing penetration and Internet subscribers to measure access to and use of the Internet is problematic. India is a country of disparate demographics. Over 40% of India's 1 billion strong population live in poverty, defined by the Indian government to be less than $.40 a day (Indiastat, 2003). In addition, literacy levels and education levels are significantly lower than in the United States (Indiastat, 2003). Internet usage, by definition, requires linguistic skills since the Internet is a written medium.

However, the recent technology boom has yielded a tech-savvy middle class numbering 300 million. In India, the appearance of this middle class and the rapid spread of independently-owned Internet kiosks—which provide affordable Internet access without computer ownership—has shifted a massive portion of the population from the have not side of the divide to the have side. Some scholars estimate that Internet users number as many as four times the number of Internet subscribers in India (Raven, Huang & Kim, 2007). A separate survey found that over 40% of those who used the Internet accessed it from public places, such as Internet cafes (Chandrasekhar, 2003).

Service Provider Infrastructure Characteristics

Organizations providing (or desiring to provide) the services necessary to build and offer Internet technology are divided by the infrastructure on which they operate. The infrastructure could be literal, in that limited connectivity and technology can prohibit the provision of such services (Seshagiri, 1999). Backbone network technology is the infrastructure that provides the bandwidth between exchange points. Backbone technology may include telephone lines (for dial-up access),

cellular towers (for mobile data access) broadband networks (such as cable, DSL or fiber optic lines) or satellite technologies. In addition to backbone technology, the infrastructure also includes last-mile or end-user services, which are access points (at home, cafes, businesses) through which end users may access the Internet. Without backbone technology, service providers are clearly highly limited in the End User services they can offer (Seshagiri, 1999). India's telephone line density, for example, is fairly low. In 2003, India had about 5 telephone lines per 100 people (Indiastat, 2003). By comparison, the United States stands at 57 telephone lines per 100 people.

The infrastructure that service providers require can also be social and legal. In India's poorer areas, basic needs such as water, electricity and sustainable agriculture often outweigh demands for digital services (Kenny, 2003). Therefore, the demand for Internet access services might be considerably lower than in urban areas where disposable personal wealth tends to be higher (Malhotra & Singh, 2007). In a quasi-free market economy, service providers are simply not incented to enter the market in rural areas. Historically, governments have used deregulation and tax incentives and exemptions to correct this market failure. Certainly, countries that offer lower levels of regulation and higher levels of tax and labor incentives provide a more attractive environment in which service providers can operate (Mistry, 2005).

This desire to avoid the burden of regulation, however, does not seem to apply to those types of regulation which protects service provider interests, such as regulation protecting intellectual property rights. Since service providers have a natural interest in protecting their intellectual property and development, particularly in competitive industries such as software development, countries with less protection seem to drive away service providers (Bagchi, 2005). The protection of intellectual property rights is also a major contributor to the digital divide. Bagchi's study, which uses interpersonal trust as a measure of this protection, concludes that the greater the interpersonal trust in society, the slower the digital divide would grow and the narrower the digital divide becomes over time. In addition, service provider avoidance of regulatory burden seems not to apply to service quality regulation (Chinn & Fairlie, 2007). This can be explained by arguing that higher service quality tends to attract and retain customers, which in turn offsets the distortion effect of the regulatory burden.

In addition, countries (like India) with low regulatory burdens and tax incentives for ICT firms attract more private industry suppliers of ICT (Mistry, 2005). Additional incentives are often required to ensure suppliers enter rural markets where education and income levels tend to be even lower than urban areas (Malhotra & Singh, 2007). Without such incentives, ICT access for those with lower education and income levels is further limited since suppliers are less likely to enter rural markets where they perceive a lack of market demand.

Thus, those who are left behind by the digital divide tend to be those with low personal income, minorities, women, those with low levels of education and literacy and those who simply do not have the ability to access ICT. Consequently, e-governance initiatives for programs whose constituents fall into the groups above may well be missing their target audience, especially if no measures are taken into account for bridging the divide.

THE DIGITAL DIVIDE AND E-GOVERNANCE: ISSUES AND SOLUTIONS

Fundamental Digital Divide Issues in E-Governance

E-government initiatives lose effectiveness when they do not account for certain digital divide-related issues. For users, these issues are lack of education, literacy, affordable access to ICT and a social context within which individuals may learn to effectively use ICT. In order to address those issues, e-government initiatives may also have to function within a policy environment where certain service provider issues are addressed – such as lack of a physical infrastructure, tax and regulatory burdens on ICT industries, protection of service provider interests in the law and regulatory burdens on associated industries. In order to effectively reach citizens on both sides of the digital divide, e-government initiatives must work within a policy context that mitigates these short and long term social equity issues.

Framing access to ICT thus as a fundamental social equity issue does not exclude or minimize the fact that a significant portion of the world's nations do not have access to basic amenities like food, clean water and personal security. Certainly, these issues must take precedence over access to ICT, as they directly impact survival. However, access to ICT can have long-reaching implications in educating and informing entire generations of those left on the far side of the digital divide. People's lives tend to be better, more self-actualized and fuller when they have access to ICT (Chandrasekhar, 2003). Understanding how to bridge the digital divide without compromising or minimizing the lower level physical needs presents a unique challenge for e-governance initiatives.

Further, any policy actions undertaken by e-governance initiatives as they relate to mitigating social equity issues become more complicated in the context of the digital divide. Traditionally, such actions would fall into the realm of technology policy. However, in the context of the digital divide, basic social policies that aim to better the education and prosperity levels of constituents can also work to mitigate the digital divide equity issues. Therefore, actions traditionally considered social or economic policies actually affect technology areas, suggesting that the boundaries between policy areas become blurred in the context of the digital divide.

E-Governance Solutions Mitigating Digital Divide

Some Indian e-governance initiatives have begun to work at mitigating the social equity issues within the digital divide, especially for programs which target rural constituents with lower levels of education, literacy and income and who have less access to ICT.

In the coastal state of West Bengal which borders the Bay of Bengal, the Indian government gives away the Simputer, a portable "simple computer" which converts text to speech in several Indian languages as well as in English to local low-income workers. The Simputer, for example, is used by fishermen in the Bay of Bengal to access weather conditions and government warnings (Meall, 2001). Thus, coastal workers who may not have high literacy levels can use Internet services, including Internet-based government outreach on public safety issues, without prohibitive literacy or linguistic challenges.

A second initiative attempting to mitigate the lack of education and literacy issues within the digital divide is one where throughout rural areas in Northern India, the government offers intermediary e-services for land use issues. These intermediary services take the form of offices or kiosks, which are fully staffed with government workers. These workers enter government transactions – such as inquiring about land boundaries, "e-post" transmission of documents, accessing databases of public records – into terminals on behalf of rural workers who might lack the education or linguistic abilities to use the terminals themselves. Since these services are provided free of charge, it is not surprising that some 4 million use these intermediary services (James, 2004).

Some e-governance initiatives also acknowledge that such initiatives have limited viability in an environment where the general physical infra-

structure for connectivity and access is lacking. In addition to lack of education and literacy, the 70% of Indians who live in rural areas generally have less access to ICT (Chinn & Fairlie, 2007; Indiastat, 2003; Lu, 2001). In an effort to bridge the gap between the availability of access in urban versus rural areas, the Indian government set up Community Information Centers (Mistry, 2005) as part of the "IT For All" initiative (Seshagiri, 1999). These centers provide subsidized Internet and telephony access in rural areas, including subsidies for suppliers with the aim of encouraging service providers to enter into rural markets.

In an effort to encourage use of ICT as part of the general social context, the Indian government, also as part of the "IT For All" initiative, has provided village schools with network and computing technologies, including providing ICT development and education in Indian languages at government schools (Mistry, 2005). In addition to the obvious advantages of promoting computer and ICT literacy, these initiatives have the added advantage of incorporating the use of ICT for daily and problem-solving usage into the social context.

In addition to intermediary services, e-governance initiatives have also relied on visual technologies to mitigate literacy concerns. The Indian e-initative "Bhoomi" in the state of Karnataka, a service which computerizes land records (the word Bhoomi translates to land or earth) provides images of land boundaries in addition to transaction information (Walsham & Sahay, 1999). In a culture which is characterized by a distrust of a potentially corrupt bureaucracy (James, 2004), using direct visual images can ameliorate any suspicion associated with using intermediary service. In the state of Gujarat, networked traffic checkpoints use visual images of plates for checks against records – and to communicate with constituents with lower levels of literacy. Associated e-governance initiatives include "Khajane" and "Therige," which are intended to provide financial services, also work to build trust and direct information flow to constituents who may not be able to access or use ICT without assistance (Mistry, 2005).

There is little doubt that long term policies to increase education levels must be put in place, in order for those on the "have not" side of the digital divide to cross to the other side (Hoffman & Novak, 1998). Education levels tend to be positively correlated with the ability of individuals to be informed, develop and actualize themselves and to generally increase both their earning potential and their quality of life. Thus, since the gap in personal wealth explains a significant portion of the digital divide (Bagchi, 2005; Chinn & Fairlie, 2007; Kiiski & Pohjola, 2002), long term investment in education which can lead to increased income potential can also lead to bridging the digital divide. In India, such investment translates to need for government spending on education infrastructure (Chandra, Fealey & Rau, 2006), which is not surprising since government investment in education in developing countries is particularly significant in predicting Internet diffusion (Kiiski & Pohjola, 2002).

E-governance initiatives cannot be successful in bridging the digital divide and reaching target constituents unless they operate in a policy environment that incents service providers to provide connectivity and access. As part of a substantial policy initiative, India's central government created the Department of Information Technology to develop the nation's technology infrastructure while also advocating a deregulated marketplace that would drive down costs to access the technology (Mistry, 2005). India's policy initiative and the special department it created helped to spark rapid growth among Internet service providers, with growth rate of 27 percent over the years (Raven, Huang & Kim, 2007). For the Indian government, market forces were key in providing low-cost Internet access to even remote areas. To accomplish this, the Indian government primed the marketplace by bringing in low-cost computers and smaller, cheaper telephone exchanges, driv-

ing down overall costs for Internet access (Raven, Huang & Kim, 2007; Walsham & Sahay, 1999).

In addition to market forces, the Indian government offered tax incentives to keep technology and Internet access as affordable as possible. These tax incentives included 60 percent depreciation allowances on hardware and 100 percent depreciation allowances on software as well as exemptions on export taxes for information-technology services (Seshagiri, 1999). These incentives complemented subsidized land costs, government fee reductions and the elimination of tariffs on information technology companies -- all of which helped to make information and technology more affordable nationwide (Mistry, 2005). The success of these policy initiatives can clearly be measured in the expansion of the information-technology export sector, which has grown annually by 35 to 44 percent (Chandrasekhar, 2003; Mistry 2005). The results of these policies on the Indian economy have had immediate and long-term effects. In the more immediate term, the expansion of information-technology has helped India increase its foreign-exchange reserve by more than tenfold since 1999. What's more, in the longer term, India stands to reap continued benefits, with one study indicating 83 percent of American companies will outsource their information-technology needs to India (Chandrasekhar, 2003).

Liberalization of India's technology market has been instrumental in this economic success. The government in India abolished all monopoly protections for Internet service providers and has offered license-fee exemptions and reduced fees where those fees still exist (Seshagiri, 1999). The next step for the government would be to liberalize the markets as they relate to information-technology backbone and end-user Internet service providers. If properly liberalized, the Indian government could spur further development and innovation in creating lower-cost backbone technology, further driving down the cost of Internet access in India. Policy actions such as these are allowing the market to not only expand access to the Internet but expand it at costs that are cheaper for the end user (Walsham & Sahay).

In India, a country divided by many languages and religious beliefs, information technology may help promote inclusiveness (James, 2003). Key to that will be providing Internet access to the rural areas, which can be accomplished by using state subsidies for service providers to build infrastructure in the more remote areas (Raven, Huang & Kim, 2007). There has been some success already. India has provided incentives to private companies and nonprofits to build everything from infrastructure to privately owned kiosks. In some cases, this infrastructure has needed to be unorthodox. As an example, a company called N-Logue has installed wireless systems to network kiosks in several villages (James, 2003). Ultimately, this type of government investment will spur economic activity in the market. By building the low-cost infrastructure, either through government contracts or with government incentives, entrepreneurs have the opportunity to establish new businesses, such as Internet kiosks in villages.

It will take years for widespread implementation of the Indian government's policies, and an even longer period of time to measure the success of those initiatives. As it is today, the majority of India's more than 1 billion people have not reaped the benefits of these initiatives. That's clear from India's e-readiness index, which measures ITC adoption in social and business environments and shows that technology access varies greatly by country (Raven, Huang & Kim, 2007). Despite technology centers in its largest metropolitan areas and success with outsourcing from the United States and Western Europe, India rates among the bottom 25 percent of countries, according to the e-readiness index.

FUTURE RESEARCH DIRECTIONS

Internet infrastructure development will always be an uphill battle, for developed countries as well as for developing nations such as India. That's due to the expanding nature of technology: Software development and the consumption of bandwidth are indelibly linked (James, 2001). Although the current capacity of India's Internet infrastructure is not in doubt (Chandrasekhar, 2003), the creation of software and devices that uses ever more bandwidth suggests backbone capacity will remain a constant challenge (Nair et al, 2005). What's more, this doesn't take into account increased demand on the infrastructure as a result of India's policies to bridge the digital divide. Simply put, the more people use the Internet, the more burden on the infrastructure; the greater the policy's success, the greater the need for a policy to address capacity. Future policy initiatives will need to find ways to not only provide Internet access, but also find ways to ensure the infrastructure's capacity can be built with expansion in mind.

What's more, globalization of information technology and the creation of so-called informational capitalism – the global economic engine related to information-technology providers -- have favored nations of the developed world (Parayil, 2005; Chary, 2007). As a result of the economic advantage of developed nations as it relates to informational capitalism, international organizations have predicted a worsening of the digital divide. In fact, the Internet is "the two edged sword that is leading the process of globalization: wounding those who don't quickly enough grasp how to use it by leaving them ever further behind," according to a United Nations Development Programme address (Brown, 2000, p.2). At the same time the Internet leaves those behind, it creates a path for better services and higher efficiency levels for those of developed nations who can take advantage of information-technology advancements (Brown, 2000 & 2003). Indeed, instead of alleviating social inequities, information technology has in some cases accentuated the detrimental effects of globalization for developing nations.

"Those on the wrong side of the digital divide are not only not better off — they are actually worse off" as a result of globalization (Chary, 2007, p. 184). Unless human rights and labor laws are considered, this trend will only continue, with the digital divide widening and deepening, particularly for those in developing nations.

Finally, expansion of Internet-based services affirms future economic benefits of both e-business (Genus & Nor, 2005) and e-governance (Hawkins & Hawkins, 2003) will continue to be healthy. Despite the short track record of Internet-based technology policy, it's clear that deregulation has been instrumental in reducing barriers to entry for Internet service providers (Wallsten, 2005). But as government policy lowers costs and fuels competition for Internet technology, the government must also use public policy to guide future growth (Riggins & Dewan, 2005) and ensure its socially responsible expansion in developing nations. The good news is that there is still time. In most developing nations, the information technology market is still in its infancy, as a result, policy actions still have time to guarantee that social equity in the developing world does not pay the price for economic growth.

CONCLUSION

The chapter has aimed to present an understanding of the global phenomenon of the digital divide as a critical factor impacting e-government initiative development and contribute to our understanding of how to evaluate and enhance e-government initiatives in the social equity context of the digital divide.

The global digital divide is defined here to mean the gap between those who have the ability to access and use information and communication technology (ICT) and those who do not. Constituents who do not have the ability to access and use ICT, meaning those who are not currently reached by e-governance initiatives are characterized by

lower levels of education, literacy and personal wealth. Several Indian e-governance initiatives have addressed these issues through policy actions that, while laudable, have not yet reached the vast majority of those constituents left on the far side of the digital divide. Initiatives aimed toward providing intermediary services, visual services and embedding use of ICT in the educational and social contexts have begun to address some of the social equity issues. E-governance initiatives can certainly have a multi-faceted role: to promote efficiency and effectiveness, while encouraging the use of ICT in the social context. However, long-term investment in education and literacy are fundamental to the continued mitigation of the social equity issues associated with the digital divide and e-governance. Clearly, improving education and literacy rates are not new policy issues that developing nations face. However, the social equity issues associated with e-governance add new immediacy to the need for such investment. In addition, e-governance initiatives cannot mitigate effects of the digital divide and reach targeted constituents unless they are operating in a policy environment that encourages the provision of technology and access.

E-governance implicitly assumes that the provision of information and services on a digital platform reduces transaction costs and increases benefits. Access to ICT can have a substantial impact on a person's quality of life, in terms of education, training and personal development (Chandrasekhar, 2003). Those who suffer from adverse effects of the digital divide (poor, illiterate, uneducated constituents) tend to fall into the same segment of the population as those who are targeted by many government social programs. As such, without solving the digital divide issue, e-governance initiatives only reach a portion of the population and most likely, not the portion of the population who most needs access to the information and services contained in those initiatives. Thus, the implications of the digital divide on social equity can be so grave that governments simply cannot afford to ignore what may be the most important social justice issue of the day. If the reach of e-governance initiatives is to be widespread and effective, governments must solve the social equity problem inherent in the digital divide.

REFERENCES

Bagchi, K. (2005). Factors contributing to global digital divide: Some empirical results. *Journal of Global Information Technology Management*, 8(3), 47–65.

Bradbrook, G., & Fisher, J. (2004). *Digital equality: Reviewing digital inclusion, activity and mapping the way forward*. Retrieved, July 8, 2007 from http://www.citizensonline.org.uk/site/media/documents/939_Digital Equaltity1.pdrf

Brown, M. M. (2000). *The challenge of information and communications technology for development*. Retrieved May 2005, from http://www.undp.org/dpa/statements/administ/2000/july/3july00.html

Brown, M. M. (2003). *Statement to World Summit on the Information Society, Geneva, 11 December*. Retrieved May, 2005 from http://www.undp.org/dpa/statements/administ/2003/ december/11dec03.html.

Chadwick, A., & May, C. (2001). *Interaction between states and citizens in the age of the Internet.: "E-Government" in the United States, Britain and the European Union*. Paper presented to the American Political Science Association annual meeting.

Chandra, A., Fealey, T., & Rau, P. (2006). National barriers to global competitiveness: the case of the IT industry in India. *Competitiveness Review*, 16(1), 12–19.

Chandrasekhar, C. P. (2003). The diffusion of information technology: The Indian experience. *Social Scientist*, 31(7/8), 42–85. doi:10.2307/3518307

Chary, M. (2007). Public Organizations in the Age of Globalization and Technology. *Public Organization Review*, 7(2), 181–189. doi:10.1007/s11115-007-0029-0

Chary, M., & Aikins, S. K. (2009). Policy as a Bridge across the Global Digital Divide. In Ferrero, E. (Eds.), *Overcoming digital divides: constructing an equitable and competitive information society*. Hershey, PA: IGI Global.

Chinn, M. D., & Fairlie, R. W. (2007). The determinants of the global digital divide: a cross-country analysis of computer and Internet penetration. *Oxford Economic Papers*, 59, 16–44. doi:10.1093/oep/gpl024

Compaine, B. M. (2001). Declare the war won. In Compaine, B. M. (Ed.), *The digital divide: Facing a crisis or creating a myth?* Cambridge, MA: MIT Press.

Cooper, M. (2006). *Expanding the digital divide and falling behind on broadband: Why a telecommunication policy of neglect is not benign*. Washington, DC: Consumer Federation of America and Consumers Union. Retrieved, May 29, 2006, from www.consumersunion.org/pub/ddnewbook.pdf

Derthick, M., & Quirk, P. (1985). *The politics of deregulation*. Washington: Brookings Institution.

Dye, T. R. (1978). *Understanding Public Policy*. Englewood Cliffs, NJ: Prentice-Hall.

Genus, A., & Mohd Ali Mohamad Nor. (2005). Socialising the digital divide: Implications for ICTs and e-business development. *Journal of Electronic Commerce in Organizations*, 3(2), 82–95.

Grondeau, A. (2007). Formation and emergence of ICT clusters in India: the case of Bangalore and Hyderabad. *GeoJournal*, 68, 31–40. doi:10.1007/s10708-007-9051-6

Hawkins, E. T., & Hawkins, K. (2003). Bridging Latin America's digital divide: Government policies and Internet access. *Journalism & Mass Communication Quarterly, 80*(3), 646–665.

Hoffman, D. L., & Novak, T. P. (1998). Bridging the racial Divide on the Internet. *Science. New Series, 280*(5362), 390–391.

IndiaStat. (2003). *Revealing India statistically.* Retrieved June 2008, from www.indiastat.com

James, J. (2001). The Global Information Infrastructure Revisited. *Third World Quarterly, 22*(5), 813–822. doi:10.1080/01436590120084610

James, J. (2002). Informational technology transaction costs and patterns of globalization in developing countries. *Review of Social Economy, 60*(4), 507–519. doi:10.1080/00346760022000028046

James, J. (2003). Sustainable Internet access for the rural poor? Elements of an emerging Indian model. *Futures, 35,* 461–472. doi:10.1016/S0016-3287(02)00092-7

James, J. (2004). Reconstruing the digital divide from the perspective of a large, poor, developing country. *Journal of Information Technology, 19,* 172–177. doi:10.1057/palgrave.jit.2000019

Kenny, C. (2003). Development's false divide. *Foreign Policy, 134,* 76–77. doi:10.2307/3183524

Kiiski, S., & Pohjola, M. (2002). Cross-country diffusion of the Internet. *Information Economics and Policy, 14,* 297–310. doi:10.1016/S0167-6245(01)00071-3

Kingdon, J. W. (2003). *Agendas, alternatives, and public policies.* New York: Longman.

Lu, M. T. (2001). Digital divide in developing countries. *Journal of Global Information Technology Management, 4*(3), 1–5.

Luyt, B. (2006). Defining the digital divide: the role of e-readiness indicators. *New Information Perspectives, 58*(4), 276–291.

Malhotra, P., & Singh, B. (2007). Determinants of Internet banking adoption by banks in India. *Internet Research, 17*(3), 323–339. doi:10.1108/10662240710758957

Meall, L. (2002). Business: The digital divide – eastern promise. *Accountancy, 129*(1303), 1–4.

Miller, R. R. (2001). Leapfrogging? India's information technology industry and the Internet. *International Finance Corporation,* Discussion Paper No.42. Washington: World Bank.

Mistry, J. J. (2005). A conceptual framework for the role of government in bridging the digital divide. *Journal of Global Information Technology Management, 8*(3), 28–47.

Nair, M., Kuppusamy, M., & Davison, R. (2005). A longitudinal study on the global digital divide problem: Strategies to closure. *The Business Review, Cambridge, 4*(1), 315–326.

Oudshoorn, N., Rommes, E., & Stienstra, M. (2004). Configuring the user as everybody: Gender and design cultures in information and communication technologies. *Science, Technology & Human Values, 29*(1), 30–63. doi:10.1177/0162243903259190

Parayil, G. (2005). The digital divide and increasing returns: Contradictions of informational capitalism. *The Information Society, 21*(1). doi:10.1080/01972240590895900

Raven, P. V., Huang, X., & Kim, B. B. (2007). E-Business in developing countries: A comparison of China and India. *International Journal of E-Business Research, 3*(1), 91–108.

Riggins, F. J., & Dewan, S. (2005). The digital divide: Current and future research directions. *Journal of the Association for Information Systems, 6*(12), 298–336.

Seshagiri, N. (1999). The informatics policy in India. *Information Systems Frontiers, 1*(1), 107–116. doi:10.1023/A:1010025130799

Smith, S. M. (2005). The digital divide: gender and racial differences in information technology education. *Information Technology, Learning and Performance Journal, 23*(1), 13–23.

US Census Bureau. (2005). Computer and Internet use in the United States: 2003. Washington, DC. Retrieved June 30, 2007 from www.census.gov/prod/2005pubs/p23-208.pdf

Vietor, R. H. K. (1994). *Contrived competition: Regulation and deregulation in America.* Cambridge, MA: Harvard University Press.

Wallsten, S. (2005). Regulation and Internet use in developing countries. *economic development and cultural change, 53*(2), 501-524.

Walsham, G., & Sahay, S. (1999). GIS for district-level administration in India: Problems and opportunities. *Management Information Systems Quarterly, 23*(1), 39–65. doi:10.2307/249409

Weimer, D., & Vining, A. (1989). *Policy analysis: Concepts and practice.* Upper Saddle River, NJ: Pearson Prentice Hall.

Wilhelm, A. G. (2004). *Toward an inclusive information society.* Cambidge, MA: MIT Press.

Yin, R. K. (1994). *Case study research: Design and methods.* Thousand Oaks, CA: Sage.

KEY TERMS AND DEFINITIONS

ICT: Information and communication technology, encompassing computing, Internet, traditional telephony and mobile telephony

Digital Divide: The gap between those who have ability to access and use ICT and those who do not.

E-Governance Initiative: government use of ICT to disseminate information or provide services

(ICT) User: Individuals who have access to and utilize ICT. Potential users are those who do not have access to and use ICT.

Service Provider: Organizations (public and private) providing backbone and end user services required for the users to access and use ICT.

Section 2
Evidence from Current Practice

Chapter 7
A Descriptive Analysis of Contents of Asian E-Government Websites

Abebe Rorissa
University at Albany, State University of New York, USA

Dawit Demissie
University at Albany, State University of New York, USA

Mohammed Gharawi
University at Albany, State University of New York, USA

ABSTRACT

Advances in information and communication technologies (ICTs) continue to drastically impact the activities of individuals, families, communities, businesses, governments, as well as other national and global entities. They often give rise to new institutions and systems such as electronic government (e-government). E-government improves the efficiency of governments' services and facilitates government-to-citizen and other types of communications. Nowhere is the impact of ICTs and e-government more pronounced than in developing countries, such as those in Asia, a continent that is home to the largest democracy in the world (i.e., India), where an appropriate use of ICTs can enable them to become part of the global information society. There had been encouraging signs in Asia with respect to e-government adoption and implementation of relevant services. Asian countries provide e-government services, mainly through websites that range from static to fully fledged web portals. However, there is a lack of e-government literature that provides detailed analyses of contents of Asian e-government services. This chapter is intended to address this. In addition to describing Asian e-government services, it also provides recommendations with respect to future works, and identifies prospects for e-government services.

DOI: 10.4018/978-1-61692-018-0.ch007

Table 1. A profile of Asia

	Asia	World
Population	3,780,819,792 (56.35%)	6,710,029,070
Land area	17.2 million sq mi (30%)	57.31 million sq mi
Internet Users	657,170,816 (41.17%)	1,596,270,108
Internet penetration (% Population)	17.4%	23.8%
Internet user growth (2000-2008)	474.9%	342.2%
E-Readiness Index	0.4467	0.4514
Web Measures index	0.3725	0.3540
Human Capital index	0.7916	0.7825
Infrastructure index	0.1670	0.2104
E-Participation index	0.2084	0.1909
Telecom infrastructure index	0.179332	0.570928

Sources: (United Nations, 2007; Internet World Stats, 2009)

INTRODUCTION

There has been an encouraging development in Asia in terms of e-government adoptions and implementations in the last few years. Asia is home to a third of the world's population and the largest democracy (India). Although it lags behind Europe and North America in rate of adoption and use of information and communication technologies (ICTs), there are more Internet users in Asia than anywhere else (Internet World Stats, 2009). However, the Internet penetration rate (as a percentage of the total population on the continent) remains one of the lowest at 17.4% (Table 1), while the number of Internet users grew by an impressive 475% over the last decade (Internet World Stats, 2009). The continent has made such remarkable strides that the question is not whether ICTs and allied technologies (like e-government) play a role in social and economic development. It is rather how effectively and efficiently they can be incorporated into every sector of society, including business/commerce, government, education, and entertainment. All of this points to the fact that Asian countries individually, and the continent as a whole, have one of the ingredients of not only successful e-government services but also of social and economic development.

Developing countries are using ICTs for governance in innovative ways. ICTs and e-government services present a number of opportunities for development of both rural and urban communities (InfoDev, 2002), albeit against some significant obstacles and challenges. Not all Asian countries are, however, taking full advantage of opportunities provided by e-Government. Such initiatives would encourage citizens to participate in government activities. They would act as participatory tools through which citizens can contribute actively toward a better government as well, thereby bolstering the core notion of democracy. Furthermore, "in economic terms, the ability of citizens to access government services anytime, anywhere helps to mitigate the transaction costs inherent in all types of government services" (Lee, Kirlidog, Lee, & Lim, 2008, p. 843). For this to happen, e-government services need to be effective, standard, impersonal, efficient, convenient, and transparent.

All Asian countries and their governments have had a significant presence on the Web. They have been providing e-government services through websites ranging from informational to full-fledged e-government web portals. Except for some analyses of Asian e-government services that were conducted as part of a global survey (e.g., United Nations, 2003, 2004, 2005, 2008; West, 2004, 2007a), existing e-government literature has, however, focused mainly on the United States and Europe (e.g., Lee, Tan, & Trimi, 2005; Olphert & Damodaran, 2007).

We are attempting to fill this gap through a comprehensive analysis of e-government web-sites. We identified 3,551 e-government service websites from 52 Asian countries (an average of 68 per country). A random sample of 1,050 web-sites (about 30%), which, after further scrutiny was reduced to 939 was further analyzed in order to determine:

- type of website (e.g., whether it is for/by a federal/national government, local government, federal/national government department, local government department, embassy, and others),
- type of service (e.g., tax filing, voter registration, application and renewal of passport, job listing/application, visa application, complaint submission, driver's license application/renewal, business license application/renewal, ordering reports/documents, grant application, application for benefits, document/trademark filing, downloading forms/documents, and others),
- available features (e.g., publications, databases, audio & video clips, foreign language access, not having ads, not having premium fees, not having user fees, disability access, having privacy policies, security policies, allowing digital signatures, an option to pay via credit cards, email contact information, areas to post comments, option for email updates, option for personalization, and PDA accessibility), and

- level of development of e-government services.

We used content analysis through a number of coding dictionaries to analyze contents of the e-government websites. This work has its limitations. It is a snapshot and not based on longitudinal data over a number of years, and only a few characteristics of the contents of the websites were considered for analysis. Our work remains significant, however, as one of a few comprehensive surveys of Asian e-government websites. It provides future researchers with rich baseline data, the lack of which is often cited as one of the hurdles in conducting cross-national comparisons (Wescott, 2004).

BACKGROUND

ICT and E-Government in Asia

In the past few decades, advances in information technologies have drastically restructured the activities of individuals, families, communities, and governments, as well as national and global institutions. These transformations strongly emphasize the importance of information, and its efficient management, as critical components of development (Dias & Brewer, 2009). Such changes are increasingly giving rise to new institutions and systems that focus on the creation, organization, use, management, and transfer of information over networked environments such as the Internet and the World Wide Web. ICTs have an enduring impact, for instance, on how governments across the globe communicate with their citizens and conduct public affairs. Since the beginning of the new millennium, the world has been increasingly wired. Consequently, information travels faster, and distance is not a major barrier. Governments are thereby confronted with citizens' demands for good governance, particularly in fighting corruption and bringing transparency in the management of public resources. Almost all governments around the world have introduced some form of e-government to their public institutions to cope with these pressures.

Electronic government has emerged as a programmatic tool for executing government operations with a key focus on offering services to citizens (United Nations, 2008). One of the benefits of e-government services is the opportunity it provides for the government to reorganize its services and make them more efficient than traditional/conventional services, both for citizens and governmental departments. The United Nations has been championing ICTs as an indispensible construct for building e-government initiatives. International institutions such as the United Nations recognize e-government as a gateway to socio-economic opportunities that eventually lead to the creation of knowledge-based societies in member states (United Nations, 2003). Various factors contribute to the successful implementations of e-government initiatives. Comparative studies show that the impact of implementing e-government is more visible in developing nations, including those in Asia, than in the developed world (Heeks, 2002).

Asian countries recognize the potential of e-government in improving government transparency and accountability while reducing corruption. The general perception toward e-government services varies widely in the continent. At one end, there is the optimistic view that e-government services are expanding and are the answer to all problems (e.g., Furuholt & Wahid, 2008; Kumar & Best, 2006). The view at the other end is that Asian countries have a long way to go to catch up with developed countries, or even to reach the level of businesses operating in the continent (e.g., Wescott, 2004).

Some (e.g., Wescott, 2004) point out that Asian governments are in the initial stages of ICT and e-government adoption. This could enable them to streamline not only the delivery of government services, allowing efficient interaction between citizens and governments, but also to enhance communication with their citizens. There is, however, pressure that comes with being a late adopter. When trying to adopt the necessary technologies and to implement their own e-government services, Asian governments are expected to mimic other countries in outsourcing vital services to public and private specialist organizations (Wescott, 2004). Information requests, license renewals, tax payments, and e-procurement are some of these vital services. Newly introduced e-government services are also likely to reflect existing structures and processes.

Previous Literature: Analyses of Contents of E-Government Websites

The definition of e-government varies from the generic: "use of ICTs and its application by the government for provision of information and public services to the people," (Curtin, 2007) to the specific: "the delivery of government information and services online through the Internet or other digital means" (West, 2004, p. 16). "A popular conception of e-government is that it is about the delivery of government services over the Internet in general and the Web in particular. At the other end of the spectrum, another school of thought defines e-government as any use of ICT in public administration and services. A pragmatic definition lies between these two extremes" (Bannister, 2007, p. 172). For this chapter, we adopted West's (2004) definition and the conception that e-government is the delivery of government services over the Web because of the nature of our data and analysis, e-government websites, and content analysis of their contents.

A number of authors, including corporate authors and international organizations, have for various reasons conducted content analysis of e-government service websites (e.g., UNDPEPA, 2002; United Nations, 2003, 2008; West 2007a, 2007b; Zhou, 2004). Some are descriptive in nature (e.g., Zhou, 2004) while others have a specific set of goals, among which is benchmarking and evaluation (United Nations, 2003, 2008; West 2007a). These content analysis studies also range from one-off snapshots (Zhou, 2004) to multiyear longitudinal surveys (West 2007a).

The studies differ with respect to their coverage as well, both in terms of sample size of e-government websites and countries. For instance, studies by the United Nations (2003, 2008) and West (2007a) include several hundreds of websites from various countries spanning the World while Zhou's (2004) work focuses on 177 Chinese e-government websites. These studies mainly focused on the type of services and features available on e-government websites. Some emphasized the importance of features available on e-government websites, especially those that allow the completion of a transaction online, as an indication of the level of their e-government service development. Although they used content analysis as the main method, some of them did not address inter-coder reliability.

A Framework for Analyses of Contents of Asian E-Government Websites

Although our work is exploratory and descriptive in nature, we employed a framework that is among the often cited in e-government literature and that has a reasonable level of consensus built around it. Others (e.g., Torres, Pina, & Acerete, 2005) have adopted an approach similar to ours and used a stages/levels-based model to study the evolution of e-government services and analyze their contents. They acknowledge, as we do, that while it is not a formal model, the framework "provides an exploratory conceptual tool that helps one understand the evolutionary nature of e-government" (Torres, Pina, & Acerete, 2005, p. 222).

In their efforts to differentiate between e-government websites that provide static information and those that are portals – and those that are in

between - researchers have attempted to formulate a common framework for the level/stage of development of e-government services available via e-government websites. For instance, Affisco & Soliman (2006) and Al-adawi, Yousafzai, & Pallister (2005) proposed a four level/stage framework: (1) publishing (web presence), (2) interacting, (3) transacting, and (4) transforming (integration). A website at the publishing level presents static information about the government agency/department; one at the interacting level allows the downloading of forms and has search facilities. At the transacting level, a user can complete an entire task online. A website at the fourth and last level integrates all services by all branches of government at all levels, and is usually a portal.

Another four-stage framework (1.cataloguing, 2.transaction, 3.vertical integration, and 4.horizontal integration) was also proposed by Layne & Lee (2001). A website at the cataloguing stage is only for online presence, catalog presentation (e.g., phone numbers and addresses), and downloading of forms. At the second stage, the website includes databases supporting online transactions (e.g., citizens may renew their licenses and pay fines online). A website is at the vertical integration stage if it links systems that run local e-government services to those running services by governments or their departments at higher-levels, such as state and federal/national (e.g., a drivers' license registration system at a state DMV may be linked to a national database of licensed truckers for cross checking). An e-government website at the fourth level combines different functions and services across a range of agencies (e.g., a business is able to pay its unemployment insurance to one state agency and its state business taxes to another state agency at the same time). The classifications by UNDPEPA (2002), Torres, Pina, & Acerete (2005), Moon (2002), and United Nations (2008) of the stages of development of e-government services have five (5) categories, albeit with different labels. Generally, the five

Table 2. A comparison of frameworks for levels/stages of development of e-government services

Torres, Pina, & Acerete, (2005); United Nations, (2008); UNDPEPA, (2002)	Layne & Lee (2001)	Affisco & Soliman, (2006); Al-adawi, Yousafzai, & Pallister, (2005)	Moon, (2002)
Emerging	Cataloguing	Publishing (web presence)	Information dissemination
Enhanced			
Interactive	Transaction	Interacting	Two-way communication
Transactional		Transacting	Transactions
Seamless/Connected	Vertical integration	Transforming (Integration)	Integration
	Horizontal integration		Political participation

categories are: (1) emerging (an official online presence is established by a government), (2) enhanced (government sites increase; information becomes more dynamic), (3) interactive (users can download forms, e-mail officials, and interact through the web), (4) transactional (users can actually pay for services and complete other transactions online), (5) seamless (full integration of e-services across administrative boundaries).

Table 2 presents a comparison of four classifications of dimensions and levels/stages of e-government service development. A closer look at these classifications reveals that they have some common elements. For instance, the technological and organizational complexities, as well as integration of services and functions, increase as the websites move from a lower level/stage to a higher one. A general four-stage framework also emerges. Hence, we used the four-stage framework proposed by Affisco & Soliman (2006) and Al-adawi, Yousafazi, & Pallister (2005) for our analysis in this chapter.

CONTENTS OF ASIAN E-GOVERNMENT WEBSITES

Identification of the Websites and Data Analysis

Even though an exhaustive list is difficult to compile, our search for relevant websites, conducted between February and May 2009, yielded a total of 3,551 e-government service websites from 52 Asian countries (an average of 68 per country). In order to have a relatively comprehensive sample of websites for each country, the authors searched the entire web, using search engines and web directories, and individual countries' portals. An initial list of e-government websites for each country in Asia was first compiled based on a list by Anzinger (2003). The authors searched for additional relevant websites until no new websites were found. For analyses purposes, a random sample of 1,050 websites (about 30%) was selected and a further examination reduced the sample to 939 (about 18 per country).

Content analyses through coding dictionaries, some of which were developed by the authors, and some used by others (e.g., West, 2007b), were initially conducted by the authors (with the help of native speakers of languages other than English and the Google translation facility, http://translate.google.com/translate_t?hl=en. According to Weber (1990), content analysis procedures usually involve four steps: (a) creating and testing a coding scheme by defining the recording units and categories, (b) assessing the accuracy of the coding, (c) revising the coding rules, and (d) coding the data set. We followed these steps with a single e-government website as our recording unit.

The content analysis was conducted to identify the type of site or body/institution responsible for its contents and services, type of services, features available on the website, number of executable services available through the website, the level of development of e-government services, as well as to compute e-government indexes for all the countries. To test inter-coder reliability for each of these variables, a graduate student coded a random sample of about 20% of the websites. Coding reliability was measured using percent agreement and Cohen's Kappa (1960), where all the values for both measures were above the often-recommended minimum of 0.70 (Neuendorf, 2002) for type of site, or body/institution responsible for its contents and services (0.88 & 0.83, respectively), type of services (0.81 & 0.75), features available on the website (0.74 & 0.71), number of executable services available through the website (0.80 & 0.71), and the level of development of e-government services (0.83 & 0.71).

Results

Body/Institution Responsible for Contents of the Website

The type of e-government website or institution responsible for its contents is one of the factors that determine its contents and types of service available to users. Of the 939 Asian e-government websites, more than half (55.17%) were federal/national government department websites, and a combined 62.84% were by federal/national governments and their departments. When websites for embassies are included, the percentage of Asian e-government websites by federal/national governments and their departments/embassies increases to 71.04%. On the other hand, the percentage of websites by local governments and their departments' websites is a mere 13.85%. These figures reflect the general composition of types of e-government websites in most developing countries and some developed countries, where countries adopt a top-down approach to e-government adoption, resulting in more e-government services at the national level than the local government.

Of course, this hinders the vertical integration of e-government services via the websites, a strong foundation for implementing higher-level e-government services, such as portals. If users are to benefit from efficient e-government services, both horizontal and vertical integration of e-government services need to be made.

The United Nations (UN) divides Asia into five sub-regions: Central, Eastern, Southern, South-Eastern, and Western Asia (http://unstats.un.org/unsd/methods/m49/m49regin.htm#asia). With respect to the number of websites by the various institutions, the trend across the sub-regions is very much similar to the continent as a whole (Figure 1). There are more websites by federal/national governments and their departments than websites by local governments and their departments (Central Asia: 2.67% vs. 0.43%; Eastern Asia: 15.02% vs. 4.69%; Southern Asia: 17.25% vs. 6.38%; South-Eastern Asia: 11.5% vs. 1.07%; and Western Asia: 16.41% vs. 1.28%). A chi-square test of independence of the number of e-government websites maintained by the different types of bodies/institutions showed that the sub-regions are not similar (χ^2 =93.5, df=12, p=0.00). There were a few cells in our contingency tables that had expected frequencies less than one, violating some of the assumptions of the chi-square test (Weinberg & Goldberg, 1990). In such cases, further chi-square tests were conducted, either by combining or deleting categories. This procedure was used for our subsequent chi-square tests, as well.

Type of E-Government Service

Governments at all levels adopt e-government and provide e-government services through websites to carry out their public responsibilities while providing efficient automated services to users. Although a higher quality e-government service should be the ultimate goal, one of the first objectives of an e-government website should be to offer the right mix of services to targeted groups of users. Out of

Figure 1. Types of the body/institution responsible for contents of Asian e-government websites by subregion

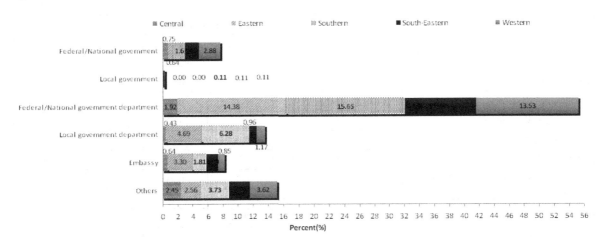

13 different types of services that are commonly provided via e-government websites, more Asian e-government service websites (53.91%) allow the downloading of forms and other documents than 12 other services (Table 3). This is because it is among the first services available through most e-government websites, even those at the initial stages of e-government service development. Asian e-government websites lack some crucial services, such as application for and renewal of drivers and business licenses or online visa application services. The number of websites that provide the different types of e-government services also differ across the five sub-regions, as confirmed by results of a chi-square test of independence (χ^2 =124.81, df=32, p=0.00).

Type of Features Present on the Websites

The number of features present on an e-government website is important to any potential user. It is also part of a framework for computing e-government indexes and producing rankings of countries with respect to e-government. According to West's (2007a) framework for computing e-government index, the higher the number of features, the higher the e-government index for a website. Eventually, the more such websites exist, the higher the e-government index and ranking for the country.

The top five features on Asian e-government websites are: "not having premium fees" (available on 17.8% of the websites), "not having user fees" (17.51%), "not having ads" (17.41%), "email contact information" (14.93%), and "foreign language access" (9.3%). They account for over three-fourths (76.95%) of the features on all the Asian e-government websites in our sample (Table 4). Among the features available on the fewest number of Asian e-government websites are audio clips (0.69%) and video clips (0.83%), crucial features that have the potential to increase the usability both of the services and the websites, given the relatively low literacy rates among the population.

The availability of the various features on Asian e-government websites was not uniform. The number of features available on e-government websites for countries in the five Asian sub-regions differed significantly (χ^2=203.54, df=52, p=0.00).

Table 3. Number of Asian e-government websites that deliver the different types of e-government services (n=52)

Type of service	Number of websites					
	Min	Max	Mean	SD	Total	%
Tax filing	0	7	0.56	1.26	29	2.25
Voter registration	0	4	0.27	0.66	14	1.08
Application and renewal of passport	0	5	0.25	0.76	13	1.01
Job listing and/or application	0	34	2.04	4.82	106	8.21
Visa application	0	7	0.46	1.24	24	1.86
Complaint submission	0	7	0.77	1.39	40	3.10
Application/Renewal of driver's license	0	5	0.37	0.95	19	1.47
Application/Renewal of business licenses	0	6	0.60	1.21	31	2.40
Order reports and other documents	0	8	0.65	1.25	34	2.63
Grant application	0	3	0.08	0.44	4	0.31
Application for benefits	0	5	0.27	0.82	14	1.08
Document and trademark filing	0	12	0.79	2.02	41	3.18
Download forms and other documents	0	172	13.38	24.88	696	53.91
Others (e.g., webmail)	0	25	4.35	5.01	226	17.51
				Total	1291*	100

*Total exceeds 939 because some websites provide more than one service (e.g., a website that provides both tax filing and voter registration services was counted twice). Min, Max = minimum and maximum number of websites per country that provide each service.

Online Executable Services Available on the Websites

The number of online executable services on an e-government website, together with the number of features present on the website, is used for computing e-government indexes and produce rankings of countries with respect to e-government (see West, 2007a). Once again, according to West's (2007a) framework, the higher the number of features, the higher the e-government index for a website and, eventually, the more such websites exist, the higher the e-government index and ranking for the country. Online executable services transform an e-government website from the first or second level of development to at least the third (transacting) stage, where users/citizens can complete an entire task online without having to travel to the relevant offices.

Asian e-government websites in our sample had a total of 1,686 online executable services, for an average of 1.8 online executable services per website, and 32.42 online executable services per country. The number of online executable services on Asian e-government websites ranged from 0 to 27. About 5.64% of the websites provide no online executable service. E-government websites for countries in Eastern (29%) and Southern Asia (28.71%) had the highest number of online executable services, with those in Western Asia (21.65%) a close third (Figure 2). Similar to results for the number of services and features on their e-government websites, websites for Central Asian countries had the fewest online executable services (4.63%).

Level/Stage of Development of E-Government Services

Centralization is effective when it comes to e-government services. A portal, which is a one-stop gateway to most e-government services and

Table 4. Type of features present on Asian e-government websites (n=52)

Type of feature	Number of websites					
	Min	Max	Mean	SD	Total	%
Publications	0	107	8.88	15.32	462	8.90
Databases	0	80	6.65	11.55	346	6.67
Audio clips	0	4	0.69	0.83	36	0.69
Video clips	0	7	0.83	1.35	43	0.83
Foreign language access	0	41	9.29	11.16	483	9.30
Not having ads	1	177	17.38	25.66	904	17.41
Not having premium fees	1	183	17.77	26.47	924	17.80
Not having user fees	1	184	17.48	26.65	909	17.51
Disability access	0	16	0.44	2.24	23	0.44
Having privacy policies	0	14	1.10	2.67	57	1.10
Security policies	0	14	1.10	2.65	57	1.10
Allowing digital signatures on transactions	0	2	0.10	0.36	5	0.10
An option to pay via credit cards	0	4	0.56	0.80	29	0.56
Email contact information	0	184	14.90	26.63	775	14.93
Areas to post comments	0	20	1.88	3.99	98	1.89
Option for email updates	0	1	0.40	0.50	21	0.40
Option for website personalization	0	2	0.08	0.34	4	0.08
PDA accessibility	0	10	0.31	1.42	16	0.31
				Total	5191*	100

* Total exceeds 939 because some websites have more than one feature

combines both horizontal and vertical integration, is much more beneficial to users than one at the lower levels of development. Government should, therefore, strive to provide e-government services through portals to realize the real potential of e-government and improve their e-government ranking. Although the trend is encouraging in this respect, there is a long way to go before Asian governments set up portals as the main source of e-government services. The majority of Asian e-government websites (94.36%) are either at the first (49.63%) or second (44.73%) stages of e-government service development (Table 5). This is in line with our finding above, where a few of all Asian e-government websites provide services that require an e-government website at higher levels of development to deliver them. Examples include application and renewal of

driver's license (1.47%), application and renewal of business licenses (2.40%), tax filing (2.25%), voter registration (1.08%), application and renewal of passport (1.01%), and visa application (1.86%).

The proportions of e-government websites by countries in the five Asian sub-regions differed significantly ($\chi^2 = 38.33$, df=8, p=0.000). In all five sub-regions, there were still significantly more e-government service websites at the first and second levels/stages than the third and fourth (Figure 3).

RECOMMENDATIONS

Asian countries should look no further for e-government initiatives than those cited as examples of best practices. The following examples

Figure 2. Percentage of online executable services on Asian e-government websites by sub-region

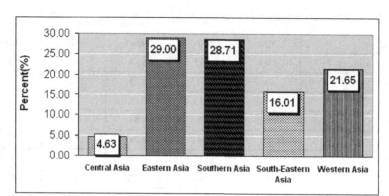

Table 5. Number of Asian e-government websites at the four levels of development (n=52)

Level	Number of websites					
	Min	Max	Mean	SD	Total	%
1. Publishing	0	84	8.96	13.02	466	49.63
2. Interacting	0	96	8.08	14.62	420	44.73
3. Transacting	0	12	0.85	1.96	44	4.69
4. Transforming	0	1	0.17	0.38	9	0.96
				Total	939	100.00

Figure 3. Percentage of Asian e-government websites at the four levels of e-government service development by sub-region

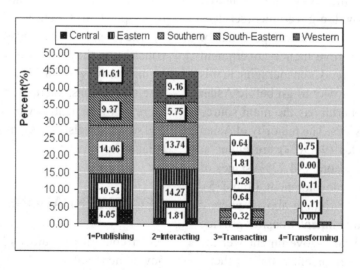

illustrate major success stories of e-government implementations in Asia (Wescott, 2003).

- In India's state of Andhra Pradesh, a computerization project involving more than 214 property deeds registration offices within the last decade reduced service time and eliminated corruption.
- In Vietnam, an electronic health insurance cards program with a goal of facilitating the expansion of health coverage to rural and poor communities improved administrative efficiency and reduced fraud.
- In the Philippines, the government put in place an online e-procurement system that allows suppliers to do public bidding which resulted in increased transparency and is highly regarded by the suppliers. Similar e-procurement systems have also been put in place in Indonesia and the Republic of Korea.
- In Indonesia, the Republic of Korea, and Pakistan, online fraud detection and investigation systems have been set up to allow citizens to monitor applications for services.

Two of the major component parts of current frameworks and procedures for the computation of e-government indices and rankings of countries are the number of features and online executable services present on e-government service websites. As the results above show, they do not prominently feature on most Asian e-government websites. This, in turn, has a negative impact on their ranking relative to countries in other parts of the world. If Asian countries are to boost their standings with respect to e-government, provided the rankings are based on web measures, they should strive to provide the right mix, number, and quality of features and online executable services through their e-government websites.

FUTURE RESEARCH DIRECTIONS

Through the findings, we have shown that the five Asian sub-regions differ significantly with respect to the types of institution responsible for contents of e-government websites, type and level of development of e-government services, number of online executable services, and number of features available via the websites. This should be expected because of the variability of underlying conditions for e-government adoption and implementation in the sub-regions. These include, but not limited to, level of economic development, e-readiness, and level of ICT adoption. Therefore, future researchers should bear this in mind and not consider the entire continent as a homogenous entity.

Creating rich e-government profiles for individual nations is important (Curtin, 2006). We believe that cross-national comparisons of the profiles among countries in a region or on a continent are essential because they make the profiles even richer. Such comparisons also allow countries to gauge their progress relative to the progress of those in the same region or continent. Researchers, therefore, should strive to get a deeper insight into why and how countries in the same/similar region(s) are implementing e-government services. This will shed more light and help us understand the nature and extent of adoption and use of e-government services at local, national, regional, and global levels.

CONCLUSION

Our goal for this work was to conduct a comprehensive analysis of contents of Asian e-government websites and present an e-government profile of the continent. We compiled a total of 3,551 e-government websites from 52 Asian countries. A random sample of 1,050 websites (about 30%) was examined for a final set of 939 sites. We employed content analyses through coding procedures similar to previous researchers (e.g., West, 2007b) and ensured coding reliability.

The general picture that emerges from our analyses is that most Asian countries have made significant efforts to adopt and implement e-government services via the World Wide Web. This is true in spite of the apparent obstacles they face, such as the lack of adequate infrastructure, cultural barriers, and type/mode of government. This could be due to the nature of e-government, which is an equal opportunity technology that any type of government can take advantage of. According to West (2007b), "nondemocratic systems are as likely as democracies to perform well on new technology initiatives. Some authoritarian countries have been successful with digital government because they have top-down political structures and are able to overcome bureaucratic and political intransigence" (p. 21). In Asia, too, a number of countries (some with undemocratic governments), have made progress with respect to e-government adoption and implementation.

Most Asian e-government websites, however, remain at the early stages of development and some Asian countries have a long way to go before they realize the full potential of e-government. For instance, while there are encouraging signs among national or federal governments, web presence at the local level are minimal. It must be noted, however, that this is also the case in most other parts of the world. The type of e-government website as well as the number, variety, and level of development of e-government services are not uniform across the five sub-regions as well. This difference can be attributed to the fact that not all Asian countries follow the same path e-government (Lee, Tan, & Trimi, 2005).

REFERENCES

Affisco, J., & Soliman, K. (2006). E-government: A strategic operations management framework for service delivery. *Business Process Management Journal, 12*(1), 13–21. doi:10.1108/14637150610643724

Al-adawi, Z., Yousafzai, S., & Pallister, J. (2005). *Conceptual model of citizen adoption of e-government*. The Second International Conference on Innovations in Information Technology. Retrieved June 24, 2009, from http://www.it-innovations.ae/iit005/proceedings/articles/G_6_IIT05-Al-Adawi.pdf

Anzinger, G. (2003). *African governments on the WWW*. Retrieved March 25, 2008, from http://www.gksoft.com/govt/en/africa.html

Bannister, F. (2007). The curse of the benchmark: An assessment of the validity and value of e-government comparisons. *International Review of Administrative Sciences, 73*(2), 171–188. doi:10.1177/0020852307077959

Cohen, J. (1960). A coefficient of agreement for nominal scales. *Educational and Psychological Measurement, 20*, 37–46. doi:10.1177/001316446002000104

Curtin, G. (2006). *Issues and challenges global e-government/e-participation models, measurement and methodology: A framework for moving forward*. Prepared for the United Nations Department of Administration and Development Management Workshop on e-participation and e-government: Understanding the present and creating the future. Budapest, Hungary. Retrieved June 25, from http://www.usc.edu/schools/sppd/private/bedrosian/Global_EGovernmentJul06.pdf

Curtin, G. (2007). *Encyclopedia of political communications*. Thousand Oaks, CA: Sage Publications.

Dias, B., & Brewer, E. (2009). How computer science serves the developing world. *Communications of the ACM, 52*(6), 74–75. doi:10.1145/1516046.1516064

Furuholt, B., & Wahid, F. (2008). E-Government challenges and the role of political leadership in Indonesia: The case of Sragen. In *Proceedings of the 41st Annual Hawaii International Conference on System Sciences* (HICSS 2008). Hawaii, US. January 7-10, 2008.

Heeks, R. (2002). E-Government in Africa: Promise and practice. *Information Polity: The International Journal of Government & Democracy in the Information Age, 7*(2/3), 97–114.

InfoDev. (2002). The e-government handbook for developing countries. Washington, DC: The World Bank. Retrieved May 1, 2009, from http://unpan1.un.org/intradoc/groups/public/documents/apcity/unpan007462.pdf

Internet World Stats. (2009). World Internet users and population stats. Retrieved June 10, 2009, from http://www.internetworldstats.com/stats.htm

Kumar, R., & Best, M. L. (2006). Impact and sustainability of e-government services in developing countries: Lessons learned from Tamil Nadu, India. *The Information Society, 22*(1), 1–12. doi:10.1080/01972240500388149

Layne, K., & Lee, J. (2001). Developing fully functional e-government: A four stage model. *Government Information Quarterly, 18*(2), 122–136. doi:10.1016/S0740-624X(01)00066-1

Lee, K. C., Kirlidog, M., Lee, S., & Lim, G. G. (2008). User evaluations of tax filing web sites: A comparative study of South Korea and Turkey. *Online Information Review, 32*(6), 842–859. doi:10.1108/14684520810923962

Lee, S. M., Tan, X., & Trimi, S. (2005). Current practices of leading e-government countries. *Communications of the ACM, 48*(10), 99–104. doi:10.1145/1089107.1089112

Moon, M. J. (2002). The evolution of e-government among municipalities: Rhetoric or reality? *Public Administration Review, 62*(4), 424–433. doi:10.1111/0033-3352.00196

Neuendorf, K. A. (2002). *The content analysis guidebook*. Thousand Oaks, CA: Sage Publications.

Olphert, W., & Damodaran, L. (2007). An evaluation of the information content of local authority websites in the UK using citizen-based scenarios. *Library and Information Research, 31*(98), 45–60.

Torres, L., Pina, V., & Acerete, B. (2005). E-government developments on delivering public services among EU cities. *Government Information Quarterly, 22*(2), 217–238. doi:10.1016/j.giq.2005.02.004

United Nations. (2003). *UN global e-government survey*. Retrieved February 20, 2008, from http://unpan1.un.org/intradoc/groups/public/documents/un/unpan016066.pdf

United Nations. (2004). *United Nations global e-government readiness report*. Retrieved February 20, 2008, from http://unpan1.un.org/intradoc/groups/public/documents/UN/UNPAN019207.pdf

United Nations. (2005). United Nations global e-government readiness report. Retrieved February 20, 2008, from http://unpan1.un.org/intradoc/groups/public/documents/un/unpan021888.pdf

United Nations. (2007). United Nations e-government readiness knowledge base. Retrieved June 10, 2009, from http://www2.unpan.org/egovkb/

United Nations. (2008). United Nations e-government survey 2008: From e-government to connected governance. Retrieved September 2, 2008, from http://unpan1.un.org/intradoc/groups/public/documents/UN/UNPAN028607.pdf

United Nations Division for Public Economics and Public Administration (UNDPEPA). (2002). *Benchmarking e-government: A global perspective*. Retrieved June 19, 2008, from http://aps.vlaanderen.be/straplan/vindplaatsen/benchmarking-e-government.pdf

Weber, R. P. (1990). *Basic content analysis* (2nd ed.). Newbury Park, CA: Sage Publications.

Weinberg, S. L., & Goldberg, K. P. (1990). *Statistics for the behavioral sciences*. New York: Cambridge University Press.

Wescott, C. G. (2003). E-Government to combat corruption in the Asia Pacific region. In Proceedings of the 11th International Anti-Corruption Conference, Seoul, Republic of Korea. Retrieved September 25, 2009, from http://www.adb.org/Governance/egovernment_corruption.pdf

Wescott, C. G. (2004). E-government in the Asia-Pacific region: Progress and challenges. *Systemics, Cybernetics and Informatics, 3*(6), 37-42. Retrieved June 25, 2009, from http://www.iiisci.org/journal/CV$/sci/pdfs/P749171.pdf

West, D. (2007b). *Digital Government: Technology and Public Sector Performance*. Princeton, NJ: Princeton University Press.

West, D. M. (2004). E-Government and the transformation of service delivery and citizen attitudes. *Public Administration Review, 64*(1), 15–27. doi:10.1111/j.1540-6210.2004.00343.x

West, D. M. (2007a). Global e-government. Retrieved February 20, 2008, from http://www.insidepolitics.org/egovt07int.pdf

Zhou, X. (2004). E-government in China: A content analysis of national and provincial web sites. *Journal of Computer-Mediated Communication, 9*(4). Retrieved September 25, 2009, from http://jcmc.indiana.edu/vol9/issue4/zhou.html.

KEY TERMS AND DEFINITIONS

Information and Communication Technologies (ICTs): A broad term that includes communication and digital technologies, media devices (cable, satellite, radio, etc.), telecom infrastructures, protocols that govern such communications, hardware (computers, information networks, etc.) and software applications.

Electronic Government (E-Government): The delivery of government information and services to citizens, businesses, and other users using information and communication technologies.

E-Government Service: A government service, including transactions and interactions, provided to the end user (e.g., citizens, businesses, etc.) with the help of information and communication technologies such as the Internet, the Web, mobile devices, and others.

Content of E-Government Website: What is available on and/or via websites created and maintained by governments at all levels (local, state, federal) to provide e-government services.

E-Government Adoption: This is a process that involves a range of steps beginning with the realization of the need for e-government to implementation and provision of e-government services and use of these services.

E-Government Index: This term refers to a numerical composite index usually employed for e-government benchmarking and rankings of countries. It is often, but not always, computed by assigning numerical values to e-government services.

Online Executable Service: An e-government service that allows users completion of a transaction partially and/or wholly online without requiring visits to government offices. Examples include online tax filing.

Chapter 8
Breaking the Bureaucratic Inertia:
E-Government, Civil Society and Mobilization of Citizens in Bangladesh

Akhlaque Haque
University of Alabama at Birmingham, USA

ABSTRACT

E-Government's effectiveness depends not on the technological supremacy of government but on how encompassing it is to reach the maximum number of citizens at the grass roots level. This requires a greater appreciation and understanding of inter-organizational and institutional factors beyond technology and human skills that shape the relationship between the government and its citizenry. Using the context of Bangladesh, the chapter highlights the promises of E-Government reform in Bangladesh with the caveat that whether at the agency level or individual level, E-Government focus should be from the ground up. Bureaucratic inertia is more prominent at the lower level of agency hierarchy than at the top. Given the successes of social entrepreneurship via civil society organizations (CSOs) in Bangladesh, the study suggests governmental partnerships with CSOs in providing E-Government services. As one of the primary communication devices of the 21st century, mobile phones offer a clear advantage to computers in bringing government to citizen's finger tips.

INTRODUCTION

In recent years, among all types of governmental reform measures, E-Government has been in the top of the list since the publication of the National Performance Review (Office of the Vice President, 1993) published during the Clinton Administration. The attraction has been due to

DOI: 10.4018/978-1-61692-018-0.ch008

a culmination of factors including the rise of the Internet and popular belief that government is in the business of satisfying customer demands in the most cost efficient and timely manner. Just as with the Internet revolution, E-Government promised to become the modern-day tool for public managers in bringing government to the doorsteps of citizens. The initial buzz that began almost sixteen years ago is now seen in the ubiquitous presence of government websites at all levels in the United States and across the globe. The United Nations and World Bank have made E-Government development a priority for developing countries with the hope that it will make governments more transparent and public managers more responsive to citizen demands. More importantly, it is seen as an empowering tool that will transform government and liberate the marginalized groups who normally are unable to participate in direct democracy.

Despite the promises, there is little evidence to suggest E-Government has lived up to them, or has followed a path of progression that could lead to transformation of governmental service delivery (David Coursey and Donald Norris, 2008; Wescott, 2001). Rather, as envisioned about technology in general (Danziger and Anderson, 2002; Kraemer, Dutton and Northrup, 1981), E-Government has taken the incremental approach—technological adoption has been slow, having only limited impact on the quantity and quality of services in routine governmental operations. Instead of transforming the way government interacts with citizens on a daily basis, E-Government adds to traditional government service delivery creating another layer catered to a smaller group of citizens. The beneficiaries have been limited to those who are privileged in society, particularly individuals and public agencies that can afford and have access to technology. Large segments of society are unable to penetrate this new layer of service delivery method or benefit from it due to various reasons including lack of operational knowledge (of its benefits) and lack of resources required to access them. The issue becomes far more complex in developing countries where bureaucratic practices and rules and customs add to the existing socioeconomic barriers (Yang & Rho, 2007). More often than not the barriers are overshadowed by the optimism espoused by E-Government enthusiasts.

Given the limitations of technology and the unequal distribution of information, understanding of E-Government applications for all populations is in order. E-Government's success can be measured by the tool's effectiveness in motivating marginalized groups to participate in governance leading to improvement in their quality of life. This requires a greater appreciation and understanding of the socio-cultural situation beyond technology, and the sheer reality that technology cannot feed the hungry or clothe the needy.

This chapter takes a step towards exploring factors that might shape the next generation of E-Government in developing democracies. First, the study assesses the E-Readiness or E-Government status of Bangladesh by looking at findings from two different surveys done in 2004 and 2008 by the Government of Bangladesh (GoB). The findings suggest notable improvement in E-Readiness in public agencies, with the central government agencies leading the way and taking advantage of the resources allocated for E-Government reform. However, the development is more prominent in the central government agencies located in the capital city compared to their local counterpart outside the capital and in the rural areas. Moreover, the E-Readiness was biased towards higher ranking officers compared to the clerical staff. This discrepancy was also clearly evident in another focus group interview conducted in 2008 among 19 senior to mid-level managers in the central government. Respondents of the focus group revealed that lower ranking officers' are less optimistic about E-Government's potential and are less likely to become pro-active in implementing E-Government reforms. We believe the apathy towards E-Government by clerical staff is not only due to unequal resource allocation but a lack of motivation towards reforms that tends to favor the ruling class and the higher administrative authority. Solutions call for a shift in the mindset about E-Government, as an elite tool for elite business-like operations, to a common tool for routine every day functions affecting the daily lives of the common people. The potential to make this an everyday tool for government service delivery may require a revolutionary agenda. Capitalizing on the large network of civil society organizations in Bangladesh, the chapter suggests an alternative E-Government model of social empowerment using innovative E-Government applications. The proven success of social entrepreneurship using civil society organizations in Bangladesh carries important implications for innovative usage of technology, such as mobile phones and internet kiosks, to bring the governments closer to the general population.

The chapter has been divided into three parts. It begins by bringing to the forefront the barriers to electronic community within the governmental bureaucracy. First, surveys from Bangladesh highlight the status of E-Government at the early stages of its development and the implications of uneven resource allocation. Second, we discuss how civil society organizations (CSOs) can become mediators to prepare the ground work for sustainable E-Government partnerships to reach out to the mass. Finally the chapter provides some examples of social entrepreneurship and future trends in E-Government knowledge networks tapping into the next generation of mobile-based devices used by people at all levels of society.

STUDY BACKGROUND

E-Government and Society in Developing Countries

The basic premise under which E-Government operates is that, through the application of information and communication technologies (computers, mobile phones, hand-held devices) governmental and non-governmental services will be delivered to citizens. Advances in information and communication technologies (ICT) have given governments the ability to provide information about public services (and the value of those services) at a much faster and cost efficient way. By opening a direct electronic communication channel between government and its citizens, E-Government promises to fulfill three main objectives in a democracy: (1) faster response to citizen demands and more efficient implementation of governmental planning than the traditional paper-based method (2) be open and transparent about its goals and the methods (or processes) by which it expects to meet the goals, and (3) dissemination and sharing of information among government units and among all people so all population will have equal access to government and its services so that any citizen can have the capacity to improve their own lives. In short, in addition to one-stop shopping for services through an electronic medium, the E-Government concept promises a trustworthy government that is dedicated to empowering its own citizens to increase the individual and common good. With this overall goal, E-Government is not merely a strategy for efficiency in government but a capacity building tool ingrained with democratic values, particularly citizen empowerment. Indeed the latter goal of E-Government has greater (perhaps break-through) implications for developing countries than was envisioned by earlier skeptics.

Although western industrialized nations and some developed Asian nations have seen unprecedented growth in E-Government in recent years, developing countries are lagging in its strides to make the best use of this tool. The greatest obstacle for E-Government is similar to the reasons cited for economic development, namely low economic resources and human development (World Bank, 2002) but also the socioeconomic, cultural and historical factors that shape the relationship between the citizens and the government (Singh, 1992). Most developing nations that lag in E-Government (less matured or providing fewer or no services online) are new democracies that received independence from colonization or a communist regime in the last 50 to 60 years.

Historically the way the administrative apparatus' evolved in the colonies has important implications for public administration in today's newly developing democracies. The colonies sought the establishment of apolitical administrative machinery for the purpose of "managing" people domestically (primarily for resource allocation, taxation and infrastructure development). After the countries became independent from the colonies in the 40s and early 50s, the newly independent states found themselves being ruled by powerful elite administrative mechanisms guided under weak democratic institutions. In well established democratic systems, public administration is expected to serve only the interest of the people (hence *public servant*). In contrast administration in colonized countries grew under the guidance that domestic administration is the representative ("servant") of the political regime (foreign rulers) and the citizenry is expected to be guided by the domestic administration. In contemporary times, however, in the absence of a foreign regime, the bureaucracy is expected to serve the interest of the politicians. The wide discretionary powers of public officials along with weak institutional and legal frameworks allow them to deviate from accepted norms of behavior to serve political ends. Because of a "master-slave" relationship between the government and the governed, the traditional mode of service delivery has built-in incentives for corruption and rent-seeking behavior (Heeks, 1998).

Obviously, to establish trust among public officials and citizens, the traditional *modus operandi* has to change. Technology can only bring them closer but the trust must be earned through a mediator and not simply from a medium. It is unlikely that the politicians will find it advantageous to mediate, leaving it to the nongovernmental or civil society organizations to take on this task. Therefore, success of E-Government is clearly a complex one and requires an understanding of the role technology might play in empowering public managers and citizens alike.

Bangladesh, a country of more than 153 million, has been under several regimes since its independence in 1972. It is one of the N-11 countries ("The Next Eleven") identified by Goldman Sachs investment bank as having a high potential of becoming one of the world's largest economies in the 21st century along with Brazil, Russia, India and China (Wilson and Stupnyska, 2007). We use Bangladesh as a case in point to evaluate the status of E-Government development and its implications for transforming the country's administrative processes.

Study Methodology

We use the findings from two surveys conducted in 2004 and 2008 by the Government of Bangladesh (GoB, 2004, 2008) assessing the E-Readiness status of the governmental agencies across Bangladesh. The surveys primary focus was the infrastructure and human development factors that affect E-Government development. We also conducted a focus group survey in 2008 to identify organizational culture, human development and computer access that might affect the implementation of E-Government within governmental agencies. Also, the survey focused on how the barriers to E-Government were intensified by the priorities based upon the existing organizational hierarchy.

E-GOVERNMENT STATUS IN BANGLADESH

ICT Survey 2004 and 2008

The recent status of E-Government in Bangladesh shows that, as one of the least developed nations, it is close to realizing connectivity within governmental institutions, showing signs of the initial phases of E-Government – connecting government-to-government online or G2G. Despite economic and political upheaval the E-Government reform movement has been kept alive. Until as recently as the last election in December 2008, the elected Prime Minister attracted the attention of the younger generation by declaring to build a "Digital Bangladesh" (Mustafa, 2008).

We discuss two recent survey reports conducted under the Support to ICT Task Force Program (SICT) in Bangladesh, to assess the status of E-Government. The survey conducted by the Government of Bangladesh in 2004 and followed up in 2008, shows that the status of E-Government at the macro level has significantly improved in the last four years in terms of infrastructure and human resource development.[1] However, training remains inadequate and is one of the most pressing priorities for government officials.

According to the 2008 survey, 80% of government agencies at all levels has a minimum of one desktop with at least 28 desktops for every 100 employees. This is a significant improvement from 2004 where only 4 desktops were available for every 100 employees at the Ministerial level (division headquarters) and one for every 100 employees at the local government (corporation) level. Computer usage is almost even among senior level managers and clerical staff in Ministries (59% vs. 56%), however, at the local level, 36% of senior officers in departments have desktops compared to 20% clerical staff. This gap has also been reduced since 2004 when only 21% of senior managers had access to computers at the local level compared to 6% of clerical staff. Whereas 29% of the clerical staff received some kind of ICT training in 2004, 46% of the clerical staff went through training in 2008. At the local level only 7% of clerical staff received training in 2004 compared to 17% in 2008. Today all Ministries and divisional headquarters have at least one active website. In 2004 only 24% of the Ministry and 60% of the Divisions had a website. Almost all websites function as billboards, providing general information about the Ministries (Departments under the Office of the Prime Minister). Bangladesh National Portal, http://www.bangladesh.gov.bd/, connects all Ministries into one platform. In addition each ministry website publishes its citizens' charter, outlining the mission, vision and the role of the ministry in the affairs of the Government and the citizens at large.

The Reports also addressed the primary barriers to E-Government as perceived by respondents (mainly heads of agencies) of the survey in 2004 and 2008 (See GoB, 2004, p. 6 and GoB, 2009, p. 49). In both the Reports, inadequate training and lack of hardware topped the list, with 65 to 69% identifying lack of adequate training and 56% to 59% identifying lack of hardware, as primary barriers to E-Government development. Lack of native language (*Bangla*) interface and frequent power failure were also identified as barriers to E-Government (22% to 35% of the respondents). Organizational culture, such as "fear of change" and "mindset against computer usage" was less of an issue in both the years. However, in 2004, whereas 19% identified 'fear of change" as a barrier, in 2004, only 8% agreed with that. Similar optimism was expressed about "mindset against computers" – 18% identified that as a barrier in 2004 compared to 9% in 2008.

The Reports provide an overall assessment of IT infrastructure and connectivity status. It suggests the Bangladesh Government has accepted the promises of E-Government and is on the path to realizing them. However, the Reports provide limited guidance on how each agency embraces E-Government to transform the process by which it interacts and provides services to citizens. Since one of the goals of E-Government is to make government more transparent, an assessment of the inter-organizational challenges is critical.

Inter-Organizational Challenges

In June 2008 a focus group survey was conducted among 19 mid-to-senior level civil service officers in Bangladesh from different Ministries (Departments under the Head of State). The purpose of the survey was to assess the status of E-Government initiatives and learn how the barriers to E-Government were intensified by the priorities placed upon the existing organizational hierarchy. The officers were heads of the department who represented their agencies on E-Government is-

Table 1. Access to technology by organizational hierarchy

Level	Have desktops (pct)	Internet connection (pct)	Use computer on routine basis (pct)	Computer literate (pct)
Clerical Staff	44	18	63	59
Managerial (mid-level)	86	82	83	65
Senior executives	98	98	76	57

Table 2. IT training among government employees

	Do you think your employees have adequate skills to utilize computer? (pct)	Do you think IT training is adequate? (pct)	Do you have dedicated budget for IT training? (pct)
Yes	36	47	6
No	63	53	94

sues. Participation varied among ministries and is not representative of all the ministries for the Government of Bangladesh. Prior to conducting the onsite survey the officers participated in a half-day workshop on E-Government.[2] The survey focused on three main organizational factors directly related to the success of E-Government: (1) status of technological infrastructure, (2) human resource skill, and (3) environmental factors (political and cultural issues).

Technological Infrastructure and Preparedness

All participants responded to having computer access in respective ministries. However access varied with hierarchy: managers at the higher level had more access and connectivity than at the lower level staff. Table 1 shows the clerical staff that are at the bottom of the hierarchy have far more limited access (44%) than mid-level managers and senior executives (86% and 98% respectively). This phenomenon is typical in developing organizations where decision makers often are the first beneficiaries of new technology and resources. When considering access to the Internet, the discrepancy is much wider – only 18% of the clerical staff has an Internet connec-

tion compared to almost all senior level managers. Senior managers, despite having access, may resist using IT because of 'computer phobia.' Table 2 shows senior executives are less computer savvy (57%) compared to clerical staff (59%). The fact that senior executives were the primary responders of the survey says much about such phobia within public offices in Bangladesh. However, senior executives who are computer literate appear to use it more regularly (76%) than clerical staff (63%).

The uneven IT resource and connectivity within organizations carry important implications for E-Government in Bangladesh. First, it suggests that E-Government is in its infancy – routine operations are paper-based rather than managed electronically. Citizens have to rely on the clerical staff (the front desk of all departments) to apply for services. Although some of the forms for seeking services may be posted online, citizens still must bring those forms to clerical staff for processing. Second, uneven interconnectivity suggests IT favors centralization of power within senior level managers. The apparent disconnect between offline and online staff further suggests creating another bureaucratic class layer that may resist E-Government initiatives given the benefits received from a non-transparent governmental structure. Finally, in the absence of digitized data

Table 3. Perceptions of e-government among government employees

Level	Pct of employees who value E-Government	Pct of Staff invited to meetings
Clerical Staff	20	11
Managerial (mid-level)	67	94
Senior executives	77	84

Table 4. Cultural barriers to innovation

Rank the Cultural barrier that plays the most important role in undermining creativity and innovation in employees	Rank (n = 19)
Low Morale (due to low compensation)	2
Lack of incentive	3
Lack of political leadership	1
Lack of coordinated procedures	4
Lack of National Strategy	5

and information in public offices, low computer literacy is not surprising. As per the phases of E-Government, when the core business of government is digitized (such as filing and storage of data) followed by digital processing (through an integrated information management system), it is expected that the digital environment will influence user's decisions to learn how to become part of the digital operation.

Human Resource Skill Factors

The survey asked if the office staff had adequate skills to utilize (make purposeful use of) computers. Table 2 shows about 63% responded their employees had inadequate skills to utilize computer applications. Also an overwhelming majority (94%) responded that their training was inadequate to conduct computer operations. More than half (53%) responded they did not have a dedicated budget for IT training.

The responders also thought upgrading the skills through training may not be enough for IT adoption. Knowledge gained from training is seldom applied because of the lack of political

interest and the absence of an environment under which E-Government can survive. For example, the survey finds 87% of computer usage is related to word processing only; about 16% use it in database management system, 7% for programming and 23% for email and Internet browsing. Because there is no integrated information management system in most departments, E-Government training exposes the concept of E-Government without the required working knowledge.

Political and Environmental Factors

The socio-political environment may be the most dominant barrier for E-Government success in Bangladesh. Table 4 shows how E-Government is valued at various staff levels. It appears clerical staff are not as enthusiastic about E-Government as their senior counter parts. Only 22% of the clerical staff may value E-Government compared to mid-level managers (67%) or senior executives (77%). The implication of low perception of E-Government is in line with the idea that, within a centralized hierarchical structure, enabling of IT is associated with downsizing the clerical and middle management (Kraemer & Dedrick, 1997). This fear may be real among the low-skilled employees who are likely to resist E-Government moves in order to protect their jobs. However current *modus operandi* of governmental agencies may not be helping to curb such fears. For example, only 11% of the clerical staff, according to the survey, are invited to staff meetings compared to 94% and 84% of senior level officers respectively (Table 3). Lack of communication is another hurdle for bringing the low-level managers under the foray of the E-governance agenda, this is particularly significant for developing countries where decision making is centralized, non-transparent and can be politically motivated.

The survey asked the managers to rank the most important cultural barriers they believe undermine creativity and innovation in their organization. The rationale here was to identify the motivating factor under which government managers must operate to take on the challenge of E-Government. This question is particularly important to determine the underlying resistance for innovative thinking – a requirement for E-Government implementation. All responders ranked "lack of political leadership" as the number one barrier to creativity and innovation in employees in their organization. "Low morale (due to primarily low compensation)" was ranked second followed by "lack of incentives to take new initiatives." Given the history of Bangladesh's political struggle in recent years, the lack of political leadership being ranked so high is not very surprising. Although National ICT strategy has almost become a requirement for formulating comprehensive E-Government programs, none of the success stories of E-Government can be found solely based on national strategy. Strong political support is necessary to implement E-Government initiatives as shown in some countries like South Korea and Singapore. This becomes more important in countries where the legal and policy framework is weak in protecting public managers who take on new initiatives. When asked "Do you believe there is necessary policy, procedures and legal framework to implement E-Government," 95% responded that they did not believe it was present.

The focus group survey described here provides us with three important findings. (1) IT infrastructure is available but distributed unevenly, favoring mostly the top level public managers. Transparency in government is not apparent due to lack of information flow (or informatization) and availability of digital records; (2) Employees

are lacking in IT training due to budgetary constraints and, despite available training, also lack hands-on working knowledge of E-Government (such as using integrated MIS system, file management and retrieval etc.). Hence, training is not helpful in building E-Government capacity within organizations. (3) Political leadership is a must for developing E-Government programs within departments. E-Government requires re-engineering of processes customized to citizen needs. In the absence of strong political support, policy directives and legal framework, empowering public managers to reach out to citizens is at best a shot in the dark.

We should be cautious about generalizing the findings because of the limitations of the focus group survey, specifically the smaller sample size and that subjects who do not fully represent the government agencies in Bangladesh. However, the caveat should not overshadow the major implications of the findings that parallel previous similar studies. For example, Jane Fountain (2001) has shown that overcoming the entrenched organizational and political divisions within the state may be the major determinant in the success of IT adoption. The factors highlighted thus far could suggest that the socio-political bias towards the technocratic class can only make the organizational processes less transparent—allowing one group to benefit from the online "connection" at the expense of the lower level clerical staff that is expected to continue taking advantage of the traditional approach to providing services to the citizens. Imposing E-Government on ad-hoc basis can not only hide the abuses under the shadow of a powerful technocratic class but also legitimize such abuse. Organizations may be technologically ready to take E-Government but may not be ready in terms of human resource skills or environmental and political issues.

Given that the majority of the population live below a subsistence level and are disconnected from the government, the main beneficiaries of E-

Government are likely to be an elite class who are connected to the elite administrative machinery. Rather than reducing the socio-economic disparity, E-Government helps to reinforce such disparity.

SOLUTIONS AND RECOMMENDATIONS

E-Government and Citizen Empowerment

While connectivity between governments is becoming apparent, connectivity by citizens is quite another issue. Among the three objectives outlined earlier, G2G serves one of the objectives by providing unidirectional one-stop services to citizens. The beneficiaries are those citizens who are part of the digital network and generally belong to the higher income group. For example, very few of us should expect a street vendor to apply for a business license or driver's license or a rickshaw puller to apply for a passport to go overseas. As premised earlier, instead of transforming the way government interacts with citizens on a daily basis, E-Government adds to traditional government service delivery by creating another layer of service delivery approaches catered toward a smaller group of citizens. The beneficiaries have been limited to those who are privileged in society, particularly those individuals and governmental agencies that can afford and have access to technology and resources. This argument holds both in the developed world and the less developed world.

Therefore, how to make E-Government relevant to the mass group to improve their livelihood? The nontraditional approach would be to find an intermediary that prepares the environment (ground rules) to empower public managers so that they can retool E-Government based on citizen needs.

Implication of Civil Society and E-Governance

As argued by Clay Wescott (2001), the clearest area where E-Government can claim success is through Non-governmental organizations or Civil Society Organizations (CSOs). The market driven approach to E-Government fails to provide the avenues for the marginalized class to participate in the process. In other words by not being able to exchange in the "E-Government market" due to lack of access or business, the significant majority remains out of touch with its government. According to World Bank Reports, CSOs have become increasingly influential actors in public policy discourse. By partnering with governmental agencies, they have been effective in development efforts, especially formulating grass-root level agendas to empower marginal groups which normally do not participate in policy discourse or engage in development efforts. It is estimated that up to $1 billion a year, or 5% of the World Bank's annual portfolio, is channeled to CSOs through the government-managed funds. Other funders of CSOs include Asian Development Bank, USAID, Canadian International Development Agency (CIDA), DFID, UNDP, Japan International Cooperation Agency (JICA), World Health Organization (WHO), Swedish International Development Agency (SIDA) and German Technical Cooperation Agency (GTZ).

Although the role of CSOs has often been undermined in political circles by labeling them as "foreign agents," some of the most ground breaking governmental reform measures in developing countries could not have been possible without their influence. For example in Bangladesh, the Right to Information (RTI) Ordinance and Citizen Charter Ordinance could not have been realized without CSOs and citizen demand.[3] Free flow of information is a precondition to protecting democratic values (and the institutions that uphold them). Such rights, that are taken for granted in the industrialized world, have to be protected, implemented and nurtured by citizens themselves. Without the help of powerful citizen groups and international civil rights organizations, they would never survive. With the passing of the RTI Act, public managers will have the necessary legislation to act as whistle blowers and curb the abuse of power by peers, supervisors or political masters. All government agencies in Bangladesh are now required to have a citizen charter that is posted on the agency website and/or in public places. The purpose of the citizen charter is to give citizens the right to demand services as outlined in the charter.

Another CSO, Institute of Governance Studies (IGS) at BRAC University, provided technical assistance to the Government of Bangladesh to develop an anti-corruption strategy to stand as the foundation of the good governance agenda. More recently USAID funded IGS for the Journalism Training and Research Initiative (JATRI). The purpose of JATRI is to train journalists on investigative reporting and to become a resource for independent journalists. Clearly, these initiatives by CSOs are in line with citizen empowerment that can only strengthen democracy.

FUTURE RESEARCH DIRECTIONS

Mobile Phone Mobilization

The advent of information technology in the developing world cannot be timelier given the ground work established by CSOs. To protect and nurture democratic values, ICT plays a significant role; particularly empowering citizens to take control of their lives. As one of the primary communication devices of the 21st century, mobile phones offer a clear advantage to computers in bringing government to citizen's finger tips. More than half of the world's population has one active mobile phone. Developing countries have twice the number of mobile phone users than industrialized countries (Heeks and Jagun, 2007). Whereas there are 1.2 computers per 100 people in Bangladesh (UNdata,

2004), there are more than 44 million mobile phone users (28% of the population) growing at the rate of 50% a year (BuddComm, 2009). The prospect of using the mobile phone for E-Government in Bangladesh is far reaching, particularly when such devices have reached across all income groups. For example, as of 2009, thousands of the rural population in cyclone prone areas will receive early warning alerts to their mobile phones during an impending storm or natural disaster (Reuters, 2009). Even two years ago, deployment of this technology could have saved thousands of people during the coastal cyclone SIDR. The micro-credit enterprise (Grameen Bank) revolutionized by Noble Laureate Dr. Yunus, has shown how connectivity through mobile phones can empower rural women to do business and earn a livelihood, by selling chickens, vegetables and farm products at a fair market price. By applying simple concepts such as peer-group motivation and connectivity, micro-credit has pulled millions out of poverty. In 2004 Bangladesh Research Development Network (D.Net) setup Rural Information Helpline. Rural women with common livelihood queries sought help by calling via mobile phones. The program was expanded to 'Mobile Ladies' initiative. Women with mobile phones in hand go door-to-door in villages, listening to common livelihood problems and advising on how best they can be solved (Raihan, 2005). In addition, by spending a marginal amount with no overhead cost or taxes, citizens can directly speak to a practicing physician, seek advice and get prescriptions. Provided by Grameen phone, such live medical service is available 24 hours a day.

Also known as m-Government applications, the mobile applications are being used to pay utility bills ("push technology"), obtain cash directly from banks ("pull technology"), and receiving grades directly on mobile phones. Also by subscribing to certain databases (housed and secured by government or CSOs) acute patients can be notified about ozone alerts, asthma attacks due to high level pollutants in the air, immunization reminders etc. Businesses can subscribe to alerts that might affect one's business, for example, new and upcoming business related regulations. Alerts can be customized so that when someone approaches a certain geographic point they are notified through mobile alert (for example, traffic jam, crime alerts and health hazards etc).

In addition to mobile E-Government deployment, the general population can also benefit from Community Information Centers (CIC). These kiosks act as information and communication hubs in remote areas providing services such as internet access, email, video conferencing to communicate with family and support to rural farmers in terms of information about pesticides, fertilizer distribution etc. In Bangladesh, The Grameen partnership with the Society for Economic and Basic Advancement (SEBA) has established CIC across rural Bangladesh. The Grameen CIC project so far has given 20 million people the chance to use the Internet and e-mail for the first time. One CIC services 40,000 people in 15 rural villages.

CONCLUSION

E-Government's effectiveness depends not on the technological supremacy of government but on how encompassing it is to reach the maximum number of citizens at the grass roots level (regardless of their socioeconomic status). Whether at the agency level or individual level, E-Government focus should be from the ground up. Bureaucratic inertia is more prominent at the lower level of agency hierarchy than at the top. Because of the fear of losing jobs (and control) E-Government investment on clerical staff should be a priority. They must be brought into the new decision making apparatus and be informed about the opportunities to move up professionally. The same is true for citizens who belong to marginal groups. More often the marginal group has a deep distrust of government machinery. Simple issues

that affect their lives are often the least priority for governments. E-Government should be used to take care of such simple issues. Clearly CSOs have stepped up to the plate to fill the void in developing countries.

The mistrust among citizens and government officials is deep rooted and historical. A knowledge network must be established to bring trust among partners (Dawes, Cresswell & Pardo, 2009). Partnering with CSOs can allow such trust to penetrate the governmental sector. Mobile phones shall be the vehicle to connect citizens with government. If a farmer can know the price of chicken in the market, a schoolteacher can also know when his or her paycheck arrives in the bank or a farmer when his fertilizer is dispatched in a remote rural village.

Transparency in bureaucratic decision making is a precondition to upholding democratic values within a society. Government websites, rather than becoming information bill boards, must become markets where citizens exchange ideas that add value to their existing knowledge. Web 2.0 technologies (blogs, wiki, tweeter etc) should be effectively utilized in websites so that E-Governance – the effective functioning of the government through online deliberation – becomes an integral part of E-Government. Market driven service delivery provision is unidirectional (citizens demands and government provides), there are no avenues for discourse for knowledge creation. Just as governments provide services to citizens, given the platform, citizens can also provide their services when demanded by the government. That makes the E-Government unique in the 21st century.

REFERENCES

BuddeComm. (2009). *Mobile Phone Data*. Retrieved July 2, 2009 from http://www.budde.com.au

Coursey, D., & Norris, D. (2008). Models of e-government: Are they correct? An empirical assessment. *Public Administration Review*, May/Jun *68*(3), 523-36.

Danziger, J., & Anderson, K. (2002). The impacts of information technology on public administration: An analysis of empirical research from the "Golden Age" of transformation. *International Journal of Public Administration, 25*(5), 591–627. doi:10.1081/PAD-120003292

Dawes, S., Cresswell, A., & Theresa, P. (2009). From "Need to Know" to "Need to Share": tangled problems information boundaries and the building of public sector knowledge networks. *Public Administration Review, 69*(3), 392–401. doi:10.1111/j.1540-6210.2009.01987_2.x

Government of Bangladesh. (2004). *Comprehensive study of e-government initiatives in Bangladesh: Final report*. Retrieved May 2009, from http://www.sict.gov.bd/digitallibrary.php

Government of Bangladesh. (2008). *e-Government initiatives in Bangladesh: A sample survey*. Retrieved May 2009, from http://www.sict.gov.bd/digitallibrary.php

Heeks, R. (1998). *Information technology and public sector corruption*. Information Systems for Public Sector Management Working Paper 4. Manchester: IDPM. Retrieved, June, 2009, from http://unpan1.un.org/intradoc/groups/public/documents/APCITY/UNPAN014658.pdf

Heeks, R., & Jagun, A. (2007). Mobile phone and development: The future in new hands. *ID21 Insights, 69*. Retrieved June 2009, from http://www.id21.org/insights/insights69/insights69.pdf

Kraemer, K., William, H., & Northrup, A. (1981). *The management of information systems*. New York: Columbia University Press.

Kraemer, K. L., & Dedrick, J. (1997). Computing and public organizations. *Journal of Public Administration: Research and Theory, 7*(1), 89–112.

Office of the Vice President. (1993). *From Red tape to results. Creating a government that works better and costs less. Report of the National Performance Review*. Washington, DC: US Government Printing Office.

Raihan, A. (2005). Mobile ladies' in Bangladesh: Connecting villagers to livelihoods information. *ID21 Insights*. Retrieved July 2009, from http://www.id21.org/insights/insights69/art02.html

Reuters. (2009). Bangladesh trials cell phone disaster alerts. Retrieved July 3, 2009 from http://www.msnbc.msn.com/id/31523970/

Sabir, M. (2008). *Bangladesh stunned by Awami victory*. BBC News. Retrieved July 2, 2009, from http://news.bbc.co.uk/2/hi/south_asia/7804040.stm

UnData. (2009). *Personal computers per 100 population*. Retrieved July 8, 2009, from http://data.un.org/Data.aspx?d=CDB&f=srID%3A29971.

Wescott, C. (2001). E-Government in the Asia-Pacific region. *Asian Journal of Political Science, 9*(2), 1–24. doi:10.1080/02185370108434189

Wilson, D., & Stupnytska, A. (2007). *The N-11: More than an acronym*. Global Economics Paper No. 153. Goldman Sachs. Economic Research from the GS. Retrieved July, 2009, from http://www.chicagobooth.edu/alumni/clubs/pakistan/docs/next11dream-march%20'07-goldmansachs.pdf

World Bank. (2002), *The e-government handbook for developing countries*. Retrieved June 2009, from http://www.cdt.org/egov/handbook/2002-11-14egovhandbook.pdf

Yang, K., & Rho, S.-Y. (2007). E-Government for Better Performance: Promises, Realities, and Challenges. *International Journal of Public Administration*, *30*(11), 1197–1217. doi:10.1080/01900690701225556

ENDNOTES

[1] Both the survey Reports can be found under SICT website at http://www.sict.gov.bd/digitallibrary.php

[2] Survey was sponsored by the Bangladesh Public Administration Training Centre (BPATC), United Nations Development Program (UNDP) and Institute of Governance Studies, BRAC University. Survey questionnaire is available from the author upon request.

[3] Although RTI was approved by the Interim-government last year, it requires ratification by the parliament members to become an Act. Currently it is waiting for final legislation by the present government. Transparency International that monitors corruption in public offices played an important role in formulating RTI.

Chapter 9
An Assessment Study of Indian State Government Portals

Debjani Bhattacharya
Northern Institute for Integrated Learning in Management, India

Umesh Gulla
Teri University, India

M. P. Gupta
Indian Institute of Technology Delhi, India

ABSTRACT

Does the e-readiness of a country or a state give any insight into the success of their e-government projects? Does scaling up of e-readiness help to measure the acceptance of e-government projects by citizens? Research has failed to provide a direct answer to these questions. While an e-readiness index summarizes the infrastructural condition of a state or country in terms of network readiness and availability of hardware facility; e-government readiness implies the acceptance of e-government projects by the citizens in a state or a country. So, the e-readiness index cannot clearly depict the e-government readiness of a country. Since e-government projects are broadly categorized as Government to Citizen, Government to Business and Government to Government, it becomes difficult to quantify the satisfaction level of the stakeholders. For analysing the acceptance of e-government business models particularly the web based ones, researchers (Yang, 2002; Kašubienė & Vanagas, 2007; Janssen, Kuk & Wagenaar, 2008; Morgeson & Mithas, 2009) often adopted the quality criteria used in evaluating service offered by of e-commerce sites. The most pervasive concept of quality in use is the extent to which a web service meets and/or exceeds a citizen's/customer's expectations. Portals at the Federal Government level in India were developed with the idea to form a 'single window' access to the facilities provided by the states or union territories to the citizens in an integrated platform. The idea behind such investment

DOI: 10.4018/978-1-61692-018-0.ch009

on state wise portals was to serve the citizens better but there was hardly any attempt from the government side to assess the acceptance of the portals. Some of the portals have counters to keep a track of visitors and email facilities have been provided to serve queries of the visitors. So the effectiveness of the portals has become a questionable issue today. In this study we have tried to concentrate on Indian State government portals and assess the service quality provided by them. It was observed that State wise Service Quality issues in e-government differ significantly when global parameters like usability, adequacy of information, navigation facility interactivity are considered. So, to evaluate the portals a conceptual framework based on previous research works was proposed. Quality dimensions were identified to assess service quality of government portals and each of the state and the union territory portal was audited based on the parameters proposed like usefulness of information, adequacy of information, citizen centric information, usability, accessibility, interaction, privacy, security and citizen participation.

INTRODUCTION

E-government or electronic government has evolved as a popular concept in public administration that supposedly ensures efficient and effective (Heeks, 2001) service delivery to the citizens and stakeholders with proper interconnectivity of related government departments. The concept also asissts in helping to enhance interactivity, decentralization and transparency in the working of government. The United Nations (UN) and American Society for Public Administration (ASPA) (2002) has defined e-government as "utilizing the Internet and the World-Wide-Web for delivering government information and services to citizens". The services of e-government also include use of other mode of ICT in addition to the Internet and the Web, such as "database, networking, discussion support, multimedia, automation, tracking and tracing, and personal identification technologies" (Jaeger, 2003). Fountain (2001) appositely termed this concept of rendering government service as 'digital government' or 'virtual state' instead of e-government.

E-government projects can be broadly classified into threee categories; Government to Citizen, Government to Business and Government to Government. As a result, the concept of e-government is perceived differently depending on the type of stakeholders who use the service. There is no universal definition of e-government, but prior research unanimously concedes that e-government involves: the automation or computerization of existing paper-based procedures that will prompt new styles of leadership, new ways of debating and deciding strategies, new ways of transacting business, new ways of listening to citizens and communities, and new ways of organizing and delivering information (Yildiz, 2007).

Since the introduction of electronic government is a relatively newer concept in a traditional democracy like India, general acceptance and frequency of use has been observed to be considerably low. Though there have been some success stories like 'e-Seva', 'SETU', 'Bhoomi' and FRIENDS, which have gained appreciation nationally and internationally, there have been many other endeavours from the Government of India that have barely received a mention in any of the platforms and are rarely used by the stakeholders.

Implementation of country level projects to achieve citizen centric government in a country like India with vast diversity has proved to be a herculean task. The following factors must be addressed: expansion of the subcontinent, menacing population growth, cultural diversity, political interference, digital divide, knowledge divide, lack of infrastructure. These are just are just a few of the problems that have thwarted the growth of e-government projects countrywide. However, the growth of ICT and the demand for direct access to government information from both inside and outside government has become an unusual phenomenon in India. To keep up with the increasing demand from the citizens and to impart effective governance, the Department of Information Technology is trying to shift most of the e-government web enabled activities from single service based websites to multiple services based portals. Government portals can be different, ranging from service portal to transaction portals or they can even serve as just information portals. The concept of a portal signifies a 'single window' approach to a wide spectrum of services. Today, India has managed to launch over more than 2000 websites and portals to render effective governance electronically.

Elaborate research in general and big investments in particular have been undertaken by the Government of India to implement web enabled e-government projects with several more projects subsequently conceived in the 11th five-year plan. Compared to the pace at which the projects have been developed, the acceptance of these projects has been quite disheartening. A service assessment has thus become imperative so that the usage of the facilities which are specifically meant for the citizens/users can be given a lift. Thorough research needs to be conducted to develop the quality criteria which can help to assess web enabled e-government projects. Though it has been argued that process evaluation is more important than impact evaluation in e-government (Wolf and Krcmar, 2005), in the area of e-service it is necessary that research provide input into the process and help to improve the implementation of existing project as well as for new projects. In this chapter we have attempted to do a select study on the effectiveness of state government portals. An empirical model has been proposed to study the service quality of government web portal. The approach which has been used to design the model is normative based on the study done by Yang, Cai, Zhou & Zhou (2005). This chapter aims to find out the relative state of ICT infrastructure existing

at federal level and delve into the fact that how far e-readiness actually influences e-government readiness of a state. While conducting the study we have also tried to find out the constraints which hinder use of the state portals in India.

BACKGROUND

Steps towards E-Government in India

Governance generally involves the process of making and implementing decisions. Therefore e-Governance is not merely employing information and communication technology to existing systems, but it emphasizes on efficient and effective dissemination of services to the stakeholders making the system transparent. Thus, in this process all the participants namely the society, various government and non-government agencies, stakeholders and the electronic media need to work in harmony having the accountability and being responsive to incorporate the primary characteristics of citizen centric governance

India took initiative in incorporating e-government with the creation of a separate ministry in 1999, the Ministry of Information Technology. The ministry approved of IT Act 2000 to promote growth of IT industry in the country. There have been isolated e-Governance initiatives in the country at the National, State, district and even block level for over a decade. Quite a few of them are successful and ready for replication across other States. Both successes and the failures of the various initiatives played an important role in shaping the e governance strategy of the country. The Government Approved the National e-Governance Plan (NeGP), comprising of 27 Mission Mode Projects (MMPs) and eight components in 2006.

The existing projects are being implemented by various Central Ministries/State departments/States and integrated service levels to create a citizen-centric and business-centric environment for governance. Apart from mission mode projects, other three major components of NeGP include, creation of State Wide Area Network, State Data Centre (SDC) and Community Service Centres (CSC) to serve villages in the country and provide a range of services. Today every state of India has an IT Policy in place and is involved in the development of e-governance.

The components of national e-government programme include (Dwivedi & Sahu, 2008):

- Awareness and communication
- Assessment
- Capacity building
- Common Service Centre
- Infrastructural and technical support
- Monitoring and evaluation
- Project and Financial appraisal
- Research and Development

The National Informatics Centre (NIC) is another such organization of the Department of Information Technology which is responsible for providing network backbone and e-Governance support to Central Government, State Governments, UT Administrations, Districts and other Government bodies. Till recently, it had offered a wide range of ICT services including Nationwide Communication Network for decentralised planning, improvement in Government services and wider transparency of national and local Governments. NIC assists in implementing Information Technology Projects, in close collaboration with Central and State Governments, in the areas of (a) Centrally sponsored schemes and Central sector schemes, (b) State sector and State sponsored projects, and (c) District Administration sponsored projects.

NIC's constant endeavour is to ensure proper planning in areas of IT and the latest technology available to government. The centre also takes care of implementation of projects to facilitate the citizens. The state and union territories' portals have been designed carefully by NIC so that users can have easy access to the portals.

The National Knowledge Commission (NKC), a high-level advisory body to the Prime Minister of India, has the objective of transforming India into a knowledge society. It covers sectors ranging from education to e-governance. National Knowledge Commission has formed a special group, to study reviews of various e-governance efforts at the Centre and State levels. Discussions with stakeholders including the Administrative Reform Commission concluded that following changes are essential:

- **Government process reengineering before any computerization:** Since most of the government processes were adapted from the British Rule, popularly known as British Raj, so restructuring of the cumbersome processes and integration between different processes have become imperative before any computerization.
- **Identification and simplification of important processes:** To have an immediate impact on citizens, it is critical to identify and simplify important processes and services, which are presently cumbersome, bureaucratic and prone to delays. These processes can be reengineered and made available as web-based services like issuance of birth certificates, death certificates, proof of residence and ration or ID cards. This approach will require each state to implement these processes in concert and learn from each other.
- **Common Standards:** Presently various state governments have selectively computerized their processes to provide e-governance facility to the stakeholders. Many of these projects have been found to be vendor dependent and lack scalability. It is a mammoth task to develop and enforce citizen/business standards uniformly over all states and central ministries and func-

tions because these standards should neither be hardware-centric nor totally vendor dependent. The standards should be defined in such a way which can enable easy participation by any State, Panchayat Institution, business, NGO or citizens. The National Knowledge Commission emphasizes the standards, templates and data formats be designed carefully by teams of experts drawn from government, IT companies, academia, R & D institutions and users/ stakeholders who understand latest trends, technology, software, user interfaces.

NIC has strived to include the guidelines given by NKC for designing the state government portals so that the citizens can use the services provided by the states in a user friendly environment.

Adoption of Portals as E-Governance Medium

To increase usability of services and impart accessibility to a wider spectrum of services effectively and efficiently; the concept of Portal or a 'single stop' medium has been implemented in the working of electronic and citizen centric government.

The government web portals should have the main objectives of:

- Providing state and national level government services digitally,
- Integrating remote regions nationwide with primary operational areas.
- Providing service to one and all indiscriminate of caste, creed, and community.

Studies conclude that Government portals serve a simple gateway that offers an opportunity to reorient services for the needs of citizens while consolidating back office responsibilities (Gupta, Kumar & Bhattacharya, 2004). So, from the user perception, e-government portals should have complete usability and allow for self service,

which can expand from searching for information to paying tax. They must ensure:

- easy-to-use services
- accessibility and availability round the clock
- cost-effectiveness
- unification across agencies
- Multilingual coverage
- consistent in appearance
- interoperability to incorporate various functionality
- Interaction with government offices

As mentioned earlier, the response to e-government projects has been bleak in India. Sarkar's (2008) study of Indian government portals concludes that mindset of users, lack of inertia to be at par with technological development, interests and changeability involved in incorporating new systems are some of the unavoidable constraints in the execution of e-government programs. The other factors which thwart the deliverability and acceptance of e-government in India can be enumerated as:

- A population of more than a billion,
- Unequal distribution of wealth
- Illiteracy
- Knowledge divide
- Cultural hindrances
- Digital divide and
- Political interference
- Insufficient infrastructure

ASSESSMENT CRITERIA FOR WEB SITES OR PORTALS

The government web portals present a significant variety of features, complexity of structure and plurality of services offered. As in the case of all information systems, evaluation serves as an aspect of their development and operation that can contribute to maximizing the return on investment

(Adelman, 1991). Moreover, website assessment can also significantly contribute to redefine the services which can satisfy user needs and meet the user expectations to the maximum possible extend. Assessment of information technology initiatives is conducted either as an ex-ante (before implementation) or ex-post (after implementation) procedure. Process re-engineering, education, revision of government policies, software and hardware requirement analysis, network setup and cost estimation are some of the aspects which need to be considered to assess an e-government project before implementation. Quality assessment of e-government projects after implementation is generally done based on the user perceived usefulness and ease of use.

In e-government, where web portals become the primary interface of connection to citizens and other stakeholders, government attempts to provide high quality web portals. Another reason for government agencies to provide high quality web portals is lack of human contact offered in e-governance, as interaction is purely accomplished through technology. However, technology fails to compensate for the aspects like courtesy, friendliness, helpfulness, care, commitment, flexibility, and cleanliness in websites or web portals. Thus, it is important that the qualities of brick and mortar service be replaced by better performance or excellence on specific web factors like website design, usability, performance and interactivity (Zeithaml, 2002; Palmer, 2002; Iwaarden, Wiele, Ball, & Millen, 2004).

Initial studies emphasized more on the website designs. According to prior research (Giudice & Goodman, 1999; Davis & Merritt, 1998; Loiacono, Watson & Goodhue, 2002), the process of developing web sites / portals consists of three fundamental stages:

- Defining the mission, goals, potential users and general strategies of the site/portals
- Designing and choosing the appropriate unified style, information architecture,

technologies, and navigation paths; and

- Producing, integrating, testing, and refining the programming, typography, editorial style, graphic design, and multimedia objects of a Web site.

Later the focus of research shifted from design perspective to the range of services that were delivered through the web sites or web portals. Concepts of service quality evolved from interactive marketing strategy and expanded in the domain of e-commerce. Several scales were developed to measure the service quality provided by web sites like WEBQUAL(Loiacono et al,2002), e-SQ(Zeithaml, Parasuraman, & Malhotra,2000) and.comQ (Wolfinbarger & Gilly, 2002), which primarily dealt with quality dimensions like web site aesthetics, reliability/ fulfillment, efficiency, privacy/security, assurance/trust, responsiveness, integrated communication and price knowledge, which are valid either for transactional sites or for interface design to enhance user perception of web sites. These attempts were not successful and confronted criticism. Most of the contemporary surveys proposed a multivariate approach because of the complexity and the multi-dimensional nature of the website quality assessment problem. Website quality aspects found in the literature, may be summarized into the following quality dimensions like content (Grose, Forsythe, Ratner, 1998; Warner, 1999; Winkler, 2001 and Nielsen, 2002), navigation (Vora,1998) personalization (Blankenship,2001, Winkler, 2001), structure and design (Virpi and Kaikkonen,2003;Shedro, 2001). Still the service quality of Web sites remained an under defined construct. Grönroos, (2001) concluded that the way in which customers are treated has a direct impact upon their perceptions of satisfaction. Aladwania & Palvia (2002) developed an instrument based on user perceived web-quality measuring four dimensions (specific content, content quality appearance and technical adequacy.

An elaborate research by Moustakis, Litos, Dalivigas, and Tsironis (2004) summarized relevant and significant set of quality features that described sufficiently user perceptions and preferences like: relevance of information, usefulness of content, reliability of information, specialization, architecture, navigability efficiency, layout, appearance animation and multimedia (Grigoroudis, Litos, Moustakis, Politis & Tsironis, 2008).

From the previous studies we can conclude that three key elements for user-centric evaluations of e-government web portals are primarily:

- Functionality,
- Usability and
- Accessibility.

Discussion on Models

Besides dimensions, different models were also suggested to structure services offered by the government web sites/ web portals and improve their effectiveness. While dimensions speak about the measurement criteria for service quality; models provide the stages where the dimensions need to be monitored. A reference model given by ISO distinguishes three domains with which design work is carried out. The domains are identified as Process Domain, Evaluation Domain and Design Domain and are described below as:

- **Process domain:** This domain incorporates the government policies and strategies designed by government officials and ministries to have interactive systems.
- **Evaluation domain:** Generally involves the techniques and methods for assessing the usability of the portals.
- **Design domain:** Technology and design to develop websites or portals to render maximum functionality is taken care of in this domain.

Hallowell (2002) stated that the link between operations' strategy and service delivery is the base for creating a "virtuous cycle". A virtuous cycle is a customer loyalty cycle, starting with navigation, and continuing through information delivery, customer support, and well maintained value chain. In the e-government paradigm, ease of navigation represents the ability of citizens, businesses, and other government agencies to navigate through a website. When ease of navigation, information dissemination, online support, and service delivery are well designed and executed, service quality is high and a favourable EGEC (e-governance experience cycle) develops, which results in increasing citizens' satisfaction and loyalty. Improved navigation leads to a decrease in citizens' support costs and service improvement.

Several other business models were given by researchers (Timmers, 1998, Mahadevan, 2000, Rayport & Jaworski, 2001; Afuah & Tucci, 2002; Chesbrough & Rosenbloom, 2002) to effectively define the services of e-government. The definitions given by the above models emphasized on dimensions like value proposition, organized and dependable resource system, profit oriented financial model and competitive strategy. None of them could satisfactorily define service in the context of e-governance. E-governance service should provide citizen empowerment, citizen satisfaction and cost efficiency in terms of money and time, thus making it more qualitative rather than quantitative.

Verdegem & Verleye (2009) developed a comprehensive model for measuring user satisfaction. This conceptual model considers the different phases that the user of e-government services must undergo and identified the stages as awareness, intension of use, access to service and actual usage.

Acceptance of technology plays a vital role in dissemination and maintenance of web based services. Therefore Davis' (1989) Technology Acceptance Model was chosen as the base model by Yang et al. (2005) for developing a model to

Table 1. Property and their purpose for evaluation of service quality of a government portal

Property	Purpose
a. Usefulness of information	Refers to value information, its reliability and accuracy along with relevance of the information to the user. Reliability necessarily means the consistency and dependability. Information provided in the web should be timely and has to be updated regularly. The information is expected to be free of error.
b. Adequacy of information	Explains the completeness of information. Government web portals should provide information for the users so that they understand the working of government agencies thus helping to promote e-governance. Research reports and hyperlinks to relevant web portals should be provided.
c. Citizen centric information	Multilingual facility, online help, cost effectiveness.
d. Usability	Refers to user friendliness. From the literature survey we know that content layout, website structure, user interface web site appearance and visual design, clarity, search facilities greatly influence user visiting the site.
e. Accessibility	It essentially refers to availability and responsiveness. All time availability of information along with speedy log-on, search, downloads
f. Ease of interaction	Interaction can be between service providers and users, users and website or between peer users. Personalized services may be expected by users can add value to the web site service
g. Privacy / Security	Secured transaction, digital signature, privacy of information which is not shared to third party.
h. Citizen Participation	Refers to customization, feedback, interaction directly with government authority.

measure user perceived service quality for information presenting web portals. Technology Acceptance Model (TAM) is a theoretical approach of information systems that depicts users' acceptance and use of a technology. The model suggests that perceived usefulness and perceived ease-of-use influence the decision when users come across any a new technical application.

Yang et al. (2005) identified two major determinants of user perceived usefulness and ease of use as information quality and system quality. It was reasoned that separating content (information) from delivery system might elucidate the process by which users evaluate service quality of a web site. These determinants were further split into five determinants (usefulness of information, adequacy of information, usability, accessibility, ease of interaction and privacy/security) to explain the concept of overall service quality through portal. The diagram of the model is given below.

E-government has also adopted the concept of service quality but services provided by e-government have a completely different approach.

Here the customers are the citizens and the ownership of services goes to government. Government faces no competition and quite often feedbacks from citizens are overlooked.

In our study of assessing service quality of government state portals, we have extended the above model by incorporating two more determinants (citizen centric information and citizen participation), to the existing determinants of this original model.

The determinants that we have considered to evaluate the state portals have been elaborated in Table 1.

India is a country of diverse culture, language, all of which poses major problems for E-government. Multilingual facility needs to be provided in the portals for common men. Since the knowledge divide is quite pronounced in the country, people from backward/rural areas need online help to navigate through the portals. All information provided by the portals should be free of cost for citizens; hence we have incorporated these dimensions in citizen centric information

Figure 1. Conceptual Model prepared to assess service quality of state web portals of India. (Adapted from model given in Development and validation of an instrument to measure user perceived service quality of information presenting Web portals by Yang et al (2005))

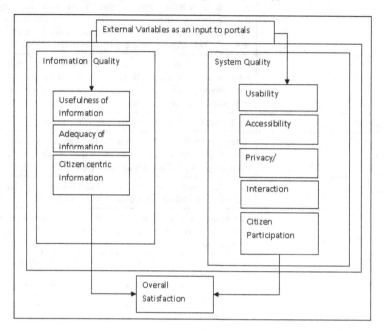

determinant. Citizen participation determinant empowers citizen to participate directly in government activities.

A diagrammatic representation of our conceptual model is as shown in Figure 1.

Methodology Used for the Study

Conceptual Model

The model proposed by Yang et al. (2005) for evaluation of IP Web Portals was used as the base model for evaluating e-government readiness of states with required modification to accommodate characteristics of government portals and incorporate satisfaction criteria of citizens. We introduced two more dimensions; citizen centric information under information quality and citizen participation under system quality. Each quality dimension was broken up into several parameters or items. A total of thirty-four items were approved by web designers, government officials and aca-

demicians. A list of the items has been provided in the Appendix 3.

Analysis

Each of the state government and union territory portals was evaluated against the parameters in a five-point Likert scale (1= *strongly disagree* and 5 = *strongly agree*). Total value for Information Quality and System Quality was then calculated individually. The weighted average of Information Quality and System Quality (appendix 5) was found for each state to rank them accordingly. Since we have considered service quality of the web portals as one of the major determinants of e-government readiness of a state, a comparative study was then made between the e-readiness index (source: India e-Readiness Assessment Report 2006 published by DIT; chapter 4, p.p.48) of each state and the service quality offered by the portal of that state.

Figure 2. E-Readiness vs. count of states and UTs (based on data given by DIT on India: e-readiness assessment report, 2006, provided in appendix 4)

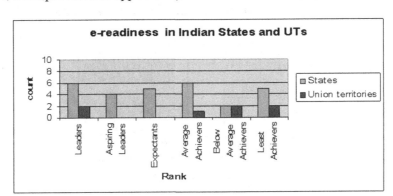

STATE GOVERNMENT PORTALS IN INDIA

India is politically divided into 28 states and seven union territories. Each state and union territory has its own portal which facilitates citizens services and different efforts taken by the government in that particular state. Names of the states and union territories with corresponding portal addresses listed in Appendix one and Appendix two respectively.

According to Economist Intelligence Unit, e-readiness is a yardstick to estimate the quality of information and communications technology (ICT) infrastructure prevailing in a country and the ability of its consumers and business and government to add value to a state or a nation as a whole by using ICT. A framework has been given by the Network Readiness Index (NRI), published by the World Economic Forum (WEF), to assess e-readiness which considers three major components to characterize e-readiness; namely environment, readiness and usage. The Department of Information and Technology (DIT), has modified the framework according to conditions prevalent in India to rank the states and union territories.

A plot showing the ranking of states in terms of e-readiness vs. count of states and union territories is given in the Figure 2.

A report published by DIT for the year 2006 on usage of ICT by Indian states and union territories depicts that only 22% of the total number of states and union territories has appreciably used the resources of ICT in government activities while others still lag behind. (see Figure 3).

It can be seen from the above figure that only 22% of the total number of states has shown a steady growth in e-readiness index. The states in the leader category has been able to implement many successful e-government projects based on PPP model like KAVERI - Computerization of sub registrar's offices in Karnataka, Khajane - Computerization of treasuries in Karnataka, eProcurement - Online tendering in Andhra Pradesh. eSeva - One stop shop for many services in Andhra Pradesh, Kerala has taken up projects like e-Srinkhala, RDNet, Fast, Reliable, Instant, Efficient Network for the Disbursement of Services (FRIENDS). Tamil Nadu has effectively implemented Rasi Maiyams – an application form related to public utility, tender notices and display.

Fourteen percent of the total capacity of India is expected to adapt to the growing pace of ICT and thus show a steady rise in its utility. Rajasthan, West Bengal, Himachal Pradesh, Chhattisgarh and Jharkhand are the states which have been categorized as expectants due to their environmental advancement and usage of existing projects. Infrastructural improvements have shown a

Figure 3. E-Readiness status of Indian states and union territories

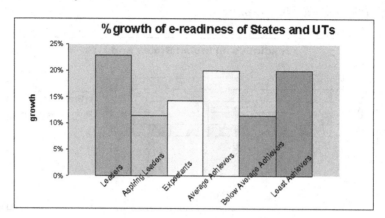

steady rise in the states. Recently Chhattisgarh has been ranked first for the portal www.choice.gov. in. Chhattisgarh Online Information for Citizen Empowerment (CHOiCE) aims at better delivery of government services at the village level.

Some of the states like Mizoram, Orissa, Puducherry, Madhya Pradesh, Sikkim, Meghalaya and Uttarakhand are striving to create a niche in the e-readiness profile list. They constitute around 20% of total number of states. Rest 33% of the states need sincere effort and cooperation from central government to reap the benefits of ICT.

Status of State Portals

To start with the assessment of state portals we first need to know the phase of development for each state.E-government project are generally classified based on four phases of development (Gil-Garcia and Martinez-Moyano, 2006; Belanger & Hiller,2006). The stages are as follows:

*   Web Presence
*   Interaction
*   Transaction and
*   Integration

In India all the states and union territories have developed their sites/portals so the initial stage of web presence for all the states and union territories has been fulfilled.

Interaction in these portals is encouraged primarily through email. Most of the web portals provide an email ID of web masters. In some portals phone numbers of high government officials have been provided. At the same time there is little evidence that most of the portals encourage interactions.

Since e-government is neither a homogeneous nor a static phenomenon, research has been conducted on the dynamics involved to integrate each system of the government (Gil-Garcia et al, 2006; Heeks & Bailur, 2006). Thus, interoperability between different systems, both internal to a department or among external departments of government, play a pivotal role in increasing the ease of access to information. Integration of inter governmental departments is needed in most of the projects like passport, income tax, property tax, death and birth registration so that complete satisfaction can be rendered to the citizens. Some of the states like Rajasthan, Maharashtra, Karnataka and West Bengal have been able to implement interoperability to a great extent while others are still struggling to attain it.

E-government readiness has a different implication from e-readiness. A study (Ray, Sirajee & Dash, 2006) of the status of Indian state was made in which e-government was measured as a weighted average of e-readiness and web-readiness. E-Government readiness analysis might vary with country or region. Al-Omari & Al-Omari (2006) studied that e-government readiness depends on organizational readiness, governance and leadership readiness, customer readiness, competency readiness, technology readiness and legal readiness. Since portals provide a window to government services and represent customer readiness, competency readiness, technology readiness and legal readiness, it is important to evaluate the success of web medium.

Another study (Velsen, Geest, Hedde & Derks, 2009) states engineering is needed to make the government portals user centric as the target group of users is highly heterogeneous because it comprises the entire population of a region. Incidental use, complicated content, interoperability and no competition make the government sites ineffective and difficult to use. Thus, e-readiness alone cannot determine the acceptability of web presence of a government

Graphical representations of the result found are explained in Figure 4.

The Network Readiness Index (NRI), published by the World Economic Forum (WEF), considers usage of ICT resources by government, business and individuals as one indicator to promote e-governance in a particular region. If a portal serves as a one stop service for citizens, then the usability of the portals also contribute to the success of e-government implementation to a large extent. In this study we have tried to examine the influence of e-readiness on information quality of a particular state. Since National Informatics Centre has been established in most of the states it is assumed that the availability of infrastructural benefits influences the design and working of the regional portal considerably.

States like Karnataka, AndhraPradesh, Kerala, TamilNadu, Haryana, Punjab and union territories like Delhi and Chandigarh lead the list of e-readiness ranking with an e–readiness index of more than 1.01. In the plot we find information

quality of the states and union territories match up to the preparedness of the region and show a growth of 73%. Haryana shows 67% growth and Punjab shows only 53% growth in information quality which is inferior to the other leaders. The aspiring leader states like Maharashtra, Gujarat, UttarPradesh have an average e-readiness index of 0.8, with information quality of 73%. Goa being in the same rank has a dip in the information quality and has a value of 54%.

In the states of HimachalPradesh, WestBengal, Rajasthan, Chhattisgarh and Jharkhand the quality of information shows considerable variation. This can be due to improper marketing of the state portals, illiteracy, reluctant attitude toward online services, inadequate information, and improper design of websites. The average achievers like Mizoram, Orissa, Puducherry, Madhya Pradesh, Sikkim, Meghalaya and Uttarakhand show a negative e-readiness index. The information quality suprisingly has a higher value for States like Bihar, Assam, Arunachal Pradesh, Tripura, Meghalaya, Andaman and Nicobar Islands, Dadra and Nagar Haveli with a range between 67% and 60%. We can conclude here that though services are provided through portals and citizens have easy access to information, the lack of proper environmental factors hinder the complete utilization of the portals.

We next study a comparative plot of e-readiness versus system quality. (see Figure 5)

In Figure 5, we observe that Andhra Pradesh leads the system quality among the leaders with a value of 80%. Close to we have Gujarat with a value of 75%. Though Gujarat is in the second ranking with respect to e-readiness, it shows a greater value compared to the leader states of Haryana, Kerala, Karnataka and Tamil Nadu. Maharashtra, Tamil Nadu and Kerala show a value of 55%. Himachal Pradesh though has an e-readiness index of 0.3. It shares the same value of system quality with Haryana, one of the leader states. West Bengal has a better system quality compared to information quality. If the system quality value of West Bengal is compared with a

Figure 4. E-Readiness vs. information quality of state government portals

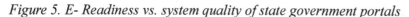

Figure 5. E- Readiness vs. system quality of state government portals

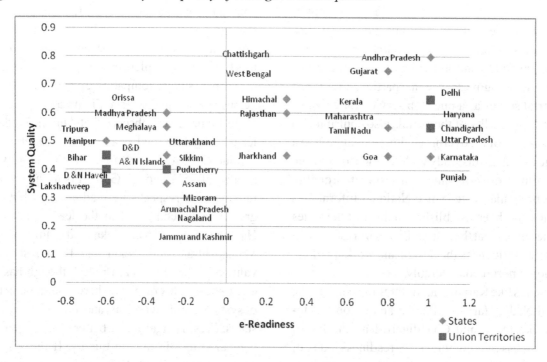

leader state like Tamil Nadu, West Bengal shows a much higher value. The deviations can be explained as perceived ease of use for citizens might not depend upon infrastructural advancement only. Portal appeal is a qualitative aspect which is partially dependent on technology.

In Figure 6, the plot suggests that overall service quality of a government portal varies linearly with improved information quality. Thus to evaluate a portal information quality need to be taken care of. Similarly we can study the variation of service quality with system quality as shown in Figure 7.

Here too we get a positive slope which indicates that overall service quality improves with improved system quality.

The system quality as well as information quality can be improved only if the e-readiness index of a region is positive. If the e-readiness index is negative the system quality and information quality can be high but will show low acceptance of portal.

SOLUTIONS AND RECOMMENDATIONS

The unrelenting effort of India to reduce the digital divide and give minimum ICT facility across the length and breadth of the country has called for huge investment. A return-on-investment (ROI) approach is essential to make the investment effective. Reports published by research institutes like NCAER, IMRB, NIC,IBM and others have focussed on the need of infrastructure and reengineering of government systems to impart successful e-government service to citizens.

Implications for Practitioners

The model gives an insight to the criteria which need to be considered while evaluating a portal or assessing service quality from user's perception. This study has tried to depict that besides the research for a basic need in ICT implementa-

tion while also focusing on user oriented service quality through web media. The stake holders (citizens, community and government) should be empowered by helping them to participate in government decision making. Since India has pronounced digital and knowledge divide, each government portal should be equipped to cater to all categories of citizens so that complete trust and satisfaction can be achieved.

Implications for Researchers

A holistic approach has been made to develop the framework to address common problems faced by citizens while using state portals. A further study can be made on issues unique to each state in India. This kind of work can help the web engineers to develop a better approach for service delivery and ensure maximum exploitation of ICT in government activities.

CONCLUSION

Analysis of state portals has been done on a theoretical framework in this study. The process analysis has been explained above. There are more than 2000 registered sites in India serving as e-government projects. The research had to be done on selective sites and thus the scope of study was limited. In the process we have cognized some added features, like contextual factors which are beyond technology, and various referent domains and ideas with much diversity. It has been observed that the delivery of service is dependent on the system quality and information quality of a particular state in India considerably. Researchers (Katre, 2006; Mitra & Gupta, 2008) have endeavoured to suggest different models, but none of them have been practically adopted. It has been observed during the study that there is a lack of clarity and lack of rigor about methods for improvement of web portal service quality in India and is taken as a general approach. Citizen

Figure 6. Information quality vs. overall service quality

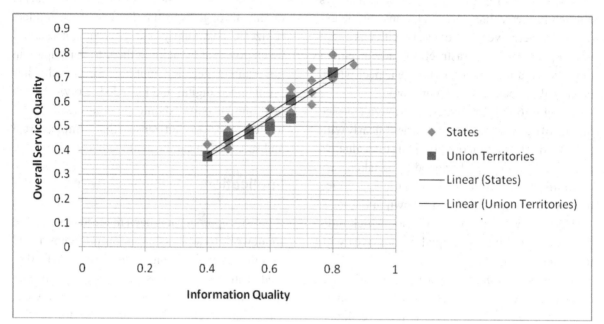

Figure 7. System quality vs. overall service quality

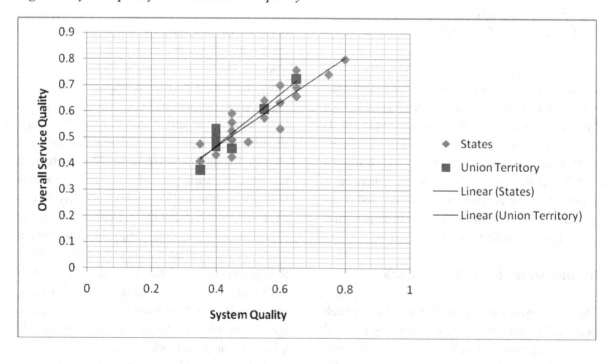

charter has given the guidelines to the web managers and design engineers but that has remained a theoretical suggestion and has not been implemented extensively. No uniformity of approach or design has been maintained in the state portals which call for more problems. Besides, illiteracy, politics, poor training, less exposure to electronic mode and multilingual problem pose a major hindrance in successful usage of e-government portals. This study also identifies the constraints that affect the service quality in different states of India. Thus the framework is expected to provide new aspects and directions for designers and web managers to maintain uniformity in portals hence promising a better service delivery through a 'single-window' approach.

REFERENCES

Afuah, A., & Tucci, C. (2002). *Internet business models and strategies*. New York: McGraw-Hill.

Al-Omari, A., & Al-Omari, H. (2006). E-Government readiness assessment model. *Journal of Computer Science, 2*(11), 841–845. doi:10.3844/jcssp.2006.841.845

Aladwania, A., & Palvia, P. (1999). Developing and validating an instrument for measuring user-perceived web quality. *Information & Management, 39*(6), 467–476. doi:10.1016/S0378-7206(01)00113-6

Baum, C., & De Maio, A. (2000). *Gartner's four phases of e-Government model.*

Belanger, F., & Hiller, J. S. (2006). A framework for e-government: privacy implications. *Business Process Management Journal, 12*(1), 48–60. doi:10.1108/14637150610643751

Blankenship, E. (2001). *Portal design vs. web design*. Retrieved September 24, 2009, from http://www.sapdesignguild.org/editions/edition3/graphic.asp

Chesbrough, H., & Rosenbloom, R. (2002). The role of the business model in capturing value from innovation: Evidence from Xerox Corporation's technology spin-off companies. *Industrial and Corporate Change, 11*(3). doi:10.1093/icc/11.3.529

Davis, F. (1989). Perceived usefulness perceived ease of use and user acceptance of information technology. *Management Information Systems Quarterly, 13*(3), 319–339. doi:10.2307/249008

Davis, J., & Merritt, S. (1998). *The web design wow book: Showcasing the best of on-screen communication*. Berkeley, CA: Peachpit Press.

Denhardt, R. (1999). The future of public administration. *Public Administration and Management, 4*(2), 279–292.

Dwivedi, P., & Sahu, G. (2009). *Challenges of e-government implementation in India. Emerging technologies in e-government*. New Delhi: GIFT Publishing.

Fountain, J. (2001). *Building the virtual state: Information technology and institutional change*. Washington, DC: Brookings Institution Press.

Gil-Garcia, J., & Martinez-Moyano, I. (2007). Understanding the evolution of e-government: The influence of systems of rules on public sector dynamics. *Government Information Quarterly, 24*, 266–290. doi:10.1016/j.giq.2006.04.005

Gil-García, J., & Pardo, T. (2005). E-government success factors: Mapping practical tools to theoretical foundations. *Government Information Quarterly, 22*, 187–216. doi:10.1016/j.giq.2005.02.001

Giudice, M., & Goodman, S. (1999, December). *Where the front and backend meet: Collaboration between designers and engineers*. Paper presented at the CNET Builder.com Live Conference, New Orleans, LA.

Grigoroudis, E., Litos, C., Moustakis, V. A., Politis, Y., & Tsironis, L. (2008). The assessment of user-perceived web quality: Application of a satisfaction benchmarking approach. *European Journal of Operational Research, 187,* 1346–1357. doi:10.1016/j.ejor.2006.09.017

Grose, E., Forsythe, C., & Ratner, J. (1998). Using web and traditional style guides to design web interfaces. In Grose, E., Forsythe, C., & Ratner, J. (Eds.), *Human factors and web development* (pp. 121–131). Mahwah, NJ: Lawrence Erlbaum Associates.

Gupta, M. P., & Jana, D. (2003). E-government evaluation: A framework and case study. *Government Information Quarterly, 20,* 365–387. doi:10.1016/j.giq.2003.08.002

Gupta, M. P., Kumar, P., & Bhattacharya, J. (2004). *Government online.* New Delhi: Tata McGraw-Hill.

Hallowell, R. (2002). Virtuous cycles: Improving service and lowering costs in e-commerce, *Harvard Business School,* Cambridge, MA, Module Teaching Note 5-802-169.

Heeks, R. (2001). Understanding e-governance for development. The University of Manchester, Institute for Development, Policy and Management Information, Systems, Technology and Government: *Working Papers Series, Number 11/2001.* Retrieved June 22, 2009, from http://www.sed.manchester.ac.uk/idpm/research/publications/wp/igovernment/igov_wp11.htm.

Heeks, R., & Bailur, S. (2006). Analyzing e-government research: Perspectives, philosophies, theories, methods, and practice. *Government Information Quarterly, 24,* 243–265. doi:10.1016/j.giq.2006.06.005

Iwaarden, J., van Wiele, T., van der Ball, L., & Millen, R. (2004). Perceptions about the quality of web sites: A survey amongst students at Northeastern University and Erasmus University. *Information & Management, 41*(8), 947–959. doi:10.1016/j.im.2003.10.002

Jaeger, P. T. (2003). The endless wire: E-Government as a global phenomenon. *Government Information Quarterly, 20*(4), 323–331. doi:10.1016/j.giq.2003.08.003

Janssen, M., Kuk, G., & Wagenaar, R. (2008). A survey of web-based business models for e-government in the Netherlands. *Government Information Quarterly, 25,* 202–220. doi:10.1016/j.giq.2007.06.005

Kašubienė, L., & Vanagas, P. (2007). Assumptions of e-government services quality evaluation. *Engineering Economics. 5* (55), *Commerce Of Engineering Decision,* 68-74.

Katre, D. (2006). Usability survey report of Indian state government web portals. *HCI Vistas,* Volume I, Article IRN-8.

Kyoung, J., & Hong, J. H. (2002). Development of an e-government service model: A business model approach. *International Review of Public Administration, 7*(2), 109–118.

Loiacono, E., Watson, R., & Goodhue, D. (2002). WebQual: A measure of website quality. Marketing Educators' Conference. *Marketing Theory and Applications, 13,* 432–437.

Mahadevan, B. (2000). Business models for internet based e-commerce. [Summer.]. *California Management Review, 42*(4), 55–69.

Mitra, R. K., & Gupta, M. P. (2008). A contextual perspective of performance assessment in eGovernment: A study of Indian police administration. *Government Information Quarterly, 25,* 278–302. doi:10.1016/j.giq.2006.03.008

Morgeson, F. III, & Mithas, S. (2009). Does e-government measure up to e-business? Comparing end user perceptions of U.S. federal government and e-business web sites. *Public Administration Review, 69*(4), 740–752. doi:10.1111/j.1540-6210.2009.02021.x

Moustakis, V., Litos, C., Dalivigas, A., & Tsironis, L. (2004). Website assessment criteria. In *Proceedings of International Conference on Information Quality, Boston: MIT*, November 5–7, 59–73.

Nielsen, J. (2002). *Designing web usability: The practice of simplicity.* Indianapolis, USA: New Riders Publishing.

Palmer, J. W. (2002). Web site usability, design, and performance metrics. *Information Systems Research, 13*(2), 151–167. doi:10.1287/isre.13.2.151.88

Ray, D. S., & Dash, S. (2006). A study on e-government readiness of Indian states. In R.K. Mitra (ed.) *E-government: macro issues* (pp. 107-122). New Delhi: GIFT Publishing.

Rayport, J., & Jaworski, B. (2001). *Cases in e-commerece.* New York: McGraw-Hill Professional.

Sarkar, S. (2008). E-government adoption and diffusion. In Sahu, G. P. (Ed.), *Adopting e-governance.* New Delhi: GIFT Publishing.

Timmers, P. (1998). Business models for electronic markets. *Electronic Markets, 8*(2), 3–8. doi:10.1080/10196789800000016

United Nations & American Society for Public Administration. (2002). *Benchmarking e-government: A global perspective.* New York: U.N. Publications.

van Velsen, L., van der Geest, T., ter Hedde, M., & Derks, W. (2009). Requirements engineering for e-Government services: A citizen-centric approach and case study. *Government Information Quarterly, 26*, 477–486. doi:10.1016/j.giq.2009.02.007

Verdegem, P., & Verleye, G. (2009). User-centered e-government in practice: A comprehensive model for measuring user satisfaction. *Government Information Quarterly, 26*, 487–497. doi:10.1016/j.giq.2009.03.005

Virpi, R., & Kaikkonen, A. (2003). Acceptable download times in the mobile internet. In *Proceedings of the 10th International Conference on Human-Computer Interaction,* (pp.1467–1472). Mahwah, NJ: Lawrence Erlbaum Associates.

Vora, P. (1998). Human factors methodology for designing web sites. In Grose, E., Forsythe, C., & Ratner, J. (Eds.), *Human factors and web development* (pp. 189–198). Mahwah, NJ: Lawrence Erlbaum Associates.

Warner, S. (1999). Internet portals, what are they and how to build a niche internet portal to enhance the delivery of information services. In *Proceedings of the 8th Asian-Pacific SHLL Conference.*

Winkler, R. (2001). Portals-The all-in-one web supersites: Features, functions, definition, taxonomy. Retrieved from http://www.sapdesignguild.org/editions/edition3/overview_edition3.asp

Wolf, P., & Krcmar, H. (2005). Process-oriented e-government evaluation. *Wirtschaftsinformatik, 47*(5), 337–346.

Wolfinbarger, M., & Gilly, M. (2002). *comQ: Dimensionalizing, measuring and predicting quality of the e-tailing experience.* MSI Working Paper Series, No. 02-100.

Yang, Z., Cai, S., Zhou, Z., & Zhou, N. (2005). Development and validation of an instrument to measure user perceived service quality of information presenting web portals. *Information & Management, 42*, 575–589. doi:10.1016/S0378-7206(04)00073-4

Yang, Z., & Jun, M. (2002). Consumer perception of e-service quality: from Internet purchaser and non-purchaser perspectives. *The Journal of Business Strategy, 19*(1), 19–41.

Yildiz, M. (2007). E-government research: Reviewing the literature, limitations, and ways forward. *Government Information Quarterly, 24,* 646–665. doi:10.1016/j.giq.2007.01.002

Zeithaml, V. (2002). Guru's view: Service excellence in electronic channels, special on service excellence. *Managing Service Quality, 12*(3), 135–138. doi:10.1108/09604520210429187

Zeithaml, V., & Parasuraman, A. & Malhotra. (2000). *A conceptual framework for understanding e-service quality: Implications for future research and managerial practice.* MSI Monograph, Report # 00-115, 2000.

Zeithaml, V., Parasuraman, A., & Malhotra, A. (2001). *A conceptual framework for understanding e-service quality: Implications for future research and managerial practice.* MSI Working Paper Series, No. 00-115, Cambridge, MA.

Zeithaml, V., Parasuraman, A., & Malhotra, A. (2002). Service quality delivery through web sites: A critical review of extant knowledge. *Journal of the Academy of Marketing Science, 30*(4), 362–375. doi:10.1177/009207002236911

KEY TERMS AND DEFINITIONS

Government Portals: They are web portals used by various government departments to ensure easy access for citizens to available government services. E-government uses this one-stop citizen centric approach to enhance transparency, effectiveness and efficiency in government activities.

States: A State in India refer to federated state forming a part of federal union of India. There are 28 such states in India. Each state holds administrative jurisdiction over a defined geographic boundary. Each state has its own legislative body and thus forms a regional government.

Union Territories: A Union Territory is a sub-national entity in federal union of India. Unlike the states of India, union territories do not have their own elected governments and are ruled directly by the federal government; the President of India appoints an Administrator or Lieutenant-Governor for each territory. There are 7 union territories in India.

Service Quality: Quality of service rendered by e-government portals to citizens in India in terms of usefulness of information and functionability of the portals.

E-Readiness: E-readiness implies the acceptability status of Information and Communication Technologies in a territory/state /country. It is generally measured by the infrastructural preparedness and usage of the technology.

E-Government Readiness: E-government readiness denotes the actual usage of e-government projects in a state/country by its citizens.

APPENDIX 1. STATES IN INDIA

SN	Name of States	Name of State Portals
1	Andhra Pradesh	www.aponline.gov.in
2	Arunachal Pradesh	www.arunachalpradesh.nic.in
3	Assam	www.assamgovt.nic.in
4	Bihar	http://gov.bih.nic.in
5	Chhattisgarh	www.chhattisgarh.nic.in
6	Goa	http://goagovt.nic.in *no search, important email*
7	Gujarat	www.gujaratindia.com
8	Haryana	http://haryana.gov.in
9	Himachal	www.himachal.nic.in
10	Jammu and Kashmir	http://jammukashmir.nic.in
11	Jharkhand	www.jharkhand.nic.in
12	Karnataka	www.karunadu.gov.in
13	Kerala	www.kerala.gov.in
14	Madhya Pradesh	www.mp.gov.in
15	Maharashtra	www.maharashtra.gov.in
16	Manipur	http://manipur.nic.in
17	Meghalaya	http://meghalaya.nic.in
18	Mizoram	http://mizoram.nic.in
19	Nagaland	http://nagaland.nic.in
20	Orissa	http://orissagov.nic.in
21	Punjab	http://punjabgovt.nic.in
22	Rajasthan	http://www.rajasthan.gov.in
23	Sikkim	http://sikkim.gov.in
24	Tamil Nadu	http://www.tn.gov.in
25	Tripura	http://tripura.nic.in
26	Uttaranchal	http://www.ua.nic.in
27	Uttar Pradesh	http://upgov.nic.in
28	West Bengal	http://www.wbgov.com

APPENDIX 2. UNION TERRITORIES IN INDIA

SN	Name of Union Territories	Name of Union Territory Portals
1	Andaman and Nicobar Islands	http://www.and.nic.in
2	Chandigarh	http://chandigarh.gov.in
3	Dadra and Nagar Haveli	http://dnh.nic.in
4	Daman & Diu	http://daman.nic.in
5	Delhi	http://delhigovt.nic.in
6	Lakshadweep	http://lakshadweep.nic.in
7	Puducherry	http://pondicherry.nic.in

APPENDIX 3. EVALUATION CRITERIA FOR THE PORTALS

Objective	Attribute	Element
Information Quality	Usefulness	Necessary information of the state
		Updated news in education, politics, employment etc
		Consistent data throughout the portal
		Highlights of new projects which are on pipeline
	Adequate Information	Search can be customized within and outside portal
		Links between India portal and State portal
		Information provided is complete in all respect/detailed daily news of state
		Well defined link to major e-government projects of the state
		Well defined link to different departments in a state
	Citizen centric information	Multilingual language option
		24/7 availability of service (if any)
		Cost effective transaction rate
		Online help/Citizen Charter/Training option
System Quality	Usability	Browser compatibility
		Sitemap availability
		Search facility
		Navigation allowed with proper prev and next option
		Indication of active link
		Usage of separate browser window whenever navigating to external link
		Drop down menu
		Standard web design with proper tables/frames /font size/animation
	Accessibility/Citizen Participation	User wise categorization of information
		Link to Home, contact and feedback provided
		Email facility, online chatting/other discussion forum
		Log on facility
		High speed download
		Facility for illiterate/handicapped/adult citizen
		Consideration of low bandwidth
	Privacy/security	Privacy of information provided
		Secured transaction facility
	Interaction	Message Board/Option for taking citizen input
		Follow up with queries of citizens/citizen to citizen interaction
		Online contact with web master
		Web directory

APPENDIX 4. RANKING OF STATES AND UNION TERRITORIES (ADAPTED FROM INDIAINDIA: E-READINESS ASSESSMENT REPORT 2006 FOR STATES/UNION TERRITORIES, A REPORT BY DEPARTMENT OF INFORMATION TECHNOLOGY)

Leaders		Aspiring Leaders	Expec-tants	Average Achievers		Below Average Achievers		Least Achievers	
Delhi	Haryana	Maha-rash-tra	Rajas-than	Pudu-cher-ry	Mizo-ram	Anda-man and Nico-bar Island	Assam	Daman and Diu	Bihar
Chandi-garh	Karna-taka	Gujarat	West Ben-gal		Orissa	Laksha-dweep	Naga-land	Dadra and Nagar Haveli	Tripura
	Punjab	Uttar Pradesh	Hima-chal Pradesh		Madhya Pradesh				Manipur
	Andhra Pradesh	Goa	Chhattis-garh		Sikkim				Jammu and Kashmir
	Kerala		Jhar-khand		Megha-laya				Arunachal Pradesh
	Tamil Nadu				Uttara-khand				

APPENDIX 5. VALUES CALCULATED FOR EACH CONSTRUCT BASED ON ITEMS MENTIONED IN APPENDIX 3

Name of States and Union Territories	Total of Information quality in %	Total of System Quality in %	e-readiness*	Overall service quality
Andhra Pradesh	0.8	0.8	1.01	0.8
Arunachal Pradesh	0.6	0.45	-0.6	0.525
Assam	0.6	0.35	-0.6	0.475
Bihar	0.6	0.45	-0.6	0.525
Chhattisgarh	0.86667	0.65	0.3	0.758333
Goa	0.53333	0.45	0.8	0.491667
Gujarat	0.73333	0.75	0.8	0.741667
Haryana	0.66667	0.65	1.01	0.658333
Himachal	0.66667	0.65	0.3	0.658333
Jammu and Kashmir	0.4	0.35	-0.6	0.375
Jharkhand	0.4	0.45	0.3	0.425
Karnataka	0.66667	0.45	1.01	0.558333
Kerala	0.73333	0.65	1.01	0.691667
Madhya Pradesh	0.46667	0.6	-0.3	0.533333
Maharashtra	0.73333	0.55	0.8	0.641667
Manipur	0.46667	0.5	-0.6	0.483333
Meghalaya	0.6	0.55	-0.3	0.575

Name of States and Union Territories	Total of Information quality in %	Total of System Quality in %	e-readiness*	Overall service quality
Mizoram	0.46667	0.35	-0.3	0.408333
Nagaland	0.46667	0.35	-0.6	0.408333
Orissa	0.66667	0.6	-0.3	0.633333
Punjab	0.53333	0.45	1.01	0.491667
Rajasthan	0.8	0.6	0.3	0.7
Sikkim	0.46667	0.4	-0.3	0.433333
Tamil Nadu	0.66667	0.55	1.01	0.608333
Tripura	0.66667	0.45	-0.6	0.558333
Uttarakhand	0.53333	0.45	-0.3	0.491667
Uttar Pradesh	0.73333	0.45	0.8	0.591667
West Bengal	0.66667	0.65	0.3	0.658333
Andaman and Nicobar Islands	0.66667	0.4	-0.6	0.533333
Chandigarh	0.66667	0.55	1.01	0.608333
Dadra and Nagar Haveli	0.6	0.4	-0.6	0.5
Daman & Diu	0.46667	0.45	-0.6	0.458333
Delhi	0.8	0.65	1.01	0.725
Lakshadweep	0.4	0.35	-0.6	0.375
Puducherry	0.53333	0.4	-0.3	0.466667

1 e-readiness value calculated based on India: e-Readiness Assessment Report 2006 by Department of Information Technology, Chapter 4,(pp 48).

Chapter 10
E–Government Gateway Development in Turkey:
Some Challenges and Future Directions for Citizen Focus

Asım Balcı
Selçuk University, Turkey

Tunç Durmuş Medeni
METU, Turkey

ABSTRACT

This chapter aims to elaborate on the development of the E-Government Gateway (EGG) in Turkey, and the underlying issues of citizen-oriented e-Government. First, background information on the academic perspective of citizen-oriented e-Government development is provided. Then the historical development and current status of e-Government in Turkey, as well as detailed information about EGG are shared, offering a country-specific and practical perspective to the literature. Future direction of EGG and e-Government development in Turkey that emphasizes the citizen perspective is also elaborated. It is hoped that the good practices, lessons-learned, suggestions and prospects regarding this EGG case will shed light on previous experience and pave the way for further progress for citizen-oriented e-Government development not only in Turkey but also in other nations.

INTRODUCTION

Masterminding a single website, which can be referred to with various names such as One-Stop-Shops, Gateways, Portals, with its front and back office operations for the provision of government services to citizens' and other stakeholders who use information and communication technologies (ICT) is a recent trend and focus in e-Government practice and academic research. As a part of this trend, Turkey has initiated its own project to establish an E-Government Gateway (EGG).

In this chapter, the main aim is to elaborate on the development of EGG in Turkey by describing some challenges that have been experienced, lessons learned from the past, and in addition enumerating some current prospects and suggestions for the future. Taking into account some basic characteristics and shortcomings of the Turkish

DOI: 10.4018/978-1-61692-018-0.ch010

public administration system, the chapter will make an evaluation of EGG. A specific focus of the chapter will be on the public sector supply of e-Government services and citizen demand for current e-services provided by the EGG. It is hoped that the good practices, lessons-learned, suggestions and prospects regarding this EGG case will shed light on previous experience and pave the way for further progress for citizen-oriented e-Government development not only in Turkey but also in other nations.

BACKGROUND

Academic Perspective on Citizen-Oriented E-Government Development

According to Arif (2008), "e-Government applications need to be citizen-oriented for the government agencies and the end users". This orientation could mean "an effective mechanism in order to ensure that development processes incorporate customer needs, an emphasis on usability, the incorporation of accessibility, the effective use of cultural markers", each of which, according to Arif, could require separate research.

Since the idea of providing citizen-oriented e-Government services has become a common issue among researchers and practitioners, a variety of approaches has been proposed to put it in place. One of the recent concepts on this issue is finding a mechanism or method to measure the degree of citizen satisfaction levels with e-Government services. This is vital to putting citizens' need and preferences first instead of those of the bureaucracy (Bekkers and Zouridis, 1999).

Another significant concept in this area is e-inclusion programs. In order to ascertain that all parts of the society enjoy the benefits of e-Government applications, certain public policy steps need to be in place. For instance, underdeveloped regions of countries, the elderly or the handicapped, and

those with low incomes should be kept in mind, when bringing public services online. The needs and expectations of these groups should be taken into account. Specific awareness and promotion campaigns focused on these groups should be conducted in order to insure that no citizen is left behind. The European Union (EU) has made its commitment to the e-inclusion concept on the basis of six sub-categories of issues as follows (European Commission, n.d.):

1. e-Accessibility
2. Age Inclusiveness
3. e-Competences
4. Socio-Cultural e-Inclusion
5. Geographical e-Inclusion
6. Inclusive e-Government

Taking a citizen-centred approach in e-Government applications is also on the agenda of the EU. The provision of high quality public services is one of the keystones of the i2010 program for achieving a European Information Society. Public services play an important role in the route to an inclusive European society. According to a recent report, "The e-Government policy environment has evolved from 'bringing public services online' to a concept of effective and user-centric service delivery in an inclusive and competitive European society". Based on this idea, the i2010 e-Government Action Plan emphasizes five priorities (Capgemini, 2007):

1. No citizen left behind
2. Making efficiency and effectiveness a reality
3. Implementing high-impact key services for citizens and businesses
4. Putting key enablers in place
5. Strengthening participation and democratic decision-making

With the advent of ICTs and e-Government applications, a kind of "buffer" (Arif, 2008) is created between the agency and the citizen. This buffer is the web or mobile interface that is used by the citizen when receiving public services.

To shed light on the development and acceptance of e-Government services works categorized as maturity models and technology adoption models are briefly discussed below in terms of their relation to citizen orientation:

1. **Maturity models:** In order to explain e-Government development, many works have tried to understand the e-Government phenomenon from an evolutionary point of view, and applied a staged approach by dividing the e-Government development process of progressive steps in a continuous process,[1] where the development starts from the 'immature' and moves to the 'mature'[2]. However, there has been no consensus among these different perspectives on the requirements for moving from one stage to another stage. Moreover, generally, these government-oriented models do not specifically address the citizen's perspective in terms of e-Participation in government policy making processes (C.E.E.S. 2009). There are also various software maturity models such as the Prince 2, ITIL, CMMI, among others, that can be applied to e-Government projects (Prince2, n.d.; ITIL, n.d.; Carnegie Mellon University, n.d.). However, these core software engineering models are generally based on code maturity and may not reflect the actual development and management of the e-Government projects. In conclusion, generally the service provision and supply of services by government is represented more than service demand and use by citizens in these maturity models – rather than citizen-oriented, they are government-oriented.

2. **Service adoption Models:** Other works focus on the adoption of services such as the technology acceptance model (TAM) developed by Davis (1989) and diffusion of in-novation (DOI) developed by Rogers (1995). "By adopting an innovation, an organization tries to show its legitimacy in order to achieve conformity with (changing) patterns of meaning in its environment" (Korteland & Bekkers, 2008, p. 74). The way in which organizations embrace various functional, political and institutional meanings influences the way in which an organization is perceived as legitimate. Such perspectives can explain how new developments in e-Government services spread into public institutions and act as not only demanders but also suppliers of e-Government services in various ways. In addition to addressing government supply side, such adoption models can then provide an understanding of the demands of users. Tassabehji and Elliman (2006), provide a summary of studies on the adoption of e-Government services from the perspective of not only government but also citizens. One major problem in most of these studies is the theoretical inconsistencies. For instance, they do not use common definitions – in certain studies, two different constructs can have too similar meanings, which creates problems in summarizing their overall impact (Kanat and Ozkan 2009). Moreover, the lack of a clear classification and thorough analysis of the motivation and needs of users remains as a gap to be filled. Thus, while service adoption perspectives can address user/citizen-orientation, there are limitations.

To sum up, there are different perspectives on e-Government studies and they underline varying issues on e-Government development and citizen orientation. For the purposes of this study, perspectives that can reflect the citizen demand more are considered further. For instance, as Carter & Belanger (2005) discuss; according to Davis' (1989) TAM, subjective constructs and assessments of users such as perceived usefulness

(PU) and perceived ease of use (PEOU) influence and determine the use of technology, because the easier a system is to use, the more useful it can be. Technology adoption will be more difficult, if users do not perceive a system as useful and easy to use. Also, according to Rogers' (1995) Diffusion of Innovation (DOI), user adoption of new technologies is influenced by certain characteristics of a new technology such as complexity (which is comparable to TAM's perceived ease of use construct), relative advantage (how it is superior to its predecessor), and compatibility, among others. Carter & Belanger (2005) also emphasize that citizens' perceptions of trustworthiness issues such as security and privacy (trust of Internet and of government) can also influence the use of e-Government services.

Tassabehji and Elliman (2006) point out that as a complex concept, trust attracts much attention from various disciplines. Pre-interactional factors regarding individual citizen behavioural attributes, institutional attributes, and interactional factors regarding service, transactional delivery and fulfilment of services, and information content attributes have a consistent impact on the building of trust. Furthermore, trust building can be linked with perceived security rather than security itself, recalling the importance of citizens' perceptions to the adoption of e-Government services as, for instance, in the TAM model. As Tassabehji and Elliman (2006, p.6) suggest, the perception of the security that is implemented within e-Government "needs to be disseminated to its citizenry (organizations as well as individuals)." Furthermore, a process trust model is based upon "trustors assimilating information, including perception of the trustee's situation; then processing the information to form a belief regarding trustworthiness of the trustee." (p. 3) "If the trustee is found to be trustworthy, then a relationship is entered into." (p.4)

Tassabehji and Elliman (2006, p.5), on the other hand, point out that individual concerns regarding "lack of trust and confidence in services provided electronically found to be a significant

barrier to the development" of e-Government. Gil-Garcia & Pardo (2005), in addition, provide a comprehensive review of barriers or challenges to the development of e-Government (Figure 1).

These challenges apply to the case in Turkey as well. Historical development and the current condition of e-Government and EGG in Turkey are discussed in the next sections.

TURKISH CASE OF E-GOVERNMENT GATEWAY DEVELOPMENT

Historical Development and Current Condition of E-Government in Turkey

E-Government initiatives in Turkey began in 1998 with the "Kamunet" project that was aimed at establishing a national information system. Soon after this in the framework or the "e-Europe plus" project Turkey prepared its own action plan named the e-Türkiye initiative in 2001. In 2006 the Information Society Strategy document published by the State Planning Organization (Devlet Planlanma Teşkilatı, DPT) continued the development of e-Government services for transforming Turkey into an information society. (DPT, 2006)

According to the Information Society Strategy in Turkey (DPT, 2006), in 2011, 70% of all the e-Government services will be ready. In the 2008 Progress Report by DPT (2008), nevertheless, it is noted that among the 111 actions defined in the strategy document, only 3 are concluded, 51 are works-in-progress, 34 are in their infancy, and 23 are yet to start. In the report, DPT (2008) highlights the idea that the priorities and objectives of the Strategy still need to be appreciated and owned by all stakeholders, and other responsible and interested entities in the society. Problems experienced in the implementation of the strategy are described in the report under the headings of Legislation (and Legal) Issues, Financial Issues, Personnel (and Human Resources) Issues, Issues of Intra- Institutional Coordination, Issues of

Figure 1. Challenges to e-government success (adapted from Gil-Garcia & Pardo, 2005)

Challenge Category	Challenge
Information and data	Information and data quality
	Dynamic information needs
Information technology	Usability
	Security issues
	Technological incompatibility
	Technology complexity
	Technical skills and experience
	Technology newness
Organizational and managerial	Project size
	Manager's attitudes and behavior
	Users or organizational diversity
	Lack of alignment of organizational goals and project
	Multiple or conflicting goals
	Resistance to change
	Turf and conflicts
Legal and regulatory	Restrictive laws and regulations
	One year budgets
	Intergovernmental relationships
Institutional and environmental	Privacy concerns
	Autonomy of agencies
	Policy and political pressures
	Environmental context (social, economic, demographic)

Inter-Institutional Coordination, and Other Issues (DPT 2008).

According to our analysis of the overall Information Society Strategy Progress Report (DPT 2008), Legislation Issues and Issues of Inter-Institutional Coordination are evaluated to have the highest (negative) impact (21%), followed by Personnel Issues (19%), Financial Issues (16%), Issues of Intra-Institutional Coordination (13%) and Other Issues (%10), which also include coordination issues, in the implementation of the Strategy. Similarly for the implementation of the individual action points/projects to pave the way for reaching Information Society within the overall strategy; Legislation Issues and Issues of Inter-Institutional Coordination are highlighted the most (19%) followed by Personnel and Financial Issues (18%), Issues of Intra-Institutional Coordination (17%) and Other Issues (9%) (Figure 2).

This analysis suggests the necessity of cross-cultural interaction among various societal entities for the integration and interoperability of e-Government services in Turkey. The European Interoperability Framework identifies three aspects of interoperability: Organizational, Semantic and Technical (European Commission, 2004). Within this framework, in order to make collaboration possible one of the basic requirements is to identify common norms and standards and develop information systems and integrated e-Government services with respect to these norms and standards. Another important issue is enabling coordination and collaboration within and among public institutions[3].

Figure 2. The problems experienced in the implementation of information society strategy

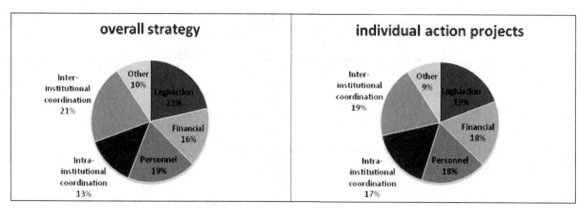

Nevertheless, according to the Organization for Economic Co-Operation and Development (OECD) report, "Turkey is making strong progress in implementing e-Government", having achieved "quick wins in the e-Government arena by prioritizing projects that make government more efficient, effective, transparent and accountable" (OECD, 2006, p. 9). Various studies confirm that in general, Turkey is at an advanced and sophisticated level with respect to e-services for businesses (Capgemini, 2007), which brings increased revenues to the state (Çayhan, 2008), and provides more Transactional and Connected services (United Nations, 2008). Services for citizens, however, are less advanced and open to development and improvement.

Currently, available e-Government applications in Turkey include passport and license application, tax return, education and banking. The work of Kutlu and Sevgi (2007) and OECD (2006) provide further information about the e-Government projects in Turkey. In terms of efficiency and effectiveness gains, ICT projects in public administration seem to be successful. In some cases despite increases in workload, costs declined after ICT applications. Consequently, the evidence shows that IT reforms have been increasing financial, administrative and technical capacities. (Kutlu & Sevgi, 2007) Moreover, while some services are effectively provided, integration and personalization are still issues.

The EU (2009) also assesses e-Government services for citizens in Turkey (Figure 3) using a stages framework on a 0-5 scale, where appropriate. Highly sophisticated services for citizens are limited, and among the services that are in the process of development, the low sophistication levels for car registration, application for building permission, certificates of birth and marriage, and health services are especially note-worthy. These assessments underline the fact that services for citizens need to be developed in Turkey.

When central and municipal governments are asked how they find out about the demand for online services counting web site hits is considered to be the most frequent way of judging demand by both levels of government. Government responses also indicate that Internet access and computer literacy are important factors that affect demand for e-services (OECD 2006). While such surveys provide valuable information about the supply side, similar information regarding citizen demand and the ordinary citizens' perspective is somewhat problematic. Government institutions confirm this fact by acknowledging that only about 30% of responding organizations use customer surveys, which is too low to assure that e-services reflect citizen demand and priorities, in other words, they are not citizen-oriented (ibid.).

Figure 3. The sophistication level of e-government services for citizens in Turkey

eGovernment Factsheet - Turkey - eServices for Citizens		
1. Income taxes: declaration, notification of assessment	: 5/5	Description: Information on all types of tax for which declaration is needed and forms which can be submitted electronically. The e-Declaration application provides acceptance of declarations; announcements and appendixes via the Internet. Integration and data exchange with external systems such as banks is also provided. The Internet Tax Office of the Revenue Administration enables taxpayers to follow their tax transactions such as accrual tax, payments-in, etc. These applications are parts of the Tax Offices Automation Project (VEDOP).
2. Job search services by labour offices	: 4/4	Description: Online job search is available.
3. Social security benefits — a. Unemployment benefits	: 3-4/5	Description: Online information about unemployment insurance but no online transactions.
b. Child allowances	: 3-4/5	Description: Information only.
c. Medical costs	: 3-4/5	Description: Online information about health insurance and application forms are available but no online transactions. However, pharmacy automation system allows on-line transactions between pharmacies and Social Security Institution.
d. Student grants	: 3-4/5	Description: Information on results for scholarship and credit applications and debt information can be reached online and application forms can be downloaded, online application facilities are available.
4. Personal documents: passport and driver's licence — a. Passport	: 2-3/4	Description: Information and online application facilities are available for 38 out of 81 provinces.
b. Driver's licence	: 2-3/4	provinces.
5. Car registration (new, used, imported cars)	1-2/4	Description: Information and online application facilities are available in Ankara. Service has not yet available in other provinces.
6. Application for building permission	: 0-1/4	Description: Some of the municipalities provide information.
7. Declaration to the police (e.g. in case of theft)	: 3/3	Description: Online declaration available. The POLNET system is a comprehensive store of information, providing a secure on-line aid to criminal investigation. The system enables police officers in the field to access national information via a police network. It also contributes to the detection of vehicle theft offenders through the Vehicles Database, and of criminals through the Criminal Records Database. It also houses important data about Terrorists and Organised Crime Groups.
8. Public libraries (availability of catalogues, search tools)	: 4/5	Description: Online catalogue search and book reservation available for a number of Turkish libraries including the National Library and most university libraries. National Library offers electronic reservation service.
9. Certificates (birth and marriage): request and delivery	: 1/4	Description: Provides information on the necessary procedures to obtain a birth or marriage certificate but will soon be able to provide more advanced services through the MERNIS system.
10. Enrolment in higher education/university	: 3/4	Description: University registration is not possible but course registration is provided in some universities.
11. Announcement of moving (change of address)	: 1/4	Description: Addresses can be checked online, but no online registration facility yet.
12. Health related services (interactive advice; appointments for hospitals)	: 0-1/4	Description: Online information is provided by hospitals through their websites. Furthermore, online appointments are available at certain hospitals. Besides, the Ministry of Health is working on an one-stop-shop mechanism for online appointments.

EGG

The EGG Project in Turkey ("e-Devlet Kapısı" or "e-Kapı") was officially launched in December 2008 and signifies a reference point for citizen-oriented service-transformation. The EGG Project is a major milestone for achieving the Information Society Strategic Goals set by Turkey, aiming to provide Turkey's 70 million citizens and business entities with a single point of access, one-stop-shop, to e-Government services. Here, e-Government basically means provision of public services through electronic means, which implies faster and cheaper access to these services.

The most effective utilization of ICT requires that the work flow of public services be redesigned to reflect the "central importance of citizens" perspectives. The EGG project in Turkey provides citizen access to public services at one single point, while also setting up the infrastructure for data-sharing and communication among public institutions. EGG is then prepared to provide state services to citizens in a way that is linked to work flows; giving priority to user needs on a 24/7 bases, uninterrupted, secure, accessible from multiple modes and integrated via a one-point portal. This portal is built for citizens reaching all electronic government services from one point by one identity confirmation using their national identity numbers.

By the completion of this project, a conceptual integrity called "integration standards" will also be ensured where security standards and data-sharing among public institutions at the international level is provided under one roof. These integration standards then contribute to the establishment of an interoperability framework according to which different systems, organizations, and services will work in a seamless and coherent way across the public sector.

The implementation process of EGG is based on service transformation. The main principle will be the consideration of user satisfaction issues when re-designing the business processes of public institutions and services delivered to citizens and enterprises. The priority in services transformation will not be merely to transfer available business processes to electronic channels without making any improvements; on the contrary, the aim will be to deliver these electronic government services, as processes which are redesigned according to user needs for integration or simplification when necessary, in an effective, uninterrupted, fast, transparent, reliable way.

Another important aspect of the EGG is related to content management. Content management is the creation, collection, management, maintenance, publication and use of data, information and knowledge in the forms of text, image or sound on web sites. Here content can be understood as information tagged with data, and used as knowledge (Balci, Kumaş, Medeni, Medeni, 2009). During the early development phase, even though initial content of the gateway has been gathered from public institutions over a long period, new content that citizens seek in the gateway, and updating the whole content to make it more citizen-oriented will take priority. If the citizens are not able to find what they seek in the gateway, they are more likely not to use the gateway in the future. For content management, a new tailored content management system (CMS) has been developed by outsourcing to a national company (Penguen-Turk). In the long-run, an in-house system under development can be expected to take-over the content management (in addition to inventory and document management) in public agencies. In the current CMS, content categorization is designed with respect to public services, rather than public institutions. Related contents from different institutions are combined into categories on the basis of life events. The content is categorized under headings from birth to death, so that citizens can easily find specific information and access public

services. In some cases, the same content has been placed under different headings to make it easier for citizens to find necessary information, since different citizens can search the same content from different places and headings. For example, "getting a birth certificate" can be found under the "birth" heading or "citizenship", it may also be found under the "health" heading which would be obtained from the Population and Citizenship Affairs Agency or Ministry of Health respectively. The search function also supports easy-access to any requested information within this content categorization. With the open publication of the EGG content user tests are being conducted for continuous improvement. In addition to the CMS as a part of EGG, a guidebook is published to support all public institutions in the development and standardization of their websites (Web Sites of Public Agencies, Kamu Kurumları Internet Siteleri (KAKIS) document, Türksat, 2009).

There is also significant work-in-progress with respect to measuring citizen satisfaction with the "Citizen Satisfaction Index." Collaboration between Türksat and Kahramanmaraş Sütçü İmam Üniversitesi has been initiated in order to develop a methodology for measuring citizen satisfaction from e-Government services. Based upon the existing literature, a draft model using variables such as trust, website quality and citizen services will be proposed. A multi-equation cause-and-effect model and Structural Equation Modeling will be used for data analysis of the relationships among the variables. Regarding the Structural Equation Modeling, "Path Analysis with Observed/Latent Variables", and "Confirmatory Factor Analysis" will be applied to the specific Turkish case, for developing indices at three different levels (e-service, e-institution, e-Government) as suggested by Bakan, Aydın, Kar, and Öz (2008, 2009). The initial results will be available at the end of 2009. In addition to this national project, an international project for citizen-oriented evaluation of e-Government services has been developed in collaboration with Brunel University, UK and

American University of Beirut, Lebanon (2008). The project will use the Data Envelope Analysis (DEA) framework, a reference process model that will allow the application of findings to Turkey as well as to other EU countries. (Lee et al., 2009)

A series of conferences and workshops at the national and international level complement this work. For instance, the National e-Government Conference was held in November 2008 in Ankara before the official launch of EGG in December 2008.[4] The conference presentations are published online and participants were contacted to give feedback and improvement suggestions on conference organization and e-Government services. Activities to get citizen feedback and improvement suggestions by participants follow:

- The establishment of ICT units within government organizations in the areas outside the big cities.
- Acknowledgement and raising awareness/consciousness of citizens, staff and managers of public institutions about e-Government applications, for instance with regard to how using the services could promote trustworthiness and provide an easier to use interface.
- Improving the effectiveness of communication across institutions by using workgroups, shared databases, seminars for the exchange of technical experience and information.
- Publicizing by (TV) advertisements, kiosks or other publicity points.
- Increasing the number of conferences where experts and representatives from different areas and segments of society can exchange ideas.

For further information, see Hezer, Medeni, and Dalbay (2009). With the official launch of EGG, a series of "International Conferences on e-Government and e-Governance (ICEGEG)", the first of which was held in March 2009 in Ankara,

have also been initiated[5]. In addition to the academic works that were published and delivered to the participants as conference proceedings, special open sessions on e-Government best practices in Turkey were held.

The CMS, national and international projects on measuring service quality and citizen satisfaction as well as national and international conferences to provide channels for sharing experiences and disseminating knowledge, have been developed, in part, as a result of the effort of Türksat's Corporate Communications department. This department was established under the responsibility and mediatory role of Türksat to enable the involvement of various stakeholders including academia, public agencies, and NGOs that represent and educate citizens. The department's role is to facilitate the necessary corporate communications for coming closer to the fulfillment of the "putting citizens first" philosophy underlying EGG in Turkey.

Such e-Government initiatives as CMS development, the development and measurement of citizen satisfaction, and the organization of national and international conferences are important for learning from Turkey's experience with EGG. At the same time these developments should be supported with other initiatives. There are major challenges such as resistance from public institutions and the digital divide. While CMS, the measurement of citizen preferences and the exchange of ideas at the national and international level seem to be progressing, managerial, organizational and legal issues lag behind and tend to retard the progress of EGG in Turkey. Until the official launch of EGG, a major concern among the developers of the EGG Türksat team, to whom the authors belong, has been to receive support from the public institutions and government agencies as the suppliers of public knowledge and services. With the official launch of EGG, especially with the addition and development of new services, more attention is paid to the citizen's demands, none-the-less the resistance of public institutions is an important concern.

As for the digital divide issue, the Ministry of Transport and Communication has been establishing public internet access points throughout the country. Also, ICT classrooms have been equipped in almost all primary and secondary schools in Turkey, financed by the universal service fund.[6] As an affiliated organization of the Ministry of Transport and Communication, Türksat has devised satellite-based internet connection to more than 5,000 schools in geographically remote areas in the country where other means of communication are unavailable[7].

Currently, Branch of IT Technologies (BITT) in Türksat is responsible for the establishment and operation of the EGG project in Turkey, while the Corporate Communication Department (CCD) supports content management. In general, the EGG provides the communication between different government institutional systems for various services. These government institutions, among which communication is provided, retain and own the data part of the system, while EGG system retains logs regarding system usage. The technical infrastructure of EGG is developed and maintained by technical units on the Türksat campus, which is located on outskirts of Ankara. Unless the issue is too technical, the corporate communications including user queries, some of which was recently outsourced, are handled by CCD the communications department located close to the capital, Ankara, city center.

With the official launch of the EGG, most of the queries were about identity authentication and control. There were also queries about the system usage, the process and contents, or requests for other forms of specific information. Some queries were irrelevant to EGG, but related to other government agencies and these were forwarded to the relevant public institutions. Interestingly, it was common for citizens to presume that the e-Government Gateway was the government per se. For instance, there were citizen queries written to the Prime Minister, requesting support for

personal issues. Some citizen queries were related with providing financial support, or finding suitable training or position for personal interest or professional employment.

There are currently more than 140 e-services integrated into EGG and new services are under development (See Appendix). Besides these services, EGG provides links to hundreds of electronic services provided by individual agencies from their own websites. Currently EGG services do not "take over" agency web site services, however it provides a trustworthy, user-friendly choice with a single sign-up mechanism to securely access all services in one place. Identity management using personal password and e-signature are integrated into the system, and limited financial transactions and higher levels of personalization are planned for the near future.

Issues of security, the management of sign-up mechanisms, back office management, handling of user problems, addressing back-up can be solved more easily and adequately in a unified way by the EGG. Nevertheless, as far as the authors, who are involved with the EGG development, are concerned, there are still public institutions that are not convinced of the benefits of the EGG to provide electronic services. One of their arguments is loss of strategic managerial power and operational control over the service. Another one is related to the additional burden, to them, by this development. Understanding which services have and will be developed and integrated will help to clarify the future direction of e-Government development in Turkey. This understanding can also provide some useful suggestions for similar projects in other countries.

FUTURE DIRECTION OF EGG AND E-GOVERNMENT DEVELOPMENT IN TURKEY

Uçkan (2009) comments that in Turkey e-Government is led by a specific community of e-Government technicians, who know the standards of this business and have fought for development based on these standards for the last 15 to 20 years. During this period there seems to have been no strong citizen demand for e-Government. Moreover, Alican (2007), and Gökmen (2009) criticize the Information Society Strategy of Turkey for having a weak social content. Specifically these authors argue that the development of Turkey's e-Government capabilities ignores underdeveloped regions and that it does not consider that more than 10% of the population is illiterate, or lack the necessary ICT capabilities. Thus, low citizen demand and a persistent digital divide remain issues that hinder e-Government development in Turkey[8]. As recently identified by research conducted by Saruç (2009), a lack of trust is another important handicap to the development of e-Government services. Fifty two percent of 650 research respondents indicate that they do not trust making payments to government offices over the Internet.

Development of new services and improvement of existing services may be an area where citizen demand and government/state supply meet. Government agencies tend to believe that Internet access and computer literacy are important factors that affect the demand for e-services. The lack of customer access to the Internet and lack of awareness of online service availability are viewed as constraints affecting the demand and web hit counts which are the most frequent way of judging demand (OECD, 2006). While information about the demand and supply side are available, information regarding the ordinary citizen's perspective on e-Government services is not available as such. Government institutions confirm this fact by acknowledging that only about 30% of responding organizations use customer surveys. This is considered to be too low to properly assess citizen demand and priorities for e-Government services (OECD, 2006).

TÜİK (2008) provides some statistics that reflect citizen priorities. In this study 40% of the respondents indicated that they use the Internet to interact with public authorities. The major types of interaction with public authorities is for obtaining information from public authorities' web sites (38%), downloading official forms/documents (11%), and sending in forms (6%).

Citizen perspectives and perceptions of e-Government services are also being studied by Türksat[9]. As a descriptive preliminary study; mainly qualitative, open-ended questions have been asked to the local youth councils' representatives of the National Youth Parliament in Turkey. This was done following a training seminar on e-Government and e-inclusion for 150 participants organized within the framework of the Youth and e-Inclusion Summit in December 2008. Thirty responses were received by e-mail from across most of the country. Responses included opinions and demands from many of the less-developed areas that also suffer from digital divide issues. The findings tend to confirm the importance of factors such as education and publicity for the adoption of e-Government services by the citizens, as about 40% of the responses included remarks on education and publicity.[10] Other issues found in the literature, as discussed above, such as factors of relative advantage, perceived usefulness and ease of use and trustworthiness are also confirmed by respondent comments. For instance, perceived ease of use for the services and content is a common comment (about 25%).

While there are some positive but shallow remarks about the perceived usefulness of the system, with respect to the issue of relative advantage, certain comments from the respondents provide some insights into possible barriers to the widespread use of e-Government services. Currently the EGG system requires citizens to go to the post offices to get their passwords, if they want to access specific services. In this regard one respondent made the following observation: "Why do I now have to bother myself with going to the Post Office to get a password for things that I can already do easily?" For this respondent, the system should enable citizens to receive services online such as getting a passport or tax number without stopping by the government agencies that are normally responsible for delivering such services. "I don't want to have to go to the government agencies in order to use the e-Government applications. According to the system currently developed, I have to go to Post Office to get my password." are the comments of another respondent that suggests the lack of any perceived relative advantage, usefulness, or ease of use.[11]

Relative advantage and ease of use is actually very much related with being able to benefit from public services without dealing with any bureaucratic obstacles. The provision of e-Government services that are easier and quicker than currently available public services is consistently emphasized by participants as can be seen in the following comments:

- Efforts should be made to reduce bureaucracy.
- The system should save us from the bureaucracy that we always complain about.
- Such applications should overcome bureaucratic obstacles and enable us to benefit from more capabilities.

These demands imply a need for transformation in bureaucratic public sector institutions. An important aspect of such transformation is the cultivation of trustworthiness between citizens and state. According to our analysis, security and trust issues with respect to e-Government services are included in the remarks of various (over 20%) respondents. Furthermore, education and publicity for such issues of trustworthiness are suggested.

Our preliminary research supports the importance of certain factors in the literature such as relative advantage, perceived ease of use, and trustworthiness for the widespread implementation of e-Government services. In addition to such factors, there are also other note-worthy issues, as comments from a couple of individual

respondents imply. For instance, personalization issues are evident such as the demand for personal record-keeping of services and benefits used and completed transactions. E-governance and e-democracy issues such as the suggestion for participatory e-governance initiatives not only for local but also the central government are among the particular comments made by certain respondents. Some respondents also made reference to previous e-banking initiatives in the private sector, suggesting material incentives such as the reduction of costs associated with using the Internet for public information and services. Perhaps cost reduction can encourage citizens to adopt e-Government applications. Finally, allocation of dedicated staff and equipment to encourage e-Government use in government agencies is also among the comments provided by respondents.

These preliminary findings can be summarized as supporting the general importance of education and publicity. Education methods range from users learning by doing on their own to users and trainers coming together in institutional settings. This includes educating young and also mature people in local areas as well as training state staffs so that they can use and publicize e-Government services. Education and publicity for the trustworthiness, usefulness and ease of use, as well as relative advantage and benefits of e-Government services can be suggested as important requirements for widespread use. Also, while the focus currently seems to be on the factors of relative advantage, ease of use, and trustworthiness, with the integration of new services to the e-Government Gateway and further sophistication new factors may well arise in the Turkish case. Currently, however, even the factors already identified in this study require cautious consideration. For instance, understanding the ease of use or trustworthiness can vary, depending on the level of knowledge (education, experience, awareness) a respondent possess. Nevertheless, these preliminary findings can be considered a step forward in incorporating citizen needs and demands for the improvement of EGG.

With the long-anticipated launch of EGG in December 2008 an important start has been made to the provision of public institutional content and services via the gateway on the web. Some important issues that have risen with respect to the introduction of EGG and actual launch experience are worthy of note. These issues are summarized below:

1. The resistance and inertia of the bureaucracy towards implementing EGG must be dealt with. Leadership from politicians and higher public officials is needed to support the ongoing efforts. At present responsibility is divided and overall ownership is not clear regarding e-Government strategy and operations. There is currently a debate regarding an enabling legal framework and establishing a central agency to take responsibility and ownership over the other agencies and institutions involved.
2. Organizational and technical management issues with the project require attention. Coordination among internal units and with external institutions, and requirements to rigorously test all components of the infrastructure system need to be strengthened.
3. Trustworthiness and security issues are evident. How the system is protected from cyber-terrorism, how the privacy of citizens is preserved, and how the misuse or abuse of data can be protected against are critical issues.
4. Interoperability issues require attention. For example, passport applications can be initiated online, but the applicant still has to apply personally to finalize the application. Also while the application is processed, the applicant may have to go to other government agencies to provide supporting documents in certain cases.
5. Combating the digital divide while attempting to bring more services online is a problem to be coped with so that all segments of the society can take advantage of e-Government services. In remote areas, various public computer use and internet access centers have been established. Some of these, however, are treated as if they are special sites to be preserved and their actual, effective use is being prevented in a misguided effort to maintain and protect them.

Some of these issues are common elsewhere, and addressed by other authors. For instance, as Bannister and Wilson (2009, p. 8) argue the increasing prominence of the concerns about trustworthiness is noted. Regarding the use of data:

...there is a strong business and technical case for single instances of public data... Why should citizens have to supply the same information to government time and time again? Why should they have to go from one agency to another in order to complete a single task...? Unfortunately, there is a tendency with such a concentration of information, to result in a concentration of power... the evidence tended to suggest that the tendency, if any, was ... towards greater centralisation and concentration of power.

Similar concerns with regard to centralization of information have also been raised in Turkey. In various public communication activities regarding EGG and e-Government the authors were often asked questions regarding government power and data security: Can the collected information about individuals be used against them? No matter how secure it could be, doesn't concentration of information and collection of data in one place cause additional security risks?

CONCLUSION

This chapter has elaborated on the development of EGG in Turkey in relation to the challenging issues and future directions for citizen-oriented e-Government. Background information on the academic perspective on citizen-oriented e-Government development has been provided. As the main part of this discussion, the historical development and current status of e-Government in Turkey, as well as some detailed information about EGG have been given. Future directions of EGG and e-Government development in Turkey that are suggested by preliminary findings on citizen perspectives have also been presented. By offering a country-specific and practical perspective to the literature, it is hoped that this EGG case - the good practices, lessons-learned, suggestions and prospects discussed - will shed light on previous experience and pave the way for further progress for citizen-focused e-Government development not only in Turkey but also in other nations.

In short, the reflection of citizen preferences should be considered a determinant of e-Government development. Not just meeting citizen demands but putting citizens first, above the needs of government institutions should be the ultimate target. While service provision should be improved and be more sensitive to citizen demand, continuous reassessment of the supply and demand match is necessary. For certain needs, citizens may demand more sophisticated services, however for other needs they may be satisfied with less sophisticated services.

What public institutions supply and what citizens need and demand in Turkey and other countries should be studied further in order to complement and improve the ongoing academic and practical work of developing government web sites. Meanwhile, perspectives of not only government staff and citizens but also businesses and other legal entities as well as foreigners/aliens as other stakeholders of e-Government service provision and development also require separate attention.

REFERENCES

Alican, F. (2007). Experts without expertise: E-society projects in developing countries – The case of Turkey. *Information Polity, 12*, 255–263.

Andersen, K. V., & Henriksen, H. Z. (2006). E-government maturity models: Extension of the Layne and Lee model'. *Government Information Quarterly, 23*, 236–248. doi:10.1016/j.giq.2005.11.008

Arif, M. (2008). Customer orientation in e-government project management: A case study. *The Electronic. Journal of E-Government, 6*(1), 1–10.

Bakan, İ. A., Aydın, H., Kar, M., & Öz, B. (2008). *T-VOHSA Project Phase 2 Report*. Submitted to Türksat

Bakan, İ. A., Aydın, H., Kar, M., & Öz, B. (2009). *T-VOHSA Project Phase 1 Report*. Submitted to Türksat

Balci, A., Kumaş, E., Medeni, T., & Medeni, İ. T. (2009). Development and implementation of e-government services in Turkey . In Cunha, M. M., Oliveira, E. F., & Antonio, J. T. (Eds.), *Handbook of Research on Social Dimensions of Semantic Technologies and Web Services*. Information Science Reference.

Balci, A., Kumas, E., Tasdelen, H., Süngü, E., Medeni, İ. T., & Medeni, T. (2008) Development and implementation of e-government services in Turkey: Issues of standardization, inclusion, citizen satisfaction, integration and interoperability *ICEGOV 2008,* November, Egypt pp 337-342.

Bannister, F., & Wilson, D. (2009). O(ver)-government: E-government and the limits of the desirable. *Proceedings of ICEGEG2009*, Turkey

Bekkers, V., & Zouridis, S. (1999). Electronic service delivery in public administration: Some trends and issues. *International Review of Administrative Sciences, 65*(2), 183–195. doi:10.1177/0020852399652004

Capgemini (2007). *The user challenge benchmarking: The supply of online public services 7th measurement*. European Commission, Directorate General Information Society and Media. Retrieved n.d. from http://74.125.93.132/search?q=cache:LcdZTz-gJFoJ:ec.europa.eu/information_society/eeurope/i2010/docs/benchmarking/egov_benchmark_2007.pdf+The+user+challenge+benchmarking:+The+supply+of+online+public+services+7th+measurement&cd=1&hl=en&ct=clnk&gl=us

Carnegie Mellon University. (n.d.). *Capability Maturity model Integration*. Retrieved August 8, 2009, from http://www.sei.cmu.edu/cmmi/

Carter, L., & Bélanger, F. (2005). The utilization of e-government services: Citizen trust, innovation and acceptance factors. *Information Systems Journal*, *15*, 5–25. doi:10.1111/j.1365-2575.2005.00183.x

Çayhan, B. E. (2008). Implementing e-government in Turkey: A comparison of online public service delivery in Turkey and the European Union. *EJISDC (2008) 35, 8*, 1-11

C.E.E.S. (2009) *Citizen-oriented evaluation of e-government services*. EU Marie Curie IAPP funded Project. Unpublished literature review as project deliverable document.

Coursey, D., & Norris, D. F. (2008). Models of e-government: Are they correct? An empirical assessment. *Public Administration Review*, (May-June): 523–535. doi:10.1111/j.1540-6210.2008.00888.x

Davis, F. (1989). Perceived usefulness, perceived ease of use and user acceptance of information technology. *Management Information Systems Quarterly*, *13*(3), 19–340. doi:10.2307/249008

Devlet Planlanma Teşkilatı. (2006). *Information society strategy document*. Devlet Planlanma Teşkilatı.

Devlet Planlanma Teşkilatı. (2008). *Information society strategy progress report*. Devlet Planlanma Teşkilatı. (in Turkish)

European Commission. (2004) *European interoperability framework for pan-european egovernment services*. Retrieved on June 12, 2008, from IDABC website: http://ec.europa.eu/idabc/servlets/Doc?id=19528

European Commission. (n.d.). *e-Inclusion policy*. Retrieved January 19, 2009, from http://ec.europa.eu/information_society/activities/einclusion/policy/index_en.htm

European Union. (2009). *epractice*. Retrieved June 5, 2009, www.epractice.eu

Gil-Garcia, J. R., & Pardo, T. A. (2005). E-government success factors: Mapping practical tools to theoretical foundations. *Government Information Quarterly*, *22*, 187–216. doi:10.1016/j.giq.2005.02.001

Gökmen, A. (2009). Developments and prospects in e–government implementations in Turkey. In *Proceedings of the ICEGEG2009*, Turkey.

Hezer, E., Medeni, T., & Dalbay, Ö. (2009). 2008 Ulusal Konferans Katilimci Anketi Sonuçlarina Dayali, Bir Türkiye'deki E-Devlet Çalişmalari Analizi. YEBKO 2009, Turkey.

Irani, Z., Al-Sebie, M., & Elliman, T. (2006). Transaction stage of e-government systems: identification of its location & importance. In *Proceedings of the 39th Hawaii International Conference on System Sciences (HICSS-39)*, Hawaii, USA.

ITIL. (n.d.). *ITIL*. Retrieved August 9, 2009, from http://www.itiltraining.com/

Kanat, İ. M., & Özkan, S. (2009). Explaining citizen adoption of government to citizen services: a model based on theory of planned behaviour (TBP). *European and Mediterranean Conference on Information Systems (EMCIS)* 2009, Turkey

Korteland, E., & Bekkers, V. (2008). The diffusion of electronic service delivery innovations in Dutch e-policing: The case of digital warning systems. *Public Management Review, 10*(1), 71–88. doi:10.1080/14719030701763195

Kutlu, Ö., & Sevinç, İ. (2007). Information technology based systems and projects in Turkish public administration: Problems and solutions. In *Proceedings of BEYKON, 2007*, Turkey.

Lee, H., Irani, Z., Osman, I., Balci, A., Ozkan, S., & Medeni, T. (2008). Research note: toward a reference process model for citizen-oriented evaluation of e-government services. *Transforming Government: People, Process and Policy, 2*(4).

Medeni, T. (2008). Turkey case. In *Proceedings of the Panel on Electronic Governance for Rural Communities, ICEGOV 2008, November*, Egypt.

Medeni, T., Balci, A., & Dalbay, Ö. (2009). Understanding citizen demands for wide-spreading e-government services in Turkey: A descriptive study *EMCIS, 2009*, July, İzmir, Turkey

Medeni, T., Medeni, İ. T., Balci, A., & Dalbay, Ö. (2009). Suggesting a framework for transition towards more interoperable e-government in Turkey: A nautilus model of cross-cultural knowledge creation and organizational learning. In *Proceedings of ICEGOV, 2009*, March, Ankara, Turkey.

OECD. (2006). *OECD e-government studies: Turkey*. OECD Prince2. n.d. Retrieved August 31, 2009, from http://www.prince2.com/

Rogers, E. (1995). *Diffusion of innovations*. New York: The Free Press.

Saruç, N. T. (2009). The factors effecting use of e-government services and perceived quality of public services: an empirical study. In *Proceedings of ICEGEG2009*, Turkey.

Tassabehji, R., & Elliman, T. (2006). Generating citizen trust in e-government using a trust verification agent *European and Mediterranean Conference on Information Systems (EMCIS)* 2006, Spain.

TÜİK. (2008). *TÜİK*. Retrieved August 1, 2009, from http://www.turkstat.gov.tr/PreIstatistikTablo.do?istab_id=46

Türksat. (2009). *Kamu kurumları internet siteleri*. Retrieved October 9, 2009 from, http://www.kakis.gov.tr

Uçkan, Ö. (2009). *Everyone is governed as they deserve*. Retrieved January 19, 2009 from, http://arsiv.sabah.com.tr/2009/01/04/pz/haber,0499516A4921456CA2DA627988C1E222.html

United Nations. (2008). *E-government survey 2008 - From e-government to connected governance*. New York: United Nations.

KEY TERMS AND DEFINITIONS

EGG: e-Government Gateway in Turkey. In general, the gateway/portal aims to enable citizens (as well as businesses & state institutions) securely and conveniently reaching all electronic government services and essential information at one single-access point.

E-Government Maturity Model(ing)s: In order to understand the e-Government phenomenon from an evolutionary point of view, applying a staged approach by dividing the e-Government development process into many stages of a given level in a continuous process, where the development focuses from the 'immature' to the 'mature'.

Service Adoption: Perspectives to explain how new developments of e-Government services spread into public institutions and citizens such as technology acceptance model (TAM) of Davis (1989) and diffusion of innovation (DOI) of Rogers (1995).

Türksat: Despite its foundation as a satellite operator of Turkey, this state-owned and privately-operated company has also been in charge of e-Government infrastructure development and project management in Turkey. Specific e-Government and ICT projects are e-Government Gateway (EGG) development, dissemination of e-Government services, secure public network, standardization of public Internet sites, among others.

ENDNOTES

[1]   (for a summary of these models, see, for instance, Coursey & Norris 2008)

[2]   (Irani, Al-Sebie & Elliman, 2006; Anderson and Henriksen, 2006 in C.E.E.S., 2009)

[3]   Please see Medeni, Medeni, Balci, Dalbay for a deeper discussion on a framework for facilitating cross-cultural interactions to support interoperability and collaboration

[4]   http://www.edevletkonferansi.org/ last access 10.09.2009

[5]   http://www.icegeg.info/ last access 10.09.2009

[6]   The Law No. 5369 on universal services was approved by Turkish Grand National Assembly in June 2005 in order to provide basic universal services such as basic Internet services, among others, to certain geographical areas to where investment is assumed non-economical by the private sector. (http://www.epractice.eu/files/Turkey_e-Inclusion%202007.pdf, last access 10.11.2009)

[7]   For a further discussion on e-Government development and e-Inclusion issues in Turkey please see Balci et. al 2008 and Medeni 2008.

[8]   Please visit http://epractice.eu/files/download/i2010_eInclusion_Reports.pdf for an e-Inclusion report done by an e-practice.eu sub-group to have a good basis of comparison for digital divide issues.

[9]   A more comprehensive analysis of this study can be found at Medeni, Balci & Dalbay (2009)

[10]   Collaboration with public institutions other than government agencies for education and development is also specifically stressed by a quarter of total respondents for the spread of e-Government services. This could be expected, as respondents represent a non-government organization of youth networks.

[11]   Moreover, the importance of providing simple information and transactions that match low levels of education and knowledge was evident in some of the responses. Meanwhile, there were also, comments that highlighted demands for the enrichment of contents and services that can satisfy more users with higher levels of education.

APPENDIX

Services Offered through EGG (By Autumn 2009)

NO	Organization and Name of Service
1	BİMER-Prime Ministry Communication Center New Application
2	Bimer Results of Internet Application
3	Ministry of Transportation Vehicle Authorization Inquiry
4	Ministry of Justice Court Case File Inquiry
5	Ministry of National Defense- ASAL Address Confirmation and Updating
6	Ministry of National Defense- ASAL Final Roll Call Information Form
7	Ministry of National Defense- ASAL Summons Period Choice
8	Ministry of National Defense- Reserve Roll Call Services
9	Ministry of National Defense- Personnel Mobilization Maneuver Inquiry
10	Ministry of National Defense- Personnel Campaign Duty Order Inquiry
11	Logistics Mobilization Data for Overland Transport Vehicles Inquiry
12	Logistics Mobilization Data for Work Machinery Inquiry
13	Ministry of Finance e-Payroll Service
14	Ministry of Internal Affairs e-Internal Affairs Project Document Follow up
15	General Directorate of Police- Driver's License Permanent Cancellation Inquiry
16	General Directorate of Police- Vehicle Status Details Inquiry
17	General Directorate of Police- Driver's License Penalty Points Inquiry
18	Ministry of National Education- MEB Examination Results Inquiry
19	Ministry of National Education- MEB Examination Venue Inquiry
20	Ministry of Industry and Trade- Consumer Organizations Inquiry
21	Arbitration Committee for Consumer Problems Inquiry
22	Authorized After-Sales Service and Qualification Certificate Inquiry
23	Ministry of Industry and Trade- Warranty Certificate Inquiry
24	Ministry of Industry and Trade- Operation Manual Inquiry
25	Undersecretariat of Shipping-International Oil Pollution Prevention Certificate
26	Firefighting Systems Examination and Testing Certificate
27	Organic Arrest Preventive System Entry
28	Certificate of Compliance for Hazardous Cargo Transportation
29	Certificate of Compliance for Solid Cargo Transportation
30	Certificate of Compliance for Grain Transportation
31	CAS Certificate of Compliance
32	Certificate to the Effect that Petroleum Tanker Operations are Safely Conducted
33	Life Saving Equipment Examination and Testing Certificate
34	Life Boat Examination and Testing Certificate
35	Lifesaving Raft Examination and Testing Certificate
36	SMC (ISM) Safety Management Certificate
37	DOC (ISM) Document of Compliance

continued on following page

NO	Organization and Name of Service
38	Passenger Ship Safety Certificate
39	Cargo Ship Building Safety Certificate
40	Cargo Ship Equipment Safety Certificate
41	Radio Safety-Radio Telephone Safety Certificate
42	International *Load* Line Certificate
43	Certificate of Exemption
44	IAPP (International Air Pollution Prevention Certificate)
45	ISPP (International Sewage Pollution Prevention Certificate)
46	ISPP (International Sewage Pollution Prevention Certificate)
47	Undersecretariat of Shipping-Ship Load Balancing Information Booklet Approval
48	Ship Load Balancing Information Booklet Approval Fee (in the event of changes)
49	Undersecretariat of Shipping-Freeboard Calculations and Plan Control and Approval
50	Freeboard Calculations and Plan Control and Approval Fee (in the event of changes)
51	Ships Fire Safety, Lifesaving Safety, Ship Plan Approval (in the event of changes)
52	Ship Poor Balance and Loading Booklet Approval Fee
53	Undersecretariat of Shipping-Load Binding Manual, SOPEP, SMPEP Approval
54	Load Binding Manual, SOPEP, SMPEP Approval Fee
55	Passenger Ships Fire Safety Plan - Life Saving Safety Plan - Ship Plan Approval
56	Undersecretariat of Shipping-Ship Poor Balance and Loading Booklet Approval
57	Undersecretariat of Shipping-Certificate of Minimum Safety for Seaman Equipment
58	Undersecretariat of Shipping-Compulsory Survey Services in Turkish Straits
59	Undersecretariat of Shipping- Surveys Made for Ships under the Turkish Flag
60	Undersecretariat of Shipping-Port State Control
61	Port and Shore Structures – Facilities Provisional Commissioning / Survey Services
62	Control&Approval of Fire & Lifesaving Equipment Test & Examination Companies
63	Undersecretariat of Shipping-Type Approval for Equipment used on Ships
64	Undersecretariat of Shipping-On-site Disassembling Survey
65	Undersecretariat of Shipping- Continuous Synopsis Record (CSR) Certificate
66	Undersecretariat of Shipping Limbo Supervision Operations
67	Undersecretariat of Shipping Condition Evaluation Survey
68	Undersecretariat of Shipping, Shipping Agency Authorization Certificate Fee
69	Shipping Agency Authorization Certificate Renewal Fee
70	Undersecretariat of Shipping, Shipping Agency Branch Authorization Certificate Fee
71	Undersecretariat of Shipping Ship Certificate
72	Assignment for Maintaining the Registered Ship Until the Ship Lifetime Ends
73	Assignment of Registered Ship against Payment or Registry Arrangements
74	Usufruct Establishment on Registered Ship against Payment
75	Undersecretariat of Shipping Liens to be Lodged on Registered Ship
76	Undersecretariat of Shipping Endorsement of Ship Contracts in the Ship Registry
77	Annulment of Transactions under the Subject of Charges
78	Undersecretariat of Shipping Ship Registry Corrections

continued on following page

NO	Organization and Name of Service
79	Copies of Documents Referring to the Ship Registry and Copies of Registry Records
80	Undersecretariat of Shipping Turkish International Registry Recording Fee
81	Undersecretariat of Shipping Annual Tonnage Charge
82	Undersecretariat of Shipping Seaworthiness Certificate
83	Undersecretariat of Shipping Measurement Certificate
84	Undersecretariat of Shipping Permission for Voyage – Port Exit Certificate
85	Undersecretariat of Shipping Ministry of Transportation Flag Certificates
86	Certification of Ship Logs by Port Authorities
87	Certificate of Qualification
88	STCW Documents
89	Cargo Ship Building Safety Certificate
90	Certificate of Exemption
91	Passenger Ship Safety Certificate
92	Radio - Telegram Safety Certificate
93	International *Load* Line Certificate
94	Cargo Ship Radio - Telephone Safety Certificate
95	Cargo Ship Equipment Safety Certificate
96	Transitlog Certificate
97	Private Yacht Certificate of Registry
98	General Directorate of Sea Trade Charged Procedures – Liner Certification Fee
99	Shipyard partial operation permit certificate fee
100	Shipyard operation permit certificate fee
101	Existing shipyard area organization and settlement plan approval fee
102	Shipyard Area Organization and Settlement Plan (Deemed Necessary to Examine)
103	On-site Examination by İTDK for the Shipyard
104	Application for Shipyard's Existing Floating Pools
105	Existing Boat Production Area Organization and Settlement Plan Approval Fee
106	New Floating Pool for Boat Production Area Application Fee
107	On-site Examination for Boat Production Area Organization and Settlement Plan
108	Undersecretariat of Shipping-Boat Production Area Operation Permit Certificate Fee
109	Boat Production Area Partial Operation Permit Certificate Fee
110	Boat Production and Boat Yard Area Operations
111	Undersecretariat of Shipping-Jet-Ski Production Authorization Certificate Issuance
112	Undersecretariat of Shipping- Jet-Ski Production Authorization Certificate Visa
113	Certificates of Exemption within the scope of International Treaties
114	Undersecretariat of Shipping-Underwater Motorcycle Registry Certificate Issuance
115	Undersecretariat of Shipping- Jet-Ski Registry Certificate Issuance
116	Undersecretariat of Shipping-Three Days and More Anchorage Fee
117	Undersecretariat of Shipping-On-Site Disassembly Survey
118	Off-Ship Disassembly Site, Ship Disassembly Authorization Certificate
119	Undersecretariat of Shipping-Private Boat Certificate Fee

continued on following page

NO	Organization and Name of Service
120	Shore Maintenance Authorization Certificate – for GMDSS Devices
121	Undersecretariat of Shipping-Ship Navigation Log
122	Book of Fuel Purchase with no Special Consumption Tax
123	Social Security Agency- SSK Service Breakdown
124	Social Security Agency- SSK Address and Bank / PTT Change
125	Social Security Agency- SGK Registry Inquiry
126	İŞKUR- Vacancy Inquiry and Job Application by Criteria
127	İŞKUR- Vacancy Inquiry and Job Application by Profiles
128	İŞKUR- Job Application Result Inquiry
129	İŞKUR- Payables to İŞKUR Inquiry
130	İŞKUR- Unemployment Compensation Application
131	İŞKUR- Unemployment Compensation Payment
132	İŞKUR- Turkish Dictionary of Professions
133	İŞKUR- Vocational Course Inquiry
134	PTT- Nearest PTT Office
135	PTT- Registered Mail Follow up
136	General Directorate of Civil Aviation- Flight Crew Licensing/Rating Application
137	TCDD- e-Ticket Reservation and Sales
138	State Meteorological Affairs General Directorate- Daily Weather Forecast
139	State Meteorological Affairs General Directorate- Seawater Temperatures
140	International Centers Weather Forecast
141	State Meteorological Affairs General Directorate- 3 Day Weather Forecast
142	Inland Revenue Service - e-Tax Sign Inquiry
143	TCMB (Central Bank) Exchange Rates
144	KOSGEB (SME Development & Support Agency) Business Status Inquiry

Chapter 11
Recovery.gov:
Small Steps toward Transparency, Interactivity, and Trust

Franz Foltz
Rochester Institute of Technology, USA

Rudy Pugliese
Rochester Institute of Technology, USA

Paul Ferber
Rochester Institute of Technology, USA

ABSTRACT

President Barak Obama's directive on transparency and open government, and the creation of the Website Recovery.gov, would seem to be concrete examples of the predictions of cyber advocates that computer-mediated communication and the Internet will change the nature of democracy and make citizens more participatory. A major goal is to try to increase the public's trust in their government. An examination of Recovery.gov, however, reveals it to be not very interactive and less than fully transparent. While it may be praised for providing information, it falls far short of the vision of cyber advocates. The state sites associated with Recovery.gov do a slightly better job by putting a personal face to the oversight of the recovery. Overall, the sites tend to provide only a limited view into the workings of the government and have a long way to go before they increase public trust in the government.

INTRODUCTION

Even before the highly-noticed Putnam study (1995, 2000) showed that public trust in government had been declining for four decades; politicians, public servants, and citizens alike had tried to reverse this trend. Many believe that we cannot rely simply on traditional media to rebuild public trust, but must take advantage of the features of new media and address citizens by involving them directly and openly. On January 21, 2009, in an attempt to increase public trust in government, President Barak Obama, addressing a campaign promise, issued a memo that called on the federal government to use the Internet to create a more transparent and open government. He declared that government should be transparent, participatory, and collaborative, and directed the Office

DOI: 10.4018/978-1-61692-018-0.ch011

of Management and Budget (OMB) to establish guidelines to promote this goal. In February 2009, *The Nation* hailed this accountability as "both good policy and necessary politics" but called for "deeper disclosure" (LeRoy, 2009. February 16, p. 15) and urged the President to adopt the best practices from cities and states while employing a system to keep a watchful eye on governors and mayors intent on squandering his Recovery Plan.

The Recovery.gov Website is one attempt to fulfill this promise and should, at least in concept, be pleasing to people who have long argued that computer-mediated communication (CMC) can serve to promote greater civic involvement. As such, the Recovery.gov Website provides useful insights into the ability of the Internet to provide transparency and public participation. By looking at the early construction and evolution of the site, a deeper understanding of the government's concept of transparency can be determined. An analysis of this site and the related state sites allows for a better understanding of the connection between transparency and e-government.

BACKGROUND

The claim that computer-mediated communications (CMC) can be used to create greater public involvement in government actually pre-dates the widespread use of the Internet, and there is a broad range in the scope of predictions as to what computer-mediated communication can or will accomplish. Some have claimed that CMC would allow citizens to interact meaningfully with each other and elected officials in a manner unencumbered by traditional political structures (Grossman, 1995). Others wonder if politicians are really willing to live in glass houses of honesty (Schudson & Haas, 2008).

Studies suggest that the creation of a transparent and participative Website could increase trust and satisfaction. Trust and use of government Websites have been strongly related at the local

level (Tolbert & Mossberger, 2006). Citizen use of government Websites is significantly related with satisfaction with e-government (Welch, Hinnant, & Moon, 2005). However, dissatisfaction with interactivity of government Websites has been reported, and those reporting greater concern regarding government responsiveness were less satisfied (Welch, Hinnant, & Moon, 2005). Consequently, these sites have to be made more responsive by increasing the levels of interactivity. Two-way interaction has been suggested as an important means of demonstrating government accountability (Roberts, 2002). Thus, transparency and interactivity are connected concepts for increasing public trust.

Recovery.gov provides an opportunity to evaluate what progress, if any, the federal government has made toward the goals of transparency, interactivity, and accountability. An understanding of Recovery.gov begins with President Obama's directive. President Obama defines his understanding of transparency and open government.

Government should be transparent. Transparency promotes accountability and provides information for citizens about what their Government is doing. Information maintained by the Federal Government is a national asset. My Administration will take appropriate action, consistent with law and policy, to disclose information rapidly in forms that the public can readily find and use. Executive departments and agencies should harness new technologies to put information about their operations and decisions online and readily available to the public. Executive departments and agencies should also solicit public feedback to identify information of greatest use to the public.

Government should be participatory. Public engagement enhances the Government's effectiveness and improves the quality of its decisions. Knowledge is widely dispersed in society, and public officials benefit from having access to that dispersed knowledge. Executive departments and agencies should offer Americans increased opportunities to participate in policymaking and to provide their Government with the benefits of their collective expertise and information. Executive departments and agencies should also solicit public input on how we can increase and improve opportunities for public participation in Government.

Government should be collaborative. Collaboration actively engages Americans in the work of their Government. Executive departments and agencies should use innovative tools, methods, and systems to cooperate among themselves, across all levels of Government, and with nonprofit organizations, businesses, and individuals in the private sector. Executive departments and agencies should solicit public feedback to assess and improve their level of collaboration and to identify new opportunities for cooperation. (Obama, 2009)

President Obama's goal of transparency is one cyber advocates are bound to view favorably. The Cyberspace Policy Research Group (CyPRG, n.d.) study, for instance, rated sites based solely on their transparency and interactivity. CyPRG argues that transparency and interactivity are the two most important properties of CMC for e-government. They define transparency as "a layman's basic map of the organization as depicted in the information on the site [and] reveals the depth of access it allows, the depths of knowledge about processes it is willing to reveal, and the level of attention to citizen response it provides" (LaPorte, Demchak, & de Jong, 2002, p. 415; Demchak, Friis, & LaPorte, 1998, p. 2000). An organization's Website demonstrates how transparent it is by allowing citizens to observe its performance (Reichard, 1998). But while transparency always seems to be a virtue, the definition of it shifts about as much as that of interactivity. The CyPRG definition of transparency, for instance, is drastically different from the one that President Obama is pushing.

CyPRG, as well as most of the studies in the early 2000s, viewed transparency primarily as the ability of users to find out who owned and controlled the content of the Website. They were interested in ownership as this helped to judge the usefulness and reliability of the information provided by the Website. If one does not know who was behind the information, how could one trust the information presented on the Website?

It is not unreasonable that today, in the age of Twitter and Facebook, many people would argue that CMC can be used to allow the public to see the actual workings of the government. We now seem to have unprecedented ability to view into people's lives. We know when they eat, work, and take a shower, 24/7. In this governmental context, transparency does not directly provide trust in the content, but instead it tries to build trust in the organization behind the Website.

Further variance in the meaning of transparency can be found in the internal focus. Some people see the Internet creating transparency within public sector organizations (McIvor, McHugh, & Cadden, 2002). The technology allows individuals from the organization to interact and powerfully encourage the free flow of information. Here transparency is internal and has no connection to people outside the organization.

Trust is a common thread in many of the discussions of transparency. Many authors (Owen & Powell, 2006; Martinez-Moyano, Samsa, Baldwin, Willke, & Moore, 2007) argue that trust is linked to a group's transparency. The more practical papers, those coming out of government organizations from around the globe, argue a connection between transparency (and interactivity) and trust. They argue that government needs to inform the public through its Websites. Many of the more academic papers also support this connection, and like Welch and Hinnant (2002), argue that simply providing information through a one-way e-government model may be insufficient for true cyber-democracy. Curtin and Meijer (2006) agree that transparency and trust (legitimacy) are related, but that governments' naïve practice of simply creating fancy Websites is not enough. The site's users need to be more than just passive observers. They need to have an active role.

President Obama's desire to make government more participatory speaks to the cyberadvocates' view of democracy, especially with its connection of transparency and interactivity. The vision of a more democratic future often draws on the interactive nature of the Web to create opportunities for constituents to interact directly with elected officials in collaboratively designing policy, and to actively participate in the governing process. But the degree of interactivity on Websites varies greatly, and the measurement of it is complicated by differing interpretations of what makes a site interactive.

Ferber, Foltz and Pugliese (2007) argue that the interactive potential of sites can be seen through a modification and addition to McMillan's model of cyber-interactivity. Given that political Websites have the potential to offer citizens an audience of active and engaged users interested in political discourse, it would appear that McMillan's (2002) model of cyber-interactivity should make provision for not just two-way communication, but three-way communication aimed at influencing other parties or, in other words, providing a mechanism for public deliberation.

The McMillan model uses two-way communication as a description of not just interpersonal communication but public communication as well. There is a difference. Two-way communication is primarily interpersonal and perhaps best illustrated by email, a feature provided by most political sites. A site's email directory allows users to contact other individuals, such as legislators, but not to post messages to the site. The difference is that users are not allowed to address the larger audience of site users. This is in contrast to allowing users to post messages to the site and facilitating public discourse by addressing a third party. Three-way communication allows unknown or yet to be identified parties to receive the mes-

sage, thus making it a publication.[1] In this sense, a publication becomes public once the message has been received by a third party.

The three-way model in Figure 1 includes "controlled response" and "public discourse." In controlled response, such as a poll or bulletin board, the site provides opportunities for users to participate, but the site retains significant control over the content. In a poll, the site determines the questions and how the results are presented. "Controlled" forums require the moderator to forward participants' comments to the site. Contrasted to that is public discourse, such as some forums, blogs, and chat rooms, where participants have an almost unrestricted opportunity to determine the content. Site control is often limited to such actions as deleting comments for libel, obscenity, or for some violation of the sites' norms. In such cases the participants have a high level of control.

Note the shifting roles of individuals and Websites in these higher-order instances of the model. In a controlled response poll, for instance, site users begin their involvement as receivers, but some of these receivers move on to be participants when they choose to provide responses to poll questions. In public discourse, where the site exerts little control over content, the site becomes a participant, as does any other user who posts comments. Thus, in order to build trust, the government needs to be both more transparent and to offer 2-way and 3-way means of interactivity.

REVIEW OF THE SITES

An evaluation of the Recovery.gov Website reveals it to be somewhat limited in transparency, relatively minimal in content, and often lacking in interactive 2- and 3-way modes of communication. The Website was initially reviewed during the last week of March 2009, when it was still fairly young. A second review was done two months later to assess its evolution. This review found a number of promising updates and improvements

Figure 1. A six-part model of cyber-interactivity

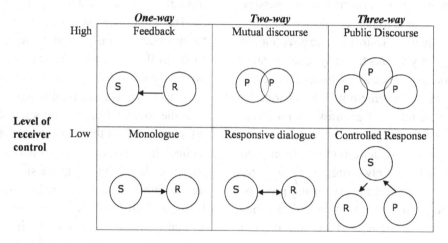

Direction of communication

S = sender, R = receiver, P = participant (where sender/receiver roles are interchangeable)

to the site. The associated recovery sites of the 50 states, as well as the District of Columbia, were also examined to see how they addressed the concepts of transparency and interactivity.

The Recovery.gov Site

The Recovery.gov Website's primary function appeared to be the provision of information to the public. As such, it is not very transparent as judged by the CyPRG definition of transparency. Originally, there was very little information concerning the ownership of the site other than a contact page reference to a *Recovery Accountability and Transparency Board*. It claimed that "The Board consists of Inspectors General from about ten major cabinet agencies – including the Departments of Justice, Treasury, and Commerce – and one of its duties will be to review the comments and questions submitted to the site." The site did not list which agencies were involved, nor who were the Inspector General's. Two months later, there was a full listing of the Recovery Accountability and Transparency Board, with the names of its chair and 12 other members, and the agencies

they represent. But despite considerably increased content and clearer identification of ownership, the site continued to be mostly 1-way communication, and lacks mechanisms that provide interaction.

The Board's stated purpose was to make sure that Recovery.gov fulfilled its mandate – to help citizens track the spending of funds allocated by the American Recovery and Reinvestment Act. An examination of the site's features and content may show how well they met this mandate. The home page provided a daily update of news stories associated with the American Recovery and Reinvestment Act, and provided links to four areas: Accountability and Transparency, Share your Recovery Story, State Progress and Resources, and Agency Progress and Resources. Two months later, the home page featured a rotating series of examples of recovery activities including graphics and a series of text-based featured news stories. Top-side links included Investments and Opportunities, along with the previously existing Home, About, Impact, News, FAQ, and Contact Us. Right-side links continued to include Accountability and Transparency, and Agency Progress and Resources, but Share your Recovery Story

Figure 2. Recovery.gov screenshot of Accountability and Transparency page

had been changed to Fraud, Waste and Abuse, and State Progress and Resources had become State, Local, Tribal and Territorial Resources.

The original "Accountability and Transparency" section (see Figure 2) simply provided information concerning the President's views on transparency and linked to the documents that ordered this site. Nothing here could be considered interactive or rising above 1-way communication. In June 2009, the Accountability and Transparency page looked very similar, but with the addition of links to the listing of the Board membership, Inspector General Findings, and Inspector General Financial Status Reports. These second two options produced lists of reports from the Inspectors General of various agencies and many downloadable documents. Another link led to downloadable reports from GAO. The volume of information was very impressive, but it was all in the nature of 1-way communication from the government to the public.

The "Share Your Story" page was simply a form to fill out and send to the Board, and the user had no sense of how this information would be used. There was no provision that this information

would be shared with the public, or any promise that the Board would contact a writer in return. Again, this was limited 1-way communication from the receiver to the site. If the stories or best stories were posted, it would have become basic 3-way communication. In June, the "Share your Recovery Story" page had become "Fraud, Waste and Abuse" (see Figure 3), which led to Whistle-blower Information, Inspectors General Fraud Hotlines (agency forms and/or phone numbers) and Tips for Identifying Collusion and Fraud. This last option provided minimal information, but did have a link to the Department of Justice's Economic Recovery Antitrust Division, which included information such as the Red Flags of Collusion.

The "State Recovery Sites" page (see Figure 4) was a little more interactive in the classic sense. Users could click on the map and the recovery activities of that state appeared. However, as one can see not all of the states had working sites in March. In many cases these sites were specific recovery sites for the state; in other cases, these pages were simply a page on the governors' site. These links would be, in most cases, 2-way communication

Figure 3. Recovery.gov screenshot of new Fraud, Waste and Abuse page

Figure 4. Recovery.gov screenshot of Interactive State Recovery Sites page

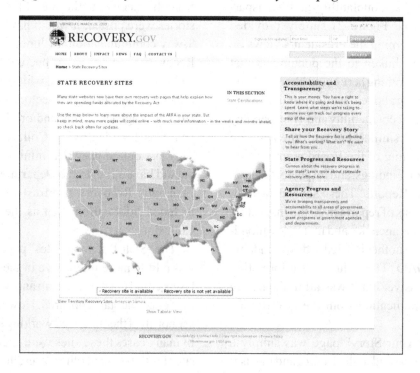

as the receiver requests specific information (a state) and gets that specified information; but aside from the user's selection of which state, the site retained total control of the content.

This pattern was continued with the revised State, Local, Tribal and Territorial Resources page, which had obviously been expanded to include more than just the previous state jurisdictions. State information included two clickable U.S. maps, leading to state recovery sites, and state certification documents. Territories did not make the map but were listed at the bottom of it. Tribal information was limited to links to a news page and to related organizations. The page's content had been increased, but its form was still basically 1-way communication with some minimal 2-way interaction involving the clickable maps.

The "Agency Recovery Sites" page was similar to the previous state page, except that it sent users to the respective federal agency/department, where they could view the agency/department page(s) concerning how money was being spent. This was simply 2-way communication and, aside from the selection of an agency, the user had no control over content. Two months late, the Agency Progress and Resources continued to include links to the recovery sites of many agencies, but also had links to agency financial and activity reports, recovery plans, and funding notifications. Many additional documents were downloadable.

In the navigation bar, there was one area of particular interest – the link for Impact. The Impact page itself was fairly nondescript. However it linked to two pages: Investments and Jobs. The investment page was definitely not interactive, though it did provide a quick illustrative summary of how the federal funds are being used. The jobs page was significantly more interesting. Again, the user would find a map of the U.S. This time when they clicked on a state, they would find the number of jobs that would be created or saved in that state due to the American Recovery and Reinvestment Act. The map listed as its source the Council of Economic Advisors, which was

reasonably specific as far as transparency and ownership go, but assumed that users understood what that organization was, as there was no explanation of its function, or list of its membership, and, for some inexplicable reason, no link to it. An option did exist to open a portable document file (PDF) file describing the estimation methods from which the job numbers were generated. In June, "Impact" still led to the clickable U.S. map which revealed jobs saved or created in each state. What used to be the second half of this page, Investments, had been moved to a separate top-line option. The options under Investments still included the distribution of money by category, as illustrated by the size of a circle, but also by state, as found in a clickable map, and by agency, as found in a list. Clicking on a state led to a list of funded programs within that state.

In June, the site also included another new option of Opportunities, which led to several paragraphs describing recovery-related jobs, career planning, and information on government loans and benefits. Embedded in the paragraphs were many links to other sites such as FedBizOpps.gov.

The final top-line option was Contact Us, which led to options of contacting the Webmaster, and reporting Fraud, Waste and Abuse, which in turn led to the same content as the right-side link of the same name. A third option was Share Your Story, where users are invited to use a form and share their recovery story. This option was present in March, but received better billing then as it was a right-side option on the home page. In June a user could stumble on it via the Contact Us link. This option still had all of the limitations found in March, as there was still no provision to share the story with the public, or any promise that a writer would be contacted in return. It was also not entirely clear as to where the story was being sent, but presumably the "we" in "We want to hear from you" is the Recovery Accountability and Transparency Board.

Recovery.gov admits that it is a work in progress, and changes from March to June show significant evolution of the site, as it gained significant heft. Transparency, in the CyPIRG sense of clear identification of site ownership was much improved. The amount of content available to users had been also been considerably increased, but the utility of the information was questionable. The amount of interactivity, however, remained minimal. The vast majority of the site was 1-way delivery of information, and minimal 2-way interaction was found only in the provision of options, clicks on lists, or on a map of the U.S.

Regarding the utility of the increased content, some information, such as clicking on a map and finding that 133,000 jobs had been created or saved in Ohio, over the next two years, was easily accessible but rather simplistic. Far more detailed information was available, but the level of skill needed to interpret it, as well as the time to understand it, increased with the complexity. Some information, in fact, was so complex that one wonders if it exceeds the capability or anticipated effort of common citizens to understand it. Such information is undoubtedly more useful to the audience of professional users, including government officials, journalists, lobbyists, and lawyers.

As for regular citizens who may lack the time to pour through complicated documents, the considerable information on the site may increase their trust in government, on the assumption that such a deluge of information must be evidence of the government being open, accountable, and trustworthy. The site certainly enables citizens to electronically bury themselves under an avalanche of documentation. Perhaps that may encourage feelings or trust, but it may also produce cynicism among citizens who view this as an electronic snow job of providing more information than they can possibly process. In the end, the role of professionals in validating or discrediting the accuracy of the information may become crucial to the site's ability to foster a feeling of open government.

The Fifty States and the District of Columbia Sites: June 2009

The Recovery.gov site linked via an interactive map to the recovery/stimulus sites of all 50 states and the District of Columbia.[2] These 51 sites provide a look at different interpretations of the role of the states in the American Recovery and Reinvestment Act of 2009 as well as differing definitions of transparency and accountability. Like the national site, they changed over the first three months of the program. Originally they were fairly thin, having very little time to get something together by the end of March. Therefore, they will only be examined as the sites appeared during the week of June 1, 2009.

Immediately noticeable on the state sites was their tendency to be more personable than the national site. The sites had many more pictures of people and events. Thirty of the sites had a picture of their governor[3], while 32 had a signed welcoming letter. Sixteen sites had a video welcome by the governor or a video of the press conference announcing the state's use of the federal funds. The most interesting video was California's.

Governor Schwarzenegger, not surprising, was very relaxed in front of the camera and seemed to be discussing the acquisition of funds with the viewer as he signed a request for funding. He clearly explained what he was doing and why California needed these funds. He also told the viewer that he would do everything in his power to get California as much funding as possible. This presentation attempted to bring two aspects of transparency to the site. First, it showed the people in charge of the site. Second, it tried to explain what they were doing and why they were doing it. Governor Schwarzenegger was signing the proper forms to guarantee California its fair share of the stimulus money and on either side of him sat administrators who were going to make sure that the money was used properly.

Overall, the state sites contained a wide range of functions. Some sites provided a number of

Figure 5. Missouri Recovery home page

different features, while others were focused into specific niches. Fifteen of the sites had sections devoted specifically to transparency and accountability, where they outlined their strategies to make sure that the funds were not misused or wasted. A number of the states called their entire sites transparent, their focus being the notion of providing transparency. One such site, Texas run by the State Comptroller, was entitled "Texas Eye on the Dollar." A dozen of the sites included a fraud hotline link to enable the public to contact the proper authority to report misuse of the money. Trust is presumably built by allowing citizens to have some level of control in the oversight of the money.

Six of the sites allowed the users to submit ideas for how the state should spend its money. In this case, the idea was to give the citizen some control over how the money was being spent. They could participate in how their state spent the money. The entire Missouri site, in particular (see Figure 5), was focused on allowing the public to input ideas and submit proposals for the money. It included little else in the way of information for the user.

Many of sites focused on providing money to their citizens. Twenty-nine had information for acquiring grants or other funds. Nine had links specifically for people looking for employment. Five sites had specific material on tax relief and another five had information specifically for businesses.

Some sites focused on providing constant updates. In this case the idea was to keep the citizen constantly informed as to how the money was being spent. That way they could see how their tax money was being used. Eighteen sites provided subscription services, so that the public would be constantly updated. Sixteen had Real Simple Syndication (RSS) feeds, and four sites provided Tweets. Two had personal digital assistant (PDA) options. Some of the sites took this idea to the extreme and seemed to provide more public relations for the governor than oversight of funding. Five of them had photo galleries of the governors at various public events, four had archived videos of key public events, and one even had MP3s of various speeches. A number of the sites also had various means of setting up appointments with the governor.

The largest function of these sites was to provide information to the public. Forty-one sites provided a running update of important happenings in the state associated with the recovery efforts. Thirty-two sites provided various amounts of downloadable documentation. A number of sites, like Alaska, simply seemed to be clearinghouses of information. In particular, 30 sites provided their certifications and other correspondence with the federal government. A number of the Republican Governors included memos listing their objections to various components of the recovery act and why or why not they took particular funds.

Figure 6. Screenshot of California's interactive map

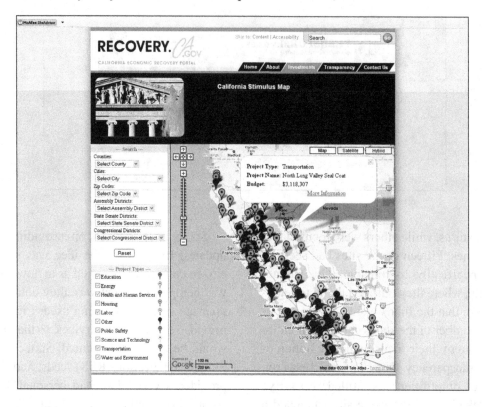

The governor[4] seemed to be the primary contact person in all but five of the states. Nineteen listed teams of individuals to help the governor. In most cases these individuals were named and some amount of contact information was available. However, in some cases the group was unnamed and unreachable. One state claimed to have a recovery board, though no one was sharing any information on it. A little over half of the sites had some form of contact information for the governor and/or those in charge. Twenty-eight had phone numbers, 27 had emails, and 21 provided regular mailing addresses.

The states sites with their pictures, videos and personal greetings did a better job of showing who was in charge of the site than the national site and thus providing the old style of transparency, or perhaps an updated video version of ownership. Sixteen state sites had pages devoted to providing organizational information. On the whole,

however, the states were no better than Recovery. gov at providing the type of transparency that President Obama requested. They had lots of information, but provided very little insight into the workings of government. As an example, 500 words explaining how a state was going to oversee federal funds did very little to convey what was to become of the money.

Turning to the aspect of transparency focusing on interactivity and public dialogue, like the national site, the state sites tended to focus on 1-way communication, providing information or in some cases acquiring information. Even though some information was requested, none of this was ever shared, and hence no 3-way communication was present on any site. Even the two sites with Blogs had only basic systems that allowed government spokespeople to post, but allowed no public discussion of their content. Also, since most sites now use forms instead of straight emails, there was no way of finding out if the emails would be responded to in some manner – hence little could be judged as to whether or not they were 2-way communication with humans.

Other features on these sites ranged from very little interactivity to, in some cases, significant 2-way communication, albeit with a machine. Fourteen states had interactive maps and 11 had timelines. The best maps showed the locations of all expenditures and when clicked would provide in-depth detail on the type of project, those involved, and the funds involved (see Figure 6). The timelines ran the gamut from basic link-less schedules for the next two years to fully interactive chronologies of projects undertaken and various levels of background information.

TRANSPARENCY AND TRUST

Even though the notion of transparency has a number of differing definitions, in all cases it deals with the idea of trust. Either trust in the information being presented by the site or trust in the organization behind the site. President Obama wanted to increase the public's trust in their government. This is a very daunting task to say the least, given that society as a whole has become more distrustful of those in power after almost 40 years of perceived abuse of power by both political and business leaders.

Empirical studies support the notion of this decline of trust in the United States over the past 40 years. The figures report a drop from about 55% of the population in 1960 feeling others could be trusted to about 35% in 2000 taking that position (Hooghe & Stolle, 2003: p.6). One of the studies often cited is the World Values Survey that reported findings from 43 societies representing 70% of the world's population. It shows that this decline in trust is not just an American problem, but that there has been a general decline of trust worldwide (Inglehart, Basanez, & Moreno, 1998).

Almost everybody agrees that trust is fundamental in social relationships and that trust is essential for cooperative behavior. For example, Jane Mansbridge (1999) writes:

A modicum of trust greases the wheels of commerce, politics, and social life. Large-scale economies and polities must generate this modicum of trust among strangers. Stranger-to-stranger transactions are most efficient if they can draw on reliable sources of situation-specific and more generalized trust, secured by social and institutional sanctions that punish breaches of trust and by a moral basis for trustworthiness in individual consciences. All this is well known. (p. 291)

The issue becomes whether a Website has the ability to reverse this trend and actually build trust. The Recovery.gov and related state sites attempt to create trust in several ways. Overall, they try to provide a view into the workings of government. People distrust what they do not know. Knowledge of the system can create trust in the system. The attempt to create this type of trust can be seen in the quantities of information and continuous updates across the various sites. The public sees what is happening or at least what the site wants them to see. An informed public is one in a better position to act than one that is in the dark. Thus, increased access to timely information should increase public trust.

This is where differing definitions of transparency must merge. Building public trust in an organization through the use of information is only as good as the trust the people have in the information provided by that organization. If the public thinks that the organization lies, then why would it assume that the information is true? Therefore the newer emphasis of transparency – trust in the organization through provision of information – is dependent, in part, on the earlier focus – trust in the information through identification of the providers of it, that is, the owners of the site. Thus, content veracity matters in both views of transparency, and the site still needs to show who is behind the information on the site.

One way to address this conundrum is by providing a human face to the government. Knowing who is in charge and what they think is another way to try to build trust. The state sites did a much better job of this than the federal site. Seeing people, both in videos and photos, allows the public to see, and perhaps establish a stronger connection to, who is responsible for the recovery money. The explanations and personal insights of government officials allow the average citizen to not only see them but also understand their thoughts. They might not completely trust the government, but they now know who is responsible and can hold them personally accountable.

Some critics may consider it to be calculated fluff, but it can be argued that the public can trust a persuasive governor more than it can a faceless bureaucratic entity. It may be one thing to reveal site ownership though a detailed listing and flowchart of names, and another to claim ownership through an engaging video from a prominent government official. In some sense this new "video ownership" borrows on the social media aspects of the later-day Internet. The downside, of course, is that the prominent official must not have a pre-existing reputation as being untrustworthy. Further, this attempted concentration of trust in one or a few individuals runs the risk of creating vanity sites, where the goal becomes less of building trust in government, and more toward the promotion of the government official(s).

Regarding trust and participation, there were a few cases where the sites appeared to provide the public with opportunities to participate in their governing. This would seem to support the notion that the government is not just the domain of a vague group of elites, but a place where any citizen has an opportunity to provide suggestions and have their voice heard. The biggest problem with this conception of trust is that overall these sites provided very little real interaction. Therefore even though a citizen could send in an idea, there

is no real evidence on how those ideas actually contributed to the governing process. A solution would be the creation of true 3-way communication. The sites need not just take in or provide access to information, but to show how the input is used. Trust through participation will be achieved only if the public sees that they are affecting the way the government runs.

Finally, many of the sites provided an opportunity for the public to play watchdog over the government. The various means for reporting fraud do not necessarily increase the public's trust in the government, but at least they allow the public a means for reacting to problems, and perhaps give them a feeling of having a role in the recovery. But whether this increases trust or provides confirmation of distrust is an open question.

CONCLUSION

In a number of studies of interactivity, some researchers defined interactivity simply as whatever people believed was interactive. It was a totally social construct – for them, there was nothing that made something inherently interactive. To a point, the new definition of transparency as a window into the workings of government is also such a construct. Perhaps a claim of transparency will be accepted if the word is repeated often enough, just as people will come to regard a site as interactive if enough people say it is. But those standards are different from those of empirically based analysis.

The review of Recovery.gov and the related state sites reveals them to be not very interactive and often less than transparent. Some would argue that the site is relatively new and that it needs time to grow. But the government has been creating Websites for a significant period of time, so it is not as if the Recovery.gov site was created without some history. If a site's primary goal is to build trust through transparency and interactivity, the Recovery.gov site left a lot to be desired. Anyone who studies media realizes that the editor has a final say in what appears—just like reality televisions shows are not truly real in any sense. A site that simply provides content or links to additional content may be about as transparent into the actual workings of government as mud.

This is not to say that Recovery.gov has not achieved anything in the goal of transparency and trust. A government that acts in the shadows and denies the public a right to know what it is doing greatly harms the ideal of democracy. One that tries to show its actions and provide some level of accountability to the public moves government toward greater democracy. If the goal is to build trust, more information is better than none. Connecting faces to what was previously faceless, has some worth, and may create a more personal feeling of trust.

Trust built through interaction and participation, however, is where these sites leave the most to be desired. Does absorption of information equate to participation? Perhaps not, although it still might build trust, if the information is believable. But what about the submission of recovery stories, suggestions, and the like? Do these expressions, perhaps acknowledged with a form response, but certainly with no sharing with fellow citizens, equate to participation? We think not, and believe that the cyberdemocrats promoting a utopian vision of democracy will take an even dimmer view. But we also see Recovery.gov as progress in the right direction.

REFERENCES

Curtin, D., & Meijer, A. (2006). Does transparency increase legitimacy? *Information Polity*, *11*(2), 109–122.

Cyberspace Policy Research Group. (n.d.). *Cyberspace Policy Research Group*. Retrieved March 7, 2009, from http://www.cyprg.arizona.edu/waes.html

Demchak, C. C., Friis, C., & La Porte, T. M. (1998). Reflections on configuring public agencies in cyberspace: A conceptual investigation, in Snellen and van de Donk., (eds.). *Public administration in an information age: A handbook*. Amsterdam: IOS Press. pp. 225-244.

Department's National Telecommunications and Information Administration. (2009). *Memorandum for the heads of executive departments and agencies*. Retrieved September 24, 2009, from http://www.whitehouse.gov/the_press_office/TransparencyandOpenGovernment/

Ferber, P., Foltz, F., & Pugliese, R. (2007). Cyberdemocracy and online politics: A new model of interactivity. *Bulletin of Science, Technology & Society*, *27*(5), 391–400. doi:10.1177/0270467607304559

Grossman, L. (1995). *The electronic republic: Reshaping American democracy in the information age*.

Hooghe, M., & Stolle, D. (2003). Introduction. In M. Hooghe & D. Stolle, D. (Eds), *Generating Social Capital: Civil society and Institutions in Comparative Perspective* (pp. 1-18). New York: Palgrave Macmillan.

Inglehart, R., Basanez, M., & Moreno, A. (1998). *A human values and beliefs – A cross-cultural sourcebook: Political religious sexual, and economic norms in 43 societies: Findings from the 1990-1993 world values survey*. Ann Arbor, MI: University of Michigan Press.

LaPorte, T. M., Demchak, C. C., & de Jong, M. (2002). Democracy and bureaucracy in the age of the Web: Empirical findings and theoretical speculations. *Administration & Society*, *34*(4), 411–446. doi:10.1177/0095399702034004004

LeRoy, G. (2009, February 16). The power of transparency. *Nation (New York, N.Y.)*, 15.

Mansbridge, J. (1999). Altruistic Trust . In Warren, M. (Ed.), *Democracy and Trust* (pp. 290–309). Cambridge: Cambridge University Press. doi:10.1017/CBO9780511659959.010

Martinez-Moyano, I. J., Samsa, M. E., Baldwin, T. E., Willke, B. J., & Moore, A. P. (2007). *Investigating the dynamics of trust in government: Drivers and effects of policy initiatives and government action.* Retrieved March 22, 2009, from http://www.dis.anl.gov/publications/articles/Trust_in_Government%202007.pdf

McIvor, R., McHugh, M., & Cadden, C. (2002). Internet technologies: Supporting transparency in the public sector. *International Journal of Public Sector Management, 15*(3), 170–187. doi:10.1108/09513550210423352

McMillan, S. J. (2002). A four-part model of cyber-interactivity. *New Media & Society, 4*(2), 271–291.

Owen, T., & Powell, J. L. (2006). Trust, professional power and social theory: Lessons from a post-Foucauldian framework. *The International Journal of Sociology and Social Policy, 26*(3/4), 110–120. doi:10.1108/014433306610657179

Prosser, W. L. (1955). *Handbook of the law of torts.* St. Paul, MN: West Publishing Company.

Putnam, R. D. (1991). Bowling alone: America's declining social capital. *Journal of Democracy, 6*(1), 65–78. doi:10.1353/jod.1995.0002

Putnam, R. D. (2000). *Bowling alone: The collapse and revival of American community.* New York: Simon & Schuster.

Reichard, C. (1998). The impact of performance management on transparency and accountability in the public sector . In Hondeghem, A. (Ed.), *Ethics and accountability in a context of governance and new public management* (pp. 123–137). Amsterdam: IOS Press.

Roberts, N. (2002). Keeping public officials accountable through dialogue: Resolving the accountability paradox. *Public Administration Review, 62*(6), 658–669. doi:10.1111/1540-6210.00248

Schudson, M., & Haas, D. (2008). Voting for glass houses. *Columbia Journalism Review, 71.*

Tolbert, C. J., & Mossberger, K. (2006). The effects of e-government on trust and confidence in government. *Public Administration Review, 66*(3), 354–369. doi:10.1111/j.1540-6210.2006.00594.x

Welch, E. W., & Hinnant, C. C. (2002). Internet use, transparency, and interactivity effects on trust in government. In *Proceedings of the 36th Hawaii International Conference on System Sciences – 2003.*

Welch, E. W., Hinnant, C. C., & Moon, M. J. (2005). Linking citizen satisfaction with e-government and trust in government. *Journal of Public Administration: Research and Theory, 15*(3), 371–391. doi:10.1093/jopart/mui021

KEY TERMS AND DEFINITIONS

Internet: The network of computers linking together many smaller computer networks worldwide. The Internet includes commercial, educational, governmental, as well as other networks.

Interactivity: The extent to which a computer program and human being seem to have a dialog.

Transparency (new): The degree that a website allows the user to see the inner workings of the organization behind the website in order to build user trust for that organization.

Transparency (old): The degree that the organization behind a website identifies themselves so that you can judge the quality of the website's content.

Websites: A connected group of pages on the World Wide Web regarded as a single entity, usually maintained by one person.

ENDNOTES

[1] This is based on the definition of publication that has evolved out of legal usage, particularly defamation law (Prosser, 1955).

[2] In order to simplify things, we will refer to the 51 sites as state sites and refrain from mentioning the District of Columbia each time.

[3] Kansas's welcome was from their former governor and not the current one.

[4] The Mayor in the case of DC.

Chapter 12
Access Indiana:
Managing a Website through a Successful Public–Private Partnership

J. Ramon Gil-Garcia
Centro de Investigación y Docencia Económicas, Mexico

Francisco R. Hernandez-Tella
Universidad Autónoma del Estado de México, Mexico

ABSTRACT

Indiana was one of the first states to build a state website. Its IT functions had strong legislative underpinnings and its central IT agency exercises a relatively high degree of authority over agency-based IT functions. In addition, Indiana's website, AccessIndiana, was the product of a long-term public-private partnership. Based on the analysis of official and public documents and some in-depth semi-structured interviews with key factors such as the general manager of Indiana Interactive and the former state CIO, this case describes the recent history and success of AccessIndiana from about 1995 to 2005. This was the period in which AccessIndiana was considered one of the most successful public-private partnerships managing a state Website. After a brief period of uncertainty, in July of 2006, the state of Indiana signed a new long-term contract with Indiana Interactive to develop and maintain its official portal. AccessIndiana offers important lessons to public agencies, particularly for state and local governments and developing nations.

INTRODUCTION

The use of information technologies (IT) in government has been considered a powerful strategy for administrative reform (Heeks, 1999; Fountain, 2001; Kramer & King, 2003; Garson, 2004; Dawes, Gregg & Agouris, 2004). Governments around the world are developing and implement-

ing IT applications in order to obtain numerous benefits such as higher quality services, more efficient government operations, greater citizen participation and transparency, or more effective public policies and programs (Dawes & Pardo, 2002; Fletcher, 2002; Scholl, 2002; Gil-Garcia & Helbig, 2006). The realization of these benefits is not always easy and many more factors other than the technology itself play an important role in this type of initiative (Carter & Belanger, 2005;

DOI: 10.4018/978-1-61692-018-0.ch012

Gil-Garcia & Pardo, 2005; Khadaroo, 2005; Luna-Reyes et al., 2005; Zhang, Faerman & Cresswell, 2006; Eglene, Dawes & Schneider, 2007). Recent literature has demonstrated that one of the most important factors is collaboration, particularly in inter-organizational efforts (Harris, 2000; Lee, 2001; Dawes & Prefontaine, 2003; Gant, 2003b; Pardo et al., 2006). This collaboration could exist among units of the same government agency, among agencies from different levels of government or between government agencies and private companies (Harris, 2000; Faerman, McCaffrey & Van Slyke, 2001; Pardo, Gil-Garcia & Burke, 2007).

Public-private partnerships are a very specific type of collaboration in which a government agency and a private company work together towards a common objective and share the risk (Gant, 2003b). Public-private partnerships could be useful in many policy domains, but they are particularly suitable in situations in which governments do not have the necessary resources (or prefer not to spend them) to start a new project or initiative (Angelelli, Guaipatín & Suaznabar, 2004; Gant, 2003a). This chapter describes a successful public-private partnership that provides services to citizens and businesses via Internet applications, known as AccessIndiana. The analysis includes a review of official and public documents and nine semi-structured interviews with key actors such as the general manager of Indiana Interactive and the former state CIO. Interviews were conducted in two different periods: one in 2001 and the other in 2005. Questions were related to several topics such as the background and history of AccessIndiana, its management structure, and the benefits and challenges of the website, among others.

We think that AccessIndiana is an interesting case and provides useful lessons about a successful public-private partnership. As mentioned before, this organizational form could be useful not only to manage government websites, but could also be applied to other policy domains or other types of services. The experience of Indiana could have relevance for any government, particularly state and local governments that want to start a highly functional website, but have little resources to do so. A public-private partnership for website development could leverage resources and it make possible to provide high quality information and services with the limited financial resources of many local governments. These lessons could also be very important for developing nations, which often still face problems in creating and maintaining their e-government applications in general and their websites in particular.

As a medium-sized state, Indiana was a good laboratory for testing the private participation model, which significantly increased the number of services and the quality of information state agencies provided to the public. For example, AccessIndiana helped the state move from providing services via a registration process with monthly charges to a more convenient credit card payment system for specific services. AccessIndiana also included a section for local governments to provide their own services and receive payments, such as property taxes. Once AccessIndiana was running in this collaborative fashion, the know-how from the private participation allowed the state to not only improve its income from internet transactions, but also the quality of the services and, consequently, the satisfaction of citizens, businesses, and other more specific customers. This organizational form is becoming increasingly popular in recent years. As of 2009, there are 23 states and 2 local governments in the US with similar organizational models and partnerships with NIC Inc., a private company that provides e-Government portals.

BACKGROUND AND HISTORY

The population of Indiana in 2000 was about 6 million people, close to the national average for states of 5.6 million. Indiana is a big potential market for e-government services. In 1999, median income per household in Indiana was $41,567 and median income per family was about $50,261. In this same year, 9.5% of the population and 6.7% of the families were considered under the poverty line. About 82% of its highly educated population has completed high school or a higher degree and about 19% have at least a bachelor's degree. Finally, computer ownership increased from 44% in 1998 to 49% in 2000. Similarly, the percentage of people with Internet access rose from 26% in 1998 to 39% in 2000.

With respect to competition and political orientation, in the gubernatorial election of 2000 the percentage of votes for Democrats was 57% and for Republicans was 42%. The governor in 2000, Frank O'Bannon, was from the Democratic Party. According to Holbrook and VanDunk (1993), the Ranney Index presents Indiana as a state with relatively high political competition between 1981 and 1988 (0.86 out of 1). At the district level, these authors also found that Indiana was among the states with high political competition between 1982 and 1986 (Indiana received a score of 44.59. The highest score was 56.58 in North Dakota). During the gubernatorial election of 2000, the difference between the percentage of votes for Democrats and for Republicans was 15%, which showed some advantage for the Democratic Party. However, in the gubernatorial election of 2004, the Republican candidate won.

Indiana has a medium-sized state economy and many of the indicators below are close to the national average for all states. For instance, the government Gross State Product (GSP) was about $19.3 billion in 2000 and $20.9 billion in 2001 (national average was $23 and $24 billion, respectively). Indiana's total revenue in 2000 was about $20.5 billions. The number of state government jobs grew slightly from 108,867 in 1998 to 110,610 in 2000. Similarly, the number of local government jobs increased from 248,361 in 1998 to 255,369 in 2000. Total earnings were about $3.8 billion for state government employees and about $9.6 billion for local government employees in

2000. Another useful way to evaluate the size of the economy is by looking at the number of jobs and private earnings in several industries such as education, communications, management and engineering, among others. Total private earnings in education services jobs were about $1.1 billion in 2000, with about 60,000 jobs. The total number of jobs in the electronic and other electric equipment industry was 52,858 and private earnings for this industry were about $2.7 billion in 2000. Similarly, the total number of jobs in the communications industry in 2000 was 23,751 and private earnings were about $1.2 billion. The total number of jobs in engineering and management services was 68,143 and private earnings were about $2.3 billion in 2000.

Access Indiana and its Environment

In Indiana, the Office of the CIO oversees two legislatively mandated organizations: (1) the Division of Information Technology (DIT) and (2) the Information Technology Oversight Commission (ITOC). The Division of Information Technology is an operations organization that provides central services to other agencies on a fee-for-service basis. The Information Technology Oversight Commission was charged with activities such as IT planning, architecture, and policy setting for the state. Table 1 shows some relevant characteristics of Indiana's website environment, including organizational structure, resources, and the institutional framework. For instance, the total number of employees at the Office of the CIO was 185 in 2001, about 13% smaller than the US average of about 213 employees. Similarly, the average budget for the centralized IT organization in the United States was about $68 million in 2001 and the Office of the CIO's budget was $62.7 million. Indiana provides accessibility and usability training for its IT employees, as do about half of the states. Indiana provided website services using both outsourcing and direct provision from the Office of the CIO. In 2001, twenty-seven

Table 1. Selected characteristics about the Indiana website environment

Characteristics	Indiana	United States
Number of employees in the IT organization	185	Mean = 213
Budget of the IT organization	62.7 million	Mean = $68.4 millions
State provides accessibility training for IT employees	Yes	24 states (Yes)
State provides usability training for IT employees	Yes	22 states (Yes)
Provision of website services (direct provision, outsourcing, or both)	Both	27 states (direct provision) 5 states (outsourcing) 15 states (both)
Centralized IT organization directly manage portal development for agencies	Yes	31 states (Yes)
Percentage of the IT Office budget devoted to maintenance	2%	Mean = 7.7%
Percentage of the IT budget revenue sources from federal funds	2%	Mean = 3.13%
State has an IT Specific Legislative Committee (House, Senate, None)	None	29 states (House) 25 states (Senate)
All state IT professionals are members of the Civil Service	No	29 states (Yes)
State has mandatory accessibility standards for state websites	Yes	34 states (Yes)
State has mandatory usability standards for state websites	No	21 states (Yes)

Source: NASCIO. (2002). *NASCIO 2002 Compendium of Digital Government in the States.* Lexington, KY: National Association of State Chief Information Officers.

states provided their website services directly and five states outsourced their service delivery. Indiana is one of the thirty-one states in which the centralized IT organization directly manages portal development for agencies; in this specific case, that management occurs through a formal relationship with Indiana Interactive, Inc.

In 2002, the percentage of the Office of the CIO's budget devoted to maintenance overall was 2%, while the national average was about 8%. Similarly, the percentage of resources from federal sources was 2% in Indiana, while the national average was 3.13 percent in 2002. Indiana does not have IT committees either in the state House of Representatives or in the State Senate and has mandatory accessibility standards for state websites. Finally, in Indiana IT professionals are not entirely members of the Civil Service. In fact, due to a public-private partnership, all employees of AccessIndiana are formally working for a private company (Indiana Interactive, Inc.), and for these employees, personnel management has the

flexibility, competitiveness, and other advantages of private sector organizations.

According to West (2000, 2001, 2002, 2003, 2004), Indiana greatly improved from 2000 to 2001 and has been among the top 15 states in e-government functionality in the last four years. Figure 1 shows the trend of Indiana in this ranking from 2000 to 2004. The contract with Indiana Interactive was renewed in 2000 and it seems that this renewal had a positive effect on the score that Indiana received in 2001. In fact, Gant (2003a, 2003b) shows that a major re-design and other important managerial and policy changes took place between 2000 and 2001. AccessIndiana was completely re-designed and organized in terms of functional categories, instead of government structures. In addition, several policies and guidelines were created to improve the communication and coordination among Indiana Interactive, the Office of the CIO, and other state agencies.

For comparability purposes, Table 2 contains five different measures of state e-government quality or functionality that were developed between

Figure 1. Position of Indiana in the rank of West, 2001-2004

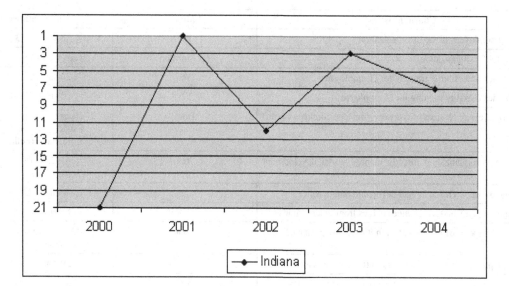

2001 and 2002. This was the only period of time in which all rankings and their methodologies were available. The overall state e-government ranking developed by Darrell West takes into consideration the greatest number of elements and attempts to evaluate complete websites. According to this more comprehensive measure, Indiana has a highly functional website, ranked 1st among all 50 states in 2001. The electronic commerce score includes mainly online services, but also some measures of information quality. It also attempts to evaluate the whole website. Gant and Gant (2002) developed the all score measure, which assessed the functionality of the state portals (only the initial pages). Finally, the number of e-commerce systems and the number of online services are simply the amount of these elements available in the state.

Evolution of AccessIndiana

In about 1994, a group of people from several Indiana state agencies started meeting regularly to talk about technology. At that time only two state agencies were providing some kind of online service and very few had any type of presence on the web. Some of the agencies represented were the Commission of Higher Education, the Department of Education, and the State Library, among others. This group began discussing the web and different strategies to bring its benefits to the State of Indiana. They explored several alternatives including the public-private partnership developed by Kansas. Basically, the model is to outsource the website development to a private company with the promise of being able to charge convenience fees for commercially viable data.

The public-private partnership model seemed to be a workable alternative for Indiana. The Intelenet Commission issued a request for proposals and Indiana Interactive, Inc. (a wholly owned subsidiary of NIC Inc.), was selected as the manager of the state website (network manager). AccessIndiana, which was the official name of Indiana's website, was made available on the World Wide Web by December 1995.

When it started in 1995, AccessIndiana did not have a common look and feel. Each agency developed its own website and they all looked different. The only thing they had in common was the third-level URL to get there (i.e., www. sos.IN.gov). State agencies were required to use

Table 2. E-Government position of Indiana (2001-2002)

Measures	Score	Rank	Source
Overall State E-Government Ranking	52.3	1	West, D. M. (2001). State and Federal E-Government in the United States, 2001. Providence, RI: Brown University.
Electronic Commerce Score	75	8	Lassman, K. (2002). The Digital State 2001. Washington, DC: The Progress & Freedom Foundation.
All Score	29	16	Gant, Diana B., Gant, Jon P. & Craig, L. Johnson (2002). State Web Portals: Delivering and Financing E-Service. E-Government Series. Arlington, VA: The PricewaterhouseCoopers Endowment for The Business in Government.
Number of E-Commerce Systems	7	19	NASCIO. (2002). NASCIO 2002 Compendium of Digital Government in the States. Lexington, KY: National Association of State Chief Information Officers.
Number of Online Services	7	10	CSG. (2002). The Book of the States. 2002 Edition, Volume 34. Lexington, KY: The Council of State Governments.

domain names that ended with IN.gov for their own websites. The initial goal was just to get every agency online. Once every agency had some presence on the Web, the Office of the CIO and Indiana Interactive started working towards two objectives: (1) identifying and developing convenience-fee transactions, and (2) applying a statewide common look and feel: "one site, one website." They achieved that goal through conversations with state agencies about the importance of having more dynamic information and providing electronic services to their constituencies. Around 1999, the home page of AccessIndiana was organized in such a way that the user needed to know which agency he or she wanted to interact with. It consisted of a window with a logo and with a few categories around it (e.g., state, local, associations). Clicking on a category took the user to a list of available links (i.e., list of all state agencies) and it was difficult for users to find the information or service they needed. In 2004, the home page was more driven by functions. The new categories in the left column attempted to capture events or functions that users wanted to perform or information they needed to find (e.g., traveling, finding a job, paying taxes).

As mentioned above, the public-private partnership model is funded through convenience fees applied to certain transactional services. Therefore, identifying several commercially viable transactions was very important. AccessIndiana started with driver's records, which are used by insurance companies and other entities on a regular basis. However, having only one source of revenue was considered very risky for a private company. Therefore, in order to diversify the sources of revenue for AccessIndiana, the partners explored other potential transactions and developed them in the following years. The Governor's Technology Taskforce helped to identify information and services that people were looking for from the website. The taskforce reviewed other states' websites, obtained information about the popularity of certain online services in other states, and discussed personal web experiences of the members of the taskforce, among other topics. Through this process, the members of the taskforce identified a variety of potential services, some of which were then developed and made available on the web. Some examples of the services identified were fishing licenses and driver's license renewals.

Initially, in order to obtain services that require a fee, users needed to be subscribed to the portal and they were billed at the end of the month. Around 1999, AccessIndiana began allowing the use of credit cards to pay for services. With this

Figure 2. Indiana Website (April 2005)

development, agencies realized that collecting fees was not as problematic as they originally thought and they became more interested in developing transactional services online.

Technology, Organization, and Outcomes

In 2005, AccessIndiana had a common look and feel. It was organized in a three-column setup with two thinner columns on each side and a larger column in the middle (see Figure 2). The column on the left was navigation and the column on the right contained direct links to information or services that people use the most. The middle column features services, either new ones or seasonal offerings such as filing taxes or hunting and fishing licenses.

Regarding the mission of AccessIndiana, one of the brochures states, "Belonging to Indiana state government, AccessIndiana is the brand name under which state agencies, boards, and commissions provide online services and information for citizens and businesses." Technical and program staff members characterized AccessIndiana in different ways. For instance, one respondent mentioned that the goal was "to provide access to citizens and businesses in an easy fashion. We do not want constituencies to have to know what agencies they need to interact with.... At the same time the goal is to make it as cost effective as possible." Talking about the mission another interviewee said, "Citizen's service at the citizen's convenience, not at our convenience... and what that really meant was that we had to have 24x7 access. We had to provide privacy and security, because people are not going to consider something convenient that puts them at risk. So, privacy and security were very important to providing that kind of citizen convenience... and then through that convenience being able to drive down the cost of doing business with government, both for government and for the individual."

Two main elements characterize the mission of AccessIndiana from the view of leaders and managers. First, AccessIndiana has to be able to help citizens, businesses, and other users to conveniently obtain the information and services they need. Second, AccessIndiana should be able to produce cost-savings not only for government agencies, but also for users. Convenient high quality services and reduced real cost are also seen as incentives for citizens and businesses to use the Website.

Services and Audiences

In AccessIndiana, information and services were organized in fourteen categories: (1) About Indiana, (2) Business, (3) Tourism and Recreation, (4) Labor and Employment, (5) Education and Training, (6) Licensing and Permits, (7) Family, Health and Safety, (8) Taxes and Finance, (9) Agriculture and Environment, (10) Travel and Transportation, (11) Law and Justice, (12) Public Assistance, (13) In Your Neighborhood, and (14) Technology. These categories are designed to help citizens, businesses, and other users to easily find the information they need; the categories also attempt to present information according to the functions that users want to perform. In addition, about three years ago, AccessIndiana partnered with Google to offer a search engine, which helps users find the material they need.

Some of the services that are available are hunting and fishing licenses, filing state taxes, renewing license plates, renewing driver's license, renewing professional licenses, and permits, among others. Searching for legislation has also become popular. In fact, an important characteristic of AccessIndiana is that all three branches of state government are represented on it. Citizens can have access to information and services from the executive, legislative, and judicial branches

through the same website. As one of the respondents said, "citizens of Indiana really do have a virtual one-stop shop. One place to go, no matter who you need information from in state government." Legislation was an important factor in accomplishing this virtual co-location.

The legislation creating AccessIndiana requires all agencies under the governor to use the portal and allows the legislative and judicial branches the option of using the portal. In addition, posting information at AccessIndiana is free for state government users from all three branches of government. When AccessIndiana started in 1995, the legislative and judicial branches did not have separate pages. From the beginning, they built their websites at AccessIndiana because the service that Indiana Interactive staff provides is equally beneficial for all three branches. Managing each branch as three separate streams of activity, the staff has been able to respect the order and priorities of the governor, the legislators, and the judiciary in regard to website services.

In 2004, the first applications for myLocal. gov were made available online. The rationale behind myLocal is that citizens do not know and do not have to know what part of government is responsible for certain information or services. They do not necessarily differentiate between the executive, legislative, and judicial branches or services provided by their city, their county, or their state. MyLocal works in the following way. There is a "local government" link at the home page (www.IN.gov). From this page, people can go to any local government website and can also perform some transactions such as paying property taxes. From a developmental point of view, the transactional services are like customizable templates on which local governments can put their name, bank account number, and other relevant information. These templates are available for use by all local governments in Indiana.

As mentioned before, one of the most important sources of revenue for AccessIndiana is driver's records. The main customer for this type of service is insurance companies, but sometimes public institutions also need the service. For example, a school may need the record of a potential school bus driver. When this is the case, the record is provided for free to the public organization. The courts also use driving records. For example, if a person is arrested for driving under the influence of alcohol and will be going to court, the prosecutor needs to know his or her previous driving record to make a better decision in the case. A digital signature application was developed to streamline this process. The commissioner needed to certify and sign all driving records before sending them to the courts. This process used to take between 6 days and 2 weeks. With the new system, the driving records are electronically signed and the whole process takes only a few minutes. AccessIndiana was also attempting to offer more integrated solutions to specific audiences (i.e., a Human Resources portal). Another important initiative is to offer information and services in multiple languages. As of 2005, they were working on a Spanish version of the website.

Website Management

AccessIndiana was designed in accordance with a three-tier architecture: (1) the presentation layer, (2) the application layer, and (3) the data layer. As the primer for AccessIndiana explains, "The presentation layer is the user interface and is what the user sees… The application layer controls the business logic and applies that logic to the user input before passing a request to the data layer… The data layer performs the request and passes the results to the application layer, which may again apply business logic before delivering the result back to the presentation layer."[1] The purpose of this separation is to reduce the complexity of managing the whole website and increase portability, scalability, and re-usability.

Figure 3 shows how the website was divided for development and management purposes. Most online transactions were hosted at AccessIndi-

ana and managed in a centralized fashion. The presentation layers are normally hosted at AccessIndiana and most of these transactions also use AccessIndiana's payment engine, but the database layer of these applications are normally the responsibility of the respective agencies. Agencies have to pay for web hosting of their database layers and these databases are maintained in different locations. Some of them are hosted at AccessIndiana, others are hosted at the Division of Information Technology, some agencies host them on their own servers, and others outsource the hosting to a private company. However, if an agency chooses to house the database layer outside of the agency or the central IT organization, they needed to get a waiver from the Technology Oversight Commission.

AccessIndiana staff attempts to be technologically eclectic and is open to many different technologies and programming languages. However, in practice, and because of the kind of applications they normally needed to create, they could be considered a Java shop. Since some agencies have already embraced specific technologies, AccessIndiana has to be ready to understand and support these platforms and software. For example, the Bureau of Motor Vehicles is adopting the "dot.net" platform and the state IT office is planning to become a Microsoft driven shop. Indiana Interactive is the state network manager and has responsibilities for daily operations, including application development, design, marketing, customer service, systems support, and infrastructure. The Enhance Data Access Review Committee (EDARC) meets every other month and the general manager of AccessIndiana presents a report of the completed work and suggestions for the next steps. This committee includes members from state agencies and some citizens appointed by the Governor's Office. EDARC has the authority to evaluate Indiana Interactive's work and authorize fees for new online services. Staff from the Office of the CIO and AccessIndiana meet regularly to

Figure 3. Website development and management strategies

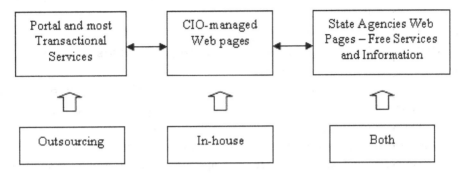

discuss the general strategy for the website and to determine the next set of statewide priorities.

AccessIndiana staff meets with state agencies to discuss the current state of their websites and potential new developments. Most state agencies rely on AccessIndiana for web applications development, especially those that will be available through the portal. This service is free for state government including the executive, legislative, and judicial branches. Normally, agencies present their requests to AccessIndiana staff and discuss the importance and priority of their current and future projects. Upon acceptance of new projects, they are put on a list that works on a first come, first serve basis.

Sometimes, agencies need an application faster (i.e., in order to meet a deadline) and they have the resources to pay for its development. In these situations, they outsource the development to another private company; once it is ready, AccessIndiana staff can web-enable it and host it. By following this process, those agencies can still get the benefits from the free hosting (or the presentation layer) and all transactions are offered in the same place. In addition, the vendor that develops the application has to follow detailed guidelines and statewide standards.[2] Some important elements included in these guidelines are common look and feel, architecture, technology standards, privacy policy, accessibility, security, and hosting. The use of these guidelines for vendors has been an important strategy to keep the website more

consistent and to enable efficient administration and maintenance.

The legislature is involved with AccessIndiana through the staff at the Legislative Services Agency. They work together with AccessIndiana staff in keeping the legislature's portion of the website up to date. There is a committee of legislators, which oversees the Legislative Services Agency and makes requests to its staff about the website and other technology related matters. During session in January, AccessIndiana helps legislators conduct surveys of citizens. Sometimes AccessIndiana staff members meet with legislators individually and talk about the services offered and how those services can be useful for the legislators' constituencies. AccessIndiana is always working with the legislature, but most of the time this involvement is about the legislative portion of the website. Legislators are normally not involved in decisions or actions about the whole website.

Regarding the content of the main page, AccessIndiana staff proposes what to include in this initial page and the objective is to change it at least every quarter. AccessIndiana staff meets with selected agencies and businesses to get their feedback. The proposed page is reviewed by the Office of the CIO and other state agency representatives, who can make suggestions about specific content changes and overall structure of this initial page. In general, the first pages of the portal are developed and managed by Indiana Interactive. All other pages can be updated by each agency through their own authorization process. If an agency does not have the necessary staff to do its updates, AccessIndiana can help with this process. AccessIndiana staff is directly involved in this process only if it is a new fee-based service or if the modifications affect the current fee structure. Currently, the content management process is done manually, but AccessIndiana is planning to acquire an automated tool in the near future.

For fee-based transactional services there are three types of fees. First, there are statutory fees, which always go back to the state agency. These are fees that agencies normally charge for providing certain kinds of services and they are specified by law. Second, enhanced access fees or convenience fees go to Indiana Interactive as the network manager of AccessIndiana. These fees are used to maintain the existing free services and to develop new projects. They are also used for management expenses such as marketing campaigns, AccessIndiana staff, new infrastructure, etc. Third, instant access fees are used to cover the costs associated with processing a credit card or an electronic check.

Feedback from users is very important to making decisions about the content and structure of AccessIndiana. Citizens and businesses can always send e-mail messages with questions or suggestions. When launching new services, AccessIndiana organizes focus groups to get feedback before making them available online. They also organize training sessions with banks, law firms, and other potential users to explain how the services work and get comments from them. AccessIndiana staff members attended trade shows and demo several of their services to different audiences such as human resources managers and health professionals, among others. A live chat is also available in the portal and users can start a session to interact with a member of AccessIndiana staff. At the end of a live chat session the user is asked to fill out a short survey. Similarly, at the end of many services there is a survey for users to provide feedback. Finally, there is also an op-portunity to share good overall experiences with AccessIndiana through a service called FanMail.

Website Policies

Due to security and control considerations, policies require that the presentation layer be hosted at AccessIndiana. This helps to keep the common look and feel and support the marketing and branding efforts. In addition, if there is a problem with the back-end system, Indiana Interactive can restrict access to the presentation layer until the problem is fixed and the application is running again. Because it offers transactions, security and privacy are especially important for AccessIndiana. The architecture of the website helps to provide security and convenience to the user. Several standards and guidelines regarding hosting, development, and other elements of the technological architecture work simultaneously to enhance convenience, but also to ensure security and privacy for AccessIndiana's users.

In addition, all state agencies are required to use IN.gov in their URLs. This policy helps people to identify Indiana's government websites and creates a sense of security about who they are interacting with. It is also useful as part of the branding and marketing efforts. Website privacy, accessibility, and security are also important policies governing AccessIndiana. In addition, some guidelines include information about required characteristics of the website as well as technology standards that have to be used by state agencies.

Benefits of the AccessIndiana Website

Convenience for citizens is one of the most important benefits of AccessIndiana. Citizens can obtain information and services 24 hours a day, 7 days a week. They do not have to stand in line in order to get government forms or to pay for government services. They can easily find information and services they need from any computer with

Internet access. The website is now organized in such a way that users do not need to know with precision which agency they need to interact with.

Using the website also helps to save money for the citizens and the state agencies. One of the goals of AccessIndiana is not only to be convenient and easy to use, but also to offer cost-savings solutions to most users. The services and fees are designed to meet users' needs and to help them to save money (such as the cost of parking, traveling, gasoline, and messengers used for in-person services). For instance, some fees have been calculated by taking into consideration the walk-in cost of obtaining that service. According to one of the interviewees, fees are always lower than the total cost of the service for citizens or businesses to get the service at a state agency's office. Technology has the potential to reduce the cost of service provision and both provider and client should benefit from it.

Another benefit is greater participation in the democratic process. This benefit is partly due to the convenience of having legislators' contact information, legislative bills, political appointees' e-mail addresses, and other information available online. The availability of information improves the perceived accessibility to representatives and government officials and helps to increase the perceived transparency of state government. Through the website, citizens can be more informed and involved in state government actions and have a sense that government is more open to the people. Citizen participation and involvement varies, but according to one of the interviewees, website use statistics show a positive trend regarding overall use of AccessIndiana over time. AccessIndiana has the potential to make state government more accessible and accountable. Talking about the relationship between citizens and governments, one respondent said, "A web portal that works well creates a community that requires both sides to be responsible and accountable."

For businesses, AccessIndiana clearly creates cost-saving benefits. Businesses use the website because they save money and they can get the information and services they need faster. As one respondent mentioned talking about the benefits for businesses, "Time is money, and the faster you can get something done, the more you have access to information, the more you can cut down that cycle and just have it finished, the better off you are. So, to me clearly it is costs-savings." In addition, many businesses used to spend a large amount of money and time sending messengers or maintaining employees whose sole job was to sit in government offices and look for certain documents or to courier documents between the company and government agencies. AccessIndiana has helped to reduce the cost and time businesses need to get specific information and services.

Local governments play at least two roles in their interaction with AccessIndiana. First, like citizens and businesses, they can be users of the information and services available at the website. In this role, they can get the same benefits that other users receive: convenience and cost-savings. Local governments can get some services such as driver's records or limited criminal histories at either no cost or for a reduced fee. In addition, local governments, like state agencies, can also provide information and services through AccessIndiana. There are several potential benefits they can achieve in this role, such as the provision of transactional services and efficiency improvements. In addition, citizens are now more willing to interact with government through the web, including local governments. Local government can take advantage of the experience of AccessIndiana and the best practices developed at the state level.

Challenges to the AccessIndiana Website

Interviewees stated that resources are limited and it is necessary to manage priorities. AccessIndiana deals with this challenge through the use of a first come, first serve strategy. However, there have been exceptions to this. For example, the

Governor's projects receive a higher priority. In these cases, agencies that were in the queue were contacted and informed about the situation. However, projects of the legislative or judicial branches have not been moved as a result of a Governor's priorities. By managing these separately, AccessIndiana respects the autonomy and authority of the three branches of state government. This separation has helped AccessIndiana to continue working with all three branches and be considered the website of the whole state government, not only the executive branch. In addition, having a private outsourcing alternative for agencies that need to meet a deadline and have financial resources for development has also been a useful strategy to deal with priorities.

State websites require complex inter-organizational processes and good coordination and communication mechanisms. However, communication between the strategic level and the operational level is often difficult. In a public-private partnership model, like AccessIndiana, communication between the responsible state agency and the vendor is very important. This communication has to take place not only at the strategic level, between the CIO and the general manager, but also at the operational level between webmasters, graphic designers, and others. In addition, the communication channels should flow not only from top to bottom, but also from bottom to top. For AccessIndiana, communication from the operational level to the strategic level has been the most challenging. Some information at the operational level could be useful to make better decisions, but generally this information does not flow as frequently as needed. Building consensus about the strategic direction for the website has also been a challenge for AccessIndiana. Developing overall strategies is a combination of understanding what state agencies need and want from the website and what the website can do for all state agencies and other stakeholders. As one respondent said, "It is a mixture of listening and leading… and you cannot do one or the other, you have to do both, because there are some people who are going to give you things that you are going to be doing. Other people who just start looking for you to provide leadership because they have no idea and you have to be able to satisfy both of those to build consensus."

Coordination among all the actors involved in the development and management of the website is an important challenge. AccessIndiana has designed different ways to develop and manage transactional services for state agencies. In order to keep the same look and feel and a more integrated website, it is necessary for AccessIndiana to work together with state agencies, legislators, courts, vendors, business users, and other important stakeholders. As of 2005, AccessIndiana was 10 years old and had over 300,000 pages of information. The management of all this content is difficult and requires work from many different actors. Until this point, content management has been done manually, but many recognize that a website of this size needs a better way to deal with this issue. AccessIndiana is planning to start using a content management automated tool. They know that the challenge will be to convince all agencies and organizations involved to migrate to this new system.

Finally, language translation was also identified as an important challenge. As of 2005, AccessIndiana used machine translation software, which provides only 60% to 70% accuracy. The problem is that for certain information and applications these levels may be enough, but for others more accurate translations are necessary. For content that needs more accuracy, the state has to make a decision about how to proceed, either to manually translate this content or to build a dictionary repository to increase the accuracy. AccessIndiana is currently working on a Spanish version of the website, but the complexity of this initiative has delayed its implementation. One respondent mentioned that initiatives like this one may require direct sponsorship by the Governor.

SOLUTIONS AND RECOMMENDATIONS

This section offers some recommendations based on the success factors found in the case study. As mentioned before, AccessIndiana was a public-private partnership in which a private company, Indiana Interactive, managed the portal and most of the transactions offered through the website. Its maintenance and improvement are not tightly linked to the state budget, but to website usage and the revenues it generates through fees. These convenience fees are the main source of financial support for AccessIndiana, and consequently Indiana has a strong focus on marketing information and services available for different types of users, including insurance companies, law firms, professionals, and the general public. This independence from the state budget and ability to generate revenue could be considered important success factors in a public-private partnership model.

AccessIndiana and its governance structure have been supported by legislation. From the very beginning, the website effort had a clear but flexible legal framework. For instance, agencies were required to participate in the website and meet certain requirements. In addition, in states that have outsourced the management of their Web portal, such as Indiana, many of the necessary staff works for the outsourcing company, which has more flexibility in hiring, assignments, and compensation. The centralized IT organization still plays an important role, but it is less operational and more strategic in nature. Developing an adequate legal framework and having flexibility in the management of human resources are important success factors.

State website financial arrangements and their importance vary according to the specific business model and management approach taken. For Indiana, the maintenance of the portal and most of the maintenance of online services are the responsibility of Indiana Interactive; therefore, resources for this activity are necessary in this organization.

Since Indiana Interactive's budget comes mainly from convenience fees and its primary goal is to develop and maintain the website, resources for these purposes are always available and do not have to compete with other state priorities. This dedicated budget played an important role in the success of AccessIndiana.

Respondents in Indiana indicated that both in-house and outsourced responsibilities were essential for a successful website. In Indiana, Indiana Interactive manages the portal and most transactional services. Even in this mostly outsourced environment, however, respondents said that in-house responsibilities are extremely important. The Office of the CIO and governance structures within the state has helped Indiana Interactive to do its part of the job. Support and commitment from state partners are two important elements for the success of a public-private partnership. For instance, strategic and operational staff members from the Office of the CIO and Indiana Interactive had regular meetings to discuss progress and future directions.

Marketing was also recognized as an important success factor. Due to the convenience-fee approach, aggressive marketing was extremely important for Indiana. Marketing efforts lead to more usage of the website, and more usage leads to more resources to continue developing AccessIndiana. As any other private company, Indiana Interactive needs to attract customers in order to stay in business. Marketing is therefore a key element of AccessIndiana's overall strategy. In fact, one of the four main areas in the organizational structure of Indiana Interactive is marketing. For Indiana Interactive, as for any private company, assessing the size of the population and therefore the size of the potential market for new e-government services was very important for the website's success.

Involvement of and feedback from agency customers and other stakeholders have also been important success factors for AccessIndiana. Formal and informal committees have been essential to its success, because involved agencies become active designers of AccessIndiana and promoters of its overall strategies. In addition, for convenience-fee models, a state partner that is committed to the success of the website is very important.

According to the National Association of State Chief Information Officers (NASCIO), the average tenure of state CIOs is about 2 years. The CIO of the state of Indiana who was in charge during this period was in her position for 7 years and the general manager of Indiana Interactive had been working for that company for 6 years. Respondents in Indiana considered the stability of the people responsible for the website as an important success factor, too. Finally, rankings are important to obtain information about what other states are doing and how AccessIndiana can be improved. When planning a redesign, among other activities, AccessIndiana staff members review available rankings. They pay close attention to the websites that ranked high and try to find areas for improvement by looking at the differences and similarities between those websites and AccessIndiana. Paying attention to current and best practices seems to be another success factor to consider.

FUTURE RESEARCH DIRECTIONS

For Indiana, the public-private partnership model was successful. Indiana was able to manage a large website with a very small government budget and coordination with Indiana Interactive was also very well executed. For instance, one of the causes for AccessIndiana's success could be the willingness of both parties, public and private, to make it work with a simple and well-coordinated strategy. However, these conditions would not be the same for other states and other countries. Future studies should analyze the effectiveness of this outsourcing model in different economic, technological, political, and national contexts. In

addition, a survey will be desirable to assess the generalizability of the benefits and challenges found in this interesting case. It would also be important to assess to what extent the success of AccessIndiana was due to the partnership model.

Research about specific topics would also be important. For instance, future challenges for AccessIndiana include the improvement of back-office processes. Leaders and managers of AccessIndiana recognize that it is relatively easy to create a good interface for a legacy system or a cumbersome back-office process. However, future improvements have to deal with bureaucratic work processes that are not always linked or efficient. This type of change is necessary in order to have a more integrated website and obtain the benefits from a more efficient government. Future studies should attempt to understand if the improvement of back-office processes is different or similar in an outsourcing environment in comparison with in-house efforts.

In general terms, AccessIndiana found ways to deal with state politics without getting too involved with or being responsive to only one of the branches. For example, regarding the development of new applications, there was a project queue that was managed on a first-come, first-serve basis. In this scheme, the governor could change the priority of the projects within the executive branch, but cannot affect the order of projects from the legislative or judicial branches. Government websites will always be surrounded by the political environment. It would be very interesting to assess how effective public-private partnerships are in considering and managing government politics and future research should focus on this issue. There are also interesting questions about other related topics such as accountability, transparency, and democracy in cases like AccessIndiana. For instance, public-private partnerships could be a good way to improve the relationships among governments, citizens, and private companies, but it is not always clear which party is accountable if something goes wrong. A private company

Figure 4. Indiana Website (October, 2009)

may be providing a public service, but it could be expected that the government is still responsible and accountable for the results of these agreements. More research is needed in this direction.

Finally, as of 2009, the official website of the state of Indiana is still managed by a public-private partnership. After a brief period of uncertainty, in July of 2006, the state of Indiana signed a new long-term contract with Indiana Interactive to develop and maintain its official portal (initially for four additional years). In 2006, Indiana's website was a finalist in the Best of the Web awards and 9th place in the Brown University eGovernment Survey. Its name is no longer AccessIndiana, but IN.gov (see Figure 4). Recently, Indiana has included more services in the myLocal section and has added services for mobile devices. Currently, Indiana's website offers many services for citizens and businesses. For citizens: (1) Driver's license renewals, (2) State of Indiana Job Bank, (3) Licensed child care center searches, (4) Income tax filings, (5) "Who's Your Legislator?" service, (6) Hunting, trapping, and fishing licenses, (7) Vehicle registration renewals, and (8) Automated legislative bill tracking. For businesses: (1) Busi-

ness entity name searches, (2) New hire reporting, (3) Limited criminal history searches, (4) File lobbyist reports, (5) Health professional license verifications, (6) Uniform Commercial Code filings and searches, (7) Notary searches, and (8) Title and lien searches. Future studies should explore the benefits of public-private partnerships at the beginning of IT initiatives and the potential benefits in the medium and long terms, both in the development and management aspects of such projects.

CONCLUSION

The public-private partnership model followed by Indiana seems to be an interesting and useful alternative for other governments to consider, especially at the local level in which there may be limited financial resources and technical expertise. Different from pure outsourcing, the public-private partnership strategy requires a greater level of coordination between the government IT central agency and the private company managing components of the information and services. This coordination can be difficult at times, but helps to obtain positive results such as high quality services, important policies, and good relationships with most agencies, the legislative, and the judicial branches. The public-private partnership strategy could promote the development of high-quality government websites, which are then managed with appropriate expertise and deliver value to citizens and to the government itself. We think that considering this model as an alternative could help other governments to better understand the costs, benefits, and challenges of managing a large and complex website, particularly at the local level and in developing nations.

More generally, the public-private partnership model could be introduced in different aspects of public management and different policy domains, providing innovative solutions (Gray, 1989; Faerman, McCaffrey & Van Slyke, 2001; Mattessich et al., 2001; Vangen & Huxham, 2003; Luna-Reyes, 2004). One example can be found in the public-private collaboration for developing small enterprises in Latin America (Angelelli, Guaipatín & Suaznabar, 2004). These authors identified certain conditions for growing collaboration: (1) the increasing need to establish consensus in order to define new priorities for scarce resource allocation, (2) the failure of supply-oriented programs, (3) the demand for accountability and transparency, (4) the competitive advantages that the private sector has in client-oriented platforms, (5) the need for generating market-based mechanisms sustainable in the medium term, (6) the need for feedback mechanisms for policy evaluation and redesign (Angelelli, Guaipatín & Suaznabar, 2004). All of these conditions can be found in many different policy domains. In addition, the International Labor Organization (ILO) considers various development opportunities facilitated by public-private collaborations, particularly the positive effect from combining private sector know-how with important public values such as gender equality, accountability, sustainability, and universal access (ILO, 2008). Therefore, we think

that some of the lessons from the AccessIndiana case could help to develop better awareness of situations in other policy domains where a public-private partnership could be a good organizational alternative.

REFERENCES

Angelelli, P., Guaipatín, C., & Suaznabar, C. (2004). *La colaboración público-privada en el apoyo a la pequeña empresa: siete estudios de caso en América Latina*. Informe de Trabajo. Departamento de Desarrollo Sostenible. International Development Bank.

Carter, L., & Belanger, F. (2005). The utilization of e-government services: Citizen trust, innovation and acceptance factors. *Information Systems Journal*, *15*, 5–25. doi:10.1111/j.1365-2575.2005.00183.x

CSG. (2002). *The book of the states. 2002 edition* (*Vol. 34*). Lexington, KY: The Council of State Governments.

Dawes, S. S., Gregg, V., & Agouris, P. (2004). Digital government research: Investigations at the crossroads of social and information science. *Social Science Computer Review*, *22*(1), 5–10. doi:10.1177/0894439303259863

Dawes, S. S., & Pardo, T. A. (2002). Building collaborative digital government systems. systematic constraints and effective practices. In McIver, W. J., & Elmagarmid, A. K. (Eds.), *Advances in digital government. technology, human factors, and policy* (pp. 259–273). Norwell, MA: Kluwer Academic Publishers. doi:10.1007/0-306-47374-7_16

Dawes, S. S., & Prefontaine, L. (2003). Understanding new models of collaboration for delivering government services. *Communications of the ACM*, *46*(1), 40–42. doi:10.1145/602421.602444

Eglene, O., Dawes, S. S., & Schneider, C. A. (2007). Authority and leadership patterns in public sector knowledge networks. *American Review of Public Administration, 37*(1), 91–113. doi:10.1177/0275074006290799

Faerman, S. R., McCaffrey, D., & Van Slyke, D. M. (2001). Understanding interorganizational cooperation: public–private collaboration in regulating financial market innovation. *Organization Science, 12*(3), 372–388. doi:10.1287/orsc.12.3.372.10099

Fletcher, P. D. (2002). Policy and portals. In McIver, W. J., & Elmagarmid, A. K. (Eds.), *Advances in digital government: Technology, human factors, and policy*. Norwell, MA: Kluwer Academic Press. doi:10.1007/0-306-47374-7_14

Fountain, J. E. (2001). *Building the virtual state. Information technology and institutional change*. Washington, DC: Brookings Institution Press.

Gant, D. B., Gant, J. P., & Craig, L. J. (2002). *State web portals: Delivering and financing e-service. E-Government Series*. Arlington, VA: The PricewaterhouseCoopers Endowment for The Business in Government.

Gant, J. P. (2003a). *Delivering e-government services through the access Indiana information network*. Albany, NY: Center for Technology in Government, University at Albany, SUNY.

Gant, J. P. (2003b). *Information sharing communications, and coordination in e-government collaborations*. Albany, NY: Center for Technology in Government, University at Albany, SUNY.

Garson, G. D. (2004). The promise of digital government. In Pavlichev, A., & Garson, G. D. (Eds.), *Digital government: Principles and best practices* (pp. 2–15). Hershey, PA: Idea Group Publishing.

Gil-Garcia, J. R., & Helbig, N. (2006). Exploring e-government benefits and success factors. In Anttiroiko, A.-V., & Malkia, M. (Eds.), *Encyclopedia of digital government* (pp. 803–811). Hershey, PA: IGI Global.

Gil-Garcia, J. R., & Pardo, T. A. (2005). Egovernment success factors: Mapping practical tools to theoretical foundations. *Government Information Quarterly, 22*(1), 187–216. doi:10.1016/j.giq.2005.02.001

Gray, B. (1989). *Collaborating: Finding common ground for multiparty problems* (1st ed.). San Francisco, CA: Jossey-Bass Inc.

Harris, N. D. (2000). Intergovernmental cooperation in the development and use of information systems. In Garson, D. (Ed.), *Handbook of Public Information Systems*. New York: Marcel Dekker.

Heeks, R. (1999). *Reinventing government in the information age. International practice in IT-enabled public sector reform*. New York: Routledge. doi:10.4324/9780203204962

Holbrook, T. M., & Van Dunk, E. (1993). Electoral competition in the American states. *The American Political Science Review, 87*(4), 955–962. doi:10.2307/2938827

ILO. (2008). *Consejo de Administración, Comisión de Cooperación Técnica. Oficina Internacional del Trabajo (International Labor Organization)*. Ginebra.

Khadaroo, M. I. (2005). An institutional theory perspective on the UK's private finance initiative (PFI) accounting standard setting process. *Public Management Review, 7*(1), 69–94. doi:10.1080/1471903042000339428

Kraemer, K. L., & King, J. L. (2003). *Information technology and administrative reform: Will the time after e-government be different?* Paper presented at the Heinrich Reinermann Schrift Fest, Post Graduate School of Administration, Speyer, Germany.

Lassman, K. (2002). *The digital state 2001.* Washington, DC: The Progress & Freedom Foundation.

Lee, J.-N. (2001). The impact of knowledge sharing, organizational capability and partnership quality on IS outsourcing success. *Information & Management, 38,* 323–335. doi:10.1016/S0378-7206(00)00074-4

Luna-Reyes, L. F. (2004). *Collaboration, trust and knowledge sharing in information-technology-intensive projects in the public sector.* (Unpublished PhD Dissertation). University at Albany, Albany, NY.

Luna-Reyes, L. F., Zhang, J., Gil-García, J. R., & Cresswell, A. M. (2005). Information systems development as emergent socio-technical change: A practice approach. *European Journal of Information Systems, 14,* 93–105. doi:10.1057/palgrave.ejis.3000524

Mattessich, P. W., Murray-Close, M., & Monsey, B. R. (2001). *Collaboration: What makes it work* (2nd ed.). Saint Paul, MN: Amherst H. Wilder Foundation.

NASCIO. (2002). *NASCIO 2002 compendium of digital government in the states.* Lexington, KY: National Association of State Chief Information Officers.

Pardo, T. A., Cresswell, A. M., Thompson, F., & Zhang, J. (2006). Knowledge sharing in cross-boundary information system development in the public sector. *Information Technology Management, 7*(4), 293–313. doi:10.1007/s10799-006-0278-6

Pardo, T. A., Gil-Garcia, J. R., & Burke, B. (2007). Sustainable cross-boundary information sharing. In Chen, H., Brandt, L., Dawes, S., Gregg, V., Hovy, E., & Macintosh, A. (Eds.), *Digital government: Advanced research and case studies.* New York: Springer.

Scholl, H. J. (2002). *Executive briefing on electronic government and business process change.* Albany, NY: Center for Technology in Government.

Vangen, S., & Huxham, C. (2003). Nurturing collaborative relations: Building trust in interorganizational collaboration. *The Journal of Applied Behavioral Science, 39*(1), 5–31. doi:10.1177/0021886303039001001

West, D. M. (2000). *State and federal e-government in the United States, 2005.* Providence, RI: Brown University.

West, D. M. (2001). *State and federal e-government in the United States, 2001.* Providence, RI: Brown University.

West, D. M. (2002). *State and federal e-government in the United States, 2002.* Providence, RI: Brown University.

West, D. M. (2003). *State and federal e-government in the United States, 2003.* Providence, RI: Brown University.

West, D. M. (2004). *State and federal e-government in the United States, 2004.* Providence, RI: Brown University.

Zhang, J., Faerman, S. R., & Cresswell, A. M. (2006). *The effect of organizational/technological factors and the nature of knowledge on knowledge sharing.* Paper presented at the 39th Hawaiian International Conference on System Sciences (Awarded Best Paper in the Conference), Hawaii.

ADDITIONAL READING

Cresswell, A. M., & Pardo, T. A. (2001). Implications of legal and organizational issues for urban digital government development. *Government Information Quarterly, 18,* 269–278. doi:10.1016/S0740-624X(01)00086-7

Cushing, J., & Pardo, T. A. (2005). Research in the digital government realm. *IEEE Computer*, *38*(12), 26–32.

Dawes, S. S., Gregg, V., & Agouris, P. (2004). Digital government research: Investigations at the crossroads of social and information science. *Social Science Computer Review*, *22*(1), 5–10. doi:10.1177/0894439303259863

Dawes, S. S., Pardo, T., & DiCaterino, A. (1999). Crossing the threshold: Practical foundations for government services on the world wide web. *Journal of the American Society for Information Science American Society for Information Science*, *50*(4), 346–353. doi:10.1002/(SICI)1097-4571(1999)50:4<346::AID-ASI12>3.0.CO;2-I

Dawes, S. S., Pardo, T. A., Simon, S., Cresswell, A. M., LaVigne, M. F., Andersen, D. F., & Bloniarz, P. A. (2004). Making Smart IT Choices: Understanding Value and Risk in Government IT Investments, http://www.ctg.albany.edu/publications/guides/smartit2.

Gil-Garcia, J. R., Chengalur-Smith, I., & Duchessi, P. (2007). Collaborative E-Government: Impediments and Benefits of Information Sharing Projects in the Public Sector. *European Journal of Information Systems*, *16*(2), 121–133. doi:10.1057/palgrave.ejis.3000673

Gil-Garcia, J. R., & Helbig, N. (2006). Exploring e-government benefits and success factors. In Anttiroiko, A.-V., & Malkia, M. (Eds.), *Encyclopedia of Digital Government*. Hershey, PA: Idea Group Inc.

Gil-Garcia, J. R., & Martinez-Moyano, I. (2007). Understanding the Evolution of E-Government: The Influence of Systems of Rules on Public Sector Dynamics. *Government Information Quarterly*, *24*(2), 266–290. doi:10.1016/j.giq.2006.04.005

Hall, R. H. (2002). *Organizations. Structures, Processes, and Outcomes*. Upper Saddle River, NJ: Prentice Hall.

Harrison, T., Pardo, T. A., Gil-Garcia, J. R., Thompson, F., & Juraga, D. (2007). Geographic Information Technologies, Structuration Theory, and the World Trade Center Crisis. *Journal of the American Society for Information Science and Technology*, *58*(14), 2240–2254. doi:10.1002/asi.20695

Luna-Reyes, L., Gil-Garcia, J. R., & Estrada-Marroquín, M. (2008). The Impact of Institutions on Interorganizational IT Projects in the Mexican Federal Government. *International Journal of Electronic Government Research*, *4*(2), 26–42.

Luna-Reyes, L. F., Gil-Garcia, J. R., & Cruz, C. B. (2006). E-Mexico: Collaborative Structures in Mexican Public Administration. *International Journal of Cases on Electronic Commerce*, *3*(2), 54–70.

Luna-Reyes, L. F., Gil-Garcia, J. R., & Cruz, C. B. (2007). Collaborative Digital Government in Mexico: Some Lessons from Federal Web-Based Interorganizational Information Integration Initiatives. *Government Information Quarterly*, *24*(4), 808–826. doi:10.1016/j.giq.2007.04.003

Luna-Reyes, L. F., Zhang, J., Gil-Garcia, J. R., & Cresswell, A. M. (2005). Information systems development as emergent socio-technical change: A practice approach. *European Journal of Information Systems*, *14*(1), 93–105. doi:10.1057/palgrave.ejis.3000524

Pardo, T. A., Cresswell, A. M., Thompson, F., & Zhang, J. (2006). Knowledge sharing in cross-boundary information system development in the public sector. *Information Technology Management*, *7*(4), 293–313. doi:10.1007/s10799-006-0278-6

Rocheleau, B. (2000). Prescriptions for public-sector information management: A review, analysis, and critique. *American Review of Public Administration*, *30*(4), 414–435. doi:10.1177/02750740022064759

Zhang, J., Cresswell, A. M., & Thompson, F. (2002). *Participant's expectations and the success of knowledge networking in the public sector.* Paper presented at the AMCIS Conference, Texas

KEY TERMS AND DEFINITIONS

Chief Information Officer (CIO): The highest job title in an information technology organization. Normally the CIO has strategic responsibilities in contrast to operational ones.

Electronic Government: Electronic government is the use of information and communication technologies to provide high quality services, improve organizational efficiency and effectiveness, and promote democratic mechanisms.

Outsourcing: It is a strategy that consists on subcontracting a service or process to a third-party company.

Portal: Portal could be understood as the main set of Web pages in a Website. Normally, a government portal has a standard way to present information and services from different agencies within a government.

Public-Private Partnership: It is a strategy to manage a Website in which there is a close relationship between the central IT organization of a government and a private company that manages some of the services or other Web pages in exchange of the opportunity to charge convenience fees.

Website: A Website is a set of Web pages which are put together around a theme, organization, or audience.

Website policies: They are a set of policies about how the Website is used and they relate to security, privacy, confidentiality, contracting, among many other topics.

ENDNOTES

[1] From "Everything you ever needed to know about AccessIndiana www.IN.gov, but didn't know who to ask. A Primer on Indiana's Official Web Portal." Available at www.in.gov/itoc/html_site/architecture/guidelines.html

[2] For more information, see "Web-Based Computing Guidelines for Prospective Vendors," available at http://www.in.gov/dpoc/html_site/Policies/ITP_00-7_Web_Based_Guidelines.pdf

Chapter 13
E-Policing:
The Value of Police Websites for Citizen Empowered Participation

Matthew A. Jones
Portland State University, USA

Melchor C. de Guzman
State University of New York, USA

ABSTRACT

This chapter provides a bridge between e-government research related to websites and the study of police organizations and strategy. In a digital age, the police need to have a strong web presence to engage in good governance by maintaining transparency and empowering citizens to participate. It is posited that web presence and citizen participation are linked to policing strategy, allowing citizens to work in tandem and co-produce public safety in their communities. This research utilized content analysis of the websites of police departments employing 250 or more sworn officers serving a municipal population. Using previously employed measures of website evaluations as well as some developed for this research, we found that police organizations have minimal web presence. Policy recommendations related to enhancing website presence are provided.

INTRODUCTION

With the increased availability and rapid development of computer hardware and software, the use of information technology is pervading in public organizations exponentially. This chapter addresses the use of information technology via organizational websites of a particular public organization—police departments. Since the police are the government's most controversial arm

(Cordner & Scarborough, 2008), comprehensive, functional, and participative websites can assist police organizations in maintaining open and transparent relationships with the community as well as empowering citizens to participate and actively co-produce public safety. Thus, a comprehensive web presence can assist American police organizations in achieving their strategic missions.

Minimal research exists related to the utilization of e-government in policing. The few studies that were available have examined the prevalence and utilization of the e-government and policing

DOI: 10.4018/978-1-61692-018-0.ch013

in India (Mitra, 2004; Mitra & Gupta, 2007) and The Netherlands (Korteland & Bekkers, 2007). In the United States where local public police departments total over 17,000 (US Department of Justice, Bureau of Justice Statistics, 2008), this issue is largely under-researched. Although some researchers have examined specific police department websites, the policing components of prior research are merely part of larger e-government projects (Holzer & Melitski, 2003) or research focused upon a specific website capability (Westbrook, 2008).

The primary goal of this chapter is to provide a comprehensive description of the current state of police websites. It summarizes the state of U.S. police departments' efforts to integrate the Internet into their operations. The second goal is to provide preliminary explanations for the existing variability in the development of police websites. Factors are identified that may explain why some department websites are so comprehensive, informative, and engaging of the community while others are rudimentary. Previous research has demonstrated that differences in practice of police organizations are largely based upon organizational and environmental factors (King, 1999; Langworthy, 1986; Maguire, 1997; 2003; Wilson, 2006). This chapter explores the relationships of these factors to the digital practices of police departments. Through these two goals an informative description on the "state of the art" of websites is provided to municipal and police administrators. Based upon this description, policy prescriptions are proposed to assist departments in the development of critical aspects of their web presence.

The third and final goal of this chapter is to provide insights to US police departments on the extent they have solicited community participation in policing through the Internet. It has been observed that community members' participation in community oriented meeting has been minimal (Grinc, 1994; Skogan, 2006). The results of the study informs administrators on how their web-

site has contributed to their community policing efforts and should guide policy makers as to the importance of the engagement of the people in governance and how the Internet can enhance that participation. Although the Internet only provides virtual participation, it may bring the community and the police closer together. Indeed, there were contrary views about the ability of technology to bring the community and the police closer together. For instance, Samuel Walker (2001) observed that technology in the Reform Era brought the police closer to the community as opposed to Wilson and Kelling's (1982) view that technology brought them apart. However, there seems to be a prevailing consensus that the Internet strengthens social relationships. Therefore, the previous contentions about the contributions of technology about social distance seem unwarranted.

BACKGROUND

Inevitably, one must ask; why should any body of e-government research focus on the police rather than any other public organization? The answer is two-fold. First, the police have a uniquely tenuous relationship with the polity in a democratic society (Bittner, 1970). The basic tenets of liberal democracy adhere to notions of protection from the arbitrary use (and abuse) of power. The mere presence of a strong organized police force can put a society in conflict with this tenet (Bittner, 1970; Caldero & Crank, 2004). As Manning (1987) has stated, the police are the most visible representatives of the state. As such, they are often counted on by the community as a twenty-four hour representative of government. Furthermore, the police have the ability (if they choose either justifiably or unjustifiably) to seize life, liberty, and property without prior adjudication (Jones, 2008). Given these propositions, the police are in a constant pursuit of legitimacy among the polity and must therefore maintain the utmost level of transparency and accountability to ensure the public against abuse of power (Bass, 2000; Herbert, 2001).

In the past, traditional media sources have played a strong role in maintaining transparency and control of police departments (de Guzman, 2001). Many police departments designated a position solely dedicated to "public information" in pursuit of these objectives. With the increased availability of the Internet, citizens are now looking to their computer for information, services, and participation from their local police departments. As previous researchers have suggested, electronic forms of government allow for the incorporation of democratic processes (Bekkers, 2003; Janssen, Rothier, & Snijkers, 2004; West, 2005). With a strong web presence, police have the ability to bolster legitimacy and maintain a strategy of democratic policing.

The nexus between strategic website development and policing also touches upon a very important democratic process, participation of the citizenry in government. An essential element of democracy is the people's ability to participate in their government. The Internet has exponentially expanded the level of ability for citizen participation. Even the current US president, Barrack Obama, has started to use this medium to solicit input from the citizens and deliver weekly addresses that were once only broadcast over the radio, which one can argue is largely an artifact of government/citizen interaction from the mid-twentieth century.

Traditionally, police departments have different mechanisms for eliciting inputs from the citizens. The most common form is the so-called reactive model (Black, 1980) where the department simply invites people to report incidents or information to the police. This is simply one-way communication where the burden is placed upon the citizen. This mode of communication is primarily how local, and subsequently national, crime statistics are calculated. These data also drive the policy and strategic directions of law enforcement.

The accurate measurement of crime has been the preoccupation of government and scholars alike. Since the establishment of the Uniform Crime Report (UCR), there has been an issue about its inability to reliably measure certain crimes such as rape or theft. The main source of its reliability is the unwillingness of victims to report crimes to the police. There are several motivations for failure to report a crime. One is the lack of anonymity in the reporting system. Second, there is a public perception that the police could not solve the crime. Third, and very feasible, is a lack of reporting alternative. Personal and telephone communications are so far the only media that the police and citizens use to interact with each other. Thus, the National Crime Victimization Survey (NCVS) was devised as an alternative to crime measurement and was intended to uncover the dark figure of crime. However, the intrusive aspect of the NCVS brings to doubt the reliability of the data especially regarding crimes of rape, incest, and domestic abuse.

Website presence assists police organizations in strategically understanding crime and its impact in their respective communities by enabling mechanisms for citizens to file criminal reports and/or make criminal complaints. Also, it may provide a more accurate estimate of crime in society.

The level of citizen participation is really constrained by the mechanisms available to them. Thus, another important process is the level of government's ability to enhance its responsiveness to people's concerns. One can assess the level of responsiveness of a police department to the people's concerns by the variability with which the departments provide access, information, and intervention through the use of the Internet.

The second form of engagement with citizens is the so-called pro-active model (Black, 1980). There are departments that initiate contact with the people and actively solicit information from their constituents. In this latter case, the method of communication is two-way where both citizens and members of the government engage each another in a partnership. This is where community-oriented policing gained prominence (Skolnick & Bayley, 1986).

Thus, the evaluation of websites is also relevant to community policing, which has become the predominant paradigm of policing in Western countries. Most studies center on the contributions of environmental and organizational factors to the implementation of community oriented policing (Giblin, 2006), yet Internet access and intervention has largely been overlooked and therefore received little exploration.

Participation is an essential component of a democracy, and all citizens should be able to participate in some meaningful way (Ferber, Foltz, & Pugliese, 2003). In recent years the concept of *good governance* has become a dominant theme in the public management literature (e.g. see United Nations Development Program), and more recently has increasingly been applied to police organizations (Dupont, 2003; Wood & Dupont, 2006; Jones, 2009). The United Nations Development Program has outlined five principles for good governance (Institute on Governance, 2003):

1. Legitimacy and voice, which includes participation.
2. Direction, which encompasses strategic vision of the organization.
3. Performance, which incorporates themes of: responsiveness, effectiveness, and efficiency.
4. Accountability, which is also comprised of the concept of transparency.
5. Fairness.

Police organizations have long been overly concerned with the first principle, that of legitimacy. To increase their legitimacy (as well as working in tandem with the other goals) they have recently placed the locus of concentration on creating mechanisms and processes that promote a strong role for citizen participation. Prior to 1980 community members largely did not have

the capability to actively participate alongside their local police departments in law enforcement activities. Police officers were viewed as the sole experts of crime control and there was no perceived need for citizen participation in police matters (Wilson & Kelling, 1982). During the shift to community based policing philosophies in the 1980s local law enforcement organizations drastically altered this viewpoint by outstretching their arms to the community and actively seeking citizen participation (Cole & Smith, 2008). The levels to which communities across the United States participated vary, but in larger cities the majority of community members did not participate in the co-production of public safety (Fung, 2004; Skogan, 2006).

Websites provide a new medium for citizens to actively engage in the promotion and maintenance of public safety in their communities. Through the use of websites, community members may actively engage their police departments anytime and anywhere it is convenient for them. This proposition is consistent with the general theme of community policing, which has been enthusiastically advocated by the Federal government. Community policing has become the desired conceptual mode by which police organizations operate. The Federal government has vigorously promoted adoption of this philosophy by allocating vast amounts of dollars to local departments.

On its most basic level, community oriented policing is geared towards the increased participation of the community in the provision of safety (Goldstein, 1990). The idea behind this co-production arrangement is to make the police more effective in addressing crime (Skolnick & Bayley, 1986) and to better address disorder in the community (Wilson & Kelling, 1982). This arrangement of community participation is called democratized policing and one of the major public safety provisions identified by Bayley and Shearing (2001) as the emerging trend of policing. Thus, police effectiveness seems to be contingent upon the democratization of its process (i.e., making the community participate in policing).

Increased participation in policing is argued as being critical to the effectiveness of the police in accomplishing its goals and mission. Indeed, Sung (2006) found that increased democratization of police tactics and strategies increases police effectiveness. Community policing was devised as a means to increase contact and participation of the citizens in the provision of safety. The central principle behind community policing was the formation of citizens as co-producers of safety (Goldstein, 1990; Skolnick & Bayley, 1986). Thus, for community policing to prosper, the police should develop ways for the community to become involved in providing safety.

Several programs and innovations have been implemented to realize this goal. Originally, the principal means of connecting with citizens was bringing the police into the midst of the citizens. Along this line, police departments started to reintroduce foot patrols (Trojanowicz & Bucqueroux, 1990; Trojanowicz & Smyth, 1983). The second wave consisted of forming community organizations and projects such as conducting community meetings, Weed and Seed, and other forms of intense community-police activities. The third wave consisted of increasing the use of technology in the analysis of neighborhood problems such as COMPSTAT (McDonald, 2002). The emerging wave is the use of computers with I-CLEAR (Skogan, Rosenbaum, Hartnett, DuBois, Graziano, & Stephens, 2005) and the use of intelligence centers (Gottschalk, 2008; White, 2008). The next wave may just be the increasing use of the Website to achieve multiple police goals of community outreach, intelligence gathering, and development of interventions for crime and disorder prevention. Despite the rapid development of interactive medium such as the Internet, very few studies have turned up in our search for the literature relative to policing.

Community policing was devised to mobilize the community. Police departments have continually devised means to reach citizens and for citizens to have the ability to reach them. The 911 system was the major innovation along this line. Despite the seeming efficiency of the 911 system, its effectiveness to address the issue of active crime reporting remains questionable (Cole & Smith, 2008). Thus, police departments started to implement a more active engagement of the citizens through the use of reverse 911 (Walker & Katz, 2005). In addition, police departments have started to conduct periodic surveys of their constituents. These efforts indicate that there is a continuing search for effectively engaging the citizens in the co-production of safety.

The Internet appears to be a potential tool to reach out to citizens and for the citizens to connect to their police department. Intelligence and information gathering is essential to problem solving and crime solving for the police. They have to develop both the internal capability of the police to gather information as well as the ability of citizens to relay information. The Internet presents a promise. Thus, this study wants to explore the extent to which the police departments have developed their websites to increase citizen participation and information about the police.

MAIN FOCUS OF THE CHAPTER

This research involves a systematic study of the websites of large police departments in the United States. The study attempted to answer the following research questions:

1. What extent do police departments develop their websites as a means of empowered participation for the citizen?
2. How do organizational and environmental factors influence the extent of website development by police departments?

We hypothesize that:

1. as organizational size increases, the level of website development of police departments increases; and
2. as population size increases, so does the level of police website developments.

To answer the first question, a descriptive narrative regarding the components of these sites is provided. The goal of the descriptive analysis is to provide a summary of practices of the web presence of American police departments. To answer the second question, and test the two hypotheses, correlation analysis is presented. However, this correlation study should be considered as exploratory rather than explanatory. Other contextual variables have not been included in the analysis to formulate an explanatory model. Despite this limitation, it is our expectation that the results of this study will assist re-engineering or re-aligning police practices.

For this study, websites from 164 municipal police departments in the United States were sampled. The sample of police departments was obtained from the 2003 Law Enforcement Management and Administrative Statistics series (LEMAS). The series contains data that are collected from a survey that the Department of Justice administers every three years. In LEMAS, all law enforcement agencies employing over 100 officers are surveyed as well as every State Police agency. For this research only the websites of municipal police organizations containing 250 or more officers were evaluated.[1] These organizations have public safety responsibilities for the largest population centers in the United States. Environmental factors existing in these large jurisdictions motivate or constrain police departments to adopt the efficiency of the Internet to reach out to their constituents. Moreover, each of these agencies is large enough to have sufficient monetary and human resources to devote to maintaining an active presence on the Web. Researchers collected data from the police websites between April and May of 2009.

This study used content analysis of current police department websites to examine the extent of website development. As with any study with social artifacts as the unit of analysis, content analysis seems to be the most appropriate research methodology (Bachman & Schutt, 2007). This study used manifest coding to determine the transparency, ability to transact, usability, and connectivity that the police provide to its citizens. We argue that each of these dimensions is related to the principles of good governance.

Transparency refers to the extent by which the police website shares information to the citizens. This concept will have as its indicators the department website's provision of information about crime statistics, complaint and case updates, and the information about the performance of the police. This concept is related to the fourth principle of good governance, accountability as previously outlined in the background of the study.

Ability to transact through websites empowers citizens to file crime complaints, report police misconduct, commend police officers, request for services such as home watch or night walks, and provide comments and suggestions to the police department. These are essential in a co-production of safety especially the reporting of crime and police misconduct. The lack of provision of these Internet accesses limits the participation of the citizens. Most often, citizens are not inclined either to report crime to the police (Cole & Smith, 2008) or to report police misconduct personally to the Chief or the police department (Walker, 2001; de Guzman & Frank, 2004). The Internet overcomes these limitations of current reporting systems. This concept is related to the first and second principles that pertain to good governance, legitimacy and voice.

Usability refers to the extent by which police websites accommodate variations in the citizen's ability to use the Internet medium. For the website to be usable it should be able to accommodate and overcome challenges to citizen participation such as language, vision, hearing, and offer the latest use of the Internet such as twitter and instant messaging capabilities. This is related to the third principle of good governance, that is, performance. The organizations should be responsive and able to meet the needs of all of its stakeholders.

Finally, the police should also be able to direct citizens to relevant government and private sector links. The provision of this service satisfies one of the tenets of community policing involving collaborative problem solving and referral of citizens to agencies that can serve their needs. Thus, connectivity refers to the availability of both governmental and non-governmental links to provide services or information to citizens. This is also related to performance in that the organization attempts to meet the needs in an efficient manner of all of its stakeholders by directing them to the most appropriate resources.

There have been several prior studies completed on the approaches to evaluating websites (e.g., Alexander & Tate, 1999; Faber, 1998; Ferber et. al, 2003; Hawkes, 1999; Henriksson et. al., 2006; Holzer, 2003; West, 2001; Kaylor, 2001). We designed an instrument drawing from previous research, yet at the same time devising new measures and revising previous measures to reflect what we contend are important components to police department websites that assist in promoting democratic participation. In this regard, we used four evaluative criteria: transparency, transaction, usability, and connectivity.

Demchak, Friis, and Laporte (1998) offered that transparency is one of the main components of organizational openness. Given the aforementioned arguments about the tenuous nature of the police/community relationship, we developed four measures specifically related to police departments that reflect a transparent organizational web presence: (1) the presence of crime statistics, (2) complaint updates, (3) case updates, and (4) department performance indicators. These measures were used to evaluate the presences of on-line

information related to the department's direct interactions with community members. Similar to the research of Cap Gemini, Ernst and Young (2004) each of the four measures were coded on a three-point scale (0=non-existent or dead link; 1=information is available; 2= user-interactive information). Examples of key concepts of this dimension coded as information available were the posting of monthly crime statistics, complaint or case updates, or performance indicators in a portable document format. These indicators represent the organization's willingness to display this data and information, often in aggregate form. Items coded as user-interactive were those that allow citizens to search for specific information based upon more specific queries. Examples of this might include websites that provide the capability for interactive crime mapping, where users can search for reported crimes based upon geographic boundaries, time, dates, and crime or complaint category. The maximum score for scale for the transparency scale was eight.

For assessing the quality of website transactions, we adopted Scott's (2005) proposed measure. As keenly noted by Scott (2005), citizen-to-government (C2G) interaction is one of the most highly touted benefits of e-government. Four measures of this dimension were developed that allowed users to interact with their local police departments through the website. These measures were: (1) crime complaints, (2) police complaint or commendation, (3) request for service, and (4) comments or feedback.

Like the dimension of transparency, each indicator for transaction was coded on a three-point scale (0= non-existent or dead link, 1= information available, 2= user-interactive). Those items coded as "information available" would, for example, be organizations that post information on how users go about initiating a crime complaint, filing a complaint or commendation about an officer or the department, or providing comments and feedback. Most often this information might appear as a phone number and/or contact person. Although the information might be available through the website, the citizen might still be required to take extra steps and use the telephone, draft a letter, or appear in-person at a physical location. Examples of websites that were considered to have user-interactive capabilities under this dimension were those that enable users to report crime/disorder complaints via an on-line reporting system, file a complaint against or commendation to an officer or the department via an on-line system, request police service directly through the website, or provide a two-way communication with a department representative as a mechanisms to provide comments and feedback. The maximum score for the transaction scale is eight.

Usability is a common dimension utilized to evaluate the quality of a government website (Ferber et al., 2003; Holzer & Melitski, 2003; Scott, 2005). Previous studies have largely operationalized this dimension as the user-friendliness of a website and its capability to reach targeted audiences. As Scott (2005) noted, a major component of a site's usability includes the ability to reach and communicate with special needs audiences. In this research websites were evaluated for their media and language options as well as having texting capabilities such as Twitter or instant messaging (IM). For media capability the site must have either video or audio options. For language options the site must have capability to translate the contents of its website into at least one language other than English. Under each of these measures we assess the site specifically for the presence (coded 1) or absence (coded 0) of: (1) crime stats, (2) complaint updates, (3) case updates, (4) crime complaint, (5) police complaint, (6) comments, (7) requests for service, and 8) performance indicators. The maximum score achieved on the usability scale is 17. Ostensibly, a recording of a higher score a department has (i.e., the sum of these dichotomous variables) would indicate that the stakeholders and clients of the department had greater ability to use utilize the resources of the website.

The final dimension utilized for this evaluation is connectivity. This measure evaluated the website for the presence, coded as 1, or the absence, coded as 0 of links to other government offices and non-governmental organizations. The maximum score for this dimension is the sum of the two dichotomous variables, which equals two. Musso, Wear, and Hale (2001) posited that the presence of local links assists users in connecting with available resources in the community. Westbrook (2008) previously explored this issue by examining police websites for information that assist victims of domestic abuse. Table 1 presents the summary of the key evaluative categories, potential ranges of scores and the key ideas for each category.

The initial analysis intended to provide a description of the extent of website development by the sampled police departments. The descriptive procedure used several steps. First, each item was analyzed using summary statistics to extract information about the website development of different police departments. Second, an index for all the four dimensions of website development was constructed by adding all the items for each dimension. Third, the total website development was derived by adding the indices of all the dimensions.

After transforming the ordinal measures into ratio level measurements, we analyzed the data applying multiple regression analyses with population and officer size as independent variables. The indices for the dimensions were used as the dependent variables. Ideally, the data for the independent variables should also come from the websites. However, we found that very few departments provided the information on their websites. This resulted in very few cases being included in the model making regression analysis inappropriate as an estimation technique. As recourse, we extracted the data for the independent variables from the 2003 LEMAS. Although the data were collected several years earlier, the number of officers and population size were not

Table 1. Summary of key evaluative categories

Category	Measures	Potential Score	Key Ideas
Transparency	1. Crime Statistics 2. Complaint Updates 3. Case Updates 4. Performance Indicators	0-8	Department is accountable, easy user access to information.
Transactions	1. Crime Complaints 2. Complaint/Commendation 3. Service Request 4. Comments/Feedback	0-8	C2G interaction

Usability	1. Media
	   a. Crime Statistics
	   b. Complaint Updates
	   c. Case Updates
	   d. Crime Complaint
	   e. Police Complaint
	   f. Comments
	   g. Request for service
	   h. Performance Indicators
	2. Language options
	   a. Crime Statistics
	   b. Complaint Updates
	   c. Case Updates
	   d. Crime Complaint
	   e. Police Complaint
	   f. Comments
	   g. Request for service
	   h. Performance Indicators
	3. Twitter/Instant Messaging
		0-17	User-Friendly, reaches targeted audiences, meets special needs of consumers.

Connectivity	1. Links to Government Services 2. Links to Non-Governmental Services (non-profits, etc.).	0-2	Website acts as an informational portal, citizens are directed to most appropriate resources.

expected to change dramatically within a six-year period especially in the absence of historical event that might produce dramatic social demographic changes. Thus, it is not probable that the time lag between the LEMAS and the website evaluation will significantly affect the reliability of the LEMAS data to measure the independent variables.

RESULTS OF THE STUDY

We present the results of the study in two sections. The first section involves a descriptive analysis of the different measures grouped by the different dimensions that were used. The second section presents the descriptive statistics of the indices created and the results for the regression analyses

conducted. Table 2 presents the descriptive evaluation of the websites of the police departments.

Data from Table 2 illustrate that the websites of police organizations could benefit from quality improvement. Although the sites have made great strides in transparency with nearly half of them having the ability for the user to interactively gather information about crime statistics (45.3%), the descriptive statistics painted a bleaker picture for the other measures. Based on the analysis, it is more likely that a department will not have case (72.8%) or complaint updates (80.1%) rather than providing that information. To their credit, almost half of the departments did post some form of performance indicator (48.1%), with almost no department having an interactive component (6.2%). More troubling is that a large proportion

Table 2. Descriptive statistics on the dimensions of website development (N=162)

Variables	Non-existent n (%)	Information Available n (%)	User interactive n (%)
Transparency			
Crime statistics	21 (13.0)	67 (41.6)	73 (45.3)
Complain updates	129 (80.1)	23 (14.3)	9 (5.6)
Case updates	118 (72.8)	32 (19.8)	12 (7.4)
Performance Indicators	74 (45.7)	78 (48.1)	10 (6.2)
Transactions			
Crime complaint	39 (24.1)	74 (45.7)	49 (30.2)
Complain/Commend officer	46 (28.4)	76 (46.9)	40 (24.7)
Request for service	50 (30.9)	95 (58.6)	17 (10.5)
Comments/Feedbacks	47 (29.0)	80 (49.4)	35 (21.6)
Usability (Media)			
Crime statistics	144 (90.0)	16 (10.0)	--
Complaint updates	156 (96.3)	6 (3.7)	--
Case updates	151 (93.8)	10 (6.2)	--
Crime complaint	153 (94.4)	9 (5.6)	--
Complain/Commend officer	157 (96.9)	5 (3.1)	--
Request for service	149 (92.0)	1 (8.0)	--
Comments	153 (94.4)	9 (5.6)	--
Performance indicators	146 (90.1)	16 (8.0)	--
Usability (Language)			
Crime statistics	149 (92.0)	13 (8.0)	--
Complaint updates	154 (95.1)	8 (4.9)	--
Case updates	152 (93.8)	1 (6.2)	--
Crime complaint	143 (88.3)	19 (11.7)	--
Complain/Commend officer	140 (86.4)	22 (13.6)	--
Request for service	144 (89.4)	17 (10.6)	--
Comments/Feedbacks	142 (87.7)	20 (12.3)	--
Performance indicators	154 (95.1)	8 (4.9)	--
Usability (Twitter/IM)	142 (87.7)	20 (12.3)	--
Connectivity			
Links to government	29 (17.9)	133 (82.1)	--
Links to non-government	64 (40.3)	95 (59.7)	

of departments failed to provide any organizational performance indicators whatsoever (45.7%).

Almost a third of the sample had the capability for on-line crime reporting (45.7%) but 24 percent of the departments did not have any link at all

for this variable. In addition, just fewer than 25 percent had an interactive component to the site for commending or initiating a complaint against an officer. Likewise, only 28.4 percent of the departments did not provide any information on

Table 3. Descriptive statistics of the police department website characteristics and total website development

Indices	N	Mean	Median	Mode
Transparency	160	2.53	2.00	2.00
Transaction	162	3.75	4.00	4.00
Usability				
Media	161	0.54	0.00	0.00
Language	161	0.68	0.00	0.00
Total	161	1.20	0.00	0.00
Connectivity	160	1.43	2.00	2.00
WebsiteDev.Index	156	8.95	8.00	9.00

commending or complaining against an officer and 30.9 percent of the departments failed to provide the user with the information regarding requests for service. This practice does not bode well for organizations that wish to enable the citizens to reach the department. Soliciting the inputs of the citizens through feedbacks and comments was also minimally practiced with barely 22 percent of the departments providing their constituents this capability. These organizations should immediately provide the minimum information possible on their websites while striving to seek an interactive approach in the near future.

The sample of organizations overwhelmingly lacked in usability. Few of the organizations had the capability to provide critical information in languages other than English or in other media formats. A sizeable number (86.4%) did not provide information for complaining or commending an officer in a non-English language. This isolates members of the community that do not speak English and provides a significant barrier for those who may wish to initiate a complaint. This lack of capability is also true with accommodating the needs of special populations. Ninety percent or more of the departments had no audio or media interactive capabilities. Neither did the departments have twitter or IM capabilities (87.7%).

The organizations fared slightly better in their connectivity. The majority of the departments pro-vided links to other government agencies (82.1%) and over half provided links to non-governmental organizations (59.7%). This illustrates that many police departments are attempting to provide pathways for citizens seeking information that may fall out of the direct services that police organizations provide.

Table 3 presents the summary of the descriptive statistics for the indices created. There were five indices created. Four of the indices were additive composite measures for each of the four dimensions of website development, namely transparency, transactions, usability, connectivity. The fifth index is an additive composite measure of the different dimensions that provided the information for the total website development index. The range of scores for each of the four dimensions has been previously reported in Table 1. The total website index of police department had a range of scores from 0-34. The total number of police departments was 162. Two departments were dropped from the analysis because their portal links were under construction or their websites were not updated for the current year. Index construction does not give partial credits. Hence, these two departments were not included in the analysis (Babbie, 2008).

The data from Table 3 suggest that police departments generally fell short in providing empowerment through the website. Except for connectivity, none of the variables reached attained

Table 4. Zero order correlations of the indices, population size, and officer size

	Transactions	Usability	Connectivity	Population Size	Number of Officers
Transparency	.43*	.42*	.26*	-.10	-.09
Transaction		.22*	.13	.03	.07
Usability			.20*	-.08	-.10
Connectivity				-.02	-.07
Population Size					.97*

* Significant at p≥.01

a mean that is equivalent to half of the total possible score. Transparency has a median score of 2.00. This means that most departments (i.e., at most half) offered mostly information and did not have an interactive website. Police departments have a fairly helpful website in terms of being able to transact business (mean = 3.75) and find links to other services (mean = 1.43). The median score for ability to transact is 4.00 indicating that at most of the departments are providing citizens the ability to transact over the net. It is also commendable that departments provide connectivity.

Police departments seem to lack provisions for greater usability of its website. The provisions of media (mean = 0.54) and language options (mean = 0.68) were hardly existent in the websites. Out of the total score of 17, the police departments registered a mean score of 1.20. This means that those who have physical and language deficiencies will have difficulty using the websites. Thus, the police had very low mean score (8.95) of website development.

None of the research hypotheses were supported in the study. Population size and number of officers showed no significant correlations with the different dimensions of website empowerment characteristics. Instead, the analysis revealed that several of the website characteristics are significantly and highly correlated with each other. Only the relationship between connectivity and ability to transact was not significant (r= .13). Controlling for population size and number of officers,

the relationship between connectivity and ability to transact became significant (r = .24).

Similarly, the results in analyzing the relationships between population size and number of officers with total website development showed the two independent variables are poor predictors of website development. Our hypotheses on their relationships were not supported by the data. The model was not able to explain any of the variance (R^2 = .004) with the standardized coefficients for population size at -.075 (Sig. = .82) and for the number of officers at .01 (Sig. = .98). These findings suggest that website development may be related to other variables that were not tapped in this study.

SOLUTIONS AND RECOMMENDATIONS

This analysis has illustrated that population and organizational size has little to do with the quality of the organization's websites. Therefore, administrators are less constrained by these environmental factors that have previously been found as influential to the operations of the department. Local police departments should see this as an historical opportunity to enhance their presence and improve their operation. Innovative police practices demands two major inputs. First, innovations require a strong leadership (Moore & Braga, 2003) that will push for the establishment of the major reforms and change the culture of the organization towards the acceptance of that reform (Paoline, 2004; Wilson, 1968). Second, a significant amount of resources is necessary to implement and maintain the innovation (Moore & Braga, 2003). Hardware investments and software developments are key components to maintaining a viable police website.

The police are facing a technological era in their operations. This is the growing trend that police departments and academic institutions should anticipate. The results of this study suggest that police departments face a huge gap in their use of the website to empower citizens. The challenge must be met with resolved determination that should emanate from the top leadership of the department. Likewise, police departments should also solicit support from its different constituents for implementation and maintenance of their websites. In the community-policing era, police departments seek the support of crime fighting activities from its citizens through citizens' patrols, night watches, and other volunteer jobs. In a technological policing era, the police could also seek volunteers from its community members who can develop and maintain their websites. In addition, they need to include plans for training their personnel in website development, maintenance and utilization. These foci will alleviate some of the demands in the use of the website.

Academic institutions should also redirect their focus towards the emerging trends in policing. As we are approaching the technological era of policing, universities and academies should include significant amount of courses on computer literacy and utilization. These courses will enable students to meet the technological challenges of their future law enforcement jobs.

FUTURE RESEARCH DIRECTIONS

As little research has entirely focused on websites of police organizations there remains much to be accomplished. Future research studies will want to focus on developing better measures of website quality. Since we argued that police organizations are quite different from other municipal organizations, police website evaluation likely requires the development of new measures. Future research should also expand the scope to determine the factors that predict a quality website. There is an inordinate amount of literature related to the implementation of new methods, strategies, and organizational arrangements in policing. Using existing theories and the collection of new data, researchers might be able to provide some explanation regarding the variations in the quality of police department websites. This will help answer one of the questions that still remains at the conclusion of this study; why is there such variation in websites across the United States. Our research has come across some stunning examples, while others are quite rudimentary. Lastly, future researchers may want to investigate for any possible relationships that exist between the quality of a police organization's website and the level of trust the community members have in this institution.

CONCLUSION

This chapter has argued that police organizations are unique from other municipal organization because of the nature of their function and tenuous relationship created between them and the polity in a liberal democracy. By enhancing website capability, police organizations create political value by engaging in good governance. Through this engagement, they are not only better able to meet the needs of the citizens they serve, but also mitigate the contentious relationship they sometimes have with the community. At no other point in history has a mechanism been available that allows for maximum engagement and interaction between the community and the police.

Police departments should be ready to meet the demands of new technology in an effort to be effective. An improperly maintained website imparts to constituents that police departments may not care about community concerns. Thus, the website can become both a blessing and a curse for the department. If they maintain it, it can become an effective communication tool for the police and the public. It may even result in developing greater trust from the public. If they are not ready to maintain the technology, it will become a source of frustration for the public who would like to try to get information and services from their police departments (Bass, 2000). Police departments might find themselves in the same quagmire similar to the Reform Era where technology became both a tool of efficiency and effectiveness but it was viewed as the source of alienation between the police and the public (Walker, 2001; Wilson & Kelling, 1982).

NOTE

The sample is taken from all agencies in the LEMAS dataset with 250 or more sworn officers categorized as municipal. Although municipally based, some agencies serve a larger metropolitan jurisdiction (e.g. Nashville metro).

REFERENCES

Alexander, J., & Tate, M. (1999). *Web wisdom: How to evaluate and create information quality of the Web*. Mahwah, NJ: Lawrence Erlbaum.

Babbie, E. R. (2008). *The practice of social research* (11th ed.). Belmont, CA: Wadsworth Publishing.

Bachman, R., & Schutt, R. K. (2007). *The practice of research in criminology and criminal justice* (3rd ed.). Thousand Oaks, CA: Sage Publications.

Bass, S. (2000). Negotiating change: Community organizations and the politics of policing. *Urban Affairs Review, 36*(2), 148–177. doi:10.1177/10780870022184813

Bayley, D. H., & Shearing, C. D. (2001). *The new structure of policing: Description, conceptualization, and research agenda*. Washington, DC: National Institute of Justice.

Bekkers, V. (2003). E-government and emergence of virtual organizations in the public sector. *Information Polity: The International Journal of Government and Democracy in the Information Age, 8*, 89–102.

Bittner, E. (1970). *The functions of police in modern society*. Washington, D.C.: US Government Printing Office.

Black, D. (1980). *The manners and customs of the police*. New York: Academic Press.

Caldero, M. P., & Crank, J. P. (2004). *Police ethics: The corruption of a noble cause* (2nd ed.). Cincinnati, OH: Anderson Publishing, Inc.

CapGemini. Ernst and Young. (2004). *Online Availability of Public Services: How is Europe Progressing? (Web-based Survey on Electronic Public Services: Report of the Fourth Measurement, October 2003), Report to the European Commission DG Information Society:* Author. Retrieved June 4, 2009, from ec.europa.eu/information_society/eeurope/2005/doc/highlights/whats_new/capgemini4.pdf de Guzman, M. C. (2001). *Integrity, legitimacy, efficiency and impact: Do all these matter in the civilian review of the police?* Unpublished Ph. D. dissertation, University of Cincinnati, Cincinnati, OH.

Cole, G. F., & Smith, C. E. (2008). *Criminal justice in America* (5th ed.). Belmont, CA: Wadsworth Publishing.

Cordner, G., & Scarborough, K. (2008). *Police administration*. Newark, NJ: Anderson Publishing.

de Guzman, M. C., & Frank, J. (2004). Using learning as a construct to measure civilian review board impact on the police: The Philippine experience. *Policing: An International Journal of Police Strategies and Management, 27*(2), 167–182.

Demchak, C., Friis, C., & La Porte, T. (1998). Reflections on configuring public agencies in cyberspace: A conceptual investigation. In Snellen, I. M., & van Donk, W. (Eds.), *Public administration in an information age: A Handbook*. Amsterdam: IOS Press.

U.S. Dept. of Justice, Bureau of Justice Statistics. LAW ENFORCEMENT MANAGEMENT AND ADMINISTRATIVE STATISTICS (LEMAS): 2003

SAMPLE SURVEY OF LAW ENFORCEMENT AGENCIES Computer file. ICPSR04411-v1. Washington, DC: Dept, U. S. of Commerce, Bureau of the Census [producer], 2006. Ann Arbor, MI: Inter-university Consortium for Political and Social Research [distributor], 2006-05-10. doi:10.3886/ICPSR04411

Dupont, B. (2003). The New Face of Police Governance in Australia. *Journal of Australian Studies, 27*(78), 15–24. doi:10.1080/14443050309387867

Faber, K. (1998). *The Internet design project: The best of graphic art on the Web*. New York, NY: Universe Publishing.

Ferber, P., Foltz, F., & Pugliese, R. (2003). The politics of state legislature web sites: Making e-government more participatory. *Bulletin of Science, Technology & Society, 23*(3), 147–167. doi:10.1177/0270467603023003002

Fung, A. (2004). *Empowered participation: reinventing urban democracy*. Princeton, NJ: Princeton University Press.

Giblin, M. (2006). Structural elaboration and institutional isomorphism: The case of crime analysis units. *Policing: An International Journal of Police Strategies & Management, 29*(4), 643–664. doi:10.1108/13639510610711583

Goldstein, H. (1990). *Problem-oriented policing*. Philadelphia, PA: Temple University Press.

Gottschalk, P. (2008). Organizational structure as predictor of intelligence strategy implementation in policing. *International Journal of Law, Crime and Justice, 36*, 184–195. doi:10.1016/j.ijlcj.2008.05.001

Grinc, R. M. (1994). Angels in marble: Problems in stimulating involvement in community policing. *Crime and Delinquency, 40*(3), 437–468. doi:10.1177/0011128794040003008

Hawkes, L. (1999). *A guide to the World Wide Web*. Upper Saddle River, NJ: Prentice-Hall.

Henriksson, A., Yiori, Y., Frost, B., & Middleton, M. (2006). Evaluation instrument for e-government websites. *Electronic Government, an International Journal, 4* (2), 204-226.

Herbert, S. (2001). Policing the contemporary city: policing broken windows or shoring up neo-liberalism . *Theoretical Criminology, 5*(4), 445–466. doi:10.1177/1362480601005004003

Holzer, M., & Melitski, J. (2003). *A comparative e-government analysis of New Jersey's 10 largest municipalities*. Newark, NJ: National Center for Public Productivity Institute on Governance. (2003). *Principles for good governance in the 21st century*. Retrieved June 16, 2006, from www.iog.ca/publications/policybrief15.pdf

Janssen, D., Rotthier, S., & Snijkers, K. (2004). If you measure it they will score: An assessment of international egovernment benchmarking. *Information Polity: The International Journal of Government and Democracy in the Information Age, 9*, 124–125.

Jones, M. (2008). *Police organizations: An empirical examination of American sheriff's offices and municipal police agencies.* Unpublished doctoral dissertation, Portland State University.

Jones, M. (forthcoming). Governance, integrity, and the police organization. *Policing: An International Journal of Police Strategies and Management.*

Kaylor, C., Deschazo, R., & Van Eck, D. (2001). Gauging e-government: A report on implementing services among American cities. *Government Information Quarterly, 18*(4), 293–307. doi:10.1016/S0740-624X(01)00089-2

Kerley, K. R., & Benson, M. L. (2000). Does community oriented policing help build better communities? *Police Quarterly, 3*(1), 46–69. doi:10.1177/1098611100003001002

King, W. R. (1999). Time, constancy, and change in American municipal police organizations. *Police Quarterly, 2*(3), 338–364. doi:10.1177/109861119900200305

Korteland, E., & Bekkers, V. (2007). Diffusion of E-government innovations in the Dutch public sector: The case of digital community policing. *Information Polity, 12*(3), 139–150.

Langworthy, R. (1986). *The structure of police organizations.* New York, NY: Praeger.

Maguire, E. (1997). Structural change in large municipal police organizations during the community policing era. *Justice Quarterly, 14*(3), 701–730. doi:10.1080/07418829700093471

Maguire, E. (2003). *Organizational structure in american police agencies: Context, complexity and control.* Albany, NY: SUNY Press.

Manning, P. (1987). *Police work: The social organization of policing.* Prospect Heights, IL: Waveland Press.

McDonald, P. (2002). *Managing Police Operations: Implementing the NYPD Crime Control Model Using COMPSTAT.* Belmont, CA: Wadsworth.

Mitra, R. K. (2004). Issues and challenges of E-governance in Indian Police: A study. Unpublished doctoral dissertation, Indian Institute of Technology, Delhi, India.

Mitra, R. K., & Gupta, M. P. (2007). Analysis of issues of e-government in Indian Police. *Electronic Government, an International Journal, 4*(1), pp. 97–125.

Moore, M. H., & Braga, A. A. (2003). Measuring and improving police performance: The lessons of COMPSTAT and its progeny. *Policing: An International Journal of Police Strategies & Management, 26*(3), 439–453. doi:10.1108/13639510310489485

Musso, J., Weare, C., & Hale, M. (2001). Designing Web technology for local governance reform: Good management or good democracy? *Political Communication, 17*(1), 1–19. doi:10.1080/105846000198486

Paoline, E. A. III. (2004). Shedding light on police culture: an examination of police officers' occupational attitudes. *Police Quarterly, 7*(2), 205–236. doi:10.1177/1098611103257074

Ratcliffe, J. (2005). The effectiveness of police intelligence management: A New Zealand case study. *Police Practice and Research, 6*(5), 435–451. doi:10.1080/15614260500433038

Scott, J. (2005). Assessing the quality of municipal government websites. *State and Local Government Review, 37*(2), 151–165.

Skogan, W. (2006). *Police and community in Chicago: A tale of three cities.* New York, NY: Oxford University Press.

Skogan, W. G., & Hartnett, S. M. (2005). The diffusion of information technology in policing. *Police Practice and Research, 6*(5), 401–417. doi:10.1080/15614260500432949

Skogan, W. G., Rosenbaum, D. P., Hartnett, S. M., DuBois, J., Graziano, L., & Stephens, C. (2005). CLEAR and I-CLEAR: A status report in new information technology and its impact on management, the organization and crime fighting strategies. Chicago, IL: The Chicago community Policing Evaluation Consortium.

Skolnick, J. H., & Bayley, D. H. (1986). *The new blue line: Innovation in six American cities*. New York, NY: Free Press.

Sung, H. (2006). Structural determinant of police effectiveness in market democracies. *Police Quarterly, 9*(1), 3–19. doi:10.1177/1098611103257061

Trojanowics, R. C., & Smyth, P. R. (1983). The foot patrol officer, the community, and the school. *Community Education Journal, II*, 18–19.

Trojanowicz, R. C., & Bucqueroux, B. (1990). *Community Policing: A Contemporary Perspective*. Cincinnati, OH: Anderson.

U.S. Department of Justice, Bureau of Justice Statistics. (2008). *Law enforcement statistics.* Retrieved May 24, 2008 from http://www.ojp.usdoj.gov/bjs/lawenf.htm.

Walker, S. (2001). Broken windows and fractured history: The use and misuse of history in recent police patrol analysis . In Dunham, R., & Alpert, G. (Eds.), *Critical issues in policing* (4th ed., pp. 480–492). Prospect Heights, IL: Waveland Press.

Walker, S., & Katz, C. M. (2005). *Police in America: An introduction* (5th ed.). Boston, MA: MacGraw Hill.

Wall, D. S., & Williams, M. (2007). Policing diversity in the digital age: Maintaining an order in virtual communities. *Criminology & Criminal Justice, 7*(4), 391–415. doi:10.1177/1748895807082064

West, D. (2001). Assessing E-Government: The Internet democracy, and service delivery by state and federal governments. *Brown University Report.* Retrieved April 28, 2009 from http://www.brown.edu/Departments/Taubman_Center/polreports/egovt01us.html.

West, D. (2005). *Digital government: Technology and public sector performance*. Princeton, NJ: Princeton University Press.

Westbrook, L. (2008). E-government support for people in crisis: An evaluation of police department website support for domestic violence survivors using "person-in-situation" information need analysis. *Library & Information Science Research, 30*, 22–38. doi:10.1016/j.lisr.2007.07.004

White, J. (2008). *Terrorism and Homeland Security* (6th ed.). Belmont, CA: Wadsworth Publishing.

Wilson, J. Q. (1968). *Varieties of police behavior: The management of law and order in eight communities*. New York, NY: Harvard University Press.

Wilson, J. Q., & Kelling, G. (1982). Broken windows, *The Atlantic Monthly*, 249 (3), pp. 29-48, Wilson, J. (2006). *Community policing in America*. New York, NY: Taylor & Francis.

Wood, J., & Dupont, B. (2006). *Democracy, society, and the governance of security*. New York, NY: Cambridge University Press. doi:10.1017/CBO9780511489358

Chapter 14

Internet–Based Citizen Participation:
Do Municipal Website Contents Reflect Officials' Beliefs and Funding?

Stephen K. Aikins
University of South Florida, USA

ABSTRACT

This chapter determines whether the deliberative features of local government websites reflect city officials' beliefs and funding for Internet-based citizen participation. Although the Internet is argued to have interactive potential to bring citizens closer to their governments, empirical evidence suggests many governments have not taken advantage of this potential. A survey was sent to Chief administrative officers of municipalities with websites, and respondents' government website contents were analyzed and audited against the survey responses. Findings from the audit reveal that in general, the deliberative features of local government websites reflect the beliefs and funding stated in the survey. The technique applied in this research could be a useful tool to investigate the degree of alignment between a government's Internet website contents and its e-government strategic goals, policy requirements and priorities, etc.

INTRODUCTION AND BACKGROUND

The purpose of this chapter is to determine whether local government officials' beliefs in Internet-based citizen participation and funding for online participation are reflected in the deliberative features of their local government websites. Advocates for citizen participation argue that citizen involvement in democracy will produce more citizen-supported decision making on the part of administrators and a better appreciation of the larger community among the public (Stivers, 1990; Oldfield, 1990; Box, 1998). Some scholars argue improved citizen participation could halt the deterioration of public trust and hostility toward the government (King and Stivers, 1998). Thomas (1995) argues citizen involvement is intended to produce better decisions, and thus more efficiency benefits to the rest of society.

The above-mentioned benefits notwithstanding, incorporating citizen input into public decision making could have social and economic costs if

DOI: 10.4018/978-1-61692-018-0.ch014

not done carefully (Irvin and Stansbury, 2004, Thomas, 1995). As argued by Thomas (1995), in spite of proven accomplishments of citizen groups in some policy areas, there is a growing body of data to support the contention that public participation which is automatic, unrestrained, or ill-considered can be dangerously dysfunctional to political and administrative systems. The case could therefore be made that the decision of local public officials to involve citizens in the policy process and in public decision making, and to fund citizen engagement, depends on the perception and beliefs of those officials regarding the relative benefits and disadvantages of participation.

The use of Internet technology to further citizen participation is believed to hold great promise to enhance citizen participation and democratic governance by allowing citizens to access public information and interact with government officials, by promoting better accountability of public officials to citizens through efficient and convenient delivery of services, and by producing fertile ground for reinvigorated civil society (Webber & Loumakis, 2005; Budge, 1996; Barber, 1984; Bimber, 1996; Scavo & Yuhang Shi, 1999; La Port et al., 2000). Consequently, some pundits and scholars have touted the Internet as a means to strengthen the political community, foster democratic renewal, and reverse the recent downward trends in civic engagement by offering a more convenient and less costly alternative to traditional outlets of citizen participation (Klotz, 2004; Johnson & Kaye, 2003; DiMaggio et al., 2001; Trippi, 2004).

Despite the interactive potential of the Internet, empirical evidence suggests that some of the promises of bridging the gap among governments and citizens through enhanced interaction between citizens and government, and between citizens themselves are yet to be fulfilled (Chadwick & May, 2001; West, 2001; Musso, Hale & Weare, 1999; Kerns, Bend & Stern, 2002; the Global e-Policy and e-Government Institute and Rutgers University e-Governance Institute, 2003, 2005).

This may be due to certain challenges inherent in the Internet as a medium of interaction. For instance, the required investment in computer hardware, monthly service fees, and computer skills can be prohibitive, especially to minorities and low income citizens. In addition, effective expressions in a text medium require a high level of education (Klein, 1999). Furthermore, improvements in citizen access to decision making and broadened participation often came at substantial cost, with those bearing the cost tending to have substantial say in setting the agenda (Arterton, 1987). Based on these constraints, it is not entirely surprising that officials at various levels of government have not taken advantage of the Internet to bring citizens closer to their governments.

If local government officials see the Internet as an important medium of communication and interaction, they will be more likely to support Internet-based citizen participation. The literature suggests that traditional citizen participation has strengths and weaknesses, and Internet-based citizen participation is plagued with opportunities and challenges. The above stated pros and cons coupled with the fact that various governments at all levels have not taken full advantage of the Internet's potential to bring citizens closer to their governments imply that there are unanswered questions as to whether city officials believe in traditional and Internet-based citizen participation and, even if they do, whether their beliefs are reflected in the deliberative features of their local government websites. Although there have been several studies on e-government, (e.g. Global e-Policy and e-Government Institute and Rutgers University e-Governance Institute, 2003, 2005; Jensen & Venkatesh 2007), municipal e-participation (Kerns, Bend & Stern, 2002) and analysis of government website contents (Hale, Musso & Weare, 1999; West, 2001, 2005) few studies are yet to determine whether the deliberative features on government websites reflect officials' thoughts and funding for online participation. Therefore, this study aims at filling this research gap by auditing local government website contents against survey responses of municipal officials to determine whether there is an alignment between officials' beliefs, funding and deliberative features of municipal websites.

CITIZEN PARTICIPATION AND THE INTERNET

Citizen participation is defined as citizen involvement in decisions making pertaining to the management of public affairs and service delivery (Langton, 1978). Participation occurs when citizens and public officials have participation needs and when participation mechanisms exist (King, Feltey & Susel, 1998). Traditional citizen participation occurs through mechanisms such as hearings, citizen forums, community or neighborhood meetings, community outreaches, citizen advisory groups, individual citizen representation, etc.

The argument over involving citizens directly in government dates back to the early days of the American government, as expressed in the federalist and Jeffersonian views of democracy. In the Federalist Papers, Hamilton and his federalist colleagues argued that direct citizen participation would not be necessary and that a sound administrative system would keep people's allegiance (Sitvers, 1990). In Federalist 63, Madison rejected a direct role for citizens and called for exclusion of the people who needed protection against their errors and decisions (Rohr, 1984). "The federalist preference for the executive branch was a faithful distrust of the people. An intelligent perception of sound public policy, in their view, could come only from well-educated men of affairs, men with trained minds and broad experience - in short from the upper class" (White, 1948, p. 410). The Jeffersonians, on the other hand, saw the administration of government as intimately connected to the problem of extending democracy to the entire nation. They thus preferred a more decentralized

approach to the executive function and sought formal legal controls on the executive to prevent abuse of power (Caldwell, 1964).

The above arguments, which exist today, have direct bearing on administrative theory in the sense that public officials and administrators, in the course of their functions and decision making, can invite direct citizen participation in developing public policy or they can discourage it (Thomas, 1995). Like the Jeffersonian founding fathers, advocates for citizen participation argue that citizen involvement in democracy will produce more citizen-supported decision making on the part of administrators and a better appreciation of the larger community among the public. Niskanen (1971) argues that public needs are not automatically served by a bureaucracy whose main motivation is the maximization of its financial inputs. Other scholars (Kaufman, 1969; Lowi, 1969) argue the needs of the general public are further compromised by special interest groups with large financial leverage to influence governmental decision making. Public participation therefore provides guidance for bureaucratic production and a balance to the influence of powerful interest groups through enhanced communication between citizens and government, thereby enabling government to understand what the public wants (Creighton, 1981, pp.11-12).

Citizen participation also allows the public to voice its needs, which provides legitimacy for government to develop publicly supported goals, missions, and service priorities (Langton, 1978, pp. 13-24). DeSario & Langton, (1984) argue an enduring task in public management is to resolve the tension between public demand and management reality. Factors such as resource availability, management complexity and urban heterogeneity limit governments' capacity to meet public demands. Through participation, citizens get the opportunity to reevaluate their demands, better understand management limitation and help to build consensus on proposed public programs and policies.

The above-mentioned benefits notwithstanding, it is not always easy to get people involved or to ensure that participants are representative of the community. In addition, expert professionals might worry about the results of sharing decision making for complex issues with the public (Thomas, 1995). For example, government officials might be reluctant to include citizens in the budget process for fear that it will increase spending expectations beyond affordable levels. Based on the literature, the case could be made that the decision of local public officials to involve citizens in the policy process and in public decision making depends on the perception and beliefs of those officials regarding the relative benefits and disadvantages of participation. Many scholars believe the Internet provides an avenue for overcoming the shortfalls of traditional citizen participation by facilitating interaction between citizens and government.

Internet-based citizen participation is the use of the Internet to facilitate citizen participation, through deliberative features such as policy discussion forums, chat rooms for citizen discussions on government policies and initiatives, online bulletin boards, online feedback and comment forms, online citizen initiated contact of government officials, online citizens survey, etc. Deliberative features of the Internet are therefore attributes that serve as democratic outreach by facilitating communication, interaction and discussion between citizens and government. The Internet is viewed as a means to strengthen the political community, democratic renewal and reversal of the recent downward trend in civic engagement by offering more convenient and less costly alternative to traditional citizen participation (Klotz, 2004; Johnson & Kaye, 2003; DiMaggio et al., 2001; Trippi, 2004). Internet technology is increasingly being applied in government organizations to help improve public services and make them less expensive to deliver, and to make organizations more responsive to citizens (West, 2001; West, 2005). Government agencies can use the Internet to seek citizen opinion on particular issues to guide policy making, and potentially help address problems with the state-citizen relationship by providing unmediated access to government officials, and thereby minimize agenda management.

The Internet is free from constraints of space and time, as well as the expense of traveling to the meeting hall. Consequently, participants do not have to assemble in a single space to communicate with each other, and communication in a non-chat room online forum does not require close synchronization between participants (Klien, 1999). These structural characteristics, which differentiate the Internet from other participation forums such as meeting halls, could serve as a motivating factor for officials of any form of government who believe in citizen participation to avail themselves of the opportunities offered by the interactive features of the technology to bring citizens closer to their governments. However, empirical evidence suggests that some of the promises of bridging the gap among governments and citizens through enhanced interaction between citizens and government, and between citizens themselves are yet to be fulfilled (Chadwick & May, 2001; West, 2001; Musso, Hale & Weare, 1999; Kerns, Bend & Stern, 2002; the Global e-Policy and e-Government Institute and Rutgers University e-Governance Institute, 2003, 2005; Needham, 2004; Jensen & Venkatesh 2007).

This may be due to certain challenges inherent in the Internet as a medium of interaction. For instance, the required investment in computer hardware, monthly service fees, and computer skills can be prohibitive, especially to minorities and low income citizens. In addition, effective expressions in a text medium require a high level of education (Klein, 1999). Furthermore, improvements in citizen access to decision making and broadened participation often came at substantial cost, with those bearing the cost tending to have substantial say in setting the agenda (Atherton, 1987). Based on these constraints, it is not entirely surprising that officials at various levels of government have not taken advantage of the Internet to bring citizens closer to their governments. If governments do not believe in taking advantage of the Internet to enhance citizen participation, they may not allocate funds for that purpose and, the degree of interactive features of their government websites should reflect this. Through the analysis of municipality website contents, this study seeks to determine whether city officials' beliefs and funding for Internet-based citizen participation is reflected in their government websites.

CONTENT ANALYSIS

Various authors have proposed formal definitions of content analysis. For example, Berelson (1952) defines content analysis as a research technique for the objective, systematic, and quantitative description of manifest content of communication. Stone et al. (1966) define it as any research technique for making inferences by systematically and objectively identifying specified characteristics within text. Krippendorff (1980) defines content analysis as a research technique for making replicative and valid inferences from data to their content. Weber (1990) argues Krippendorff is right to emphasize the relationship between the content of texts and their institutional, societal, or cultural contexts.

Whatever the variation in definitions, it seems clear that content analysis uses a set of procedures to determine the presence of certain words, concepts, themes, phrases, characters, features, or sentences within texts or set of texts in order to make valid inferences about the sender(s) of the message, the message itself, or the audience of the message. Texts can be broadly defined to include books, book chapters, essays, interviews, discussions, newspaper headlines and articles, historical documents, speeches, conversations, advertising, theater, informal conversation, or really any occurrence of communicative language (Palmquist, 2002). From this definition, one can

infer that texts include electronic documents such as content of Internet web sites.

There are two general categories of content analysis: conceptual analysis and relational analysis. Conceptual analysis can be thought of as establishing the existence and frequency of concepts in a text. Relational analysis builds on conceptual analysis by examining the relationships among concepts in a text. To conduct a content analysis on a text, the text is coded, or broken down into manageable categories on a variety of levels and then examined using one of the content analysis basic methods.

Nachimias and Nachimias (1981) suggest a critical step in content analysis is to develop categories, which are both relevant to the purpose of the research and clearly defined. The three requirements for content categories are that they be appropriate, exhaustive and mutually exclusive. These are especially crucial to reliability and validity (Budd, Thorp & Donohew, 1967). Categories are considered valid if they measure the definition that the researcher wanted to measure (Bengston & Fan 1999). Clearly defined rules, procedures and definitions improve validity and facilitate replication and reliability (Roth, 1996). Categories that are exhaustive and exclusive contain all aspects relevant to the subject of the study and ensure each item is addressed in only one area within the groups of categories respectively (Nachimias & Nachimias, 1981). Budd, Thorp and Donohew (1967) suggest adding some limited miscellaneous comment category to help achieve an exhaustive analysis. While many content analysis projects are focused on the message produced, their object may be to find links between the message and other parts of the environment. In such studies, content analysis is considered a tool to be used in combination with other techniques.

The literature reviewed suggest that traditional citizen participation has strengths and weaknesses, and Internet-based citizen participation is plagued with opportunities and challenges. Additionally, various governments at all levels have not taken full advantage of the Internet's potential to bring citizens closer to their governments. These imply that there are unanswered questions as to whether city officials believe in traditional and Internet-based citizen participation, and whether their beliefs are reflected in their local government website contents through the presence of deliberative features. As a tool in this study, content analysis is used in combination with survey research to determine the extent to which local government officials' beliefs and resource allocation for online citizen participation are reflected in their government website contents. That is, if local government officials believe strongly in Internet-based citizen participation and they fund it, we should expect to see deliberative features on city websites that are consistent with such beliefs and funding. Therefore, this study aims at answering the following research questions:

1. What do local government officials believe about Internet-based citizen participation compared to traditional citizen participation?
2. To what extend do local government officials fund Internet-based citizen participation?
3. Do local government officials' beliefs and funding reflect the deliberative features of their government websites?

METHODOLOGY

This study uses a mixed methodology consisting of survey research and website content analysis. Cities with web sites in five mid-western states were identified and sampled to select those to which a survey was sent, and content analysis of their web sites performed. These five states are (IA, KS, MN, MO, and NE). Together, they have a total of 3,906 municipalities (2002 Census of Governments) of which 548 had functioning websites as of December 30, 2005 according to information obtained from the online directory of official state, county and city web sites. They were

selected because they have similar geographic and economic environment, and Minnesota communities serve as a national model for electronic democracy.

A stratified random sample was drawn from the web sites of city governments within the five states. The stratification was based on the following category of city population sizes: Less than 5,000, 5,000-24,999, 25,000-49,999, 50,000-74,999, 75,000-99,999 and 100,000 and above. The 2000 U.S. census data was utilized to determine the population sizes of cities in the sample. The sampling frame consists of the list of all cities with official web sites (in the five selected mid-western states) obtained from the online directory of official state, county and city government web sites. Although the online directory is updated daily, a potential problem inherent in the sampling frame is incomplete and inaccurate information. To avoid inaccuracies in the sampling frame, the list of all cities in the selected Mid-western states was thoroughly examined to detect any of the above-mentioned potential problems before stratification and random selection were performed. In addition, the list was reviewed for multiple listings of domain names. To minimize the potential problem of omitted eligible domain names, multiple sources of lists of municipal government domain names were used. For example, the list of all cities was cross checked against a list from the respective official state web sites.

A mail survey was sent in 2004 to 218 municipal Chief Administrative Officers of the stratified random sample of the cities drawn from the web sites of the five Midwestern states, and 117 returned the survey, representing a 54% response rate. Local government officials are the appropriate subjects for this study because local government is the tier of public authority to which citizens first look to solve their immediate problems. It is also the level of democracy in which the citizen has the most effective opportunity to actively and directly participate in decisions made for all of society. The first two parts of the survey measured several variables of interest on a seven point Likert Scale. The variables measured include the extent of respondents' beliefs in activities that enhance traditional citizen participation, and in activities that enhance Internet-based citizen participation. This allowed for the comparison of responses pertaining to the beliefs in traditional and Internet-based citizen participation for the chief administrative officers of the cities within the different population ranges in our sample.

The following city officials' beliefs were specifically measured from the perspective of traditional and Internet-based citizen participation: Inform and educate citizens on policy issues; include citizens in discussion of policy prior to any final decisions; solicit and take citizens' opinion into account in making decisions; inform citizens about services city provided; include citizens in discussion of city services provided; provide feedback to citizens on their inputs and inquiries. For example, regarding citizen participation in policy decisions, respondents were asked whether they believe citizens should be included in discussion of policy before final decision, and whether they believe city web sites should be used to stimulate citizen discussion of policy prior to final decision. Part III measured the extent of resources allocated by the city officials toward Internet-based citizen participation. Part IV measured official specific variables such as the percentage of information technology (IT) budget spent on electronic government and citizen participation

Once the questionnaire was returned, a content analysis of the municipality's web site was performed to identify and score those features that support citizen participation in governance. The emphasis of the content analysis was on the evaluation of the contents of the 117 survey respondents' official city websites in order to audit them against survey responses regarding local government officials' beliefs and funding for Internet-Based Citizen Participation. The official city web sites used for this study included homepages and related web pages containing

information about city administration and online services provided by the city, as well as information about the city council. Separate homepages for city agencies and departments that are linked to the above-mentioned homepages were also included in this study.

A follow-up content analysis was performed between late 2005 and early 2006. The web site content analyses involved an examination of the 117 survey respondents' official local government web sites from across the five selected mid-western states. The examination consisted of searching for elements of four key categories of deliberative features within each web site that would facilitate citizen participation through the communication and interaction between government and citizens, and among citizens. The categories examined include: online government information and services, online news and bulletin boards, and online feedback and discussion forums.

The elements reviewed in the respective categories are as follows: information and services category - online contact information, local government minutes and budgets, administrative services provided, and frequently asked questions and answers; news and bulletin board category - online news and events, policies under current debate, newsletter, and webcast; feedback and discussion forum category – online feedback and comment form, chat room, policy discussion forum and customer satisfaction survey. These categories were selected because together, they strengthen public accountability through communication, interaction and feedback between citizens and government, as well as citizen participation in the local governance process.

Conceptual analysis was used to examine the presence of sentences, themes and features that relate to the elements in the categories and coded for their existence in each web site. The concept here was the presence of the key elements within the dimensions of deliberative features. To increase validity, several sources were consulted to assist with developing categories that are both

Table 1. Mean scores for belief variables measured

Belief Variables and Constructs	N	Mean	Std. Deviation
Inform and educate citizens about policy issues	117	6.25	.887
Include citizens in discussions of policy prior to any final decision	117	5.84	.871
Take citizen opinion into account in making decisions	117	5.95	.808
Inform and educate citizens about administrative services provided by city	117	6.35	.802
Include citizens in discussion of administrative services provided	117	5.65	.894
Provide feedback to citizens on their inputs and inquiries	117	6.09	.877
Average Belief in Traditional Citizen Participation	**117**	**6.02**	**.615**
Use city website to inform and educate citizens issues policy issues	117	6.00	1.098
Use city website to stimulate online public discussion on policy	117	4.58	1.416
Use city website to solicit and take citizen opinion into account in making decisions	117	4.80	1.347
Use city website to inform and educate citizens on services	117	6.00	1.099
Use city website to stimulate online public discussion on services	117	4.58	1.414
Use city website to offer feedback to citizens	117	5.29	1.352
Encourage citizens to contact city officials Using the city website	117	5.65	1.309
Average Belief in Internet Based Citizen Participation	**117**	**5.27**	**1.0765**

pertinent and in sufficient quantity to be exhaustive. Questions and categories to identify web page contents followed those suggested by Cooke (1999) in evaluating the quality of organizational web pages, and DeConti (1998) in an evaluation of U.S. State government sites. In the analysis section of this study, the results of the content analysis are audited against the survey responses to discern any relationship.

FINDINGS

Reliability analysis was performed to determine the extent to which the variables measured are free from error and therefore yield internal consistency. Nunnally (1978) and Churchill (1979) suggest that constructs with coefficient alpha equal to or greater than 0.70 have adequate internal consistency. The Cronbach coefficient for all the variables measured had alpha coefficient above 0.700.

Beliefs in Participation

Means and standard deviations were computed to determine respondent's average agreement to questions eliciting their beliefs in several areas of citizen participation. The following detailed scores were used for the responses: 1 = Completely Not believe, 2 = Strongly Not Believe, 3 = Somewhat Not Believe, 4 = Neutral, 5 = Somewhat Believe, 6 = Strongly Believe, and 7 = Completely Believe. Table 1 shows that the mean scores of the belief variables measured in the Traditional Citizen Participation construct range from the score of 5.65 for "include citizens in discussion of administrative services provided" to 6.35 for "inform and educate citizens on administrative services provided by the city." The table also shows an average mean score of 6.02 for all the belief variables measured in the Traditional Citizen Participation construct, and an average standard deviation of 0.615.

The result in Table 1 shows that in general, all the 117 respondents *strongly believe* that city public officials should: inform citizens about policy and administrative services provided, include citi-

Table 2. Resource deployment summary statistics

Questions on Resource Deployment	N	Yes	No	Not Sure	Total
Does your city allocate funds specifically for citizen participation?	117	29%	70%	1%	100%
Does your city allocate funds specifically for city's web site?	117	82%	19%	1%	100%
Does your city provide funds for web site features that facilitate citizen participation?	117	38%	60%	2%	100%
Has your city set up electronic kiosks to broaden access to the Internet?	117	6%	87%	7%	100%
Does your city publicize its city web site to citizens?	117	92%	8%	-	100%
Does your city offer educational materials about government on its city web site?	117	66%	33%	1%	100%
Does your city offer training so that citizens may use the Internet?	117	20%	80%	-	100%
Does your city run its own web site?	117	67%	32%	1%	100%
If your city runs its own web site, does it have a designated personnel to maintain the site?	117	99%	1%	-	100%

zens in the discussion of policy and administrative services provided prior to any final decision, take citizens opinions into account in making decisions, and provide feedback to citizens on their inputs and inquiries. Table 1 also shows that the mean scores for the belief variables measured in the Internet-Based Citizen Participation construct range from 4.58 for "use city web site to stimulate online public discussion on service and policy issues" to 6.00 for "use city web site to inform and educate citizens on policy and services." The table also shows an average mean score of 5.27 for all the belief variables measured in the Internet-Based Citizen Participation construct, and an average standard deviation of 1.078.

The above result for Belief in Internet-Based Citizen Participation shows that in general, all the 117 respondents *somewhat believe* that city public officials should use city web site to: solicit citizen opinion, inform and educate citizens on policy and services, stimulate online public discussion on policy and services, offer feedback to citizens, and encourage citizens to contact city officials. This modest belief in Internet-Based Citizen Participation pales in comparison to the strong belief in Traditional Citizen Participation noted above. This implies that although city government officials strongly believe in engaging in activities

that enhance citizen participation without the use of Internet technology, such belief is reduced if they are to use Internet technology to engage in the same activities.

Funding for Internet-Based Citizen Participation

Table 2 illustrates the percentages of respondents who indicated their city governments allocate funds specifically for citizen participation, for their city web sites, and for their city web site features that enhance citizen participation. Table 3 also illustrates the percentage ranges of city IT budgets spent on E-Government, the percentage ranges of E-Government budgets spent on enhancing city web site features to support citizen participation, and the corresponding percentages of respondents who indicated the percentage ranges spent in the two cases.

The results illustrated in Table 2 shows 70% of the respondents stated their city governments do not allocate funds specifically for citizen participation, compared to the 29% whose city governments allocate funds for that purpose. This result appears to be consistent with the results illustrated in Table 3, which shows 55% of respondents' city governments spend less than 5% of IT budget on

Table 3. Percentage of IT budget spent on e-gov, and of e-gov budget spent on internet-based citizen participation (N =117)

Percentage Responding	Less Than 5%	5% -14%	15-24%	25%-34%	35%- or More	Don't Know	Total
Percentage responding for % of IT budget spent on E-Government	55%	15%	8%	3%	6%	13%	100%
Percentage responding for % of E-Gov budget devoted to web site enhancement for citizen participation	61%	13%	5%	2%	5%	15%	100%

E-Government and 61% spend less than 5% of E-Government budget on city web site features that support citizen participation. This implies that overall, at least 55% of the local governments whose officials were surveyed spend less than 0.25% (0.05x0.05 = 0.0025 = 0.25%) of their IT budget on city web site features that support citizen participation.

Table 2 also illustrates that although 82% of cities allocate funds specifically for the city web site, only 38% provide funds for web site features that facilitate citizen participation. In addition, while 92% publicize their city web site to citizens, and 66% offer educational materials about government on their city web sites, only 20% offer any training so that citizens may use the Internet, and only 6% do provide electronic kiosks to broaden access to the Internet. These results are not surprising, considering the limited amount of E-government budgets spent to enhance website features to enable online citizen participation.

Audit of Website Contents Against Survey Findings

Online Government Information and Services

Contact Information: The results of the content analysis reveal that 100% of the web sites reviewed had at least one form of official contact information – email, telephone number, and mailing address - on their web sites. Ninety six percent

(96%) had any two of the contact information, and fifty percent (50%) had all three forms of contact information. Table 4 provides a comparison between the survey findings and the web site content analysis findings for three of the variables measured under Online Government Information and Services. The table has three main sections – "Variables Measured," "Survey Findings" and "Content Analysis Findings." The contents of the columns in the "Survey Findings" and "Content Analysis Findings" sections in Table 4 illustrate comparisons of the research results for each of the three variables measured. The variables are: (1) belief in encouraging citizens to use city web sites to contact city officials, (2) offering of educational materials about government on city web sites, (3) belief in using city web sites to inform and educate citizens about policy and services.

In Table 4, (and in all the other tables in the content analysis section of this chapter), the intersection of each row of the variables measured and the applicable column under "Survey Findings" and "Content Analysis Findings" indicates the survey and the content analysis findings that are compared to determine consistencies and interrelationships. For example, the row containing the variable "belief in encouraging citizens to use city web sites to contact city officials" intersects with the "Fair Belief" cell in the column titled "Encourage use of Site for Contact" under "Survey Findings" and also with the "100%" cell in the column titled "Contact Information" under "Content Analysis Findings." As shown in Table

Table 4. Comparison of survey findings and contents analysis findings: Online govt. information and services

Measured Variables	Survey Findings			Content Analysis Findings (% of Web Sites Evaluated That Provide):		
	Encourage use of Site for Contact	Education Materials on Site	Use Site to Inform on Services	Contact Information	Minutes and or Budgets	Admin Services
Belief in encouraging citizens to use city web sites to contact city officials	Fair Belief (Mean Score = 5.27)			100%		
Does your city offer educational materials about government on its web site? (Percentage responding Yes)		66%			90%	
Belief in using city web site to inform and educate citizens on policy and services			Strong Belief (Mean Score = 6.0)			100%

4, although city government officials stated in the survey that they fairly believe in encouraging citizens to use city web sites to contact city officials (mean score = 5.65), results of the content analysis indicates 100% of respondents' cities provide at least one form of contact information on their web sites.

Minutes and Budgets: The comparison in Table 4 shows while the survey finding indicates 66% of the cities offer educational materials about government on their web sites, the content analysis reveals 90% of the city web sites have some form of minutes and budget information to educate citizens on city council legislative and financial priorities. However, the analysis revealed some of these educational materials are buried under layers of information in many of the websites reviewed, and required the use of search engines for easy retrievals. Further analysis revealed forty eight percent (48%) of the web sites reviewed had search engine in addition to either minutes/ agenda or budget/financial report. Considering the fact that only 20% of the cities provide training for citizens to use the Internet, and less than half of the city web sites provide search engines for access to additional materials to educate the public, one could make the case that the overall content analysis results are consistent with the

survey results regarding resource allocation for educational materials on city web sites.

Administrative Services Provided: As indicated in Table 1 above, the variable 'belief in using city websites to inform and educate citizens about administrative services provided' has a score of 6.0 on a 7.0 scale, reflecting officials' strong belief in this activity. The comparison in Table 4 shows this is consistent with the content analysis finding, which reveals 100% of the web sites analyzed have information on some form of administrative services provided. Detailed analysis not shown in Table 4 indicates 45% of the web sites had just a list of the administrative services provided. Another 38% had the capability to download service and permit applications in addition to the list of services provided. Additional 11% had the capability for citizens to apply for services or permits online, and additional 5% allowed users to pay for fine or services online.

Online News and Bulletin Boards

Bulletin Boards for Policies Under Current Debate: We may recall from Table 1 that although city officials strongly believe in providing feedback to citizens (mean score = 6.09), they only somewhat believe in using the city website for

Table 5. Comparison of survey findings and content analysis findings: Online news and bulletin board

Variables Measured	Survey Findings		Content Analysis Findings (% of Web Sites Evaluated That Provide):			
	Use site to Provide Feedback	Information by Bulletin Board	Bulletin Board for Debates	Online Notice Board	Online Newsletter	Online Web cast
Belief in using city web site to provide feedback to citizens	Modest Belief (Mean Score = 5.29)	2%	4%	79%	34%	2%

such activity (mean score = 5.29). Table 5 provides a comparison between the survey findings and the web site content analysis findings for the variable measured under Online News and Bulletin Boards - belief in using city web site to provide feedback to citizens. The content analysis examined the presence of features or dimensions of online news and bulletin boards that reflect this belief. Bulletin boards for issues under current debate constitute one web site feature identified to reflect belief in using city web sites to provide feedback to citizens.

The content analysis results show only 4% of the web sites provided bulletin board for polices under current debate, and 2% invited citizen comments on the policies or issues in addition to posting them on the bulletin board. In addition, another 2% posted the citizen comments with the policies/issues on the bulletin board. The comparison in Table 5 reveals consistency between the survey finding regarding city government officials modest belief in using city web sites to provide feedback to citizens, and the content analysis finding which reveals only 4% of the city web sites provide bulletin boards for issues under current debate. The content analysis result is also consistent with the analysis of the result in Table 3 which revealed that at least 55% of local governments surveyed spend less than 0.25% of their annual IT budget to enhance web site features that facilitate citizen participation.

Online News and Notice Board: As indicated in Table 5, results of the content analysis reveal 79% of the web sites reviewed did post some form

of news and notices online, although many of these were not posted on formal bulletin boards. However, detailed reviews of the news and notices posted on the web sites revealed they were primarily information about current or upcoming events in the cities rather than notices regarding feedback to citizens. From this standpoint, the higher percentage of the notices is not entirely inconsistent with the city government officials' modest belief in using city web sites to provide feedback to citizens.

Online Newsletter: This relates to a means of city officials providing information to citizens such as informing about how the government is addressing their needs. As indicated in Table 5, the results of the content analysis indicates only 34% of the city web sites reviewed did have online city newsletter. The comparison reveals consistency with local government officials' modest belief in using city web sites to provide feedback to citizens (mean score =5.29). Further analysis not shown in Table 5 indicates ten percent (10%) of the web sites had newsletters in HTML format, and another 19% had newsletter in formats that can be downloaded.

Online Video/Web Cast: The content analysis results revealed only 2% of the web sites did have web cast for broadcasting public events, compared to the 98% who neither had asynchronous nor synchronous web casts. This finding is, again, not only consistent with the modest belief of city officials but also with the fact that the city governments spend less than 0.25% of annual IT

Table 6. Comparison of survey findings and content analysis findings: Online feedback and discussion forum

Variables Measured	Survey Findings			Content Analysis Findings (% of Web Sites Evaluated that Provide):			
	Use Site to Stimulate Discussion	Use site to Solicit Citizen Opinion	IT Budget for Internet-based Participation	Chat Room	Online Discussion Forum	Online Feedback Form	Online Satisfaction Survey
Belief in using city web site to stimulate online discussion of policy and services	Very Weak Belief (Mean Score = 4.58)		< 0.25%	1%	1%		
Belief In using city web site to solicit citizen opinion		Weak Belief (Mean Score = 4.80)	< 0.25%	1%	1%	29% (Departments) 9% (Elected Officials)	9%
Percentage of annual IT budget spent to enhance Internet-based participation (at least 55% responded this way)			< 0.25%	1%	1%	29% (Departments) 9% (Elected Officials)	9%

budget in enabling interactive features for citizen participation.

Online Feedback and Discussion Forum

An interesting but not surprising finding in Table 1 is that officials' average belief in including citizens in discussion about policy and service ranks low among all the variables measured both for both traditional (mean scores= 5.84 for policy discussions and = 5.65 for service discussions) and Internet-based (mean score = 4.58 for both policy and service discussions) citizen participation. Additionally, while officials almost strongly believe in soliciting citizens' opinion in decision making (mean score = 5.95), they do not have the same strong desire when it comes to using city website for the same purpose (mean score = 4.80). Thus, the mean scores for both policy and service discussions as well as citizens' opinion are weak when it comes to the use of city websites. Table 6 provides a comparison between the survey findings and the web site content analysis findings for the

variables measured under Online Feedback and Discussion Forum. The variables measured are: (1) belief in using city web site to stimulate online discussion of policy and service, and (2) belief in using city web site to solicit citizen opinion. Additionally, the Table also provides comparison for the variable 'percentage of IT budget spent to enhance Internet-based citizen participation' to help put the entire findings in perspective. The four web site features measured in this section are availability of a chat room, online policy discussion forum, online feedback form and online satisfaction survey

Chat Room: As illustrated in Table 6, the content analysis results indicate only 1% of the city web sites reviewed did have a chat room where any citizen can post ideas or comments or opinion without a specific discussion topic. This is consistent with the weak beliefs of officials revealed in the survey findings regarding online stimulation of public discussion and solicitation of citizen opinion. Additionally, the findings reflect the third survey result in Table 6 which indicates at least 55% of local governments surveyed spend less than 0.25% of their annual IT budget to enhance web site features that facilitate citizen participation. Considering the low IT budget spent to enhance Internet-based citizen participation, and the fact that, as shown in Table 2, 60% of local governments do not provide funds for web site features that facilitate citizen participation, this result is not surprising.

Online Policy Discussion Forum: Results of the content analysis also indicates only 1% of the city web sites reviewed did have online policy discussion forum where citizens participate in discussion of specific policy proposals. The analysis for this finding is the same as that for chat room. This finding is comparable to the survey finding indicating city government officials very weakly believe in the use of city web site to stimulate online discussion of policy and administrative services. As indicated earlier, the mean score of 4.58 for this variable was the lowest among the scores for the use of city web site to support the use of the Internet for citizen participation.

Comments and Feedback to Individual Departments and elected officials: The results of the content analysis reveal a total of 29% of the web sites had online feedback forms to enable citizens to provide feedback and comments to city department officials. Additionally, 9% of the web sites provided online feedback form and contact information to elected officials. The comparison in Table 6 indicates these findings are also consistent with the survey finding regarding city government officials' non enthusiastic belief in the use of city web sites to solicit citizens' opinion (mean score = 4.80). The findings are also not surprising, as they appear consistent with the finding in Table 2, which shows that only 38% of cities provide funds for web site features that facilitate citizen participation. Furthermore, they constitute a reflection of the very small percentage of annual IT budget spent on deliberative features. Detailed results not shown in Table 6 also indicate 31% of the city web sites analyzed did not invite comments or feedback to elected officials. Additionally, 14%

of the web sites reviewed had only department telephone numbers for feedback and comments, 6% had only department email links, while 51% had both department numbers and email links for communication with the departments.

Online Satisfaction Survey: Results reveal only 9% of the city web sites analyzed did have online citizen satisfaction surveys. Again, this finding reflects the analysis from the survey finding that at least 55% of cities spend less than 0.25% of their annual IT budget to support the use of the Internet for citizen participation.

DISCUSSION

The analysis presented in this chapter clearly indicates some consistencies and interrelationships between city officials' beliefs in Internet-Based Citizen Participation, resource allocation and the contents of the web sites evaluated. Simply put, deliberative features of local government web sites reflect city officials' beliefs and funding to support Internet-based citizen participation. The findings in this study have theoretical and practical implications for public administration and e-government research.

From theoretical perspective, the audit of government website contents against survey responses represents a fundamental shift in focus from previous e-government research. While several studies involving the evaluation of government web sites have been performed in recent years, very few are yet to focus on auditing the findings of the web site content analysis against survey responses pertaining to beliefs, or against policy requirements, organizational missions, strategic goals and objectives that impact the contents of the websites. The application of the research technique used in this study could be instrumental in identifying the degree to which government website contents reflect key e-government policy requirements, missions, strategic goals, priorities, preferences, etc, and the extent to which e-government related expenditures reflect the intended goals of public agencies, as well as the purpose of funding.

The key findings from this research suggest that the degree of deliberative contents of local government websites studied do consistently reflect city officials' perceptions about Internet-based citizen participation and the amount of funding committed for such purpose. From a practical perspective, the findings have implications for public administrators and other public sector managers in the sense that they help to affirm the importance of leadership commitment to organizational change. To many traditionalists within public organizations, the adoption of Internet technology and use of the Internet to support citizen participation constitute a major organizational change. Without the beliefs and commitments of the Chief Administrative Officers and other leaders to the processes and outcomes of Internet-based citizen participation initiatives, adequate resources and funding could not be deployed for successful outcomes, hence the consistency between the website contents, officials believes and funding.

The commitment of government leaders to the processes and outcomes of Internet-based citizen participation also has implications for successful outcome of e-government and e-participation initiatives. As indicated in the findings section, although 92% of survey respondents' governments publicize their websites, only 38% of provide funds for website features that facilitate citizen participation. Additionally, only 6% provide electronic kiosks to broaden access to the Internet and 20% provide training so that citizens may use the Internet. Considering the fact that knowing the availability of Internet services in government is one of the significant factors influencing citizens' acceptance and use of e-government services (Sæbø, Rose, & Flak, 2008), the high rate of website publicity is in order. However, the fewer number of governments who fund or provide resources for deliberative features, electronic kiosks and Internet usage training appear consistent with arguments by scholars such as Olphert & Demo-

daran (2007), who suggest current e-government practices take technocratic approach of e-services with minimal involvement of citizens. This supply-side approach to e-government may be the reason why 48% of Internet users rarely or never visit government websites (Accenture 2004).

The research results also show that city officials prefer to engage citizens through traditional means than through the medium of the Internet. As stated earlier, this preference is not only backed up by the low spending on features that could facilitate online citizen engagement, but is also reflected in the contents of city government websites in terms of the presence of deliberative features. These findings confirm the findings from many other studies (e.g. Kerns, Bend & Stern, 2002; the Global e-Policy and e-Government Institute and Rutgers University e-Governance Institute, 2003, 2005; Jensen & Venkatesh 2007) which suggest that some of the promises of bridging the gap among governments and citizens through enhanced interaction between citizens and government are yet to be fulfilled. Additionally, they seem to confirm the argument by Thomas (1995) that traditionally, public managers have shied away from orchestrating or promoting citizen participation in the policy process, due in part to a belief that elected officials are the appropriate conduit for gauging public opinion and in part to a fear that engaging the public will complicate policy-making and program management efforts.

This research is limited by the effects of the dynamic nature of the Internet, and the fast pace of technological advancement in communication and deliberative features on the reproducibility of the results of the web site content analysis. The analysis of survey respondents' city web sites was performed in a six month period from February 2004 through July 2004, with follow ups done in late 2005 and early 2006. As cities modify the design of their web sites, the contents and deliberative features of those web sites could be altered, with potential adverse effect on inter-coder consistency. Thus, rapid changes in the web site contents and features could lead a subsequent researcher using the same coding techniques to arrive at a somewhat different conclusion. Although this problem was minimized by using the standard coding technique in previous research and by moving back and forth between the web site contents and the output of the content analysis, the potential impact of changes in web site designs on deliberative features should not be under estimated. This study only included cities with functioning websites. As a result, the beliefs of, and resource allocation by, officials in cities without websites in supporting Internet-based citizen participation are not represented. Furthermore, the sample size in this study may limit the generalization of the results on global basis. Despite the above-mentioned limitations, the findings are useful because, as stated earlier, the examination of e-government from the perspective of auditing government website contents against survey findings regarding official believes, or for that matter, policy requirements or strategic goals, is a relatively young research technique and very little empirical research is available in this area.

Further studies are required to determine whether changes in websites contents and the broadening of the research sample to include municipalities in other parts of the United States as well as other countries could make a difference in the results. Another area for further study is the impact of organizational factors such as the presence or absence of e-government strategy, policy requirement, organizational missions, stated goals and objectives and organizational culture on local government adoption of Internet-based citizen participation, the contents of local websites, and the implication for public policy. As part of the data analysis for such a study, the findings in the web site content analysis could be audited against policy requirements, organizational mission, or stated goals and objectives, etc. This could provide empirical evidence regarding the degree of alignment between a government's Internet website contents and its e-government strategic goals, and policy priorities.

CONCLUSION

Overall, the findings suggest deliberative contents of local government websites constitute a reflection of city officials' beliefs and funding for the use of the Internet to support citizen participation. Deliberative features of the local government websites reviewed are low because the officials seem to be more willing to engage citizens through the traditional means. Considering the interactive potential of the Internet to bring citizens closer to their governments by allowing citizens to access public information, to interact with government officials and to promote better accountability of officials to citizens, its significance as a tool for participatory governance and vision building for e-government initiatives cannot be overlooked. However, as the findings from this study reveal, it is through the beliefs and commitments of the responsible officials in government to the processes and outcomes of online participation initiatives, and funding for those initiatives, that could truly make the Internet the tool for participatory governance.

REFERENCES

Accenture (2004). *2004 eGovernment report: High performance, maximum value*. Retrieved January 14, 2006, from http://www.accenture.com/NR/rdonlyres/D7206199-C3D4-4CB4A7D8846C94287890/0/gove_egov_value.pdf

Arterton, C. (1987). *Teledemocracy: Can technology protect democracy?* Newbury Park, CA: Sage Publications.

Barber, B. (1984). *Strong democracy: Participatory politics for a new age*. Berkeley: University of California Press.

Bengston, D. N., & Fan, D. (1999). An innovative method for evaluating strategic goals in public agency. *Evaluation Review, 23*(1), 77+. Retrieved February 5, 2000, from EBSCO Database (Academic Search Elite 1531559) http://www.ebsco.com

Berelson, B. (1952). *Content analysis in communication research*. New York: Free Press.

Box, R. C. (1998). *Citizen governance: Leading American communities into the 21st century*. Thousand Oaks, CA: Sage Publications.

Budd, R. W., Thorp, R. K., & Donohew, L. (1967). *Content analysis of communications*. New York: Macmillan Company.

Budge, I. (1996). *The new challenge of direct democracy*. Oxford, UK: Policy Press.

Caldwell, L. (1964). *Administrative theories of Hamilton and Jefferson*. New York: Russell & Russell.

Chadwick, A., & May, C. (2001). *Interaction between states and citizens in the age of the Internet: "E-Government" in the United States, Britain and the European Union*. Paper presented to the American Political Science Association annual meeting.

Cooke, A. (1999). *Neal-Schuman authoritative guide to evaluating information on the Internet*. New York: Neal-Schuman Publishers.

Creighton, J. L. (1981). *The public involvement manual*. Cambridge, MA: Abt.

Deconti, L. (1998). *Planning and creating a government web site: Learning from the experience of U.S. states* (Working Paper No.2). Manchester, UK.

DeSario, J., & Langton, S. (1984). *Citizen Participation in public decision making*. New York: Greenwood Press.

Dimaggio, P., Hargttai, E., Neuman, W. R., & Robinson, J. P. (2001). Social implications of the Internet. *Annual Review of Sociology, 27*, 307–336. doi:10.1146/annurev.soc.27.1.307

Hale, M., Musso, J., & Weare, C. (1999). Developing digital democracy: Evidence from California municipal web pages. In Hague, B. N., & Loader, B. D. (Eds.), *Digital democracy: Discourse and decision making in the information age*. London: Routledge.

Irvin, R. A., & Stansbury, J. (2004). Citizen participation in decision making: Is it worth the effort? *Public Administration Review, 4*(1), 55–65. doi:10.1111/j.1540-6210.2004.00346.x

Jensen, M., & Venkatesh, A. (2007). Government websites and political engagement: Facilitating Citizen entry into the policy process. In B. Thossen (Ed.). *Schriftenreihe Informatic*: Vol. 23. *Towards Electronic Democracy Conference Proceedings* (pp. 55-65). Linz, Austria: Trauner Verlag.

Johnson, T. J., & Kaye, B. K. (2003). A boost or bust for democracy: How the Web influenced Political attitudes in the 1996 and 2000 presidential elections. *Harvard Journal of Press/ Politics, 8*, 9-34.

Kaufman, H. (1969). Administrative decentralizations and political power. *Public Administration Review, 29*(1), 3–15. doi:10.2307/973980

Kearns, I., Bend, J., & Stern, B. (2002). *E-participation in local government*. Retrieved July 12, 2003 from www.ippr.org

King, C., & Stivers, C. (1998). *Government is us: Public administration in an anti-government era*. Thousand Oaks, CA: Sage Publication.

King, S. K., Feltey, K. M., & Susel, B. O. (1998). The question of participation: Toward authentic participation in public administration. *Public Administration Review, 58*(4), 317–326. doi:10.2307/977561

Klien, H. K. (1999). Tocqueville in cyberspace: Using the Internet for citizen associations. *The Information Society, 15*, 213–220. doi:10.1080/019722499128376

Klotz, R. (2004). *The politics of Interne communication.* Lanham, MD: Rowman & Littlefield.

Krippendorff, K. (1980). *Content Analysis: An Introduction to Its methodology.* Beverly Hill, CA: Sage.

La Port, T., Demchak, C., & de Jong, M. (2000). *Democracy and bureaucracy in the age of the web: Empirical findings and Theoretical speculations.* Paper presented at the International Political Science Association, August, 5, 2000.

Langton, S. (1978). What is citizen participation? In Langton, S. (Ed.), *Citizen participation in America* (pp. 13–24). Lexington, MA: Lexington Books.

Lowi, T. J. (1969). *The end of liberalism.* New York: Norton.

Nachimias, D., & Nachimias, C. (1981). *Research Methods in Social Sciences* (2nd ed.). New York: St Martin's Press.

Needham, C. (2004). The citizen as a consumer: E-government in the United Kingdom and United States. In Gibson, R. (Eds.), *Electronic democracy: Mobilization, organization, and participation via new ICTs* (pp. 43–69). New York: Routledge.

Niskanen, W. A. Jr. (1971). *Bureaucracy and representative government.* Chicago: Aldine-Artherton.

Nunnally, J. (1978). *Psychometric theory* (2nd ed.). New York: McGraw Hill.

Oldfield, A. (1990). *Citizenship and community: Civic republicanism and the modern world.* London: Routledge Publishing.

Olphert, W., & Damodaran, L. (2007). Citizen participation and engagement in the design of e-government services: The missing link in effective ICT design and delivery. *Journal of the Association for Information Systems, 8*(9), 491–507.

Palmquist, M. (2002). *Content Analysis.* Retrieved September 30 2002, from http://fiat.gslis.utexas.edu/~palmquis/courses/content.html

Rohr, J. A. (1984). Civil servants and second class citizens. *Public Administration Review, 44*, 135–140. doi:10.2307/975553

Roth, M. S. (1996). Patterns in direct-to-consumer prescription drug print advertising and their public policy implications. *Journal of Public Policy and Marketing.*

Sæbø, Ø., Rose, J., & Flak, L. S. (2008). The shape of e-participation: Characterizing an emerging research area. *Government Information Quarterly, 25*, 400–428. doi:10.1016/j.giq.2007.04.007

Stivers, C. (1990). The public agency as poll: Active citizenship in the administrative state. *Administration & Society, 22*(1), 86–105. doi:10.1177/009539979002200105

Stone, P. J., Dunphy, D. C., Smith, M. S., & Ogilvie, D. M. (1966). *The general inquirer: A computer approach to content analysis.* Cambridge: MIT Press.

The Global e-policy and e-governance institute & Rutgers University e-governance institute. (2003). *Assessing websites and measuring e-government index among 100 world cities.* Study sponsored by the division of public administration and development, department of economics And social affairs, United Nations.

The Global e-policy and e-governance institute & Rutgers University e-governance institute. (2005). *Assessing websites and measuring e-government index among 100 world cities.* Study sponsored by the division of public administration and development, department of economics And social affairs, United Nations.

Thomas, C. J. (1995). *Public participation in public decisions.* San Francisco, CA: Jossey-Bass Publishers.

Trippi, J. (2004). *The revolution will not be televised: Democracy, the Internet, and the overthrow of everything*. New York: HaperCollins.

Weber, L. M., & Loumakis, A. (2005). Who participates and why? An analysis of citizens on The Internet and the mass public. *Social Science Computer Review*, *21*(1), 26–42. doi:10.1177/0894439302238969

Weber, R. P. (1990). *Basic content analysis* (2nd ed.). Newbury Park, CA: Sage Publications.

West, D. M. (2001). *E-Government and the transformation of public sector service delivery*. Paper presented at the annual meeting of the American Political Science Association. San Francisco CA. August, 30 –September, 2, 2001.

West, D. M. (2005). *State and Federal governments in the United States, Providence, RI: Center for Public Policy, Brown University*. Retrieved September 30, 2006, from http://www.insidepolitics.org/egovt05us.pdf

White, L. D. (1948). *The Federalists*. New York: Macmillan.

KEY TERMS AND DEFINITIONS

Local Government: A level of government that constitutes administrative office lower than a state or national government. Local governments usually have fewer powers than state or national governments. They usually have some powers to raise taxes, although this may be limited by central government legislation. In some countries, local governments are wholly or partly funded by subventions from the central or national government.

Internet: A global network connecting millions of computers. The Internet is decentralized by design and each computer (host) on the Internet is independent. The World Wide Web (WWW) is a technology that sits on top of the Internet to allow for communication enabled by web browsers such as Internet Explorer, Netscape and Firefox. The Internet generally consists of the WWW, electronic mail (e-mail), file transfer protocol (FTP), Internet Relay Chat (IRC), and USENET.

Website: A collection of related web pages, images, videos or other digital assets that are addressed by a domain name or IP address in an Internet-based protocol network. A website is hosted on at least one web server, accessible via the Internet or private local area network. The pages of a website can usually be accessed from a single Uniform Resource Locator (URL) called the homepage. A web page is a document, typically written in plain text interspersed with formatting instructions of Hypertext Markup Language (HTML, XHTML).

Content Analysis: A research technique for the objective, systematic, and quantitative description of manifest content of communication. Content analysis is used for making replicative and valid inferences from data to their content by systematically and objectively identifying specified characteristics within text. For the purpose of content analysis, texts can be broadly defined to include books, book chapters, essays, interviews, discussions, newspaper headlines and articles, historical documents, electronic documents, speeches, conversations, advertising, theater, informal conversation, or really any occurrence of communicative language

Resource Deployment: The means provided to support a specific project or goal such as provision of Internet access and design of deliberative features for online citizen participation. Such means may include allocation of funds for the technological infrastructure, assignment of support personnel, access provision (e.g. electronic kiosks) and connectivity, Internet usage training, promotion of city web site, and availability of education materials on the Internet.

Citizen Participation: Citizen involvement in decision-making pertaining to the management of public affairs, including public policy deliberations. Traditional citizen participation occurs through mechanisms such as hearing, citizen forums, community or neighborhood meetings, community outreaches, citizen advisory groups, individual citizen representation, etc.

Internet-Based Citizen Participation: The use of the Internet to support active citizen involvement in decision making pertaining to the management of public affairs, including public policy deliberations. This includes using government web sites to solicit citizens' opinion on policies and administrative services, to allow citizens to provide online feedback to administrative agencies and the legislature, and to stimulate online public discussions on policy and the political process.

Internet Deliberative Features: Attributes that serve as democratic outreach by facilitat-

ing communication, interaction and discussions between citizens and government. These include online discussion forums and feedback forms.

E-Government: Government's use of information and communication technology (ICT) to exchange information and services with citizens, businesses, and other arms of government. E-government may be applied by legislature, judiciary, or administration, in order to improve internal efficiency, the delivery of public services, or processes of democratic governance. Components are e-services, e-management, e-democracy and e-commerce.

Section 3
Future Directions

Chapter 15
A Review of Standardization Frameworks for Electronic Government Service Portals

Demetrios Sarantis
National Technical University of Athens, Greece

Dimitris Askounis
National Technical University of Athens, Greece

ABSTRACT

E-Government service portals have a challenging and unique mission, focused on public access, for an unknown group of users who vary greatly in terms of the information and services they seek, as well as their education, background, and access to technology. Within this context public organizations at central, regional or local level initiate many efforts towards the development of government portals in order to offer electronic services to citizens and businesses. However, even if these efforts are in most cases successful, the portals that are developed do not follow a common set of specifications. On the contrary, each public agency follows its own design, set its own functional and technical specifications and most of all put its own needs before the needs of its users. The need for e-Government frameworks, as a prerequisite supporting tool for e-Government portals implementation becomes more apparent worldwide, when considering the added complexity of procedures, information needs and systems, technologies used, security aspects, legal frameworks, organizational structures, and other special issues which have to be taken into account. In this chapter a comparison framework is proposed, extending and adopting existing approaches, to the national standardization framework's needs. Applying the proposed comparison framework an assessment and extended review of some of the most significant standardization efforts undertaken worldwide are considered in an attempt to assist decision makers, politicians, public and IT managers to design their own Standardization Framework for Electronic Government Service Portals.

DOI: 10.4018/978-1-61692-018-0.ch015

INTRODUCTION

As yet, there is no generally accepted definition of a portal and the definition and characteristics of a government portal are even less well specified; no existing definition fits the unique requirements of a government portal. Government service portals are not the same as public portals that have a strong commercial aspect and they provide structured access to web sites across the whole of the World Wide Web. They are not vertical portals that attempt to provide comprehensive access to information on a defined topic or function to a defined audience, even though there are vertical specialist portals in the government sector. Although they may focus exclusively on government information and services, government has much broader scope than does the normal range of a specialist portal. They have a challenging and unique mission, focused on public access, for an unknown group of users who vary greatly in terms of the information and services they seek, as well as their education, background, and access to technology. Within this context government portals must try to channel users and inquiries through hundreds of thousands, and in some cases millions, of web pages, with maximum efficiency and with user satisfaction.

The number of public sector web sites has mushroomed in recent years and governments worldwide have published a stream of web site guidance, addressed to a range of audiences. Implementing public sector web sites involves a complex bundle of interrelated activities with decisions about management, organization, structure, content, security and legal issues, as much as about surface, or the 'interface'. Discovering who the web site's potential users are, finding out their requirements, using this to decide what information to include on the site, how to structure it and what to call it, and designing navigation paths through it that are as clear as possible, are all part of design. These days, it is also essential to ensure information is accessible to as many different people as possible. Many of the best practices, rules and standards regarding some of those processes are proposed from international standardization bodies' (ISO, W3C, Oasis, OMG etc.), which affect research in areas related to e-Government but are not particularly readable.

In the second section of this chapter we present the need behind the development of standardization frameworks for electronic government service portals (SF) and we propose a framework against which, some of the most remarkable government frameworks worldwide, will be examined in section three. In section 4 the results are discussed and finally we present our conclusions and some thoughts about the necessity, usability and applicability of a standardization framework for electronic government service portals (SF).

Positioning of Standardization Framework in National E-Government Strategy

Government administrations at the central, regional or local level initiate many efforts towards the development of government portals in order to offer electronic services to citizens and businesses. However, even if these efforts are in most cases successful, the portals that are developed do not follow a common set of specifications. On the contrary, each public agency follows its own design, set its own functional and technical specifications and most of all puts its own needs before the needs of its customers (i.e. citizens and businesses). These rather dispersed, uncoordinated and heterogeneous efforts for the development of government service portals resulted in several problems and discrepancies for both public agencies and citizens and businesses. More specifically, different solutions were adopted for issues such as content organization and presentation, navigation, search functions, accessibility, domain name registration, type of users' identification, or personal data protection. On top of these issues, and probably the most significant area that raises difficulties for national governments is the identification of organizational structures, public policies and marketing issues regarding the development and management of public administration portals. In many cases, e-Government services are not either well designed or not suitably promoted by public agencies that provide them, resulting in a very low level of usage. National Standardization Frameworks for Electronic Government Service Portals aim at providing effective and efficient solutions to the above issues defining strategic directions, standards and specifications for the design, development and support of the operation of government portals that offer electronic services to citizens and businesses.

E-Government portals reflect the entry point of citizens and businesses to electronic public services and information thereof. In order to design such e-Government portals, several preconditions and general requirements have to be met. Some countries attempt to adopt holistic e-Government development frameworks other propose to public organizations the use of specific web sites guidelines.

The need for e-Government frameworks, as a prerequisite for joined-up e-Government services becomes more apparent worldwide, when considering the added complexity of procedures, information needs and systems, technologies used, legal frameworks, language and other special regional needs between different countries and the thousands of front and back-office systems which have to be taken into account in order to achieve this. E-Government frameworks provide a systematic disambiguation of this strategy towards actual application-to-application interoperable systems' deployment.

Different dimensions, such as issues related to processes, users, data, technology, security, laws, organization, social and political aspects, have to be investigated during the implementation of a standardization framework for electronic government service portals (SF). There exist already many discussions on which factors should be considered

from a standardization framework for electronic government service portals (Garzotto et al, 1995).

For assessing the sophistication of national standardization frameworks we propose a framework that applies five different clusters of requirements (Figure 1). The proposed framework extends the GIF layers (UNDP, 2007a) and adopts them properly to cover the national standardization framework's needs in terms of providing a comparative analysis framework for national SFs. Existing approaches and frameworks for implementing (Wimmer & Holler, 2003; Klaassen et al., 2006) and evaluating (Panopoulou et al., 2008; Lee, 2003; Eschenfelder, 2004) public web sites have been considered in order to identify the relative aspects regarding a public authority's portal implementation. The identified aspects are filtered through the optics of a national standardization framework and classified in relative clusters. Each cluster consists of a specific number of aspects. Each proposed cluster along with its aspects are analyzed in detail as follows.

Content Cluster: This cluster includes all the information which is displayed by a public organization's web portal such as information or data and instructions regarding an e-Government process. It includes data and metadata on the offered services such as the needed documents, the process structure, legal grounding of the process, fees, preconditions, etc. It further contains information about e.g. the forms, procedures and descriptions about legal background. The content concept refers mainly to the completeness of information provided online (West, 2007; Henriksson et al., 2006), to relevancy, accuracy, reliability and usefulness of information (Garcia et al., 2005; Smith, 2001), to frequent updating and currency of the provided information (Smith, 2001; Holzer & Kim, 2005) and to the consistency of information and its clear formulation according to the audience Garcia et al., 2005; Smith, 2001). This cluster also includes process workflow support of the user within a running public service from the invocation of the service until its completion.

Figure 1. Standardization framework's clusters

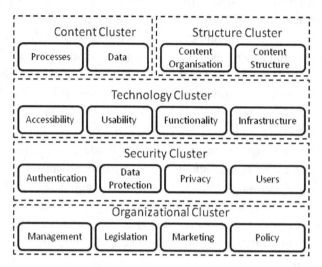

Structure Cluster: The public organization's provided content (information, public services) should be organized in a structure that facilitates the management of it and suits the users' needs (Gant & Gant, 2002). For virtual administrations, the concept of appropriately structuring their content according to life episodes (Sarantis et al., 2008) and business situations and to bundle related public services appropriately has become quite popular in recent time. Each service should be designed in a clear way that the users can easily find out what it is good for and how it works. At best, it is represented in a way that a user knows intuitively how to use it, but there should be help topics available if needed. Especially for non-expert user groups of e-Government portals, the interface must give the user the feeling that it is easy to use and that the system operates intuitively. Hence, an important requirement is that the requested information structure at the portal is visualized appropriately and intuitively (Følstad et al., 2004).

Technology Cluster: The technology cluster considers accessibility, usability, functionality and infrastructure aspects of the web portals. Adequate standards must be selected enabling reuse, ensuring interoperability (UNDP, 2007b),

implementing human-computer interfaces and socio-linguistic problems (Traunmüller & Wimmer, 2003), as well as ensuring long-term usability (Davis, 1989; DeLone & Mclean, 1992) while minimizing constraints. Technology incompatibility has also been identified as one difficult challenge to e-Government portals (Chengalur-Smith & Duchessi, 1999; Brown, 2001). Systems that are very different and sometimes very old increase the complexity of e-Government portals, especially information integration initiatives (Burbridge, 2002).

Here, the process flow and content for a specific public service are integrated and visualized to the user through the interface. How users interact with individual parts of information (e.g. control the active media till playing) and how they move among them are treated in this cluster. In terms of navigation, web site design and general ease of use, the relevant literature suggests that the pages of the site should be consistent in terms of layout, coloring and terminology (Smith, 2001; Henriksson et al., 2006; Garcia et al., 2005). Moreover, features like user menus (Smith, 2001), site maps, RSS feeds and search tools (Holzer & Kim, 2005; Smith, 2001; Henriksson et al., 2006) FAQs and help documentation (Henriksson et al., 2006; Garcia et al., 2005) should be present. E-Government processes require the workflow and a series of interfaces to back-office systems and databases. It contains all information on the online request, the portal functionality and the description of the E-Government online offer. The accessibility concept addresses any kind of accessibility problems relevant to providing access to the disabled (West, 2007; Garcia et al., 2005; Smith, 2001; Holzer & Kim, 2005; Henriksson et al., 2006), to technical compatibility in terms of both hardware and software (Henriksson et al., 2006; Smith, 2001) and web site loading speed (Smith, 2001), as well as to supporting multiple languages (West, 2007; Henriksson et al., 2006; Holzer and Kim, 2005).

Infrastructure aspects focus on technologies that should be in place before E-Government services can be offered reliably and effectively to the public. The potential of these technologies is to support and integrate the operations of information systems and applications across organizations by offering the necessary standards and protocols through network and communication infrastructure approaches (e.g. intranet, extranet, and internet).

Security Cluster: Since public administration portals require a clear, unique and trusted identification of the applicant, identification and authentication mechanisms like login, digital identity and functionality for intermediaries are necessary. Encryption, security and authenticity of data should be ensured. E-Government processes deal with rather sensible and personal data and documents, which are transmitted via an insecure Internet. Security and encryption mechanisms have to be provided between the user, the portal and the back-office to secure data and documents and to ensure that these are not manipulated, wiretapped and object to fraud.

All sources include privacy and security as an important component of a government web site; the site should provide a clear privacy statement (Smith, 2001; Holzer and Kim, 2005; Henriksson

et al., 2006; West, 2007), protection of citizen information sent through encryption mechanisms (Smith, 2001; Holzer and Kim, 2005; Henriksson et al., 2006; Garcia et al., 2005) and protection of citizen data from the public authority and any other third parties (Holzer and Kim, 2005; Henriksson et al., 2006; West, 2007).

Organizational Cluster: Undoubtedly, the size of the web portal and the diversity of its users are two of the main challenges to public administration web portal initiatives (McFarlan, 1981; Davis, 1982). Alignment between organizational goals and the web portal should take place (Dawes & Nelson, 1995). The interaction between a user of the public administration's portal and the authority in charge of delivering a specific public service has to be implemented adequately without hampering legal grounding (e.g. data protection, access rights) and in order to be able to fully exploit the potential of virtual public administrations. Restrictive laws and regulations developed prior to or in ignorance of technologies relevant to E-Government can affect the success of government portals. One strategy for responding to these challenges is to invest in changes to the regulatory environment that allow for or enable adoption of emerging technologies (Barret & Green, 2001; Dawes & Nelson, 1995). Digital signature technologies, for example, required statutory changes in most jurisdictions before they could be adopted for use. Developing appropriate government-wide IT policies and standards can also provide and adequate framework for E-Government initiatives to be successful. In this regard, state governments are developing IT policies and standards and making them available through their official Web sites.

National Standardization Frameworks Analysis

At the present time, building a Standardization Framework for Electronic Government Service Portals must oppose the tendency to "reinvent the wheel" and requires examination and extended review of related research and standardization efforts undertaken worldwide. Focusing on work achieved in the UK, the USA, Australia, New Zealand, India and Greece their relative standardization frameworks are analyzed and compared. The specific span of countries has been selected on the basis that their specifications are available in English, are adopted at national level and have reached a certain level of maturity. The most recent version of each country's standardization framework has been thoroughly considered in order to extract its fundamental features. Each standardization endeavor brings a remarkably different approach to the task of designing and implementing Electronic Government Service Portals defining its own guidelines, best practices, characteristics, and having its own strengths and weaknesses. Having considered analytically the provided guidelines of the above frameworks we could classify them in specific categories. The following subsections present key observations about the national standardization frameworks for electronic government service portals that have been analyzed. The intent here is not to give exhaustive analyses, but rather to highlight and contrast the most salient features and aspects of these frameworks.

United Kingdom

United Kingdom appears as a pioneer in implementing a standardization framework. Central Office of Information, reporting to the Minister for the Cabinet Office has been issued web standards and guidelines (Cabinet Office, UK, 2009) to ensure a high quality and consistent user experience of the public sector online. These guidelines are intended for all involved in the delivery of public sector web content. They have been designed to ensure that online services conform to legal and industry standards meet the requirements and expectations of public organizations and citizens and contribute to effective communication and service delivery strategies. The guidelines cover the following sections:

- **Accessibility, usability and design:** This section sets out the minimum standard of accessibility for public sector web content and web authoring tools. It recommends a user-centered approach to accessibility, taking account of user needs in the planning and procurement phases of web design projects.

- **Marketing communications:** It describes the basic principles of buying and selling advertising and entering into a sponsorship relationship with a third party. It also contains the eligibility rules governing .gov.uk registrations.

- **Legal and technical requirements:** This guidance covers the principal laws relating to electronic communications, for example the Data Protection Act, Crown Copyright and the Welsh Language Act. Specimen terms and conditions for web sites are also provided.

- **Structured content:** This section explains the purpose of, and provides guidance for, the deployment of XML Sitemaps on UK Public Sector Web sites. Joined-up government needs joined-up information systems. The e-Government Metadata Standard (e-GMS) lays down the elements, refinements and encoding schemes to be used by government officers when creating metadata for their information resources or when designing search systems for information systems.

- **Measuring quality and value:** This guidance equips central government departments with a common method for measuring the cost of web sites, providing the first step in determining value for money. It also facilitates the development of performance measures for use in the planning, design and evaluation of web sites.

- **Platforms and devices:** It is designed to ensure that your web site works on as many browsers and devices as possible.
- **Social media and Web 2.0:** It proposes that participation online results should be permanently available and open to being republished in other media using social media and web 2.0 technologies.

United States

The US Framework is based on Web Design & Usability Guidelines (Department of Health and Human Services, U.S.A., 2009). Although this is a collaborative effort involving many federal agencies, the Web Communications Division in the U.S. Department of Health and Human Services' Office of the Assistant Secretary for Public Affairs has primary responsibility for managing this effort. This site was developed to specifically assist web managers, designers, usability specialists, and others create web sites that are highly responsive, easy-to-use, and useful. This is the primary government source for information on usability and user-centered design. It provides guidance and tools on how to make web sites and other communication systems more usable and useful. Topics include a step-by-step guide on how to plan, analyze, design, and usability test a highly usable web site, quick access to the latest usability methods, an introduction to usability, how to get started, and what it costs, the latest research-based web design guidelines, templates and examples for assessing audience needs, writing a usability test report. The content of the framework is based on the results of research that have been completed in the individual sectors that are related with the design and implementation of web sites. The guidelines are allocated in the following categories:

- **Design process and evaluation:** The most important usability-related issues, methods, and procedures that require careful

consideration when designing and developing web sites are presented in this section.

- **Optimizing the user experience:** Instructions are provided in order web sites to be designed in order to facilitate and encourage efficient and effective human-computer interactions.
- **Accessibility:** Web sites should be designed to ensure that everyone, including users who have difficulty seeing, hearing, and making precise movements, can use them. All United States Federal Government web sites must comply with the Section 508 Federal Accessibility Standards.
- **Hardware and software:** Designers should identify the hardware and software used by primary and secondary audiences and their design should maximize the effectiveness of the web site.
- **The homepage:** A homepage should clearly communicate the site's purpose, and show all major options available on the web site.
- **Page layout:** All items should be appropriately aligned on the pages and pages length should be long enough to adequately convey the information, but not so long that excessive scrolling becomes a problem.
- **Navigation:** A web site's navigation scheme and features should allow users to find and access information effectively and efficiently.
- **Scrolling and paging:** Generally, designers should ensure that users can move from page to page as efficiently as possible.
- **Headings, titles, and labels:** Designers should strive to use unique and descriptive headings, and to use as many headings as necessary to enable users to find what they are looking for-it is usually better to use more rather than fewer headings.

- **Links:** To ensure that links are effectively used, designers should use meaningful link labels (making sure that link names are consistent with their targets), provide consistent clickability cues (avoiding misleading cues), and designate when links have been clicked.
- **Text appearance:** There are several issues related to text characteristics (fonts, background, headings etc.) that can help ensure a web site communicates effectively with users.
- **Lists:** Each list should be clearly introduced and have a descriptive title.
- **Screen–based controls:** Entry fields are used when completing forms and entering text into search boxes. Designers should try to minimize the amount of information entered by users and apply appropriately buttons.
- **Graphics, images, and multimedia:** When images must be used, designers should ensure that the graphics do not substantially slow page download times.
- **Writing Web content:** When preparing prose content for a web site, use familiar words and avoid the use of jargon. If acronyms and abbreviations must be used, ensure that they are clearly understood by typical users and defined on the page.
- **Content organization:** Organizing content includes putting critical information near the top of the site, grouping related elements, and ensuring that all necessary information is available without slowing the user with unneeded information.
- **Search:** The site's search capability should be designed to respond to terms typically entered by users.
- **Usability:** It should be ensured that the best possible method for usability testing is used and to ensure that an iterative approach is used.

Australia

Australia's web publishing guide (Australian Government Information Management Office, 2009) helps Australian government agencies to manage their web sites, and to identify their legal and policy obligations. The web publishing site brings together Australian government resources for web site management. It makes it easy for Australian Government agencies to discern their legal and policy obligations and to access policies, guidance and examples of better practice. The site is managed by the Australian Government Information Management Office in the Department of Finance and Deregulation. These guidelines are organized in the following categories:

- **E-Government policy:** Policies that affect the enterprise landscape of Australian Government web sites and web publishing.
- **Planning:** Advice on agency and project level strategic and planning business processes.
- **Types of sites:** There are specific requirements for some types of web sites.
- **Users:** Understand the importance of consulting and engaging users.
- **Marketing:** The effective marketing of e-Government improves the awareness, acceptance and usage of e-Government products and services.
- **Visual design and branding:** Improve citizen interactions through a consistent user experience and improved visual presentation.
- **Legal issues:** Aspects of information law that affect web sites.
- **Managing content:** Requirements for specific content types.
- **Web 2.0:** These guidelines are being developed as part of trials of online consultation being conducted by the Australian Government. They will be expanded and developed on the basis of the experience

of the trials and incorporated into the Web Publishing Guide.

- **Types of content:** This section presents information about approaches to content management and content architecture, including information management.
- **Accessibility and equity:** Ensuring that all citizens can fully participate in the information economy is a high priority for the Australian Government.
- **Technical development:** This section presents information about the technical aspects of web and electronic publications deployment and the influence of legislation on their use.
- **Archiving and preservation:** Archiving is just the first step in a complex series of processes to ensure long-term access to government information in electronic formats. Preservation strategies must be put in place so that electronic information will stay accessible over time.
- **Maintaining and evaluating:** Best practice support of web initiatives is backed by a rigorous, quality driven cycle of web and electronic content maintenance and support activities including the regular measurement of site performance to understand when sites become irrelevant and are ready for decommissioning or upgrade.

New Zealand

New Zealand's web guide (Information & Communications Technology branch, New Zealand, 2009) aims to support government web development from a number of angles. Government Web Standards (version 2.0) are divided in four categories:

- **Strategy and operations:** Agencies must have a formal web strategy. When outsourcing web development, agencies must include a requirement for compliance

with the New Zealand Government Web Standards in all relevant RFPs, RFIs and contracts. They concern mainly content people and project managers who deal with business cases, archiving, analytics and social media management.

- **Technical:** The W3C's Web Content Accessibility Guidelines 2.0 (WCAG2.0) has been adopted as the New Zealand Government's technical standards. These include New Zealand-specific requirements. They concern mainly developers who deal with development issues of WCAG2.0, accessibility, content, multimedia, security, mobile and others.
- **Content and design standards:** Agency web sites must contain specific pages or sections (homepage, contact information, legal and policy information, publicly available reports, media releases and other public information, site owner is clearly identified) and a respective minimum content is specified. They concern mainly content and communications people who deal with issues of using audio and video, printing pages, usability and others.
- **Legal and policy:** Minimum requirements are defined regarding issues of copyright, copyright of third parties, privacy statement, disclaiming content and terms of use. They concern mainly content people, project managers and others who deal with issue regarding guides to issues covered by the standards and to those covered by the other standards, policy and legislation.

India

The Department of Information Technology of Ministry of Communications and Information Technology, Government of India has published guidelines for development and management of government web sites and Portals in India. The primary objective of these guidelines is to ensure that Indian Government web sites, belonging to any constituent of the Government, at any level, are citizen centric and visitor friendly. These guidelines address common policy issues and practical challenges that government departments face during development and management of their web sites. The guidelines aim to assist the departments in ensuring that their web site conforms to a consistently high standard. This is expected to enhance the trust level of the citizens while accessing Government information and availing services online. The main issues that the framework deals with are the following:

- **Government of India identifiers:** Web sites and portals belonging to the Indian Government Domain is important to convey in some way to the visitors that Indian Government officially sponsors and owns the information and services being provided in the concerned web site.
- **Building confidence:** It is implied that the original information put up on the web site by a Government Department is by default a copyright of the owner Department and may be copied, reproduced, republished, uploaded, posted, transmitted, or distributed only if the copyright policy of the concerned Department allows so. Every Indian Government web site must have a comprehensive and clear-cut hyperlinking policy defined and spelt out for those who wish to hyperlink content from any of its sections.
- **Scope of content:** The content of a Government web site is its soul as the citizens rely heavily upon a Government web site to access authentic and up-to-date information. Ideally, an Indian Government web site should have a minimum content and information that should be avoided is defined.
- **Quality of content:** Indian Government web sites should be oriented towards

their prospective audience. Information Architecture is concerned with how information is organized, structured, labeled, and presented for maximum access. The content of a Government web site or any web site per se, has to be structured in such a way that the target audience is able to access the desired information with minimum effort.

- **Design:** Design in the broad sense is a process that achieves the end result of enhancing the user experience by presenting the content in a form that is easily understandable, navigable and searchable by the user, in addition to being visually appealing. Page layout is a significant consideration in the overall design interface of any web site and specific guidelines are defined.
- **Development:** Departments are advised to follow W3C and open standards for developing their web applications. Government web sites should therefore provide access to documents in appropriate file formats that are based on open standards and do not impose an unnecessary burden of downloading or acquiring specific software on the intended audience. Application developers should however be sensitive about security aspects, as a lot of security threats arise due to vulnerability of application software code.
- **Web site hosting:** While it is extremely important to develop web sites using state-of-the-art technologies, hosting infrastructure plays a crucial role in the performance, availability and accessibility of these web sites to end users with varying set-ups. Hence, configuration of hosting server infrastructure as well as facilities at Data Centers is an important aspect to review, prior to hosting.
- **Web site promotion:** The existence of any Government site lying inaccessible on the web is meaningless. For this purpose

a conscious and concentrated effort has to be made to increase the reach of the web site. Therefore, the importance of web site promotion, especially in the context of Government web sites which aim to reach the largest possible number of citizens and stakeholders cannot be emphasized over.

- **Web site management:** The success of any endeavor depends upon the backing of a strong and enthusiastic team. In case of a Government web site, the role of a Web site management team assumes paramount importance in ensuring its credibility amongst its patrons.

Greece

The Greek SF is part of the Greek e-Government Framework (Ministry of Interior, Greece, 2009), which aims at meeting the demands of the Greek Digital Strategy, contribute to the Lisbon economic and societal objectives and harmonize with the pan-European policies and directions of i2010 (EU, 2006). The e-Government Framework also complies with the recommendations for national interoperability frameworks issued by the European Interoperability Framework (IDABC, 2004). Finally, the E-Government Framework takes into account the results of standardization efforts performed by international organizations and initiatives such as W3C, OASIS, IETF, etc. The SF consists of 4 areas:

The *portal administration and optimization* part of the SF tries to regulate all issues related to the roles and the procedures that the public agency-owner of the portal should establish in order to assure that the portal is functioning properly. So, this part describes the roles and the procedures for content management, e-Government services support, and content, e-services and web site evaluation. The procedures and measures used for the registration of users to E-Government services as well as their authentication to them are also described in this section.

The second major group, *content organization and presentation*, of SF's guidelines refer to the organization and the presentation aspects of the content hosted in governmental portals (Wimmer & Holler, 2002). First of all, it is very important that the content of governmental portals meets the needs of its users (Gant & Gant, 2002). To this direction, the SF includes guidelines about the actual content of the portals (i.e. what information should exist on a governmental portal and how it should be organized).

The selection of a domain name and the accessibility of a governmental portal are two topics that the SF regulates. Compliance with World Wide Web's Web Accessibility Initiative (WAI, 2009) (W3C/WAI) and Web Content Accessibility Guidelines (WCAG, 2008) version 2.0 is defined.

A fundamental part of the SF is the *E-Government services support & interoperability* section. This section provides guidelines about the way of presenting and granting access to services via government service portals and how the portals should communicate and exchange data with back office systems (Hammer, 1990). Since interoperability and authentication are the two concepts hidden behind the words here, the SF simply describes the basic requirements and cross-references to other parts of the Greek E-Government Framework.

Guidelines for *security requirements and legal issues* are included in the Greek SF. Service Level Agreements are also introduced in case a government portal is hosted in an ISP's or an ASP's premises. The protection of personal user data in respect to Data Protection Act is a very important issue when delivering electronic services to constituents. Therefore, public agencies should take the appropriate measures in order to conform to the above Law and publish the respective security policy on the web site. In case intellectual property rights (IPR) exist on all or part of the web site's content or there are limitations on the use of the content or services of the portal, public agencies should also care for the publication of IPR, terms of use or disclaimers on the web site, contributing this way to the transparency, credibility and trustfulness of the portal.

Results Discussion

The standardization frameworks for electronic government service portals usually consist as part of the national overall E-Government framework, which usually, except the web site standardization framework, includes parts related to interoperability and security and authentication issues.

Most approaches to advance E-Government web portals are concentrated mainly on technical specifications of the proposed systems (e.g. data integration, metadata, XML repositories, security, confidentiality and delivery channels), providing guidance on system design. Only some (United Kingdom's e-GIF Registry and the Danish Info-StructureBase) EU Member States have some partial implementations of the appropriate infrastructures, such as repositories of XML schemas for the exchange of specific-context information throughout the public sector.

In Table 1 we present a comparison among the above mentioned standardization frameworks considering the coverage of each of the identified clusters' aspects (Figure 1). Each SF characteristic receives a coverage mark ($\sqrt{}$), or a no coverage mark (blank). In order to classify the features of each of the considered national SF in the relative cluster and aspect, the full text of each one's guidelines has been thoroughly considered and analyzed. The documents elaboration included not only search of specific keywords but also detailed content analysis took place in order to detect the actual correspondence between the parts of the SFs and the proposed framework.

All the standardization frameworks can be definitely awarded as a positive effort and they should be considered a point of departure and a solid basis for future public sector web site design. As shown by the analysis, most of the frameworks deal with issues regarding the technology cluster (accessibility, usability, design) but they bear

substantial differences on the coverage of issues such as content structure, marketing, legal issues, security issues, operations, web site policy and planning and supporting organizational structure.

In most of the frameworks there is no presentation of best practices exploitation and reuse. For public authorities transferring knowledge means a continuous and effective exchange of experience. Best practice is the pivot around which public sector web site implementation could spin. Landmark projects as model cases are the starting point from where public organization could find suitable model cases, evaluate the feasibility of a specific project and embark on learning processes and transfer mechanisms.

In principle, the frameworks sets out government support for user-centered design for web sites, putting the user (citizen, business, government) at the center of the design process. The framework is a good idea in principle, but usually is poorly executed. In most of the cases there is no any enforcement for the framework's application. The usage of the national standardization framework is optional and usually its application depends on each public organization's good will.

Responsible national organizations for the standardization frameworks have been pushing usability up the E-Government agenda and the framework is another welcome example of its advocacy. It would more efficient and more effective if the standardization framework was expressed in a simpler - more usable - form so that it is understood as widely as possible. The provision of the SF in a simplified form (e.g. compliance matrix) could be easily used, from each public organisation, as a checklist of mandatory guidelines outlined in the framework during the portal implementation. Public agencies may use this checklist to validate their web sites against these guidelines and make necessary modification to ensure compliance.

And for a framework about making the best use of new media, it makes surprisingly little use of online resources. Instead, we have many of-

Table 1. Framework coverage

Cluster/ Country	UK	USA	Australia	New Zealand	India	Greece
Content						
Process			√			√
Data			√	√	√	√
Structure						
Content Organization	√	√	√		√	√
Content Structure	√					
Technology						
Accessibility	√	√		√	√	√
Usability	√	√		√		√
Functionality	√	√	√	√	√	√
Infrastructure	√	√	√	√	√	
Security						
Authentication						√
Data Protection	√		√	√		√
Privacy				√		√
Users						√
Organizational						
Operations					√	√
Legislation	√		√	√		√
Policy			√	√		
Marketing	√		√		√	

fline references to academic papers; what online resources are included are often out-of-date. The Framework is a document about the Web. So why not link to online resources? In fact, why not create an online resource that supports the advice given and that can be easily updated? A standardization framework on-line based on continuous update by the responsible organization will be clearly more usable and handy.

CONCLUSION

Around the world, there are several governmental attempts, by means of new information - and communication technologies to regenerate the relationship between citizen/business and governments.

The development of standardization frameworks for electronic government service portals seems to be still in its infancy, and those working in the field predict a new generation of government portals with enhanced capabilities. Framework developments are dependent on technologies that are already available and are starting to be used in some of the most advanced commercial, educational and enterprise-based portals; they are being tentatively applied to government portals. However, on top of all reasons, it is the political willingness of each country that will drive the effort of developing a standardization framework for electronic government service portals. Governments that have realized the anarchy in the electronic facet of public administration have the opportunity to correct the situation, or at least try to improve it, by issuing a standardization framework that defines a common set of principles, rules and guidelines to be considered by all public agencies when they design and develop their portals.

The understanding of e-Government portal standardization framework by public sector organizations is a significance strategic phase toward reliable and effective E-Government adoption. The standardization framework defines standards, identifies the portal content, the portal structure, infrastructure components, applications, technologies, policies, management procedures that are the guidelines for E-Government portal implementation. The purpose of the standardization framework is to reduce any confusion surrounding the E-Government portals in the public sector, by understanding the implementation process, identifying the requirements of ICT tools, highlighting the importance of the organizational and management resources. The structure of the standardization framework of e-Government portals can be divided into five clusters:

1. Content
2. Structure
3. Technology
4. Security
5. Organizational

The framework guides decision makers, politicians, public and IT managers to recognize the technological and organizational requirements for e-Government portal implementation in public sector organizations. The awareness of these clusters and the relative aspects is important for any e-Government standardization framework since they will alert the e-Government project team with any problems or challenges might be existed during the implementation process so they will be ready to overcome them.

An increasing number of governments worldwide establishes and promotes the use of standardization frameworks as an essential part of their E-Government strategies. This article explores some of the most important endeavors regarding public sector standardization frameworks that attempt to transform functionally specialized governmental agencies into a more coherent and integrated network administration. The countries selected for this study are governments because of their closeness and level of expertise concerning framework implementation. Methodologically, the article is based on an interpretative policy analysis where data has been derived through studies of policy documents.

The review revealed that usually governments adopt standards, set specific rules, principles and guidelines according to their needs and requirements. As the needs and requirements across these governments are similar, it comes as no surprise that the frameworks' content is similar. Despite the similarities however, there are still differences between frameworks depending on the extant of the national frameworks and the issues that they attempt to cover. The reasons may be because, first, although the public sector type of portals is of same type the content coverage of the framework are considered differently, based on each country's national E-Government strategy. Second, governments are usually more committed with technical issues. With respect to content structure, security, organizational issues, significant differences between countries were found. In many countries a lot has been done to ensure successful public sector portals implementation, however with different speed of development and emphasis. This paper develops a framework that allows evaluation and comparison of standardization frameworks. Broadly, this research offers several contributions:

1. It provides a framework for evaluating and comparing national standardization frameworks for electronic government service portals;

2. It provides sufficient knowledge about the content of the most important existing national frameworks;

3. Decision makers, politicians, public manager could use the research as a baseline beginning their own standardization framework endeavor;

4. It sheds light on which are the main differences between national frameworks.

Moreover, a longitudinal study could enrich the findings. Similar studies at different countries are likely to enhance the review. Therefore, in future research, reviewing more national frameworks from different countries could provide a more international perspective to the subject.

REFERENCES

Andersen, D. F., & Dawes, S. S. (1991). *Government Information Management. A Primer and Casebook*. Englewood Cliffs, NJ: Prentice Hall.

Australian Government Information Management Office. (2009). *Web Publishing Guide*. Retrieved June 20, 2009 from http://webpublishing.agimo.gov.au

Barret, K., Green, R., & Katherine Greene, K. (2000). *Powering Up. How Public Managers Can Take Control of Information Technology*. Washington, DC: CQ Press.

Brown, M. M. (2001). The benefits and costs of information technology innovations: An empirical assessment of a local government agency. *Pubic Performance and Management Review*, *24*(4), 351–366. doi:10.2307/3381224

Burbridge, L. (2002). Accountability and MIS. *Public Performance and Management Review*, *25*(4), 421–423. doi:10.1177/15357602025004013

Cabinet Office. UK. (2009). *Web standards and guidelines*. Retrieved June 20, 2009 from http://www.cabinetoffice.gov.uk/government_it/web_guidelines.aspx

Chengalur-Smith, I., & Duchessi, P. (1999). The initiation and adoption of client–server technology in organizations. *Information & Management*, *35*(2), 77–88. doi:10.1016/S0378-7206(98)00077-9

Davis, F. D. (1989). Perceived usefulness, perceived ease of use and user acceptance of information technology. *Management Information Systems Quarterly*, *13*(3), 319–330. doi:10.2307/249008

Davis, G. B. (1982). Strategies for information requirements determination. *IBM Systems Journal*, *21*(1), 4–30. doi:10.1147/sj.211.0004

Dawes, S. S., & Nelson, M. R. (1995). Pool the risks, share the benefits: Partnerships in IT innovation . In Keyes, J. (Ed.), *Technology Trendlines. Technology Success Stories from Today's Visionaries* (pp. 125–135). New York: Van Nostrand Reinhold.

Deci, E. L., & Ryan, R. M. (1991). A motivational approach to self: Integration in personality. In R. Dienstbier (Ed.), *Nebraska Symposium on Motivation*: *Vol. 38. Perspectives on motivation* (pp. 237-288). Lincoln: University of Nebraska Press.

DeLone, W., & Mclean, E. (1992). Information systems success: The quest for the dependent variable. *Information Systems Research*, *3*(1), 60–95. doi:10.1287/isre.3.1.60

Department of Health and Human Services. U.S. (2009). *Research Based Web Design & Usability Guidelines*. Retrieved June 20, 2009, from http://www.usability.gov

Eschenfelder, K. (2004). How do government agencies review and approve text content for publication on their Web sites? A framework to compare Web content management practices. *Library & Information Science Research*, *26*, 463–481. doi:10.1016/j.lisr.2004.04.007

EU. i2010 eGovernment Action Plan, Commission of the European Communities (CEC), i2010 e-Government Action Plan: Accelerating e-Government in Europe for the Benefit of All, COM (2006) *173 final*. Retrieved June 20, 2009 from http://ec.europa.eu/idabc/servlets/Doc?id=25286

Følstad, A., Jørgensen, H. D., & Krogstie, J. (2004). User involvement in e-government development projects. In *Proceedings of the third Nordic conference on Human-computer interaction*. Tampere, Finland.

Gant, J. P., & Gant, D. B. (2002). Web portal functionality and State government E-service. In *Proceedings of the 35th Hawaii International Conference on System Sciences*.

Garcia, A. C. B., Maciel, C., & Pinto, F. B. (2005). A quality inspection method to evaluate e-government sites. In M.A. Wimmer, R. Traunmuller, A. Gronlund, & K.V. Andersen, (Eds.), *Proceedings of Electronic Government: 4th International Conference, EGOV 2005*: Lecture Notes in Computer Science, Vol. 3591, Copenhagen, Denmark, pp. 198-209.

Garzotto, F., Mainetti, L., & Paolini, P. (1995). Hypermedia design, Analysis, and Evaluation Issues. *Communications of the ACM, 38*(8), 74–86. doi:10.1145/208344.208349

Hammer, M. (1990). Reengineering Work: Don't Automate, Obliterate. *Harvard Business Review*, 104–112.

Henriksson, A., Yi, Y., Frost, B. & Middleton, M. (2007). Evaluation instrument for e-government web sites. *Electronic Government, an International Journal, 4*(2), 204-226.

Holzer, M., & Kim, S.-T. (2005). *Digital Governance in Municipalities Worldwide, A Longitudinal Assessment of Municipal Web sites throughout the World, The e-Governance Institute*. Retrieved June 20, 2009 from http://unpan1.un.org/intradoc/groups/public/documents/aspa/unpan022839.pdf

IDABC. (2004). *European Interoperability Framework for pan-European eGovernment Services, Version 1.0*. Retrieved June 20, 2009 from http://ec.europa.eu/idabc/en/document/2319

Information & Communications Technology branch, New Zealand. (2009). *New Zealand Government Web Standards*. Retrieved June 20, 2009 from http://www.e.govt.nz/standards/web-guidelines

Klaassen, R., Karreman, J., & van der Geest, T. (2006). Designing Government Portal Navigation Around Citizens' Needs, M.A. Wimmer et al. (Eds.), *EGOV 2006, LNCS 4084*, 162–173, Springer-Verlag Berlin Heidelberg.

Lee, J. (2003). A model for monitoring public sector Web site strategy. *Internet Research, 13*(4), 259–266. doi:10.1108/10662240310488942

McFarlan, F. W. (1981). Portfolio approach to information systems. *Harvard Business Review, 59*, 142–150.

Ministry of Communications and Information Technology, Government of India. (2009). *Guidelines for Indian Government websites*. Retrieved June 20, 2009, from http://web.guidelines.gov.in

Ministry of Interior. Greece. (2009). *Greek e-Government Framework*. Retrieved June 20, 2009, from http://www.ermis.gov.gr

Panopoulou, E., Tambouris, E., & Tarabanis, K. (2008). A framework for evaluating web sites of public authorities. *Aslib Proceedings, 60*(5), 517–546. doi:10.1108/00012530810908229

Sarantis, D., Tsiakaliaris, C., Lampathaki, F., & Charalabidis, Y. (2008). A Standardization Framework for Electronic Government Service Portals. In *Proceedings 17th International Conference on Information Systems Development*. Paphos, Cyprus.

Smith, A. G. (2001). Applying evaluation criteria to New Zealand government web sites. *International Journal of Information Management, 21*(2), 137–149. doi:10.1016/S0268-4012(01)00006-8

Traunmüller, R., & Wimmer, M. A. (2003). E-Government at a decisive moment: Sketching a roadmap to excellence. In G. Goos, J. Hartmanis, & J. van Leeuwen (Eds.), *Proceedings of Electronic Government: 2th International Conference, EGOV 2003*: Lecture Notes in Computer Science, Vol. 2739, Prague, Check Republic, pp. 1073.

United Nations Development Programme (UNDP). (2007a). *e-Government Interoperability: A Review of Government Interoperability Frameworks in Selected Countries*. Retrieved from http://www.apdip.net/projects/gif/GIF-Review.pdf

United Nations Development Programme (UNDP). (2007b). *e-Government Interoperability: Guide*. Retrieved from http://www.apdip.net/projects/gif/GIF-Guide.pdf

Web, C. A. G. (WCAG) 2.0. (2008). *WCAG*. Retrieved June 20, 2009 from http://www.w3.org/TR/WCAG20/

West, D. M. (2007). *Global E-government 2007, Inside Politics*. Retrieved June 20, 2009, from http://www.insidepolitics.org/egovt07int.pdf

Wimmer, M. A., & Holler, U. (2003). Applying a Holistic Approach to Develop User-Friendly, Customer-Oriented E-government Portal Interfaces, N. Carbonell, C. Stephanidis (Eds.): *User Interfaces for All, LNCS 2615*, pp. 167–178. Berlin, Germany: Springer-Verlag.

World Wide Web's Web Accessibility Initiative. (2009). *World Wide Web's Web Accessibility Initiative*. Retrieved June 20, 2009 from http://www.w3.org/wai

KEY TERMS AND DEFINITIONS

Government: A body that has the power to make, and the authority to enforce rules and laws within a civil, corporate, religious, academic, or other organization or group.

E-Government: ICT use for the purposes of government processes improvement. ICT usage in administrative activities Categories of electronic instruments for improving interactions between government and citizens (G2C), government and business enterprises (G2B), and between agencies themselves (G2G) are internationally recognized.

Standards: In the context of information technology, standards are guidelines for allowing disparate devices and applications to communicate and work together.

Standardization Framework for Electronic Government Service Portals (SF): A framework for the definition of standardized principles, rules, guidelines, protocols, technologies, procedures and standards selection for implementing and managing e-Government web portals.

Chapter 16
Web 2.0 Applications and Citizen Relations through E–Government Websites

Heasun Chun
The State University of New York at Buffalo, USA

Daejoong Kim
The State University of New York at Buffalo, USA

ABSTRACT

This research will focus on constructing an analytical model for Web 2.0 applications through making a systematic analysis on emerging web practices, to talk about a strategic, systematic plan of Web 2.0 in e-government Web sites. To achieve this mission, we suggest applying dialogic communication theory (Kent & Taylor, 1998) that has been developed in public relations, to create an analytic model of the various types of Web 2.0 applications for building better e-government Web sites.

INTRODUCTION

In recent years, we have witnessed a series of new Web applications change the way that people communicate and build relationships with others. The emerging applications, generally called social Web or Web 2.0, encapsulate the idea of the proliferation of interconnectivity and interactivity of Web-delivered content by accelerating users' participation in online communities. The Web sites embracing Web 2.0 capabilities can facilitate two-way communication, information-sharing, and collaborative work in virtual space.

Thus, to build positive relationships with citizens, many IT vendors and service providers are making widespread investments to embrace Web 2.0 capabilities on Web sites. For instance, according to a recent survey of executives worldwide (Bughin & Manyika, 2007), more than three fourths say that they are already investing in Web 2.0 trends and planning to increase their investment in the near future.

Although Web 2.0 technologies are becoming mainstream both in consumer and business contexts, many practitioners involved in e-government Web sites are still skeptical. Web 2.0 is an important phenomenon that should not be ignored as hype or a passing fad. This chapter will help governments understand Web 2.0 and its potential so that

DOI: 10.4018/978-1-61692-018-0.ch016

governments can harness Web 2.0 effectively in the context of e-government Web sites.

Up until now, however, only a few research essays have talked about the emerging applications in building e-government Web sites, therefore an applicable analytical framework and systematic plan to help governments develop e-government Web sites are lacking. Thus, this research will focus on constructing an analytical model for Web 2.0 applications through systematically analyzing emerging Web practices, to talk about a strategic and systemic Web 2.0 plan in constructing e-government Web sites. To achieve this mission, we suggest applying dialogic communication theory (Kent & Taylor, 1998), which was developed in public relations, to create an analytic model of the various types of Web 2.0 applications to build a better e-government environment and better relationships with the public.

This chapter consists of two main sections. The first section provides a brief overview about the definition of and the technological characteristics of Web 2.0 in comparison with its predecessor, Web 1.0. Then, the section discusses how the improved interactivity and user's controllability of Web 2.0 are changing the paradigm of Web-mediated communication by reviewing the approach to indexing and retrieval methods of information, the role of actors, the concept of Web design, and communication type. The second section attempts to introduce dialogic theory (Kent & Taylor, 1998) that has been developed in public relations, to create an analytic model of the various types of Web 2.0 applications for building better e-government Web sites. Three sub-sections organize this chapter: (1) theoretical ideas of dialogic theory, (2) five dialogic principles, and (3) categorization of the web 2.0 features. The last section includes the potential of encompassing Web 2.0 capabilities in e-government Web sites by five dialogic principles.

BACKGROUND

Recently, the term Web 2.0 has become one of the most frequently used buzzwords. The term, first presented by Tim O'Reilly in 2004, has clearly taken hold, with more than 140 million citations in Google. Web 2.0 has largely been popularized by IT professionals, business, and Web users to name a quickly growing set of Web-based applications. However, despite the huge popularity of the term, there is still disagreement about what Web 2.0 means. Most people believe that Web 2.0 is the next generation of the Web, but there is no exact universally accepted definition. Disagreement exists mainly because the term Web 2.0 is too nebulous and broad to be summarized in a specific, uniform concept. Web 2.0 covers a wide array of Web applications that share little in common, from advanced search engines, syndication technologies, and social networking to virtual reality.

Thus, instead of a uniform definition, the core tenets of broadly defined Web 2.0 technologies should be found, and both technological and sociological aspects of Web 2.0 should be considered to define what Web 2.0 stands for. To find the shared tenets of various Web 2.0 technologies, this section first explores the concepts related to the use of Web 2.0 tools, in particular comparing the technological differences with its predecessor, Web 1.0. We then move to a discussion of the challenges and opportunities of Web 2.0 for governments to interact with their citizens through the Internet.

What is Web 2.0?

Most of the recent attempts to define Web 2.0 derive from the original texts of Tim O'Reilly, an inventor of the term and president of O'Reilly Media Inc. When Tim O'Reilly suggested the term at a conference brainstorming session, he used the term to emphasize the advantages of new technologies supporting collaboration based on the Internet. Therefore, he defined Web 2.0 as a platform that is built on an "architecture of participation," in which "the service acts primarily as an intelligent broker, connecting the edges to each other and harnessing the power of the users themselves" (O'Reilly, 2005, p. 22). The architecture of participation is facilitated by Ajax (Asynchronous JavaScript+ XML) technologies that enable multidimensional interactions between Web servers and end-users. Similarly to O'Reilly's definition, Maness (2006) pointed out that the key elements of Web 2.0 are user-centered participation, social interactions, and rich communication between users. For a more technology-oriented definition, Nielsen (2007) suggested four technological components encapsulating Web 2.0: RIA (Rich Internet Application), community features or social networks, mashups, and advertising. These definitions certainly capture some technical aspects of various Web 2.0 tools, but are still insufficient to grasp the social aspects of Web 2.0.

Other observers have approached Web 2.0 as a social phenomenon facilitated by a cluster of quickly growing Web technologies. From the sociological perspective, Hoegg et al. (2006) defined Web 2.0 as a philosophy of "mutually maximizing collective intelligence and added value for each participant by formalized and dynamic information sharing and creation (p.15)." For Birdsall (2007), Web 2.0 is an entirely sociological term that refers to several new trends in Web-mediated communication, summarized by such keywords as democratic, respect for users, user-orientated, community building, collaborative, interaction, participative, sharing, and social networking.

The most significant catchword in the above definitions is the improved ability of users' controllability of the Web. Web 2.0 cedes control over applications from organizations to individual users, enabling users to extract and reuse the data in a flexible way. Therefore, Web 2.0 can harness the Web in a more interactive and collaborative manner, which emphasizes users' social interaction and collective intelligence. For this reason, Web

2.0 is often called the wisdom Web, people-centric Web, or participative Web.

Symmetric Dialogue Model of Web 2.0

To get a better understanding of Web 2.0, it is important to observe how new Web technologies are transforming the paradigm of mediated communication. As a whole, Web 2.0 is transforming the paradigm of mediated communication from the asynchronous publishing model to the synchronous dialogue model. In this section, we will discuss how Web 2.0 is different from its old version of the same Web in more detail to present the paradigm shift of Web-mediated communication. As previously mentioned, the key distinction of Web 2.0 is users' improved ability to control Web information. The improvement can change Web-mediated communication in terms of the approach to indexing and retrieval methods of information, the role of actors, the concept of Web design, and the communication type.

Indexing and Retrieval Methods of Information

Web 2.0 is associated with the approach to indexing and retrieval methods of information. In Web 1.0, information is classified by taxonomy, which is a top-down classification system. Taxonomy is a hierarchical structure of keywords that is predetermined by website designers or administrators before being published. Therefore, information on Web sites has a static content that is organized by the authority in control. This traditional approach has tended to see information as something independent from users, which can be accessed, stored, classified, and managed by reference to its objective characteristics.

Web 2.0, however, treats information with folksonomy. Folksonomy refers to user-generated keywords for indexing and retrieving information. A key difference between folksonomy and taxonomy is the nonhierarchical structure of keywords, in which all tags are horizontally distributed in a flat namespace without any clearly defined relationships with other tags. In the hierarchical structure of taxonomy, the relationships between keywords are professionally controlled according to structured directories. The nonhierarchical structure of folksonomy, by contrast, allows individual Web users to easily add free forms of tags to Web content for retrieving and sharing the content along natural axis of the tags. Folksonomy treats information as things constructed in the interaction between users and the Web or between users (Tredinnick, 2006), making the Web more efficient and quickly responsive to an individual user's need than does taxonomy. In sum, Web 2.0 is presented as a process of ceding control over applications to users, enabling users to extract information and data and reuse that information and data in a flexible way.

The Role of Actors

The enhanced interactivity of Web 2.0 is changing the role of Internet users. Although the initial Web also provided some degree of interactivity, most communication via the Internet was asymmetric in which one who has information distributes the information to anonymous masses through a one-way broadcasting approach. In this traditional approach, the information published on Web sites is static and unchangeable, and Web users passively consume information. Therefore, those who access the information are named audiences who cannot edit the original Web content.

In contrast to the traditional approach, Web 2.0 places a greater emphasis on the user's role in Web-based communication.

The idea of Web 2.0's open architecture is to free data from corporate control, allowing anyone to engage in adding, creating, and sharing information to meet his or her own needs. Therefore, by using collaborative Web sites such as wikis and online video forums, people can directly post

comments and information resources to the Web to share and discuss information. For instance, Wikipedia, an online collaborative encyclopedia, has gained more than 75,000 voluntary contributors, from experts to casual readers, who add content and revise others' work online without claiming any authority over or ownership of the content.

In Web 2.0, all Web users can be consumers as well as producers of information. Therefore, it is almost impossible to make a clear distinction between consumers and producers of information; thus, the users in Web 2.0 turn into "pro-sumers" (Sentinelli, Marfia, Gerla, & Kleinrock, 2007). Prosumer is the term for an active participant who gets more involved in the process of information creation in mediated communication. Prosumers generate the value of information in social interactions between users and interactions between users and Web sites. Web 2.0 information reflects the collaborative knowledge that a number of prosumers create over time in dynamic interactions and discussion, rather than an organization's preferred view (Tredinnick, 2006). For instance, the initial Web pages of Wikipedia are blank and not prepared before their use, which means they have no value at all. However, once a user posts information on the Web and another user reads it, the Web pages create some value and knowledge in the use of that information. In recent years, we have observed the tremendous increase in quantity and diversity of Web 2.0 resources on the Web. The quantity of information and content produced in Web 2.0 has exponentially increased. In a word, the key to Web 2.0 is "harnessing the ways in which users use [the] information sources that they use" (Tredinnick, 2006, p. 232), and the value of the networks and information that is created by their use.

Allowing users to participate in the process of information creation, Web 2.0 tools improve the ability of individuals to exercise their right to communicate in Web-mediated communication. The right to communicate is defined as the basic human right to active participation in the communication processes (Birdsall, 2007; Richstad & Anderson, 1981), making it possible for any individual or group to talk to whomever they want to talk to and create a social network according to their own interests and purposes. The concept of the right to communicate differs from earlier concepts of freedom of information. Whereas freedom of information assumes that users are passive receivers of information predetermined by authors or publishers, the right to communicate assumes that users are active participants who add some value to the published information or create new information in collaborative work with other users. Web sites such as collaborative Web sites or audio/video-sharing Web sites such as YouTube, MySpace.com, and Wikipedia are the main enablers of this phenomenon, freeing the Web from corporate control and allowing anyone to participate in creating and sharing information and knowledge (Barsky, 2006).

As the role of users changes from audiences or receivers of information to active participants, the role of Web designers and administrators is also changing from a publisher of Web content or a regulator of mediated communication to a communication partner of Web users or a protector of users' right to communicate. O'Reilly (2005) explained that these changing roles of actors reflect that the participatory model of Web 2.0 is superseding the predominant publishing model of mediated communication.

The Concept of Web Designs

As Web 2.0 has been making mediated communication more dialogic and dynamic in nature, the concept of Web design has also evolved from task-oriented to experience-oriented approaches. Task-oriented approaches to design are the best fit for traditional Web sites, emphasizing functionality and efficiency in the execution of user tasks. This approach, Nielson (2007) argued, regards the Web designer or administrator as the hero

and the user as a victim to be saved by designer intervention.

However, experience-oriented approaches are a more recent concept of Web design, called "experience design" or "emotional design" (Zappen, Harrison, & Watson, 2008). Many researchers agree that this recent concept places increased attention on users' interactivity with Web sites and on other users (Corry, Frick, & Hansen, 1997; Zappen, et al., 2008). Since the goal of this approach is the total user experience that Zappen et al. named user's satisfaction, the approaches focus on users' engagement, the quality of the user experience, and the interactivity between users and Web sites. Zappen et al. argued that users' satisfaction comes when the users exercise control over Web sites. The authors explained that people feel satisfaction when they experience "not the sense of being in control, but the sense of exercising control in difficult situations" (Zappen, et al., 2008, p. 19). That means a Web designer should consider the users' motivations and interests throughout the whole design process to facilitate users' participation in web-mediated communication.

In making this transition to experience-oriented approaches, web designers should consider how to encompass all of the social features of Web 2.0 such as interactivity, community building, and participation within the Web. Since users' participation is helpful and essential to Web design, Web designers are required to encourage users' contributions "not by replacing those innovations with centralized solutions, but by helping to design systems that workers can modify" (Spinuzzi, 2003, pp. 4-5).

Communication Type

Web 2.0 is transforming the paradigm of mediated communication from the asynchronous publishing model to the synchronous dialogue model. As the key distinctions between Web 1.0 and Web 2.0 presented in Table 1 suggest, the technological

Table 1. Comparison between Web 1.0 and Web 2.0

Index	Web 1.0	Web 2.0
Indexing and Retrieval of Information	Hierarchical Classification (Taxonomies)	Non-Hierarchical Classification (Tags or Folksonomies)
Information Flow	Top-down	Horizontal or Bottom-up
The level of Interactivity	One-way or Asymmetric Two-way	Asymmetric or Symmetric Two-way
Role of Users	Audience	Participant
Role of Web Administrator	Publisher	Partner or Protector
The Goal of Communication	Efficient Delivery of Information	Efficient Delivery, Mutual Understanding
Communication Type	Publishing Model	Dialogue Model

improvement of Web 2.0, such as increased interactivity and flexibility, is empowering individual users to actively participate in Web-mediated communication and is changing the role of Web administrators from authoritative publishers to partners or protectors of users' right to communicate. Such a change is called a personalization of the Web. Web 2.0 is providing users with greater flexibility in control of their Web experiences, which allows users to have rich dialogue with others with whom they can identify (Mayes & de Freitas, 2007). For example, personalized Web sites such as iGoogle and MyYahoo allow users to customize the layout of a Web page by choosing modules that are relevant to the users' needs. Seltzer and Mitrook (2007) observed that the structural features of Web 2.0 are making mediated communication more dialogic and dynamic in nature.

APPLICABILITY OF DIALOGIC THEORY IN E-GOVERNMENT WEBSITES

Interactivity and Dialogic Communication Theory

Encompassing Web 2.0 capabilities, e-government Web sites can facilitate new forms of interaction between government and citizens. Many scholars anticipated that the arrival of the Internet would transform traditional bureaucracy by shifting the focus of governance to its external relationship with citizens (Bennett, 2003; Fountain, 1999; Ho, 2002; Lilleker & Jackson, 2008). They believed that the Internet would gradually mature into a user-friendly platform (Ho, 2002) for the citizens to participate in public discourses and political discussion.

However, in contrast to the early anticipation on the capacity of the Internet for enhancing democracy, technical difficulties until now have made it impossible for citizens to participate in policy-making process. Without real interactive communication tools at the initial stage of Web development, the public sector's use of the Internet would focus heavily on managerial or transactional aspects of the Internet (Chadwick & May, 2003; Layne & Lee, 2001). In this stage, practitioners used government Web sites as a simple delivery tool for government information or a cost-saving transaction tool providing payment options. In this initial Web environment, the major concern of Web site designers and practitioners was the efficiency of mass delivery. Also, in this stage, the level of interactivity was simply asymmetric. Therefore, e-government Web sites functioned as nothing more than a simple electronic version of brochures having payment options. Thus, many initial government Web sites were simply designed to suit informational or transactional orientations, and dialogic interactive functions were not fully facilitated.

The emergence of Web 2.0 is changing the traditional model of e-government Web sites. Web 2.0 provides practitioners and Web site designers with more diverse communication options from one-way asymmetric to two-way symmetric communication channels, creating a new opportunity for e-government Web sites. Central to the capacity of Web 2.0 as a facilitator of participatory democracy is the enhanced interactivity (Chadwick & May, 2003; Lilleker & Jackson, 2008). The enhanced interactivity is especially useful to heighten the levels of a user's involvement and engagement in Web sites because interactivity serves as a motivational factor that encourages users to construct their own messages and therefore to become involved in the Web-mediated communication (Kirk, 2001; Schlosser, 2000).

Dialogic communication theory is one of the most widely used theories in the field of public relations and Web-mediated communication to explain the capacity of Web interactivity in users' involvement. The main idea of dialogic communication theory is that enhanced interactivity of Web-mediated communication facilitates positive organization-public relationship building because the enhanced interactivity on Web sites positively influences the frequency of communication, improves user satisfaction, and strengthens the trust between the user and the organization (Kirk, 2003). This idea is applicable to the relationship between government and citizens in Web 2.0 environments. In the context of e-government Web sites, as the enhanced interactivity of Web 2.0 shifts the editorial power from governments to the citizen, it expands the public's opportunities to participate in public sphere and contributes to the establishment of the deliberative democracy (Chadwick, 2008; Chadwick & May, 2003; Coleman & Gotze, 2003).

Dialogic communication theory, suggested by Kent and Taylor (1998), provides a useful framework for understanding how organizations build and maintain public relations, in particular in online public relations. Particularly, the five dialogic principles (Kent & Taylor, 1998; Kent, Taylor, & White, 2003; Taylor, Kent, & White, 2001) formulated under dialogic communication theory offer practical guidelines for organizational Web site design committed to achieving successful public relations.

Dialogic communication theory is deeply rooted in the disciplines of philosophy, psychology, and relational communication. In the tradition of philosophy, dialogue is regarded as an effort to acknowledge the value of the other, and thus holds the ethical values of reciprocity, mutuality, involvement, and openness while interacting with others (Kent & Taylor, 1998). Similarly, the psychological tradition conceptualized dialogue as unconditional positive regard for others. According to the psychological tradition, holding the stance would eventually enhance the development of a relationship between interactants involved in the dialogue (Kent & Taylor, 1998). Synthesizing the concepts in both fields, the concept of dialogue is extended to relational management that voluntarily obliges mutual understanding, unconditional positive regard, and equality while in dialogue in the field of communication (Kent & Taylor, 1998). Based on traditions from a variety of academia, Kent and Taylor (1998) theorized dialogic communication as a process of two-way, open, and negotiated discussion where participants are able to exchange ideas and opinions freely.

Although dialogic communication theory was developed in the field of public relations, this theory gives valuable insight into constructing e-government Web sites as an essential in relationship building between governments and the public. From the viewpoint of government–citizen relations, dialogic communication theory provides both concepts imperative to government–citizen relations and procedural means whereby governments and citizens can communicate interactively as well. Dialogic communication theory properly provides us with the analytic framework for assessing the capacity of e-government Web sites that encompass the enhanced interactivity of Web 2.0.

The Basics of Five Dialogic Principles

Dialogic communication theory suggests that it is important for organizations (or governments in the e-government context) to create effective government-citizen communication channels, if organizations are willing to interact with citizens in an honest and ethical way. In this regard, the Internet has already been used as a popular communication channel bridging the gap between governments and citizens via Web sites. According to Taylor, Kent, and White (2001), even though dialogic communication theory is applied as a framework for interpersonal relationships, it can also be used to understand mediated relationships created by Web communication. The authors argued that Web sites strategically designed based on sound principles may encourage governments and citizens to engage in two-way dialogic relationships.

The five principles described by Kent and Taylor (1998) can be actual guidelines to help foster Web communication relationships in an honest and ethical way. The five dialogic principles include a dialogic loop, the usefulness of information, generation of return visits, ease of the interface, and conservation of visitors.

First, a dialogic loop refers to the opportunities for feedback from citizens and governments' response to citizens' questions, concerns, and problems. Kent and Taylor (1998) suggested that because it is not enough for Web sites to play a role as an information provider, they should also play a central role as an opinion receiver from citizens about their concerns, problems, and inquiries. In the Web 1.0 era, this principle has been usually accomplished by providing an e-mail address, online surveys of issues, and feedback boxes for users/customers' comments or reviews.

The second principle that is necessary for dialogic relationship is the usefulness of the information. The principle does not refer to general information that is useful only for general citizens. Along with general information, the Web site should include information of interest to each specific citizen. In addition to seeking citizens' satisfaction for information needs, this principle also claims that information should be delivered promptly with various types of multimedia formats to help citizens understand the information. In the Web 1.0 era, the principle was achieved by incorporating audio/visual capacity (e.g., audio/video streaming services), downloadable graphics, and archives for news releases for the press and stakeholders.

The generation of return visits, the third principle, centers on the notion that Web sites should contain features that make them useful and attractive for repeat visits on a regular basis. According to Taylor et al. (2001), relationships can be established and maintained by repeated interactions, not by a one-time contact, because relationship building and maintenance in pursuit of trust requires time. Encouraging visitors to return to the Web site can be fulfilled by incorporating such Web 1.0 features as, bookmarking, downloadable information (e.g., downloadable pdf documents or image files), and automatic delivery of information to citizens by e-mail.

The fourth principle is the ease of the interface. This means that Web sites should be easy for visitors to use. To achieve this principle, Taylor et al. (2001) suggested that Web sites should be designed to be intuitive enough so that visitors and even inexperienced visitors do not spend too much time navigating a site and finding information. The authors also suggested that construction of an easy-to-use interface is a prerequisite for creating a genuine dialogue using a Web-mediated communication channel. Placing such Web 1.0 features as a site map, search engine, and image maps into a site interface has fulfilled the principle of ease of the interface.

The fifth principle, the rule of conservation of visitors, suggests that a Web site should be cautiously organized to try to keep visitors on the page, without leading visitors off to third-party Web sites. The caution here is that although visitors are willing to stay on the Web site, they may leave the Web site and not return to the page because of visitors' unfavorable experiences while opening the first page of the Web site such as long loading time, annoying pop-up windows, nothing new, and no time stamp for updated postings on the front page. Accordingly, this principle has been accomplished by minimizing site loading time (in general, less than 4 seconds), and posting important information with the last updated time and date on the front page of the Web site.

Numerous studies have explored how organizations incorporate the five principles on Web sites in different organizational contexts. For example, Kent and Taylor (2001) examined 100 environmental organization Web sites to see if they incorporated dialogic features in the Web sites. The authors found that most environmental organization Web sites include technical and design features involved in dialogic communication, but do not fully employ the features in relation to the dialogic loop, which is a key component in the five dialogic principles. In another study of the dialogic principles for community college Web sites, McAllister and Taylor (2007) also found that college Web sites showed high scores for the principles of the usefulness of information and ease of the interface but low scores for the principles of conservation of visitors and dialogic loop.

More importantly, the authors argued that in particular interactive features for the dialogic loop were very limited on the Web sites. A recent study yielded the same results of a lack of dialogic loop capacity in organizations' Web sites. Ingenhoff and Koelling (2009) found that the potential of Web sites for dialogic communication is not used efficiently by most nonprofit organizations in Switzerland. The findings of previous studies provide empirical insight into how better Web

sites can be created for relationship building and maintenance between government and citizens by incorporating advanced Web 2.0 technologies in the Web sites.

Categorization of the Web 2.0 Features to the Five Dialogic Principles

This chapter reviewed a variety of Web 2.0 technologies, and technological features in detail. In addition, this chapter also assessed dialogic communication theory and the five dialogic principles as practical guidelines for Web site design. Next, we will discuss the potential of Web 2.0 technology features for government–citizen relationship building in conjunction with the five dialogic principles. Then, we will discuss how the dialogic functionality of Web 2.0 tools can be utilized in the context of e-government.

Dialogic Loop

First, the principle of the dialogic loop can be robust with the use of such Web 2.0 features as live Web chat and text comments boxes included on blogging and video/photo-sharing Web services. Above all, the feature of live Web chat can provide citizens with the opportunity for direct interaction with governments about questions, concerns, and problems in relation to citizens' benefits. The live Web chat can be regarded as a dialogic communication tool in that citizens can get a direct real-time response from governments to their questions. In comparison with the live Web chat, citizens can deliver indirect feedback to governments by leaving comments or messages regarding the material (e.g., news, articles, and audio/video stuff) posted on government blogs or video/photo-sharing sites created by governments.

In a study that compared responsiveness between Web sites and blogs (Seltzer & Mitrook, 2007), the results showed that Weblogs rather than Web sites are significantly higher in responsiveness. Furthermore, most government Web sites do not provide electronic message board systems where citizens can exchange opinions on issues. In this regard, lack of interactivity in government Web sites can be overcome by fully employing dialogic features embedded in either blogs or video/photo-sharing services.

Usefulness of Information

The second principle, usefulness of information, can be fulfilled with the utilization of collaboration tools such as wikis, video/photo-sharing services, and audio/podcasting features. In fact, this principle entails not simply the generation of useful information to citizens but also prompt delivery of the information to citizens in a variety of multimedia formats. In the Web 1.0 era, as mentioned earlier, most information was delivered to citizens in different types of texts, audio, and videos by plug-in software such as Window Media player, QuickTime player, or RealPlayer. However, the current online bandwidth is not enough to deliver audio/video content to citizens in real time. As a consequence, users often experience long waits or frequent pauses for buffering while using multimedia format files, especially when using video format files. In comparison with Web 1.0 technologies, Web 2.0 technologies have the capacity to quickly deliver information to citizens with various arrays of multimedia formats files when photo/video-sharing services provided by numerous third-party Internet services are adopted (e.g., Flickr.com for photo-sharing services and Youtube.com or Google Video for video-sharing services).

Wikis can accommodate large numbers of collaborative pages that can be edited by anyone with access to them. Wikis provide several advantages in terms of the quantity and diversity of information (Kennedy, et al., 2007). For example, Wikipedia, the best known wiki, currently contains more than 1.9 million entries in its English version.

Audio/podcasting describes the distribution of digital multimedia files using syndicated Internet feeds. Users can subscribe to individual feeds and listen or watch the downloaded podcasts on MP3 players or personal computers' for later playback. Audio/podcasting provides e-government Web sites with diverse ways to get messages out in a conversational voice (Godwin, 2008).

Generation of Return Visits

To encourage the third principle of the generation of return visits, e-government Web sites can employ the Web 2.0 technologies of RSS, widgets, or social bookmarking embedded in social networking tools. RSS is the easiest way to receive information from government Web sites in a totally automatic way, substituting the function of automatic information delivery of e-mail in Web 1.0 technologies. Since RSS offers users a simple headline (sometimes with a short summary) with a link to the main body content of the Web sites, RSS might lead to driving subscribers to visit the Web sites.

Bookmarking in Web 1.0 technologies was a way of saving users' favorite Web pages on users' Web browsers so that users can find them again later. While the bookmarking function in the Web 1.0 era provided a limited function, accessibility from only users' personal computers, social bookmarking in the Web 2.0 era offers a wide range of methods and the flexibility to store, organize, and manage bookmarks of Web pages (e.g., delicious.com and diigo.com) as well as remote accessibility to users' sets of bookmarks from various locations. To help users easily add bookmarks, e-government Web sites can consider incorporating a bookmarking tool directly linked to social bookmarking service sites.

Another Web 2.0 feature, widgets, has the potential to increase citizens' awareness of the organization, and thus might lead to future citizens' visits to Web sites. A widget is a generic term that refers to the part of a Graphical User Interface that displays information and allows users to interact with the application and operating system in different ways.

Ease of Interface

For the principle of ease of interface, governments can utilize the Web 2.0 features of advanced search engines. Advanced search engines provide users with opportunities to find relevant information with the option to search by keyword, time period, subject, and file format within Web sites, while search engines in the Web 1.0 era offered opportunities to retrieve documents, files, or data from a database mostly by keyword search. In addition, search engines should function as a tool to integrate government information scattered across multiple locations (e.g., blogs and social network service Web sites) in various formats (e.g., texts, images, audios, and videos). Recently, some popular search engines (e.g., Google.com and Yahoo.com) have been adopted as a basic search tool in many organizations' Web sites. Because the search engines give extended search options, governments should think of using them strategically.

Virtual worlds also contribute to improving the ease of interface. Virtual worlds are the simulated three-dimensional places of environments and people where users can socialize, connect, and create (Oberlander, Karakatsiotis, Isard, & Androutsopoulos, 2008; Wyld, 2008). The core difference between the traditional Web interface and virtual worlds can be found in the interface design. A traditional interface is a surface forming a boundary between the screen of the monitor and the person accessing the information, while cyberspace enables the person to pass through the barrier of the computer screen to feel as if he or she is "inside" the virtual world (Bricken, 1991).

Conservation of Visitors

The principle of conservation of visitors does not entail technological facets. Rather, the principle places emphasis on design elements such as minimizing the loading time of the first page by the reduction of pop-up windows and the simple design of the first page. In Web 2.0 technologies, however, it is worth considering using the mashup feature. Since mashup technology integrates data or functionality from external sources into one Web page or service, this technology can minimize the chance for users visiting other Web sites to look for relevant information and provide users with an integrated experience. In addition to utilization of mashup technology, it is still necessary for governments to adopt the same strategies as those created in Web 1.0 technologies such as short loading time and minimizing pop-up windows.

DIALOGIC CAPACITY OF WEB2.0 IN E-GOVERNMENT WEB SITES

Many expect that the dialogic feature of Web 2.0 applications will improve the convenience and accessibility of government services and information to citizens as well as civic engagement (Chadwick & May, 2003; de Kool & van Wamelen, 2008; Francq, 2009; Osimo, 2008). In addition, these Web 2.0 features are expected to increase the level of interaction between governments and citizens, making e-government Web sites more responsive to citizens' interests and needs. In this sense, some e-government Web sites are already experimenting with blogs, wikis, chat rooms, podcasts, Really Simple Syndication (RSS), and other social software (social networking and videos/images) on their Web interfaces.

However, few studies have done that discuss the potential benefits of encompassing Web 2.0 capabilities in e-government Web sites. Therefore, in this section, we review in what way Web 2.0 tools, categorized by the five dialogic principles,

Table 2. Categorization Web 2.0 features to the five dialogic principles

Five principles	Web 1.0 features	Web 2.0 features
Dialogic loop	Email address, online survey, user comment	Live web-chat, Blogging, comment boxes embedded in video/photo sharing services
Usefulness of information	Audio/video streaming services, downloadable graphics, archives for press release	Video/photo sharing services, audio/podcasting, social news sharing services
Generation of return visits	Bookmarking, FAQ, links to other Web sites, downloadable information, automatic information delivery by email	Social bookmarking, widgets, RSS
Ease of interface	Search engine, sitemap, major links to rest of site	Advanced search engine
Conservation of visitors	Short loading time, minimizing pop-up windows	Mash-ups

are likely to have an impact on e-government and what e-government activities are likely to be affected.

Dialogic Loop

The Web 2.0 tools for creating a dialogic loop are social networking sites and blogs. In terms of the opportunities for feedback from citizens and dialogic interactions between citizens, social networking sites such as Facebook and MySpace also help to enhance the dialogic loop of Web sites. On social networking sites, people create and customize personal Web sites to share personal information such as detailed profiles or pictures of themselves. The idea of offering social connections with others is important to establish the dialogic feature of communication online because these Web sites enable people to exercise their right to communicate online. That is, using blogs or other social networking tools, citizens can have a more direct contact with and keep track of politicians or governmental officials (Osimo, 2008). For instance, web chat that is incorporated into blogs or social networking sites provide much of the interactivity and person to person contact, enabling users to chat online with and submit paperwork to government personnel (United Nations, 2008). From the perspective of e-government practitioners, the Web 2.0 tools can

help them to gain interest and feedback from the citizens (Lilleker & Jackson, 2008).

Technologically, social networking sites and blogs obviate the need for dedicated Web-publishing software and replace professional software with a combination of Web forms for inputting information and a template for displaying the information. Due to the ease of Web publishing, social networking sites and blogs allow anyone with only a little technological savvy to participate in the discursive space of the Internet.

Usefulness of Information

Promoting collaboration works across governmental agencies and inviting citizens to join policy-decision processes can encourage government modernization (Osimo, 2008). The benefits of collaborative tools are at least three folds.

First, collaboration tools support coordinated cooperation within and across different agencies. Public services like CAISI (Client Access to Integrated Services and Information) and Alaska social services are recently experimenting collaboration tools for this purpose. CAISI and Alaska social services department are using collaboration tools to coordinate the delivery of services from different social health service providers to help the homelessness.

Second, collaboration tools efficiently collect information and draft intelligence for supporting the internal and external policy-making process. In order to create collaborative information and knowledge within and across governmental agencies, officials from 16 U.S spy agencies recently construct a wiki-based platform named as 'Intellipedia.' Intellipedia enables the direct collaboration by 3,600 intelligence professionals to produce joint reports (Shrader, 2006). According to Michael McConnell (2007), Intellipedia has been widely used among analysts to pool their knowledge, form virtual teams, and make assessments.

Third, the collaboration tools also help governments to invite their citizens to engage in policy-making processes. Using collaboration tools such as wikis and audio/video sharing sites, governments can make it possible for citizens and officials to contribute to policy-making processes (Francq, 2009; Osimo, 2008). For instance, governments can utilize video/audio sharing sites to allow citizens to create and post video/audio for self-expression. It would help build community for all to share their information and knowledge involved in governmental processes. In addition, if e-government Web sites encompass the sharing services, governments can play a role as a protector for the public sphere and e-democracy. That is, collaboration tools can encourage citizen to engage in the public sphere, which is a strategic tool for facilitating e-democracy and e-participation initiatives.

Multimedia software like Audio/Podcasting also satisfies one of the key objectives of e-government, efficient delivery of government information to citizens. Audio/podcasting service in Web 2.0 can distribute digital multimedia files to targeted audience using syndicated internet feeds. Therefore, the services convey more dynamic and customized information to the end audience and help the audience to be informed. Currently, a number of podcasts are available in the public sector at the White House, NASA, the USA.gov federal podcast library, and Webcontent.gov. As

wikis fulfill usefulness of information by making a number of multimedia resources available to other users over a network, so does audio/podcasting.

Generation of Return Visits

The Web 2.0 tools for generation of return visits include RSS, widget, and social bookmarking. In the context of e-government, RSS can be very useful for formal announcements by pulling content together across government sources. RSS provides citizens with a convenient way to return to government Web sites that users would like to be connected with. For example, the USS.gov Federal RSS Library is utilizing RSS feeds to provide citizens with tailored feeds of national and regional news for automated notification of frequent updates.

Widgets are small applications and code in Web pages or for desktop use. Widgets bring content to the user's homepage and can increase awareness, which attracts users to return to the Web sites again. Widgets are widely used in public agencies such as the FBI, Veterans Affairs, and the U.S. Census. For example, the FBI provides citizens with four widget services: Wanted by the FBI, FBI News, Predators and Missing Persons, and FBI History.

Ease of Interface

Virtual town halls or virtual school systems can reach a wider audience without geographical or physical restrictions. Several governmental agencies are experimenting with Second Life, an online 3-D community. Currently, some government agencies such as the Centers for Disease Control and Prevention, the National Oceanic and Atmospheric Administration (NOAA), and the National Library of Medicine are experimenting with Second Life and other virtual worlds for a wide variety of purposes, including informational outreach, education, and emergency preparedness (Wyld, 2008).

Another example is Missouri state government that hired its first IT employee at a Second Life job fair. For the public agency, Second Life can be a useful and money-saving employee recruitment tool that can reach the target audience in a geographically wide area (Towns, 2008).

Conservation of Visitors

Incorporating Web 2.0 tools like mashups, e-government Web sites can provide citizens with easy access to government information at one stop. Since mashups support a link-rich one-stop service, they can keep visitors on the Web pages and satisfy the principle of conservation of visitors. From the perspective of e-government practitioners, development and use of mashups improve access to and understanding of data, and save time. Currently, several public agencies such as Housing and Urban Development (HUD), the California Health Care Foundation (CHCF), and Virtual Earth are beginning to utilize mashups (Farnham, 2008). For example, HUD provides a single entry point to local housing data with the Google Maps API (which allows site developers to embed Google Maps on their sites) and internally developed geocoding. The Web site integrates multiple resources such as basemaps, operational data, and analysis into one service. USA Search (USASearch.gov) also uses mashups to integrate several government data sources with search results.

CONCLUSION AND FUTURE RESEARCH

This chapter investigated the features of Web 2.0, dialogic communication theory, five dialogic principles, and the potential for the application of Web 2.0 features to e-government Web site design for better relationships between governments and its citizens. The chapter concludes that Web 2.0 technologies have a strong potential to foster dialogic communications between governments and citizens in several ways. Above all, the promise that the Web 2.0 technology holds are in agreement with those of dialogic theory in that both seek better communication and more efficient interaction with citizens. If the features of Web 2.0 technologies are applied properly to e-government Web sites, there is no question that Web 2.0 technologies will make a significant contribution to positive relationship building between governments and its citizens.

Additional research is needed, however, to more fully demonstrate the manner in which Web 2.0 technologies can contribute to the construction of better e-government Web sites. More recently, with the popularity of Web 2.0 applications, the topic of citizen engagement has come into the spotlight in the field of e-government research. Although some exploratory studies attempt to explain the potential of Web 2.0 in e-democracy, most of the studies focus on the capacity of the new technology instead of on relationship building between governments and citizens (Chadwick & May, 2003; de Kool & van Wamelen, 2008; Francq, 2009; Osimo, 2008). Thus, additional research should be conducted in other domains such as issues on the cost of maintaining blogs and audio/video-sharing service Web sites, and an information discrepancy posted between official government Web sites and other blogs/social network service Web sites outside. Furthermore, future research should suggest a way to compensate the discrepancy between what practitioners believe their Web sites can accomplish in terms of relationship building and how Web site design actually facilitates relationship building.

As many e-government Web sites incorporate Web 2.0 technologies, future studies need to examine the progress and effectiveness of the new technologies in facilitating citizen's political participation. Practitioners and Web site designers should further promote adoption of the best Web 2.0 practices in the field of e-government and develop user-friendly interfaces that efficiently serve the user's needs. Special emphasis should be placed on a comprehensive analysis of user's needs for the interactivity in various service features. In addition, a comparative assessment of Web 2.0 adoptions among federal, regional, and local governments should be followed in the future to address how new technologies contribute to construct deliberative democracy.

SOLUTIONS AND RECOMMENDATION

The current study attempted to examine the challenges and opportunities of Web 2.0 features for e-government Web sites. Obviously, Web 2.0 technology offers government more communication options from one-way asymmetric to two-way symmetric communication with citizens. However, many challenges need to be met. Among these challenges, the following three issues are fundamental ones governments have to take into consideration to construct efficient and effective e-government Web sites for relationship building with citizens.

The first thing to consider is communication channel choice. As Web 2.0 features offer various communication channels to interact with citizens, it becomes an important question to determine what is the best channel choice corresponding to a communication goal. For example, if a government wants to get citizens' opinions on public services or policies in a more friendly way, blogging may be an appropriate communication channel because it offers a channel for more intimate communication and provides an easy way for citizens' receive immediate feedback. A live Web-chat as a tool replacing face-to-face or telephone communication can be used in persuasion and gaining social support for government policies.

Another issue in constructing e-government Web sites is related to the technological expertise of governments and costs. Adoption of Web 2.0 features may require additional staff to assist the

services associated with them. Just the use of Web 2.0 features would not guarantee a successful e-government Web site unless governments allocate sufficient human resources to carry out the services stemmed from Web 2.0 features. For example, when using a live web-chat, citizens always expect that they can contact government staff immediately at anytime. If governments fail to meet this expectation, it might cause trust to deteriorate between governments and citizens. Accordingly, in the design stage of the e-government Web site, governments need to consider carefully the cost of human resources to guarantee future stable operations.

The third reality to consider carefully is the digital divide. The digital divide refers to the gap between those who have effective use and access to information technology and those who do not. Although the penetration rate of Internet use has rapidly grown during the past decade, large portions of people are still unable to access e-government Web sites for various reasons. Adoption of some Web 2.0 features that require high bandwidth and technological standards may cause people who do not have appropriate devices or high-speed Internet connections difficulty in accessing e-government Web site. Practitioners and Web site designers have to design e-government Web sites incorporating Web 2.0 features in a user-friendly fashion to increase user's accessibility. For example, if e-government Web sites provide users e-manual systems allowing for online access to electronic instruction manuals about Web 2.0 features, it would help increase user's understanding and use of Web 2.0 features and their services.

In addition, contents, images, and Web 2.0 features should be balanced appropriately for short loading time, particularly on a front page. Allocation of too many Web 2.0 features into a front page often results in long page loading time as does too much content and too many images. It may lead visitors to browse other Web sites as they search for information. For this reason, it is recommended not to allocate Web 2.0 features that require long loading times to the front page. Instead, it is suggested that Web 2.0 features move to subpages or be accessed through links to the front page.

REFERENCES

Barsky, E. (2006). Introducing Web 2.0: RSS trends for health librarians. *JCHLA / JABSC, 27*, 7-8.

Bennett, L. (2003). Communicating global activism: Strengths and vulnerabilities of networked politics. *Information Communication and Society, 6*(2), 143–168. doi:10.1080/1369118032000093860

Birdsall, W. F. (2007). Web 2.0 as a social movement. *Webology, 4*(2). Retrived from June 12th, 2009, from http://www.webology.ir/2007/v4n2/a40.html

Bricken, M. (1991). Virtual worlds: No interface to design . In Benedikt, M. (Ed.), *Cyberspace: First Steps* (pp. 363–382). Cambridge, MA: MIT Press.

Bughin, J., & Manyika, J. (2007). *How businesses are using web 2.0: A McKinsey global survey*. San Francisco, CA: McKinsey & Company.

Chadwick, A. (2008). Web 2.0: New challenges for the study of e-democracy in an era of Informational exuberance. *A Journal of Law and Policy for the Information Society, 51*, 9-42.

Chadwick, A., & May, C. (2003). Interaction between states and citizens in the age of the Internet: "e-Government" in the United States, Britain, and the European Union. *Governance: An International Journal of Policy, Administration, and Institutions, 16*(2), 271–300.

Coleman, S., & Gotze, J. (2003). *Bowling together: Online public engagement in policy deliberation*. London, UK: Hansard Society.

Corry, M., Frick, T., & Hansen, L. (1997). User-centered design and usability testing of a web site: An illustrative case study. *Educational Technology Research and Development, 45*(4), 65–76. doi:10.1007/BF02299683

de Kool, D., & van Wamelen, J. (2008). *Web 2.0: A new basis for e-government?* Paper presented at the 3rd International Conference on Information and Communication Technologies, Damascus, Turkey.

Farnham, K. (2008). *Use of Mashups in the US Government*. Retrieved May 03, 2009, from http://blog.programmableweb.com/2008/10/23/use-of-mashups-in-the-us-government/

Fountain, J. (1999). The Virtual State: Toward a Theory of Federal Bureaucracy in the 21st Century . In Kamarch, E., & Nye, J. (Eds.), *Democracy.com? Governance in a Networked World* (pp. 133–156). Hollis, NH: Hollis Publishing Company.

Francq, P. (2009). E-democracy: the social software perspective . In Lytras, M., Tennyson, R., & Pablos, P. (Eds.), *Knowledge Network* (pp. 61–73). Hershey: IGI Publishing. doi:10.4018/978-1-59904-976-2.ch005

Godwin, B. (2008). Matrix of web 2.0 technology and government. Retrieved June 9th, 2009, from http://www.usa.gov/webcontent/documents/Web_Technology_Matrix.pdf

Ho, A. (2002). Reinventing local governments and the e-government initiative. *Public Administration Review, 62*(4), 434–444. doi:10.1111/0033-3352.00197

Kennedy, G., Dalgarno, B., Gray, K., Judd, T., Waycott, J., Benett, S., et al. (2007). *The net generation are not big users of web 2.0 technologies: Preliminary findings*. Paper presented at the ascilite, Singapore.

Kent, M., & Taylor, M. (1998). Building dialogic relationships through the world wide web. *Public Relations Review, 24*(3), 321–334. doi:10.1016/S0363-8111(99)80143-X

Kent, M., Taylor, M., & White, W. (2003). The relationship between Web site design and organizational responsiveness to stakeholders. *Public Relations Review, 29*(1), 63–77. doi:10.1016/S0363-8111(02)00194-7

Kirk, H. (2001). Strategic media planning: Toward an integrated public relations media model practitioner. In R. L., Heath & G. Vasquez (Eds), *Handbook of public relations* (pp. 461-470). Thousands Oaks, CA: Sage Publications.

Kirk, H. (2003). *A Model for assessing Web sites as tools in building organizational-public relationships*. Paper presented at the annual meeting of the International Communication Association, San Diego, CA.

Layne, K., & Lee, J. (2001). Developing fully functional E-government: A four stage model. *Government Information Quarterly, 18,* 122–136. doi:10.1016/S0740-624X(01)00066-1

Lilleker, D., & Jackson, N. (2008). *Politicians and Web 2.0: the current bandwagon or changing the mindset?* Paper presented at the Politics: Web 2.0 International Conference, London, UK.

Maness, J. (2006). Library 2.0 theory: Web 2.0 and its implications for libraries. *Webology,* Retrieved April 28th, 2009, from http://www.webology.ir/2006/v3n2/a25.html

Mayes, T., & de Freitas, S. (2007). Learning and e-learning: the role of theory . In Beetham, H., & Sharpe, R. (Eds.), *Rethinking Pedagogy for a digital age: Designing and delivering for e-learning* (pp. 13–25). London: Routledge.

McConnell, M. (2007). *Confronting the Terrorist Threat to the Homeland: Six Years after 9/11*. Retrived June 15th, 2009, from http://hsgac.senate.gov/index.cfm?Fuseaction=Hearings.Detail&HearingID=479

O'Reilly, T. (2005). What Is web 2.0: Design patterns and business models for the next generation of software. *Communications & Strategies, 65*(1), 17–31.

Oberlander, J., Karakatsiotis, G., Isard, A., & Androutsopoulos, I. (2008). *Building an adaptive museum gallery in Second Life*. Proceedings of the Museums and the Web, Montreal, Quebec, Canada.

Osimo, D. (2008). *Web 2.0 in government: Why and how?* Seville, Spain: Joint Research Center, European Commission.

Richstad, J., & Anderson, M. H. (1981). Policy context for news and a new order . In Richstad, J., & Anderson, M. H. (Eds.), *Crisis in International News: Policies and Prospects* (pp. 26–27). New York: Columbia University Press.

Schlosser, A. (2000). Harnessing the power of interactivity: implications for consumer behavior in online environments . In Hoch, S. J., & Meyer, R. J. (Eds.), *Advances in consumer research, 27* (p. 79). Valdosta, GA: Association for Consumer Research.

Sentinelli, A., Marfia, G., Gerla, M., & Kleinrock, L. (2007). Will IPTV Ride the Peer-to-Peer Stream? *IEEE Communications Magazine, 45*(6), 86–92. doi:10.1109/MCOM.2007.374424

Shrader, K. (2006, November 2nd). Over 3,600 Intelligence professionals tapping into "intellipedia". *The Associated Press*. Retrieved June 20, 2009, from http://www.usatoday.com/tech/news/techinnovations/2006-11-02-intellipedia_x.htm

Spinuzzi, C. (2003). *Tracing Genres through Organizations: A Sociocultural Approach to Information Design (Acting with Technology).* Cambridge, MA: MIT Press.

Taylor, M., Kent, M. L., & White, W. J. (2001). How activist organization are using the Internet to build relationship. *Public Relations Review, 27,* 263–284. doi:10.1016/S0363-8111(01)00086-8

Towns, S. (2008, September 25). *Missouri Hires First Employee from Second Life.* Retrieved June 12th, 2009, from http://www.govtech.com/gt/418153

Tredinnick, L. (2006). Web 2.0 and Business: A pointer to the intranets of the future? *Business Information Review, 23*(4), 228–234. doi:10.1177/0266382106072239

United Nations. (2008). *UN E-government survey 2008 - From e-government to connected governance. New York: The Department of Economic and Social Affairs of the United Nations Wyld, D. C. (2008). Government in 3D: How Public Leaders Can Draw on Virtual Worlds.* Washington, D.C.: IBM Center for the Business of Government.

Zappen, J., Harrison, T., & Watson, D. (2008). *A new paradigm for designing e-government: web 2.0 and experience design.* Paper presented at the 9th Annual International Digital Government Research Conference, Montreal, Canada.

KEY TERMS AND DEFINITIONS

Conservation of Visitors: Web functionality that is organized to try to keep visitors on the page, without leading visitors off to third-party Web sites.

Dialogic Communication: A process of two-way, open, and negotiated discussion where participants are able to exchange ideas and opinions freely.

Dialogic Loop: The opportunities for feedback from citizens and the government's response to citizens' questions, concern, and problems.

Interactivity: The extent that a user can alter the form and content of message in Web-mediated communication.

Two-way Symmetric Communication: Any system in which data speed or quantity is the same in both directions, allowing both parties to involve in transmitting, creating, and sharing information.

User-Centric System: A system that recognizes that users are helpful and even essential contributors to the design process.

Web 2.0: The Web applications that improve the user's ability and controllability of the web with architecture of participation.

Chapter 17
Benefits and Barriers of Using XML in Government Websites

J. Ramon Gil-Garcia
Centro de Investigación y Docencia Económicas, Mexico

Jim Costello
University at Albany, SUNY, USA

Donna S. Canestraro
University at Albany, SUNY, USA

Derek Werthmuller
University at Albany, SUNY, USA

ABSTRACT

Electronic government can be understood as the use of information technologies in public sector organizations. One of the most visible strategies of electronic government is the development of Websites. As these government Websites have grown in size, complexity, and prominence, Website management, content management, maintenance costs, and accessibility have become growing concerns for federal, state, and local governments. Government webmasters and system administrators have come to realize that the technologies and strategies used in the past to build most Websites are designed to produce individual Web pages. However, they do not provide a structure to easily maintain entire Websites, keep them responsive to changing needs, or manage the workflow involved in Web content production and maintenance; nor do they facilitate the sharing and reuse of Website content. Based on semi-structured interviews and a survey to program and IT staff from five government agencies, this paper examines the potential of XML (Extensible Markup Language) for Website content management in government settings.[1] It identifies expected benefits and perceived barriers. It also provides some examples and explanations about the usefulness of XML for Website content management in government.

DOI: 10.4018/978-1-61692-018-0.ch017

INTRODUCTION

Previous research has identified electronic government as a strategy for administrative reform (Heeks, 1999; Kraemer & King, 2003). Improved service quality, cost savings, productivity gains, and more effective policies and programs are some examples of potential benefits from e-government initiatives (Brown, 2001; Kim & Kim, 2003; OECD, 2003). Electronic government has been conceptualized in different ways ranging from the provision of services only through the Internet to the use of any information and communication technologies in government settings (Gil-Garcia & Luna-Reyes, 2003; 2006; Schelin, 2003). Many of the current e-government applications involve the use of Internet and related Web technologies. Among these applications, one of the most pervasive, are government Websites. As these Websites have grown in size, complexity, and prominence, Website management, content management, maintenance costs, and accessibility have become growing concerns (Costello, Adhya, Gil-Garcia, Pardo, & Werthmuller, 2004; Kerer, Kirda, Jazayeri, & Kurmanowytsch, 2001).

Despite the Web's promise for ease of use and access, creativity, and efficiency, agency managers and leaders are finding their Websites increasingly present challenges of inflexibility, inconsistency, workflow bottlenecks, and new costs. Consequently, government agencies are losing the ability to be responsive and flexible in providing new information and services. In addition, the costs of maintaining complex Websites could become prohibitive (Costello, 2002). Government webmasters and system administrators have come to realize that the technologies and strategies used in the past to build most Websites are designed to produce individual Web pages. However, they do not provide a structure to easily maintain entire Websites, keep them responsive to changing needs, or manage the workflow involved in Web content production and maintenance; nor do they facilitate the sharing and reuse of Website content.

One approach to address the above Website management problems has been to implement Content Management Systems (CMS) that can be acquired through a vendor or as an open-source solution or via an internally developed system. This paper does not focus on the relative merits of CMS, but rather on the underlying content (data) structure on which CMS operate. If that underlying source content is structured and formatted in XML, this paper makes the case that the content lends itself to more efficient management. If that underlying source content is structured and formatted in HTML, then management becomes increasingly problematic. Use of a CMS is more of a strategic choice based on an agency's workflow. This paper argues that many content management benefits can be accrued through implementation of XML alone. The addition of a CMS or use of a CMS based on XML is not opposed to these benefits, but reinforces and enhances them.

Dealing with some of the limitations of HTML, XML offers a viable solution to these Website management problems. However, it is not clear what benefits government agencies can expect from XML, given the particular characteristics of government settings. In addition, the use of XML could have differentiated impacts depending on the type or organization and the process in which it is used. Similarly, it is important to understand whether XML initiatives are expected to face the same or different barriers and challenges in comparison with other government IT initiatives. Based on semi-structured interviews and a survey to program and IT staff from five government agencies, this chapter identifies the main benefits of and barriers to the adoption of XML for Website content management in government. The paper also provides some explanations related to the main benefits and barriers and highlights some differences in perceptions about these benefits and barriers between technical and program staff. Finally, this chapter suggests a set of solutions and recommendations to deal with the main barriers and obtain the expected benefits.

The chapter is organized in seven sections, including the foregoing introduction. Section two presents how XML has been characterized in the literature as a useful tool for Website content management. This section highlights some of the main benefits and challenges of using XML, paying special attention to its application for Website content management. In section three, the research design and methods are briefly described. This chapter is based on a study that uses semi-structure interviews, a survey, and the analysis of relevant documents. Section four identifies the most important benefits of and barriers to XML based on the survey and several semi-structured interviews with program and technical staff from five state agencies. Section five provides some practical lessons to help public managers to understand and, potentially, adopt XML for managing their agency Websites. Section six present some ideas for future research directions in this topic, with particular attention to government Websites. Finally, section seven provides some concluding remarks and final comments.

BACKGROUND: XML FOR WEBSITE CONTENT MANAGEMENT

XML is generally understood to be a new technology that supports effective data exchange between applications (Costello et al., 2006). This is probably the most known application of XML (Gil-Garcia et al., 2007). However, XML has another value that is much less exploited and understood. It offers an innovative long-term solution to many of the shortcomings of current Website design tools and techniques (e.g., HTML), because it structures and describes Web content in a meaningful way (Costello et al., 2004; Rockley Group, 2005; Costello et al., 2006). HTML tools and techniques may work well for individual Web pages, but present serious challenges when used for managing complex Websites (Kerer et al., 2001; Costello et al., 2007).

Converting and updating documents for the Web can be not only time consuming, but also produce important delays and inconsistencies across an agency Website (Costello et al., 2004). This is, at least in part, because content authors are not able to markup documents for the Web and the task falls on a few members of agency technical staff, for whom, in many cases, the maintenance of the Website is just a small part of their overall responsibilities. In addition, a very simple change to an HTML-based Website may mean the need to change dozens of single Web pages, because the same information may be presented in multiple places in an agency Website (Costello et al., 2004). Despite clear advantages, government agencies confront many obstacles to the adoption and implementation of XML-based Website management. These include the need for technical training and infrastructure readiness, but more important are the needs for solid business case justifications, understanding the impact of organizational change, leadership buy-in, and a firm understanding of where to begin (Costello et al., 2007).

Benefits from XML

XML's properties allow for the separation of a document's content, structure, and display. The separation of these three elements of content production and distribution provide organizations with the ability to manage Websites more effectively (Costello, 2002). The single source document concept of the XML technology is frequently cited as a major benefit of using the tool. The principle behind single source is that one document contains all the content independent of display attributes. The source document is eventually combined with an XSL (Extensible Stylesheet Language) to produce a variety of publication outputs including HTML pages, PDFs (Print Document Format), and RTFs (Rich Text Format). This technique is frequently referred to as re-purposing content. Having the ability to create a variety of outputs from a single source can save on time and thus have a direct return on investment (Ethier, 2002).

In addition to re-purposing content, XML's single source capability decreases errors in content and ensures consistency of format throughout entire Websites and between formats for multiple devices (Ethier, 2002). With the fast pace of information, changes to content can be frequent and since content often appears in more than one place on a Website executing those changes can also be challenging (Kerer et al., 2001). Without a single content source, a webmaster might not be able to update all instances of the outdated content and thus risk inconsistency of presentation. The use of a single source document can also foster collaboration between staff in organizations, which would not be accomplished as easily with HTML (Rockley Group, 2005). When XML is implemented properly, a single authoritative source document is created and maintained for specific content. This content may then be rendered as various outputs: PDF, RTF, RSS feed (Real Simple Syndication / Rich Site Summary), XHTML web page, portions may appear on a home page listing and as links in margins on all pages. The important point is that all these outputs come from one source: the XML document. Multiple versions of this original content do not exist in various locations and various forms corresponding to the outputs. Therefore, version control is simplified because you are only maintaining one source document, not several. This not only ensures that multiple authors do not have different versions, but also that no one individual has ownership of the content to the exclusion of all other individuals. All stakeholders involved in the publication process need to work together and design a workflow that allows the benefits of XML use to be realized.

In addition to content management, there are other general benefits that can be obtained by using XML. XML's data structure requirements provide an effective and fast method to share and exchange data (Boeri, 2002; Chen, 2003; Cingil,

Dogac, & Azgin, 2000; Hibbard & Dalton, 1999; Kendall & Kendall, 1999). Data exchange is fostered by the development of a common set of tags that describe and structure the data. Unlike HTML, however, XML requires strict adherence to a formal set of standards or else Web pages will not display on browsers (the XML parser will prevent a document that is not well-formed from getting to the point of being rendered as XHTML or PDF or any intended output format). Similar to other standards, using XML has a direct effect on accessibility. As the Web continues to grow in size and prominence, accessibility to data is paramount (Lawrence, 1999). Sites that contain several images may delay content from appearing on a Web page. This situation is still true today for despite widespread, high-speed access to the Internet, such access is not universal or equitable. Government Websites, in particular, serve a variety of citizens, many of whom have limitations on their Internet access. XML's defined structure requirements make data more accessible. The tags allow search engines to pull out data based on the definition tags, without knowledge of the specific data (Silver, 2005).

Another benefit of XML is that it is device independent (Kerer et al., 2001; Lie & Saarela, 1999). As wireless devices gain popularity, this feature will be especially important to reach consumers. XML/XSL can deliver to PDAs (Personal Digital Assistant), cell phones, and other wireless devices with the same ease as desktop computers. Furthermore, XML also allows for the potential to personalize data (Ryan, 2002). Because XML separates content from style, various stylesheets can be applied to customize data for different audiences. Finally, XML increases the speed and aggregation of content (Fichter, 2000). For instance, a related technology RSS, can locate and update content immediately. RSS is based on a simple XML markup that structures content into a "headline" format (with titles, descriptions, URL's, and dates) that makes this content available to everyone across the Web. Thus, without going to individual Websites, you can retrieve these RSS "feeds" from multiple locations and make your own RSS content available to everyone else. RSS is typically used for breaking news, press release, updates to information, etc. RSS is easily created via a variety of software packages and services or by an XSL transformation of existing XML content.

Barriers to XML Adoption and Implementation

Chen, LaBrie, & Shao (2003) proposed a framework for managers when considering XML adoption. This framework includes the diffusion process, costs associated with the technology, and technology acceptance within the organization. Evaluating both benefits and barriers can help managers mitigate potential risks associated with information technologies (Andersen & Dawes, 1991; Bloniarz et al., 2000; Gil-García & Pardo, 2005). However, while XML technology is an improvement to managing data, it is still not a universal solution to all data problems (Yen, Huang, & Ku, 2002). In addition, many of the barriers organizations may face with using XML are common to other IT projects and fall under organizational and policy categories, not technical data handling.

For instance, one of the key barriers to many technology projects is the lack of understanding about workflow processes (Rockley Group, 2005). This is especially important with XML because the content management process includes several areas and multiple actors in an organization. Some of the stakeholders that must be considered in the case of XML adoption include: policy makers, who set the guidelines for document creation and the approval process; content creators, who input data; content reviewers, who ensure the data meets established criteria; and of course, technical staff, who markup and upload the Web pages (whether they do this "by hand," via a Website editing platform, or a CMS).

Due to XML's structured authoring environment, an important barrier is authors' resistance to accept and adopt the new method of document creation (Ethier, 2002). XML requires strict adherence to rules guiding document structure. Since the structure of a document is predetermined, authors may lose some control over formatting. The strict environment can be a challenge, but with time and training can also be beneficial to the workflow process. XML allows organizations to define document displaying rules without impacting the author (Dunn, 2003). The organizational rules attached to XML documents can even decrease the complexity of the authoring process by reducing the need to format. Authors can spend a significant amount of time adjusting the size of headings, paragraph alignment and dealing with other formatting issues.

Another potential barrier to stakeholder acceptance may be the inability for the average user to differentiate between a system designed with XML and another type of system. XML's ability to transform data into various formats including HTML, makes XML technology difficult to detect (Fichter, 2000). Even if an individual were to view the source of a Web page they would not see the entire XML schema; they would see the HTML generated by the XSL/XML documents. The technology and its potential impact on a business should be explained to stakeholders. Providing training and demonstrations can mitigate potential resistance and other barriers.

Lastly, there is a learning curve associated with adopting XML technology. Similar to other technologies, individuals will need time to understand XML as well as its impact on the organization. A key step to ensuring the success of any technology is building a case. Analyzing the organization's information management needs along with the technology can be a great start to planning. If organizations follow steps to ensure that stakeholders understand the technology and information management process as well as the risks associated with its adoption, barriers can

Table 1. XML benefits and barriers

Benefits	Barriers
• Multiple publication outputs • Cost savings • Improved consistency (less errors) • Collaboration among staff members • Effective data sharing and exchange • Improved accessibility • Same content in multiple devices • Personalized data • Increased speed and aggregation of content	• Lack of understanding about workflow processes • Multiple stakeholders with different priorities and interests • Individual resistance • Some results of using XML are not evident • Learning curve for understanding and adopting XML

Source: Elaborated by the authors based on previous studies.

be mitigated and benefits can be achieved (Gil-Garcia & Pardo, 2005). Table 1 summarizes the main XML benefits and barriers found in recent literature.

RESEARCH DESIGN AND METHODS

The study uses multiple research methods such as semi-structured interviews, surveys, and analysis of relevant documents. Five NYS government agency teams were selected, looking for a mixture of several aspects such as technological expertise, organizational capabilities, and organization size, among others. The agencies represented a mix of small, medium and large scale agencies (based on the number of full time employees employed.) The policy domains represented by the agencies were: employee relations, information technology, civil service, housing, higher education, culture, and prevention of domestic violence. Within this study, the composition of the agency team was very important. The technical expertise was not as important to the research design as was the fact that all roles within the Web content development process had to be represented. Some had previously attended a one-day XML training; others were slightly familiar with the potential XML could provide. And still others were only familiar with XML from a data exchange perspective. Many had access to information technology expertise while others had minimal support. Each

team was comprised of program and technology staff as well as the Public Information Officer from each agency.

Thirty individual program and technical staff members from each agency team participated in the survey and were also interviewed. The survey captured participants' perceptions about their current website management and workflow processes and technologies, and about the potential of XML as an alternative technology for website management in public sector organizations. The items in the survey were initially developed based on existing literature about the benefits of and barriers to XML. However, since this literature was still in the emerging stage, the survey development was also informed by more general literature about IT adoption and success in government settings. The items were measured with a seven-point scale ranging from 1 = "Not at all to be achieved to" 7 = "Very likely to be achieved for the benefits" and from 1 = "Not a barrier" to 7 = "A severe barrier for barriers". The results of the survey were analyzed with basic statistical techniques such as descriptive statistics and tests for differences between means. These results were complemented with information from the interviews and the analysis of documents.

For the semi-structured interviews, a research team member visited the interviewees in their offices to have an individual conversation. Interviews were recorded and transcribed. Then, the research team looked for specific categories

Table 2. Top 10 expected benefits from the use of XML in Website content management

Rank	Item	Mean	Standard Deviation
1	Information will be more consistent across Web pages and non-Web deliveries (print publications, memos, etc.).	5.45	0.961
2	Duplicate data and content sources will be reduced	5.29	1.101
3	Duplicate data and content handling will be reduced	5.16	1.098
4	Website (s) will be more compatible with new devices and formats (e.g., mobile devices, integrated call systems, etc.)	5.03	1.581
4	Internet and Intranet Website users will have better information for their own use.	5.03	1.329
6	Participating departments or organizations will provide more responsive service to their clients through the Website.	4.97	0.912
7	Participating departments or organizations will provide more timely, accurate, and effective information to their Website users.	4.94	0.854
7	Elements of a shared information infrastructure (such as standards and common data definitions) will be built.	4.94	1.209
9	Participating departments or organizations will become more cost-efficient in Website and content management.	4.84	1.036
10	Publications and information will be better coordinated among the participating departments and organizations.	4.74	1.032

Notes: Based on a seven-point rating scale: 1 = Not at all likely to be achieve, 7 = Very likely to be achieved.

in the transcripts. Categories such as benefits, challenges, and barriers were analyzed looking for patterns, relationships, and relevant processes. This multi-method approach helped to answer multiple interrelated research questions and practical concerns such as: (1) What are the main expected benefits from using XML in Website management?, (2) What are the main barriers that public agencies perceive in using XML for Website management?, (3) How do perceived benefits, barriers, and problems differ from one context to another depending on project organizational and environmental characteristics?, and (4) How do these expectations differ between teams, job positions, and roles in the organization?

BENEFITS AND BARRIERS OF USING XML: ANALYSIS AND RESULTS

This section presents the results from our study. The benefits and barriers are organized in order

of importance for the program and technical staff members who participated in the project. Since the scale of the items had seven points, we decided to select all benefits and barriers with means higher than the expected middle point of the scale (4). Examining the results, it was decided that a natural cutoff point was about 4.5 and, considering this, 10 benefits and 10 barriers were selected. In addition to identifying the top 10 XML benefits and the top 10 barriers to XML adoption as reported by participants, this section presents some of the rationales of their importance. It also provides some recommendations to help obtaining the benefits and for dealing with the barriers when using XML.

Expected Benefits from the Use of XML

Table 2 shows the top 10 expected benefits from the use of XML in Website content management. The first 4 benefits align with the benefits articulated in the literature, specifically the reduction of errors, ensuring consistency, and flexibility of changes. All of these benefits increase the efficiency and effectiveness of organizations allowing them to be more responsive to their constituents. These benefits focus on the technological benefits obtained from using XML in Website development and the remaining 6 focus on the improvement of services provided to the end users of the content – better access, more responsive to changes, and more timely.

More Consistent Information across Web Pages and Non-Web Deliveries

Information consistency means consistency of content independent of display mechanism. Whether it is in print, Web (various browsers), wireless devices, or within a word processing format – the information displayed needs to be consistent. Consistency is critical because you do not want to be presenting inaccurate, incomplete, or conflicting information on a Website. At best, it is embarrassing; at worst, it could lead to litigation. XML can enhance consistency in two ways. The first is XML's single-source of content which means that regardless of where or how often the same information appears across a Website, it always comes from the same source. The second way XML ensures consistency comes from its ability to produce multiple HTML and PDF pages from single XML/XSL files. This turns an overwhelming task into one that is highly manageable.

Reduced Duplicate Data and Content Sources

Duplicate data and content sources mean that identical text, images, and other content that may appear in multiple locations and in multiple formats across a Website are actually duplicate source files for those locations and formats. This duplication may even extend beyond the Website to "original sources" such as Word documents where the content originated. Duplicate data is a problem

similar in nature to information consistency. But it can also bloat your Website by requiring multiple copies of the same files (increasing overall file size). XML can eliminate the duplication of data because the XML file serves as the single-source of the data or content. Its various manifestations throughout a Website and beyond (HTML, Word, PDF, etc.) are produced via the XML stylesheets (called XSL) which transform and present the XML single-source content in the format and location desired, without modifying or copying that original XML data source.

Reduced Duplicate Data and Content Handling

Duplicate data implies multiple copies of a "source file" duplicated in many locations. By definition, this requires that the "same" content be handled in several locations, probably by different people, and across time. Without a single source, you create potential for "version differences" between the duplicates, manual tracking and maintenance of all the locations of the duplicated data, and different technical skills needed for handling of data in its various guises (e.g., Word, HTML, database, etc.). XSL "handles" the content and produces the output so XML/XSL not only eliminates the duplication of data, it also manages how that data is handled through its various manifestations.

Better Website Compatibility with New Devices and Formats

The Web is relatively young (about 15 years) and the surrounding technology advances at incredible speeds. Devices barely imagined in the early days of the Web (PDA's, cell phones, MP3 Players, etc.) are becoming commonplace and newer unimagined devices will be arriving. XML has one big advantage over HTML in this regard because XML is a content specification standard (a meta-language of rules for how data can and should be described). It is not tied to any output format as HTML is to producing pages on a Web browser. And because XML is an open standard, it can easily adapt and integrate with new devices and formats. In the simplest sense, it only requires an XSL stylesheet to format the output to a particular device such as XHTML which seems to be a standard around which many newer devices (iPod Touch, iPhone) are standardizing or a simpler, text-based HTML page for older devices.

Better Information for Internet and Intranet Website Users

This relates to timely, accurate, and effective information. Basically, since the Internet and Intranet are the primary vehicles for getting information to your user base, you want to get as much information as you can, in ways that are most useful to those users. Since XML offers a much more flexible structure for information and delivery of that information, it provides easier dissemination of information across Internet and Intranet Websites.

More Responsive Service to Clients through the Website

Organizations use their Websites as a primary vehicle for information and services. Clients of the Website increasingly expect high levels of service from it. As Websites continue to grow in importance, clients continue to become more savvy and demanding customers. When service does not live up to those expectations, the threat of alienating or losing those customers increases. Because an XML-based Website offers the opportunity to shift many of the time-consuming menial maintenance tasks to activities that improve the quality and responsiveness of the Website, it can produce more customer-oriented benefits.

More Timely, Accurate, and Effective Information to Website Users

In many, if not most, cases, Websites are an organization's primary vehicle for delivering information. Timely, accurate and effective information means that what appears on the Website is not out-of-date or inaccurate and that it is easy to find and understand. From a business and public service sense, it is important that the information be timely, accurate, and effective. Because XML dramatically reduces the amount of time required for the maintenance of Web pages (due to enhanced consistency and reduced duplication), it frees up time to ensure that the actual content on the site is timely, accurate, and effective.

New Elements of a Shared Information Infrastructure

Data sharing, collaboration, and integration are dominant topics in today's IT world. Organizations need to share data within their own organization and across organizations throughout the world. The costs of developing and maintaining interfaces and middleware to communicate data across different formats can be prohibitive and shortsighted. It is far more advisable to have data formats that are open, standard, easily communicable, and that persist over time. XML is first and foremost an open, standards-based, data formatting specification. By using XML – especially by adopting industry-wide standards within XML such as DocBook, EAD (Encoded Archival Description), and other data definition schemas – users are building the elements of a shared information structure.

Cost-Efficiency in Website and Content Management

Cost efficiency in Website and content management mean that organizations are not "paying twice or more" for the same function. With HTML cost efficiencies are inversely tied to the size of the

Table 3. Top 10 perceived barriers to the use of XML in Website content management

Rank	Item	Mean	Standard Deviation
1	Organizational resistance to change.	5.03	1.602
2	Different priorities among the participating departments and organizations.	4.94	1.340
3	Individual resistance to change.	4.68	1.514
3	Program and service staff lack knowledge of technology.	4.68	2.120
5	Goals that are too ambitious for the people and money available.	4.61	1.564
5	Reluctance to abandon current technologies and procedures.	4.61	1.564
5	Turf battles and Conflicts.	4.61	1.783
8	Lack of common publishing and communications standards.	4.58	1.822
9	Overlapping or conflicting missions among participating departments and organizations.	4.55	1.650
10	Lack of agreement about the overall goals.	4.35	1.582

Notes: Based on a seven-point rating scale: 1 = Not a barrier, 7 = A severe barrier.

Website. It can be very cost-efficient to maintain a small site in HTML (especially when using good HTML editing software), but as the site grows, those efficiencies decrease because there are more individual pages and duplicated iterations of content to manage. The more the site grows, the less efficient it becomes to manage. With XML, just the opposite occurs. Since the many pages of a Website are generated by a very small number of XSL files, the number of files to manage stays constant as the occurrence of individual Web pages increases. For instance, an XML-based site with 20 XSL stylesheets may produce 100, 1,000, or 10,000 HTML Web pages.

Publications and Information Will be Better Coordinated

Publications can present particular difficulties to Websites due to their number of pages, unique formatting and layout, and navigation/paging requirements. In addition, most publications are created and maintained in a format that is "foreign" to HTML, such as word processing or desktop publishing software. Things that are taken for granted in many publications such as a table of contents, tables, graphics, and footnotes can be

very difficult to recreate in HTML pages. Likewise, a single publication may have many incarnations on its way to the Web – from a word processing document (the "original") to a desktop published document (the "printer's original") to a series of individual HTML pages (the "Web original") to a PDF file (on the Web and in print). XML/XSL provides perhaps its biggest benefits in its ability to better coordinate publications.

Perceived Barriers to XML Adoption and Implementation

Table 3 shows the top 10 perceived barriers to the use of XML in Website content management as reported by program and IT staff from five different government agencies. It is interesting that in general benefits were rated higher than barriers, which may indicate that public managers perceived more benefits and see most of the following factors as surmountable barriers. The first three barriers are organizational in nature and represent the resistance to change and to trying new technologies and processes. One of them highlights the importance of dealing with different organizational priorities as one of the most important barriers. The fourth barrier talks about the importance of having basic knowledge about XML in substantive and strategic terms. Program and service staff should have this knowledge in order for them to appreciate the benefits of XML for their own activities and for the organization as a whole.

In general, the barriers could be classified in three groups. The first group is related to individual and organizational resistance to change. Here we have also the reluctance to abandon current technologies. The second group includes two barriers related to technology and processes: lack of knowledge about technology and lack of common publishing and communications standards. These two barriers could be considered as technical or process-oriented. Finally, the larger group includes five barriers related to the inter-departmental or inter-organizational nature of using XML. These barriers recognize the differences in priorities, goals, and missions among participating department or organizations. Here, turf battles and conflicts could be a difficult barrier to overcome if the real problems among organizations are not identified and the diversity is not recognized and taken into consideration in the development of the initiative.

Organizational Resistance to Change

This refers to the general characteristic of many organizations' resistance to change of any kind. It is important to recognize organizational resistance to change because any innovation requires change, so this general resistance will always have to be addressed. In regard to changes precipitated by converting to XML for Website management, it is important to recognize that the changes required will lead to more efficient processes, better service and products, and less work down the line, so there is an incentive to change from an organizational perspective. However, it is also important to note that the changes will be felt throughout an entire organization, or at least the areas involved in developing and bringing content to the Web. So,

you cannot address the factor of change only in the IT or Web unit.

Different Priorities among the Participating Departments

Many different departments are involved in Web content (e.g., individual business or program units, public information offices, IT, Web unit, etc.) and all these units have their own priorities and missions both in regard to the Web and outside of it. Therefore, it is important to recognize these differing priorities to balance them among one another and with overall organizational priorities. Again, an XML based Website can help to align priorities by stressing the single-source content and demonstrating how everyone benefits from keeping the content consistent, timely, and accurate.

Individual Resistance to Change

This refers to the general characteristic of some individuals to resist change, particularly change derived from IT initiatives. It is important to recognize and address individual resistance to change. In regard to changes precipitated by converting to XML for Website management, for some individuals there is an incentive to change. However, it is also important to recognize that certain individuals will resist change no matter what, so workarounds or accommodations may need to be made.

Program and Service Staff Lack Knowledge of Technology

This is a common situation in which staff simply does not know enough about a technology to evaluate or use it. This lack of knowledge can be a barrier on two levels. First, it may hamper a clear understanding of how an unfamiliar technology such as XML can provide benefits, thus making an evaluation or acceptance of it difficult to achieve. Second, it may short-circuit implementation when staff just does not feel up to the task. Since XML is not really a technology, but rather an open, standards-based data formatting specification, that makes other processes and technologies (such as data transfer, document management, etc.) easier, it is really not that difficult from a technological perspective. While it has a steep learning curve due to its requiring a change in mindset as to how organizations manage content, that learning curve is also short because XML/XSL itself is quite simple to use, and not highly technical. In addition, when integrating XML with existing platforms, staff needs to have knowledge not only about XML, but also about the current technological infrastructure.

Goals that are too Ambitious for the People and Money Available

Redesigning part or a complete Website (either via XML or not) can be a huge undertaking for an organization and involve far more people, areas, and resources than anticipated. It is important to evaluate the appropriateness of goals for two reasons. First, if they are too ambitious, public managers can be ready and scale back accordingly. Second, public managers should not confuse the ambitiousness of the goals with the "doability" of the project, and wrongly conclude that XML cannot be implemented in their agencies. XML for Website management offers good flexibility for scaling back projects to fit an organization's capabilities, while still delivering benefits.

Reluctance to Abandon Current Technologies and Procedures

Like resistance to change, this is a common situation for organizations and individuals – but with the added elements of technical comfort and monetary investment in technologies. If people have technologies and procedures that they are used to and that work for them, regardless of how inefficient they may appear to an impartial

observer, it is difficult to convince them to change their behavior on a promise. Because of its non-proprietary, open standard nature, XML does not always present an either/or situation. It can be, and is, integrated with existing technologies and procedures. On the other side, because of the efficiencies it brings to content management and the "creation to Web workflow processes," XML can offer a strong argument for replacing cherished technologies and procedures.

Turf Wars and Conflicts

This is again a general organizational problem whereby different units or individuals have certain "turf" (programs, people, priorities) that they want to protect and which they may perceive as being threatened by other initiatives. Turf wars and conflicts can threaten any innovation because they are not based on any reasonable ground that can be evaluated and argued. Thus, stressing potential benefits may have no impact upon these turf loyalties. On the other hand, some negotiation may be necessary and useful to obviate the impact of the conflicts. These are human relations and organizational issues that need to be addressed in order to better achieve the benefits from XML.

Lack of Common Publishing and Communications Standards

Publications often exist and are produced in a variety of formats within an organization depending on how they will be delivered or what the creator is familiar with. The lack of standards creates a large workflow barrier as individuals continually reinvent the wheel along each step of the publication process or with each new publication. It can lead to "version control" issues whereby it becomes difficult to identify the authoritative source document. Because XML is a specification for defining content structure, it addresses common publishing and communication standards at the root. The innate structure of XML-based

Table 4. Expected benefits from the use of XML in Website content management with differences between technical and program staff

No.	Items	Mean Tech	Mean Prog	Sig. Test P-value
3	Information will be more consistent across Web pages and non-Web deliveries (print publications, memos, etc.).	5.72	5.08	.064
7	Participating departments or organizations will provide more timely, accurate, and effective information to their Website users.	5.17	4.62	.076

Notes: Based on a seven-point rating scale: 1 = Not at all likely to be achieve, 7 = Very likely to be achieved.

documents lends itself to procedures and standards that capitalize on this structure and streamline the publishing flow.

Overlapping or Conflicting Missions among Participating Departments

One department's "mission" may be to have its material on the Web as soon as possible in a prominent location, while another department's mission may be to make sure that the material is in a format that is Web-accessible and positioned properly among all the elements of the Website. It's important to recognize these differing missions in order to balance them among one another and with overall organizational priorities. Again, an XML based Website can help to align missions by stressing the single-source document and demonstrating how everyone benefits from keeping the content consistent, timely, and accurate. Conversely, conflicting missions can threaten XML initiatives by taking resources away or focusing in different directions.

Lack of Agreement about the Overall Goals

Different individuals and departments have different understandings of what is important and what results are desired as well as different levels of awareness of the workflow processes they are involved in. Because Website management cuts across so many organizational areas and involves so many different perspectives, it is important to articulate and clarify overall goals so that everyone is not pulling in opposite directions. Because XML-based management of a Website addresses workflow processes and standardizes how content gets from creation to the Web, it requires a certain level of agreement about goals.

Different Perceptions between Technical and Program Staff

Identifying benefits and barriers to the adoption of XML for Website content management is very important to plan for this type of transition. Technical and program staff may have different understandings, and therefore, different perceptions about XML, as well as its benefits and barriers. As one member of a team stated "I think it's just a matter of our internal customers, our staff, people from the various different offices, who are not really aware of what all it takes to present this information... I think they have a lack of understanding of how it happens, how it goes from Point A to Point B to Point C —there's a vacuum there." Using t tests for difference between means, the views of program and technical staff regarding benefits and barriers of XML for Website content management were compared. Tables 4 and 5 show the benefits and barriers that were perceived significantly different by program and technical staff. Given the exploratory nature of this study, the significance level of 0.1 was selected for these tests.

Table 5. Perceived barriers to the use of XML in Website content management with differences between technical and program staff

No.	Items	Mean Tech.	Mean Prog.	Sig. Test P-Value
3	Funding that is inappropriately allocated among the participants.	3.12	4.31	.039
13	Fear that XML is just the latest "flavor of the month."	2.67	4.00	.035
19	Technology changes too often for all parties to keep up.	3.67	4.54	.093
27	Current level of investment in HTML.	2.72	3.92	.040
32	One-year-budget restrictions.	3.00	4.08	.069
33	Difficult intergovernmental relationships.	2.88	3.85	.059

Notes: Based on a seven-point rating scale: 1 = Not a barrier, 7 = A severe barrier.

In general, there were very few differences in how technical and program staff members perceive the benefits. The two benefits that were perceived differently are related to the consistency and quality of Website information. In both cases, technical staff perceived that these two benefits are more likely to be achieved than program staff. The mean for technical staff was greater than the mean for program staff in both cases. This may be because technical staff members have more knowledge about the capabilities of XML, and because they are more optimistic about achieving the benefits of information technology solutions. In contrast, program staff may be less optimistic and, based on past experiences, consider that technologies rarely provide the expected benefits. It could also be that both program and technical staff have very similar expectations about the benefits from XML and, therefore, they consistently evaluate some benefits high and some benefits low, not having significant differences between them.

There were more differences in the perceived barriers. In general terms, program people identified six factors as more severe barriers than technical staff. For all items with significant differences, the mean for program staff was higher than the mean for technical staff. There seem to be two main topics in this group of barriers: financial resources and technology acceptance. Program staff members seem to be more concerned about the availability of adequate financial resources than technical staff. This may be because technical staff members are more knowledgeable or optimistic about the real cost of the transition from HTML to XML. As one technical staff member mentioned "...costs of transitioning from HTML into XML--I don't think those costs are terribly high to begin with. And I think we have enough commitment that that's not going to be a real big issue." The second group includes caution of technology changes and the pace of technological change. Program staff considers this to be a more severe barrier than technical staff members.

Solutions and Recommendations

Government managers are facing new challenges in managing their Websites. XML is a new technology that can help to manage these government Websites better and, subsequently, improve how government serves citizens and other stakeholders. In addition, XML is a flexible technology and provides excellent opportunities for innovation in public service, as well as the capacity to improve how government managers make use of their IT and program employees. Here are some practical recommendations.

Communicate the Benefits of XML to Different Stakeholders through the Use of a Business Case

To mitigate the barriers and exploit the benefits of XML it is important to consider any initiative from the basis of what value it will bring to the organization and the participants. XML is a relatively new technology and its use for Website content management is not as extended as other uses such as data exchange. Therefore, it is very important to communicate the benefits of XML to different stakeholders by discussing how these changes will impact their workflow for the better. They should be able to see how the use of XML will help them with their own activities, interests, and objectives.

Deal Directly with Organizational and Individual Resistance to Change

In addition, to the communication of benefits, it is very important to deal with organizational and individual resistance to change. Most of the time resistance is caused by fear of the unknown regarding how changes will impact an individual's work. Unfortunately many times technology is implemented without consideration of how it will impact others outside of the technology unit. Failures of IT systems are often the result of not taking into account the various stakeholders who are either upstream or downstream from the technology. Public managers need to communicate directly with the various stakeholders to understand the workflow issues and understand the impacts to all organizational units.

Consider the Project from a Workflow Perspective vs. a Department Perspective

Content many times is not proprietary to one unit or another within an organization. Content that is displayed on a Website is the property of the organization. One way to mitigate the turf battles and resistance to change is to look at the workflow process that is required to create the content. This cross-organizational perspectives many times allow for barriers to be brought down and a common vision to be created. Bring together the individuals who are part of the process to discuss the 'life' of the Web content as it passes through each organizational unit. By focusing on the process versus the units ownership allows for groups to work together and create a new more efficient way of delivering content to Web.

The Involvement of Stakeholders is Very Important

Similar to some of the previous recommendations, public managers should find ways to involve all relevant stakeholders. In the case of using XML, involving stakeholders is important, as in other IT initiatives, because it is a way to generate ideas and get buy-in in general for the initiative. Using XML requires changes in behavior of these stakeholders, since many of them are in different ways involved in the Website content management process.

Provide Strategic and Technical Training about XML

Training is very important for using XML for Website content management. This training is not only for technical staff members, but also strategic training about the substantive benefits of XML for program staff and executives. Basic technical training for program staff is also useful for them to better understand the technology and being able to better communicate with technical staff when working together.

Establish Realistic Goals and Periodic Milestones

XML allows public managers to decide the size of the project or to plan for several phases. A complete Website could be converted to XML or a small section could be used as the first step in a more comprehensive initiative. In addition, executives, policy makers, and other stakeholders may lose interest in the initiative if they do not see results relatively soon. It is therefore very important not only to establish realistic goals, but also to have milestones that clearly measure the progress of the initiative.

Promote Standards for Managing Information across Organizations or Departments

Using XML for Website content management requires having common standards for managing information across departments (or organizations). Public managers should understand the processes and the information flows that exist in their organizations. They should then promote standards that help to exchange and manage information, particularly the information related to the Website.

FUTURE RESEARCH DIRECTIONS

This study has identified the main benefits of and barriers to using XML for Website content management. The study is based on a survey and semi-structured interviews with program and IT staff from five government agencies in New York State. Future studies should explore how different or similar are the expected benefits and perceived barriers in other contexts, particularly other countries, local government, or federal agencies. Given the case study nature of this research, another important research direction would be to conduct a survey with the purpose of testing and generalizing the initial results. A potential next step would be an in-depth case study that attempts to understand the implementation process and, therefore, to compare the expected benefits with the real benefits achieved and the perceived barriers with the real barriers faced by government managers. Finally, it would be very important to evaluate the results in different settings and identify in which situations XML has better results, how the benefits vary from one situation to another, and how generalizable are the solutions and recommendations.

CONCLUSION

This chapter has shown that XML is an important alternative for managing government Websites. The separation of content and format of XML allows for new ways of managing content and understanding the flow of information. XML has several important benefits for government agencies. Some of these benefits are technical and more specific to the management of Website content, but others are organizational and have impacts on the users of information or the agency as a whole. There are also some barriers that could hinder or even neutralize the potential benefits. Most of these barriers are organizational in nature and are related to resistance to change and the difficulty of managing multiple goals, missions, and priorities. There are ways to deal with the barriers and obtain the benefits of XML. Therefore, using XML for Website content management in government organizations seems to be a very good alternative and a great investment in the long term. Websites are now the main communication channel for many governments and XML can help public managers to have more responsive, efficient, and higher quality government Websites.

REFERENCES

Andersen, D. F., & Dawes, S. S. (1991). *Government Information Management. A Primer and Casebook*. Englewood Cliffs, NJ: Prentice Hall.

Bloniarz, P., Canestraro, D., Cook, M., Cresswell, T., Dawes, S., LaVigne, M., et al. (2000). *Insider's Guide to Using Information in Government*, [Website]. Center for Technology in Government, University at Albany, SUNY. Retreived from www.ctg.albany.edu/publications/online/insider_guide?sub=online

Boeri, R. (2002). XML publishing 2002: state of the TOOLS. *EMedia Magazine, 14*(12), 61–64.

Brown, M. M. (2001). The Benefits and Costs of Information Technology Innovations: An Empirical Assessment of a Local Government Agency. *Pubic Performance & Management Review, 24*(4), 351–366. doi:10.2307/3381224

Chen, A. N. K., LaBrie, R. C., & Shao, B. B. M. (2003). An XML Adoption Framework for Electronic Business. *Journal of Electronic Commerce Research, 4*(1), 1–14.

Chen, M. (2003). Factors Affecting the Adoption and Diffusion of XML and Web services Standards for E-Business Systems. *International Journal of Human-Computer Studies, 58*, 259–279. doi:10.1016/S1071-5819(02)00140-4

Cingil, I., Dogac, A., & Azgin, A. (2000). A Broader Approach to Personalization. *Communications of the ACM, 43*(8), 136–141. doi:10.1145/345124.345168

Costello, J., Adhya, S., Gil-García, J. R., Pardo, T. A., & Werthmuller, D. (2004, August 6-11). Beyond Data Exchange: XML as a Website Workflow and Content Management Technology. Paper presented at the 2004 Annual Meeting of the Academy of Management: Creating Actionable Knowledge, New Orleans, LA, USA.

Costello, J., Canestraro, D. S., Ramón Gil-Garcia, J., & Werthmuller, D. (2007). *Using XML for Website Management: Lessons Learned Report*. Albany, NY: The Research Foundation of State University of New York.

Costello, J., Canestraro, D. S., Werthmuller, D., Ramon Gil-Garcia, J., & Baker, A. (2006). *Using XML for Website Management: Getting Started Guide*. Albany, NY: Center for Technology in Government, University at Albany, SUNY.

Costello, J., Canestraro, D. S., Werthmuller, D., Ramon Gil-Garcia, J., & Baker, A. (2007). *Using XML for Website Management: An Executive Briefing on streamlining workflow, reducing costs, and enhancing organizational value*. Albany, NY: The Research Foundation of State University of New York.

Costello, J., Werthmuller, D., & Apte, D. (2002). *XML: A new website architecture*. Albany, NY: Center for Technology in Government.

Dunn, M. (2003). *Single Source Publishing with XML*. IT Pro(Jan/Feb), 51-54.

Ethier, K. (2002). *Managing Content from Creation to Delivery with XML: Case studies*. Paper presented at the XML Conference and Exposition 2002, Baltimore, MD.

Fichter, D. C., F. (2000). Documents, Data, Information Retrieval, & XML. *Online, 24*(6), 30–36.

Gil-Garcia, J. R., Costello, J., Pardo, T. A., & Werthmuller, D. (2007). Invigorating Website Management through XML: An E-Government Case from New York State. *International Journal of Electronic Governance, 1*(1), 52–78. doi:10.1504/IJEG.2007.014343

Gil-García, J. R., & Luna-Reyes, L. F. (2003). Towards a Definition of Electronic Government: A Comparative Review . In Mendez-Vilas, A., Mesa Gonzalez, J. A., Mesa Gonzalez, J., Guerrero Bote, V., & Zapico Alonso, F. (Eds.), *Techno-legal Aspects of the Information Society and New Economy: An Overview*. Badajoz, Spain: Formatex.

Gil-Garcia, J. R., & Luna-Reyes, L. F. (2006). Integrating conceptual approaches to e-government . In Khosrow-Pour, M. (Ed.), *Encyclopedia of E-Commerce, E-Government and Mobile Commerce*. Hershey, PA: Idea Group Inc.

Gil-García, J. R., & Pardo, T. A. (2005). E-Government Success Factors: Mapping Practical Tools to Theoretical Foundations. *Government Information Quarterly*, *22*(2), 187–216. doi:10.1016/j.giq.2005.02.001

Heeks, R. (1999). *Reinventing Government in the Information Age. International Practice in IT-Enabled Public Sector Reform*. New York: Routledge. doi:10.4324/9780203204962

Hibbard, J., & Dalton, G. (1999, March). XML Gains Ground. *Informationweek*, 18-19.

Kendall, J. E., & Kendall, K. E. (1999). Information Delivery Systems: An Exploration of Web Pull and Push Technologies. *Communications of the AIS*, *1*(14), 1–43.

Kerer, C., Kirda, E., Jazayeri, M., & Kurmanowytsch, R. (2001, October 8-12). *Building and Managing XML/XSL-powered Websites: an Experience Report*. Paper presented at the 25th Annual International Computer Software and Applications Conference, Chicago, IL.

Kim, S., & Kim, D. (2003). South Korean Public Officials' Perceptions of Values, Failure, and Consequences of Failure in E-Government Leadership. *Public Performance and Management Review*, *26*(4), 360–375. doi:10.1177/1530957603026004004

Kraemer, K. L., & King, J. L. (2003, September 29). *Information Technology and Administrative Reform: Will the Time After E-Government Be Different?* Paper presented at the Heinrich Reinermann Schrift fest, Post Graduate School of Administration, Speyer, Germany.

Lawrence, S. G. (1999). Accessibility of information on the web. *Nature*, *400*(6740), 107. doi:10.1038/21987

Lie, H. W., & Saarela, J. (1999). Multiporpuse Web Publishing. Using HTML, XML, and CSS. *Communications of the ACM*, *42*(10), 95–101. doi:10.1145/317665.317681

OECD. (2003). *The e-Government Imperative*. Paris, France: Organisation for Economic Co-operation and Development.

Rockley Group. (2005). *The Role of Content Standards and Content Management*. 18.

Ryan, D. (2002). The Role of XML in Content Management. *XML Journal, 6*.

Schelin, S. H. (2003). E-Government: An Overview . In Garson, G. D. (Ed.), *Public Information Technology: Policy and Management Issues* (pp. 120–137). Hershey, PA: Idea Group Publishing.

Silver, B. (2005). *Content in the Age of XML. Intelligent Enterprise*. Retrieved from http://www.intelligententerprise.com/print_article.jhtml?articleID=163100779

Yen, D. C., Huang, S.-M., & Ku, C.-Y. (2002). The impact and implementation of XML on business-to-business commerce. *Computer Standards & Interfaces*, *24*, 347–362. doi:10.1016/S0920-5489(02)00019-3

ADDITIONAL READING

Cresswell, A. M., & Pardo, T. A. (2001). Implications of legal and organizational issues for urban digital government development. *Government Information Quarterly, 18,* 269–278. doi:10.1016/S0740-624X(01)00086-7

Cushing, J., & Pardo, T. A. (2005). Research in the digital government realm. *IEEE Computer, 38*(12), 26–32.

Dawes, S. S., Gregg, V., & Agouris, P. (2004). Digital government research: Investigations at the crossroads of social and information science. *Social Science Computer Review, 22*(1), 5–10. doi:10.1177/0894439303259863

Dawes, S. S., Pardo, T., & DiCaterino, A. (1999). Crossing the threshold: Practical foundations for government services on the world wide web. *Journal of the American Society for Information Science American Society for Information Science, 50*(4), 346–353. doi:10.1002/(SICI)1097-4571(1999)50:4<346::AID-ASI12>3.0.CO;2-I

Dawes, S. S., Pardo, T. A., Simon, S., Cresswell, A. M., LaVigne, M. F., Andersen, D. F., & Bloniarz, P. A. (2004). *Making smart IT choices: Understanding value and risk in government IT investments*. Retrieved from http://www.ctg.albany.edu/publications/guides/smartit2

Ethier, K. (2004, Sept. 15 2004). *Introduction to structured content management with XML*. CMS Watch, 5. Retrieved from http://www.cmswatch.com/Feature/112

Foley, M. J. (2006). Open things up, *Microsoft. eWeek, 23*(35).

Gil-Garcia, J. R., Chengalur-Smith, I., & Duchessi, P. (2007). Collaborative e-government: Impediments and benefits of information sharing projects in the public sector. *European Journal of Information Systems, 16*(2), 121–133. doi:10.1057/palgrave.ejis.3000673

Gil-Garcia, J. R., Costello, J., Pardo, T. A., & Werthmuller, D. (Forthcoming). Invigorating website management through XML: An e-government case from New York State. *International Journal of Electronic Governance.*

Gil-Garcia, J. R., & Helbig, N. (2006). Exploring e-government benefits and success factors . In Anttiroiko, A.-V., & Malkia, M. (Eds.), *Encyclopedia of Digital Government*. Hershey, PA: Idea Group Inc.

Gil-Garcia, J. R., & Martinez-Moyano, I. (2007). Understanding the evolution of e-government: The influence of systems of rules on public sector dynamics. *Government Information Quarterly, 24*(2), 266–290. doi:10.1016/j.giq.2006.04.005

Hall, R. H. (2002). *Organizations structures processes and outcomes*. Upper Saddle River, NJ: Prentice Hall.

Harrison, T., Pardo, T. A., Gil-Garcia, J. R., Thompson, F., & Juraga, D. (2007). Geographic information technologies structuration theory and the World Trade Center crisis. *Journal of the American Society for Information Science and Technology, 58*(14), 2240–2254. doi:10.1002/asi.20695

Jones, R., & Andrew, T. (2005). Open access, open source and e-theses: the development of the Edinburgh Research Archive. *Program: electronic library and information systems, 39*(3), 198 -212.

Long, S. A. (2006). Exploring the wiki world: the new face of collaboration. *New Library World, 107*(3). doi:10.1108/03074800610654934

Luna-Reyes, L., & Gil-Garcia, J., J. R., & Cruz, C. B. (2006). E-Mexico: collaborative structures in Mexican public administration. *International Journal of Cases on Electronic Commerce, 3*(2), 54–70.

Luna-Reyes, L., Gil-Garcia, J. R., & Estrada-Marroquín, M. (2008). The Impact of institutions on interorganizational IT projects in the Mexican Federal government. *International Journal of Electronic Government Research, 4*(2), 26–42.

Luna-Reyes, L. F., Gil-Garcia, J. R., & Cruz, C. B. (2007). Collaborative digital government in Mexico: Some lessons from federal web-based interorganizational information integration initiatives. *Government Information Quarterly, 24*(4), 808–826. doi:10.1016/j.giq.2007.04.003

Luna-Reyes, L. F., Zhang, J., Gil-Garcia, J. R., & Cresswell, A. M. (2005). Information systems development as emergent socio-technical change: A practice approach. *European Journal of Information Systems, 14*(1), 93–105. doi:10.1057/palgrave.ejis.3000524

Pardo, T. A., Cresswell, A. M., Thompson, F., & Zhang, J. (2006). Knowledge sharing in cross-boundary information system development in the public sector. *Information Technology Management, 7*(4), 293–313. doi:10.1007/s10799-006-0278-6

Report, G. (2002). *The role of XML in content management* (Volume 10, No. 8): Retrieved from http://www.gilbane.com/gilbane_report.pl/82/The_Role_of_XML_in_Content_Management.html

Robertson, J. (2003). *XML and content management systems*. Australia: Step two designs. Retrieved from http://www.steptwo.com.au/papers/kmc_xmlandcms/

Rocheleau, B. (2000). Prescriptions for public-sector information management: A review, analysis, and critique. *American Review of Public Administration, 30*(4), 414–435. doi:10.1177/02750740022064759

Salz, P. A. (2006). Collaboration rules. *EContent, 29*(9).

Zhang, J., Cresswell, A. M., & Thompson, F. (2002). *Participant's expectations and the success of knowledge networking in the public sector.* Paper presented at the AMCIS Conference, Texas.

KEY TERMS AND DEFINITIONS

Attribute: A qualifier on an XML element that provides additional information. For example, in the element <slide title="My Slide">, title is an attribute, and My Slide is its value.

Content Management: Managing information and content, particularly from a Website in such a way that the costs are adequate for the benefits obtained.

HTML (Hyper Text Markup Language): It is the most common language used to build Web pages. It uses labels to describe content and format. It is not a good solution for managing large complex Websites.

Interoperability: The ability for machines to exchange data without the intervention of human agents.

Open Standards: simple language data descriptions that are uniform in a discipline so that other programmers and machines can understand their logic.

Re-Purposing Content: The adaptation of content for a new purpose either within a Website or in a different medium.

Schema: Schemata for describing the structure and constraining the contents of XML documents and associating data types with XML element types and attributes. Schemas permit either tighter or looser constraints over documents than DTDs while still allowing them to be validated.

Website: Set of Web pages created by an organization or individual with various purposes.

Well-Formed: A well-formed XML document is syntactically correct. To be well-formed, an XML document needs to contain one or more elements nested properly within each other and all contained within the element root.

XHTML (Extensible HyperText Markup Language): A reformulation of HTML 4.0 in XML 1.0. XHTML is the successor to, and the current version of, HTML. The need for a more strict version of HTML was felt primarily because World Wide Web content now needs to be delivered to many devices (like mobile devices).

XML (Extensible Markup Language): Modification of the Standard Generalized Markup Language (SGML). In contrast to SGML documents, XML documents may exist without having their schema described in a DTD. XML documents consist (mainly) of text and tags, and the tags (elements and attributes) impose a tree structure upon the document. It was developed to combine the flexibility of SGML (minus its complexity) with the widespread applicability of HTML.

XML for Website Management: The use of XML to manage Website content; accomplished by separating content from style, which allows publication of content in various formats.

XSL (Extensible Stylesheet Language): A standard from the W3C for describing a stylesheet for XML documents. It is the XML counterpart to the Cascading Stylesheets (CSS) in HTML and is also compatible with CSS2.

ENDNOTE

[1] A previous version of this chapter was presented at the 67th ASPA National Conference, organized by the American Society for Public Administration, Denver, CO, April 1-4, 2006.

Chapter 18
Integrating Budget Transparency into E-Government Websites

M. Ernita Joaquin
University of Nevada-Las Vegas, USA

Thomas J. Greitens
Central Michigan University, USA

ABSTRACT

This chapter provides a basic template that governments can use when integrating budgetary information into any type of e-government website. Building on previous scholarship on citizen participation, budgeting, and budgetary transparency in e-government, the template divides budgetary information into two broad categories: process-based information that gives citizens a better understanding of budget decision-making and their avenues of participation, and outcome-based information that shows citizens the types of revenue collected by the government and how those revenues are used. We examine these two categories of budgetary information on state governmental websites in the United States and find that as governments increase the technological presentation of budgetary outcomes on their websites, a decline in the presentation of some types of budgetary process information occurs. We suggest that regardless of the sophistication of the e-government website, governments must present information on both the budgetary process and outcomes for true budgetary transparency via e-government to occur.

INTRODUCTION

If greater citizen participation can enhance democratic decision making, then enlarging the scope of participation by using technology to increase transparency should be a worthy aim of electronic government. Our chapter shows practitioners and scholars how to incorporate greater budget

DOI: 10.4018/978-1-61692-018-0.ch018

transparency into electronic government (or e-government) and why such fiscal transparency is necessary in a democracy. Over the last decade, most governments have steadily enhanced their e-government services from billboard-type websites that simply provide information to citizens to interactive portal systems, wherein citizens can search for and access different services and communicate with their elected officials (Garson, 2006; Ho, 2002; West, 2005). While it is debatable whether this progression will continue into some type of interactive, online citizen democracy (Coursey & Norris, 2008), what is not debatable is that most government websites have continuously increased in sophistication since the 1990s. Today, most governments offer more information and more services on their e-government websites.

While the trend toward greater website development and use accelerates, budgetary information on many governmental websites has not shown a similar pattern of evolution. A cursory glance at most budget homepages shows that governments typically display budget data in large portable document formats (PDFs) that are often hard to understand and difficult to download. Even when governments try to enhance their budget homepages by utilizing newer technologies to create searchable online budgetary database systems for citizens, the information is still often hard to search through and difficult for citizens to understand. This is unfortunate since the budget is one of the most important public documents for citizen engagement. It directly communicates to the public how their government collects revenue and where those revenues are allocated and eventually spent. It showcases historical spending, the political priorities of the day, and planned spending and anticipated income for the near future. By making budget information more accessible on e-government websites, citizens can hold their policymakers accountable for budgetary decisions. With more of this type of accountability, governments can make more responsive budgeting decisions (Benito & Bastida, 2009).

In this chapter, we provide a basic template that governments can follow when posting budget information to any type of budget website; from basic "billboard" websites that just display information to interactive online databases. Our template emphasizes budget transparency by emphasizing the budget process and budgetary outcomes. Making this information transparent to citizens is important since it increases accountability over the budget and encourages meaningful citizen participation in the budget process beyond simply informing them of budgetary timetables and actions (Berner, 2001). In addition, we provide a brief analysis of state governmental websites to assess their effectiveness in regards to budget transparency. Our results indicate that some aspects of budget transparency become minimized as budget websites increase in complexity from a basic billboard website to an interactive online database. Thus, this chapter has three primary objectives: (1) to link budget transparency to e-government and show how that link enhances citizen participation in a democracy, (2) to assess the state of budget transparency on e-government websites of American state governments, and (3) to develop a simple template that all governments can follow, regardless of website sophistication, to help ensure budget transparency on their e-government websites.

BACKGROUND

E-government has become one of the primary ways of providing services to citizens and enhancing public accountability of governments. To provide these things to citizens through e-government, governments often put more information and services online over time. Based on this pattern of development, scholars conceived of e-government on a five-stage scale based on how information and services were offered. These stages included: an emerging web presence with only one-way communication; an enhanced web presence with more forms of communication such as e-mail and links to other governmental agencies; an interactive portal or gateway web presence with limited transactions; a transactional web presence that allowed for all types of secure transactions; and a seamless web presence where a user could log in to one central portal system and access multi-governmental responses (Garson, 2006; Ho, 2002; United Nations and American Society for Public Administration, 2002). Typically, governments first used a website to offer general information to citizens such as organizational data that introduced government officials and services. Over time, as technology improved and citizens increased their demand for online services, governments used websites to offer more dynamic services such as accessing services online. The last stage of website development, which exists in a variety of forms in many governments, allowed the citizen to log in to one portal system and access a variety of governmental services across agencies and across levels of government.

Darrell West (2005) revised this initial classification when he examined a number of governmental websites in an attempt to categorize their website activity. He concluded that four stages of government websites existed: billboards, partial service-deliveries, portals, and interactive democracy (West, 2005). In the billboard stage, governments use their websites to provide information to citizens. These are basic websites commonly found in smaller local governments, single-purpose governments, and some legislative entities. In the partial service-delivery stage, websites typically have more interactivity with advanced search functions and a limited number of online services such as hyperlinked documents, advanced search features, and guided email communications. Expanding on the partial service-delivery stage, a portal type of website allows government to offer a variety of services online. All a citizen has to do is log in to the portal and then they can perform a variety of activities from ordering governmental publications, paying a governmental fine or fee, and communicating directly to policymakers and bureaucrats. However, while all these website types make some service delivery more convenient for citizens and more efficient for government, they do not really transform the way citizens interact with their government. Instead, the transformational power of e-government begins to take shape in the final stage of governmental websites: interactive democracy. With an interactive democracy website, a citizen can directly

participate in governmental decision-making and directly hold policymakers and bureaucrats accountable on a variety of decisions (West, 2005). In this way, interactive democracy websites place more emphasis on public feedback and democratic deliberation instead of service delivery.

This evolutionary approach to e-government website development is not without controversy. As some scholars have noted, e-government website development faces significant political, technical, financial, and legal barriers; and even when governments overcome those barriers the ultimate outcomes of enhancing e-government websites are often unclear (Coursey & Norris, 2008). This demonstrates that e-government website development does not always proceed in a linear fashion and a future where e-government websites are the facilitator for interactive democracy is by no means assured. However, if e-government websites are to reach the stage of interactive democracy, then online budget transparency will have to be ensured since budgets are the primary instrument of accountability in government (Rubin, 2006). When actual government budgets and other types of budgetary information such as financial reports are publicly presented, citizens are given knowledge of how their tax dollars are spent and which departments/programs receive more funding and which receive less. If citizens are to participate in government through online interactive democracy, then they need this type of budgetary information to be present on the webpage. In order to participate in government at a very basic level, citizens have to be knowledgeable of governmental decisions. The governmental budget provides that type of knowledge. As a result, if e-government is to have value in regards to interactive democracy or citizen participation, online budget transparency will have to be ensured.

Most websites have not yet reached the stage of interactive democracy; however, the integration of some aspects of online budget transparency into e-government websites is occurring at different levels of government. For example, in the

United States the Recovery Accountability and Transparency Board maintains the site <www. recovery.gov> to show citizens how economic stimulus funds from the American Recovery and Reinvestment Act of 2009 are being spent. Citizens can go to the website and see where the stimulus money is going (e.g., compare disbursements by state) and who is receiving stimulus money (e.g., identify the contractors that actually receive the disbursements for providing some type of service). In addition, states like Alaska <http://fin.admin. state.ak.us/dof/checkbook_online>, Missouri <http://mapyourtaxes.mo.gov>, and Oklahoma <http://www.ok.gov/okaa> maintain websites that let citizens search through expenditure data by agency, budget category, or contractor (Perlman, 2009). Internationally, countries like Russia, South Africa, and Thailand use online budgeting in a similar manner to inform citizens of past budgetary decisions (Krylova, 2007; Shall, 2007; Suwanmala, 2007). However in Brazil, a country with a history of participatory budgeting that allows direct citizen involvement in the budget process, citizens use e-government budget websites to input their demands for certain projects (Wampler, 2007). In this manner, citizens can directly control certain aspects of governmental expenditures.

Unfortunately, the examples listed above are not typical of most e-government websites since online budget transparency is often marginalized on most e-government websites today. Even though the budget is one of the key documents produced by government, studies on e-government indicate that budget homepages often perform poorly in providing information and services (West, 2005, p. 68). Important budget documents and information on budget processes are not consistently posted online despite the assumption that electronic access could facilitate transparency and accountability (Perlman, 2009). The challenge is successfully integrating budget information into the e-government setting. A positive transformation between citizen and government should occur

if governments can use e-government to increase budget transparency and citizen participation in the process. Previous studies found some evidence for this type of effect. For instance, Tolbert & Mossberger (2006) concluded that governmental websites and their use by citizens can increase their trust in government. Benito and Bastida (2009) also discovered that when the budget is more transparent, policymakers make better budgeting decisions and citizens expand their participation in government activities. In addition, as Parker (1968) cautioned years before, fiscal problems only grow in complexity and citizens "need help to understand the issues (p. 129)."

When integrated with budget transparency, e-government can support the democratic role of citizens and ensure greater citizen participation in the budget process and thus more accountability over budgetary decisions. This is therefore one of the most meaningful uses of e-government websites: citizen participation. For example, some federal agencies have added e-rulemaking to their websites. This allows citizens to access the agency's website, input their comments on draft agency rules, and monitor how those comments influenced the final rules promulgated by the agency (Schulman, 2005). E-rulemaking makes it easier for citizens to participate in the governmental rule-making process. In addition, state agencies in New York are now required to webcast public meetings so that citizens can view them and hopefully participate in deliberations at the next meeting (Dawes, 2008).

To be sure, expanding citizen participation in this way faces significant challenges. Expense is one of the major challenges confronting any government attempting to promote citizen participation. The cost of encouraging citizen participation can even potentially take needed resources from policy implementation and impair programs (Irvin & Stansbury, 2004). This question of cost becomes magnified when considered against what is actually accomplished due to citizen participation. Some authors show that citizen input during city council meetings and school board meetings does not directly influence policy decisions made by the governing body. Yet, these minimal efforts give citizens an opportunity to send information to officials, network with other citizens, and set future agendas (Adams, 2004). This means that many types of citizen participation efforts, such as public meetings, may function more as a political tool for citizens rather than as a tool for deliberative democracy. In addition, researchers have discovered online citizen participation efforts might actually make participation more exclusive rather than inclusive (Rethemeyer, 2006). Perhaps because of these challenges, research on e-government and citizen participation reveals that governmental websites often lack adequate mechanisms to support public involvement (Scott, 2006).

For online citizen participation efforts to truly consider citizen input, governments may have to engage in innovative participation strategies, spend more resources, and change existing organizational cultures. Once implemented, such efforts often have immediate benefits for the community as citizens amplify their knowledge of government and increase their trust with governmental officials (Berman, 1997; Bland & Rubin, 1997; Kathlene & Martin, 1991; Webler & Tuler, 2000). While citizen participation is often hard to implement, a case can be made that it is necessary; especially if governments are to reach the transformative stage of interactive democracy via e-government.

As mentioned previously, governments desiring to reach this transformative stage of interactive democracy via e-government have a number of hurdles to overcome. Many of these hurdles will be politically based since some policymakers may not want to encourage democratic participation and deliberation through a website. It could potentially reduce the influence of personality-based efforts that many politicians prize as a means to stay relevant in public affairs. Many of the hurdles will also be financial. In an era of cutbacks, policymakers may deemphasize the importance of expanding governmental websites in this way

simply because of financial constraints. However, the most significant hurdle to citizen participation may well be transparency, particularly about the budget. How can governments make their public budget more accessible online in order to give citizens the information they need to participate in interactive democracy?

The answer is not by providing volumes of inconsistent and generalized budgetary information in newer, technically complex homepages. Rather, the answer is by providing a template for budget information that can be used on any type of e-government website: from billboards to interactive online database. Practitioners and scholars alike need this template to help achieve not just greater budget transparency, but the promise of better democracy. Implicit in this kind of template is the view that budget transparency on e-government websites is a primary component of citizen participation. If governments make budgeting more transparent, then budgetary decision makers should benefit from greater feedback, increased citizen trust on government, and a greater degree of civic involvement. Over time, this could lead to the interactive democracy transformation that scholars discuss.

MAIN FOCUS OF THE CHAPTER

The greatest problems in integrating budget transparency into e-government websites to promote citizen participation are maintaining citizen interest and promoting citizen understanding. Perhaps due to the time constraints of modern society, most citizens seemingly do not value online citizen engagement (Vigoda-Gadot, 2007). For example, most citizens seemingly do not notice or care about budget transparency especially when considering measures of budgetary performance that should help them better understand budgetary outcomes (Lynn Jr., Heinrich, & Hill, 2000; Swindell & Kelly, 2000). And when governments design innovative budgeting websites to increase citizen participation, the results are usually disappointing with no discernable increase in citizen interest or participation in the budget process (Walters, 2009).

The digital divide also remains a significant problem. Regardless of the time and money spent on enhancing an e-government website, many citizens still face significant hurdles accessing the internet (Norris, 2001; Mossberger, Tolbert, & Stansbury, 2003). An even greater concern for the future is that the pace of technology advancement now occurs so rapidly that incorporating new technological features on a governmental website can make e-government confusing for those unfamiliar with the new technology. Due to this, a different type of digital divide may be occurring where citizens access an e-government website so overloaded with information, services, and newer online tools for access, that they cannot understand anything on the website (Mossberger, Tolbert, & Stansbury, 2003).

This type of digital divide is especially pertinent in the world of budgeting. When confronted with budgetary information such as certified annual financial statements (CAFRs), statements of net assets, or even an executive budgeting proposal on an e-government website, most citizens either do not have the expertise to sift through the information in those documents or do not want to spend the time to sift through that information. As a result, governments may have to use e-government to re-categorize specific budgetary information into packets and formats that citizens can understand and quickly access. At a basic level, this revision occurs by viewing budgeting as consisting of two broad categories: the *budget process* and *budget outcomes* (Colorado Fiscal Policy Institute, 2003; Greitens, Joaquin, Bernick, & Gatti, 2009; GFOA, 1998, 2000). The budget process refers to the established system of making budgetary decisions. This includes decisions by the executive and their budget office, the legislature, and even the public on which expenditures to fund and which revenues to raise (Rubin, 2006). Through the use of budget hearings, budget summits, and legal deadlines on budget preparation and submission, the budget process structures the activities of policymakers and the public regarding public budgeting decisions. Making the budget process electronically transparent allows citizens to participate in government decision-making.

Governments can make the budget process transparent on e-government websites beginning with an explanation of how the budget process works and how public monies are collected and spent (Colorado Fiscal Policy Institute, 2003; Greitens, Joaquin, Bernick, & Gatti, 2009; GFOA, 1998, 2000). To help in this task, they can publish a primer on the budget process that explains the statutorily defined roles of the executive and the legislature. They can also publish a frequently asked questions (FAQ) section that explains budgeting terminology or processes. But perhaps most importantly, they can publish information on legislative budget hearings. Legislative budget hearings represent the point where citizens can become directly involved in the budget process. At these hearings agencies, interest groups, and citizens testify before the legislature regarding the most pressing budgetary matters, from revenue increases to expenditure cuts. Governments can therefore use e-government to better publicize this information so that a greater number of citizens know beforehand when budget hearings occur and how they can testify or submit some sort of comment to the budget hearings. Typically, e-government websites do this by using a calendar system indicating when future budget hearings occur, publishing a PDF document of the budget hearing proceeding, and/or actually showing the budget hearings in audio or video streaming format.

Budget outcomes are more tangible. They refer to the revenues collected by government, and expenditures made by government. This information is available in the final budget document passed by government. Consequently, most e-government websites show budget outcomes by just publicizing a PDF of the final, enacted budget document.

However, budgetary outcomes can also be shown using financial statements, audit results, or even performance results (for those governments that utilize performance based budgeting). Additionally, within the last few years, governments are constructing searchable online databases of budget outcomes that allow the public to search for specific revenue and expenditure decisions by geographic area, agency, and other specific search parameters (Perlman, 2009).

Thus, our template for online budget transparency includes a budget process category and a budget outcome category. In the budget process category, e-government websites should use budget FAQs/glossaries, budget process primers, budget calendars, and have online access to the proceedings of budget hearings. And perhaps most importantly for the world of e-government, that information should be easy to find. So, there should be some link on the e-government homepage that can easily direct the citizen to budget information. In the budget outcome category, e-government websites should have some presentation of the government budget that shows revenue and expenditure decisions. Ideally, this type of budget data should be presented in a way that is easy for citizens to understand.

For a basic analysis of these categories of online budget transparency, we examined state government websites in the United States. We developed a limited coding protocol based on budgetary process information and budgetary outcome information. Utilizing previous research on the topic (Colorado Fiscal Policy Institute, 2003; Greitens, Joaquin, Bernick, & Gatti, 2009; GFOA, 1998, 2000), we constructed a five-question, nominal-level protocol for process information (see Table 1).

We also examined budgetary outcomes. We assumed that most state government websites would have some presentation of budgetary outcomes, usually in the form of the proposed or enacted budget on the budget homepage. Rather than examine what specific types of outcomes

Table 1. Online budget transparency variables

Budget Process
i. Does the government have budget information on its home page?
ii. Is a current budget calendar present?
iii. Is a primer on the budget process present?
iv. Is a budget glossary or FAQ present?
v. Are the proceedings of the budget hearings accessible online?
Budget Outcomes
i. How are budgetary outcomes presented?
- No information on budget outcomes
- PDF billboards
- Hyperlinked sections
- Online Database

were reported, we simply examined the actual presentation of those outcomes. Building on the evolutionary approach to governmental websites promoted by West (2005), we constructed an ordinal-based question that determined how budgetary outcomes were presented. Responses to that question could range from no budgetary outcome information present, to budgetary outcome information presented in a billboard website with no hyperlinked sections (e.g., usually a PDF scan of the proposed or enacted budget), to budgetary outcome information divided by hyperlinked sections (e.g., hyperlinked sections for departments or for specific revenues or expenditures), to an online searchable database of budgetary outcomes that allows the citizen to obtain search results for specific budgetary inquiries (e.g., how much Department X spent on salary). Using this approach, we examined the 50 state government websites from January through February 2009.

Table 2 shows our findings. We report the number and percentage of states with budget process information on their websites categorized by how the website presented budgetary outcome information. Our coding of the 50 state government websites revealed a number of interesting findings. First, when considering all the states we find that on average, they do a poor job of making the proceedings of budget hearings accessible online. For example, when all states are considered, only

Table 2. Number of states with budget process variables categorized by presentation of budgetary outcomes (with state percentages in parentheses)

States' Presentation of Budgetary Outcomes	Sample (n)	Home Page Link	Calendar	Budget Primer	Budget FAQ	Budget Hearings
No Information	5	0 (0.00%)	0 (0.00%)	0 (0.00%)	0 (0.00%)	0 (0.00%)
PDF Billboard	28	7 (25.00%)	14 (50.00%)	7 (25.00%)	16 (57.14%)	1 (3.57%)
Hyperlinked	13	8 (61.54%)	6 (46.15%)	5 (38.46%)	4 (30.77%)	3 (23.08%)
Online Database	4	2 (50.00%)	1 (25.00%)	3 (75.00%)	3 (75.00%)	2 (50.00%)
All States	*50*	*17 (34.00%)*	*21 (42.00%)*	*15 (30.00%)*	*23 (46.00%)*	*6 (12.00%)*

Table 3. Online budget transparency template (citizen participation elements correspond to online budget elements that e-government websites should adopt to ensure online budget transparency)

	Citizen Participation Element	Online Budget Element
Budget Process	Effective Information Dispersal Hearings Administrative Support Administrative Benevolence Authentic Citizen Participation	*Link to budgeting information on governmental homepage* *Use some type of budget calendar that advertizes budget hearings well in advance* *Put a budget process primer and a budget FAQ or glossary* *Put a budget process primer and a budget FAQ or glossary* *Online access to the proceedings of the budget hearing*
Budget Outcomes	Issue Pertinence	*Show some representation of the budget document*

six states (or 12% of all the states) make their budget hearings accessible online. On average, the states did a better job on the other process questions, indicating that many states put some type of budget information on their homepage, utilize a budget calendar on their websites, and place a budget primer and a budget FAQ on their sites. However, the results from these other questions are still somewhat disappointing. With the total number of states displaying each process variable below 50.00%, our results indicate that a majority of states are not incorporating process-based budgeting information on their e-government websites.

The results are better for budgetary outcomes. We find that only five states did not have any information regarding budgetary outcomes. The other 45 states all had budgetary outcomes on their websites but presented that information in different ways. For instance, 28 states present budgetary outcomes in PDF-billboard types of websites. That is, they just publish a PDF scan of either the executive's budget proposal or the final enacted budget. 13 states present budgetary outcomes in hyperlinked sections that divide budgetary outcomes by hyperlinked sections increased usability. Four states present budgetary outcomes in online, searchable databases.

When we categorize state government websites by their presentation of budgetary outcomes and then compare percentages for the budget process questions some interesting findings emerge. For one, we find that state government websites that present their budgetary outcomes in more sophisticated ways (moving from a PDF billboard presentation to an online database presentation), have an increase in some types of budgetary process information. That is, as state websites increase in sophistication from PDF billboards to online databases there are greater average scores for the home page link question, the budget primer question, and the budget hearings question. Generally, this indicates that states with increasing sophistication in the presentation of their budgetary outcomes are more likely to have a link to budgetary information directly on the state homepage, a budget primer that helps to explain the budget process, and budget hearings that are accessible in print, audio, or video format.

However, a different type of relationship is observed between the presentation of budgetary outcomes and other types of budgetary process information. State websites that increase in sophistication from PDF billboards to online database have lower scores for the calendar variable and the budget FAQ variable. For the calendar variable, 14 of the 28 states with PDF billboard websites (or 50.00% of the states with PDF billboard websites) had a budget calendar while only one of the four states with an online database website (or 25.00% of the states with an online database website) had a budget calendar on their website. This means that on average, state government websites with increasing levels of sophistication in the presentation of their budgetary outcomes have less information on budget calendars when compared to simpler state government websites. For the budget FAQ variable, 16 of the 28 states with a PDF billboard website (or 57.14% of the states with PDF billboard websites) had a budget glossary/budget FAQ present, four of the 13 states with hyperlinked websites (or 30.77% of the states with hyperlinked websites) had a budget glossary/ budget FAQ present, and three of the four states with online database websites (or 75.00% of the states with online database websites) had a budget glossary/budget FAQ present.

Because of sample size concerns (e.g., there are only four states with a searchable, online database of budgetary outcomes), determined conclusions from this analysis are difficult. Perhaps the most important finding is that, on average, state government websites are doing a poor job of integrating all types of budget process information onto their websites at a time when demand for information is increasingly met by bloggers, watchdogs, and non-governmental entities. Percentages from all states consistently revealed that budget process

information is not accessible on a majority of state websites. In addition, when states increase the sophistication of their presentation of budgetary outcomes it does not automatically translate into greater budget transparency since certain types of budget process information are often not included. As a result, citizens may have a way to search through budgetary outcomes, but have trouble interpreting those outcomes (since no budget FAQ or glossary exists) and have no idea when budget hearings occur (since budget calendars are often missing from these more sophisticated websites). This may help to explain why citizens do not express more interest in budgetary matters.

SOLUTIONS AND RECOMMENDATIONS

To help meet this challenge, we suggest that governments follow two basic steps when integrating budgetary information onto an e-government website. First, governments should realize that online budget transparency consists of two important components: budget process and budget outcomes. Our results indicate that state government websites are focused too much on budgetary outcomes, inhibiting understanding of what brought about those outcomes in the first place. For example, while no standard list of "best practices" exists for putting budget information online, save for a few recommendations by the GFOA, bureaucrats and scholars generally feel that online budget information succeeds when it is comprehensive in nature, frequently updated, focused on expenditures, and made freely available to the public (Organization for Economic Co-operation and Development, 2001; Perlman, 2009). This often results in citizens easily viewing some presentation of budgetary outcomes on a governmental website, but because there is typically a lack of process-based information, citizens may not comprehend outcome information or learn how they can participate in the budget process. Governments with more sophisticated websites with searchable online databases should be especially aware of this as our results also give some indication that increasing sophistication may come at the expense of putting some types of process-based information online.

In addition, we suggest that governments start assessing the integration of budget information onto e-government websites in terms of the characteristics of successful citizen participation efforts. While each citizen participation effort is unique, certain common characteristics or elements for successful efforts exist. For e-government endeavors related to budget transparency, six fundamental elements seem especially pertinent. The first is effective communication with citizens. This element requires governments to publicize information about pertinent policy issues such as budgetary revisions, committee or council hearing times, and minutes from meetings. In our basic template, this element is represented by the process category and is best exemplified by having a link to budgetary information on the homepage.

The second element is the use of hearings. Generally, hearings are used to elicit public comment regarding proposed legislation or administrative action (Checkoway & Van Til, 1978). Citizens and interest groups can go to these hearings and offer input on the issue at hand. Administrators and/or policymakers then consider that input when they make their final decision. While the effectiveness of hearings on policymaking is always in question (Cole & Caputo, 1984), it is important that citizens and interest groups know of important budgetary hearings as funding decisions can easily affect several policy issues at once that directly influence citizens' lives. Even though the use of secretive budget summits may be eroding the value of open budget hearings (Rubin, 2006), we strongly advocate openness as a fundamental value in the world of budgeting. In our basic template, this element is represented by the process category and could include having a budget calendar on the website to alert citizens of hearings ahead of time and by

making the proceedings of the budget hearings accessible online.

Administrative support from the government must also occur for citizen participation efforts to succeed. Specifically, officials must take any input gleaned from citizens seriously, and actively use the information in the decision-making calculus (Daniels, 1999). Such "buy in" can be hard to develop within an administration. After all, citizen input is often uncontrollable and can produce much uncertainty within an organization over policy development (Lando, 2003). In addition, some administrators feel that input from citizens cannot even be realistically incorporated into decision-making (Callahan, 2000). In our template, this element is represented in the process category and could include an e-government website having a budget primer and a budget FAQ or glossary present on the e-government website because governments that buy in to the concept of citizen participation in budgeting would want to educate citizens on how the process works. Without this level of education, citizens would not be able to participate meaningfully.

The next elements are closely related. Benevolence, or the idea of implementing policies that are best for the citizens, is the fourth element of successful citizen participation. By actively soliciting input from citizens, policymakers are able to make decisions that are more efficient, economic, and equitable (Frederickson, 1997). Without the benevolence construct, narrow interests that do not reflect the true will of a community's public can commandeer the citizen participation process. Such a scenario could theoretically lead to residents protesting a policy decision or even residents leaving a particular community. The fifth element is assuring that "authentic citizen participation" occurs. This requires the government to develop within the entire community the capacity to participate and provide input. As a result, the citizen participation process is not just controlled by a subset of a community or by a few interested groups (Foley, 1998). This element ensures that citizens are actively engaged in the policy debate and that a culture of deliberation results in the community (Box & Sagen, 1998). Previous researchers have also identified this element as "fairness" when attempting to craft a theory of public participation (Webler & Tuler, 2000). The final element of successful citizen participation is pertinence. For citizen participation to be successful at this level, citizens must feel that the issue is important to their lives. Many citizens feel this way about budget issues. Ultimately, budget issues can influence population size (especially at the local level of government), economic strength, and the welfare of individual citizens. This makes budget issues among the most important policies impacting citizens.

These final elements are represented in our template in the outcome and process categories. By providing online access to the proceedings of the budget hearing and having a budget primer and a budget FAQ or glossary present on the e-government website, governments show that they want to educate citizens on how the budget process works. Without this level of education, meaningful involvement would not occur. And with some presentation of budgetary outcomes, citizens can theoretically view final budget decisions to determine the impact of their participation efforts.

When considered altogether, these citizen participation elements help structure our basic template on online budget transparency. Note that many of these elements are complementary. For instance, ensuring that authentic citizen participation occurs can be the sign of a benevolent administration. Likewise, an administration that buys in to a citizen participation effort can become a benevolent administration if the effort reflects criteria of efficiency and equitability. Yet, following these elements can be difficult. This is especially true in light of the expense of constructing online budgeting efforts and the question of what exactly is accomplished with such efforts.

FUTURE RESEARCH DIRECTIONS

One weakness to our approach is that it is very basic. Yet our findings suggest that at this point in the world of online budget transparency, such a basic approach is needed. State governments have seemingly emphasized the presentation of budgetary outcomes over the presentation of the budgetary process. This has left citizens in the dark regarding public budgeting. However, by following the basic template outlined in this chapter, governments can take the first step toward making budgeting more transparent. Once that is achieved, more specific templates can be devised regarding which types of budgeting information to present online and how to present that information on the e-government website.

For instance, future researchers can discuss openness of government contracting (for services and goods) and ways to make public expenditures on contracts more transparent on websites. In addition, further studies could analyze the types of financial documents that should form part of a budget website (e.g., legislative appropriations, executive budget proposals, enacted budgets, financial statements, audits, etc.) and how to integrate those different types of documents on an e-government website. While many of those documents currently exist on e-government websites, they are often not integrated on one budget homepage, their relationships to one another are often unexplained, and their usefulness to inform citizen feedback remains a task that government has seemingly not yet fully considered. Thus, here we advocate a sort of double-loop learning (Argyris & Schon, 1974) wherein an organization – in this case a local or higher level of government - does not merely provide information but feedback is designed and employed to improve the provision of pertinent knowledge to citizens. Only by initiating steps to open up budgeting through electronic government could agencies learn how best to make their websites more useful to both government and the public's purposes.

Future researchers may also suggest ways of using technology to change the process – and consequently, the outcomes - of budgeting. Much as bureaucratic rulemaking now often has an e-rulemaking component, we look forward to a new era of e-budgeting wherein citizens can download real-time information, submit online comments, or directly testify at budget hearings via an e-government website, and then receive periodic updates via information and communication technology tools on the status of the budget. As experience accumulates, both government and citizens will learn which avenues work and which do not work. The process of participation, and ultimately budgetary decision making through the use of e-government will likely evolve over time and hopefully generate better outcomes for citizens. These types of changes help lead e-government toward a future of interactive democracy.

CONCLUSION

In this chapter we provided a basic template that governments can use to better integrate budget transparency into their e-government websites. The template divides online budgetary information into two general types: budget process information and budgetary outcome information. Budget process information includes descriptions on how the budget process works, how citizens can become involved in that process, and definitions that allow citizens to better understand budgeting. Budgetary outcome information includes descriptions of how the government spent public monies and collected public revenues. Budgetary outcome information typically includes budget documents as well as certain types of financial statutes or audits.

Using this basic template on state government websites, we discovered that while most state governments do integrate budgetary outcome information into their e-government websites, many of them do not integrate budget process information. In fact, some of our results indicate that governments that increase the sophistication of their presentation of budgetary outcomes, from PDF billboard presentations to searchable online databases, sometimes have even less process-based information when compared to governments that do not increase the sophistication of the presentation of their budgetary outcomes. This disjuncture between process and outcomes may help explain why many citizen engagement efforts over the budget fail.

To help solve this problem, we suggest that governments treat citizen participation as an integral element of online budgetary endeavors. Incorporating traditional citizen participation concepts such as effective information dispersal, hearings, administrative support, administrative benevolence, authentic citizen participation, and issue pertinence into a basic template provides a way for governments to evaluate online budget transparency and provide more value for citizens wanting to become a part of the budgeting process.

REFERENCES

Adams, B. (2004). Public meetings and the democratic process. *Public Administration Review, 64*(1), 43–54. doi:10.1111/j.1540-6210.2004.00345.x

American Recovery and Reinvestment Act of 2009. (2009). Pub. L. No. 115-5, Section 901, 123 Stat. 115.

Argyris, C., & Schön, D. (1978). *Organizational learning: A theory of action perspective*. Reading, MA: Addison Wesley.

Benito, B., & Bastida, F. (2009). Budget transparency, fiscal performance, and political turnout: An international approach. *Public Administration Review, 69*(3), 403–417. doi:10.1111/j.1540-6210.2009.01988.x

Berman, E. (1997). Dealing with cynical citizens. *Public Administration Review, 57*(2), 105–112. doi:10.2307/977058

Berner, M. (2001). Citizen participation in local government budgeting. *Popular Government,* (Spring): 23–30.

Bland, R., & Rubin, I. (1997). *Budgeting: A guide for local governments.* Washington, DC: International City/County Management Association.

Box, R., & Sagen, D. (1998). Working with citizens: Breaking down barriers to citizen self-governance . In King, C., & Stivers, C. (Eds.), *Government is us: Public administration in an anti-government era* (pp. 158–172). Thousand Oaks, CA: Sage Publications, Inc.

Callahan, K. (2000). Citizen participation run amok. *Public Productivity and Management Review, 23*(3), 394–398. doi:10.2307/3380727

Checkoway, B., & Van Til, J. (1978). What do we know about citizen participation? A selective review of research . In Langton, S. (Ed.), *Citizen participation in America* (pp. 25–42). Lexington, MA: Lexington Books.

Cole, R., & Caputo, D. (1984). The public hearing as an effective citizen participation mechanism: A case study of the general revenue sharing program. *The American Political Science Review, 78*(2), 404–416. doi:10.2307/1963372

Colorado Fiscal Policy Institute. (2003). *The transparency of Colorado's budget process: Is it open, understandable, and accessible to Coloradans? Prepared by J. Zelenski, October.* Denver, CO: Colorado Center on Law and Policy.

Coursey, D., & Norris, D. (2008). Models of e-government: Are they correct? An empirical assessment. *Public Administration Review, 68*(3), 523–536. doi:10.1111/j.1540-6210.2008.00888.x

Daniels, T. (1999). *When city and county collide: Managing growth in the metropolitan fringe.* Washington, DC: Island Press.

Dawes, S. (2008). The evolution and continuing challenges of e-governance. *Public Administration Review, 68,* 86–102.

Foley, D. (1998). We want your input: Dilemmas of citizen participation . In King, C., & Stivers, C. (Eds.), *Government is us: Public administration in an anti-government era* (pp. 140–156). Thousand Oaks, CA: Sage Publications, Inc.

Frederickson, H. G. (1997). *The spirit of public administration.* San Francisco, CA: Jossey-Bass Inc., Publishers.

Garson, G. D. (2006). *Public information technology and e-governance: Managing the virtual state.* Sudbury, MA: Jones and Bartlett Publishers.

Government Finance Officers Association (GFOA). (1998). *Recommended budget practices.* Chicago, IL.

Greitens, T. J., Joaquin, M. E., Bernick, E. L., & Gatti, J. (2009). *Political culture and online access to state and county budgets.* Paper presented at the Annual Conference of the American Society for Public Administration. March. Miami, Florida.

Ho, A. T. (2002). Reinventing local government and the e-government initiative. *Public Administration Review, 62,* 434–444. doi:10.1111/0033-3352.00197

Irvin, R., & Stansbury, J. (2004). Citizen participation in decision making: Is it worth the effort? *Public Administration Review, 64*(1), 55–65. doi:10.1111/j.1540-6210.2004.00346.x

Kathlene, L., & Martin, J. (1991). Enhancing citizen participation: Panel designs, perspectives, and policy formation. *Journal of Policy Analysis and Management, 10*(1), 46–63. doi:10.2307/3325512

Krylova, E. (2007). Russia: Civic participation in subnational budgeting . In Shah, A. (Ed.), *Participatory budgeting* (pp. 67–90). Washington, DC: The World Bank.

Lando, T. (2003). The public hearing process: A tool for citizen participation, or a path toward citizen alienation. *National Civic Review, 93*(1), 73–82. doi:10.1002/ncr.7

Lynn, L. Jr, Heinrich, C., & Hill, C. (2000). Studying governance and public management: Challenges and prospects. *Journal of Public Administration: Research and Theory, 10*(2), 233–261.

Mossberger, K., Tolbert, C., & Stansbury, M. (2003). *Virtual inequality: Beyond the digital divide*. Washington, DC: Georgetown University Press.

Norris, P. (2001). *Digital divide: Civic engagement, information poverty, and the internet worldwide*. NY: Cambridge University Press.

Organisation for Economic Co-operation and Development. (2001). OECD best practices for budget transparency. *OECD Journal on Budgeting, 1*(3), 7–14. doi:10.1787/budget-v1-art14-en

Parker, A. (1968). Government finances and citizen responsibility. *The Annals of the American Academy of Political and Social Science, 379*, 123–131. doi:10.1177/000271626837900114

Perlman, E. (2009). See thru government: When it comes to spending taxpayer dollars, how much transparency is enough? *Governing*, (May): 34–37.

Rethemeyer, R. (2006). Policymaking in the age of the internet: Is the internet tending to make policy networks more or less inclusive? *Journal of Public Administration: Research and Theory, 17*(2), 259–284. doi:10.1093/jopart/mul001

Rubin, I. (2006). *The politics of public budgeting: Getting and spending, borrowing and balancing* (5th ed.). Washington, DC: CQ Press.

Schulman, S. W. (2005). E-rulemaking: Issues in current research and practice. *International Journal of Public Administration, 28*, 621–641. doi:10.1081/PAD-200064221

Scott, J. K. (2006). "E" the people: Do U. S. municipal government web sites support public involvement? *Public Administration Review, 66*(3), 341–353. doi:10.1111/j.1540-6210.2006.00593.x

Shall, A. (2007). South Africa: Citizen participation in local government policy making and budget processes . In Shah, A. (Ed.), *Participatory budgeting* (pp. 91–126). Washington, DC: The World Bank.

Suwanmala, C. (2007). Thailand: Civic participation in subnational budgeting . In Shah, A. (Ed.), *Participatory budgeting* (pp. 127–154). Washington, DC: The World Bank.

Swindell, D., & Kelly, J. (2000). Linking citizen satisfaction data to performance measures: A preliminary evaluation. *Public Productivity and Management Review, 24*(1), 30–52.

Tolbert, C. J., & Mossberger, K. (2006). The effects of E-government on trust and confidence in government. *Public Administration Review, 66*(3), 354–369. doi:10.1111/j.1540-6210.2006.00594.x

United Nations and American Society of Public Administration. (2002). *Benchmarking e-government: A global perspective assessing the UN member states*. Washington, DC: American Society for Public Administration and the United Nations.

Vigoda-Gadot, E. (2007). Revitalizing democracy? New avenues for citizen participation in the era of information technology. *Public Administration Review, 67*(4), 789–791. doi:10.1111/j.1540-6210.2007.00763.x

Walters, J. (2009, April 1). O citizen, where art thou? Getting public input into the budget writing process sounds easier than it is. *Governing*. Retrieved June 20, 2009, from http://www.governing.com/article/o-citizen-where-art-thou

Wampler, B. (2007). *Participatory budgeting in Brazil: Contestation, cooperation, and accountability*. University Park, PA: Pennsylvania State University Press.

Webler, T., & Tuler, S. (2000). Fairness and competence in citizen participation: Theoretical reflections from a case study. *Administration & Society, 32*(5), 566–595. doi:10.1177/00953990022019588

West, D. M. (2005). *Digital government: Technology and public sector performance*. Princeton, NJ: Princeton University Press.

Chapter 19
Achieving Transparency in State Lottery Websites

Charles E. Menifield
University of Memphis, USA

Joy A. Clay
University of Memphis, USA

ABSTRACT

Accountability, ethics, and transparency are buzz words that have permeated politics and administration over the decade, becoming increasingly prominent as political and business scandals have been occurring far too frequently. Given democratic need for an informed public and the need to build public trust, achieving transparency continues to grow as an important dimension of effective governance. We developed a model that assesses the level of transparency in government web sites. The model contains three constructs, Policy, Management, and Information, which are subsequently applied to five southern state lottery web sites. We chose this policy arena for two reasons. First, the number of state lotteries has increased over time due to declining revenue streams and citizen dissatisfaction with increasing taxes. Second, fungibility issues have been raised as general fund contributions to education budgets have made only marginal increases despite large sums of lottery funds. Our analysis reveals that states that began using the lottery in more recent years learned from the mistakes that occurred in earlier years. As a result, web site development in the latter years was more transparent and suggests the likelihood that not only do programs become similar as administrators learn from the experiences of others but administrative expectations of transparency are integrated in the adopted programmatic design.

INTRODUCTION

Transparency is a fundamental concept for professionals involved in financial reporting. Accounting standards require that reported financial information be transparent, that is, the profession expects reported financial numbers to be clear and accurate, assumptions explained, timeframes internally logical and consistent, etc. (Bennis, Goleman, & O'Toole, 2008). Reacting to the highly visible failure of WorldCom and Enron, pressure on the private sector for better transparency of

DOI: 10.4018/978-1-61692-018-0.ch019

financial performance has grown as corporate leaders recognize the damage to public trust when executives obfuscate, collude, or lie about financial performance. Reacting to decades long bashing of government performance, professional associations, such as the International City/County Management Association (ICMA), Governmental Accounting Standards Board (GASB), Government Finance Officers Association (GFOA), National Performance Review (NPR) and American Society for Public Administration (ASPA) are similarly exerting pressure on the public sector to improve financial and performance reporting quality (Piotrowski, 2007).

Although very important, high quality and transparent financial reporting is but one aspect of public accountability. In a web site devoted to transparency, the site argues convincingly that:

transparency is far more than the obligation to disclose basic financial information. People and institutions that interact with firms are gaining unprecedented access to all sorts of information about corporate behavior, operations, and performance. Armed with new tools to find information about matters that affect their interests, stakeholders now scrutinize the firm as never before. (www. ageoftransparency.com)

Moreover, Tapscott and Ticoll in their popular book, *The Naked Corporation* (2003), argue that achieving transparency, that is, acting ethically and being open and truthful, is an opportunity for organizations to succeed and thrive. From a similar perspective, we argue that effective democratic governance in today's fast-paced, high tech world requires that government actions, policies, and decisions all must become significantly more transparent. As governments have been working to better report on performance (financial, productivity, and outcomes), e-government is making it easier for agencies to use technology to make this information more readily accessible as well as much more interactive.[1] Increased access to information about government actions can "broaden the base of political participation" and be customized to individual citizen interests (Zinkhan, DeLorme, Peters, & Watson, 2007, p. 367) as well as give an edge in global market competition (Relly & Sabharwal, 2009). However, Garson argues that "all the hardware, network connections, and computer competence in the world will mean little if the government is not able and willing to provide electronic information in a usable form (2006, p. 119).

The emergent challenge for public administrators is in determining what is required to become transparent, both from the perspective of 1) substance, type and content of public information, and 2) technology, structure and procedures that make the information readily available to the public (Oliver, 2004; Blanton, 2007). The continuing challenge is to not only sustain but to improve upon the transparency level achieved as the agency and its programs evolve and technology advances.

The objective of this chapter is to not only make a convincing argument for greater transparency in government but to help public officials and administrators proactively and systematically think about transparency features as they engage in e-government and design systems and processes. We apply the E-Transparency model, composed of the policy, management and information architectures, to the gaming industry in five southern states, analyzing the information available on their official web sites. We anticipate that the model can be easily replicated to other policy arenas and are conducting research to test the model's replicability.[2]

The chapter begins by first examining research literature on state lotteries in the United States. Second, we provide a rationale for our research by discussing the underpinning and foundation of the E-Transparency model through an examination of relevant literature. In the next sections of the chapter, we discuss the data and methods and examine the details of each of the five states we consider and then provide the analysis and results of the study. Lastly, the final section provides conclusions and recommendations as well as offering potential directions for future research.

BACKGROUND ON STATE LOTTERIES

From a policy accountability perspective, researchers have questioned: whether state lotteries act as an implicit regressive tax (Clotfelter and Cook, 1987; Hansen, Miyazki, & Sprott, 2000; Pirog-Good and Mikesell, 1995; Price & Novak, 2000; Price & Novak, 1999; Borg & Mason, 1990; Brinner & Clotfelter, 1975), anticipated net revenues actually occur (Davis, Filer, & Moak 1992); how the lottery structure affects demand and revenue (Vrooman, 1976); lottery revenue earmarked for education actually results in positive effects on education expenditures (Spindler, 1995; Dee, 2004; Campbell, 2003; Land & Alsikafi, 1999; Stanley & French, 2003; Miller & Pierce, 1997; McCrary & Condrey, 2003) or lottery revenues become more of a legislative "shell game" (Perlman, 1998; Allen, 1991); and whether the states' purported purpose to maximize revenue occurs, especially over time (Garrett, 2001; Laschober, 1989; Mikesell, 1994; Mikesell & Zorn, 1986; Mikesell & Zorn, 1988; McCrary & Condrey, 2003). This important body of research addresses important political and economic issues. However, programmatic-level accountability of state lottery program administration, processes and procedures, has received limited research attention.

Currently, 43 states and the District of Columbia, U.S. Virgin Islands and Puerto Rico operate a state lottery. The number of states cashing in on this industry has snowballed over the last ten years. Given the size of the monetary windfall that fiscally-challenged states have experienced from implementing successful gaming venues, the reasonable moral challenge to the notion of government supported gambling, and the tension between the need for an unfettered, profit-maximizing administrative apparatus with an expectation of sound oversight of a government monopoly, complex questions of policy, program, performance, process, and legality accountability (www.seagov.org) are raised.

Rather than market forces driving legalized gambling, the National Gambling Commission argues that "the shape and operation of legalized gambling has been largely a product of government decisions and that this is most obvious for state lotteries "where governments have not just sanctioned gambling but have become its enthusiastic purveyors, legislating themselves an envied monopoly . . ." (National Gambling Impact Study Commission Report, 1999, p. 1-4). Criticizing the lack of federal action and coordination among governments, the Commission noted that "rivalry and competition for investment and revenues have been far more common factors in government decision making regarding gambling than have any impulses toward joint planning" (National Gambling Impact Study Commission Report, 1999, pp. 1-5). At the same time, the Commission noted that states faced resistance to tax increases while citizens demanded more or improved services so that revenues from legalized gambling were viewed "as a relatively painless method" to increase state coffers (National Gambling, 1999, pp. 1-5). Thus, the adoption process of state lottery programs has led to researchers identifying it as a mix of diffusion and state characteristics (Nelson & Mason, 2003-04).

LITERATURE REVIEW

Information technology (IT) and electronic government in the United States has grown tremendously since the federal government instituted initiatives during the Clinton and Obama administrations to establish and improve online service systems and the dissemination of electronic information.[3] Moon (2002) suggests that this dramatic growth is viewed not only as improving efficiencies but has helped to overcome barriers to providing government services (2002, 424). Similar growth has likewise been witnessed in other populous countries such as China, India and the United Kingdom (Relly & Sabharwal, 2009; La Porte et al., 2002). Thus, electronic government has opened up many opportunities for improving the quality of public service and service delivery to citizens. Concomitantly, the literature in this arena has grown dramatically since the internet began in 1992. Hence, rather than look at the IT and e-government literature in general, we focus attention on research that specifically examines the growth of e-government and web site evaluations.

The Growth of E-Government

Karen Layne and Jungwoo Lee (2001) developed one of the earliest models outlining the developmental growth process of e-government. The Layne and Lee four stage model includes: Catalogue, Transaction, Vertical Integration, and Horizontal Integration. As one moves from one stage to the next, the level of complexity in the web site increases since it includes all of the services in the lower levels as well as new services. Cataloging (stage 1), in simple terms, involves presenting information about government activities on the web. Since communications occur in one direction, transactions are not possible in this stage. In stage two, Transaction, citizens can transact business directly with the government. Transactions would include activities such as paying fines and renewing driver's licenses. The level of desirability by the public for such functions are viewed as offering positive benefits, improved access, information and procedural knowledge, coordination, and use of staff time (Stowers, 1999; Moon, 2002). Clearly, well-developed e-government can be an effective and efficient mechanism for government and warrants continued consideration.

Vertical Integration, stage three, is the ability of a user to use a web site to connect with local, state and federal governments from one web site. For example, once a person is married and the records are sent to the local court house, the records could then be sent to the state as well as to a national database. Horizontal Integration, stage four, is defined as, "integration across different functions and services" (p. 125). For instance, a local business person would be able to go online and pay his/her sales tax receipts to the state and at the same time conduct other financial transactions with other state agencies because each of them communicate with each other and work from the same database systems. This four-stage model captures an important dynamic of e-government, fluidity and evolution, faced by decision-makers as they allocate resources to advancing their e-government attributes.

Hiller and Belanger (2001) offer a similar staged-model, but their model is based on the premise of growth with respect to the major types of e-government relationships. Relationship one involves the government establishing and maintaining a relationship in order to deliver a service or benefit. For example, a citizen may request information on a government program. Relationship two links the government to individuals concerning the political process. This would include items such as voting online for a referendum or an elected official. The third relationship is between the government and business such as where businesses can directly pay taxes online. The fourth relationship is government to business in the market place and is particularly true for procurement-related processes. The fifth relationship is between governments and employees. This would include the provision of the intranet for employee information. The final relationship is government to government where government agencies must work in partnership and provide information and services to each other. The collaborative efforts of the sub units under the Department of Homeland Security provide an ideal example of this final type of relationship described by Hiller and Belanger.

Moon (2002) also framed web site development as progressive. Using ICMA data, Moon examines the use of e-government in U.S. municipalities, applying a five stage framework. At the early stage, a city may simply use a web site as a one-way communication tool where as in stages 4 and 5 the city uses the web site for financial transactions as well as a mechanism for consumer registration. The research findings suggest that the size of a municipality and type of government are significant factors in the implementation and development of electronic government. That is, larger governments are more likely to advance e-government. Moon also found that many local governments use web sites to post information or to provide a mechanism for two-way communication. In fact, most web sites fell into stage 1 or 2. Last, he found that a lack of technical personnel and financial capacities is a major barrier to e-government development.

Web Site Examination

As the research literature has grown in sophistication, a natural progression from examining the maturation of a web site is to evaluate web site content and quality. This body of literature provides a variety of frameworks and models that allow for cross comparisons, assessment of the breadth and depth of content, and level of interactivity.

One of the earliest studies examining web sites was conducted by Genie N. L. Stowers (1999). Using content analysis, Stowers examined state and local (cities over 100,000) government web sites with the objective of identifying the current level and type of public sector activities. In her analysis, she used 103 variables with dichotomous responses (64 information and service and 39 policy development questions). For the vast majority, state and local government web sites provided basic information (branches of government, health/human services, tourism, email addresses, etc.). From a policy perspective, she

found that most states (80%) posted proposed policies on their web site while only 42% of local governments used their web site for this purpose. Last, very few states and local governments used their web sites to enhance or promote policy discussion or to seek voter input or approval. West (2001) conducted a similar study of web sites for the seventy largest cities in the U.S. The research noted an increase in the amount of information available on the web sites over time in general and particularly with respect to executable online services. Requesting services and information, paying traffic fines, and filing complaints were the most commonly used services.

Also using content analysis, Kaylor and colleagues (2001) examined web site development in U.S. cities by creating an e-score barometer which allows the user to compare one city's online presence to another city. The model used a twelve key attribute rubric that allowed the user to compare cities based on the functions and services provided. For example, can users pay their taxes online, apply for a business license, communicate directly with an agency, and participate in online polls. Undoubtedly, content analysis has served as a model to build foundational knowledge of e-government attributes.

A recent study by Ho (2002) links the evolutionary literature with content analysis. Ho focuses more on the later stages of the Layne and Lee (2001) model. Using content and survey methods, Ho found that larger cities have a greater propensity to engage in vertical and horizontal interactions. Thus, the new direction for web site development is to focus on coordinated network building, external collaboration and customer service. However, the move towards this "new e-government paradigm" is not without problems. Ho notes that insufficient staff, lack of funding, and the problem of the digital divide among the races has hindered efforts.

La Porte and colleagues (2002) examine "governmental openness" in their cross-country analysis. That is, "the extent to which an organization provides comprehensive information about its attributes and maintains timely communications with its various publics" using a web site (p. 415). Using the WAES methodology[4] the authors use two models to assess the impact of web site usage around the world at the country level. The *transparency model* is based on five sub elements: Ownership, who manages the web site; Contact Information, the level of contact between the user and persons within the organization; Organizational or Operational Information, the level of information about the organization's operations and ties to other related organizations; Citizen Consequences, "elements that defines what the organization requires of a citizen to comply with regulations or laws," etc.; and Freshness, the extent to which the web site is updated.

The *interactivity model* uses a four pronged approach. The first factor is Ownership, the use of a clickable email address; Reachability, ability to contact staff inside the organization; Organizational or Operational Information, availability of organization information on the web site; and Response, extent of interaction between the user and the organization. Although, La Porte and his colleagues (2002) use the model to test their hypothesis, we are primarily interested in the development of their model. They found that empirical factors such as national income, central government expenditures, cultural values, etc. were not the best indicators of openness, but organizational behavior regardless of these other factors seem to best describe openness.

Finally, Reddick (2004) conducted a comprehensive assessment of the level of growth in e-government in U.S. cities. Using data from the 2002 ICMA electronic government survey, the data revealed that 76% of the cities that responded had a web site and were at least in stage 1 of e-government growth. Users were capable of communicating with elected and appointed and elected officials at a high rate, but the ability to pay taxes online, utility bills, etc. was less than 5%. Hence, the stage 2 (transactions) level of advancement

was fairly low in on-line requests for services. However, 56% of the web sites allowed forms to be downloaded for manual completion. Reddick found that the development of government to business relationships was mixed in terms of reviewing product offerings online and purchasing property, equipment or supplies online.

To facilitate accessing the research literature, Table 1 provides the factors commonly evaluated by researchers with respect to web site analysis and evaluation. It should be noted that these factors are not equal in nature. As Moon (2002) points out, web site development occurs in stages and the level of sophistication increases as governments advance in stages. With this maturation, Verdegem and Verleye (2009) also make a convincing argument for a more user-centered paradigm that should drive the next stages of advancement of e-government strategies. The Layne and Lee Model described earlier in the chapter provides the organizing framework for the web site variables in Table 1.

DEVELOPING AN E-TRANSPARENCY MODEL

As previously noted, it is the objective of this chapter to create a transparency model that can be applied to various types of government web sites. This idea emanated from concern about the lack of government transparency in general and the growing demand by the public to be informed about policy actions. By applying the model to state lottery web sites, the model highlights the key components of web site design and serves as a structured inquiry to assess stakeholders' information interests about policy and program implementation. In sum, we recommend that as government programs are designed and implemented officials should purposefully set goals about desired transparency levels. Thus, mechanisms that facilitate transparency should be examined systematically and adopted if the

Table 1. Commonly evaluated web site variables by Layne and Lee's stages of development

Stage 1 Cataloguing	
Information Dissemination	Stowers 1999; Moon 2002; Thomas and Streib 2003; Eschenfelder 2004; Welch, Hinnant and Moon 2004; Reddick 2004; Gathegi 2005
Web Site Ownership	La Porte et al. 2002; Eschenfelder 2004
Web Site Format	La Porte et al. 2002; Eschenfelder 2004
Contact Information	La Porte et al. 2002; Moon 2002; Welch, Hinnant and Moon 2004; Reddick 2004; Cuillier and Piotrowski 2009
Online Databases	Stowers 1999
Stage 2 Transaction	
Organization of Information	Stowers 1999; La Porte et al. 2002; Reddick 2004
Reachability	Hiller and Belanger 2001; La Porte et al. 2002
Interactive Forms	Stowers 1999; La Porte et al. 2002; Reddick 2004
Two-Way Communication	Stowers 1999; Hiller and Belanger 2001; Moon 2002; Welch, Hinnant and Moon 2004
Service and Financial Transaction	Hiller and Belanger 2001; Moon 2002; Thomas and Streib 2003; Reddick 2004
Political Participation	Stowers 1999; Moon 2002; Thomas and Streib 2003
Stage 3 & 4 Vertical and Horizontal Integration	
Vertical and Horizontal Integration	Hiller and Belanger 2001; Moon 2002; Ho 2002; Reddick 2004; Kim, Kim, & Lee 2009

administrative burden is feasible and reasonable.

The issues raised by the Tennessee Comptroller and in the research literature on state lotteries were used to help develop the questions of interest for the policy and administrative components. Research conducted by Stowers (1999; 2002; 2004), West (2004), La Porte, Demchak, and Weare (2005) and Garson (2006) on e-government helped us to identify questions of interest regarding the policy and information architecture. As government leaders attend to lottery competition across states (Nelson & Mason, 2003-2004), we hypothesize that there is a transfer of knowledge and innovation within a region as state lottery program officials adopt best practices and conduct comparative benchmarking. Thus, we anticipate that we will find similarity in the information architectures, but more variation in the policy and administrative (management) architectures.

As Stowers convincingly argues, "Governments are clearly becoming "cyberactive" but are emphasizing information and services for business and other economic development activities rather than dissemination of policy information, encouraging policy discussions, or delivering public services" (1999, p.111). Examination of the information available on a state lottery program's policy architecture should provide insights into the degree of transparency of important policy information, that is, the implementation context. Examination of the information about the management architecture of a state lottery program's management architecture should provide insights into the degree of transparency of important managerial processes and procedures. Finally, examination of the information architecture should provide insights into how effectively a state lottery program disseminates information and enables access to important program information. The bottom line question is: What information about a state lottery's program is readily available by citizens, researchers, students, and other interested publics to learn about the state's program? If the governance goal is to achieve a climate of openness, candor, ethical behavior, public program leaders must not only attend to operational needs and demands but also the expectation of transparency, an important component of accountability.

THE FOUNDATION OF E-TRANSPARENCY

To test our construct of E-Transparency, we examine five southern state lottery programs. From a research methodology perspective, state lotteries offer a public program that is clearly defined and not overly complex. As a government monopoly with huge revenues and expenses, an expectation of transparency appears highly reasonable. Unlike most government programs, state lotteries have a bottom line and consequently have clear financial reporting expectations. Although lotteries may vary in the details from state to state, overall they have similar attributes and face the same policy and management pressures. And, finally, this high dollar, and very visible public program would seem on its face to justify examination.

As the most recent adopter of a state lottery, Tennessee presents the opportunity to examine what policy architecture and management architecture insights a late adopter gains and whether they benefit from lessons learned. Early in 2003, the Comptroller of the Treasury issued an extensive report, "Building Tennessee's Lottery: Considerations for Policymakers." The methodology used by the Comptroller's staff was multi-pronged and extensive. The study included:

1. "A review of peer-reviewed research on the management and impact of state lotteries;
2. analysis of data from currently operating state lotteries;
3. a review of state laws and regulations governing state lotteries in other states;
4. a survey of active state lotteries;
5. a review of audits of active state lotteries;
6. interviews with lottery administrators and auditors in other states" (2003, p. 1).

Recognizing the importance of clear directives and instructions by policymakers (Patton and Sawicki, 1986), the Tennessee Comptroller's report argues that the legislature should clarify policy choices and write these goals into statute. The report authors suggest that these policy choices will affect the policy outcomes of the state lottery and recommend that the state legislature deliberate upon the following policy issues:

1. Profit maximization
2. Meeting existing demand
3. Reducing lottery regressivity
4. Minimizing compulsive gambling
5. Minimizing underage playing

The policy choices presented by the comptroller recognize the tension between establishing effective external controls with the need to allow sufficient freedom for the lottery to succeed, that is, maximize profit. This can be seen in the discussion of establishing formal limits on marketing and administrative overhead expenses versus the need for lottery administrators to be able to respond to market dynamics; the need to exempt the lottery corporation from existing state contract laws (learning from Florida's experience when lax bid protest requirements resulted in lost revenue), but to require formal contracting procedures approved by the Department of Finance and Administration and/or Office of the Comptroller (to assure a level of check and balance); exempt the lottery program from some or all of personnel laws to allow for commissions and bonuses and to allow for timely termination of ineffective employees; allow the corporation to participate in multi-jurisdictional games (this would reduce regressivity since it broadens player base); establish penalties for retailers who sell tickets without requiring a valid ID; and to check lottery winners for delinquent child support payments prior to prize distribution.

Figure 1. E-transparency model

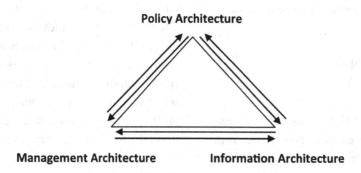

Policy Architecture

Management Architecture   **Information Architecture**

The Three Legs of E-Transparency

We propose a three-legged program construct, using three separate but linked programmatic components: *policy, management, and information architectures*[5] to examine transparency. The first leg of the construct is *policy architecture*, the statutory and policy decisions and framework that guide program implementation choices and decisions. The second component of the model is *management architecture*, the managerial processes and procedures created to manage and control public programs. The third and final program component is the agency's *information architecture,* the structure/technology that provides access to program data and information and facilitates communication with program officials. Using these three respective constructs, we can examine the degree of programmatic transparency.

As shown in Figure 1, these three constructs are separate and dynamic, but operate within a feedback system. If one program component changes, it is likely to have a ripple affect on the remaining two components. This process essentially serves as a check on the system.

DATA AND METHODOLOGY

Initially, we developed a list of question for each leg of the transparency model. The questions were developed based on information gleaned from available literature, the policies in place for lottery implementation, and an evaluation of numerous state lottery web sites. In developing our model, we determined that it is possible for a gaming institution to achieve a degree of transparency at any one level of the architecture while not doing so at another level. Unless indicated otherwise, all of our data come directly from each state's lottery web site, email contact with lottery officials, and through readily available paper documents.

Each of the questions used in the model uses a dichotomous variable.[6] The variable was assigned a score of 1 or 0 with a 1 indicating the presence of the attribute and a 0 indicating the absence of the attribute. The policy architecture has 15 questions addressing two attribute areas (enabling statute and program attributes). The management architecture contains 30 questions covering seven different attribute areas that Gulick (1987) uses in his managerial activities model (planning, organizing, staffing, directing, coordinating, reporting, and budget and finance). Last, the information architecture contains 31 questions covering five attribute areas (site structure, information access, dialogue and/or inquiry, user features to benchmark,[7] and style and presentation). Therefore, the highest possible score that a state can achieve is 76 indicating that they were perfect in each of the three categories. Hence, each level of our models operates as a standalone unit. That is, a state can be completely transparent at one level and lack transparency in the other two levels. The analysis of the web sites was conducted during the summer of 2007. The complete list of questions used in our model appears in the appendix.

In order to be completely transparent, we posit that government officials must achieve transparency in all three program components. We argue that a sophisticated and stylish agency web site that has minimal policy information is simply a marketing tool. The existence of detailed programmatic and evaluative reports is of limited use unless stakeholders can readily access them. Knowledge of policy decisions without linkage to actual managerial actions/processes provides an incomplete picture of actual program implementation and performance. Thus, all three program components require transparency in order for the government program to be transparent. Without transparency, the ability of the public to independently examine program quality and performance is seriously jeopardized. Thus, without achieving transparency, program accountability is genuinely deficient.

The next section provides detailed information concerning each of the five states that we examined in our model. More specifically, we elaborate on the legal procedures used to create the state lottery, the purpose of the lottery, and the entity created to oversee the administration of the lottery.

Five Southeastern States' Lottery Programs

Florida: Florida voters approved a constitutional amendment authorizing a state lottery in 1986. Thus, of the five state lotteries studied, the Florida lottery has the longest history. Ticket sales began in January 1988 and the first week's ticket sales exceeded $95 million (www.flalottery.com/lottery/faq/history.shtml). The Florida Public Education Lottery Act established the Department of the Lottery as a state agency and set two purposes

for the lottery, to generate revenue for education and to have the "best" lottery games available. Originally, the enabling statute established a State Lottery Commission composed of five members appointed by the Governor with private sector perspective to provide oversight of the program. The Commission, however, was abolished by the legislature in 2001 ("Reaching for the Sky: Florida Lottery, 2000-2001 Annual Report" (2001) (www.flalottery.com/lottery/faq/history.shtml).

Georgia: Georgia voters approved a constitutional amendment in November 1992 authorizing a state lottery. The Georgia Lottery for Education Act established the Georgia Lottery Corporation to operate and manage the state lottery program. Eight months after enactment (June 1993), the first lottery tickets were sold (Lauth and Robbins 2002; www.lotteryinsider.com; www.galottery.com). Clearly, the program was in high customer demand as sales in the first two days reached $18.6 million (www.galottery.com). The lottery's product mix includes a variety of ticket formats, including instant and on-line products. Although the Georgia lottery is one of the youngest of the five state lottery programs with sales in 2003, this lottery program has been very successful in generating over $300 billion in funds for the Hope Scholarship education program.

Net lottery proceeds are held in a separate account for education purposes with the General Assembly determining the purposes and amounts in accordance with the statutory requirement that the net proceeds are used for improvements and enhancements, not for supplanting existing educational resources. Georgia Code requires that at least 45% of actual lottery sales be made available for prizes (as of June 2003, 54.3%) and that that net proceeds be at least 35%; 13.1 cents of each dollar of total income was used for operating expenses with 33.3 cents for HOPE financial aid (www.galottery.com). Net proceeds must be transferred quarterly. Also, Georgia Code requires two restricted reserve funds to provide contingency funding in case of any program deficiencies, specifically a scholarship shortfall reserve and a general shortfall reserve. The unrestricted reserve is available for appropriation by the General Assembly.

Kentucky: In a November 1988 referendum, Kentucky voters approved a state lottery. The legislature, in special session, established the Kentucky Lottery Corporation as a quasi-governmental organization. The enabling legislation sets two goals for the corporation: the lottery is to be managed so that citizen benefit from the profits and enjoy the best possible games. Six months later (April 1989), the first tickets were sold. By statute the Corporation is overseen by a seven-member board of directors who are appointed by the Governor with confirmation by the state senate. The State Treasurer is a voting member of the Board.

The state legislature exerts oversight through several legislative committees and the program is audited annually by an independent firm. As a result of the 1993 audit, sweeping changes were made by the Kentucky lottery in management personnel and management practices (www.naspl.org). Lottery profits are used to support college grants, childhood reading and adult literacy programs, and the general fund (www.kylottery.com).

Louisiana: In October 1990, voters approved a constitutional amendment to establish a state lottery. The first ticket sales occurred on September 6, 1991. The legislature established a corporation to manage the program with the governor, state legislature, and legislative auditor having oversight. The Governor appoints a nine-member Board to oversee the Corporation with senate confirmation. The State Treasurer serves as an ex-officio non-voting member of the board.

According to the lottery web site, less than ten percent of sales are used for administrative overhead (www.louisianalottery.com).

Tennessee: After a 3 year unsuccessful drive for a state lottery, Tennessee citizens voted to remove the state constitutional prohibition in November 2002. The constitutional amendment only allows the General Assembly to use lottery profits to fund college loans and scholarships, capital outlays for K-12 education facilities, and early learning and after school programs (Constitution of the State of Tennessee, Article XI, Section 5). The amendment explicitly authorizes a lottery of the type such as in Georgia, Kentucky, and Virginia (of interest, these are all contiguous states). The legislation was signed by the Governor on June 11, 2003 (www.lotteryinsider.com). By statute, the state allowed for the creation of a corporation, requiring it to be known as the Tennessee Education Lottery Corporation. The June 2004 lottery report indicated sales of $427,686,000. In 2006, they reported ticket sales of $995,845,000.

By statute, the corporation is required to submit quarterly and annual reports to the governor, general assembly, treasurer and comptroller of the treasury. The corporation is subject to an annual audit by the state comptroller.

ANALYSIS AND RESULTS

Table 2 provides a summary of each states gaming commission information. The table shows that Florida has the largest number of staff employed by the lottery commission at 466. Georgia and Kentucky follow with 257 and 201 respectively. Tennessee (166) and Louisiana (145) have the smallest number of staff. Each of the state lotteries: is run by a non state agency with the exception of Florida; has a governing board; and is audited internally by the state auditor. Last, Florida and Kentucky uses a private firm for external audits, while the remaining states uses state employees.

The third table contains descriptive information relative to legislative issues. Although the data shows that only two states allocate lottery proceeds to education, all of the states in the study use a substantial proportion of these proceeds for educational purposes. Florida contributes the largest percentage of lottery proceeds to the designated location at 39%. Kentucky and Tennessee are the lowest at 27%. All of the states have statutory

Table 2. Gaming commission information

	Number of Staff	Type of Bureaucratic Structure	Governing Board and Member	Lottery Run by State Agency	Internal Audit Structure	External Audit Structure
Florida	466	Agency	FLC (5)*	Yes	State Auditor	Private
Georgia	257	QPC	GLC (7)	No	State Auditor	State
Kentucky	201	QPC	KLC (7)	No	State Auditor	Private
Louisiana	145	QPC	LLC (9)	No	State Auditor	State
Tennessee	166	QPC	TLC (6)	No	State Auditor	State

*Abolished in 2001

Table 3. Legislative information

	Designated Location for Lottery Proceeds	% of Lottery Fund used for Administrative Cost	% of Lottery Funds used For Designated Fund
Florida	Education	11%	39%
Georgia	General Fund/GA Treas.	13	33
Kentucky	General Fund	7.3	27
Louisiana	General Fund	10	35
Tennessee	Education	1.6	27
	Statutory Spending Controls in Place	Have Statutes Been Modified From Original Form?	
Florida	Yes	Yes	
Georgia	Yes	Yes	
Kentucky	Yes	Yes	
Louisiana	Yes	Yes	
Tennessee	Yes	Yes	

limits in place for spending and have modified the original statutes.

The results of the transparency analysis are found in Table 4. The data shows that Louisiana has the highest policy architecture score (12), followed by Tennessee (11) and Georgia (8). Florida and Kentucky have the lowest scores (6). The difference in these scores lies in the enabling statute questions. That is, can the user find the original legislation creating the lottery as well as the statutes that followed? This information was not available on the Florida and Kentucky web sites.

The data for the management architecture reveals that Louisiana has the highest score (22), followed by Georgia (21) and Tennessee (20).

Again, Kentucky (10) and Florida (8) have the lowest scores. States that received lower scores in this architecture were the result of a lack of information in the areas of budgeting and finance, coordinating, and staffing procedures.

The data for the information architecture shows that Louisiana has the highest score (26). Tennessee, Georgia, and Florida are in a distinct secondary group with scores of 20, 19, and 18 respectively. The greatest difference in scores was the presence or lack of attributes in the site structure and information access categories. Louisiana's lottery web site excelled in both information access and user features.

Table 4. State lottery web sites transparency scores

	FL	GA	KY	LA	TN
1. *Policy Architecture*					
Enabling	0	2	0	3	2
Program	6	6	6	9	9
Sub Total	6/15	8/15	6/15	12/15	11/15
2. *Management Architecture*					
Planning	3	4	3	4	4
Organizing	1	4	0	3	2
Staffing	0	2	0	2	2
Directing	1	3	3	3	3
Coordinating	0	2	0	3	2
Reporting	3	5	4	5	5
Budgeting and Finance	0	1	0	2	2
Sub Total	8/30	21/30	10/30	22/30	20/30
3. *Information Architecture*					
Site Structure	0	2	0	2	2
Information Access	6	6	2	8	5
Dialogue	4	3	3	4	3
User Features	7	6	5	10	8
Style	1	2	1	2	2
Sub Total	18/31	19/31	11/31	26/31	20/31
Raw Total	**32/76**	**48/76**	**27/76**	**60/76**	**51/76**
Percentage Total	**42%**	**63%**	**36%**	**79%**	**67%**

Overall, Louisiana had the highest transparency score (79%) and finished first in each of the three categories. Tennessee had a score of 67% and finished no worse than second in each of the architectures. Georgia (63%) rounded out the second tier, and Florida (42%) and Kentucky (36%) were in the last tier.

CONCLUSION AND RECOMMENDATIONS

State lottery performance and programmatic accountability warrant attention. It would seem especially sensible to investigate the policy outcomes of what many view as a morally-questionable program, that is, government sponsored and sanctioned gambling. Already serving to help researchers better understand program dissemination across states, state lotteries also offer a practical insights into e-government progression as they are a revenue-generating, business-oriented public program and realistically can be held to generally accepted business operating and accounting principles. Hopefully, the research examining the transparency of state lottery programs in the South and other states will continue to provide insights into important public administration questions: Do states learn best policy architecture and administrative practices from the states that preceded them? Is there diffusion of administrative practice across programs? Are later adopters instituting internal and external controls to avoid mistakes experienced in earlier state programs?

The transparency of program performance and outcomes should be a high priority for government officials and program leaders. As Holzer and his colleagues suggest "ill-managed governmental operations and wasteful spending make people less likely to believe government is trustworthy" (Holzer, Hu, Kang, & Zhang 2003, p. 23).

Our analysis provides some clarity to the above questions. First, our data suggests that states that formed lotteries more recently scored higher in the transparency model, suggesting that mistakes made earlier were avoided. This also suggests that states do in fact seek out best practices in order to streamline the process. The state lottery in Louisiana began in 1990, after Florida and Kentucky and before Georgia and Tennessee. The state had the highest transparency score using our model. In fact, the state's lottery web page had the highest score in each of the three architectures. Tennessee and Georgia rounded out the top three respectively. Despite the fact that each of the states used in our analysis display a lot of the same administrative and legislative procedures, it does not translate to the same level of transparency.

We do not argue that the questions used in our model cover every single aspect of transparency. However, we would argue that it provides a model that others can use as a beginning point in an understudied field. State gaming institutions that achieve high levels of accountability are more likely to withstand the scrutiny of external and internal evaluations at every level. The study also only examined five state lotteries. Although justified by the focus on how states learn from each other, the small size of the study sample also limits generalizability. Consequently, follow up research is needed to test the full impact of the model's power.

FUTURE RESEARCH DIRECTIONS

The possible use of technology in improving government service appears to have no end. How-ever, despite the wide spread use of technology, the future of transparency is uncertain. This is complicated by the vagaries of both citizens and governments. First, a large number of citizens do not know how to react to this new generation of technology when called upon to make choices. That is, they all too often become aware of "what to ask for" when a scandal occurs. Hence, it is difficult to design, redesign, and improve upon technology relative to transparency to suit citizen needs and public service expectations when the evolution of e-government is inherently fluid in nature and dependent on resource priorities. Second, politicians appear to be equally bound. How much information to disclose to the public is sufficient and how do we determine this moving target? This seemingly basic question demonstrates the challenge faced by governments as they balance information access with the cost of transparency. Agency administrators also are vulnerable to grounding decisions more on self-serving criteria rather than providing full citizen access to policy information (that is, protecting image over fullness of information).

Further, evidence suggests that a large number of the entities that we want/need policy information from lobby Congress and state legislatures not to require disclosure. The fact that Congress still debates how to improve corporate financial disclosure is one such example. Other recent examples include labeling foods with caloric and nutritional information, labeling drugs with clear side effects, and openly discussing war tactics. In the first two examples it took years for proponents to successfully get Congress to authorize improvements in food product labeling. With respect to war tactics we are still waiting for the final answer and will likely wait for some time. Further, continued research attention to the ethical implications of the revolution in information technology is warranted. Citizens are concerned about threats to privacy and data security. Although vertical and horizontal integration may bring access and other benefits, such integration can also be viewed as potentially intrusive and threatening (Zinkhan, DeLorme, Peters, & Watson, 2007). Attention to transparency offers an important lens for systematically thinking through the potential for harm as e-government progresses and evolves.

Nonetheless, the level of transparency in government is improving but more research is needed to better understand the competing values that push for and pull against transparency, to develop explicit and clear models to guide administrative decisions on transparency, and to measure the actual effect upon perception and realized accountability. We also need to better understand how internal agency dynamics, political-administration relations, and staff perceptions affect e-government evolution. Since we are only in the early-mid stages of progression of the information age in terms of improving policies and service, future research offers the promise of a fuller and richer understanding about the impact of technology on citizens. That is, specific research questions that should be of interest include: how effective are transparency policies in disseminating information to citizens? What kinds of information have priority? Does increased and improved interactivity of policy information enhance government legitimacy and citizen satisfaction and trust? And, more specifically, how do laws on transparency compare with other regulatory tools and do these formal requirements show a pattern from one state to another and one sector to another or from one policy arena to another?

REFERENCES

Bennis, W., Goleman, D., & O'Toole, J. (2008). *Transparency: How leaders create a culture of candor*. San Francisco, CA: Jossey Bass.

Blanton, T. (2007). The Struggle for openness in the international financial institutions. In Florini, A. (Ed.), *The right to know: Transparency in an open world* (pp. 243–276). New York, NY: Columbia University Press.

Borg, M. O., & Mason, P. M. (1990). Earmarked lottery revenues: Positive windfalls or concealed redistribution mechanisms? *Journal of Education Finance, 15*, 289–301.

Brinner, R. E., & Clotfelter, C. T. (1975). An economic appraisal of state lotteries. *National Tax Journal, 28*(4), 395–404.

Campbell, N. D. (2003). Do lottery funds increase educational expenditure? Evidence from Georgia's lottery for education. *Journal of Education Finance, 28*, 383–402.

Clotfelter, C. T., & Cook, P. J. (1987). Implicit tax in lottery finance. *National Tax Journal, 40*, 533–546.

Cuillier, D., & Piotrowski, S. J. (2009). Internet information-seeking and its relation to support for access to government records. *Government Information Quarterly, 26*, 441–449. doi:10.1016/j.giq.2009.03.001

Davis, J. R., Filer, J. E., & Moak, D. L. (1992). The lottery as an alternative source of state revenue. *Atlantic Economic Journal, 20*, 1–10. doi:10.1007/BF02298871

Dee, T. S. (2004). Lotteries, litigation and education finance. *Southern Economic Journal, 70*, 584–599. doi:10.2307/4135332

Eschenfelder, K. R. (2004). Behind the web site: An inside look at the production of web-based textual government information. *Government Information Quarterly, 21*, 337–358. doi:10.1016/j.giq.2004.04.004

Garrett, T. A. (2001). The Leviathan lottery? Testing the revenue maximization objective of state lotteries as evidence for Leviathan. *Public Choice, 109*, 101–117. doi:10.1023/A:1012081307920

Garson, G. D. (2006). *Public information technology and E-Governance: Managing the virtual state*. Sudbury, MA: Jones and Bartlett.

Gathegi, J. N. (2005). Democracy through access to legal information for newly democratizing nations: The Kenyan perspective and lessons from the American experience. *Government Information Quarterly, 22,* 108–121. doi:10.1016/j.giq.2004.10.004

Gulick, L. (1987). Notes on the theory of organizations . In Shafritz, J. M., & Ott, J. S. (Eds.), *Classics of organizational theory* (pp. 87–97). Pacific Grove, CA: Brooks/Cole.

Hansen, A., Miyazaki, A. D., & Sprott, D. E. (2000). The tax incidence of lotteries: Evidence from five states. *The Journal of Consumer Affairs, 34,* 182–203.

Hiller, J. S., & Belanger, F. (2001). *Privacy strategies for electronic government. E-Government Series*. Arlington, VA: PricewaterhouseCoopers Endowment for the Business of Government.

Ho, A. T. (2002). Reinventing local government and the e-government initiative. *Public Administration Review, 62*(4), 434–444. doi:10.1111/0033-3352.00197

Holzer, M., Hu, L.-T., Kang, Y. C., & Zhang, M. (2003, March). *Trust, performance and the pressures for productivity in the public sector*. Paper presented at the annual meeting of the American Society for Public Administration, Washington, D.C.

Kaylor, C., Deshazo, R., & Eck, D. V. (2001). Gauging e-government: A report on implementing services among American cities. *Government Information Quarterly, 18,* 293–307. doi:10.1016/S0740-624X(01)00089-2

Kim, S., Kim, H. J., & Lee, J. (2009). An institutional analysis of an e-government system for anti-corruption: The case of OPEN. *Government Information Quarterly, 26,* 42–50. doi:10.1016/j.giq.2008.09.002

La Porte, T. M., Demchak, C. C., & Jong, M. D. (2002). Democracy and bureaucracy in the age of the web: Empirical findings and theoretical speculations. *Administration & Society, 34,* 411–446. doi:10.1177/0095399702034004004

La Porte, T. M., Demchak, C. C., & Weare, C. (2005). Governance in the era of the world wide web: An assessment of organizational openness and government effectiveness, 1997-2001 . In Garson, G. D. (Ed.), *Handbook of public information systems*. Boca Raton, FL: Taylor and Francis.

Land, V. Q., & Alsikafi, M. H. (1999). A lottery's impact on instructional and noninstructional expenditures and unrestricted revenues for education. *Journal of Education Finance, 25,* 149–174.

Laschober, M. A. (1989). Is the Illinois state lottery a winning ticket for the state? A financial overview. *Illinois Business Review, 46,* 3–8.

Lauth, T. P., & Robbins, M. D. (2002). The Georgia lottery and state appropriations for education: Substitution or additional funding? *Public Budgeting & Finance, 22,* 89–100. doi:10.1111/1540-5850.00082

Layne, K., & Lee, J. (2001). Developing fully functional e-government: A four stage model. *Government Information Quarterly, 18,* 122–136. doi:10.1016/S0740-624X(01)00066-1

Mazmanian, D. A., & Sabatier, P. A. (1983). *Implementation and public policy*. Glenview, IL: Scott Foresman.

McCrary, J., & Condrey, S. E. (2003). The Georgia lottery: Assessing its administrative, economic, and political effects. *Review of Policy Research, 20,* 691–711. doi:10.1046/j.1541-1338.2003.00047.x

Mikesell, J. L. (1994). State lottery sales and economic activity. *National Tax Journal, 47*(1), 165–171.

Mikesell, J. L., & Zorn, C. K. (1986). State lotteries as fiscal savior or fiscal fraud. *Public Administration Review, 46*(4), 311–320. doi:10.2307/976304

Mikesell, J. L., & Zorn, C. K. (1988). State lotteries for public revenue. *Public Budgeting & Finance, 8*, 38–47. doi:10.1111/1540-5850.00772

Miller, D. E., & Pierce, P. A. (1997). Lotteries for education: Windfall or hoax? *State and Local Government Review, 29*(1), 34–42.

Moon, J. M. (2002). The evolution of e-government among municipalities: Rhetoric or Reality. *Public Administration Review, 62*(4), 424–433. doi:10.1111/0033-3352.00196

National Gambling Impact Study Commission Report. (1999). *National Gambling Impact Study Commission Report* Retrieved from http://govinfo.library.unt.edu/ngisc/index.html

Nelson, M., & Mason, J. L. (2003-2004). The politics of gambling in the South. *Political Science Quarterly, 118*(4), 645–669.

O'Toole, L. J. Jr. (2000). Research on policy implementation: Assessment and prospects. *Journal of Public Administration: Research and Theory, 10*(2), 263–288.

Oliver, R. W. (2004). *What is transparency?* New York: McGraw Hill.

Patton, C. V., & Sawicki, D. S. (1986). *Basic methods of policy analysis and planning*. Englewood Cliffs, NJ: Prentice Hall.

Perlman, E. (1998). The game of mystery bucks. *Governing, 11*, 20.

Piotrowski, S. J. (2007). *Governmental transparency in the path of administrative reform*. Albany, NY: SUNY Press.

Pirog-Good, M., & Mikesell, J. L. (1995). Longitudinal evidence of the changing socio-economic profile of a state lottery market. *Policy Studies Journal: the Journal of the Policy Studies Organization, 23*, 451–465. doi:10.1111/j.1541-0072.1995.tb00523.x

Price, D. I., & Novak, E. S. (1999). The tax incidence of three Texas lottery games: Regressivity, race, and education. *National Tax Journal, 52*, 741–751.

Price, D. I., & Novak, E. S. (2000). The income redistribution effects of Texas state lottery games. *Public Finance Review, 28*, 82–92. doi:10.1177/109114210002800105

Reddick, C. G. (2004). A two-stage model of e-government growth; Theories and empirical evidence for U.S. cities. *Government Information Quarterly, 21*, 51–64. doi:10.1016/j.giq.2003.11.004

Relly, J. E., & Sabharwal, M. (2009). Perceptions of transparency of government policymaking: A cross-national study. *Government Information Quarterly, 26*, 148–157. doi:10.1016/j.giq.2008.04.002

Spindler, C. J. (1995). The lottery and education: Robbing Peter to pay Paul. *Public Budgeting & Finance, 15*, 54–61. doi:10.1111/1540-5850.01046

Stanley, R. E., & French, P. E. (2003). Can students truly benefit from state lotteries: A look at lottery expenditures towards education in the American states. *Social Science Quarterly, 40*, 327–333.

Stowers, G. N. L. (1999). Becoming cyberactive: State and local governments on the world wide web. *Government Information Quarterly, 16*(2), 111–127. doi:10.1016/S0740-624X(99)80003-3

Stowers, G. N. L. (2002). *The state of federal web sites: The pursuit of excellence*. Washington, D.C.: Center for the Business of Government.

Stowers, G. N. L. (2004). *Measuring the performance of E-government*. Washington, D.C.: Center for the Business of Government.

Tapscott, D., & Ticoll, D. (2003). *The naked corporation: How the age of transparency will revolutionalize business*. New York, NY: Free Press.

Verdegem, P., & Verleye, G. (2009). User-centered e-government in practice: A comprehensive model for measuring user satisfaction. *Government Information Quarterly, 26*, 487–497. doi:10.1016/j.giq.2009.03.005

Vrooman, D. J. (1976). An economic analysis of the New York State lottery. *National Tax Journal, 29*(4), 482–489.

Welch, E. W., Hinnant, C. C., & Moon, M. J. (2004). Linking citizen satisfaction with e-government and trust in government. *Journal of Public Administration: Research and Theory, 15*(3), 371–391. doi:10.1093/jopart/mui021

West, D. M. (2004). *Assessing E-government: The internet, democracy and service delivery*. Providence, Rhode Island: Brown University.

Zinkhan, G. M., DeLorme, D. E., Peters, C. O., & Watson, R. T. (2007). Information sources and government research: Ethical conflicts and solutions. *Public Integrity, 9*(4), 363–376. doi:10.2753/PIN1099-9922090404

ENDNOTES

[1] Increasingly governments not only have program information, but direct services readily available and accessible on agency and jurisdictional web sites (West 2004; Stowers 2002; Stowers 2004).

[2] La Porte et al. (2005) used an empirical model to examine organizational openness in different countries based on the WAES methodology. The main components of the WAES model are: Ownership, Contact Information, Organizational or Operational Information, Issue Information, Citizen Consequences, Privacy and Security, Reachability, and Responsiveness. See also La Porte, Chris C. Demchak and Christopher Weare 2005. "Governance in the Era of the World Wide Web: An Assessment of Organizational Openness and Government Effectiveness, 1997-2001." In the *Handbook of Public Information Systems*. 2nd Edition. Edited by G. David Garson. Taylor and Francis: Boca Raton, FL.

[3] Clinton called for the creation of a web site (www.firstgov.gov) to house all online resources offered by the federal government in one location in 2000. Obama signed two executive orders in early in 2009 requiring government agencies to be more open to providing public access to government records per the Freedom of Information Act.

[4] The WAES (Web Site Attribute Evaluation System) methodology assigns a 1 when an attribute is present and a 0 when the attribute is absent.

[5] The American Accounting Association in 1970 suggested that there are five levels of accountability, policy, program, performance, process, and legality (www.seagov.org). As we operationalize the three program components, we attempted to identify program data that would address each of these levels of accountability.

[6] See Todd M. La Porte, Chris C. Demchak and Christopher Weare. (2005). "Governance in the Era of the World Wide Web: An Assessment of Organizational Openness and Government Effectiveness, 1997-2001." In the Handbook of Public Information Systems. 2nd Edition. Edited by G. David Garson. Taylor and Francis: Boca Raton, FL. See also, G. David Garson. 2006. *Public Information Technology and E-Governance*. Jones and Bartlett: Sudburry, MA.

[7] One question in our information architecture required us to email lottery officials in each state to examine response rates. On July 9, 2007 we sent officials at each of the web sites an email with the following question: How many questions do you receive concerning the web site on an average monthly basis? We coded a response received in one to two days as a 3, three to four days as a 2, and five to six days as a 1. Responses longer than six days and a lack of response were coded as a 0.

APPENDIX

Questions and Coding Scheme

A. Policy Architecture
    1. Enabling Statute
        A. Is the original legislation available? 0=No, 1=Yes
        B. Are amendments available? 0=No, 1=Yes
        C. Are there supplementary explanations, in lay language, of the program requirements available? 0=No, 1=Yes
    2. Program Requirements
        A. Is the authorized structure explained (state agency; quasi-governmental corporation)? 0=No, 1=Yes
        B. Are the purposes of the lottery clearly explained (general fund; education; gambling variety; customer-orientation)? 0=No, 1=Yes
        C. Are the purposes of the lottery focused (maximize profit; variety of product mix)? 0=No, 1=Yes
        D. Are the authorized products described (what can and can't be sold)? 0=No, 1=Yes
        E. Are reporting requirements defined (frequency, type of information; public reporting required)? 0=No, 1=Yes
        F. Is the distribution of profits mandated? 0=No, 1=Yes
        G. Is an oversight structure required and explained? 0=No, 1=Yes
        H. Are there any social responsibilities of the program mandated (Is the program supposed to address regressiveness of the lottery; address compulsive gambling; minimize under-age playing; or check for delinquent child support)? 0=No, 1=Yes
        I. Are there any requirements regarding vendor transparency (enrollment procedures; complaint procedures; or background checks)? 0=No, 1=Yes
        J. Are contracting procedures and processes explained (Follow state contracting rules or are they exempt; or a modified process)? 0=No, 1=Yes
        K. Are HR policies explained (civil service or not; salary ceilings; bonus guidelines)? 0=No, 1=Yes
        L. Is the salary of the chief executive set or based on performance? 0=No, 1=Yes
B. Management Architecture
    1. Planning
        A. Is the product mix based on market research? 0=No, 1=Yes
        B. Is there a reported market research process that appears to influence decision making? 0=No, 1=Yes
        C. Has there been an evolution of product mix? 0=No, 1=Yes
        D. Has there been an increase in sales over time? 0=No, 1=Yes
    2. Organizing
        A. Is the structure mandated in place? 0=No, 1=Yes
        B. Has it changed over time? 0=No, 1=Yes
        C. Has the structure been challenged? 0=No, 1=Yes
        D. Is there a formal relationship with other state agency officials? 0=No, 1=Yes
        E. Is there a direct relationship with the legislature? 0=No, 1=Yes

3. Staffing
    A. Is the leadership structure clear? 0=No, 1=Yes
    B. Are their roles and responsibilities clear? 0=No, 1=Yes
    C. Is their a system in place to recruit and retain high performing employees? 0=No, 1=Yes
    D. Is there a formal ethics program in place? 0=No, 1=Yes
    E. Does this include an explicit attention to conflict of interest? 0=No, 1=Yes
4. Directing
    A. Is the product marketed widely? 0=No, 1=Yes
    B. Are audit process and procedures in place? 0=No, 1=Yes
    C. Are there retailer procedures in place to establish quality control? 0=No, 1=Yes
5. Coordinating
    A. Are there other state agencies or officials that lottery officials work with to accomplish its mission? 0=No, 1=Yes
    B. Is there a formal oversight body that can exert formal oversight? 0=No, 1=Yes
    C. Is there a formal process to this oversight? 0=No, 1=Yes
6. Reporting
    A. Are winners profiled? 0=No, 1=Yes
    B. Are beneficiaries profiled? 0=No, 1=Yes
    C. Are required financial reports accomplished? 0=No, 1=Yes
    D. Are financial reports available? 0=No, 1=Yes
    E. Do program officials report program news regularly? 0=No, 1=Yes
7. Budgeting and Finance
    A. What procedures are in place to track and control expenses? 0=No, 1=Yes
    B. Is the state lottery program integrated into the state's budgetary processes? 0=No, 1=Yes
    C. Are procedures in place to ensure that transfer of funds occurs in accordance with state policy? 0=No, 1=Yes
    D. Are performance measures reported as part of the budget process? 0=No, 1=Yes
    E. Is performance linked to bonuses and commissions? 0=No, 1=Yes

C. Information Architecture
    1. Site Structure
        A. Is there a site map available (or index)? 0=No, 1=Yes
        B. Are the subsections labeled clearly? 0=No, 1=Yes
        C. Does the site have pop up ads? 0=No, 1=Yes
    2. Information access
        A. Are there downloadable forms to facilitate accessibility? 0=No, 1=Yes
        B. Are there downloadable reports to improve communication? 0=No, 1=Yes
        C. Are there links to other sites? 0=No, 1=Yes
        D. Are there links to publications/research? 0=No, 1=Yes
        E. Is there a link to the home State? 0=No, 1=Yes
        F. Is there a link to the lottery page from the State homepage? 0=No, 1=Yes
        G. Are there links for the media? 0=No, 1=Yes
        H. Are there links to other lottery sites? 0=No, 1=Yes
        I. Are there links for researchers or students to facilitate examination? 0=No, 1=Yes

3. Dialogue and/or inquiry
    A. Is there a link to contact officials (email)? 0=No, 1=Yes
    B. Is there clear contact information (address, phone contact; 800 number) available? 0=No, 1=Yes
    C. Is there a link to lodge comments, concerns or complaints? 0=No, 1=Yes
    D. Is there a forum to facilitate dialogue? 0=No, 1=Yes
4. User features to benchmark:
    A. Ease of navigating? 0=Very Difficult, 1=Difficult, 2=Average, 3= Easy, 4=Very Easy
    B. Is a User Search function available? 0=No, 1=Yes
    C. Is a User Help function available? 0=No, 1=Yes
    D. Does the system Freeze when accessing information? 0=No, 1=Yes
    E. Is there a Frequency Asked Questions feature? 0=No, 1=Yes
    F. Is there a News Feature? 0=No, 1=Yes
    G. Are provisions made for Non-English Speakers? 0=No, 1=Yes
    H. Are security and privacy policies explicit? 0=No, 1=Yes
    I. Is there disability access? 0=No, 1=Yes
    J. Are other user services provided? 0=No, 1=Yes
    K. How responsive are lottery officials to inquiries? 3=1-2 Days, 2= 3-4 Days, 1 = 5-6 day, and 0 = >6 days or no response
5. Style and presentation features to consider:
    A. Are the colors distracting? 0=No, 1=Yes
    B. Is the font size too small? 0=No, 1=Yes
    C. Are graphics used? 0=No, 1=Yes
    D. Are narratives used? 0=No, 1=Yes

Chapter 20
E–Government and its Potential to Facilitate Citizen Participation in State Budget Deliberations

Kenneth A. Klase
University of North Carolina at Greensboro, USA

Michael John Dougherty
West Virginia University Extension Service, USA

ABSTRACT

State legislative websites have potential both to inform the citizenry and increase their participation in the governing process. This is particularly the case with respect to budget deliberations, which tradition-ally have been shrouded in mystery. Previous studies as well as a direct review of websites over the last few years have shown an increasing amount of data available. It ranges from basic information such as member lists and calendars to full documentation of events via transcripts and archived audio or video. A survey of state fiscal officials confirmed the utility of these websites for providing information. Thus, the websites have reached half their potential. However, the web sites do not appear to have enhanced citizen participation in the process. Opportunities for feedback and interaction are minimal at best. The implementation of such tools would enable the websites to reach their full e-government potential.

INTRODUCTION

This chapter focuses on state legislative web sites and the information they provide about the budget process in state government. The development of such e-government web sites in recent years offers the potential for greater accessibility to informa-tion not just about the budget itself but even more importantly about the budget deliberations that occur in the process of developing and approv-ing the budget by state legislatures. When these e-government web sites provide information on budget deliberations, they create a context with the potential to enhance civic engagement. The degree to which that potential is realized depends on the nature of the information on budget delib-erations conveyed by these e-government web

DOI: 10.4018/978-1-61692-018-0.ch020

sites. It also depends not only on what information is made available but also the degree to which that information is accessible through the web site for the use of citizens, institutional actors and other stakeholders with an interest in state budget outcomes. The ability of these web sites to actually enhance citizen participation depends on the capability of the public to use the information provided to provide constructive feedback in the political process as a part of on-going budget deliberations. Once the budget is passed by the legislature, the opportunity is lost for participatory democracy to have any effect on budget outcomes encompassed in the budget.

The research presented in this chapter analyzes the availability and accessibility of information on state budget deliberations provided through state legislative web pages.

Since budget deliberations in state legislatures occur primarily in legislative committees, the focus is on examining the extent to which information is available about the budget deliberations of state legislative committees and how accessible that information is for multiple purposes. In addition to providing an assessment of these state legislative web sites for these purposes, this research also evaluates how these e-government web sites could better enhance citizen participation and thus their value for civic engagement.

PREVIOUS RESEARCH ON BUDGET DELIBERATIONS

Budget deliberations occur during the budget process after budget information has been presented in some form to legislative decision-makers, and it is the discussion and negotiation that occurs in this step in the process that inform budgetary decisions about how resources are allocated in budget outcomes. The focus of research in this area has been on linking budget deliberations to budget outcomes. Previous research examining budget deliberations has focused on the effects

of the way budget information is organized, the budget format, on subsequent budgetary decisions. Grizzle (1986) was among the first to review the deliberations of budget committees in state legislatures. Examining selected Florida and North Carolina legislative committee hearings, she described a two-step process in which budget format would influence the content of discussions in the budget review process, and the content of budget deliberations would influence the budget decisions that determine how much money is appropriated. She found that budget format is an important factor influencing the nature of budget deliberations. She viewed this initial step as an intervening link between budget format and ultimate appropriations decisions that needed to be better understood before trying to understand the second step linking deliberations under different formats to appropriations decisions.

Only a few other studies of budget deliberations have occurred at the state and federal levels. Stanford (1992) built upon Grizzle's research by reviewing budget deliberations for 1982, 1983, 1984, and 1987 in Florida. She reviewed over 12,000 questions asked by legislators during those four years. She found discernable patterns reflecting distinct orientations in legislative deliberations over agency budget requests. These patterns varied depending on factors such as fiscal conditions, agency mission, and type of funding sources. Implicit in these findings is the fact that the participation of legislators in the budgetary process appears to be more involved and more strategic than previously considered. In examining Congressional budget deliberations in selected subcommittees, Pettijohn and Grizzle (1997) and Ahmad, Grizzle, and Pettijohn (2003) found that information presented in a particular format becomes the object of deliberation during the subcommittee hearings. This in turn influences the budget deliberations.

Regardless of the unit of analysis – state or federal – this type of research has used primary data from committee hearings. At the federal level, the information is readily available through transcriptions of the Congressional hearings. Conversely at the time of their research, Grizzle (1986) and Stanford (1992) found that such information on budget deliberations at the state level was not available in a readily useable form. As previous research involving the examination of budget deliberations indicates, examination of the details of budget deliberations has occurred rather sparingly. Problems related to the availability and analysis of data has traditionally made such efforts problematic, but advances in technology in recent years could significantly change that situation.

Changes in data availability may permit an in-depth study of something that rarely even receives cursory attention – state-level budget deliberations. The lack of research in this area should not be a surprise. Rubin (2005) noted that there had been little discussion on the relationship between legislatures and agencies in her review of 25 years of articles in *Public Budgeting & Finance*. Rubin asked, *"What are the legislators' budgetary concern? When they get involved in budgetary decision making, to what extent are they just interested in distributive pork projects, or protecting constituents from program cuts, and to what extent are they active in formulating and debating public policy?"* (p. 59)

Traditionally, the focus of budgeting analysis has been on activity at the federal level. Widlavsky (1964) started this with his seminal work, *The Politics of the Budget Process* and continued looking at fiscal matters from a national perspective for over three decades in the subsequent versions of his classic (1984, 1992). Other authors followed his lead, including scholars, staffers, and pracademics. For example, LeLoup's *Budgetary Politics* (1980), Shuman's *Politics and the Budget* (1992), and Schick's *The Capacity to Budget* each looked at federal budgeting. The foci included the relationship between the President and Congress and the gamesmanship between the two branches of government.

This is not to say that there have not been some works that have looked at budgeting from a state perspective. Rubin (1997) included both state and local governments in her synopsis of the budgeting process, including the dynamics, execution, and political relationships. With respect to the state (and local) governments, however, the information presented is more historical and comparative as opposed to analytical. Some other studies have had a somewhat different focus. Thurmeier and Willoughby (2001) look at the roles played by state budget officers and examiners during the budgetary process, but they do not examine the legislative budgetary process per se. This appears to have been an outgrowth of some previous research as Thurmaier and Gosling (1997) looked at changing roles of state budget officers and found they played both policy and control roles.

Some work has focused on different perspectives of state budgeting. Willoughby and Melkers (2000) looked at performance budgeting from both a legislative and an executive perspective when they examined performance-based budgeting at the state level. Subsequent research by Willoughby (2004) looked at how budgets have been balanced through action by both governors and legislators. However, in both cases, the source of the information has been budgetary staff.

Most recently, Ryu et al. (2008) brought this research full circle. They used a framework put forth by Davis, Dempster, and Wildvasky (1966) as a guide to doing similar research on the state level while looking at agency-level budgets. They found that, while external and environmental factors held some influence over the budgetary process, as expected, the actors had the preponderance of influence. Thus, governors and legislators/legislatures were found to be the driving force behind budget decisions for state agencies. However, it should be noted that the data to support this conclusion came from a survey of state agency heads – rather than the governors or legislators themselves.

Thus legislators are key actors who influence budgetary outcomes. The key to understanding how decisions about budget allocations are made is understanding what goes on in budget deliberations between the time that legislators receive budget information and decisions are made about how to allocate resources. Research about budget deliberations at the state level has occurred rarely in the past because of lack of available data. Advances in technology have begun to change that situation. State legislatures now have websites which have begun to make information about budget deliberations available in a variety of ways. Advancements in e-government capabilities have set the stage for multiple mechanisms for provision of information about the budgetary process and for the potential that citizens might actively engage in budget deliberations.

RESEARCH ON E-GOVERNMENT CAPABILITY IN THE STATES

Governments at every level have been improving their e-government capabilities in recent years. Most government jurisdictions in the United States are commonly thought to be making effective use of the Web at least in the provision of information (Holden et al, 2003; Moon, 2002; Reddick, 2004).

Several years ago, West (2005) reported on the improving level of capability of state and federal web sites, indicating the presence of a range of features and significant levels of accessibility. A range of demographic (e.g., income, education) and non-demographic (e.g., perceived usefulness, uncertainty, and civic mindedness) audience characteristics can influence the adoption by governments of e-government information and services (Dimitrova and Chen, 2006). Notwithstanding these considerations, the staffs of state government agencies also play a large role in determining what content is included in web pages, and this in turn has important implications for information usability, costs, citizen participa-

tion, government transparency, and public trust in government (Eschenfelder, 2004).

In addition to the importance of staff professionalism for the growth of e-government, state institutional capacity is a significant factor accounting for change in digital government policy innovation over time. Institutional capacity is associated with reinvention in state governments, a more general orientation toward government reform and modernization, and the institutionalization of information technology. Thus reinvention and e-government have been linked, and modernization of state institutions may facilitate innovation (Tolbert et al., 2008).

E-government is often linked to reinvention and reform of government processes to produce greater efficiency or to enhance communication and participation (Norris, 2001; Seifert and Peterson, 2002). Entrepreneurial aspects of e-government which emphasize customer service and efficiency mirror private sector use of e-commerce (Fountain, 2001; Ho, 2002; Moon, 2002). E-government was promoted as a part of federal level reforms in the mid-1990's encompassed in the National Performance Review (Fountain, 2001; West 2005).

E-government research has typically described improvements and initiatives in e-government as occurring along a continuum (Justice et al, 2004). Moon (2002) describes five stages of e-government: information dissemination, two-way communication, services and financial transactions, information systems integration, and political participation. This typology describes a developmental continuum for e-government consisting of stages which progress from initially providing static information to processing transactions and eventually to engaging citizens in public discourse.

The innovations and changes in government web sites over time reflect improvement in the instrumental processes of government and in their capacity to convey mainly information. A study by Ferber et al. (2003) examined state legislative web sites on criteria seeking to determine their ability to facilitate higher level functions. They focused in particular on capacity to facilitate citizen partici-pation, which many had predicted e-government would provide. They rated state legislative web sites using evaluative criteria including content, usability, interactivity, transparency, and audi-ence. They evaluated sites based on these five components each measured on a ten-point scale: content in terms of information provided by the website; usability measuring site design, ease of navigation, and ability to access information; interactivity in terms of features that promoted user-government communication; transparency related to knowledge about who owns and controls the content of the site; and audience evaluating how well the site services both citizen and expert users. They considered content and usability as the two most critical evaluative criteria.

They found that state legislative web sites had some useful information, links, and even audio and video feeds and archives in some instances. Usability was limited by currency or timeliness of information and difficulties in site navigation. Interactivity, or the provision of means for citi-zens to use the web to participate in meaningful ways, was lacking. E-mail contact was generally available, but there were no public forums, chat rooms or group listservs where users could discuss issues. They concluded that state legislative web sites provided a wealth of information but did not offer new methods for citizens to participate in governing in their states. Their impact was in dissemination of information and facilitating participation by simply providing passive content to users (Ferber et al, 2003).

While Ferber et al. (2003) focused on state legislative web sites and a general range of infor-mational content, almost no research has focused specifically on the fiscal content of government web sites. In one of the only studies of e-govern-ment and fiscal accountability and responsiveness, Justice et al. (2004) focused on assessing the degree to which web sites implemented govern-mental budget dissemination, financial reporting, and citizen participation in resource allocation.

It examined the web sites of recipients of GFOA awards for budget presentations and financial reporting to see if they made available documents or applications for promoting fiscal transparency and participation. Only two states were included in the sample of 104 jurisdictions at the state and local level. They found the government web sites did not display a great degree of sophistication or thoroughness in web content related to fiscal accountability and participation and were not fully realizing even the potential for information dissemination (Justice et al., 2004).

These studies looking at state legislative web sites highlight the criticality of content and usability in the design of web sites. There is significant ambiguity about how to examine government websites, and no agreement about what is the best method to evaluate and analyze them on criteria, such as content and usability (Mofleh and Wanous, 2009). These criteria are difficult to define precisely because of difficulty in defining typical users and typical tasks because of the diverse audience of users, the wide variety of potential measurement methodologies, and the dynamic nature of constantly changing website content. In an early attempt to solve this dilemma, the National Institute of Standards and Technol-ogy (NIST) addressed these issues in their project that used collections of evaluation results from expert usability evaluations together with NIST web metrics to derive benchmarks of usability methodologies (NIST, 2001). Nonetheless, the concept of usability continues to remain a very broad concept and is frequently defined differently in different studies, and there has not been a clear framework on how benchmarking techniques can be applied to web evaluation (Hassan and Li, 2005). Hassan and Li (2005) developed a possible framework for evaluating usability and content usefulness of websites by using a benchmark-ing approach based on identified metrics. Their analysis indicates that studies of usability all tend to agree on relevant dimensions of usability, including aspects of effectiveness, efficiency, learnability, and user satisfaction, but they seem to vary on whether content coverage should be included as an element of usability. This may be less of a concern because satisfaction is indirectly related to content quality and includes both ease of use and usefulness. They used content analysis of literature on web usability to determine factors for the framework, and found web usability and content usefulness clustered around seven main factors: screen appearance, accessibility for target users, navigation, media use (availability of multi-media elements like sound, graphics, images, audio, and video), interactivity (two-way communication and features which allow users to give feedback and comments on issues raised by the website), consistency, and content. Their framework then suggests determining metrics for whichever of the seven major factors are determined to be relevant in identifying and selecting appropriate benchmarking websites against which to evaluate your own website. Based on analysis of benchmarking data and any determined gap, they recommend redesigning websites and monitoring progress. Tarafdur and Zhang (2005) also considered similar factors in determining usability from the standpoint of website design parameters. Their analysis of 200 websites found that the factors that most influenced website usability were information content, navigation, download speed, and availability. Thus usability and content are significantly linked in evaluating websites. Especially when the focus is on these critical factors, e-government websites are found lacking. Chondine and Ghinea (2005) evaluated a cross-section of e-government web sites on a set of performance metrics and found a wide variation in content of information and services, significantly off the mark for best practice. What e-government websites seem to be missing is more user-centered website design and usability testing that would better serve the needs of diverse users (Cory, Frick, and Hansen, 1997). Clearly a focus on usability remains critical to realizing the power of e-government websites.

The power of the e-government is its potential to educate and inform. E-government has the potential to increase civic engagement and improve connections with citizens, businesses, and other governments (Bimber, 1999; Seifert and Peterson, 2002; Thomas and Streib, 2003; West, 2005). For governments, this translates into the potential to inform citizens about decisions – what they are, how they are made, and what they mean. The development of e-government would be expected to have particular benefits with respect to providing information regarding state budgetary deliberations. What once occurred in hidden committee rooms now could be brought into the open through the use of technology. E-government holds the potential to diminish barriers to fiscal accountability and responsiveness (Justice et al, 2004). Research indicates that use of e-government can improve citizen confidence in government and enhance trust in government (Tolbert and Mossberger, 2006; Welch, Hinnant, and Moon, 2006). While e-government even promises the potential to provide a means for citizen participation in budget deliberation, information provision and service delivery have been much more common than opportunities for citizen participation (Chadwick and May, 2003; Musso, Weare and Hale, 2000; West 2003). Before these benefits can be realized, state governments must develop web pages that make information available about budget deliberations in a manner that makes this information accessible to the general public and promotes genuine opportunities for citizen involvement in deliberation and participation in budgetary decision making (Ebdon and Franklin, 2004; Simonsen and Robbins, 2000). The research that is the main focus of this chapter examines availability and accessibility of information about state budget deliberations on state legislative web pages and how well state legislative web pages are achieving their potential to facilitate citizen participation in budget deliberations and enhance civic engagement.

AVAILABILITY AND ACCESSIBILITY OF INFORMATION ABOUT STATE BUDGET DELIBERATIONS ON LEGISLATIVE WEB SITES

In order to assess the availability of information on state budget deliberations and the level of accessibility to that information, a survey of state legislatures about these issues was undertaken. As an initial investigation of these issues, our intention was to determine the degree to which individual state legislatures allowed access to legislative committee hearings concerning the budget, kept records of the proceedings of these hearings, and made these records accessible or available. The method employed to obtain this information was a survey of web sites for state legislatures. A review of the web sites for state legislatures was undertaken to determine if the state legislatures had information on their web sites that indicated that they had information available about legislative committee hearings, what type of records were kept about these hearings, and to what degree these records were available or accessible. A review of web sites for state legislatures allows for an assessment of overall availability of information on budget deliberations by state legislatures to the extent this information is made available through the internet by state legislatures. A review of web sites for state legislatures on the availability of information on state budget deliberations was performed in 2005 and 2009; thus a comparison between years on availability of information on budget deliberations in the states is possible based on data collected.

In addition to the information obtained through a review of web sites for state legislatures on the availability of information about budget deliberations in state legislative committee hearings, survey research methods were also employed to confirm the results of the initial review of web sites for state legislatures and to uncover additional information about accessibility of committee hearings and availability of records relating to them. A web survey was prepared to obtain feedback from e-mail contacts in legislative research offices of state legislatures. Legislative research offices or equivalent units in state legislatures are typically charged with providing legislative support related to committee hearings and budget deliberations. At least two contacts were selected as potential respondents from each of the state legislative research offices and included the executive directors, associate directors, or fiscal analysts from these offices with responsibilities for providing support for House and Senate committees. Multiple respondents from each legislative research office were selected to help insure a response from each state and as a measure of reliability for information obtained. Thus the sample of state legislative research analysts from all states included over 100 state legislative research analysts, mostly senior level managers and analysts in these offices. The purpose of the survey was to verify and expand upon factual information about accessibility of and availability of information about budget deliberations contained on the web sites of state legislatures.

The brief survey questionnaire was composed as a web survey document, and respondents were e-mailed a request to respond to the survey at the web address for the web survey document. Respondents were asked to select the answers to questions that applied to their state legislature or provide a brief comment where appropriate. The ten questions contained in the brief web survey document concerned the availability of information about state budget deliberations and access to state legislature committee hearings involving the budget, finance, or appropriations. The first part of the questionnaire asked questions about the committees in which deliberation occurs concerning the budget: whether an open meetings or sunshine law applies to House/Senate committee hearings for budget, appropriations, and finance and the extent to which committee hearings for budget, appropriations, and finance are open. The second part of the questionnaire concerned records relat-

Figure 1. Level or degree of access to budget/appropriations information

Level or Degree of Access	2005		2009	
	Number of States (Percent)	States Included	Number of States (Percent)	States Included
Significant	7 (14%)	CA, CT, ID, MN, NJ, SD, TN	17 (34%)	AK, AZ, CA, CT, GA, KY, LA, MN, MT, NJ, OR, SD, TN, TX, UT, WA, WI
Moderate	4 (8%)	LA, OR, UT, VA	3 (6%)	NH, PA, WY
Limited	14 (28%)	AK, AZ, CO, FL, KS, ME, MT, NC, NV, ND, OK, SC, TX, VT	16 (32%)	CO, FL, ID, IN, KS, ME, MA, MI, MS, NC, ND, NM, NV, NY, OK, VT
Minimal or None	25 (50%)	AL, AR, DE, GA, HI, IA, IL, IN, KY, MA, MD, MI, MO, MS, NE, NH, NM, NY, OH, PA, RI, WA, WV, WI, WY	14 (28%)	AL, AR, DE, HI, IA, IL, MD, MO, NE, OH, RI, SC, VA, WV

Source: Authors (Survey of State Legislature Web Site Information).

ing to the committee hearings: whether records are maintained, the form in which those records exist, whether those records are open and in what form they may be available to the public, and whether fees are required in order to obtain these records.

The survey of state legislative web sites was undertaken to determine the availability of records on budget deliberations and changes in availability over time. The survey of state legislative research offices sought to confirm availability of records of committee hearings and to determine accessibility to committee hearings on the budget. Together the web survey and the survey of state legislative research offices provide a basis for assessing the availability of information about budget deliberations in state legislative committee hearings and the degree of accessibility to committee hearing on the budget. Thus the findings from these complimentary survey approaches provide a greater understanding of the information context in which state budget deliberations occur and the degree to which state legislative web pages provide available and accessible information on state budget deliberations.

Research Findings

Figure 1 summarizes the results of the 2005 and 2009 surveys of state legislative web pages. The surveys ascertained the access to committee hearings related to the state budget and appropriations in 2005 and 2009 for each state. They found the level of access to information on budget deliberations in legislative committee hearings, the type of access, and period of time in which available.

The table is divided into four categories to reflect the level or degree of access to budget and appropriation committee information in 2005 and 2009 respectively. The determination of appropriate category for individual state legislative websites was a subjective judgment about the extent of access and availability of information about budget deliberations. In reviewing the websites, a four-part typology was utilized to categorize the level or degree of access to budget/appropriations information: "significant," "moderate," "limited," and "minimal or none." Those websites which provided information allowing the interested user to fully follow all of the actions of budgetary committees relating to budget deliberations were rated

Figure 2. 2009 level or degree of access

The darker the color, the higher level or degree of access.

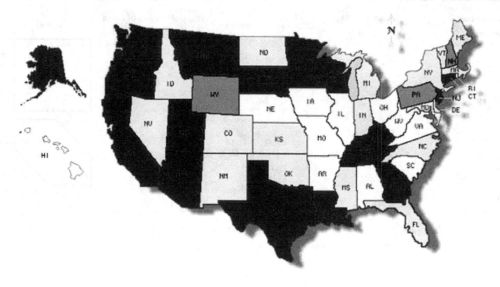

Source: Authors (Survey of State Legislature Web Site Information).

"significant." These included having complete (or near complete) transcripts or archives (audio or video) of committee hearings, as well as standard information such as membership, calendars, agendas, and minutes. In addition, there was usually access to at least some historical information from previous sessions. Websites which had some or selected transcripts or archives or less complete other information were rated "moderate." Websites which had almost no transcripts or archives but did provide general information were rated as "limited." And those websites which had no (or virtually no) information other than memberships and schedules were rated "minimal or none."

The table shows that in 2005 only seven states (CA, CT, ID, MN, NJ, SD, TN) had a significant level or degree of availability of information about budget deliberations in legislative committee hearings and that only another four states (LA, OR, UT, VA) had moderate levels of information availability. Meanwhile, 14 states had limited access to budget deliberation information in 2005.

Also, 25 states (half of all states) had minimal or no access to this information in 2005.

The analysis of state legislature web pages indicated that only 11 states (less than one-quarter of all states) provided any meaningful level of access to information on budget deliberations. Meanwhile, the other 39 states (more than three-quarters of all states) provide limited information at best.

By 2009, this situation had improved considerably. Figure 1 shows that 17 states (AK, AZ, CA, CT, GA, KY, LA, MN, MT, NJ, OR, SD, TN, TX, UT, WA, WI) – more than one-third of all states – had a significant level or degree of availability of information about budget deliberations in legislative committee hearings. Another three states (NH, PA, WY) had moderate levels of information availability. Together, this means that 20 states (two-fifths of all states) provided a meaningful access to budgetary information. Meanwhile, 16 states had limited access to budget deliberation information in 2009. Another only 14 states had minimal or no access to this information.

Figure 3. Type of information available

Type of Information	2005		2009	
	Number of States (Percent)	States Included	Number of States (Percent)	States Included
Archived Audio/Video/DVD	6 (12%)	CA, ID, MN, NJ, SD, TN	16 (32%)	AK, AZ, CA, GA, KY, LA, MN, MT, NJ, OR, SD, TN, TX, UT, WA, WI
Live Video/ Webcast	1 (2%)	CA	16 (32%)	AZ, CO, IN, KS, KY, LA, ME, MI, MN, NC, NJ, NV, OK, OR, TN, WI
Some Audio	6 (12%)	LA, ME, NC, OH, OR, UT	2 (4%)	NH, WY
Full Transcripts	3 (6%)	CA, CT, NJ	1 (2%)	CT
Some Transcripts	1 (2%)	VA	2 (4%)	PA, WY
Minutes	11 (22%)	AK, AZ, ID, KS, MN, MT, NV, ND, OH, SD, VT	12 (24%)	AK, AZ, CT, ID, KS, MT, NV, OK, OR, SD, TX, UT
Notes, Reports, Explanations, Agendas, or Summaries	8 (16%)	CO, DE, FL, NC, ND, MT, SC, VA	10 (20%)	CO, FL, IA, MA, MI, MS, NY, RI, VA, WV
Schedules or Listings of Members	28 (56%)	AL, AR, DE, FL, GA, HI, IL, IN, IA, MA, MD, MI, MO, MS, NE, NH, NM, NY, OH, OR, PA, RI, TX, VT, WA, WV, WI, WY	10 (20%)	AL, AK, DE, HI, IL, MD, MO, NE, OH, SC
None	1 (2%)	KY	0 (0%)	

Source: Authors (Survey of State Legislature Web Site Information.)

The analysis of state legislature web pages in 2009 indicated that a substantial proportion of states (40 percent) provide a considerable level of access to information on budget deliberations, although most states (60 percent) of states still provide only limited or minimal information. Figure 2 shows the level or degree of access in 2009. This marked an 18 percentage point improvement between 2005 and 2009. In addition, 19 states provided substantially more information in 2009 than they had in 2005 (AK, AZ, GA, IN, KY, LA, MA, MI, MT, NH, NY, NM, PA, OR, TX, UT, WA, WI, WY). This included four states that went from providing minimal data to (nearly) complete information related to the budgetary deliberation process over the four year period (GA, KY, WA, WI). Conversely, only three states (ID, SC, VA) provided less information in 2009 than in 2005.

The change in level or degree of access over the four-year period is particularly apparent at the extremes. The number of states at the "significant" level more than doubled – going to 17 in 2009 from just 7 in 2005. This reflected a movement of states to make audio or video of budgetary deliberations available. Likewise, 11 fewer states fell into the "minimal" category – dropping to 14 in 2009 from 25 in 2009. Nevertheless, even with this movement to increased access to state budget and appropriation information, there was still an overwhelming majority of states continue to provide limited or meager access to this information.

The details of the types of information found on the websites about budget deliberations in legislative committee hearings in 2005 and 2009 are listed on Figure 3. The table indicates a range of possible types of format in which information is made available by state legislatures, ranging from archived audio or video or DVDs to only schedules and listings of committee members or virtually nothing available. Figure 3 indicates the states which fell into each category or type of format, based upon an analysis of the website survey data.

The table shows that in 2005 only six states (CA, ID, NJ, MN, SD, TN) provided archival audio and video (including DVDs). This is the most complete type of information on budget deliberations, though for research purposes it is not as useful as archived transcripts. A total of seven states (CA, LA, ME, NC, OH, OR, UT) provided live video or some live audio in 2005. Just three states (CA, CT, NJ) provided transcripts of all committee hearings, while one state (VA) provided some transcripts.

A range of other types of format for partial information is represented in Figure 3. As might be expected, the most commonly provided information was the least descriptive data. Overall, 28 states provided schedules and listings of members (this information could also be found through extended searches on other states' web pages). Also, 11 states had meeting minutes available. A total of eight states provided notes, reports, explanations, agendas, or summaries. Finally, it should also be noted that one state (KY) provided no useful information in 2005.

Thus the analysis of state legislature web pages indicated that only a very modest number of states in 2005 provided information in a format that is complete, readily accessible, or useful for research and analysis by citizens interested in following the outcomes of the budget process. The overwhelming majority of states provided virtually nothing that would aid in analysis of budget deliberations or provide any record of the proceedings of committee hearings about the budget or appropriations after the fact according to analysis of state legislative web sites.

By 2009, the situation had improved somewhat. As indicated in Figure 3, 16 states (AK, AZ, CA, GA, KY, LA, MN, MT, NJ, OR, SD, TN, TX, UT, WA, WI), more than double the number from four years earlier, provided archived audio/video/DVD. An additional 18 states (AZ, CO, IN, KS,

KY, LA, ME, MI, MN, NC, NH, NJ, NV, OK, OR, TN, WI, WY) provided live video or some audio, again more than twice the number that offered that format of access in 2005. However, just three states (CT, PA, WY) provided transcripts of some or all committee hearings in 2009, one state fewer than previously.

The major categories or types of information available through the state legislatures about budget deliberations in legislative committee hearings in 2009, has shifted as well. More states offered archived audio or video than reports or schedules. There was also an increase in live video/webcast. Thus the situation has gone from where almost all states (47 states) offered mostly minimal information to one where more than two-thirds of states (34 states) offered some form of audio or video presentation of deliberations and proceedings. As a result of all these offerings, all 50 states provided at least some information on legislative budgetary deliberations and decision-making.

Meanwhile, the distribution of states across categories of access has definitely shifted between 2005 and 2009, rather dramatically toward providing substantially more information that would aid in analysis of budget deliberations and provide an historical record of the proceedings of committee hearings about the budget or appropriations after the fact. Thus, the analysis of state legislative web pages indicates that a significantly increased percentage of states provide information in 2009 in a format that is much more readily accessible and potentially useful. In particular, the large increase in archived audio, video, and DVDs is important. Access of this nature is particularly helpful for long-range perspective and analysis for citizens and researchers alike. The increase in live video and some audio is meaningful while the meeting or hearing is occurring. But it is not as useful as an historical record that can later be used for analysis purposes.

The importance of having access to this type of information can be seen in the results of a 2005 survey of state legislative research offices.

Figure 4. Legislative committees for budget deliberations

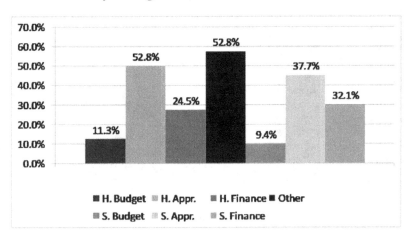

Notes: 53 of 55 respondents answered this question. Multiple answers per respondent permitted.
Source: Authors (Survey of State Legislature Officers)

Invitations to participate in a web-based surveys were sent to approximately 100 officials (two from each state – some substitutes for the potential respondents in the original sampling frame were added to ensure that two officials from each state received the invitation). A total of 55 officials completed the questionnaire, providing a 55% response rate. Officials from 44 states responded, 11 states had two respondents, and only six states had no respondents (IA, MA, MI, NC, NY, and VA).

The survey started by inquiring as to the location of budgetary deliberation. Respondents were asked to indicate all legislative committees where this occurred. As seen in Figure 4, Appropriations committees were the most popular with 52.8% of respondents saying the House Appropriations Committee and 37.7% saying the Senate Committee. Finance Committees were somewhat popular while Budget Committees were not generally cited as a location for debate. Most surprisingly though, slightly more than half the respondents (52.8%) indicated that budgetary and related discussions also occurred in other House or Senate committees.

The survey next asked about open meeting (or sunshine laws). All respondents reported their states had such laws and 92.5% of respondents said those laws applied to the budgetary, appropriations, and finance committees. Related to that, all respondents said such meetings were open to the general public and open to those conducting research. And 86% of those responding to the question said the meetings were open to those wishing to record the committee proceedings.

The remainder of the questions in the survey inquired about the records kept about legislative committee hearings relating to the budget. As seen in Figure 5, a variety of different types of records were reported as being maintained by legislative research analysts. An overwhelming majority (66.7%) said their states maintained audio records of proceedings in hearings involving the budget, finance, and/or appropriations committees. In addition, 60.8% indicated that their state maintained minutes on these proceedings. All other methods to record these hearings were reported being used in their states by less than two-fifths of the respondents. Also, it is important to note that all respondents said that these records were open to the public.

Since the public has access to these records, it is crucial to know how they can be accessed. As seen in Figure 6, the records are made available to the public in a variety of ways – closely

Figure 5. Records kept for appropriations, budget, & finance committees

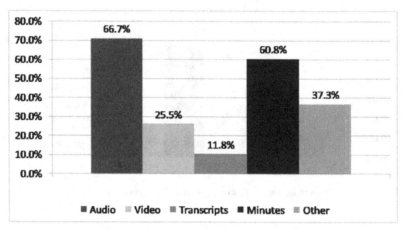

Notes: 51 of 55 respondents answered this question. Multiple answers per respondent permitted.
Source: Authors (Survey of State Legislature Officers)

related to the reported methods of record keeping discussed above. Most often, audio recordings are made as a total of 59.2% of respondents said their state makes those available. Meanwhile, 55.1% of respondents said that minutes of the meetings were made available. All other methods were reported as being used in their states by less than two-fifths of the respondents.

For those records that are made available, there was almost an even split as to whether or not a fee was required. Slightly more respondents said their respective states did not charge a fee than said their states did (56.8% vs. 43.2%).

The results of the survey of state legislative research offices allow an expanded and confirmative perspective on information availability and legislative committee accessibility and a comparison to the results of the survey of state legislative web sites.

From these results concerning the availability of information about budget deliberations in legislative committee hearings, there is a very clear indication that information (audio or video, especially where archived) has become increasingly more readily available in the last several years. The comparison of surveys of state legislative web sites portrays a substantial increase in

availability of this type of information from 2005 to 2009. The results of the survey of state legislative research offices indicates in some respects an even more promising picture of information availability than the survey of state legislative web sites would indicate. It seems to indicate that information on legislative committee hearings might be more readily available in audio form than state legislature web sites would indicate, which prompts the question why audio is not being made more available on the state legislative web sites. Similarly, the results indicate that information is somewhat more readily available in transcript form and the same questions apply with respect to this format as well.

Implications of Findings for Citizen Participation in Budget Deliberations

The results reported under research findings in this chapter tend to indicate that information about budget deliberations in legislative committee hearings is available to a degree, and in a form, that may be useful to a variety of users, and it has become increasingly more available over the last several years. These results expand on the findings of Ferber et al (2003) and West (2000 and 2004)

Figure 6. Format of committee deliberations records available to public

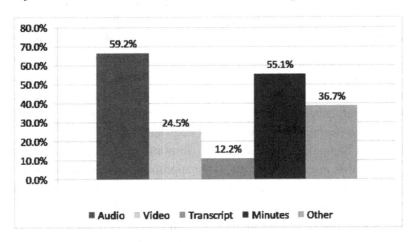

Notes: 49 of 55 respondents answered this question. Multiple answers per respondent permitted.
Source: Authors (Survey of State Legislature Officers).

in focusing specifically on information about budget deliberations on state websites. This study provides a longitudinal perspective on changes in state websites over the period studied, which expands on years covered in previous studies. The results of the research reported in this chapter also provide valuable new information on the continued growth in budget information on state websites. In addition, it also allows analysis of the characteristics of the current webpage content in this area to determine its usefulness in the broader context of citizen participation and civic engagement. Thus the results allow an analysis of the current status of state legislative webpage content against the high-level functional content that models of e-government would predict and which seem elusive in practice (Coursey and Norris, 2008).

The availability of current information and historical records in a form (live video, audio or video, or archived audio and video) that can serve as the basis for review and analysis about budget deliberations provides greater dissemination of that information. This is quite valuable since there has been little information available in any form in the past about this phase of the budget process. The provision of this information can be viewed

as enhancing accountability and transparency by providing direct access to current proceedings and historical records of budget deliberations. Achieving these objectives is not trivial in its potential benefits. However even in these instances, the information provided must be in a form usable for realizing these purposes, which may be doubtful in this case.

Unfortunately, the current availability of information on budget deliberation on state legislative websites does not necessarily make it accessible or readily useable for citizen participation. In spite of the increasing level of quantity and types of information being made available on state legislative web sites, the results of our surveys of legislative web sites are not inconsistent with the findings of Ferber et al. (2003). This research similarly found as that state legislative web pages have some useful information, links, and audio and video feeds and archives in many cases, but usability issues relate to timeliness and difficulty in site navigation in some cases. With respect to information about state budget deliberations, the state legislative web pages essentially provide some live video of legislative sessions and some committee hearings and, in an increasing number of cases, warehousing of extensive video archives of committee hearings. The video archives as historical records are potentially valuable for accountability and transparency in government; however, to utilize these videos requires slogging through hours of recordings, a task which only the most inveterate researcher would undertake. While available and generally accessible, their use by the general public in the aftermath of committee hearings is at best problematical. As Justice et al. (2004) found, and this research supports, government web sites often do not realize even their potential for information dissemination. The case of information on state budget deliberations exemplifies the significant lack of interactivity which is one of the principal factors constraining the potential of state legislative web pages from fuller citizen participation. The state legislative web pages provide few if any means for citizens to use the web to participate in meaningful ways. In almost all cases, citizens can get e-mail contact information if they want to contact their elected representative or government officials, but the potential that the web provides for other forms of dialogue and feedback are lacking. The evidence from the research findings reported in this chapter clearly indicates that the content currently being provided about budget deliberations on state legislative websites is unlikely to realize the potential of these state websites to facilitate citizen participation in budget deliberation as the analysis in the next section based on the budget information needs of citizens and usability considerations indicates.

HOW STATE LEGISLATIVE WEBSITES COULD BETTER ACHIEVE THEIR POTENTIAL TO ENHANCE CITIZEN PARTICIPATION IN STATE BUDGET DELIBERATIONS

The content provided by state legislative websites about budget deliberations fails to provide information that users would need to participate in budget deliberations.

In considering what users of state legislative websites might want or need related to budget deliberation, an important consideration is when deliberation occurs in the budget process. Deliberation occurs in the budget process after legislators have been presented with budget information and before decisions are made about appropriations in the budget. This intervening period between provision of budget information and appropriation decisions is where deliberation occurs, and not very much is known about what occurs during this intervening period or influences the decision calculus that occurs here. The important considerations for website users related to budget deliberations concern access to information about ongoing budget deliberations, availability of information that can be useful in understanding the relevant issues, and availability of means that would allow users to be actively engaged in the deliberation process.

State legislative web pages should provide a range of information for users that would help them better understand what policies and issues are being considered by the legislature, how decisions about those policies will be made, how their preferences can be considered, and what those decisions might mean in terms of their implications for citizens. Users of state legislative websites with interest in legislative decision-making about the budget will likely want to have timely information about budget proposals being considered and analysis about the merits of those proposals and alternatives to them. They need the information provided in a form that keys in on issues and critical controversies and highlights alternatives being considered. For example, the current emphasis on performance management in almost all state agencies should allow relevant information on performance measures reported to legislatures to be readily available for users to analyze with respect to its applicability to resource allocation decisions. Information of this type should be readily available by designated links on state legislative websites. State websites need to provide means for discussion of policies, issues, alternatives and other pertinent information to budget deliberations so users can be better informed about issues and different points of view. To be truly invested in a deliberative process, users need to do more than just discuss, they need to be able to engage in dialogue with their legislators in ways that will allow them to communicate their preferences and receive feedback from legislators about their reactions and responses. This could occur through group listservs, chat rooms, public forums, or blogs where discussions would be monitored by legislators and their staff for feedback on what issues need clarification or areas for further analysis as budget deliberation proceeds. Finally, users need to be informed about budget decisions that have been made. The needs of users in this vein can only be accommodated by state websites that are dynamic in providing continuously changing information and organic in growing in functionality and scope of content to meet changing and evolving user demands – even anticipating and encouraging the development of avenues of user engagement to enable them to participate more fully in budget deliberations and consequently enhancing civic engagement.

The ability of users to participate in state budget deliberations depends not only on the availability of information content on state legislative websites that users need in order to constructively participate but also on the usability of the website in providing them means to participate. The earlier section on e-government capability in the states provides the outlines of developing consensus on a framework for usability that can gauge the degree to which this objective is met. In general, the framework for evaluating usability and content usefulness identifies webmetrics on relevant dimensions or factors, which generally include screen appearance, accessibility for target users, navigation, media use (including sound, graphics, images, audio, and video), interactivity involving two-way communication and feedback, consistency, and content. Ratings on the metrics for these factors then form the basis for determining appropriate benchmarking. Significant factors focus on user-centered web design, especially information content and interactivity (Hassan and Li, 2005; Tarafdur and Zhang, 2005). A comparison of the content and usability of state legislative websites to these parameters clearly indicates the degree to which the websites fall short of meeting usability and content usefulness which will allow citizen participation in budget deliberations.

Since the development of the Internet in the 1990s, the Web has been seen as promoting technological change in government. It seemingly has the potential to alter the relationship between citizens and government because it may provide a way to make government more responsive and accessible using Web-based technology. Garson and Pavlichev (2004) advocated that governments pursue an e-government strategy because of its transformational potential. Some of the reasons to do so related to the topic of this chapter include making citizen access more convenient, combating perceptions of public disaffection for government, and reinforcing public sector freedoms and civil liberties (p.2-4).

To change the state of legislative web pages as described in the research reported in this chapter will require legislatures to overcome barriers to implementing more successful e-government approaches with respect to their legislative web pages. This will likely necessitate additional financial resources and improved technological expertise through education and training on the part of legislative staff and legislators themselves. In order to realize e-government's transformational impact, legislative leaders will have to embrace technology and the implementation of e-government strategies that will enable legislative web pages to move from just disseminating information in limited forms to their potential for enhancing citizen participation through implementation of greater interactivity.

The change during the four-year period covered by this study shows that improvements in state legislative web sites in content related to budget deliberations is occurring at a substantial rate, but not yet in ways that are meaningful for providing citizens information that they need to constructively participate in budget deliberations. For state legislative websites to accomplish the lofty goal of achieving greater citizen participation in budget deliberations, the rapid expansion of information availability about the legislative budgetary process observed in the research reported in this chapter will need to be focused in the future on meeting user needs for information rather than just providing information warehousing as evidence of transparency and accountability. Most importantly, state legislative websites will need to undertake new innovations in interactivity that will further facilitate citizen participation.

FUTURE RESEARCH DIRECTIONS

On the more general topic of state legislative web sites, research has identified interactivity as one of the central problems in enhancing the potential of these web sites to facilitate citizen participation and civic engagement. Future research needs to investigate the factors that are preventing state government web sites from initiating innovations that would provide greater interactivity. The culture of legislatures themselves may be a principal impediment since as legislative bodies they tend to adhere to time honored traditions and are slow to adopt innovations, technological or otherwise. On the specific topic of information on budget deliberations, developing a model for interactivity will require significant innovation and institutional change by state legislatures.

While perhaps technologically possible, moving from budget deliberations in hidden committee rooms to a more open dialogue in the budget process will likely require overcoming obstacles which are more institutional and organizational than technological. Research needs to focus on determining the impediments that prevent creating the environment in which technological innovations can occur in legislative bodies. Investigating what factors have facilitated best practices among state legislative web pages may be enlightening in developing paradigms for innovation and change in web page development. Chief among those factors may be the commitment of top leadership and the level of expertise of legislative staff and legislators. Determining the facilitative factors is only one of the research challenges. Of equal importance may be studying citizen behavior and what factors would better encourage their active involvement in participatory opportunities. A related concern is the potential disparity in utilization of e-government by different socio-economic groups which would necessarily be a concern in facilitating greater civic engagement.

CONCLUSION

Budget deliberation in the budget process determines budget outcomes or how resources are allocated in the budget. As a critical legislative decision-making responsibility, providing information on budget deliberations fosters accountability and transparency. E-government would seemingly provide the means to enhance these values by making information on budget deliberations readily available and accessible on state legislative web sites. The research reported in this chapter examined state legislative web sites to determine the degree to which information on budget deliberations is available and accessible. It provides a comparative analysis of state legislative web sites in 2005 and 2009 on these factors. It also reports on a web survey of legislative research offices to confirm results obtained in the survey of legislative web sites.

The results of the comparative analysis of state legislative web sites concerning availability of information about budget deliberations in legislative committee hearings clearly indicates that information in audio and video form, and even archived, has become increasingly available between 2005 and 2009. There is evidence that there have been substantial increases in the availability of this type of information over this period. The web survey of state legislative research offices confirms these results.

Notwithstanding the evidence of increased dissemination of information on budget deliberations in this form, the availability of this information is more an example of warehousing of information than a means to facilitate citizen participation in budget deliberations. State legislative web sites continue to lack interactivity, which is essential for the development of the true potential of e-government to enhance civic engagement in budget deliberations or any other legislative decision-making. The increasing level of provision of different types of information on state budget deliberations on state legislative web sites provides hope that continuing e-government innovations by state legislatures will eventually result in realizing the potential of state web sites to truly facilitate citizen participation in state budget deliberations.

REFERENCES

Ahmad, A. A., Grizzle, G. A., & Pettijohn, C. D. (2003). Patterns of change: Information change and congressional budget deliberations revisited. *Journal of Public Budgeting, Accounting &. Financial Management, 15*(1), 1–22.

Bimber, B. (1999). The internet and citizen communication with government: Does the medium matter? *Political Communication, 16*(4), 409–428. doi:10.1080/105846099198569

Chadwick, A., & Christopher, M. (2003). Interaction between States and Citizens in the age of the internet: "E-Government" in the United States, Britain, and the European Union. *Governance, 16*(2), 271–300. doi:10.1111/1468-0491.00216

Chondine, J., & Gheorghita, G. (2005). Integrated views of e-government website usability: perspectives from users and web diagnostic tools. *Electronic Government, 2*(3), 318.

Cory, M. D., Frick, T. W., & Hansen, L. (1997). User-centered design and usability testing of a websites: An illustration case study. *Educational Technology, 45*(4), 65.

Coursey, D., & Norris, D. F. (2008). Models of E-Government: Are They Correct? An Empirical Assessment. *Public Administration Review, 68*(3), 523–536. doi:10.1111/j.1540-6210.2008.00888.x

Davis, O. A., Dempster, M. A. H., & Wildvasky, A. (1966). A Theory of the Budgetary Process. *The American Political Science Review, 60*(3), 529–547. doi:10.2307/1952969

Dimitrova, D. V., & Chen, Y. (2006). Profiling the adopters of e-government information and *services*: The influence of psychological characteristics, civic mindedness, and information channels. *Social Science Computer Review, 24*(2), 172–188. doi:10.1177/0894439305281517

Ebdon, C., & Franklin, A. (2004). Searching for a role for citizens in the budget process. *Public Budgeting & Finance, 24*(1), 32–49. doi:10.1111/j.0275-1100.2004.02401002.x

Eschenfelder, K. R. (2004). Behind the web site: An inside look at the production of web-based textual government information. *Government Information Quarterly, 21*(3), 337–358. doi:10.1016/j.giq.2004.04.004

Ferber, P., Foltz, F., & Pugliese, R. (2003). The politics of state legislative web sites: Making e-government more participatory. *Bulletin of Science, Technology & Society, 23*(3), 157. doi:10.1177/0270467603023003002

Fountain, J. (2001). *Building the virtual state: Information technology and institutional change.* Washington, DC: Brookings Institution Press.

Garson, G. D., & Pavlichev, A. (Eds.). (2004). *Digital government: Principles and best practices.* London: Idea Group, Inc.

Grizzle, G. A. (1986). Does budget format really govern the actions of budget makers? *Public Budgeting & Finance, 6*(1), 60–70. doi:10.1111/1540-5850.00707

Hassan, S., & Li, F. (2005). Evaluating the usability and content usefulness of websites: A benchmarking approach. *Journal of Electronic Commerce in Organizations, 3*(2), 46–68.

Ho, A. T.-K. (2002). Reinventing local governments and the e-government initiative. *Public Administration Review, 62*(4), 434–445. doi:10.1111/0033-3352.00197

Holden, S. H., Norris, D. F., & Fletcher, P. D. (2003). Electronic government at the local level: Progress to date and future issues. *Public Performance and Management Review, 26*(4), 325–344. doi:10.1177/1530957603026004002

Justice, J. B., Melitski, J., & Smith, D. L. (2004). E-government as an instrument of fiscal accountability and responsiveness. *American Review of Public Administration, 36*(3), 301–322. doi:10.1177/0275074005283797

LeLoup. L. T. (1980). *Budgetary politics, 2nd ed.* Brunswick, Ohio: King's Court Communications, Inc.

Mofleh, S. I., & Wanous, M. (2009). Reviewing existing methods for evaluating e-government websites. *Electronic Government, 6*(2), 129–142. doi:10.1504/EG.2009.024438

Moon, M. J. (2002). The evolution of e-government among municipalities: Rhetoric or reality? *Public Administration Review, 62*(4), 424–443. doi:10.1111/0033-3352.00196

Musso, J. A., Weare, C., & Hale, M. C. (2000). Designing web technologies for local governance reform: Good management for good democracy? *Political Communication, 17*(1), 1–19. doi:10.1080/105846000198486

National Institute of Standards and Technology (NIST). (2001). NIST develops benchmarking website usability methodologies. *Journal of Research of the National Institute of Standards and Technology, 106*(3), 495.

Norris, P. (2001). *Digital divide: Civic engagement, information poverty, and the internet worldwide.* New York: Cambridge University Press.

Pettijohn, C. D., & Grizzle, G. A. (1997). Structural budget reform: Does it affect budget deliberations? *Journal of Public Budgeting, Accounting, &. Financial Management, 9*(1), 26–45.

Reddick, C. G. (2004). A two-stage model of e-government growth: Theories and empirical evidence in U.S. cities. *Government Information Quarterly, 21*(1), 51–64. doi:10.1016/j.giq.2003.11.004

Rubin, I. S. (1993). *The Politics of Public Budgeting: Getting and Spending, Borrowing and Balancing* (2nd ed.). Chatham, NJ: Chatham House.

Rubin, I. S. (1997). *The politics of public budgeting: Getting and spending borrowing and balancing* (3rd ed.). Chatham, NJ: Chatham House.

Rubin, I. S. (2005). The state of state budget research. *Public Budgeting & Finance, 25*(Special), 46–67. doi:10.1111/j.1540-5850.2005.00003.x

Ryu, J. E., Bowling, C. J., Cho, C.-L., & Wright, D. S. (2008). Exploring explanations of state agency budgets: Institutional budget actors or exogenous environment. *Public Budgeting & Finance, 28*(3), 23–47. doi:10.1111/j.1540-5850.2008.00909.x

Schick, A. (1990). *The capacity to budget.* Washington, DC: The Urban Institute Press.

Seifert, J. W., & Peterson, R. E. (2002). The promise of all things E? Expectations and challenges of emergent electronic government. *Perspectives on Global Development and Technology, 1*(2), 193–212. doi:10.1163/156915002100419808

Shuman, H. E. (1992). *Politics and the budget: The struggle between the president and the congress* (3rd ed.). Englewood Cliffs, N.J: Prentice-Hall, Inc.

Simonsen, W., & Robbins, M. D. (2000). *Citizen participation in resource allocation.* Boulder, CO: Westview Press.

Stanford, K. A. (1992). State budget deliberations: Do legislators have a strategy? *Public Administration Review, 52*(1), 16–26. doi:10.2307/976542

Tarafdur, M., & Zhang, J. (2005). Analyzing the influence of website design parameters on website usability. *Information Resources Management Journal, 18*(4), 62–81.

Thomas, J. C., & Streib, G. (2003). The new face of government: Citizen-initiated contacts in the era of e-government. *Journal of Public Administration: Research and Theory, 13*(1), 83–101. doi:10.1093/jpart/mug010

Thurmaier, K. M., & Gosling, J. J. (1997). The shifting roles of state budget offices in the midwest: Gosling revisited. *Public Budgeting & Finance, 17*(4), 48–70. doi:10.1111/1540-5850.01116

Thurmaier, K. M., & Willoughby, K. G. (2001). *Policy and politics in state budgeting.* Armonk, NY: M.E. Sharpe.

Tolbert, C. J., & Mossberger, K. (2006). The effects of e-government on trust and confidence in government. *Public Administration Review, 66*(3), 354–370. doi:10.1111/j.1540-6210.2006.00594.x

Tolbert, C. J., Mossberger, K., & McNeal, R. (2008). Institutions, policy innovation, and e-government in the American states. *Public Administration Review, 68*(3), 549–563. doi:10.1111/j.1540-6210.2008.00890.x

Welch, E. W., Hinnant, C. C., & Moon, M. J. (2006). Linking citizen satisfaction with e-government and trust in government. *Journal of Public Administration: Research and Theory, 15*(3), 371–191. doi:10.1093/jopart/mui021

West, D. M. (2000). *State and federal e-government in the United States, 2000.* Providence, RI: Brown University.

West, D. M. (2003). *State and federal e-government in the United States, 2003.* Providence, RI: Brown University.

West, D. M. (2004). *State and federal e-government in the United States, 2004.* Providence, RI: Brown University.

West, D. M. (2005). E-government capabilities Improving. *Government Finance Review, 21*(6), 8.

Wildavsky, A. (1964). *The politics of the budgetary process.* Boston: Little, Brown & Co.

Wildavsky, A. (1984). *The politics of the budgetary process* (4th ed.). Boston: Little, Brown & Co.

Wildavsky, A. (1992). *The new politics of the budgetary process* (2nd ed.). New York: Harper-Collins Publishers.

Willoughby, K. G. (2004). Performance measurement and budget balancing: State government perspective. *Public Budgeting & Finance, 24*(2), 21–39. doi:10.1111/j.0275-1100.2004.02402002.x

Willoughby, K. G., & Melkers, J. E. (2000). Implementing PBB: Conflicting views of success. *Public Budgeting & Finance, 20*(1), 105–120. doi:10.1111/0275-1100.00006

Compilation of References

Abhichandani, T., & Horan, T. A. (2006). Toward a new evaluation model of e-government satisfaction: Results of structural equation modeling. *Paper presented at the 12th America's Conference on Information Systems (AMCIS 2006)*. Acapulco, Mexico.

Abhijit, J., Mandviwalla, M., & Banker, R. D. (2007). Government as catalyst: Can it work again with wireless internet access? *Public Administration Review*, 67(6), 993–1005. doi:10.1111/j.1540-6210.2007.00790.x

Accenture (2004). *2004 eGovernment report: High performance, maximum value*. Retrieved January 14, 2006, from http://www.accenture.com/NR/rdonlyres/D7206199-C3D4-4CB4A7D8846C94287890/0/gove_egov_value.pdf

Accenture (2006). *Leadership in customer service: Building the trust*. Retrieved April 30, 2009, from http://www.accenture.com

Accenture (2007). *Leadership in customer service: Delivering on the promise*. Retrieved March 12, 2008, from http://www.accenture.com

Accessibility, N. Z. (2008). *Consider the ease of reading, and language level*. Retrieved March 18, 2009, from http://accessibility.net.nz/blog/ease-of-reading-language-level/

Adams, B. (2004). Public meetings and the democratic process. *Public Administration Review*, 64(1), 43–54. doi:10.1111/j.1540-6210.2004.00345.x

Affisco, J., & Soliman, K. (2006). E-government: A strategic operations management framework for service delivery. *Business Process Management Journal*, 12(1), 13–21. doi:10.1108/14637150610643724

Afuah, A., & Tucci, C. (2002). *Internet business models and strategies*. New York: McGraw-Hill.

Ahmad, A. A., Grizzle, G. A., & Pettijohn, C. D. (2003). Patterns of change: Information change and congressional budget deliberations revisited. *Journal of Public Budgeting, Accounting &. Financial Management*, 15(1), 1–22.

Al-adawi, Z., Yousafzai, S., & Pallister, J. (2005). *Conceptual model of citizen adoption of e-government*. The Second International Conference on Innovations in Information Technology. Retrieved June 24, 2009, from http://www.it-innovations.ae/iit005/proceedings/articles/G_6_IIT05-Al-Adawi.pdf

Aladwania, A., & Palvia, P. (1999). Developing and validating an instrument for measuring user-perceived web quality. *Information & Management*, 39(6), 467–476. doi:10.1016/S0378-7206(01)00113-6

Alexander, J. E., & Tate, M. A. (1999). *Web wisdom: how to evaluate and create information quality on the web*. Mahwah, NJ: Lawrence Erlbaum Associates.

Alexander, J., & Tate, M. (1999). *Web wisdom: How to evaluate and create information quality of the Web*. Mahwah, NJ: Lawrence Erlbaum.

Alican, F. (2007). Experts without expertise: E-society projects in developing countries – The case of Turkey. *Information Polity*, 12, 255–263.

Al-Omari, A., & Al-Omari, H. (2006). E-Government readiness assessment model. *Journal of Computer Science, 2*(11), 841–845. doi:10.3844/jcssp.2006.841.845

Alshawi, S., Alahmary, A., & Alalwany, H. (2008). E-government evaluation factors: Citizen's perspective. *Paper presented at the European and Mediterranean Conference on Information Systems 2007 (EMCIS 2007).* Spain.

American Recovery and Reinvestment Act of 2009. (2009). Pub. L. No. 115-5, Section 901, 123 Stat. 115.

Andersen, K. V., & Henriksen, H. Z. (2006). E-government maturity models: Extension of the Layne and Lee model'. *Government Information Quarterly, 23,* 236–248. doi:10.1016/j.giq.2005.11.008

Andersen, D. F., & Dawes, S. S. (1991). *Government Information Management. A Primer and Casebook.* Englewood Cliffs, NJ: Prentice Hall.

Angelelli, P., Guaipatín, C., & Suaznabar, C. (2004). *La colaboración público-privada en el apoyo a la pequeña empresa: siete estudios de caso en América Latina.* Informe de Trabajo. Departamento de Desarrollo Sostenible. International Development Bank.

Anzinger, G. (2003). *African governments on the WWW.* Retrieved March 25, 2008, from http://www.gksoft.com/govt/en/africa.html

Argyris, C., & Schön, D. (1978). *Organizational learning: A theory of action perspective.* Reading, MA: Addison Wesley.

Arif, M. (2008). Customer orientation in e-government project management: A case study. *The Electronic. Journal of E-Government, 6*(1), 1–10.

Arterton, C. (1987). *Teledemocracy: Can technology protect democracy?* Newbury Park, CA: Sage Publications.

Arzoz, X. (2007). The Nature of Language Rights. *Journal on Ethnopolitics and Minority Issues in Europe,* 2. Retrieved August 21, 2009, from http://www.ecmi.de/jemie/download/2-2007-Arzoz.pdf

Australian Government Information Management Office. (2009). *Web Publishing Guide.* Retrieved June 20, 2009 from http://webpublishing.agimo.gov.au

Babbie, E. R. (2008). *The practice of social research* (11th ed.). Belmont, CA: Wadsworth Publishing.

Bachman, R., & Schutt, R. K. (2007). *The practice of research in criminology and criminal justice* (3rd ed.). Thousand Oaks, CA: Sage Publications.

Bagchi, K. (2005). Factors contributing to global digital divide: Some empirical results. *Journal of Global Information Technology Management, 8*(3), 47–65.

Bakan, İ. A., Aydın, H., Kar, M., & Öz, B. (2008). *T-VOHSA Project Phase 2 Report.* Submitted to Türksat

Bakan, İ. A., Aydın, H., Kar, M., & Öz, B. (2009). *T-VOHSA Project Phase 1 Report.* Submitted to Türksat

Balci, A., Kumaş, E., Medeni, T., & Medeni, İ. T. (2009). Development and implementation of e-government services in Turkey. In Cunha, M. M., Oliveira, E. F., & Antonio, J. T. (Eds.), *Handbook of Research on Social Dimensions of Semantic Technologies and Web Services.* Information Science Reference.

Balci, A., Kumas, E., Tasdelen, H., Süngü, E., Medeni, İ. T., & Medeni, T. (2008) Development and implementation of e-government services in Turkey: Issues of standardization, inclusion, citizen satisfaction, integration and interoperability *ICEGOV 2008,* November, Egypt pp 337-342.

Bannister, F. (2007). The curse of the benchmark: An assessment of the validity and value of e-government comparisons. *International Review of Administrative Sciences, 73*(2), 171–188. doi:10.1177/0020852307077959

Bannister, F., & Wilson, D. (2009). O(ver)-government: E-government and the limits of the desirable. *Proceedings of ICEGEG2009,* Turkey

Barber, B. (1984). *Strong democracy: Participatory politics for a new age.* Berkeley: University of California Press.

Barnes, S. J., & Vidgen, R. T. (2004). Interactive e-government services: modelling user perceptions with eQual. *Electronic Government, an International Journal, 1*(2), 213-228.

Barret, K., Green, R., & Katherine Greene, K. (2000). *Powering Up. How Public Managers Can Take Control of Information Technology*. Washington, DC: CQ Press.

Barsky, E. (2006). Introducing Web 2.0: RSS trends for health librarians. *JCHLA / JABSC, 27,* 7-8.

Bass, S. (2000). Negotiating change: Community organizations and the politics of policing. *Urban Affairs Review, 36*(2), 148–177. doi:10.1177/10780870022184813

Basu, A. (2003). Context-driven assessment of commercial websites. *Paper presented at the 36th Hawaii International Conference on System Sciences (HICSS '03)*. Big Island, Hawaii.

Bauer, C., & Scharl, A. (2000). Quantitative evaluation of website content and structure. *Internet Research: Electronic Networking Applications and Policy, 10*(1), 31–43. doi:10.1108/10662240010312138

Baum, C., & De Maio, A. (2000). *Gartner's four phases of e-Government model.*

Bayley, D. H., & Shearing, C. D. (2001). *The new structure of policing: Description, conceptualization, and research agenda*. Washington, DC: National Institute of Justice.

Bekkers, V., & Zouridis, S. (1999). Electronic service delivery in public administration: Some trends and issues. *International Review of Administrative Sciences, 65*(2), 183–195. doi:10.1177/0020852399652004

Bekkers, V. (2003). E-government and emergence of virtual organizations in the public sector. *Information Polity: The International Journal of Government and Democracy in the Information Age, 8,* 89–102.

Belanger, F., & Hiller, J. S. (2006). A framework for e-government: privacy implications. *Business Process Management Journal, 12*(1), 48–60. doi:10.1108/14637150610643751

Bengston, D. N., & Fan, D. (1999). An innovative method for evaluating strategic goals in public agency. *Evaluation Review, 23*(1), 77+. Retrieved February 5, 2000, from EBSCO Database (Academic Search Elite 1531559) http://www.ebsco.com

Benito, B., & Bastida, F. (2009). Budget transparency, fiscal performance, and political turnout: An international approach. *Public Administration Review, 69*(3), 403–417. doi:10.1111/j.1540-6210.2009.01988.x

Benkler, Y. (2006). *The wealth of networks: How social production transforms markets and freedom*. New Haven, CT: Yale University Press.

Bennett, L. (2003). Communicating global activism: Strengths and vulnerabilities of networked politics. *Information Communication and Society, 6*(2), 143–168. doi:10.1080/1369118032000093860

Bennis, W., Goleman, D., & O'Toole, J. (2008). *Transparency: How leaders create a culture of candor*. San Francisco, CA: Jossey Bass.

Berelson, B. (1952). *Content analysis in communication research*. New York: Free Press.

Berman, E. (1997). Dealing with cynical citizens. *Public Administration Review, 57*(2), 105–112. doi:10.2307/977058

Berner, M. (2001). Citizen participation in local government budgeting. *Popular Government*, (Spring): 23–30.

Bertot, J. C., & Jaeger, P. T. (2006). User-centered e-government: Challenges and benefits for government web sites. *Government Information Quarterly, 23*(2), 163–168. doi:10.1016/j.giq.2006.02.001

Bertot, J. C., & Jaeger, P. T. (2008). The e-government paradox: Better customer service doesn't necessarily cost less. *Government Information Quarterly, 25*(2), 149–154. doi:10.1016/j.giq.2007.10.002

Bimber, B. (1999). The internet and citizen communication with government: Does the medium matter? *Political Communication, 16*(4), 409–428. doi:10.1080/105846099198569

Birdsall, W. F. (2007). Web 2.0 as a social movement. *Webology, 4*(2). Retrived from June 12th, 2009, from http://www.webology.ir/2007/v4n2/a40.html

Bittner, E. (1970). *The functions of police in modern society*. Washington, D.C.: US Government Printing Office.

Black, D. (1980). *The manners and customs of the police*. New York: Academic Press.

Bland, R., & Rubin, I. (1997). *Budgeting: A guide for local governments*. Washington, DC: International City/County Management Association.

Blankenship, E. (2001). *Portal design vs. web design*. Retrieved September 24, 2009, from http://www.sap-designguild.org/editions/edition3/graphic.asp

Blanton, T. (2007). The Struggle for openness in the international financial institutions. In Florini, A. (Ed.), *The right to know: Transparency in an open world* (pp. 243–276). New York, NY: Columbia University Press.

Blau, P. M. (1960). *Exchange and power in social life*. New York: John Wiley & Sons, Inc.

Bloniarz, P., Canestraro, D., Cook, M., Cresswell, T., Dawes, S., LaVigne, M., et al. (2000). *Insider's Guide to Using Information in Government*, [Website]. Center for Technology in Government, University at Albany, SUNY. Retreived from www.ctg.albany.edu/publications/online/insider_guide?sub=online

Blumler, J. G., & Katz, E. (1974). *The uses of mass communications: Current perspectives on gratifications research*. Beverly Hills, CA: Sage.

Boeri, R. (2002). XML publishing 2002: state of the TOOLS. *EMedia Magazine, 14*(12), 61–64.

Bolivar, M., Perez, C., & Hernandez, A. (2007). E-government and public financial reporting: The case of Spanish regional governments. *The American Review of Public Administration, 37*(2), 142-177. Retrieved March 23, 2009, from http://arp.sagepub.com/cgi/reprint/37/2/142

Borg, M. O., & Mason, P. M. (1990). Earmarked lottery revenues: Positive windfalls or concealed redistribution mechanisms? *Journal of Education Finance, 15*, 289–301.

Bovaird, T. (2007). Beyond engagement and participation: User and community coproduction of public services. *Public Administration Review, 67*(5), 846–860. doi:10.1111/j.1540-6210.2007.00773.x

Box, R. C. (1998). *Citizen governance: Leading American communities into the 21st century*. Thousand Oaks, CA: Sage Publications.

Box, R., & Sagen, D. (1998). Working with citizens: Breaking down barriers to citizen self-governance. In King, C., & Stivers, C. (Eds.), *Government is us: Public administration in an anti-government era* (pp. 158–172). Thousand Oaks, CA: Sage Publications, Inc.

Boyte, H. C. (2005). Reframing democracy: Governance civic agency, and politics. *Public Administration Review, 65*(5), 536–546. doi:10.1111/j.1540-6210.2005.00481.x

Bradbrook, G., & Fisher, J. (2004). *Digital equality: Reviewing digital inclusion, activity and mapping the way forward*. Retrieved, July 8, 2007 from http://www.citizensonline.org.uk/site/media/documents/939_Digital Equaltity1.pdrf

Bricken, M. (1991). Virtual worlds: No interface to design. In Benedikt, M. (Ed.), *Cyberspace: First Steps* (pp. 363–382). Cambridge, MA: MIT Press.

Brinner, R. E., & Clotfelter, C. T. (1975). An economic appraisal of state lotteries. *National Tax Journal, 28*(4), 395–404.

Brown, M. M. (2001). The benefits and costs of information technology innovations: An empirical assessment of a local government agency. *Pubic Performance and Management Review, 24*(4), 351–366. doi:10.2307/3381224

Brown, M. M. (2001). The Benefits and Costs of Information Technology Innovations: An Empirical Assessment of a Local Government Agency. *Pubic Performance & Management Review, 24*(4), 351–366. doi:10.2307/3381224

Brown, M. M. (2000). *The challenge of information and communications technology for development*. Retrieved May 2005, from http://www.undp.org/dpa/statements/administ/2000/ july/3july00.html

Brown, M. M. (2003). *Statement to World Summit on the Information Society, Geneva, 11 December.* Retrieved May, 2005 from http://www.undp.org/dpa/statements/administ/2003/december/11dec03.html.

Brugger, W. (1996). The Image of the Person in the Human Rights Concept [Electronic version]. *Human Rights Quarterly, 18*(3), 594–611. doi:10.1353/hrq.1996.0034

Brynjolfsson, E. (1994). Information assets, technology and organization. *Management Science, 40*(12), 1645–1662. doi:10.1287/mnsc.40.12.1645

Budd, R. W., Thorp, R. K., & Donohew, L. (1967). *Content analysis of communications.* New York: Macmillan Company.

BuddeComm. (2009). *Mobile Phone Data.* Retrieved July 2, 2009 from http://www.budde.com.au

Budge, I. (1996). *The new challenge of direct democracy.* Oxford, UK: Policy Press.

Bughin, J., & Manyika, J. (2007). *How businesses are using web 2.0: A McKinsey global survey.* San Francisco, CA: McKinsey & Company.

Burbridge, L. (2002). Accountability and MIS. *Public Performance and Management Review, 25*(4), 421–423. doi:10.1177/15357602025004013

Bystrom, K., & Jarverlin, K. (1995). Task complexity affects information seeking and use. *Information Processing & Management, 31*(2), 191–213. doi:10.1016/0306-4573(94)00041-Z

C.E.E.S. (2009) *Citizen-oriented evaluation of e-government services.* EU Marie Curie IAPP funded Project. Unpublished literature review as project deliverable document.

Cabinet Office. UK. (2009). *Web standards and guidelines.* Retrieved June 20, 2009 from http://www.cabinetoffice.gov.uk/government_it/web_guidelines.aspx

Caldero, M. P., & Crank, J. P. (2004). *Police ethics: The corruption of a noble cause* (2nd ed.). Cincinnati, OH: Anderson Publishing, Inc.

Caldwell, L. (1964). *Administrative theories of Hamilton and Jefferson.* New York: Russell & Russell.

Callahan, K. (2000). Citizen participation run amok. *Public Productivity and Management Review, 23*(3), 394–398. doi:10.2307/3380727

Campbell, N. D. (2003). Do lottery funds increase educational expenditure? Evidence from Georgia's lottery for education. *Journal of Education Finance, 28,* 383–402.

Cap Gemini. (2006). *Online Availability of Public Services: How Is Europe Progressing? Web Based Survey on Electronic Public Services – Report of the 6th Measurement.* London: Cap Gemini.

Cap Gemini. (2007). *The User Challenge: Benchmarking the Supply of Online Public Services – 7th Measurement.* London: Cap Gemini.

Cap Gemini (2007). *The user challenge benchmarking: The supply of online public services 7th measurement.* European Commission, Directorate General Information Society and Media. Retrieved n.d. from http://74.125.93.132/search?q=cache:LcdZTz-gJFoJ:ec.europa.eu/information_society/eeurope/i2010/docs/benchmarking/egov_benchmark_2007.pdf+The+user+challenge+benchmarking:+The+supply+of+online+public+services+7th+measurement&cd=1&hl=en&ct=clnk&gl=us

Cap Gemini. Ernst and Young. (2004). *Online Availability of Public Services: How is Europe Progressing? (Web-based Survey on Electronic Public Services: Report of the Fourth Measurement, October 2003), Report to the European Commission DG Information Society:* Author. Retrieved June 4, 2009, from ec.europa.eu/information_ society/eeurope/2005/doc/highlights/whats_new/capgemini4.pdf de Guzman, M. C. (2001). *Integrity, legitimacy, efficiency and impact: Do all these matter in the civilian review of the police?* Unpublished Ph. D. dissertation, University of Cincinnati, Cincinnati, OH.

Carnegie Mellon University. (n.d.). *Capability Maturity model Integration.* Retrieved August 8, 2009, from http://www.sei.cmu.edu/cmmi/

Carrizales, T. (2008). Critical factors in an electronic democracy: A study of municipal managers. *The Electronic Journal of e-Government, 6*(1), 23-30. Retrieved March 25, 2009, from http://www.ejeg.com/volume-6/vol6-iss1/Carrizales.pdf

Carter, L., & Bélanger, F. (2005). The utilization of e-government services: Citizen trust, innovation and acceptance factors. *Information Systems Journal, 15*, 5–25. doi:10.1111/j.1365-2575.2005.00183.x

Çayhan, B. E. (2008). Implementing e-government in Turkey: A comparison of online public service delivery in Turkey and the European Union. *EJISDC (2008) 35, 8*, 1-11

Chadwick, A., & May, C. (2003). Interaction between states and citizens in the age of the Internet: "e-Government" in the United States, Britain, and the European Union. *Governance: An International Journal of Policy, Administration, and Institutions, 16*(2), 271–300.

Chadwick, A., & Christopher, M. (2003). Interaction between States and Citizens in the age of the internet: "E-Government" in the United States, Britain, and the European Union. *Governance, 16*(2), 271–300. doi:10.1111/1468-0491.00216

Chadwick, A. (2008). Web 2.0: New challenges for the study of e-democracy in an era of Informational exuberance. *A Journal of Law and Policy for the Information Society, 51*, 9-42.

Chadwick, A., & May, C. (2001). *Interaction between states and citizens in the age of the Internet.: "E-Government" in the United States, Britain and the European Union.* Paper presented to the American Political Science Association annual meeting.

Chandra, A., Fealey, T., & Rau, P. (2006). National barriers to global competitiveness: the case of the IT industry in India. *Competitiveness Review, 16*(1), 12–19.

Chandrasekhar, C. P. (2003). The diffusion of information technology: The Indian experience. *Social Scientist, 31*(7/8), 42–85. doi:10.2307/3518307

Charilas, E. D., Markaki, I. O., Psarras, J., & Constantinou, P. (2009). Application of fuzzy ahp and ELECTRE to network selection. *Paper presented at the 1st International Conference on Mobile Lightweight Wireless Systems (MOBILIGHT 2009).* Athens, Greece.

Chary, M. (2007). Public Organizations in the Age of Globalization and Technology. *Public Organization Review, 7*(2), 181–189. doi:10.1007/s11115-007-0029-0

Chary, M., & Aikins, S. K. (2009). Policy as a Bridge across the Global Digital Divide. In Ferrero, E. (Eds.), *Overcoming digital divides: constructing an equitable and competitive information society.* Hershey, PA: IGI Global.

Checkoway, B., & Van Til, J. (1978). What do we know about citizen participation? A selective review of research. In Langton, S. (Ed.), *Citizen participation in America* (pp. 25–42). Lexington, MA: Lexington Books.

Chen, A. N. K., LaBrie, R. C., & Shao, B. B. M. (2003). An XML Adoption Framework for Electronic Business. *Journal of Electronic Commerce Research, 4*(1), 1–14.

Chen, M. (2003). Factors Affecting the Adoption and Diffusion of XML and Web services Standards for E-Business Systems. *International Journal of Human-Computer Studies, 58*, 259–279. doi:10.1016/S1071-5819(02)00140-4

Chengalur-Smith, I., & Duchessi, P. (1999). The initiation and adoption of client–server technology in organizations. *Information & Management, 35*(2), 77–88. doi:10.1016/S0378-7206(98)00077-9

Chesbrough, H., & Rosenbloom, R. (2002). The role of the business model in capturing value from innovation: Evidence from Xerox Corporation's technology spin-off companies. *Industrial and Corporate Change, 11*(3). doi:10.1093/icc/11.3.529

Chinn, M. D., & Fairlie, R. W. (2007). The determinants of the global digital divide: a cross-country analysis of computer and Internet penetration. *Oxford Economic Papers, 59*, 16–44. doi:10.1093/oep/gpl024

Chondine, J., & Gheorghita, G. (2005). Integrated views of e-government website usability: perspectives from users and web diagnostic tools. *Electronic Government, 2*(3), 318.

Cingil, I., Dogac, A., & Azgin, A. (2000). A Broader Approach to Personalization. *Communications of the ACM, 43*(8), 136–141. doi:10.1145/345124.345168

City of Tampa. (2009). *Tampa Announcements*. Retrieved 9 June 2009 from: http://www.tampagov.net/appl_tampa_announcements/default.asp?page=1&hide=yes&VF=0&numResults=10&typeID=WEB&searchDate=6%2F9%2F2009+1%3A41%3A25+PM

Clinton, W. J. (2000). *Executive Order 13166*. Retrieved May 10, 2009 from http://www.usdoj.gov/crt/cor/Pubs/eolep.php

Clotfelter, C. T., & Cook, P. J. (1987). Implicit tax in lottery finance. *National Tax Journal, 40*, 533–546.

Coase, R. H. (1988). *The firm the market and the law*. Chicago: University of Chicago Press.

Cohen, J. (1960). A coefficient of agreement for nominal scales. *Educational and Psychological Measurement, 20*, 37–46. doi:10.1177/001316446002000104

Cole, G. F., & Smith, C. E. (2008). *Criminal justice in America* (5th ed.). Belmont, CA: Wadsworth Publishing.

Cole, R., & Caputo, D. (1984). The public hearing as an effective citizen participation mechanism: A case study of the general revenue sharing program. *The American Political Science Review, 78*(2), 404–416. doi:10.2307/1963372

Coleman, S., & Gotze, J. (2003). *Bowling together: Online public engagement in policy deliberation*. London, UK: Hansard Society.

Colorado Fiscal Policy Institute. (2003). *The transparency of Colorado's budget process: Is it open, understandable, and accessible to Coloradans? Prepared by J. Zelenski, October*. Denver, CO: Colorado Center on Law and Policy.

Compaine, B. M. (2001). Declare the war won. In Compaine, B. M. (Ed.), *The digital divide: Facing a crisis or creating a myth?* Cambridge, MA: MIT Press.

Compeau, D., Higgins, C., & Huff, S. (1999). Social cognitive theory and individual reactions to computing technology: A longitudinal study. *Management Information Systems Quarterly, 23*(2), 145–158. doi:10.2307/249749

Cooke, A. (1999). *Neal-Schuman authoritative guide to evaluating information on the Internet*. New York: Neal-Schuman Publishers.

Cooper, T. L. (Ed.). (2005). Articles from the civic engagement initiative conference. *Public Administration Review, 65*(5), 534–623. doi:10.1111/j.1540-6210.2005.00480.x

Cooper, T. L. (1990). *The responsible administrator: An approach to ethics for the administrative role* (3rd ed.). San Francisco: Jossey-Bass.

Cooper, M. (2006). *Expanding the digital divide and falling behind on broadband: Why a telecommunication policy of neglect is not benign*. Washington, DC: Consumer Federation of America and Consumers Union. Retrieved, May 29, 2006, from www.consumersunion.org/pub/ddnewbook.pdf

Cordner, G., & Scarborough, K. (2008). *Police administration*. Newark, NJ: Anderson Publishing.

Corry, M., Frick, T., & Hansen, L. (1997). User-centered design and usability testing of a web site: An illustrative case study. *Educational Technology Research and Development, 45*(4), 65–76. doi:10.1007/BF02299683

Costello, J., Canestraro, D. S., Ramón Gil-Garcia, J., & Werthmuller, D. (2007). *Using XML for Website Management: Lessons Learned Report*. Albany, NY: The Research Foundation of State University of New York.

Costello, J., Werthmuller, D., & Apte, D. (2002). *XML: A new website architecture*. Albany, NY: Center for Technology in Government.

Costello, J., Adhya, S., Gil-García, J. R., Pardo, T. A., & Werthmuller, D. (2004, August 6-11). Beyond Data Exchange: XML as a Website Workflow and Content Management Technology. Paper presented at the 2004 Annual Meeting of the Academy of Management: Creating Actionable Knowledge, New Orleans, LA, USA.

Costello, J., Canestraro, D. S., Werthmuller, D., Ramon Gil-Garcia, J., & Baker, A. (2006). *Using XML for Website Management: Getting Started Guide*. Albany, NY: Center for Technology in Government, University at Albany, SUNY.

Coursey, D., & Norris, D. (2008). Models of e-Government: Are they correct? An empirical assessment. *Public Administration Review*, *68*(3), 523–536. doi:10.1111/j.1540-6210.2008.00888.x

Coursey, D., & Norris, D. F. (2008). Models of e-government: Are they correct? An empirical assessment. *Public Administration Review*, (May-June): 523–535. doi:10.1111/j.1540-6210.2008.00888.x

Creighton, J. L. (1981). *The public involvement manual*. Cambridge, MA: Abt.

CSG. (2002). *The book of the states. 2002 edition* (*Vol. 34*). Lexington, KY: The Council of State Governments.

Cuillier, D., & Piotrowski, S. J. (2009). Internet information-seeking and its relation to support for access to government records. *Government Information Quarterly*, *26*, 441–449. doi:10.1016/j.giq.2009.03.001

Curtin, G. (2007). *Encyclopedia of political communications*. Thousand Oaks, CA: Sage Publications.

Curtin, D., & Meijer, A. (2006). Does transparency increase legitimacy? *Information Polity*, *11*(2), 109–122.

Curtin, G. (2006). *Issues and challenges global e-government/e-participation models, measurement and methodology: A framework for moving forward*. Prepared for the United Nations Department of Administration and Development Management Workshop on e-participation and e-government: Understanding the present and creating the future. Budapest, Hungary. Retrieved June 25, from http://www.usc.edu/schools/sppd/private/bedrosian/Global_EGovernmentJul06.pdf

Cyberspace Policy Research Group. (n.d.). *Cyberspace Policy Research Group*. Retrieved March 7, 2009, from http://www.cyprg.arizona.edu/waes.html

Daft, R. L., & Lengel, R. H. (1986). Organizational information requirements, media richness and structural design. *Management Science*, *32*(5), 554–571. doi:10.1287/mnsc.32.5.554

Daft, R. L., Lengel, R. H., & Trevino, L. K. (1987). Message equivocality, media selection, and manager performance: Implications for information support systems. *Management Information Systems Quarterly*, *11*, 355–366. doi:10.2307/248682

Daniels, T. (1999). *When city and county collide: Managing growth in the metropolitan fringe*. Washington, DC: Island Press.

Danziger, J., & Anderson, K. (2002). The impacts of information technology on public administration: An analysis of empirical research from the "Golden Age" of transformation. *International Journal of Public Administration*, *25*(5), 591–627. doi:10.1081/PAD-120003292

Davis, F. D. (1989). Perceived usefulness, perceived ease of use and user acceptance of information technology. *Management Information Systems Quarterly*, *13*(3), 319–340. doi:10.2307/249008

Davis, J., & Merritt, S. (1998). *The web design wow book: Showcasing the best of on-screen communication*. Berkeley, CA: Peachpit Press.

Davis, G. B. (1982). Strategies for information requirements determination. *IBM Systems Journal*, *21*(1), 4–30. doi:10.1147/sj.211.0004

Davis, J. R., Filer, J. E., & Moak, D. L. (1992). The lottery as an alternative source of state revenue. *Atlantic Economic Journal*, *20*, 1–10. doi:10.1007/BF02298871

Davis, O. A., Dempster, M. A. H., & Wildvasky, A. (1966). A Theory of the Budgetary Process. *The American Political Science Review*, *60*(3), 529–547. doi:10.2307/1952969

Dawes, S., Cresswell, A., & Theresa, P. (2009). From "Need to Know" to "Need to Share": tangled problems information boundaries and the building of public sector knowledge networks. *Public Administration Review*, *69*(3), 392–401. doi:10.1111/j.1540-6210.2009.01987_2.x

Dawes, S. S., Gregg, V., & Agouris, P. (2004). Digital government research: Investigations at the crossroads of social and information science. *Social Science Computer Review, 22*(1), 5–10. doi:10.1177/0894439303259863

Dawes, S. S., & Prefontaine, L. (2003). Understanding new models of collaboration for delivering government services. *Communications of the ACM, 46*(1), 40–42. doi:10.1145/602421.602444

Dawes, S. (2008). The evolution and continuing challenges of e-governance. *Public Administration Review, 68*, 86–102.

Dawes, S. S., & Nelson, M. R. (1995). Pool the risks, share the benefits: Partnerships in IT innovation. In Keyes, J. (Ed.), *Technology Trendlines. Technology Success Stories from Today's Visionaries* (pp. 125–135). New York: Van Nostrand Reinhold.

Dawes, S. S., & Pardo, T. A. (2002). Building collaborative digital government systems. systematic constraints and effective practices. In McIver, W. J., & Elmagarmid, A. K. (Eds.), *Advances in digital government. technology, human factors, and policy* (pp. 259–273). Norwell, MA: Kluwer Academic Publishers. doi:10.1007/0-306-47374-7_16

de Guzman, M. C., & Frank, J. (2004). Using learning as a construct to measure civilian review board impact on the police: The Philippine experience. *Policing: An International Journal of Police Strategies and Management, 27*(2), 167–182.

de Kool, D., & van Wamelen, J. (2008). *Web 2.0: A new basis for e-government?* Paper presented at the 3rd International Conference on Information and Communication Technologies, Damascus, Turkey.

Deci, E. L., & Ryan, R. M. (1991). A motivational approach to self: Integration in personality. In R. Dienstbier (Ed.), *Nebraska Symposium on Motivation*: Vol. 38. *Perspectives on motivation* (pp. 237-288). Lincoln: University of Nebraska Press.

Deconti, L. (1998). *Planning and creating a government web site: Learning from the experience of U.S. states* (Working Paper No.2). Manchester, UK.

Dee, T. S. (2004). Lotteries, litigation and education finance. *Southern Economic Journal, 70*, 584–599. doi:10.2307/4135332

DeLone, W., & Mclean, E. (1992). Information systems success: The quest for the dependent variable. *Information Systems Research, 3*(1), 60–95. doi:10.1287/isre.3.1.60

DeLuca, D. C., & Valacich, J. S. (2008). Situational synchronicity for decision support. In Adam, F., & Humphreys, P. (Eds.), *Encyclopedia of decision making and decision support technologies* (*Vol. II*, pp. 790–797). Hershey, PA: Information Science Reference.

Demchak, C., Friis, C., & La Porte, T. (1998). Reflections on configuring public agencies in cyberspace: A conceptual investigation. In Snellen, I. M., & van Donk, W. (Eds.), *Public administration in an information age: A Handbook*. Amsterdam: IOS Press.

Denhardt, R. (1999). The future of public administration. *Public Administration and Management, 4*(2), 279–292.

Dennis, A. R., & Valacich, J. S. (1999). Rethinking Media Richness: Towards a theory of media synchronicity. In HICSS-32, *32nd Annual Hawaii International Conference on System Sciences*. Los Alamitos CA: IEEE Computer Society.

Department of Health and Human Services. U.S. (2009). *Research Based Web Design & Usability Guidelines*. Retrieved June 20, 2009, from http://www.usability.gov

Department's National Telecommunications and Information Administration. (2009). *Memorandum for the heads of executive departments and agencies*. Retrieved September 24, 2009, from http://www.whitehouse.gov/the_press_office/TransparencyandOpenGovernment/

Derthick, M., & Quirk, P. (1985). *The politics of deregulation*. Washington: Brookings Institution.

DeSario, J., & Langton, S. (1984). *Citizen Participation in public decision making*. New York: Greenwood Press.

Devlet Planlanma Teşkilatı. (2006). *Information society strategy document*. Devlet Planlanma Teşkilatı.

Devlet Planlanma Teşkilatı. (2008). *Information society strategy progress report*. Devlet Planlanma Teşkilatı. (in Turkish)

Dias, B., & Brewer, E. (2009). How computer science serves the developing world. *Communications of the ACM*, *52*(6), 74–75. doi:10.1145/1516046.1516064

Dimaggio, P., Hargttai, E., Neuman, W. R., & Robinson, J. P. (2001). Social implications of the Internet. *Annual Review of Sociology*, *27*, 307–336. doi:10.1146/annurev. soc.27.1.307

Dimitrova, D. V., & Chen, Y. (2006). Profiling the adopters of e-government information and *services*: The influence of psychological characteristics, civic mindedness, and information channels. *Social Science Computer Review*, *24*(2), 172–188. doi:10.1177/0894439305281517

Downey, E. (2008). A conceptual framework for considering the value of e-government. In Anttiroiko, A. V. (Ed.), *Electronic government concepts methodologies tools and applications* (pp. 843–852). Hershey, PA: IGI Global.

Downs, A. (1962). The public interest: It's meaning in a democracy. *Social Research: An International Quarterly of Political and Social Science*, 1-36.

Drake, B., Yuthas, K., & Dillard, J. (2000). Its only words: Impacts of information technology on moral dialogue. *Journal of Business Ethics*, *23*(1), 41–59. doi:10.1023/A:1006270911041

Dunn, M. (2003). *Single Source Publishing with XML*. IT Pro(Jan/Feb), 51-54.

Dupont, B. (2003). The New Face of Police Governance in Australia. *Journal of Australian Studies*, *27*(78), 15–24. doi:10.1080/14443050309387867

Dwivedi, P., & Sahu, G. (2009). *Challenges of e-government implementation in India. Emerging technologies in e-government*. New Delhi: GIFT Publishing.

Dye, T. R. (1978). *Understanding Public Policy*. Englewood Cliffs, NJ: Prentice-Hall.

Ebbers, W. E., Pieterson, W. J., & Noordman, H. N. (2008). Electronic government: Rethinking channel management strategies. *Government Information Quarterly*, *25*(2), 181–201. doi:10.1016/j.giq.2006.11.003

Ebdon, C., & Franklin, A. (2004). Searching for a role for citizens in the budget process. *Public Budgeting & Finance*, *24*(1), 32–49. doi:10.1111/j.0275-1100.2004.02401002.x

Eglene, O., Dawes, S. S., & Schneider, C. A. (2007). Authority and leadership patterns in public sector knowledge networks. *American Review of Public Administration*, *37*(1), 91–113. doi:10.1177/0275074006290799

Eirinaki, M., & Vazirgiannis, M. (2003). Web mining for web personalization. *ACM Transactions on Internet Technology*, *3*(1), 1–27. doi:10.1145/643477.643478

Erakovich, R., Kavran, D., & Wyman, S. (2006). A normative approach to ethics training in Central and Eastern Europe. *International Journal of Public Administration*, *29*(13), 1229–1257. doi:10.1080/01900690600928060

Erakovich, R., & Wyman, S. (2009). Implications of organizational influence on ethical behavior: An analysis of the perceptions of public managers. In Cox, R. W. III, (Ed.), *Ethics and integrity in public administration: Concepts and cases* (pp. 77–91). Armonk, NY: M. E. Sharpe, Inc.

Eschenfelder, K. (2004). How do government agencies review and approve text content for publication on their Web sites? A framework to compare Web content management practices. *Library & Information Science Research*, *26*, 463–481. doi:10.1016/j.lisr.2004.04.007

Eschenfelder, K. R. (2004). Behind the web site: An inside look at the production of web-based textual government information. *Government Information Quarterly*, *21*, 337–358. doi:10.1016/j.giq.2004.04.004

Estabrook, L., Witt, E., & Rainie, L. (2007). *Information searches that solve problems: How people use the Internet, libraries, and government agencies when they need help*. Pew Internet and American Life Project. Retrieved May 1, 2009 from http://www.pewinternet.org

Ethier, K. (2002). *Managing Content from Creation to Delivery with XML: Case studies*. Paper presented at the XML Conference and Exposition 2002, Baltimore, MD.

EU. i2010 eGovernment Action Plan, Commission of the European Communities (CEC), i2010 e-Government Action Plan: Accelerating e-Government in Europe for the Benefit of All, COM (2006) *173 final*. Retrieved June 20, 2009 from http://ec.europa.eu/idabc/servlets/Doc?id=25286

European Commission. (2004) *European interoperability framework for pan-european egovernment services*. Retrieved on June 12, 2008, from IDABC website: http://ec.europa.eu/idabc/servlets/Doc?id=19528

European Commission. (n.d.). *e-Inclusion policy*. Retrieved January 19, 2009, from http://ec.europa.eu/information_society/activities/einclusion/policy/index_en.htm

European Communication. (2006). *i2010 e-government action plan: Accelerating egovernment in europe for the benefit of all. COM(2006) 173 final*. Brussels, Belgium: Commission of the European Communities.

European Union. (2009). *epractice*. Retrieved June 5, 2009, www.epractice.eu

Faber, K. (1998). *The Internet design project: The best of graphic art on the Web*. New York, NY: Universe Publishing.

Faerman, S. R., McCaffrey, D., & Van Slyke, D. M. (2001). Understanding interorganizational cooperation: public–private collaboration in regulating financial market innovation. *Organization Science*, *12*(3), 372–388. doi:10.1287/orsc.12.3.372.10099

Fallows, J. (2007, April). One-button translation. *The Atlantic*. Retrieved March 24, 2009 from: http://www.theatlantic.com/doc/200704/fallows-translators

Farnham, K. (2008). *Use of Mashups in the US Government*. Retrieved May 03, 2009, from http://blog.programmableweb.com/2008/10/23/use-of-mashups-in-the-us-government/

Fei, J., Yao, R., & Yu, L. (2008). Fuzzy analytic hierarchy process application to e-government performance evaluation. *Paper presented at the 5th International Conference on Fuzzy Systems and Knowledge Discovery (FSKD '08)*. Jinan, China.

Ferber, P., Foltz, F., & Pugliese, R. (2007). Cyberdemocracy and online politics: A new model of interactivity. *Bulletin of Science, Technology & Society*, *27*(5), 391–400. doi:10.1177/0270467607304559

Ferber, P., Foltz, F., & Pugliese, R. (2003). The politics of state legislature web sites: Making e-government more participatory. *Bulletin of Science, Technology & Society*, *23*(3), 147–167. doi:10.1177/0270467603023003002

Fichter, D. C., F. (2000). Documents, Data, Information Retrieval, & XML. *Online*, *24*(6), 30–36.

Fletcher, P. D. (2002). Policy and portals. In McIver, W. J., & Elmagarmid, A. K. (Eds.), *Advances in digital government: Technology, human factors, and policy*. Norwell, MA: Kluwer Academic Press. doi:10.1007/0-306-47374-7_14

Florida Center for Community Design + Research, School of Architecture and Community Design, University of South Florida (2005). *Hillsborough Community Atlas: City of Tampa*. Retrieved 9 June 2009, from http://www.hillsborough.communityatlas.usf.edu/demographics/default.asp?ID=1205771000&level=mncplty#elp

Foley, D. (1998). We want your input: Dilemmas of citizen participation. In King, C., & Stivers, C. (Eds.), *Government is us: Public administration in an anti-government era* (pp. 140–156). Thousand Oaks, CA: Sage Publications, Inc.

Følstad, A., Jørgensen, H. D., & Krogstie, J. (2004). User involvement in e-government development projects. In *Proceedings of the third Nordic conference on Human-computer interaction*. Tampere, Finland.

Fountain, J. E. (2001). *Building the virtual state: Information technology and Institutional change*. Washington, DC: The Brookings Institution.

Fountain, J. (1999). The Virtual State: Toward a Theory of Federal Bureaucracy in the 21st Century. In Kamarch, E., & Nye, J. (Eds.), *Democracy.com? Governance in a Networked World* (pp. 133–156). Hollis, NH: Hollis Publishing Company.

Francq, P. (2009). E-democracy: the social software perspective. In Lytras, M., Tennyson, R., & Pablos, P. (Eds.), *Knowledge Network* (pp. 61–73). Hershey: IGI Publishing. doi:10.4018/978-1-59904-976-2.ch005

Frederickson, H. G. (1997). *The spirit of public administration*. San Francisco, CA: Jossey-Bass Inc., Publishers.

Fung, A. (2004). *Empowered participation: reinventing urban democracy*. Princeton, NJ: Princeton University Press.

Furuholt, B., & Wahid, F. (2008). E-Government challenges and the role of political leadership in Indonesia: The case of Sragen. In *Proceedings of the 41st Annual Hawaii International Conference on System Sciences* (HICSS 2008). Hawaii, US. January 7-10, 2008.

Gant, D. B., Gant, J. P., & Craig, L. J. (2002). *State web portals: Delivering and financing e-service. E-Government Series*. Arlington, VA: The PricewaterhouseCoopers Endowment for The Business in Government.

Gant, J. P., & Gant, D. B. (2002). Web portal functionality and State government E-service. In *Proceedings of the 35th Hawaii International Conference on System Sciences*.

Garcia, A. C. B., Maciel, C., & Pinto, F. B. (2005). A quality inspection method to evaluate e-government sites. In M.A. Wimmer, R. Traunmuller, A. Gronlund, & K.V. Andersen, (Eds.), *Proceedings of Electronic Government: 4th International Conference, EGOV 2005*: Lecture Notes in Computer Science, Vol. 3591, Copenhagen, Denmark, pp. 198-209.

Gardner, J. W. (1990). *On leadership*. NY: The Free Press.

Garrett, T. A. (2001). The Leviathan lottery? Testing the revenue maximization objective of state lotteries as evidence for Leviathan. *Public Choice, 109*, 101–117. doi:10.1023/A:1012081307920

Garson, G. D. (2006). *Public information technology and e-governance: Managing the virtual state*. Sudbury, MA: Jones and Bartlett Publishers.

Garson, G. D., & Pavlichev, A. (Eds.). (2004). *Digital government: Principles and best practices*. London: Idea Group, Inc.

Garson, G. D. (2003). Toward an information technology research agenda for public administration. In Garson, G. D. (Ed.), *Public information technology: Policy and management issues* (pp. 331–357). Hershey, PA: Idea Group Publishing.

Garson, G. D. (2004). The promise of digital government. In Pavlichev, A., & Garson, G. D. (Eds.), *Digital government: Principles and best practices* (pp. 2–15). Hershey, PA: Idea Group Publishing.

Garzotto, F., Mainetti, L., & Paolini, P. (1995). Hypermedia design, Analysis, and Evaluation Issues. *Communications of the ACM, 38*(8), 74–86. doi:10.1145/208344.208349

Gathegi, J. N. (2005). Democracy through access to legal information for newly democratizing nations: The Kenyan perspective and lessons from the American experience. *Government Information Quarterly, 22*, 108–121. doi:10.1016/j.giq.2004.10.004

Gehrke, D., & Turban, E. (1999). Determinants of successful website design: Relative importance and recommendations for effectiveness. *Paper presented at the 32nd Hawaii International Conference on System Sciences (HICSS'99)*. Maui Island, Hawaii.

Genus, A., & Mohd Ali Mohamad Nor. (2005). Socialising the digital divide: Implications for ICTs and e-business development. *Journal of Electronic Commerce in Organizations, 3*(2), 82–95.

Giblin, M. (2006). Structural elaboration and institutional isomorphism: The case of crime analysis units. *Policing: An International Journal of Police Strategies & Management, 29*(4), 643–664. doi:10.1108/13639510610711583

Gil-Garcia, J., & Martinez-Moyano, I. (2007). Understanding the evolution of e-government: The influence of systems of rules on public sector dynamics. *Government Information Quarterly, 24,* 266–290. doi:10.1016/j.giq.2006.04.005

Gil-Garcia, J. R., & Pardo, T. A. (2005). E-government success factors: Mapping practical tools to theoretical foundations. *Government Information Quarterly, 22,* 187–216. doi:10.1016/j.giq.2005.02.001

Gil-Garcia, J. R., Costello, J., Pardo, T. A., & Werthmuller, D. (2007). Invigorating Website Management through XML: An E-Government Case from New York State. *International Journal of Electronic Governance, 1*(1), 52–78. doi:10.1504/IJEG.2007.014343

Gil-Garcia, J. R., & Helbig, N. (2006). Exploring e-government benefits and success factors. In Anttiroiko, A.-V., & Malkia, M. (Eds.), *Encyclopedia of digital government* (pp. 803–811). Hershey, PA: IGI Global.

Gil-Garcia, J. R., & Luna-Reyes, L. F. (2006). Integrating conceptual approaches to e-government. In Khosrow-Pour, M. (Ed.), *Encyclopedia of E-Commerce, E-Government and Mobile Commerce.* Hershey, PA: Idea Group Inc.

Gil-García, J. R., & Luna-Reyes, L. F. (2003). Towards a Definition of Electronic Government: A Comparative Review. In Mendez-Vilas, A., Mesa Gonzalez, J. A., Mesa Gonzalez, J., Guerrero Bote, V., & Zapico Alonso, F. (Eds.), *Techno-legal Aspects of the Information Society and New Economy: An Overview.* Badajoz, Spain: Formatex.

Giudice, M., & Goodman, S. (1999, December). *Where the front and backend meet: Collaboration between designers and engineers.* Paper presented at the CNET Builder.com Live Conference, New Orleans, LA.

Godwin, B. (2008). Matrix of web 2.0 technology and government. Retrieved June 9th, 2009, from http://www.usa.gov/webcontent/documents/Web_Technology_Matrix.pdf

Gökmen, A. (2009). Developments and prospects in e-government implementations in Turkey. In *Proceedings of the ICEGEG2009,* Turkey.

Goldstein, H. (1990). *Problem-oriented policing.* Philadelphia, PA: Temple University Press.

Gordon, P. (1977). *Public administration in the public interest.* Paper presented at the National Conference of the American Society for Public Administration, Atlanta, GA.

Gortner, H. F. (1991). *Ethics for public managers.* New York: Praeger.

Gottschalk, P. (2008). Organizational structure as predictor of intelligence strategy implementation in policing. *International Journal of Law, Crime and Justice, 36,* 184–195. doi:10.1016/j.ijlcj.2008.05.001

Gourville, J. (2004). Why consumers don't buy: The psychology of new product adoption. *Harvard Business School Note #504-056.*

Government Finance Officers Association (GFOA). (1998). *Recommended budget practices.* Chicago, IL.

Government of Bangladesh. (2004). *Comprehensive study of e-government initiatives in Bangladesh: Final report.* Retrieved May 2009, from http://www.sict.gov.bd/digitallibrary.php

Government of Bangladesh. (2008). *e-Government initiatives in Bangladesh: A sample survey.* Retrieved May 2009, from http://www.sict.gov.bd/digitallibrary.php

Gramlich, E. M. (1990). *A Guide to benefit-cost analysis* (2nd ed.). Englewood Cliffs, NJ: Prentice Hall.

Grant, G., & Chau, D. (2005). Developing a generic framework for e-government. *Journal of Global Information Management, 13,* 1–30.

Gray, B. (1989). *Collaborating: Finding common ground for multiparty problems* (1st ed.). San Francisco, CA: Jossey-Bass Inc.

Gregory, R. J. (1999). Social capital theory and administrative reform: Maintaining ethical probity. *Public Administration Review, 59*(1), 63–75. doi:10.2307/977480

Greitens, T. J., Joaquin, M. E., Bernick, E. L., & Gatti, J. (2009). *Political culture and online access to state and county budgets*. Paper presented at the Annual Conference of the American Society for Public Administration. March. Miami, Florida.

Grigoroudis, E., Litos, C., Moustakis, V. A., Politis, Y., & Tsironis, L. (2008). The assessment of user-perceived web quality: Application of a satisfaction benchmarking approach. *European Journal of Operational Research, 187,* 1346–1357. doi:10.1016/j.ejor.2006.09.017

Grinc, R. M. (1994). Angels in marble: Problems in stimulating involvement in community policing. *Crime and Delinquency, 40*(3), 437–468. doi:10.1177/0011128794040003008

Grizzle, G. A. (1986). Does budget format really govern the actions of budget makers? *Public Budgeting & Finance, 6*(1), 60–70. doi:10.1111/1540-5850.00707

Grondeau, A. (2007). Formation and emergence of ICT clusters in India: the case of Bangalore and Hyderabad. *GeoJournal, 68,* 31–40. doi:10.1007/s10708-007-9051-6

Grose, E., Forsythe, C., & Ratner, J. (1998). Using web and traditional style guides to design web interfaces. In Grose, E., Forsythe, C., & Ratner, J. (Eds.), *Human factors and web development* (pp. 121–131). Mahwah, NJ: Lawrence Erlbaum Associates.

Grossman, L. (1995). *The electronic republic: Reshaping American democracy in the information age.*

Gulick, L. (1987). Notes on the theory of organizations. In Shafritz, J. M., & Ott, J. S. (Eds.), *Classics of organizational theory* (pp. 87–97). Pacific Grove, CA: Brooks/Cole.

Gummesson, E. (2000). *Qualitative Methods in Management Research (2nd)*. Thousand Oaks, CA: Sage.

Gupta, M. P., & Jana, D. (2003). E-government evaluation: A framework and case study. *Government Information Quarterly, 20,* 365–387. doi:10.1016/j.giq.2003.08.002

Gupta, M. P., Kumar, P., & Bhattacharya, J. (2004). *Government online*. New Delhi: Tata McGraw-Hill.

Hale, M., Musso, J., & Weare, C. (1999). Developing digital democracy: Evidence from California municipal web pages. In Hague, B. N., & Loader, B. D. (Eds.), *Digital democracy: Discourse and decision making in the information age*. London: Routledge.

Hallowell, R. (2002). Virtuous cycles: Improving service and lowering costs in e-commerce, *Harvard Business School*, Cambridge, MA, Module Teaching Note 5-802-169.

Hammer, M. (1990). Reengineering Work: Don't Automate, Obliterate. *Harvard Business Review*, 104–112.

Hansen, A., Miyazaki, A. D., & Sprott, D. E. (2000). The tax incidence of lotteries: Evidence from five states. *The Journal of Consumer Affairs, 34,* 182–203.

Harris, N. D. (2000). Intergovernmental cooperation in the development and use of information systems. In Garson, D. (Ed.), *Handbook of Public Information Systems*. New York: Marcel Dekker.

Hart, D. K. (1984). The virtuous citizen, the honorable bureaucrat and public administration. *Public Administration Review*, 111–120. doi:10.2307/975550

Hassan, S., & Li, F. (2005). Evaluating the usability and content usefulness of websites: A benchmarking approach. *Journal of Electronic Commerce in Organizations, 3*(2), 46–68.

Hawkes, L. (1999). *A guide to the World Wide Web*. Upper Saddle River, NJ: Prentice-Hall.

Hawkins, E. T., & Hawkins, K. (2003). Bridging Latin America's digital divide: Government policies and Internet access. *Journalism & Mass Communication Quarterly, 80*(3), 646–665.

Heeks, R. (2002). E-Government in Africa: Promise and practice. *Information Polity: The International Journal of Government & Democracy in the Information Age, 7*(2/3), 97–114.

Heeks, R., & Bailur, S. (2006). Analyzing e-government research: Perspectives, philosophies, theories, methods, and practice. *Government Information Quarterly, 24*, 243–265. doi:10.1016/j.giq.2006.06.005

Heeks, R. (1999). *Reinventing government in the information age. International practice in IT-enabled public sector reform.* New York: Routledge. doi:10.4324/9780203204962

Heeks, R. (1998). *Information technology and public sector corruption.* Information Systems for Public Sector Management Working Paper 4. Manchester: IDPM. Retrieved, June, 2009, from http://unpan1.un.org/intradoc/groups/public/documents/APCITY/UNPAN014658.pdf

Heeks, R. (2001). Understanding e-governance for development. The University of Manchester, Institute for Development, Policy and Management Information, Systems, Technology and Government: *Working Papers Series, Number 11/2001.* Retrieved June 22, 2009, from http://www.sed.manchester.ac.uk/idpm/research/publications/wp/igovernment/igov_wp11.htm.

Heeks, R., & Jagun, A. (2007). Mobile phone and development: The future in new hands. *ID21 Insights, 69.* Retrieved June 2009, from http://www.id21.org/insights/insights69/insights69.pdf

Henriksson, A., Yiori, Y., Frost, B., & Middleton, M. (2006). Evaluation instrument for e-government websites. *Electronic Government, an International Journal, 4* (2), 204-226.

Herbert, S. (2001). Policing the contemporary city: policing broken windows or shoring up neoliberalism. *Theoretical Criminology, 5*(4), 445–466. doi:10.1177/1362480601005004003

Hezer, E., Medeni, T., & Dalbay, Ö. (2009). 2008 Ulusal Konferans Katilimci Anketi Sonuçlarina Dayali, Bir Türkiye'deki E-Devlet Çalişmalari Analizi. YEBKO 2009, Turkey.

Hibbard, J., & Dalton, G. (1999, March). XML Gains Ground. *Informationweek*, 18-19.

Hillen, M. (2008, February 18). Housing voucher forms go on Web. *Arkansas Democrat-Gazette, 9*(11).

Hiller, J. S., & Belanger, F. (2001). *Privacy strategies for electronic government. E-Government Series.* Arlington, VA: PricewaterhouseCoopers Endowment for the Business of Government.

Ho, A. (2002). Reinventing local governments and the e-government initiative. *Public Administration Review, 62*(4), 434–444. doi:10.1111/0033-3352.00197

Ho, A., & Ni, A. (2004). Explaining the adoption of e-government features: A case study of Iowa county treasurers' offices. *The American Review of Public Administration, 34*(2), 164-180. Retrieved March 27, 2009, from http://arp.sagepub.com/cgi/reprint/34/2/164

Hoffman, D. L., & Novak, T. P. (1998). Bridging the racial Divide on the Internet. *Science. New Series, 280*(5362), 390–391.

Holbrook, T. M., & Van Dunk, E. (1993). Electoral competition in the American states. *The American Political Science Review, 87*(4), 955–962. doi:10.2307/2938827

Holden, S. H., Norris, D. F., & Fletcher, P. D. (2003). Electronic government at the local level: Progress to date and future issues. *Public Performance and Management Review, 26*(4), 325–344. doi:10.1177/1530957603026004002

Holzer, M., & Kim, S. T. (2007). *Digital governance in municipalities worldwide: A longitudinal assessment of municipal web sites throughout the world.* Newark, N.J.: E-Governance Institute, Rutgers University.

Holzer, M., Manoharan, A., Shick, R., & Stowers, G. N. L. (2009). *U.S. municipalities e-governance survey 2008: An assessment of municipal websites.* Newark, N.J.: E-Governance Institute National Center for Public Performance School of Public Affairs and Administration. Rutgers University.

Holzer, M., Manoharan, A., Shick, R., & Stowers, G. (2009). *U.S. municipalities e-governance report (2008): An assessment of municipal websites.* Newark, N.J.: National Center for Public Performance, Rutgers University.

Holzer, M., & Kim, S.-T. (2005). *Digital Governance in Municipalities Worldwide, A Longitudinal Assessment of Municipal Web sites throughout the World, The e-Governance Institute*. Retrieved June 20, 2009 from http://unpan1.un.org/intradoc/groups/public/documents/aspa/unpan022839.pdf

Holzer, M., & Melitski, J. (2003). *A comparative e-government analysis of New Jersey's 10 largest municipalities*. Newark, NJ: National Center for Public Productivity Institute on Governance. (2003). *Principles for good governance in the 21ˢᵗ century*. Retrieved June 16, 2006, from www.iog.ca/publications/policybrief15.pdf

Holzer, M., Hu, L.-T., Kang, Y. C., & Zhang, M. (2003, March). *Trust, performance and the pressures for productivity in the public sector*. Paper presented at the annual meeting of the American Society for Public Administration, Washington, D.C.

Homans, G. C. (1958). Social behavior as exchange. *American Journal of Sociology*, *63*(May), 597–606. doi:10.1086/222355

Hooghe, M., & Stolle, D. (2003). Introduction. In M. Hooghe & D. Stolle, D. (Eds), *Generating Social Capital: Civil society and Institutions in Comparative Perspective* (pp. 1-18). New York: Palgrave Macmillan.

Horrigan, J. (2004). *How Americans get in touch with government. The Pew Internet and American Life Project*. Retrieved May 1, 2009, from http://www.pewinternet.org

Huang, C. J. (2003). *Usability of e-government websites for people with disabilities. Paper presented at the 36ᵗʰ Hawaii International Conference on System Sciences (HICSS'03)*. Big Island, Hawaii.

IDABC. (2004). *European Interoperability Framework for pan-European eGovernment Services, Version 1.0.* Retrieved June 20, 2009 from http://ec.europa.eu/idabc/en/document/2319

ILO. (2008). *Consejo de Administración, Comisión de Cooperación Técnica. Oficina Internacional del Trabajo (International Labor Organization)*. Ginebra.

IndiaStat. (2003). *Revealing India statistically*. Retrieved June 2008, from www.indiastat.com

InfoDev. (2002). The e-government handbook for developing countries. Washington, DC: The World Bank. Retrieved May 1, 2009, from http://unpan1.un.org/intradoc/groups/public/documents/apcity/unpan007462.pdf

Information & Communications Technology branch, New Zealand. (2009). *New Zealand Government Web Standards*. Retrieved June 20, 2009 from http://www.e.govt.nz/standards/web-guidelines

Inglehart, R., Basanez, M., & Moreno, A. (1998). *A human values and beliefs – A cross-cultural sourcebook: Political religious sexual, and economic norms in 43 societies: Findings from the 1990-1993 world values survey*. Ann Arbor, MI: University of Michigan Press.

Internet World Stats. (2009). World Internet users and population stats. Retrieved June 10, 2009, from http://www.internetworldstats.com/stats.htm

Irani, Z., Al-Sebie, M., & Elliman, T. (2006). Transaction stage of e-government systems: identification of its location & importance. In *Proceedings of the 39ᵗʰ Hawaii International Conference on System Sciences (HICSS-39)*, Hawaii, USA.

Irvin, R. A., & Stansbury, J. (2004). Citizen participation in decision making: Is it worth the effort? *Public Administration Review*, *4*(1), 55–65. doi:10.1111/j.1540-6210.2004.00346.x

ITIL. (n.d.). *ITIL*. Retrieved August 9, 2009, from http://www.itiltraining.com/

Iwaarden, J., van Wiele, T., van der Ball, L., & Millen, R. (2004). Perceptions about the quality of web sites: A survey amongst students at Northeastern University and Erasmus University. *Information & Management*, *41*(8), 947–959. doi:10.1016/j.im.2003.10.002

Jaeger, P. T. (2003). The endless wire: E-Government as a global phenomenon. *Government Information Quarterly*, *20*(4), 323–331. doi:10.1016/j.giq.2003.08.003

James, J. (2001). The Global Information Infrastructure Revisited. *Third World Quarterly*, *22*(5), 813–822. doi:10.1080/01436590120084610

James, J. (2002). Informational technology transaction costs and patterns of globalization in developing countries. *Review of Social Economy*, *60*(4), 507–519. doi:10.1080/0034676022000028046

James, J. (2003). Sustainable Internet access for the rural poor? Elements of an emerging Indian model. *Futures*, *35*, 461–472. doi:10.1016/S0016-3287(02)00092-7

James, J. (2004). Reconstruing the digital divide from the perspective of a large, poor, developing country. *Journal of Information Technology*, *19*, 172–177. doi:10.1057/palgrave.jit.2000019

Jansen, A. (2005). Assessing e-government progress – why and what. In B.J. Tessem and G. Iden og, (Eds), *Proceedings of Christensen (red) NOKOBIT 2005.*

Janssen, M., Kuk, G., & Wagenaar, R. (2008). A survey of web-based business models for e-government in the Netherlands. *Government Information Quarterly*, *25*, 202–220. doi:10.1016/j.giq.2007.06.005

Janssen, D., Rotthier, S., & Snijkers, K. (2004). If you measure it they will score: An assessment of international egovernment benchmarking. *Information Polity: The International Journal of Government and Democracy in the Information Age*, *9*, 124–125.

Janssen, D. (2003). Mine's bigger than yours: assessing international e-government benchmarking. In F. Bannister and D. Remenyi (Eds.), *3rd European Conference on e-Government* (pp. 209-218). London: MCIL.

Jensen, M., & Venkatesh, A. (2007). Government websites and political engagement: Facilitating Citizen entry into the policy process. In B. Thossen (Ed.). *Schriftenreihe Informatic*: Vol. 23.*Towards Electronic Democracy Conference Proceedings* (pp. 55-65). Linz, Austria: Trauner Verlag.

Johnson, T. J., & Kaye, B. K. (2003). A boost or bust for democracy: How the Web influenced Political attitudes in the 1996 and 2000 presidential elections. *Harvard Journal of Press/ Politics*, *8*, 9-34.

Jones, M. (2008). *Police organizations: An empirical examination of American sheriff's offices and municipal police agencies.* Unpublished doctoral dissertation, Portland State University.

Justice, J. B., Melitski, J., & Smith, D. L. (2004). E-government as an instrument of fiscal accountability and responsiveness. *American Review of Public Administration*, *36*(3), 301–322. doi:10.1177/0275074005283797

Kanat, İ. M., & Özkan, S. (2009). Explaining citizen adoption of government to citizen services: a model based on theory of planned behaviour (TBP). *European and Mediterranean Conference on Information Systems (EMCIS)* 2009, Turkey

Kašubienė, L., & Vanagas, P. (2007). Assumptions of e-government services quality evaluation. *Engineering Economics. 5* (55), *Commerce Of Engineering Decision, 68-74.*

Kathlene, L., & Martin, J. (1991). Enhancing citizen participation: Panel designs, perspectives, and policy formation. *Journal of Policy Analysis and Management*, *10*(1), 46–63. doi:10.2307/3325512

Katre, D. (2006). Usability survey report of Indian state government web portals. *HCI Vistas*, Volume I, Article IRN-8.

Kaufman, H. (1969). Administrative decentralizations and political power. *Public Administration Review*, *29*(1), 3–15. doi:10.2307/973980

Kaylor, C., Deschazo, R., & Van Eck, D. (2001). Gauging e-government: A report on implementing services among American cities. *Government Information Quarterly*, *18*(4), 293–307. doi:10.1016/S0740-624X(01)00089-2

Kearns, I., Bend, J., & Stern, B. (2002). *E-participation in local government*. Retrieved July 12, 2003 from www.ippr.org

Kendall, J. E., & Kendall, K. E. (1999). Information Delivery Systems: An Exploration of Web Pull and Push Technologies. *Communications of the AIS, 1*(14), 1–43.

Kennedy, G., Dalgarno, B., Gray, K., Judd, T., Waycott, J., Benett, S., et al. (2007). *The net generation are not big users of web 2.0 technologies: Preliminary findings.* Paper presented at the ascilite, Singapore.

Kenny, C. (2003). Development's false divide. *Foreign Policy, 134,* 76–77. doi:10.2307/3183524

Kent, M., & Taylor, M. (1998). Building dialogic relationships through the world wide web. *Public Relations Review, 24*(3), 321–334. doi:10.1016/S0363-8111(99)80143-X

Kent, M., Taylor, M., & White, W. (2003). The relationship between Web site design and organizational responsiveness to stakeholders. *Public Relations Review, 29*(1), 63–77. doi:10.1016/S0363-8111(02)00194-7

Kerer, C., Kirda, E., Jazayeri, M., & Kurmanowytsch, R. (2001, October 8-12). *Building and Managing XML/XSL-powered Websites: an Experience Report.* Paper presented at the 25th Annual International Computer Software and Applications Conference, Chicago, IL.

Kerley, K. R., & Benson, M. L. (2000). Does community oriented policing help build better communities? *Police Quarterly, 3*(1), 46–69. doi:10.1177/1098611100003001002

Khadaroo, M. I. (2005). An institutional theory perspective on the UK's private finance initiative (PFI) accounting standard setting process. *Public Management Review, 7*(1), 69–94. doi:10.1080/1471903042000339428

Kiiski, S., & Pohjola, M. (2002). Cross-country diffusion of the Internet. *Information Economics and Policy, 14,* 297–310. doi:10.1016/S0167-6245(01)00071-3

Kim, S., & Kim, D. (2003). South Korean Public Officials' Perceptions of Values, Failure, and Consequences of Failure in E-Government Leadership. *Public Performance and Management Review, 26*(4), 360–375. doi:10.1177/1530957603026004004

Kim, S., Kim, H. J., & Lee, J. (2009). An institutional analysis of an e-government system for anti-corruption: The case of OPEN. *Government Information Quarterly, 26,* 42–50. doi:10.1016/j.giq.2008.09.002

King, W. R. (1999). Time, constancy, and change in American municipal police organizations. *Police Quarterly, 2*(3), 338–364. doi:10.1177/109861119900200305

King, C., & Stivers, C. (1998). *Government is us: Public administration in an anti-government era.* Thousand Oaks, CA: Sage Publication.

King, S. K., Feltey, K. M., & Susel, B. O. (1998). The question of participation: Toward authentic participation in public administration. *Public Administration Review, 58*(4), 317–326. doi:10.2307/977561

Kingdon, J. W. (2003). *Agendas, alternatives, and public policies.* New York: Longman.

Kirk, H. (2001). Strategic media planning: Toward an integrated public relations media model practitioner. In R. L., Heath & G. Vasquez (Eds), *Handbook of public relations* (pp. 461-470). Thousands Oaks, CA: Sage Publications.

Kirk, H. (2003). *A Model for assessing Web sites as tools in building organizational-public relationships.* Paper presented at the annual meeting of the International Communication Association, San Diego, CA.

Klaassen, R., Karreman, J., & van der Geest, T. (2006). Designing Government Portal Navigation Around Citizens' Needs, M.A. Wimmer et al. (Eds.), *EGOV 2006, LNCS 4084,* 162–173, Springer-Verlag Berlin Heidelberg.

Klien, H. K. (1999). Tocqueville in cyberspace: Using the Internet for citizen associations. *The Information Society, 15,* 213–220. doi:10.1080/019722499128376

Klotz, R. (2004). *The politics of Interne communication.* Lanham, MD: Rowman & Littlefield.

Kohlberg, L. (1981). *Philosophy of moral development.* New York: Harper and Row Publishers.

Korteland, E., & Bekkers, V. (2008). The diffusion of electronic service delivery innovations in Dutch e-policing: The case of digital warning systems. *Public Management Review, 10*(1), 71–88. doi:10.1080/14719030701763195

Korteland, E., & Bekkers, V. (2007). Diffusion of E-government innovations in the Dutch public sector: The case of digital community policing. *Information Polity, 12*(3), 139–150.

Kraemer, K., William, H., & Northrup, A. (1981). *The management of information systems.* New York: Columbia University Press.

Kraemer, K. L., & Dedrick, J. (1997). Computing and public organizations. *Journal of Public Administration: Research and Theory, 7*(1), 89–112.

Kraemer, K. L., & King, J. L. (2003). *Information technology and administrative reform: Will the time after e-government be different?* Paper presented at the Heinrich Reinermann Schrift Fest, Post Graduate School of Administration, Speyer, Germany.

Kraemer, K. L., & King, J. L. (2003, September 29). *Information Technology and Administrative Reform: Will the Time After E-Government Be Different?* Paper presented at the Heinrich Reinermann Schrift fest, Post Graduate School of Administration, Speyer, Germany.

Krippendorff, K. (1980). *Content Analysis: An Introduction to Its methodology.* Beverly Hill, CA: Sage.

Krylova, E. (2007). Russia: Civic participation in subnational budgeting. In Shah, A. (Ed.), *Participatory budgeting* (pp. 67–90). Washington, DC: The World Bank.

Kumar, N., & Vragov, R. (2009, January). Active Citizen Participation Using ICT Tools. *Communications of the ACM, 52*(1), 118–121. doi:10.1145/1435417.1435444

Kumar, R., & Best, M. L. (2006). Impact and sustainability of e-government services in developing countries: Lessons learned from Tamil Nadu, India. *The Information Society, 22*(1), 1–12. doi:10.1080/01972240500388149

Kutlu, Ö., & Sevinç, İ. (2007). Information technology based systems and projects in Turkish public administration: Problems and solutions. In *Proceedings of BEYKON, 2007,* Turkey.

Kyoung, J., & Hong, J. H. (2002). Development of an e-government service model: A business model approach. *International Review of Public Administration, 7*(2), 109–118.

La Porte, T. M., Demchak, C. C., & Jong, M. D. (2002). Democracy and bureaucracy in the age of the web: Empirical findings and theoretical speculations. *Administration & Society, 34,* 411–446. doi:10.1177/0095399702034004004

La Porte, T. M., Demchak, C. C., & Weare, C. (2005). Governance in the era of the world wide web: An assessment of organizational openness and government effectiveness, 1997-2001. In Garson, G. D. (Ed.), *Handbook of public information systems.* Boca Raton, FL: Taylor and Francis.

La Porte, T. (2001). Politics and inventing the future: Perspectives in Science and government. In W. Bruce (Ed.), *Classics of administrative ethics* (393-409). Boulder, CO: Westview.

Lambe, C., Wittmann, C., & Spekman, R. (2001, July). Social Exchange Theory and Research on Business-to-Business Relational Exchange. *Journal of Business-To-Business Marketing, 8*(3), 1. doi:10.1300/J033v08n03_01

Land, V. Q., & Alsikafi, M. H. (1999). A lottery's impact on instructional and noninstructional expenditures and unrestricted revenues for education. *Journal of Education Finance, 25,* 149–174.

Lando, T. (2003). The public hearing process: A tool for citizen participation, or a path toward citizen alienation. *National Civic Review, 93*(1), 73–82. doi:10.1002/ncr.7

Langton, S. (1978). What is citizen participation? In Langton, S. (Ed.), *Citizen participation in America* (pp. 13–24). Lexington, MA: Lexington Books.

Langworthy, R. (1986). *The structure of police organizations.* New York, NY: Praeger.

Laschober, M. A. (1989). Is the Illinois state lottery a winning ticket for the state? A financial overview. *Illinois Business Review, 46*, 3–8.

Lassman, K. (2002). *The digital state 2001*. Washington, DC: The Progress & Freedom Foundation.

Lauth, T. P., & Robbins, M. D. (2002). The Georgia lottery and state appropriations for education: Substitution or additional funding? *Public Budgeting & Finance, 22*, 89–100. doi:10.1111/1540-5850.00082

Lawrence, S. G. (1999). Accessibility of information on the web. *Nature, 400*(6740), 107. doi:10.1038/21987

Layne, K., & Lee, J. (2001). Developing fully functional e-government: A four stage model. *Government Information Quarterly, 18*(2), 122–136. doi:10.1016/S0740-624X(01)00066-1

Lee, K. C., Kirlidog, M., Lee, S., & Lim, G. G. (2008). User evaluations of tax filing web sites: A comparative study of South Korea and Turkey. *Online Information Review, 32*(6), 842–859. doi:10.1108/14684520810923962

Lee, S. M., Tan, X., & Trimi, S. (2005). Current practices of leading e-government countries. *Communications of the ACM, 48*(10), 99–104. doi:10.1145/1089107.1089112

Lee, J.-N. (2001). The impact of knowledge sharing, organizational capability and partnership quality on IS outsourcing success. *Information & Management, 38*, 323–335. doi:10.1016/S0378-7206(00)00074-4

Lee, J. (2003). A model for monitoring public sector Web site strategy. *Internet Research, 13*(4), 259–266. doi:10.1108/10662240310488942

Lee, H., Irani, Z., Osman, I., Balci, A., Ozkan, S., & Medeni, T. (2008). Research note: toward a reference process model for citizen-oriented evaluation of e-government services. *Transforming Government: People, Process and Policy, 2*(4).

LeLoup. L. T. (1980). *Budgetary politics, 2nd ed*. Brunswick, Ohio: King's Court Communications, Inc.

LeRoy, G. (2009, February 16). The power of transparency. *Nation (New York, N.Y.)*, 15.

Lie, H. W., & Saarela, J. (1999). Multiporpuse Web Publishing. Using HTML, XML, and CSS. *Communications of the ACM, 42*(10), 95–101. doi:10.1145/317665.317681

Lilleker, D., & Jackson, N. (2008). *Politicians and Web 2.0: the current bandwagon or changing the mindset?* Paper presented at the Politics: Web 2.0 International Conference, London, UK.

Lippman, W. (1955). *Essays in the public philosophy*. Boston: Little, Brown and Co.

Loiacono, E., Watson, R., & Goodhue, D. (2002). WebQual: A measure of website quality. Marketing Educators' Conference. *Marketing Theory and Applications, 13*, 432–437.

Lowi, T. J. (1969). *The end of liberalism*. New York: Norton.

LRG Research Studies. (2009). *Leichtman Research Group*. Retrieved June 1, 2009, from www.leichtmanresearch.com/research.html#studies

Lu, M. T. (2001). Digital divide in developing countries. *Journal of Global Information Technology Management, 4*(3), 1–5.

Lucas, E. (2008, February 16). The electronic bureaucrat: A special report on technology and government. *The Economist*, 3-18.

Luna-Reyes, L. F., Zhang, J., Gil-García, J. R., & Cresswell, A. M. (2005). Information systems development as emergent socio-technical change: A practice approach. *European Journal of Information Systems, 14*, 93–105. doi:10.1057/palgrave.ejis.3000524

Luna-Reyes, L. F. (2004). *Collaboration, trust and knowledge sharing in information-technology-intensive projects in the public sector*. (Unpublished PhD Dissertation). University at Albany, Albany, NY.

Luyt, B. (2006). Defining the digital divide: the role of e-readiness indicators. *New Information Perspectives, 58*(4), 276–291.

Lynn, L. Jr, Heinrich, C., & Hill, C. (2000). Studying governance and public management: Challenges and prospects. *Journal of Public Administration: Research and Theory, 10*(2), 233–261.

Maguire, E. (1997). Structural change in large municipal police organizations during the community policing era. *Justice Quarterly, 14*(3), 701–730. doi:10.1080/07418829700093471

Maguire, E. (2003). *Organizational structure in american police agencies: Context, complexity and control*. Albany, NY: SUNY Press.

Mahadevan, B. (2000). Business models for internet based e-commerce. [Summer.]. *California Management Review, 42*(4), 55–69.

Mahmoodzadeh, S., Shahrabi, J., Pariazar, M., & Zaeri, M. S. (2007). Project selection by using fuzzy ahp and topsis technique. *International Journal of Human and Social Sciences, 1*(3), 25.

Malhotra, P., & Singh, B. (2007). Determinants of Internet banking adoption by banks in India. *Internet Research, 17*(3), 323–339. doi:10.1108/10662240710758957

Maness, J. (2006). Library 2.0 theory: Web 2.0 and its implications for libraries. *Webology,* Retrieved April 28th, 2009, from http://www.webology.ir/2006/v3n2/a25.html

Manning, P. (1987). *Police work: The social organization of policing*. Prospect Heights, IL: Waveland Press.

Mansbridge, J. (1999). Altruistic Trust. In Warren, M. (Ed.), *Democracy and Trust* (pp. 290–309). Cambridge: Cambridge University Press. doi:10.1017/CBO9780511659959.010

Martinez-Moyano, I. J., Samsa, M. E., Baldwin, T. E., Willke, B. J., & Moore, A. P. (2007). *Investigating the dynamics of trust in government: Drivers and effects of policy initiatives and government action*. Retrieved March 22, 2009, from http://www.dis.anl.gov/publications/articles/Trust_in_Government%202007.pdf

Matsuo, Y., & Yamamoto, H. (2009). Community gravity: Measuring bidirectional effects by trust and rating on online social networks. *International World Wide Web Conference*. Retrieved June 1, 2009, from http://www2009.eprints.org/76/1/p751.pdf

Mattessich, P. W., Murray-Close, M., & Monsey, B. R. (2001). *Collaboration: What makes it work* (2nd ed.). Saint Paul, MN: Amherst H. Wilder Foundation.

Mayes, T., & de Freitas, S. (2007). Learning and e-learning: the role of theory. In Beetham, H., & Sharpe, R. (Eds.), *Rethinking Pedagogy for a digital age: Designing and delivering for e-learning* (pp. 13–25). London: Routledge.

Mazmanian, D. A., & Sabatier, P. A. (1983). *Implementation and public policy*. Glenview, IL: Scott Foresman.

McConnell, M. (2007). *Confronting the Terrorist Threat to the Homeland: Six Years after 9/11*. Retrived June 15th, 2009, from http://hsgac.senate.gov/index.cfm?Fuseaction=Hearings.Detail&HearingID=479

McCrary, J., & Condrey, S. E. (2003). The Georgia lottery: Assessing its administrative, economic, and political effects. *Review of Policy Research, 20*, 691–711. doi:10.1046/j.1541-1338.2003.00047.x

McDonald, P. (2002). *Managing Police Operations: Implementing the NYPD Crime Control Model Using COMPSTAT*. Belmont, CA: Wadsworth.

McFarlan, F. W. (1981). Portfolio approach to information systems. *Harvard Business Review, 59*, 142–150.

McIvor, R., McHugh, M., & Cadden, C. (2002). Internet technologies: Supporting transparency in the public sector. *International Journal of Public Sector Management, 15*(3), 170–187. doi:10.1108/09513550210423352

McMillan, S. J. (2002). A four-part model of cyber-interactivity. *New Media & Society, 4*(2), 271–291.

Meall, L. (2002). Business: The digital divide – eastern promise. *Accountancy, 129*(1303), 1–4.

Medeni, T. (2008). Turkey case. In *Proceedings of the Panel on Electronic Governance for Rural Communities, ICEGOV 2008, November,* Egypt.

Medeni, T., Balci, A., & Dalbay, Ö. (2009). Understanding citizen demands for wide-spreading e-government services in Turkey: A descriptive study *EMCIS, 2009*, July, İzmir, Turkey

Medeni, T., Medeni, İ. T., Balci, A., & Dalbay, Ö. (2009). Suggesting a framework for transition towards more interoperable e-government in Turkey: A nautilus model of cross-cultural knowledge creation and organizational learning. In *Proceedings of ICEGOV, 2009,* March, Ankara, Turkey.

Migration Policy Institute. (2007). *MPI Data Hub: Migration Facts, Stats, and Maps.* Retrieved January 28, 2009, from http://www.migrationinformation.org/DataHub/charts/6.1.shtml

Mikesell, J. L. (1994). State lottery sales and economic activity. *National Tax Journal, 47*(1), 165–171.

Mikesell, J. L., & Zorn, C. K. (1986). State lotteries as fiscal savior or fiscal fraud. *Public Administration Review, 46*(4), 311–320. doi:10.2307/976304

Mikesell, J. L., & Zorn, C. K. (1988). State lotteries for public revenue. *Public Budgeting & Finance, 8,* 38–47. doi:10.1111/1540-5850.00772

Mikhailov, L., & Tsvetinov, P. (2004). Evaluation of services using a fuzzy analytic hierarchy process. *Applied Soft Computing, 5*(1), 23–33. doi:10.1016/j.asoc.2004.04.001

Miller, D. E., & Pierce, P. A. (1997). Lotteries for education: Windfall or hoax? *State and Local Government Review, 29*(1), 34–42.

Miller, R. R. (2001). Leapfrogging? India's information technology industry and the Internet. *International Finance Corporation,* Discussion Paper No. 42. Washington: World Bank.

Ministry of Communications and Information Technology, Government of India. (2009). *Guidelines for Indian Government websites.* Retrieved June 20, 2009, from http://web.guidelines.gov.in

Ministry of Interior. Greece. (2009). *Greek e-Government Framework.* Retrieved June 20, 2009, from http://www.ermis.gov.gr

Mistry, J. J. (2005). A conceptual framework for the role of government in bridging the digital divide. *Journal of Global Information Technology Management, 8*(3), 28–47.

Mitra, R. K., & Gupta, M. P. (2008). A contextual perspective of performance assessment in eGovernment: A study of Indian police administration. *Government Information Quarterly, 25,* 278–302. doi:10.1016/j.giq.2006.03.008

Mitra, R. K. (2004). Issues and challenges of E-governance in Indian Police: A study. Unpublished doctoral dissertation, Indian Institute of Technology, Delhi, India.

Mitra, R. K., & Gupta, M. P. (2007). Analysis of issues of e-government in Indian Police. *Electronic Government, an International Journal, 4* (1), pp. 97–125.

Mofleh, S. I., & Wanous, M. (2009). Reviewing existing methods for evaluating e-government websites. *Electronic Government, 6*(2), 129–142. doi:10.1504/EG.2009.024438

Moon, M. J. (2002). The evolution of e-government among municipalities: Rhetoric or reality. *Public Administration Review, 62*(4), 424–433. doi:10.1111/0033-3352.00196

Moon, M. J., & deLeon, P. (2001). Municipal reinvention: Municipal values and diffusion among municipalities. *Journal of Public Administration: Research and Theory, 11*(3), 327–352.

Moon, M. J. (2002). The evolution of e-government among municipalities: Rhetoric or reality? *Public Administration Review, 62*(4), 424–433. doi:10.1111/0033-3352.00196

Moon, M. J., & Welch, E. W. (2005). *Same bed, different dreams: A comparative analysis of citizen and bureaucrat perspectives on e-government. Paper presented at the 37th Hawaii International Conference on System Sciences (HICSS'04).* Big Island, Hawaii.

Moore, M. H., & Braga, A. A. (2003). Measuring and improving police performance: The lessons of COMP-STAT and its progeny. *Policing: An International Journal of Police Strategies & Management, 26*(3), 439–453. doi:10.1108/13639510310489485

Moore, M. H. (1981). Realms of obligation and virtues. In Fleishman, J. L., Liebman, L., & Moore, M. H. (Eds.), *Public duties: The moral obligation of government officials* (pp. 1–15). Cambridge, MA: Harvard Press.

Morgeson, F., & Mithas, 2. (2009). Does e-government measure up to e-business? Comparing end user perceptions of U.S. federal government and e-business web sites. *Public Administration Review, 69*(4), 740–752. doi:10.1111/j.1540-6210.2009.02021.x

Morgeson, F. III, & Mithas, S. (2009). Does e-government measure up to e-business? Comparing end user perceptions of U.S. federal government and e-business web sites. *Public Administration Review, 69*(4), 740–752. doi:10.1111/j.1540-6210.2009.02021.x

Mossberger, K., Tolbert, C., & Stansbury, M. (2003). *Virtual inequality: Beyond the digital divide*. Washington, DC: Georgetown University Press.

Moustakis, V., Litos, C., Dalivigas, A., & Tsironis, L. (2004). Website assessment criteria. In *Proceedings of International Conference on Information Quality, Boston: MIT*, November 5–7, 59–73.

Musso, J. A., Weare, C., & Hale, M. C. (2000). Designing web technologies for local governance reform: Good management for good democracy? *Political Communication, 17*(1), 1–19. doi:10.1080/105846000198486

Nachimias, D., & Nachimias, C. (1981). *Research Methods in Social Sciences* (2nd ed.). New York: St Martin's Press.

Nair, M., Kuppusamy, M., & Davison, R. (2005). A longitudinal study on the global digital divide problem: Strategies to closure. *The Business Review, Cambridge, 4*(1), 315–326.

NASCIO. (2002). *NASCIO 2002 compendium of digital government in the states*. Lexington, KY: National Association of State Chief Information Officers.

National Gambling Impact Study Commission Report. (1999). *National Gambling Impact Study Commission Report* Retrieved from http://govinfo.library.unt.edu/ngisc/index.html

National Institute of Standards and Technology (NIST). (2001). NIST develops benchmarking website usability methodologies. *Journal of Research of the National Institute of Standards and Technology, 106*(3), 495.

Needham, C. (2004). The citizen as a consumer: E-government in the United Kingdom and United States. In Gibson, R. (Eds.), *Electronic democracy: Mobilization, organization, and participation via new ICTs* (pp. 43–69). New York: Routledge.

Nelson, M., & Mason, J. L. (2003-2004). The politics of gambling in the South. *Political Science Quarterly, 118*(4), 645–669.

Neuendorf, K. A. (2002). *The content analysis guidebook*. Thousand Oaks, CA: Sage Publications.

Nielsen, J. (2000). *Designing web usability: The practice of simplicity*. Indianapolis, IN: New Riders Publishing.

Nielsen, J. (2002). *Designing web usability: The practice of simplicity*. Indianapolis, USA: New Riders Publishing.

Niskanen, W. A. Jr. (1971). *Bureaucracy and representative government*. Chicago: Aldine-Artherton.

Norris, D. F., & Moon, M. J. (2005). Advancing e-government at the grassroots: Tortoise or hare? *Public Administration Review, 65*(1), 64–75. doi:10.1111/j.1540-6210.2005.00431.x

Norris, P. (2001). *Digital divide: Civic engagement, information poverty, and the internet worldwide*. NY: Cambridge University Press.

Nunnally, J. (1978). *Psychometric theory* (2nd ed.). New York: McGraw Hill.

O'Toole, L. J. Jr. (2000). Research on policy implementation: Assessment and prospects. *Journal of Public Administration: Research and Theory, 10*(2), 263–288.

Oberlander, J., Karakatsiotis, G., Isard, A., & Androutso-poulos, I. (2008). *Building an adaptive museum gallery in Second Life.* Proceedings of the Museums and the Web, Montreal, Quebec, Canada.

OECD. (2003). *OECD, the e-government imperative.* Paris: OECD e-government studies.

OECD. (2005). *OECD, e-government for better government.* Paris: OECD e-government studies.

OECD. (2006). *OECD e-government studies: Turkey.* OECD Prince2. n.d. Retrieved August 31, 2009, from http://www.prince2.com/

Oeter, S. (2007). Minority Language Policy: Theory and Practice. *Journal on Ethnopolitics and Minority Issues in Europe*, 2. Retrieved August 21, 2009, from http://www.ecmi.de/jemie/download/2-2007-Oeter-Introduction.pdf

Office of Immigration Statistics. (2008). *2008 Yearbook of Immigration Statistics.* Washington DC: Department of Homeland Security. Retrieved August 25, 2009, from http://www.dhs.gov/xlibrary/assets/statistics/yearbook/2008/ois_yb_2008.pdf

Office of the Vice President. (1993). *From Red tape to results. Creating a government that works better and costs less. Report of the National Performance Review.* Washington, DC: US Government Printing Office.

Oldfield, A. (1990). *Citizenship and community: Civic republicanism and the modern world.* London: Routledge Publishing.

Oliver, R. W. (2004). *What is transparency?* New York: McGraw Hill.

Olphert, W., & Damodaran, L. (2007). An evaluation of the information content of local authority websites in the UK using citizen-based scenarios. *Library and Information Research*, *31*(98), 45–60.

O'Reilly, T. (2005). What Is web 2.0: Design patterns and business models for the next generation of software. *Communications & Strategies*, *65*(1), 17–31.

Organisation for Economic Co-operation and Development. (2001). OECD best practices for budget transparency. *OECD Journal on Budgeting*, *1*(3), 7–14. doi:10.1787/budget-v1-art14-en

Osimo, D. (2008). *Web 2.0 in government: Why and how?* European Commission Joint Research Center. Retrieved August 28, 2009 from http://ftp.jrc.es/EURdoc/JRC45269.pdf

Oudshoorn, N., Rommes, E., & Stienstra, M. (2004). Configuring the user as everybody: Gender and design cultures in information and communication technologies. *Science, Technology & Human Values*, *29*(1), 30–63. doi:10.1177/0162243903259190

Owen, T., & Powell, J. L. (2006). Trust, professional power and social theory: Lessons from a post-Foucauldian framework. *The International Journal of Sociology and Social Policy*, *26*(3/4), 110–120. doi:10.1108/01443330610657179

Palmer, J. W. (2002). Web site usability, design, and performance metrics. *Information Systems Research*, *13*(2), 151–167. doi:10.1287/isre.13.2.151.88

Palmquist, M. (2002). *Content Analysis*. Retrieved September 30 2002, from http://fiat.gslis.utexas.edu/~palmquis/courses/content.html

Panopoulou, E., Tambouris, E., & Tarabanis, K. (2008). A framework for evaluating websites of public authorities. *Aslib Proceedings: New Information Perspectives*, *60*(5), 517–546.

Paoline, E. A. III. (2004). Shedding light on police culture: an examination of police officers' occupational attitudes. *Police Quarterly*, *7*(2), 205–236. doi:10.1177/1098611103257074

Parayil, G. (2005). The digital divide and increasing returns: Contradictions of informational capitalism. *The Information Society*, *21*(1). doi:10.1080/01972240590895900

Pardo, T. A., Cresswell, A. M., Thompson, F., & Zhang, J. (2006). Knowledge sharing in cross-boundary information system development in the public sector. *Information Technology Management*, *7*(4), 293–313. doi:10.1007/s10799-006-0278-6

Pardo, T. A., Gil-Garcia, J. R., & Burke, B. (2007). Sustainable cross-boundary information sharing. In Chen, H., Brandt, L., Dawes, S., Gregg, V., Hovy, E., & Macintosh, A. (Eds.), *Digital government: Advanced research and case studies*. New York: Springer.

Parker, A. (1968). Government finances and citizen responsibility. *The Annals of the American Academy of Political and Social Science*, *379*, 123–131. doi:10.1177/000271626837900114

Patton, C. V., & Sawicki, D. S. (1986). *Basic methods of policy analysis and planning*. Englewood Cliffs, NJ: Prentice Hall.

Perlman, E. (2009). See thru government: When it comes to spending taxpayer dollars, how much transparency is enough? *Governing*, (May): 34–37.

Perlman, E. (1998). The game of mystery bucks. *Governing*, *11*, 20.

Perri 6 (2004). *E-governance styles of political judgment in the information age polity*. New York: Palgrave McMillan.

Peters, M. R., Janssen, M., & Van Engers, M. T. (2004). Measuring e-government impact: existing practices and shortcomings. *Paper presented at the 6th International Conference on Electronic Commerce (ICEC'04)*. Delft, The Netherlands.

Pettijohn, C. D., & Grizzle, G. A. (1997). Structural budget reform: Does it affect budget deliberations? *Journal of Public Budgeting, Accounting, &. Financial Management*, *9*(1), 26–45.

Pieterson, W., & van Dijk, J. (2006). Governmental service channel positioning. In A. Gronlund, H. Scholl, K. V. Andersen, and M. A. Wimmer (Eds.), *Communication Proceedings of the Fifth International EGOV Conference 2006*. Krakow, Poland: Trauner Druck.

Pieterson, W., & van Dijk, J. (2007). Channel choice determinants: An exploration of the factors that determine the choice of a service channel in citizen initiated contacts. In *Proceedings of the 8th annual international conference on digital government research: bridging disciplines & domains*. Digital Government Society of North America, Vol. 228, 173-182.

Piotrowski, S. J. (2007). *Governmental transparency in the path of administrative reform*. Albany, NY: SUNY Press.

Pirog-Good, M., & Mikesell, J. L. (1995). Longitudinal evidence of the changing socio-economic profile of a state lottery market. *Policy Studies Journal: the Journal of the Policy Studies Organization*, *23*, 451–465. doi:10.1111/j.1541-0072.1995.tb00523.x

Portnry, K. (2005). Civic engagement and sustainable cities in the United States. *Public Administration Review*, *65*(5), 534–623.

Price, D. I., & Novak, E. S. (1999). The tax incidence of three Texas lottery games: Regressivity, race, and education. *National Tax Journal*, *52*, 741–751.

Price, D. I., & Novak, E. S. (2000). The income redistribution effects of Texas state lottery games. *Public Finance Review*, *28*, 82–92. doi:10.1177/109114210002800105

Prosser, W. L. (1955). *Handbook of the law of torts*. St. Paul, MN: West Publishing Company.

Putnam, R. D. (1991). Bowling alone: America's declining social capital. *Journal of Democracy*, *6*(1), 65–78. doi:10.1353/jod.1995.0002

Putnam, R. D. (2000). *Bowling alone: The collapse and revival of American community*. New York: Simon & Schuster.

Raihan, A. (2005). Mobile ladies' in Bangladesh: Connecting villagers to livelihoods information. *ID21 Insights*. Retrieved July 2009, from http://www.id21.org/insights/insights69/art02.html

Ratcliffe, J. (2005). The effectiveness of police intelligence management: A New Zealand case study. *Police Practice and Research*, 6(5), 435–451. doi:10.1080/15614260500433038

Raven, P. V., Huang, X., & Kim, B. B. (2007). E-Business in developing countries: A comparison of China and India. *International Journal of E-Business Research*, 3(1), 91–108.

Ray, D. S., & Dash, S. (2006). A study on e-government readiness of Indian states. In R.K. Mitra (ed.) *E-government: macro issues* (pp. 107-122). New Delhi: GIFT Publishing.

Rayport, J., & Jaworski, B. (2001). *Cases in e-commerece*. New York: McGraw-Hill Professional.

Reddick, C. G. (2004). A two-stage model of e-government growth; Theories and empirical evidence for U.S. cities. *Government Information Quarterly*, 21, 51–64. doi:10.1016/j.giq.2003.11.004

Reddick, C. G. (2004). A two-stage model of e-government growth: Theories and empirical evidence in U.S. cities. *Government Information Quarterly*, 21(1), 51–64. doi:10.1016/j.giq.2003.11.004

Reichard, C. (1998). The impact of performance management on transparency and accountability in the public sector. In Hondeghem, A. (Ed.), *Ethics and accountability in a context of governance and new public management* (pp. 123–137). Amsterdam: IOS Press.

Relly, J. E., & Sabharwal, M. (2009). Perceptions of transparency of government policymaking: A cross-national study. *Government Information Quarterly*, 26, 148–157. doi:10.1016/j.giq.2008.04.002

Rethemeyer, R. (2006). Policymaking in the age of the internet: Is the internet tending to make policy networks more or less inclusive? *Journal of Public Administration: Research and Theory*, 17(2), 259–284. doi:10.1093/jopart/mul001

Reuters. (2009). Bangladesh trials cell phone disaster alerts. Retrieved July 3, 2009 from http://www.msnbc.msn.com/id/31523970/

Richstad, J., & Anderson, M. H. (1981). Policy context for news and a new order. In Richstad, J., & Anderson, M. H. (Eds.), *Crisis in International News: Policies and Prospects* (pp. 26–27). New York: Columbia University Press.

Riggins, F. J., & Dewan, S. (2005). The digital divide: Current and future research directions. *Journal of the Association for Information Systems*, 6(12), 298–336.

Robert, L., & Dennis, A. (2005). Paradox of richness: A cognitive model of media choice. *IEEE Transactions on Professional Communication*, 48(1), 10–21. doi:10.1109/TPC.2004.843292

Roberts, N. (2002). Keeping public officials accountable through dialogue: Resolving the accountability paradox. *Public Administration Review*, 62(6), 658–669. doi:10.1111/1540-6210.00248

Rockley Group. (2005). *The Role of Content Standards and Content Management*. 18.

Rogers, E. M., & Shoemaker, F. (1971). *Communication of Innovation: A Cross-Cultural Approach* (2nd ed.). New York: Free Press.

Rogers, E. (1995). *Diffusion of innovations*. New York: The Free Press.

Rohr, J. A. (1984). Civil servants and second class citizens. *Public Administration Review*, 44, 135–140. doi:10.2307/975553

Roth, M. S. (1996). Patterns in direct-to-consumer prescription drug print advertising and their public policy implications. *Journal of Public Policy and Marketing*.

Rubin, I. (2006). *The politics of public budgeting: Getting and spending, borrowing and balancing* (5th ed.). Washington, DC: CQ Press.

Rubin, I. S. (1993). *The Politics of Public Budgeting: Getting and Spending, Borrowing and Balancing* (2nd ed.). Chatham, NJ: Chatham House.

Rubin, I. S. (1997). *The politics of public budgeting: Getting and spending borrowing and balancing* (3rd ed.). Chatham, NJ: Chatham House.

Rubin, I. S. (2005). The state of state budget research. *Public Budgeting & Finance, 25*(Special), 46–67. doi:10.1111/j.1540-5850.2005.00003.x

Ryan, D. (2002). The Role of XML in Content Management. *XML Journal, 6.*

Ryu, J. E., Bowling, C. J., Cho, C.-L., & Wright, D. S. (2008). Exploring explanations of state agency budgets: Institutional budget actors or exogenous environment. *Public Budgeting & Finance, 28*(3), 23–47. doi:10.1111/j.1540-5850.2008.00909.x

Saaty, L. T. (2008). Relative measurement and its generalization in decision making: Why pairwise comparisons are central in mathematics for the measurement of intangible factors. The Analytic Hierarchy/Network Process. *Review of the Royal Spanish Academy of Sciences, Series A. Mathematics, 102*(2), 251–318.

Sabir, M. (2008). *Bangladesh stunned by Awami victory.* BBC News. Retrieved July 2, 2009, from http://news.bbc.co.uk/2/hi/south_asia/7804040.stm

Sæbø, Ø., Rose, J., & Flak, L. S. (2008). The shape of e-participation: Characterizing an emerging research area. *Government Information Quarterly, 25,* 400–428. doi:10.1016/j.giq.2007.04.007

Sakowicz, M. (2007). *How to evaluate e-government: Different methodologies and methods. Paper presented at the 11th Annual NISPA Conference.* Bucharest, Romania.

SAMPLE SURVEY OF LAW ENFORCEMENT AGENCIES Computer file. ICPSR04411-v1. Washington, DC: Dept, U. S. of Commerce, Bureau of the Census [producer], 2006. Ann Arbor, MI: Inter-university Consortium for Political and Social Research [distributor], 2006-05-10. doi:10.3886/ICPSR04411

Sarantis, D., Tsiakaliaris, C., Lampathaki, F., & Charalabidis, Y. (2008). A Standardization Framework for Electronic Government Service Portals. In *Proceedings 17th International Conference on Information Systems Development.* Paphos, Cyprus.

Sarkar, S. (2008). E-government adoption and diffusion. In Sahu, G. P. (Ed.), *Adopting e-governance.* New Delhi: GIFT Publishing.

Saruç, N. T. (2009). The factors effecting use of e-government services and perceived quality of public services: an empirical study. In *Proceedings of ICEGEG2009,* Turkey.

Savoie, D. (2004, Spring). 2004). Searching for accountability in a government without boundaries. *Canadian Public Administration, 47*(1), 1–26. doi:10.1111/j.1754-7121.2004.tb01968.x

Schelin, S. H. (2003). E-Government: An Overview. In Garson, G. D. (Ed.), *Public Information Technology: Policy and Management Issues* (pp. 120–137). Hershey, PA: Idea Group Publishing.

Schick, A. (1990). *The capacity to budget.* Washington, DC: The Urban Institute Press.

Schlosser, A. (2000). Harnessing the power of interactivity: implications for consumer behavior in online environments. In Hoch, S. J., & Meyer, R. J. (Eds.), *Advances in consumer research, 27* (p. 79). Valdosta, GA: Association for Consumer Research.

Scholl, H. J. (2002). *Executive briefing on electronic government and business process change.* Albany, NY: Center for Technology in Government.

Schudson, M., & Haas, D. (2008). Voting for glass houses. *Columbia Journalism Review, 71.*

Schulman, S. W. (2005). E-rulemaking: Issues in current research and practice. *International Journal of Public Administration, 28,* 621–641. doi:10.1081/PAD-200064221

Schumpeter, J. (1942). *Capitalism, socialism and democracy.* New York: Free Press.

Schware, R., & Deane, A. (2003). Deploying e-government programs: the strategic importance of "i" before "e". *Info-The Journal of Policy. Regulation and Strategy for Telecommunications, 5*(4), 10–19. doi:10.1108/14636690310495193

Scott, J. (2005). Assessing the quality of municipal government websites. *State and Local Government Review*, *37*(2), 151–165.

Scott, J. K. (2006). "E" the people: Do U. S. municipal government web sites support public involvement? *Public Administration Review*, *66*(3), 341–353. doi:10.1111/j.1540-6210.2006.00593.x

Seifert, J. W., & Peterson, R. E. (2002). The promise of all things E? Expectations and challenges of emergent electronic government. *Perspectives on Global Development and Technology*, *1*(2), 193–212. doi:10.1163/156915002100419808

Sentinelli, A., Marfia, G., Gerla, M., & Kleinrock, L. (2007). Will IPTV Ride the Peer-to-Peer Stream? *IEEE Communications Magazine*, *45*(6), 86–92. doi:10.1109/MCOM.2007.374424

Seshagiri, N. (1999). The informatics policy in India. *Information Systems Frontiers*, *1*(1), 107–116. doi:10.1023/A:1010025130799

Shall, A. (2007). South Africa: Citizen participation in local government policy making and budget processes. In Shah, A. (Ed.), *Participatory budgeting* (pp. 91–126). Washington, DC: The World Bank.

Sharma, S. (2009). *The ethics driven spatial management in multiculturalism through ICTs.* Unpublished paper.

Short, J., Williams, E., & Christie, B. (1976). *The social psychology of telecommunications*. London: John Wiley.

Shrader, K. (2006, November 2nd). Over 3,600 Intelligence professionals tapping into "intellipedia". *The Associated Press*. Retrieved June 20, 2009, from http://www.usatoday.com/tech/news/techinnovations/2006-11-02-intellipedia_x.htm

Shuman, H. E. (1992). *Politics and the budget: The struggle between the president and the congress* (3rd ed.). Englewood Cliffs, N.J: Prentice-Hall, Inc.

Silver, B. (2005). *Content in the Age of XML. Intelligent Enterprise*. Retrieved from http://www.intelligententerprise.com/print_article.jhtml?articleID=163100779

Simonsen, W., & Robbins, M. D. (2000). *Citizen participation in resource allocation*. Boulder, CO: Westview Press.

Skogan, W. (2006). *Police and community in Chicago: A tale of three cities*. New York, NY: Oxford University Press.

Skogan, W. G., & Hartnett, S. M. (2005). The diffusion of information technology in policing. *Police Practice and Research*, *6*(5), 401–417. doi:10.1080/15614260500432949

Skogan, W. G., Rosenbaum, D. P., Hartnett, S. M., DuBois, J., Graziano, L., & Stephens, C. (2005). CLEAR and I-CLEAR: A status report in new information technology and its impact on management, the organization and crime fighting strategies. Chicago, IL: The Chicago community Policing Evaluation Consortium.

Skolnick, J. H., & Bayley, D. H. (1986). *The new blue line: Innovation in six American cities*. New York, NY: Free Press.

Smith, A. G. (2001). Applying evaluation criteria to New Zealand government websites. *International Journal of Information Management*, *21*(2), 137–149. doi:10.1016/S0268-4012(01)00006-8

Smith, S. M. (2005). The digital divide: gender and racial differences in information technology education. *Information Technology, Learning and Performance Journal*, *23*(1), 13–23.

Smith, A. G. (2001). Applying evaluation criteria to New Zealand government web sites. *International Journal of Information Management*, *21*(2), 137–149. doi:10.1016/S0268-4012(01)00006-8

Smith, A. (2010). Government online. *The Pew Internet and American Life Project*. Retrieved May 1, 2010, from http://www.pewinternet.org.

Soufi, B., & Maguire, M. (2007). Achieving usability within e-government websites illustrated by a case study evaluation. In Smith, M. J., & Salvendy, G. (Eds.), *Human interface and the management of information. Interacting in information environments* (pp. 777–784). Berlin, Germany: Springer. doi:10.1007/978-3-540-73354-6_85

Spindler, C. J. (1995). The lottery and education: Robbing Peter to pay Paul. *Public Budgeting & Finance, 15*, 54–61. doi:10.1111/1540-5850.01046

Spinuzzi, C. (2003). *Tracing Genres through Organizations: A Sociocultural Approach to Information Design (Acting with Technology)*. Cambridge, MA: MIT Press.

Stanford, K. A. (1992). State budget deliberations: Do legislators have a strategy? *Public Administration Review, 52*(1), 16–26. doi:10.2307/976542

Stanley, R. E., & French, P. E. (2003). Can students truly benefit from state lotteries: A look at lottery expenditures towards education in the American states. *Social Science Quarterly, 40*, 327–333.

Stivers, C. (1990). The public agency as poll: Active citizenship in the administrative state. *Administration & Society, 22*(1), 86–105. doi:10.1177/009539979002200105

Stone, R., & Henry, J. (2003). Identifying and developing measures of information technology ethical work climates. *Journal of Business Ethics, 46*(4), 337–350. doi:10.1023/A:1025632614084

Stone, P. J., Dunphy, D. C., Smith, M. S., & Ogilvie, D. M. (1966). *The general inquirer: A computer approach to content analysis*. Cambridge: MIT Press.

Stowers, G. N. L. (1999). Becoming cyberactive: State and local governments on the world wide web. *Government Information Quarterly, 16*(2), 111–127. doi:10.1016/S0740-624X(99)80003-3

Stowers, G. N. L. (2002). *The state of federal web sites: The pursuit of excellence*. Washington, D.C.: Center for the Business of Government.

Stowers, G. N. L. (2004). *Measuring the performance of E-government*. Washington, D.C.: Center for the Business of Government.

Streib, G., & Navarro, I. (2007). Citizen demand for interactive e-government: The case of Georgia consumer services. *The American Review of Public Administration, 36*(3), 288-300. Retrieved March 29, 2009, from http://arp.sagepub.com/cgi/reprint/36/3/288

Sung, H. (2006). Structural determinant of police effectiveness in market democracies. *Police Quarterly, 9*(1), 3–19. doi:10.1177/1098611103257061

Suwanmala, C. (2007). Thailand: Civic participation in subnational budgeting. In Shah, A. (Ed.), *Participatory budgeting* (pp. 127–154). Washington, DC: The World Bank.

Svara, J. (2007). *The ethics primer for public administrators in government and nonprofit organizations*. Sudbury, MA: Jones and Bartlett.

Swindell, D., & Kelly, J. (2000). Linking citizen satisfaction data to performance measures: A preliminary evaluation. *Public Productivity and Management Review, 24*(1), 30–52.

Tapscott, D., & Ticoll, D. (2003). *The naked corporation: How the age of transparency will revolutionize business*. New York, NY: Free Press.

Tarafdur, M., & Zhang, J. (2005). Analyzing the influence of website design parameters on website usability. *Information Resources Management Journal, 18*(4), 62–81.

Tassabehji, R., & Elliman, T. (2006). Generating citizen trust in e-government using a trust verification agent *European and Mediterranean Conference on Information Systems (EMCIS)* 2006, Spain.

Taylor, M., Kent, M. L., & White, W. J. (2001). How activist organization are using the Internet to build relationship. *Public Relations Review, 27*, 263–284. doi:10.1016/S0363-8111(01)00086-8

The Global e-policy and e-governance institute & Rutgers University e-governance institute. (2003). *Assessing websites and measuring e-government index among 100 world cities*. Study sponsored by the division of public administration and development, department of economics And social affairs, United Nations.

The Global e-policy and e-governance institute & Rutgers University e-governance institute. (2005). *Assessing websites and measuring e-government index among 100 world cities*. Study sponsored by the division of public administration and development, department of economics And social affairs, United Nations.

Thomas, J., & Streib, G. (2003). The new face of government: Citizen-initiated contacts in the era of e-government. *Journal of Public Administration: Research and Theory, 13*(1), 83–102. doi:10.1093/jpart/mug010

Thomas, C. J. (1995). *Public participation in public decisions*. San Francisco, CA: Jossey-Bass Publishers.

Thurmaier, K. M., & Gosling, J. J. (1997). The shifting roles of state budget offices in the midwest: Gosling revisited. *Public Budgeting & Finance, 17*(4), 48–70. doi:10.1111/1540-5850.01116

Thurmaier, K. M., & Willoughby, K. G. (2001). *Policy and politics in state budgeting*. Armonk, NY: M.E. Sharpe.

Timmers, P. (1998). Business models for electronic markets. *Electronic Markets, 8*(2), 3–8. doi:10.1080/10196789800000016

Tolbert, C. J., & Mossberger, K. (2006). The effects of e-government on trust and confidence in government. *Public Administration Review, 66*(3), 354–369. doi:10.1111/j.1540-6210.2006.00594.x

Tolbert, C. J., Mossberger, K., & McNeal, R. (2008). Institutions, policy innovation, and e-government in the American states. *Public Administration Review, 68*(3), 549–563. doi:10.1111/j.1540-6210.2008.00890.x

Torres, L., Pina, V., & Acerete, B. (2005). E-government developments on delivering public services among EU cities. *Government Information Quarterly, 22*(2), 217–238. doi:10.1016/j.giq.2005.02.004

Towns, S. (2008, September 25). *Missouri Hires First Employee from Second Life*. Retrieved June 12th, 2009, from http://www.govtech.com/gt/418153

Traunmüller, R., & Wimmer, M. A. (2003). E-Government at a decisive moment: Sketching a roadmap to excellence. In G. Goos, J. Hartmanis, & J. van Leeuwen (Eds.), *Proceedings of Electronic Government: 2th International Conference, EGOV 2003*: Lecture Notes in Computer Science, Vol. 2739, Prague, Check Republic, pp. 1073.

Tredinnick, L. (2006). Web 2.0 and Business: A pointer to the intranets of the future? *Business Information Review, 23*(4), 228–234. doi:10.1177/0266382106072239

Trippi, J. (2004). *The revolution will not be televised: Democracy, the Internet, and the overthrow of everything*. New York: HaperCollins.

Trojanowics, R. C., & Smyth, P. R. (1983). The foot patrol officer, the community, and the school. *Community Education Journal, II*, 18–19.

Trojanowicz, R. C., & Bucqueroux, B. (1990). *Community Policing: A Contemporary Perspective*. Cincinnati, OH: Anderson.

TÜİK. (2008). *TÜİK*. Retrieved August 1, 2009, from http://www.turkstat.gov.tr/PreIstatistikTablo.do?istab_id=46

Türksat. (2009). *Kamu kurumları internet siteleri*. Retrieved October 9, 2009 from, http://www.kakis.gov.tr

U. S. Department of Justice. (2002, June 18). Guidance to Federal Financial Assistance Recipients Regarding Title VI Prohibition Against National Origin Discrimination Affecting Limited English Proficient Persons. *Federal Register, 67*(117).

U.S. Census Bureau. (2008). *2005-2007 American community survey 3-year estimates* Washington, DC: US Department of Commerce. Retrieved January 30, 2009, from http://factfinder.census.gov/servlet/DatasetMainPageServlet?_program=ACS&_submenuId=&_lang=en&_ts=

U.S. Department of Justice, Bureau of Justice Statistics. (2008). *Law enforcement statistics*. Retrieved May 24, 2008 from http://www.ojp.usdoj.gov/bjs/lawenf.htm.

U.S. Department of Justice, Civil Rights Division. (2001). *Departmental plan implementing Executive Order 13166*. Retrieved January 25, 2009, from http://www.usdoj.gov/crt/cor/lep/dojimp.php

U.S. Department of Justice. (2002). Guidance to federal financial assistance recipients regarding Title VI prohibition against national origin discrimination affecting limited English proficient persons. *Federal* Register 67:117, 41455-41472. Retrieved 25 January 2009 from http://www.usdoj.gov/crt/cor/lep/DOJFinLEPFRJun182002.pdf

U.S. General Services Administration. (2005). *Citizens' service-level expectations: Final report. (USGSA Publication No. 99-D-00005)*. McLean, VA: MITRE Corporation.

Uçkan, Ö. (2009). *Everyone is governed as they deserve*. Retrieved January 19, 2009 from, http://arsiv.sabah.com.tr/2009/01/04/pz/haber,0499516A4921456CA2DA627988C1E222.html

UnData. (2009). *Personal computers per 100 population*. Retrieved July 8, 2009, from http://data.un.org/Data.aspx?d=CDB&f=srID%3A29971.

United Nations & American Society for Public Administration. (2002). *Benchmarking e-government: A global perspective*. New York: U.N. Publications.

United Nations. (2008). *E-government survey 2008 - From e-government to connected governance*. New York: United Nations.

United Nations and American Society of Public Administration. (2002). *Benchmarking e-government: A global perspective assessing the UN member states*. Washington, DC: American Society for Public Administration and the United Nations.

United Nations Division for Public Economics and Public Administration (UNDPEPA). (2002). *Benchmarking e-government: A global perspective*. Retrieved June 19, 2008, from http://aps.vlaanderen.be/straplan/vindplaatsen/benchmarking-e-government.pdf

United Nations. (2003). *UN global e-government survey*. Retrieved February 20, 2008, from http://unpan1.un.org/intradoc/groups/public/documents/un/unpan016066.pdf

United Nations. (2004). *United Nations global e-government readiness report*. Retrieved February 20, 2008, from http://unpan1.un.org/intradoc/groups/public/documents/UN/UNPAN019207.pdf

United Nations. (2005). United Nations global e-government readiness report. Retrieved February 20, 2008, from http://unpan1.un.org/intradoc/groups/public/documents/un/unpan021888.pdf

United Nations. (2007). United Nations e-government readiness knowledge base. Retrieved June 10, 2009, from http://www2.unpan.org/egovkb/

United Nations. (2008). *United Nations e-government survey 2008: From e-government to connected governance*. Retrieved June 23, 2009 from http://unpan1.un.org/intradoc/groups/public/documents/UN/UNPAN028607.pdf

US Census Bureau. (2005). Computer and Internet use in the United States: 2003. Washington, DC. Retrieved June 30, 2007 fromwww.census.gov/prod/2005pubs/p23-208.pdf

van Dijk, J. A. G. M., Peters, O., & Ebbers, W. (2008). Explaining the acceptance and use of government Internet services: A multivariate analysis of 2006 survey data in the Netherlands. *Government Information Quarterly*, *25*(3), 379–399. doi:10.1016/j.giq.2007.09.006

van Velsen, L., van der Geest, T., ter Hedde, M., & Derks, W. (2009). Requirements engineering for e-Government services: A citizen-centric approach and case study. *Government Information Quarterly*, *26*, 477–486. doi:10.1016/j.giq.2009.02.007

Van Wart, M. (1998). *Changing public sector values*. New York: Garland Publishing, Inc.

Vangen, S., & Huxham, C. (2003). Nurturing collaborative relations: Building trust in interorganizational collaboration. *The Journal of Applied Behavioral Science*, *39*(1), 5–31. doi:10.1177/0021886303039001001

Venkatesh, V., & Davis, F. D. (2000). A theoretical extension of the technology acceptance model: Four longitudinal field studies. *Management Science, 46*(2), 186–204. doi:10.1287/mnsc.46.2.186.11926

Venkatesh, V., Morris, M. G., Davis, G. B., & Davis, F. D. (2003). User acceptance of information technology: Toward a unified view. *Management Information Systems Quarterly, 27*(3), 425–478.

Verdegem, P., & Verleye, G. (2009). User-centered e-government in practice: A comprehensive model for measuring user satisfaction. *Government Information Quarterly, 26*(3), 487–497. doi:10.1016/j.giq.2009.03.005

Victor, B., & Cullen, J. B. (1987). A theory and measure of ethical climate in organizations. *Research in Corporate Social Performance and Policy, 9*, 51–71.

Vietor, R. H. K. (1994). *Contrived competition: Regulation and deregulation in America.* Cambridge, MA: Harvard University Press.

Vigoda-Gadot, E. (2007). Revitalizing democracy? New avenues for citizen participation in the era of information technology. *Public Administration Review, 67*(4), 789–791. doi:10.1111/j.1540-6210.2007.00763.x

Virpi, R., & Kaikkonen, A. (2003). Acceptable download times in the mobile internet. In *Proceedings of the 10th International Conference on Human-Computer Interaction,* (pp.1467–1472). Mahwah, NJ: Lawrence Erlbaum Associates.

Vora, P. (1998). Human factors methodology for designing web sites. In Grose, E., Forsythe, C., & Ratner, J. (Eds.), *Human factors and web development* (pp. 189–198). Mahwah, NJ: Lawrence Erlbaum Associates.

Vrooman, D. J. (1976). An economic analysis of the New York State lottery. *National Tax Journal, 29*(4), 482–489.

W3C (2008). *Web content accessibility guidelines 2.0.* Retrieved March 20, 2009, from http://www.w3.org/TR/WCAG20/

W3C (2009). *Web Accessibility Initiative (WAI) Highlights.* Retrieved March 20, 2009 from http://www.w3.org/WAI/

W3C. (1999). *Web content accessibility guidelines 1.0.* Retrieved June 8, 2009, from http://www.w3.org/TR/WCAG10/

WALDO, D. (1974). Reflections On Public Morality. *Administration & Society, 6*, 267–283. doi:10.1177/009539977400600301

Walker, S., & Katz, C. M. (2005). *Police in America: An introduction* (5th ed.). Boston, MA: MacGraw Hill.

Walker, S. (2001). Broken windows and fractured history: The use and misuse of history in recent police patrol analysis. In Dunham, R., & Alpert, G. (Eds.), *Critical issues in policing* (4th ed., pp. 480–492). Prospect Heights, IL: Waveland Press.

Wall, D. S., & Williams, M. (2007). Policing diversity in the digital age: Maintaining an order in virtual communities. *Criminology & Criminal Justice, 7*(4), 391–415. doi:10.1177/1748895807082064

Wallsten, S. (2005). Regulation and Internet use in developing countries. *economic development and cultural change, 53*(2), 501–524.

Walsham, G., & Sahay, S. (1999). GIS for district-level administration in India: Problems and opportunities. *Management Information Systems Quarterly, 23*(1), 39–65. doi:10.2307/249409

Walters, J. (2009, April 1). O citizen, where art thou? Getting public input into the budget writing process sounds easier than it is. *Governing.* Retrieved June 20, 2009, from http://www.governing.com/article/o-citizen-where-art-thou

Wampler, B. (2007). *Participatory budgeting in Brazil: Contestation, cooperation, and accountability.* University Park, PA: Pennsylvania State University Press.

Wang, L., Bretschneider, S., & Gant, J. (2005). *Evaluating web-based e-government services with a citizen-centric approach. Paper presented at the 38th Hawaii International Conference on System Sciences (HICSS'05)*, Big Island, Hawaii.

Warner, S. (1999). Internet portals, what are they and how to build a niche internet portal to enhance the delivery of information services. In *Proceedings of the 8th Asian-Pacific SHLL Conference*.

Weare, C., Musso, J., & Hale, M. (1999). Electronic democracy and the diffusion of municipal web pages in California. *Administration & Society, 31*(1), 3–27. Retrieved from http://aas.sagepub.com/cgi/reprint/31/1/3. doi:10.1177/009539999400935475

Web, C. A. G. (WCAG) 2.0. (2008). *WCAG*. Retrieved June 20, 2009 from http://www.w3.org/TR/WCAG20/

Weber, R. P. (1990). *Basic content analysis* (2nd ed.). Newbury Park, CA: Sage Publications.

Weber, L. M., & Loumakis, A. (2005). Who participates and why? An analysis of citizens on The Internet and the mass public. *Social Science Computer Review, 21*(1), 26–42. doi:10.1177/0894439302238969

Weber, R. P. (1990). *Basic content analysis* (2nd ed.). Newbury Park, CA: Sage Publications.

Webler, T., & Tuler, S. (2000). Fairness and competence in citizen participation: Theoretical reflections from a case study. *Administration & Society, 32*(5), 566–595. doi:10.1177/00953990022019588

Weimer, D., & Vining, A. (1989). *Policy analysis: Concepts and practice*. Upper Saddle River, NJ: Pearson Prentice Hall.

Weinberg, S. L., & Goldberg, K. P. (1990). *Statistics for the behavioral sciences*. New York: Cambridge University Press.

Welch, E. W., Hinnant, C. C., & Moon, M. J. (2005). Linking citizen satisfaction with e-government and trust in government. *Journal of Public Administration: Research and Theory, 15*(3), 371–391. doi:10.1093/jopart/mui021

Welch, E. W., Hinnant, C. C., & Moon, M. J. (2004). Linking citizen satisfaction with e-government and trust in government. *Journal of Public Administration: Research and Theory, 15*(3), 371–391. doi:10.1093/jopart/mui021

Welch, E. W., Hinnant, C. C., & Moon, M. J. (2006). Linking citizen satisfaction with e-government and trust in government. *Journal of Public Administration: Research and Theory, 15*(3), 371–191. doi:10.1093/jopart/mui021

Welch, E. W., & Hinnant, C. C. (2002). Internet use, transparency, and interactivity effects on trust in government. In *Proceedings of the 36th Hawaii International Conference on System Sciences – 2003*.

Welch, E., & Wong, W. (2001). Global information technology pressure and government accountability: The mediating effect of domestic content on website openness. *Journal of Public Administration Research and Theory, 11*(4), 509-538. Retrieved March 14, 2009, from http://jpart.oxfordjournals.org/cgi/reprint/11/4/509

Wescott, C. (2001). E-Government in the Asia-Pacific region. *Asian Journal of Political Science, 9*(2), 1–24. doi:10.1080/02185370108434189

Wescott, C. G. (2003). E-Government to combat corruption in the Asia Pacific region. In Proceedings of the 11th International Anti-Corruption Conference, Seoul, Republic of Korea. Retrieved September 25, 2009, from http://www.adb.org/Governance/egovernment_corruption.pdf

Wescott, C. G. (2004). E-government in the Asia-Pacific region: Progress and challenges. *Systemics, Cybernetics and Informatics, 3*(6), 37-42. Retrieved June 25, 2009, from http://www.iiisci.org/journal/CV$/sci/pdfs/P749171.pdf

West, D. M. (2004). E-Government and the transformation of service delivery and citizen attitudes. *Public Administration Review, 64*(1), 15–27. doi:10.1111/j.1540-6210.2004.00343.x

West, D. M. (2001). *State and federal e-government in the United States, 2001*. Providence, RI: Brown University.

West, D. M. (2002). *State and federal e-government in the United States, 2002*. Providence, RI: Brown University.

West, D. M. (2003). *State and federal e-government in the United States, 2003*. Providence, RI: Brown University.

West, D. M. (2004). *State and federal e-government in the United States, 2004*. Providence, RI: Brown University.

West, D. (2005). *Digital government: Technology and public sector performance*. Princeton, NJ: Princeton University Press.

West, D. M. (2004). *Assessing E-government: The internet, democracy and service delivery*. Providence, Rhode Island: Brown University.

West, D. M. (2000). *State and federal e-government in the United States, 2000*. Providence, RI: Brown University.

West, D. M. (2005). E-government capabilities Improving. *Government Finance Review, 21*(6), 8.

West, D. M. (2007). Global perspectives on e-government. In Mayer-Schonberger, V., & Lazer, D. (Eds.), *Governance and information technology: From electronic government to information government*. Cambridge, MA: MIT Press.

West, D. (2001). Assessing E-Government: The Internet democracy, and service delivery by state and federal governments. *Brown University Report*. Retrieved April 28, 2009 from http://www.brown.edu/Departments/Taubman_Center/polreports/egovt01us.html.

West, D. M. (2001). *E-Government and the transformation of public sector service delivery*. Paper presented at the annual meeting of the American Political Science Association. San Francisco CA. August, 30 –September, 2, 2001.

West, D. M. (2005). *State and Federal governments in the United States, Providence, RI: Center for Public Policy, Brown University*. Retrieved September 30, 2006, from http://www.insidepolitics.org/egovt05us.pdf

West, D. M. (2007). *Global E-government 2007, Inside Politics*. Retrieved June 20, 2009, from http://www.insidepolitics.org/egovt07int.pdf

Westbrook, L. (2008). E-government support for people in crisis: An evaluation of police department website support for domestic violence survivors using "person-in-situation" information need analysis. *Library & Information Science Research, 30*, 22–38. doi:10.1016/j.lisr.2007.07.004

White, J. (2008). *Terrorism and Homeland Security* (6th ed.). Belmont, CA: Wadsworth Publishing.

White, L. D. (1948). *The Federalists*. New York: Macmillan.

Wigand, R. T. (1997). Electronic commerce: Definition, theory and context. *The Information Society, 13*(3), 1–16. doi:10.1080/019722497129241

Wigand, D. (2007). Building on Leavitt's diamond model of organizations: The organizational interaction diamond model and the impact of information technology on structure people and tasks. *AMCIS 2007 Proceedings*. Paper 287. Retrieved from http://aisel.aisnet.org/amcis2007/287

Wildavsky, A. (1964). *The politics of the budgetary process*. Boston: Little, Brown & Co.

Wildavsky, A. (1984). *The politics of the budgetary process* (4th ed.). Boston: Little, Brown & Co.

Wildavsky, A. (1992). *The new politics of the budgetary process* (2nd ed.). New York: HarperCollins Publishers.

Wilhelm, A. G. (2004). *Toward an inclusive information society*. Cambridge, MA: MIT Press.

Williamson, O. (1995). Transaction cost economics and organization theory. In Williamson, O. (Ed.), *Organization theory from chester barnard to the present and beyond* (pp. 207–256). New York: Oxford University Press.

Willoughby, K. G. (2004). Performance measurement and budget balancing: State government perspective. *Public Budgeting & Finance, 24*(2), 21–39. doi:10.1111/j.0275-1100.2004.02402002.x

Willoughby, K. G., & Melkers, J. E. (2000). Implementing PBB: Conflicting views of success. *Public Budgeting & Finance, 20*(1), 105–120. doi:10.1111/0275-1100.00006

Wilson, J. Q. (1968). *Varieties of police behavior: The management of law and order in eight communities.* New York, NY: Harvard University Press.

Wilson, D., & Stupnytska, A. (2007). *The N-11: More than an acronym.* Global Economics Paper No. 153. Goldman Sachs. Economic Research from the GS. Retrieved July, 2009, from http://www.chicagobooth.edu/alumni/clubs/pakistan/docs/next11dream-march%20'07-goldmansachs.pdf

Wilson, J. Q., & Kelling, G. (1982). Broken windows, *The Atlantic Monthly*, 249 (3), pp. 29-48, Wilson, J. (2006). *Community policing in America.* New York, NY: Taylor & Francis.

Wimmer, M. A., & Holler, U. (2003). Applying a Holistic Approach to Develop User-Friendly, Customer-Oriented E-government Portal Interfaces, N. Carbonell, C. Stephanidis (Eds.): *User Interfaces for All, LNCS 2615*, pp. 167–178. Berlin, Germany: Springer-Verlag.

Winkler, R. (2001). Portals-The all-in-one web supersites: Features, functions, definition, taxonomy. Retrieved from http://www.sapdesignguild.org/editions/edition3/overview_edition3.asp

Wolf, P., & Krcmar, H. (2005). Process-oriented e-government evaluation. *Wirtschaftsinformatik*, *47*(5), 337–346.

Wolfinbarger, M., & Gilly, M. (2002). *comQ: Dimensionalizing, measuring and predicting quality of the e-tailing experience.* MSI Working Paper Series, No. 02-100.

Wood, J., & Dupont, B. (2006). *Democracy, society, and the governance of security.* New York, NY: Cambridge University Press. doi:10.1017/CBO9780511489358

World Bank. (2002), *The e-government handbook for developing countries.* Retrieved June 2009, from http://www.cdt.org/egov/handbook/2002-11-14egovhandbook.pdf

World Wide Web's Web Accessibility Initiative. (2009). *World Wide Web's Web Accessibility Initiative.* Retrieved June 20, 2009 from http://www.w3.org/wai

Yang, K., & Rho, S.-Y. (2007). E-Government for Better Performance: Promises, Realities, and Challenges. *International Journal of Public Administration*, *30*(11), 1197–1217. doi:10.1080/01900690701225556

Yang, Z., Cai, S., Zhou, Z., & Zhou, N. (2005). Development and validation of an instrument to measure user perceived service quality of information presenting web portals. *Information & Management*, *42*, 575–589. doi:10.1016/S0378-7206(04)00073-4

Yang, Z., & Jun, M. (2002). Consumer perception of e-service quality: from Internet purchaser and non-purchaser perspectives. *The Journal of Business Strategy*, *19*(1), 19–41.

Yen, D. C., Huang, S.-M., & Ku, C.-Y. (2002). The impact and implementation of XML on business-to-business commerce. *Computer Standards & Interfaces*, *24*, 347–362. doi:10.1016/S0920-5489(02)00019-3

Yildiz, M. (2007). E-government research: Reviewing the literature, limitations, and ways forward. *Government Information Quarterly*, *24*, 646–665. doi:10.1016/j.giq.2007.01.002

Yin, R. (2003). *Case Study Research: Design and Methods (3rd).* Thousand Oaks, CA: Sage.

Yin, R. K. (1994). *Case study research: Design and methods.* Thousand Oaks, CA: Sage.

Zadeh, L. A. (1965). Fuzzy sets. *Information and Control*, *8*, 338–353. doi:10.1016/S0019-9958(65)90241-X

Zappen, J., Harrison, T., & Watson, D. (2008). *A new paradigm for designing e-government: web 2.0 and experience design.* Paper presented at the 9th Annual International Digital Government Research Conference, Montreal, Canada.

Zeithaml, V. (2002). Guru's view: Service excellence in electronic channels, special on service excellence. *Managing Service Quality*, *12*(3), 135–138. doi:10.1108/09604520210429187

Zeithaml, V., Parasuraman, A., & Malhotra, A. (2002). Service quality delivery through web sites: A critical review of extant knowledge. *Journal of the Academy of Marketing Science, 30*(4), 362–375. doi:10.1177/009207002236911

Zeithaml, V., & Parasuraman, A. & Malhotra. (2000). *A conceptual framework for understanding e-service quality: Implications for future research and managerial practice.* MSI Monograph, Report # 00-115, 2000.

Zhang, J., Faerman, S. R., & Cresswell, A. M. (2006). *The effect of organizational/ technological factors and the nature of knowledge on knowledge sharing.* Paper presented at the 39th Hawaiian International Conference on System Sciences (Awarded Best Paper in the Conference), Hawaii.

Zhou, X. (2004). E-government in China: A content analysis of national and provincial web sites. *Journal of Computer-Mediated Communication, 9*(4). Retrieved September 25, 2009, from http://jcmc.indiana.edu/vol9/issue4/zhou.html.

Zinkhan, G. M., DeLorme, D. E., Peters, C. O., & Watson, R. T. (2007). Information sources and government research: Ethical conflicts and solutions. *Public Integrity, 9*(4), 363–376. doi:10.2753/PIN1099-9922090404

About the Contributors

Ed Downey is an Associate Professor in the Department of Public Administration at The College at Brockport, State University of New York. He holds a Doctorate in Public Administration from the University at Albany, State University of New York and has private sector experience in Human Resources and as the CEO of a software firm in the health care industry. His primary teaching and research interests are in the areas of productivity improvement and computer applications in organizations and he has worked under grants from the Ford Foundation and Brookings Institution. Ed's recent research is on the evaluation of E-Government web site content. He has just completed a study on the economic and political value of New York State county web sites.

Carl D. Ekstrom holds an MPA, Syracuse University; and Ph.D. in Public Administration, University at Albany. He has forty-seven years of professional experience in governmental and nonprofit administration and teaching and research in Public Administration at twenty-three colleges and universities in the U. S. and internationally. Carl is currently semi-retired but retaining relations with the University of Nebraska at Omaha, Wichita State University, Nova Southeastern University and Western Iowa Community College.

Matthew A. Jones is currently an Assistant Professor of the Hatfield School of Government, Department of Public Administration at Portland State University. He is also a Leadership Fellow for the Executive Leadership Institute located at Portland State University. Matthew's primary research interests revolve around public safety strategic management and the intersection of technology and policing. He has been a trainer and educator to public safety employees for a number of years. Part of his experience includes holding an appointment as an Assistant Professor of Public Safety Management at the State University of New York, Brockport College. Matthew has served as a consultant for public safety agencies in Oregon, Washington and New York. His key interests are strategic planning, leadership development, operations management and performance measurement within the public safety environment. His roles have included serving as: a methodological advisor, strategic planning facilitator, and trainer.

* * *

Stephen K. Aikins is a faculty member in the Department of Government and International Affairs. He holds graduate degrees in Public Administration, Information Systems Management and Business Administration. He is a Certified Public Accountant, a Certified Information Systems Auditor and a Certified Business Manager. He has published in the areas of information security and e-government. His research interests include risk management policy, government auditing and public economics.

Dimitrios Askounis is an Assistant Professor of Management Information and Decision Support Systems in the School of Electrical and Computer Engineering of the National Technical University of Athens (NTUA). He obtained his Diploma in Electrical Engineering and his PhD in Production Control Systems. He has acquired over 15 years of experience in the areas of e-business and e-government, business and data modelling, interoperability and decision support and has published over 80 papers in scientific journals and international conference proceedings.

Asim Balci is the director of the Corporate Communications Director at Turksat. He also holds the positions of Associate Professor in the Department of Public Administration, Selçuk University, Turkey, Prof. Balci was an advisor in the Turkish Ministry of Health with various consultative and administrative responsibilities between 2003 and 2006, having received his Doctorate degree from the Department of Political Science and Public Administration, Middle East Technical University, Turkey. Professor Balci has published numerous books and contributed to various journal publications and conference proceedings in the fields of public administration, as well as TQM and e-Government.

Debjani Bhattacharya, is an Assistant Professor in Northern Institute for Integrated Learning in Management, Centre for Management Studies, New Delhi. Her area of interest in research includes e-governance, web service and e-commerce. She has been into research and consultancy for five years.

Donna Canestraro has been a program manager at the Center for Technology in Government (CTG) for more than 10 years, providing management and technology support for projects. Her current work focuses on the policy, management and technology issues related to inter- and intra-organizational information integration, enterprise IT Governance, and business process analysis. Donna brings more than 25 years of professional experience in project management, education, and information technology to CTG's partnership projects. She works with agency partners on problem definition, process analysis, and business case development. She also participates in defining technology issues, conducting investigations of relevant technologies, managing best practices research, and evaluating organizational, process, and technology solutions for the Center's projects. She is highly experienced in facilitation, group decision conferences, and all facets of collaborative work. Donna also has experience in the fields of education and training, marketing, management, and customer service.

Dimitris Charilas is a PhD candidate in the Department of Electrical Engineering of the National Technical University of Athens (NTUA). He received his MBA in Techno-Economic Systems in 2008 and his Diploma in Electrical Engineering from NTUA in 2006. He has worked as a Research Assistant in the Telecommunications Laboratory of the Institute of Communication and Computer Systems (ICCS-NTUA). He is currently with the Mobile Radiocommunications Laboratory of ICCS-NTUA. His research interests include mobile services, quality of service, wireless communications, resource allocation and game theory applications.

Meena Chary holds a PhD in Public Administration, as well as degrees in Electrical Engineering, Economics and Management. She is a methodologist and a public policy scholar researching in the areas of human rights and information technology. She is part of the faculty of the Public Administration Program within the Department of Government and International Affairs at the University of South Florida.

Heasun Chun (PhD Candidate, University at Buffalo, the State University of New York) is a doctorate student in the Department of Communication at University at Buffalo, the State University of New York. Her research focuses on the social and policy implications of information and communication technologies with a particular interest in how the new technologies improve user's welfare and social engagement.

Joy A. Clay is Professor of Public Administration and Associate Dean for Interdisciplinary Studies in the College of Arts and Sciences at the University of Memphis. Her research and engaged scholarship focuses on administrative theory, performance, accountability, evaluation and public health (especially maternal health), and collaborative dynamics. Dr. Clay worked for the Veterans Administration in Washington, D.C. for thirteen years prior to becoming an academic and has extensive experience in the nonprofit sector as a board member and volunteer. She has published articles in a variety of public administration journals. She has served as a Tennessee Quality Award and Greater Memphis Quality Award Examiner and worked with the Office of Finance, City of Memphis on their performance measurement processes. She serves on the editorial board of *Public Administration Review* and the *Journal of Health and Human Services Administration*.

Jim Costello is the Webmaster and Web Applications Developer at the Center for Technology in Government (CTG). Prior to joining CTG, he had his own web design and development company and worked for several private and public organizations, including KeyCorp, the Professional Development Program of Rockefeller College, Coopers & Lybrand, and the Office of Data Processing, Human Resources Administration, City of New York. He has been an editor, technical writer, trainer, computer-based training designer, and manager of Web applications and distance learning. He has worked for the past eight years on the benefits and challenges of using XML. He has developed curriculum and delivered training on XML and has co-authored an article on XML in the *International Journal of Electronic Governance*. Dr. Costello has a PhD in English and American Literature.

Dawit Demissie is a PhD candidate in the Informatics (INF) PhD program at the College of Computing and Information, University at Albany, State University of New York. He received a BA in Computer/Information Science from State University of New York at Oswego, and an MS in Telecommunications & Network Management from Syracuse University. Before joining the INF PhD program, he had been a Software Engineer in Test and prior to that, he had served as a System Consultant and Information Technology Specialist at various organizations in New York. He also had been an Instructor at State University of New York (SUNY) at Albany, Hudson Valley Community College, Bryant & Stratton College, Syracuse University, and SUNY Oswego. He has published and presented in major journals and conference proceedings, and his research interests include empirical testing of models and theories of information technology, Human computer Interaction, e-Government index computation, and knowledge management.

Michael Dougherty has been an Extension Specialist with West Virginia University Extension Service since 1995. Dougherty received his BA degree in Government from the College of William and Mary in 1985, a Master's of Urban Affairs from Virginia Tech in 1989, and a PhD in Planning from Virginia Tech in 1995. Dougherty has published articles dealing with budgeting, financial management, local government information technology, and related issues in several academic journals. He has written conference papers on benchmarking, performance measurement, strategic planning, local government issues assessment, community planning, citizen involvement, and service learning. He is editor of the occasional academic series *CD Practice* web-published by the Community Development Society. Dougherty has worked with local governments and community organizations in over 40 West Virginia counties on a strategic plans, comprehensive planning, leadership training, financial administration, and general operations. He is also the Course Director of the Community Development Institute East.

Rodney Erakovich is assistant professor of management and public administration in the School of Business Administration at Texas Wesleyan University, Fort Worth Texas. He has worked with international and local public organizations in ethics, visioning and culture change with US cities and in local governments Ukraine, Serbia and Montenegro. He has presented at the American Society for Public Administration, Mount Kopaonik School of Natural Law in Serbia, The Network of Institutes and Schools of Public Administration in Central and Eastern Europe (NISPAcee), International Atlantic Economic Conference and numerous regional conferences. He has published several articles in *PA Times, International Journal of Public Administration, Journal of Business Inquiry and the Ukraine Social Science Journal* and co-author of the chapter, *Implications of Organizational Influence on Ethical Behavior: An Analysis of the Perceptions of Public Managers* in the 2009 publication of *Ethics and Integrity in Public Administration: Concepts and Cases.*

Paul Ferber graduated from George Washington University in 1986, with a PhD in Political Science. His major area of study was American Government, with a minor field in Quantitative Methodology. While in graduate school he worked as a consultant in survey research, with clients such as *The Washington Post*, and the National Science Foundation. He was also a Research Associate at the Woodrow Wilson International Center for Scholars. Professor Ferber has been a member of the faculty at Rochester Institute of Technology since 1981. Currently, he is the chair of the Political Science Department. His major research interest has been in political communication. He has produced over two dozen peer reviewed articles and conference papers on the topic of cyber-democracy.

Franz Foltz graduated from Rensselaer Polytechnic Institute with a Ph.D. in Science and Technology Studies in 1996, where he studied under Susan Cozzens, currently at the School of Public Policy at Georgia Tech. He spent a summer working in the Office of Policy Support at NSF as a Policy Analyst conducting research on customer service, Fastlane, and the Peer Review system. He's been on the faculty at Virginia Tech and Penn State University before coming to the Science, Technology, and Society/ Public Policy Department at the Rochester Institute of Technology. He is the graduate Coordinator for the Science, Technology, and Public Policy graduate Program at RIT. He is also a Contributing Editor for the Bulletin of Science, Technology, and Society. His research interests focus on technology and democratic participation. He has produced over two dozen peer reviewed articles and conference papers on the topic of cyber-democracy.

Mohammed Gharawi is currently an Information Science PhD student at the State University of New York (SUNY) at Albany. He received his BS degree in Information Systems from King Saud University in Riyadh, Saudi Arabia in 1997 and his MS degree in Computer Science from the University of South Florida in 2001. After the completion of his MS degree, he worked for the Institute of Public Administration in Saudi Arabia as an instructor and consultant for various government agencies. He is a graduate assistant at the Center for Technology in Government at SUNY at Albany. His area of specialization is Information, Government, and Democratic Societies. His research interests include comparative e-government research, IT governance, and cross-boundaries information sharing and integration.

J. Ramon Gil-Garcia is an Assistant Professor in the Department of Public Administration and the Director of the Data Center for Applied Research in Social Sciences at Centro de Investigación y Docencia Económicas (CIDE) in Mexico City. Dr. Gil-Garcia is the author or co-author of articles in *The International Public Management Journal, Government Information Quarterly, Journal of the American Society for Information Science and Technology, European Journal of Information Systems, Journal of Government Information, International Journal of Electronic Government Research, International Journal of Cases on Electronic Commerce,* and *International Journal of Electronic Governance,* among others. His research interests include collaborative electronic government, inter-organizational information integration, adoption and implementation of emergent technologies, digital divide policies, education policy, new public management, public policy evaluation, and multi-method research approaches. Dr. Gil-Garcia has a PhD in Public Administration and Policy with a concentration in Information Strategy and Management. He is also a former Fulbright Scholar.

Thomas J. Greitens is an Assistant Professor of Public Administration at Central Michigan University. He researches how e-government can be used to both increase transparency in public budgeting and enhance citizen involvement in governmental decisions. He received his PhD from Northern Illinois University and has completed research published in the journals *Administration & Society and Public Performance & Management Review.* He is currently researching the impact of fiscal retrenchment on citizen participation efforts.

Umesh Gulla, is an Associate Professor in the Department of Policy Studies, Teri University, New Delhi. He has his PhD in 'The study on Information Systems Outsourcing in Indian Banking Sector' from IIT, Delhi. His interest areas in research are Information Systems Management, Electronic Commerce/Business, E-Governance and Enterprise Resource Planning.He has executed more than thirty consultancy projects in industry.

M. P. Gupta is Chair-Information Systems Group & Coordinator-Center for Excellence in E-gov at the Department of Management Studies, Indian Institute of Technology (IIT Delhi). His research interests lies in the areas of IS/ IT planning and E-government. Prof. Gupta has authored acclaimed book *"Government Online"* and edited two others entitled *"Towards E-Government"* and *"Promise of E-Government"*, published by McGraw Hill, 2005. His research papers have appeared in National and International Journals/Conference Proceedings. He was the recipient of the prestigious Humanities & Social Sciences (HSS) fellowship of Shastri Indo Canadian Institute, Calgary (Canada) and a Visiting Fellow at the University of Manitoba. He supervised e-government portal "Gram Prabhat" which won the IBM Great Mind Challenge Award for the year 2003. He has steered several seminars and also founded the International Conference on E-governance (ICEG) in 2003 which running into seventh year. He is on the jury of Computer Society of India (CSI) E-gov Awards and also a member of Program Committee of several International Conferences. He is life member of Global Institute of Flexible Systems Management (GIFT), Systems Society of India (SSI) and Computer Society of India.

Melchor C. de Guzman is currently an assistant professor of the Department of Criminal Justice at the College of Brockport, State University of New York. He holds a doctorate degree in criminal justice from the University of Cincinnati. Dr. de Guzman was a former committee secretary for the Senate Committee on Defense and National Security in the Philippines. He was also a former director of the Philippine Veterans Affairs Office. He was also a former lecturer at the National Police College of the Philippines, the Phillipine Public Safety College, and several police academies in the United States. His research interests include community participation in policing, comparative justice systems, community policing, police organizations, and controlling police behaviors.

Akhlaque Haque, PhD is Associate Professor and Director of Graduate Studies in Public Administration at the University of Alabama at Birmingham, USA. His major areas of research have focused on public sector information management, democratic theory and decision behavior, use of GIS for decision making in local government, surveillance and mapping technology, urban/rural health and GIS. He is a Co-PI in several Federal grants focusing on community health and health disparity for the urban and rural population. His work appears in leading public administration and health journals including Public Administration Review, Administration and Society and Public Administration Quarterly. He has served in editorial boards of leading public administration journals, and served in expert panel in Congressional Briefing related to GIS in local government. He is currently working on a book manuscript on E-Government at the Grassroots.

Maria Ernita Joaquin studies the dynamics of bureaucratic adaptation, ethics, fiscal stress, performance assessment and multi-party governance. She was a researcher on local government affairs at the University of the Philippines. She studied at University of Manchester before getting her PhD at Northern Illinois University. Her publications include books and book chapters on organizational learning, fiscal decentralization, and gender in public administration. Her essays and journal articles appeared in Public Integrity, Publius, the PA Times and the American Review of Public Administration. A forthcoming work appears in Administration Society. She is currently involved in community action research in Southern Nevada.

Daejoong Kim (PhD Candidate, University at Buffalo, the State University of New York) is a doctorate student in the Department of Communication at University at Buffalo, the State University of New York. His research interest is focused around online public relations and social media relations in connection with interpersonal communication.

Kenneth A. Klase is an Associate Professor and Director of the Master of Public Affairs (MPA) program in the Department of Political Science at the University of North Carolina at Greensboro and teaches courses in budgeting and fiscal administration, public personnel management and federalism and intergovernmental relations. He received a BA from the Ohio State University, an M.B.A from Auburn University and a D.P.A from the University of Georgia. His research interests are in public budgeting and finance, public financial management and state and local government administration. His research has appeared in *Public Administration Review, Public Budgeting & Finance, Journal of Public Budgeting, Accounting & Financial Management, State and Local Government Review, International Journal of Public Administration, and Public Administration Quarterly.*

Ourania Markaki is a PhD candidate in the field of e-government in the Department of Electrical and Computer Engineering of the National Technical University of Athens (NTUA). She received her MBA in Techno-Economic Systems in 2008 and her Diploma in Electrical Engineering from NTUA in 2006. She has worked as a Research Assistant in the Telecommunications Laboratory of the Institute of Communication and Computer Systems (ICCS-NTUA); and since 2008, she is a Researcher in the Decision Support Systems Laboratory of NTUA. Her research interests include e-government evaluation, e-participation and multicriteria decision-making.

J. Scott McDonald is Associate Director of the Institute for Policy and Economic Development and Professor in Leadership Studies at the University of Texas El Paso. Previously he coordinated the Center for Applied Research at Valdosta State University (Georgia). He has authored or coauthored more than 50 refereed and governmental publications focused primarily on economic development and community development and extending into issues of transportation, quality of life, and environmental matters. He has conducted projects for a wide range of federal, state, regional, and local entities.

Tunc D. Medeni is a full-time researcher in Turksat and also affiliated to various academic institutions as a part-time staff. He was awarded a PhD degree from the Japan Advanced Institute of Science and Technology (JAIST), Japan; his MS degree from Lancaster University in the UK; and his BS degree from Bilkent University, Turkey. He has contributed to various (close to 60 in number) conference presentations, book chapters, and journal articles in his interest areas such as knowledge management, cross-cultural learning, and e-government. He has been awarded scholarships and funding from Nakayama Hayao Foundation, JAIST, Japanese State (Mombukagakusho) in Japan, Lancaster University in UK, and Bilkent University in Turkey for his education and research activities.

Charles E. Menifield is an Associate Professor in the Division of Public and Nonprofit Administration where he teaches graduates courses in budgeting and financial management, research methods, public management information systems and urban administration. Over his thirteen year career he has published 14 articles and book chapters and four books. The subjects include voting behavior among minority groups, health care, natural disasters, redistricting, minority group elections, infant mortality, public administration accreditation issues, and budget and finance. His recent research has appeared in the *Journal of Health and Human Services Administration*, *Journal of Public Affairs Education*, *Journal of Public Management and Social Policy*, and the *Journal of Public Budgeting, Accounting, and Financial Management*. In addition, he has published two award winning books on minority politics and two books on public budgeting. Last, he serves on the executive councils to NASPAA and the Association for Budgeting and Financial Management.

Gerald A. Merwin Jr. is Associate Professor of Public Administration at Valdosta State University. He has authored or coauthored refereed articles on a variety of topics and a book chapter on the way local governments promote economic development on the Web. He has traced the changes in information management applications used by local governments over the past eight years. He has also designed and developed Web sites for nonprofit organizations and educational institutions.

Keith A. Merwin is a principal in Merwin Associates, a consulting firm providing strategic technology analysis, planning, and development and change management services. He has 25 years experience developing software and providing training for customer service operations in government and for-profit organizations including meeting the needs of multilingual users.

Rudy Pugliese graduated from Temple University in 1991 with a Ph.D. in mass communications. He is currently a professor of communication at Rochester Institute of Technology and the graduate coordinator of the master's degree program in Communication & Media Technologies. His dissertation, an investigation of retention factors in distance education was funded by a grant from the Corporation for Public Broadcasting. Thomas Gordon, editor of *Communication Abstracts*, directed the study. His research interests include digital media as they relate to politics and pedagogy. He has produced over two dozen peer reviewed articles and conference papers on the topic of cyber-democracy.

Abebe Rorissa is an Assistant Professor at the Department of Information Studies, University at Albany, State University of New York (SUNY). He has over 21 years of experience working in four countries and consulted for academic institutions, national governments, and international organizations on information and communication technologies as well as information organization. Dr. Rorissa is widely published and his works appear in the *Journal of the American Society for Information Science & Technology, Information Processing and Management*, and *Government Information Quarterly*. His research interests include adoption, use, & impact of information and communication technologies (ICTs); multimedia information organization and retrieval; and human information behavior. Dr. Rorissa served on program committees of international conferences and edited some proceedings.

Demetrios Sarantis holds an MSc in Operational Research and Information Systems from London School of Economics and Political Science and he is a senior researcher of e-Government in the Decision Support Systems Laboratory at the National Technical University of Athens, Greece. His research interests include e-Government standardization frameworks, organization and implementation issues in transformational government, public sector management, process modelling and reengineering in public sector. He has ten-year professional experience as analyst and software engineer in information systems implementation in private and public sector.

Francisco R. Hernández Tella is a Full Time Professor in the Anthropology Faculty at the Autonomous University of the State of Mexico, Instructor for the Institute for Public Administration in the State of México and Professor for the Albert Einstein University. His research interests include electronic government, multiculturalism and impact of new technologies in traditional cultures. Has studies in MA in Political Science and currently is enrolled in a peace studies and development masters.

Derek Werthmuller, as the Director of Technology services, manages the Technology Solutions Laboratory and the Technology Services Unit to maintain the CTG's technology infrastructure, conduct technology investigations, and support electronic products. Derek brings more than 15 years of experience to his position as director of technology services. He brings experience building networks, automating system management and system deployment, and evaluating sustainable software systems. He is the co-author, along with Jim Costello, of the white paper "XML: A New Web Site Architecture", published in September, 2002, which detailed the Center for Technology in Government's migration to an XML-based website. He has made several presentations over the past five years on the benefits of using XML for Web site management.

Dianne Lux Wigand is an Assistant Professor and Master of Public Administration Graduate Program Coordinator in the Institute of Government at the University of Arkansas at Little Rock. Wigand researches information management in the public sector, e-government issues, multi-channel communication strategies, Web 2.0 and social media use in government. Her research interests lie at the intersection of information and newer information and communication technologies and their impact on public sector organizations. Wigand taught at Syracuse University, Arizona State University (ASU), and Texas Tech University. She had a 17 year university administrative career at ASU. She has served on editorial boards and as a reviewer for leading journals, the National Science Foundation and conferences for the Association of Information Systems such as ICIS, ECIS, and AMCIS, and the Bled International Conference on E-Commerce. Moreover, she was a guest editor for a special issue on E-Government for the Journal of Information Systems Management.

Index